BRITISH SOURCES OF INFORMATION

A Subject Guide and Bibliography

Paul Jackson

ROUTLEDGE & KEGAN PAUL
London and New York

To Rose and Phil Jackson
For Liz, Kathy and Judy

First published in 1987 by
Routledge & Kegan Paul Ltd
11 New Fetter Lane, London EC4P 4EE

Published in the USA by
Routledge & Kegan Paul Inc.
in association with Methuen Inc.
29 West 35th Street, New York, NY 10001

Set in Linotron Sabon
by Input Typesetting Ltd London
and printed in Great Britain
by Richard Clay Ltd, Bungay, Suffolk

Library of Congress Cataloging in Publication Data

Jackson, Paul, 1944–
   British sources of information.

   1. Great Britain—Bibliography.   2. Reference books—
Great Britain—Bibliography.   3. Great Britain—
Information services—Directories.   4. Great Britain—
Study and teaching—Audio-visual aids—Catalogs.
I. Title.
Z2001.J33   1987   [DA27.5]   016.941   86–26125

British Library CIP Data also available

ISBN 0–7102–0696–8

CONTENTS

Contents

Contents

Contents

PREFACE

This subject guide to books and sources aims to provide assistance above all to the general reader but also to the student and teacher in locating texts, information and teaching resources for work on major aspects of British life, society and culture.

Part I is a select bibliography of relevant and accessible publications covering forty key areas.

Part II lists periodicals, journals and magazines which provide general or specialised coverage of major topics.

Part III is a compilation of organisations and institutions which stock information on particular fields; it also contains places of study and research which provide facilities for work in these areas.

Part IV lists sources of further printed material, films, video cassettes and audio-visual aids for use in teaching areas of British life and culture.

The guide has been developed to serve a threefold requirement: the need to make information currently less accessible to the general reader more readily available; the need to overcome the traditional subject divisions by enabling readers in a particular area to explore ancillary or apparently remoter specialisations; the need to encourage a more innovative approach to traditional studies by subverting boundaries that render us all 'amateurs' outside our own fields. It is hoped that the guide to books and sources on Britain will go some way to meeting these aims, but also providing a useful general reference work for library and home use.

The lists of books should not be misunderstood as definitive bibliographies on all aspects of the topic. The sections and sub-sections into which the titles have been ordered have been kept deliberately broad without, I hope, sacrificing accuracy. Publications have only been included in so far as they relate to specifically British aspects of the area. For instance, 'Commonwealth and Empire' has omitted studies of Commonwealth countries; 'Science and Technology' is inevitably limited to questions of British science policy or science history; 'Education' is weighted heavily towards the sociology rather than the psychology of education.

It is the experience of all compilers that comprehensiveness and systematic rigour on the one hand and utility and convenience on the other can become mutual impediments. The scope and complexity of an unselective guide would have produced an impractical aggregation of encyclopaedic reference. So, common sense and practical considerations have been allowed to dictate both the ordering of subject divisions and the range of material chosen for inclusion. The topics indicated by the section headings are those felt to be of interest for most forms of everyday work and study. Inevitably, though, some distinctions such as those between 'Economics and Finance' and 'Industry and Commerce', or between 'Parliament', 'Politics' and 'Political Parties' may be convenient rather than precise.

The sources of information—selective, like the reading lists—are as accurate and up-to-date as it was possible to make them, but readers must occasionally allow for the stealthy obsolescence which may creep in subsequent to publication.

In the many cases where my own competence has been rapidly exhausted I have had recourse to other authorities. The limitations of the guide are nonetheless those of its compiler.

Paul Jackson
University of Mannheim

ACKNOWLEDGMENTS

Both the scope and selectivity of this guide have made it necessary to consult others and to supplement my guesswork with their professional judgment. My indebtedness ranges from the considerable to the infinite. But I remain solely responsible for any inaccuracies or errors of judgment that may occur.

I should like to thank the following in particular for their assistance and encouragement: J. D. Allen, A. J. Coulson, J. C. Beard, H. Fischer, A. J. Groom, H.-J. Hacker, D. Howell, R. Koster, G. Langley, D. Martin, E. Langmuir, P. M. Larby, T. Noble, C. Parry, N. Platz, B. D. Renton, A. Stevens, M. J. Stevenson, E. A. Stuart, T. Stemmler, P. Westcott, L. White, E. D. Willmott, D. Young.

I am also indebted to the editors of Routledge & Kegan Paul for their painstaking work on my manuscript.

PART I
SELECT BIBLIOGRAPHY

The following select bibliography covers forty major areas of British society, life and culture. The lists include introductory material, textbooks, comprehensive studies and reference works. The books are cited by author, editor or publisher. In the case of new editions or reprints the copy listed is the latest available.

The principles of selection underlying the bibliography have led to the following choice: works that can be recommended as useful introductions or as authoritative studies on a given topic; works which are for the most part accessible and likely to be available through libraries; relatively recent publications which reflect the state-of-the-art in each field and also provide readers with references to previous research.

The brief notes at the beginning of each section are intended to direct readers to reference material, handbooks, surveys, detailed studies or introductory reading on particular aspects of the general area.

At the end of most sections readers are given cross-references to other headings.

1 GENERAL REFERENCE

For general factual reference works which are regularly updated see: *Encyclopedia Britannica*, 32 vols, 1986; Her Majesty's Stationery Office (publisher), *Britain: An Official Handbook*, annually; Pelham Books (publisher), *Pears Cyclopaedia*, annually; Whitaker (publisher), *Whitaker's Almanack*, annually.

The major sources of bibliographical information on books and other publications are as follows: British Library, *British National Bibliography*, annually; British Library of Economic and Political Science, *A London Bibliography of the Social Sciences*, annually; Higgens, G., *Printed Reference Material*, 1984; Library Association, *British Humanities Index*, annually; Walford, A. J. (ed.), *Guide to Reference Material, vol. 1, Science and Technology*, 1980; Walford, A. J. (ed.), *Guide to Reference Material, vol. 2, Social and Historical Sciences*, 1982; Walford, A. J. (ed.), *Guide to Reference Material, vol. 3., Generalities, Languages, the Arts and Literature*, 1985; Walford, A. J. (ed.), *Walford's Concise Guide to Reference Material*, 1981.

For guides to official and government publications the following should be consulted: Butcher, D., *Official Publications in Britain*, 1982; HMSO, *Guide to Official Statistics*, annually; Richard, S., *A Directory of British Official Publications: A Guide to Sources*, 1984.

The following are standard guides to organisations: Anderson, I. G. (ed.), *Councils, Committees and Boards: A Handbook of Advisory, Consultative, Executive and Similar Bodies in British Public Life*; 1985; Codlin, E. M. (ed.), *ASLIB Directory, vol. 1, Information Sources in Science, Technology and Commerce*, 1982; Codlin, E. M. (ed.), *ASLIB Directory, vol. 2, Information Sources in the Social Sciences, Medicine and the Humanities*, 1984; Henderson, G. P. and Henderson, S. P. A. (eds), *Directory of British Associations and Associations in Ireland*, 1986.

For information on libraries, archives and museums see: Brink, A. and Watkins, D., *The Libraries, Museums and Art Galleries Year Book*, annually; British Library, *Guide to Government Department and Other Libraries*, 1984; Downs, R. B., *British and Irish Library Resources: A Bibliographical Guide*, 1982; Foster, J. and Sheppard, J., *British Archives: A Guide to Archive Resources in the United Kingdom*, 1983; Hudson, K. (ed.), *The Directory of Museums*, 1985; Roberts, S. et al., *Research Libraries and Collections in the U.K.: A Selective Inventory and Guide*, 1978.

The following books are useful selective guides to obtaining information of a general nature: Chandler, G., *How to Find Out: A Guide to Sources of Information for All*, 1982; Hoffmann, A., *Research: A Handbook for Writers and Journalists*, 1979; Walker, R., *First Clue: The A-Z of Finding Out*, 1983.

Allen & Unwin (publisher), *Scientific and Learned Societies of Great Britain: a Handbook Compiled from Official Sources*, London, 1964.

Anderson, I. G. (ed.), *Councils, Committees and Boards: a Handbook of Advisory, Consultative, Executive and Similar Bodies in British Public Life*, Beckenham, Kent, CBD Research, 1985.

Anderson, I. G. (ed.), *G. P. Henderson's Current British Directories: a Guide* to the Directories Published in Great Britain, Ireland, the British Commonwealth and South Africa, Beckenham, Kent, CBD Research, 1985.

Association Of Assistant Librarians, *Fiction Index*, London, annually.

Benn Publications (publisher), *Benn's Press Directory*, Tonbridge, Kent, annually.

Black (publisher), *Who's Who: an Annual Biographical Dictionary*, London, annually.

Black (publisher), *Writers' and Artists' Yearbook*, London, annually.

Bowker (publisher), *Irregular Serials and Annuals: An International Directory*, London, biennially.

Bowker (publisher), *Books in Print*, New York, London, annually.

Bowker (publisher), *Subject Guide to Books in Print*, New York, London, annually.

Bowker (publisher), *Ulrich's International Periodicals Directory: A Classified Guide to Current Periodicals, Foreign and Domestic*, London, New York, annually.

Brink, A. and Watkins, D., *The Libraries, Museums and Art Galleries Year Book*, Cambridge, annually.

British Library, *Guide to Government Department and Other Libraries*, London, 1986.

British Library, *British National Bibliography*, London, annually.

British Library, *Current Research in Britain: Social Sciences*, Boston Spa, annually.

British Library, *Serials in the British Library*, formerly British Union Catalogue of Periodicals, Boston Spa, quarterly.

British Library of Economic and Political Science, *A London Bibliography of the Social Sciences*, London and New York, Mansell, annually.

British Museum, *Guide to its Public Services*, London, 1970.

Burkett, J., *Library and Information Networks in the United Kingdom*, London, ASLIB, 1979.

Burkett, J. (ed.), *Government and Other Related Library and Information Services in the United Kingdom*, London, 1974.

Butcher, D., *Official Publications in Britain*, London, Bingley, 1982.

Cabinet Office, *Public Bodies*, London, HMSO, 1984.

Chadwyck-Healey Ltd (publisher), *Catalogue of British Official Publications not Published by HMSO*, Cambridge, 1980 –.

Chandler, G., *How to Find Out: A Guide to Sources of Information for All*, Oxford, Pergamon, 1982.

Codlin, E. M. (ed.), *ASLIB Directory. Vol. 1, Information Sources in Science, Technology and Commerce*, London, ASLIB, 1982.

Codlin, E. M. (ed.), *ASLIB Directory. Vol. 2, Information Sources in the Social Sciences, Medicine and the Humanities*, London, ASLIB, 1984.

Collinson, R. L., *Bibliographies, Subject and National: A Guide to their Contents, Arrangement and Use*, London, Lockwood, 1968.

Dewe, A. and Colyer, M. (eds), *British Information Services not Available Online*, London, ASLIB, 1980.

Downs, R. B., *British and Irish Library Resources; A Bibliographical Guide*, London, Mansell, 1982.

Encyclopedia Britannica (publisher), *Britannica Book of the Year*, Chicago, London, annually.

Encyclopedia Britannica (publisher), *Encyclopedia Britannica*, 32 vols, Chicago, London, 1986.

Esdaile, A. (ed.), *Student's Manual of Bibliography*, Metuchen, N.J., Scarecrow Press, 1982.

Europa Publications (publisher), *International Who's Who*, London, annually.

Europa Publications (publisher), *World of Learning*, 2 vols, London, annually.

Facts on File (publisher), *Facts on File*, New York, weekly.

Government Statistical Service, *Government Statistics: A Brief Guide to Sources*, London, HMSO, 1977.

Harvey, J. M., *Sources of Statistics,*

London, Bingley, 1971.

Henderson, G. P. and Henderson, S. P. A. (eds), *Directory of British Associations and Associations in Ireland*, Beckenham, Kent, CBD Research, 1986.

Her Majesty's Stationery Office (publisher), *Britain: An Official Handbook*, London, annually.

Her Majesty's Stationery Office (publisher), *Civil Service Handbook*, London, annually.

Her Majesty's Stationery Office (publisher), *Government Publications: Catalogue*, London, annually.

Her Majesty's Stationery Office (publisher), *Government Publications*, Sectional Lists, London.

Her Majesty's Stationery Office (publisher), *Guide to Official Statistics*, London, annually.

Her Majesty's Stationery Office (publisher), *Guide to the Contents of the Public Records Office*, 3 vols, London, 1963–8.

Higgens, G., *Printed Reference Material*, London, Library Association, 1984.

Hoffmann, A., *Research: A Handbook for Writers and Journalists*, London, Black, 1979.

Hudson, K. and Nicholls A. (eds), *The Directory of Museums*, London, Macmillan, 1985.

Keesing (publisher), *Keesing's Contemporary Archives*, Bristol, weekly.

Library Association, *British Humanities Index*, London, annually.

Library Association, *Libraries in the United Kingdom and the Republic of Ireland*, London, 1984.

Macmillan (publisher), *Statesman's Year Book*, London, annually.

Millard, P. (ed.), *Trade Associations and Professional Bodies in the United Kingdom*, Oxford, Pergamon, 1980.

National Union of Teachers, *Treasure Chest for Teachers: Services Available to Teachers and Schools*, Kettering, 1984.

Oxford University Press (publisher), *Dictionary of National Biography:*

From Earliest Times to 1900, 22 vols, London, 1908–9.

Oxford University Press (publisher), *Dictionary of National Biography, 1901–80*, 8 vols, London, 1920–86.

Oxford University Press (publisher), *Concise Dictionary of National Biography*, 2 parts, London, 1906, 1982.

Pelham Books (publisher), *Pears Cyclopaedia*, London, annually.

Pemberton, J. E., *British Official Publications*, Oxford, Pergamon Press, 1973.

Richard, S., *Directory of British Official Publications: A Guide to Sources*, London Mansell, 1984.

Roberts, S., Cooper, A. and Gilder, L., *Research Libraries and Collections in the U.K.: A Selective Inventory and Guide*, London, Bingley, 1978.

Sheppard, J. and Foster, J., *British Archives: A Guide to Archive Resources in the United Kingdom*, London, Macmillan, 1984.

Stavely, R. and Piggott, M., *Government Information and the Research Worker*, London, Library Association, 1965.

Stevenson, B. (ed.), *Reader's Guide to Great Britain*, London, National Book League, 1977.

Thomas Skinner Directories (publisher), *Willing's Press Guide*, East Grinstead, annually.

Thorne, J. O. (ed.), *Chambers Biographical Dictionary*. 2 vols, London, Chambers, 1984.

Times Newspapers (publisher), *The Times Index*, London, annually.

University of Birmingham (publisher), *Bibliographical Information in the Social Sciences and Humanities. A Guide to the Periodical Sources*, Birmingham, 1978.

Walford, A. J. (ed.), *Guide to Reference Material. Vol. 1, Science and Technology*, London, Library Association, 1980.

Walford, A. J. (ed.), *Concise Guide to Reference Material*, London, Library Association, 1981.

Walford, A. J. (ed.), *Guide to Reference*

Material. Vol. 2, Social and Historical Sciences, Philosophy and Religion, London, Library Association, 1982.

Walford, A. J. (ed.), *Guide to Reference Material. Vol 3, Generalities, Languages, the Arts and Literature*, London, Library Association, 1987.

Walford, A. J. (ed.), *Guide to Current British Periodicals Vol. 1; Humanities and Social Sciences*, London, Library Association, 1985.

Walker, R., *First Clue: The A-Z of Finding Out*, London, Pan, 1983.

Whitaker (publisher), *British Books in Print*, London, annually.

Whitaker (publisher), *Publishers in the UK and their Addresses*, London, annually.

Whitaker (publisher), *Whitaker's Almanack*, London, annually.

Wilson (publisher), *Bibliographic Index: A Cumulative Bibliography of Bibliographies*, New York, annually.

2 BUILDINGS AND ARCHITECTURE

For bibliographical and reference guides to buildings and architecture in Britain see Colvin, H. M. (ed.), *English Architectural History: A Guide to the Sources*, 1976; Hall, R. De Z. (ed.), *A Bibliography of Vernacular Architecture*, 1972; Kamen, R. H., *British and Irish Architectural History: A Bibliography and Guide to Sources of Information*, 1981.

Guides and surveys covering architecture and historical buildings in England are provided by Pevsner, N. (ed.), *Buildings of England*, 46 vols, 1951–74; Richards, J. M., *The National Trust Book of English Architecture*, 1981.

The following provide authoritative surveys of British architectural history: Allsopp, B. and Clark, U., *English Architecture: An Introduction to the Architectural History of England from the Bronze Age to the Present Day*, 1979; Betjeman, J., *A Pictorial History of Ennglish Architecture*, 1972; Kidson, P. et al., *History of English Architecture*, 1965; Pragnell, H., *The Styles of English Architecture*, 1984, Richards, J. M., *The National Trust Book of English Architecture*, 1981; Watkin, D., *English Architecture: A Concise History*, 1979; Yarwood, D., *The Architecture of Britain*, 1976.

For introductory reading on particular areas of architecture the following can be recommended:

Castles   Johnson, *The National Trust Book of British Castles*, 1981; Sorrell, A., *British Castles*, 1973.

Cathedrals   Anderson, W. and Hicks, C., *Cathedrals in Britain and Ireland*, 1978; Clifton-Taylor, A., *The Cathedrals of England*, 1967.

Churches   Child, M., *English Church Architecture: A Visual Guide*, 1981; Ison, L. and Ison, W., *English Church Architecture through the Ages*, 1973.

Country Houses   Chamberlin, R., *Great English Houses*, 1983; Cook, O., *The English Country House*, 1974.

Houses and Cottages   Aslet, C. and Powers, A., *The National Trust Book of the English House*, 1985; Cook, O. and Smith, E., *The English House through Seven Centuries*, 1968; Evans, T. and Green, C. L., *English Cottages*, 1982.

REFERENCE

Colvin, H. M. (ed.), *English Architectural History: A Guide to the Sources*, London, Pinhorns, 1976.

Curl. J. S., *English Architecture: An Illustrated Glossary*, Newton Abbot, David and Charles, 1977.

Fedden, R. and Joekes, R., *The National Trust Guide*, London, Cape, 1977.

Fedden, R. (ed.), *Treasures of the National Trust*, London, Cape, 1976.

Fleming, J. et al. (eds), *The Penguin Dictionary of Architecture*, Harmondsworth, Penguin, 1970.

Hall, R. de Z. (ed.), *A Bibliography of Vernacular Architecture*, Newton Abbot, David and Charles, 1972.

Harvey, J., *English Medieval Architects: A Biographical Dictionary down to 1550*, Gloucester, Sutton, 1985.

Holmes, M. (comp.), *The Country*

House Described: An Index to the
Country Houses of Great Britain and
Ireland, London, Victoria and Albert
Museum, 1985.

Kamen, R. H., *British and Irish
Architectural History: A Bibliography
and Guide to Sources of Information*,

London, Architectural Press, 1981.

National Book League, *Books on
Historical Buildings and Places*,
London, NBL, 1975.

Pevsner, N. et al., *A Dictionary of
Architecture*, London, Allen Lane,
1975.

GENERAL

Airs, M., *Buildings of England: Tudor
and Jacobean*, London, Barrie and
Jenkins, 1982.

Allsopp, B. and Clark, U., *English
Architecture: An Introduction to the
Architectural History of England from
the Bronze Age to the Present Day*,
Stocksfield, Oriel Press, 1979.

Ayres, J., *The Shell Book of the Home
in Britain*, London, Faber, 1981.

Betjeman, Sir J., *A Pictorial History of
English Architecture*, London,
Murray, 1972.

Braun, H., *Introduction to English
Medieval Architecture*, London,
Faber, 1968.

Braun, H., *Elements of English
Architecture*, Newton Abbot, David
and Charles, 1973.

Brunskill, R. W., *An Illustrated Book of
Vernacular Architecture*, London,
Faber, 1978.

Burke, J., *The English Inn*, London,
Batsford, 1981.

Clark, Sir K., *The Gothic Revival: An
Essay in the History of Taste*,
London, Murray, 1974.

Clifton-Taylor, A., *The Pattern of
English Building*, London, Faber,
1972.

Dixon, R. and Muthesius, S., *Victorian
Architecture*, London, Thames and
Hudson, 1978.

Downes, K., *English Baroque
Architecture*, London, Zwemmer,
1966.

Eastlake, Sir C. L., *A History of the
Gothic Revival*, Leicester, Leicester
University Press, 1970 (reprint).

Esher, L., *A Broken Wave: The
Rebuilding of England, 1940–1980*,
Harmondsworth, Penguin, 1983.

Harvey, N., *A History of Farm Buildings
in England and Wales*, London,
Batsford, 1974.

Jackson, A., *The Politics of Architecture:
A History of Modern Architecture in
Britain*, London, Architectural Press,
1970.

Jordan, R. F., *Victorian Architecture*,
Harmondsworth, Penguin, 1966.

Kidson, P. et al., *History of English
Architecture*, Harmondsworth,
Penguin, 1965.

Landau, R., *New Directions in British
Architecture*, London, Studio Vista,
1968.

Lyall, S., *The State of British
Architecture*, London, Architectural
Press, 1980.

McIntyre, A., *The Shell Book of British
Buildings*, Newton Abbott, David and
Charles, 1983.

Macleod, R., *Style and Society:
Architectural Ideology in Britain,
1835–1914*, London, RIBA, 1971.

Maxwell, R., *New British Architecture*,
London, Thames and Hudson, 1972.

Morrice, R., *Buildings of England:
Stuart and Baroque*, London, Barrie
and Jenkins, 1982.

Murray, P. and Trombley, S. (eds),
*Modern British Architecture since
1945*, London, Muller, 1984.

Nellist, J. B., *British Architecture and its
Background*, London, Macmillan,
1967.

Norwich, J. J. (ed.), *Britain's Heritage*,
London, Granada, 1983.

Norwich, J. J., *The Architecture of
Southern England*, London,
Macmillan, 1985.

Pevsner, N. (ed.), *Bedfordshire and the
County of Huntingdon and*

Peterborough, Harmondsworth, Penguin, 1968, Buildings of England.

Pevsner, N. (ed.), *Berkshire*, Harmondsworth, Penguin, 1966, Buildings of England.

Pevsner, N. (ed.), *Buckinghamshire*, Harmondsworth, Penguin, 1960, Buildings of England.

Pevsner, N. (ed.), *Cambridgeshire*, Harmondsworth, Penguin, 1970, Buildings of England.

Pevsner, N. (ed.), *Cornwall*, Harmondsworth, Penguin, 1971, Buildings of England.

Pevsner, N. (ed.), *Cumberland and Westmorland*, Harmondsworth, Penguin, 1970, Buildings of England.

Pevsner, N. (ed.), *Derbyshire*, Harmondsworth, Penguin, 1978, Buildings of England.

Pevsner, N. (ed.), *Essex*, Harmondsworth, Penguin, 1974. Buildings of England.

Pevsner, N. (ed.), *Herefordshire*, Harmondsworth, Penguin, 1973, Buildings of England.

Pevsner, N. (ed.), *Hertfordshire*, Harmondsworth, Penguin, 1977, Buildings of England.

Pevsner, N. (ed.), *Leicestershire and Rutland*, Harmondsworth, Penguin, 1970, Buildings of England.

Pevsner, N. (ed.), *Lincolnshire*, Harmondsworth, Penguin, 1970, Buildings of England.

Pevsner, N. (ed.), *London, vol. 1., Cities of Westminster and London*, Harmondsworth, Penguin, 1973, Buildings of England.

Pevsner, N. (ed.), *North East Norfolk and Norwich*, Harmondsworth, Penguin, 1970, Buildings of England.

Pevsner, N. (ed.), *North Lancashire*, Harmondsworth, Penguin, 1969, Buildings of England.

Pevsner, N. (ed.), *North Somerset and Bristol*, Harmondsworth, Penguin, 1958, Buildings of England.

Pevsner, N. (ed.), *North West and South Norfolk*, Harmondsworth, Penguin, 1962, Buildings of England.

Pevsner, N. (ed.), *Northamptonshire*, Harmondsworth, Penguin, 1974, Buildings of England.

Pevsner, N. (ed.), *Northumberland*, Harmondsworth, Penguin, 1970, Buildings of England.

Pevsner, N. (ed.), *Nottinghamshire*, Harmondsworth, Penguin, 1979, Buildings of England.

Pevsner, N. (ed.), *Shropshire*, Harmondsworth, Penguin, 1958, Buildings of England.

Pevsner, N. (ed.), *South and West Somerset*, Harmondsworth, Penguin, 1958, Buildings of England.

Pevsner, N. (ed.), *South Lancashire*, Harmondsworth, Penguin, 1969, Buildings of England.

Pevsner, N. (ed.), *Staffordshire*, Harmondsworth, Penguin, 1974, Buildings of England.

Pevsner, N. (ed.), *Suffolk*, Harmondsworth, Penguin, 1975, Buildings of England.

Pevsner, N. (ed.), *Wiltshire*, Harmondsworth, Penguin, 1975, Buildings of England.

Pevsner, N. (ed.), *Worcestershire*, Harmondsworth, Penguin, 1970, Buildings of England.

Pevsner, N. (ed.), *Yorkshire: East Riding*, Harmondsworth, Penguin, 1972, Buildings of England.

Pevsner, N. (ed.), *Yorkshire: North Riding*, Harmondsworth, Penguin, 1970, Buildings of England.

Pevsner, N. (ed.), *Yorkshire: West Riding*, Harmondsworth, Penguin, 1970, Buildings of England.

Pevsner, N. and Hubbard, E. (eds), *Cheshire*, Harmondsworth, Penguin, 1971, Buildings of England.

Pevsner, N. and Nairn, I. (eds), *Surrey*, Harmondsworth, Penguin, 1971, Buildings of England.

Pevsner, N. and Nairn, I. (eds), *Sussex*, Harmondsworth, Penguin, 1970, Buildings of England.

Pevsner, N. and Newman, J. (eds), *Dorset*, Harmondsworth, Penguin, 1972, Buildings of England.

Pevsner, N. and Sherwood J. (eds), *Oxfordshire*, Harmondsworth, Penguin, 1974, Buildings of England.

Pevsner, N. and Wedgwood, A. (eds),

Warwickshire, Harmondsworth, Penguin, 1966, Buildings of England.

Pragnell, H., *The Styles of English Architecture*, London, Batsford, 1984.

Richards, J. M., *The National Trust Book of English Architecture*, London, Weidenfeld and Nicolson, 1981.

Service, A., *Edwardian Architecture and its Origins*, London, Architectural Press, 1978.

Service, A., *Buildings of Britain: Anglo-Saxon and Norman*, London, Barrie and Jenkins, 1982.

Summerson, Sir J. N., *Architecture in Britain, 1530–1830*, Harmondsworth, Penguin, 1969.

Taylor, H. M. and Taylor, J., *Anglo-Saxon Architecture*, Cambridge, Cambridge University Press, 1965.

Watkin, D., *English Architecture: A Concise History*, London, Thames and Hudson, 1979.

Watkin, D., *Buildings of England: Regency*, London, Barrie and Jenkins, 1982.

Webb, G., *Architecture in Britain: The Middle Ages*, Harmondsworth, Penguin, 1975.

Yarwood, D., *The Architecture of Britain*, London, Batsford, 1976.

Yarwood, D., *Outline of English Architecture*, London, Batsford, 1977.

CHURCH AND CATHEDRAL ARCHITECTURE

Anderson, W. and Hicks, C., *Cathedrals in Britain and Ireland from Early Times to the Reign of Henry VIII*, London, Macdonald and Jane's, 1978.

Betjeman, Sir J., *A Pocket Guide to English Parish Churches*, 2 vols, London, Collins, 1975.

Bony, J., *The English Decorated Style: Gothic Architecture Transported, 1250–1350*, Oxford, Phaidon, 1979.

Braun, H., *Parish Churches: Their Architectural Development in England*, London, Faber, 1970.

Braun, H., *English Abbeys*, London, Faber, 1971.

Butler, L. and Given-Wilson, C., *Medieval Monasteries of Great Britain*, London, Michael Joseph, 1979.

Child, M., *English Church Architecture: A Visual Guide*, London, Batsford, 1981.

Clifton-Taylor, A., *The Cathedrals of England*, London, Thames and Hudson, 1967.

Clifton-Taylor, A., *English Parish Churches as Works of Art*, London, Batsford, 1974.

Foster, R., *Discovering English Churches*, London, BBC, 1981.

Harvey, J., *The Cathedrals of England and Wales*, London, Batsford, 1974.

Hutton, G. and Cook, O., *English Parish Churches*, London, Thames and Hudson, 1976.

Ison, L. and Ison, W., *English Church Architecture through the Ages*, London, Barker, 1973.

Johnson, P., *British Cathedrals*, London, Weidenfeld and Nicolson, 1980.

Little, B., *Abbeys and Priories in England and Wales*, London, Batsford, 1979.

Morris, R., *Cathedrals and Abbeys of England and Wales*, London, Dent, 1979.

New, A., *A Guide to the Cathedrals of Britain*, London, Constable, 1980.

New, A., *A Guide to the Abbeys of England and Wales*, London, Constable, 1985.

Pevsner, N. and Metcalf, P., *The Cathedrals of England*, 2 vols, Harmondsworth, Viking, 1985.

Platt, C., *The Abbeys and Priories of Medieval England*, London, Secker and Warburg, 1984.

Spence, K., *Cathedrals and Abbeys of England and Wales*, London, Benn, 1985.

Thorold, H., *Collins Guide to the Cathedrals, Abbeys and Priories of England and Wales*, London, Collins, 1986.

CASTLES AND HOUSES

Adair, J. *Royal Palaces of Britain*, London, Thames and Hudson, 1981.

Addy, S. O., *The Evolution of the English Country House*, London, E. P. Publishing, 1975.

Aslet, C. and Powers, A., *The National Trust Book of the English House*, Harmondsworth, Viking, 1985.

Bailey, B., *English Manor Houses*, London, Hale, 1983.

Bence-Jones, M., *The National Trust Book of Ancestral Houses*, London, Weidenfeld and Nicolson, 1984.

Braun, H., *Old English Houses*, London, Faber, 1968.

Brown, R. J., *The English Country Cottage*, London, Hale, 1979.

Burton, N. (ed.), *The Historic Houses Handbook*, London, Macmillan, 1981.

Cave, L. F., *The Smaller English House: Its History and Development*, London, Hale, 1981.

Chamberlin, R., *Great English Houses*, London, Weidenfeld and Nicolson, 1983.

Colvin, H. M., *The History of the King's Works*, 6 vols, London, HMSO, 1963–73.

Colvin, H. M. and Harris, J. (eds), *The Country Seat: Studies in the History of the British Country House*, London, Allen Lane, 1970.

Cook, O., *The English Country House*, London, Thames and Hudson, 1974.

Cook, O., *English Cottages and Farmhouses*, London, Thames and Hudson, 1982.

Cook, O., *The English House through Seven Centuries*, Harmondsworth, Penguin, 1984.

Darley, G., *The National Trust Book of the Farm*, London, Weidenfeld and Nicolson, 1981.

Evans, T. and Green, C. L., *English Cottages*, London, Weidenfeld and Nicolson, 1982.

Fedden, R. and Kenworthy Browne, J. (eds), *The Country House Guide*, London, Cape, 1979.

Flower, S. J., *The Stately Homes of Britain*, London, Hamish Hamilton, 1982.

Gascoigne, C., *Castles of Britain*, London, Thames and Hudson, 1975.

Harris, J., *The Design of the English Country House*, London, Trefoil Books, 1985.

Her Majesty's Stationery Office, *Castles: England and Wales*, London, 1973.

Hogg, G., *Castles of England*, Newton Abbot, David and Charles, 1970.

Howard, P., *The Royal Palaces*, London, Hamish Hamilton, 1970.

Hussey, C., *English Country Houses*, 3 vols, London, Country Life, 1955–8.

Johnson, P., *The National Trust Book of British Castles*, London, Panther, 1981.

Mercer, E., *English Vernacular Houses: A Study of Traditional Farmhouses and Cottages*, London, HMSO, 1979.

Muthesius, S., *The English Terraced House*, New Haven, Yale University Press, 1982.

Nicolson, N., *The National Trust Book of Great Houses of Britain*, London, Weidenfeld and Nicolson, 1978.

Oliver, P. et al., *Dunroamin: The Suburban Semi and its Enemies*, London, Barrie and Jenkins, 1981.

Platt, C., *The Castle in Medieval England and Wales*, London, Secker and Warburg, 1981.

Powell, C., *Discovering Cottage Architecture*, Aylesbury, Shire Publications, 1984.

Quiney, A., *House and Home: A History of the Small English House*, London, BBC, 1986.

Reid, R., *The Shell Book of Cottages*, London, Michael Joseph, 1977.

Renn, D., *Norman Castles in Britain*, London, Black, 1973.

Royal Commission on Historical Monuments, *English Vernacular Houses: Study of Traditional Farmhouses and Cottages*, London, HMSO, 1980.

Simpson, W. D., *Castles in England and Wales*, London, Batsford, 1969.

Sorrell, A., *British Castles*, London, Batsford, 1973.

West, T., *The Timber Frame House in England*, Newton Abbot, David and Charles, 1970.

Wood, M., *The English Medieval House*, London, Ferndale Editions, 1983.

3 CITIES

The most accessible sources of information on local and municipal matters are the official handbooks, brochures and publicity material issued by city and town councils. These are available from press or publicity departments. For a list of city and town councils see pages 347–356.

In some cases lists on local affairs are provided by city libraries, (see pages 347–356) and local history societies and museums (see pages 438–453). Further possible sources of information are the chambers of commerce (see pages 347–356) and tourist information centres (see pages 428–430).

For municipal and urban history studies consult the reference works listed below.

REFERENCE

Gross, C., *A Bibliography of British Municipal History*, Leicester, Leicester University Press, 1966.

Helps, W. W. (ed.), *Urban and Regional Research: A Directory of Organisations*, London, Department of the Environment Library, 1978.

Martin, G. H. and McIntyre, S., *A Bibliography of British and Irish Municipal History*, Leicester, Leicester University Press, 1972.

Reeder, D. A. (ed.), *Urban History Yearbook*, Leicester, Leicester University Press, annually.

BATH

Coard, P., *Vanishing Bath*, Bath, Kingsmead Press, 1973.

Cunliffe, B. W., *Roman Bath Discovered*, London, Routledge & Kegan Paul, 1971.

Haddon, J., *Portrait of Bath*, London, Hale, 1982.

Little, B., *Bath Portrait: The Story of Bath, its Life and its Buildings*, Bristol, Burleigh Press, 1968.

Neale, R. S., *Bath, 1680–1850: A Social History*, London, Routledge & Kegan Paul, 1981.

Robertson, C., *Bath: An Architectural Guide*, London, Faber, 1975.

Sheppard, E. J., *Bath in the Eighteenth Century*, London, Longman, 1962.

Sitwell, E., *Bath*, Bristol, Redcliffe, 1983.

Whiteman, V., *Bath: City and Countryside*, Golden Hart Guide, Sidgwick and Jackson, 1984.

BELFAST

Bardon, J., *Belfast: An Illustrated History*, Belfast, Blackstaff Press, 1982.

Bardon, J. and Conlin, S., *Belfast: 1,000 Years*, Belfast, Blackstaff Press, 1985.

Beckett, J. C. and Glasscock, R. E. (eds), *Belfast: The Origin and Growth of an Industrial City*, London, BBC, 1967.

Ulster Museum, *The Changing Face of Belfast*, Belfast, 1968.

BIRMINGHAM

Allen, G. C., *The Industrial Development of Birmingham and the*

Black Country 1860–1927, London, Cass, 1966.

Bird, V., *Portrait of Birmingham*, London, Hale, 1979.

Brooks, J. A., *Birmingham Past and Present*, Norwich, Jarrold, 1969.

Dent, R. K., *Birmingham Old and New*, London, E.P. Publishing, 1973.

Eley, G. and Zuckerman, J., *Birmingham Heritage*, London, Croom Helm, 1979.

McKenna, J., *Birmingham As It Was*, Nelson, Hendon Publishing, 1979.

Newton, K., *Second City Politics: Democratic Process and Decision Making in Birmingham*, London, Oxford University Press, 1976.

Price, S., *Birmingham Old and New*, London, E.P. Publishing, 1976.

Sanders, J., *Birmingham*, London, Longman, 1969.

Sutcliffe, A. and Smith, R., *Birmingham, 1939–1970*, London, Oxford University Press, 1974.

Timmins, S. (ed.), *Birmingham and the Birmingham Hardware District*, London, Cass, 1967.

Whybrow, J. and Waterhouse, R., *How Birmingham Became a Great City*, Birmingham, J. Whybrow, 1976.

BRADFORD

Fieldhouse, J., *Bradford*, Bradford, P. Shardlow, 1978.

Hird, H., *Bradford in History*, Bradford, Horace Hirst, 1968.

Richardson, C., *Geography of Bradford*, University of Bradford, 1976.

Slack, M., *Portrait of West Yorkshire*, London, Hale, 1984.

Wright, D. G. and Jowitt, J. A., *Victorian Bradford*, Bradford, City of Bradford Metropolitan Libraries, 1982.

BRISTOL

Ballard, C. M., *Bristol: Sea Port City*, London, Constable, 1966.

Brace, K. *Portrait of Bristol*, London, Hale, 1976.

Gomme, A. H. et al., *Bristol: An Architectural History*, London, Lund Humphries, 1979.

Macinnes, C. M., *Bristol: Gateway of Empire*, Newton Abbot, David and Charles, 1968.

Shipside, F. and Eason, H., *Bristol: Profile of a City*, Bristol, Redcliffe Press, 1981.

Smith, B. S. and Ralph, E., *A History of Bristol and Gloucestershire*, Aylesbury, Phillimore, 1982.

Walker, F., *The Bristol Region*, London, Nelson, 1972.

Wells, C., *Bristol's History*, 2 vols, Bristol, R. Winstone, 1975–80.

CAMBRIDGE

Benstead, C. R., *Portrait of Cambridge*, London, Hale, 1968.

Gloucester, R. and Hobhouse, H., *Oxford and Cambridge*, London, Macdonald, 1980.

Grant, M., *Cambridge*, London, Weidenfeld and Nicolson, 1966.

Heaton, O. S. J., *The Colleges of Oxford and Cambridge*, London, Ariel Press, 1963.

Hedley, O., *Cambridge: The City and the Colleges*, London, Pitkin, 1971.

Mason, M., *Oxford and Cambridge, Blue Guide*, London, Benn, 1982.

Reeve, F. A., *Cambridge*, London, Batsford, 1976.

Sidgwick and Jackson, (publisher), *Cambridge*, Golden Hart Guide, London.

Tibbs, R., *University and Colleges of Cambridge*, Sudbury, T. Dalton, 1972.

CANTERBURY

Boyle, J., *Portrait of Canterbury*, London, Hale, 1980.

Church, R. T., *Portrait of Canterbury*, London, Hutchinson, 1968.

Keates, J. and Hurnack, A., *Canterbury Cathedral*, London, R. Wilson, 1980.

Moorman, J. R. H. et al., *Canterbury: Christian City of Pilgrims*, London, Pitkin, 1970.
Somner, W., *Antiquities of Canterbury*, London, E.P. Publishing, 1977.
Waddams, H. M., *City of Canterbury*, London, Pitkin, 1968.
Woodman, F., *Architectural History of Canterbury Cathedral*, London, Routledge & Kegan Paul, 1982.

CARDIFF

Dicks, B., *Portrait of Cardiff*, London, Hale, 1984.
Hilling, J. B., *Cardiff and the Valleys: Architecture and the Townscape*, London, Lund Humphries, 1973.
Rees, W., *Cardiff: A History of the City*, Cardiff Corporation, 1969.
Williams, S., *Cardiff Yesterday*, 3 vols, Barry, S. Williams, 1980–1.

CHESTER

Bethell, D., *A Portrait of Chester*, London, Hale, 1980.
Clopper, L. E. (ed.), *Chester*, Manchester, Manchester University Press, 1980.
Harris, B., *Chester*, Edinburgh, Bartholomew, 1979.
Jarmann, C. E., *Chester: Cathedral and City*, Norwich, Jarrold, 1975.
Mason, E. H., *The City of Chester*, London, Pitkin, 1963.
Thomas, H., *A Stranger's Handbook to Chester and its Environs*, Manchester, E. J. Morton, 1972.
Ward, T. E., *Chester as it Was*, Nelson, Hendon Publishing, 1980.

COVENTRY

Gilbert, V., *Coventry as it Was*, Nelson, Hendon Publishing, 1973.
Newbold, E., *Coventry Old and New*, London, E.P. Publishing, 1974.
Newbold, E., *Portrait of Coventry*, London, Hale, 1982.

Prest, J. M., *The Industrial Revolution in Coventry*, London, Oxford University Press, 1960.
Richardson, K., *Twentieth Century Coventry*, London, Macmillan, 1972.
Williams, H., *Guide to Coventry Cathedral*, Derby, English Life, 1980.

EDINBURGH

Armstrong, N., *Edinburgh As it Was*, Nelson, Hendon Publishing, 1977.
Barclay, J. B., *Edinburgh from the Earliest Times to the Present Day*, London, Black, 1965.
Birrell, J. F., *An Edinburgh Alphabet*, Edinburgh, Mercat Press, 1980.
Bruce, G., *The City of Edinburgh*, London, Pitkin, 1973.
Cameron, C. W., *Curiosities of Old Edinburgh*, Edinburgh, Albyn Press, 1975.
Catford, E. F., *Edinburgh: The Story of a City*, London, Hutchinson, 1975.
Chambers, R., *Traditions of Edinburgh*, Edinburgh, Chambers, 1967.
Cruft, C., *Edinburgh Old and New*, London, E.P. Publishing, 1975.
Daiches, D., *Edinburgh*, London, Hamish Hamilton, 1978.
Daiches, D., *Edinburgh: A Traveller's Companion*, London, Constable, 1986.
Gifford, J. et al., *Edinburgh, Buildings of Scotland*, Harmondsworth, Penguin, 1984.
Kersting, A. F., and Lindsay, M., *Buildings of Edinburgh*, London, Batsford, 1981.
Linklater, E., *Edinburgh*, London, Newnes, 1960.
Luger, K. and Lacombe, S., *Edinburgh Illustrated*, Edinburgh, Chambers, 1979.
Minto, C. S. and Armstrong, N., *Edinburgh Past and Present*, London, Oxford University Press, 1980.
Molendinar Press (publisher), *Discovering Edinburgh*, Glasgow, 1981.
Nimmo, I., *Portrait of Edinburgh*, London, Hale, 1975.

Pennycook, A., *Literary and Historical Landmarks of Edinburgh*, London, Albyn Press, 1973.

Ritchie, W. K., *Edinburgh in its Golden Age*, London, Longman, 1967.

Scott-Montcrieff, G., *Edinburgh*, Edinburgh, Oliver and Boyd, 1965.

Smith. W. G., *Edinburgh*, London, Collins, 1979.

EXETER

Barlow, F. (ed.), *Exeter and its Region*, Exeter, University of Exeter, 1969.

Hoskins, W. G., *Two Thousand Years in Exeter*, Chichester, Phillimore, 1969.

Little, B., *Portrait of Exeter*, London, Hale, 1983.

Thurmer, J., *Exeter: Cathedral and City*, Norwich, Jarrold, 1976.

GLASGOW

Barr, W., *Discovering Glasgow*, Glasgow, Molendinar Press, 1980.

Checkland, S. G., *The Upas Tree: Glasgow 1875–1975: A Study in Growth and Contraction*, Glasgow, University of Glasgow Press, 1976.

Corrance, D., *Glasgow*, London, Collins, 1981.

Daiches, D., *Glasgow*, London, Deutsch, 1977.

Doak, A. M. et al., *Glasgow at a Glance*, London, Hale, 1983.

Gibb, A., *Glasgow: The Making of a City*, London, Croom Helm, 1983.

Gomme, A. and Walker, D. W., *The Architecture of Glasgow*, London, Lund Humphries, 1968.

House, J., *Glasgow Old and New*, London, E.P. Publishing, 1974.

Lindsay, M., *Portrait of Glasgow*, London, Hale, 1981.

Moss, M. S. and Hume, J. R. (eds), *Glasgow as it Was*, 3 vols, Nelson, Hendon Publishing, 1975–6.

Oakley, C. A., *The Second City*, Glasgow, Blackie, 1975.

Young, A. M. and Doak, A. M. (eds), *Glasgow at a Glance: An Architectural Handbook*, Glasgow, Collins, 1965.

GLOUCESTER

Evans, S. J. A., *Gloucester Cathedral*, London, Pitkin, 1969.

Thurlow, G., *The City of Gloucester*, London, Pitkin, 1981.

Verey, D. and Welander, D., *Gloucester Cathedral*, Gloucester, A. J. Sutton, 1979.

HULL

Broadhead, I., *Portrait of Humberside*, London, Hale, 1983.

Calvert, H., *A History of Hull*, Chichester, Phillimore, 1978.

Gillet, E. and Macmahon, K. A., *A History of Hull*, Hull, Hull University Press, 1985.

LEEDS

Broadhead, I. E., *Exploring Leeds: A Guided Tour*, Warley, Tetradon Publications, 1981.

Feather, J. W., *Leeds: The Heart of Yorkshire*, Leeds, Basil Jackson Publications, 1967.

Fraser, D., *A History of Modern Leeds*, Manchester, Manchester University Press, 1982.

Nelson, B., *The Woollen Industry of Leeds*, Leeds, J. Thornton, 1980.

Nuttgens, P., *Leeds*, Otley, Stile, 1979.

Payne, B. and Payne, D., *Leeds As it Was*, Nelson, Hendon Publishing, 1974.

Thompson, B., *Portrait of Leeds*, London, Hale, 1971.

Thornton, J. *Picture Story of the City of Leeds*, Leeds, J. Thornton, 1983.

LEICESTER

Brown, A. E. (ed.), *The Growth of Leicester*, Leicester, Leicester University Press, 1970.

Elliot, M., *Leicester: A Pictorial History*, Chichester, Phillimore, 1984.

Ellis, C. D. B., *History in Leicester*, Leicester City Publicity Department, 1976.

Pye, N. (ed.), *Leicester and its Region*, Leicester, Leicester University Press, 1972.

Simmons, J., *Leicester, Past and Present*, 2 vols, London, Methuen, 1974.

LINCOLN

Dunlop, D. C., *Lincoln Cathedral*, London, Pitkin, 1959.

Elvin, L., *Lincoln as it Was*, Nelson, Hendon Publishing, 1981.

Hill, F., *Mediaeval Lincoln*, Cambridge, Cambridge University Press, 1948.

Hill, F., *Georgian Lincoln*, Cambridge, Cambridge University Press, 1966.

Hill, F., *Victorian Lincoln*, Cambridge, Cambridge University Press, 1974.

Hill, F., *City of Lincoln*, London, Pitkin, 1975.

LIVERPOOL

Bagley, J. J., *The Story of Merseyside*, 2 vols, Liverpool, Parry, 1968–9.

Body, G. (ed.), *Liverpool and Manchester; A Photographic Essay*, Weston-super-Mare, Avon Anglia Publications, 1980.

Brack, A., *Liverpool: The Official Book of the City*, Liverpool, City of Liverpool Public Relations Office, 1978.

Chandler, G., *An Illustrated History of Liverpool*, Liverpool, Rondo, 1972.

Channon, H., *Portrait of Liverpool*, London, Hale, 1976.

Harris, J. R. (ed.), *Liverpool and Merseyside: Essays in the Economic and Social History of the Port and its Hinterland*, London, Cass, 1969.

Hyde, F. E., *Liverpool and the Mersey: The Development of a Port, 1700–1970*, Newton Abbot, David and Charles, 1971.

Midwinter, E. C., *Old Liverpool*, Newton Abbot, David and Charles, 1971.

Muir, R., *A History of Liverpool*, Wakefield, S. R. Publishers 1970 (reprint).

Vigier, F., *Change and Apathy: Liverpool and Manchester during the Industrial Revolution*, London, MITP, 1971.

Waller, P., *Democracy and Sectarianism: The Political and Social History of Liverpool, 1868–1939*, Liverpool, Liverpool University Press, 1981.

LONDON

Aldous, T., *London's Villages*, London, Secker and Warburg, 1980.

Allison, R., *Greater London*, London, Hodder and Stoughton, 1978.

Ashley, M., *Life in Stuart London*, London, Batsford, 1964.

Barker, F. and Jackson, P., *London: 2000 Years of a City and its People*, London, Macmillan, 1983.

Barker, T. C. and Robbins, M., *A History of London Transport*, London, Allen and Unwin, 1976.

Barltrop, R. and Wolveridge, J., *The Muvver Tongue*, London, Journeyman Press, 1980.

Booker, C. and Green, C. L., *Goodbye London: An Illustrated Guide to its Threatened Buildings*, London, Collins, 1973.

Borer, M. C., *The City of London: A History*, London, Constable, 1977.

Bourne, R. *Londoners*, London, Dent, 1981.

Brooke, C. and Keir, G., *London, 800–1216: The Shaping of a City*, London, Secker and Warburg, 1975.

Brown, I. J. C., *London: An Illustrated History*, London, Studio Vista, 1965.

Buchanan, M. et al., *Transport Planning for Greater London*, Farnborough, Saxon House, 1980.

Clarke, N. and Evans, P., *London for Beginners*, London, Writers and Readers, 1984.

Clayton, R., *Portrait of London*, London, Hale, 1980.

Clout, H. (ed.), *Changing London*, Slough, University Tutorial Press, 1978.

Cunningham, P., *Handbook of London, Past and Present*, London, E.P. Publishing, 1978.

Dalzell, W. R., *Shell Guide to the History of London*, London, Michael Joseph, 1981.

Denney, M., *London's Waterways*, London, Batsford, 1977.

Donnison, D. and Eversley, G., *London: Urban Patterns, Problems and Policies*, London, Heinemann, 1973.

Eades, G. E., *Historic London: The Story of a City and its People*, London, Queen Anne Press, 1966.

Gardiner, G., *The Changing Life of London*, London, Stacey, 1973.

Gaunt, W., *London*, London, Batsford, 1961.

Gibson-Jarvie, R., *The City of London: A Financial and Commercial History*, Cambridge, Woodhead-Faulkner, 1979.

Gray, R., *A History of London*, London, Hutchinson, 1978.

Greater London Council, *Historic Buildings in London*, London, 1975.

Green, B., *London*, London, Oxford University Press, 1984.

Grimes, W. F., *The Excavation of Roman and Medieval London*, London, Routledge & Kegan Paul, 1968.

Hall, J. M., *London: Metropolis and Region*, London, Oxford University Press, 1976.

Hanson, M., *2000 Years of London: An Illustrated Survey*, London, Country Life, 1967.

Haynes, J., *London: A Pictorial History*, London, Batsford, 1969.

Hibbert, C., *London: the Biography of a City*, Harmondsworth, Penguin, 1980.

Jarvis, S., *Around the Historical City of London*, London, Bell and Hyman, 1981.

Jones, E. and Woodward, C., *Guide to the Architecture of London*, Weidenfeld and Nicolson, 1983.

Kent, W., *An Encyclopaedia of London*, London, Dent, 1970.

Manley, L., *London in the Age of Shakespeare*, London, Croom Helm, 1986.

Marcan, P. (ed.), *London's Local History: An Annotated Catalogue of Publications and Resources*, High Wycombe, Marcan Publications, 1983.

Marsden, P., *Roman London*, London, Thames and Hudson, 1980.

Merrifield, R., *The Roman City of London*, London, Benn, 1965.

Mitchell, R. J. and Leys, M. D. R., *A History of London Life*, London, Longman, 1958.

Mulgan, C., *London: An Illustrated History*, London, Arnold, 1979.

Museum of London, *Roman London*, London, HMSO, 1985.

Olsen, D., *The Growth of Victorian London*, Harmondsworth, Penguin, 1979.

Rayns, A. W., *The London Region*, London, Bell, 1971.

Rudé, G., *Hanoverian London, 1714–1808*, London, Secker and Warburg, 1971.

Service, A., *Architects of London and their Buildings from 1066 to the Present Day*, London, Architectural Press, 1979.

Sheppard, F., *London, 1808–1970: The Infernal Wen*, London, Secker and Warburg, 1971.

Summerson, J., *Georgian London*, Harmondsworth, Penguin, 1962.

Weightman, G. and Humphries, S., *The Making of Modern London, 1914–1939*, 2 vols, London, Sidgwick and Jackson, 1983–4.

Weinreb, B. and Hibbert, C. (eds), *The London Encyclopaedia*, London, Macmillan, 1984.

Williams, G. A., *Medieval London: From Commune to Capital*, London, Athlone, 1963.

Young, K. and Garside, P., *Metropolitan London: Politics and Urban Change, 1837–1981*, London, Arnold, 1982.

MANCHESTER

Archer, J. H. (ed.), *Art and Architecture of Victorian Manchester*, Manchester, Manchester University Press, 1985.

Aston, J., *A Picture of Manchester*, Manchester, E. J. Morton, 1969.

Atkins, P., *A Guide across Manchester*, Manchester, Civic Trust for the North West, 1976.

Body, G., (ed.), *Liverpool and Manchester: A Photographic Essay*, Weston-super-Mare, Avon Anglia Publications, 1980.

Frangopulo, N. J. (ed.), *Rich Inheritance: A Guide to the History of Manchester*, Manchester, Manchester Education Committee, 1962.

Kennedy, M., *Portrait of Manchester*, London, Hale, 1970.

Krieger, E., *Bygone Manchester*, Chichester, Phillimore, 1984.

Makepeace, C., *Manchester as it Was*, 5 vols, Nelson, Hendon Publishing, 1972–6.

Messinger, G. S., *Manchester in the Victorian Age: The Half-Known City*, Manchester, Manchester University Press, 1985.

Mullineux, F., *Manchester Old and New*, London, E.P. Publishing, 1975.

Sharp, D., *Manchester*, London, Studio Vista, 1969.

Thompson, W. H., *A History of Manchester to 1852*, Altrincham, Sherratt, 1968.

White, H. P. (ed.), *The Continuing Conurbation: Change and Development in Greater Manchester*, Aldershot, Gower, 1980.

NEWCASTLE UPON TYNE

Allsopp, B. and Clark, U., *Historic Architecture of Northumberland and Newcastle upon Tyne*, London, Routledge & Kegan Paul, 1977.

Bourne, H., *The History of Newcastle upon Tyne*, Newcastle upon Tyne, Graham, 1979.

Fraser, C. M. and Emsley, K., *Tyneside*, Newton Abbot, David and Charles, 1974.

Hepple, L., *A History of Northumberland and Newcastle upon Tyne*, Chichester, Phillimore, 1976.

McCord, N., *North East England: An Economic and Social History*, London, Batsford, 1979.

Middlebrook, S., *Newcastle upon Tyne: Its Growth and its Achievements*, Wakefield, S.P. Publishers, 1969.

NORWICH

Davis, J. F., *Norwich: A Market Town*, London, Oxford University Press, 1964.

Day, J. W., *Norwich through the Ages*, Ipswich, East Anglian Magazine, 1976.

Green, R. and Young, R. H. R., *Norwich: The Growth of a City*, Norwich Castle Museum.

Hepworth, P., *Norwich as it Was*, Nelson, Hendon Publishing, 1974.

Newcombe, L., *Historic Norwich*, Norwich, Cotman House, 1981.

Thurlow, G., *The City of Norwich*, London, Pitkin, 1970.

Thurlow, G., *Norwich Cathedral*, London, Pitkin, 1973.

NOTTINGHAM

Bryson, W. E., *Portrait of Nottingham*, London, Hale, 1982.

Church, R. A., *Economic and Social Change in a Midland Town: Victorian Nottingham 1815–1900*, London, Cass, 1966.

Denison, G. M., *Nottingham, Old and New*, London, E.P. Publishing, 1973.

Edwards, K. C. (ed.), *Nottingham and its Region*, Nottingham, British Association for the Advancement of Science, 1966.

Rogers, A. (ed.), *Approaches to Nottingham's History*, Nottingham, University of Nottingham, 1972.

Thomis, M. I., *Old Nottingham*, Newton Abbot, David and Charles, 1968.

Wood, A. C., *A History of Nottingham*, London, E.P. Publishing, 1971.

OXFORD

Ashdown, J. and Kersting, A., *The Buildings of Oxford*, London, Batsford, 1979.

Balsdon, D., *Oxford Now and Then*, London, Duckworth, 1970.

Cassell (publisher), *Berlitz Travel Guide to Oxford and Stratford*, London, 1981.

Cheetham, H., *Portrait of Oxford*, London, Hale 1971.

Cordeaux, E. H. and Merry, D. H., *A Bibliography of Printed Works relating to the City of Oxford*, Oxford, Oxford Historical Society, 1977.

Gaunt, W., *Oxford*, London, Batsford, 1965.

Gloucester, R. and Hobhouse, H., *Oxford and Cambridge*, London, Macdonald and Jane's, 1980.

Graham, M., *Oxford Old and New*, London, E.P. Publishing, 1976.

Green, V. H., *A History of Oxford University*, London, Batsford, 1974.

Heaton, O. S. J., *The Colleges of Oxford and Cambridge*, London, Ariel Press, 1963.

Heyworth, P., *The Oxford Guide to Oxford*, Oxford, Oxford University Press, 1981.

Hinton, D. A., *Oxford Buildings from Medieval to Modern*, Oxford, Ashmolean, 1977.

Hurst, H., *Oxford Topography*, Oxford, Oxford Historical Society, 1900.

Judge, C. W. (ed.), *Oxford Past and Present*, Oxford, Oxford University Press, 1972.

Mason, M., *Oxford and Cambridge, Blue Guide*, London, Benn, 1982.

Morris, J., *Oxford*, London, Oxford University Press, 1978.

Neville, R. G. and Sloggett, T., *Oxford as it Was*, Nelson, Hendon Publishing, 1979.

Rowse, A. L., *Oxford in the History of the Nation*, London, Weidenfeld and Nicolson, 1975.

Salter, H. E. (ed.), *Survey of Oxford*, 2 vols, Oxford, Oxford Historical Society, 1956–66.

Sidgwick and Jackson (publisher), *Oxford*, Golden Hart Guide, London.

Smith, C. G. (ed.), *Oxford and its Region*, London, Oxford University Press, 1982.

Thackrah, J. R., *The University Colleges of Oxford*, Sudbury, T. Dalton, 1981.

Trench, N. (ed.), *Oxford Guide*, London, Oxford University Press, 1979.

Ward, W. R., *Georgian Oxford*, Oxford, Oxford University Press, 1958.

Ward, W. R., *Victorian Oxford*, London, Cass, 1965.

Wood, A., *The History of the City of Oxford*, 3 vols, Oxford, Oxford Historical Society, 1889–99.

PLYMOUTH

Gili, C., *Plymouth: A New History*, 2 vols, Newton Abbot, David and Charles, 1966–79.

Trewin, J. C., *Portrait of Plymouth*, London, Hale, 1973.

PORTSMOUTH

Brown, R., *A Guide Book to Portsmouth and Southsea*, Portsmouth, Milestone Publications, 1982.

Brown, R., *Portsmouth Guidebook: An Historical Guide for Visitors*, Portsmouth, Milestone Publications, 1983.

Lipscomb, F. W., *Heritage of Sea Power: The Story of Portsmouth*, London, Hutchinson, 1967.

SHEFFIELD

Bunker, B., *Portrait of Sheffield*, London, Hale, 1972.

Derry, J., *The Story of Sheffield*, Ilkley, Scolar Press, 1971.

Harvey, P., *Sheffield*, Sheffield, Sheaf Publishing, 1980.

Hawson, H. K., *Sheffield: The Growth of a City, 1893–1926*, Sheffield, Northend, 1968.

Hinchcliffe, B. (ed.), *Sheffield as it Was*, Sheffield, Turntable Publications, 1974.

Pybus, S. M. (ed.), *Basic Books on Sheffield History*, Sheffield City Libraries, 1976.

Vickers, J. E., *Sheffield Old and New*, London, E.P. Publishing, 1980.

Vickers, J. E., *Popular History of Sheffield*, London, E.P. Publishing, 1982.

SOUTHAMPTON

Gadd, E. W. *The Changing Face of Southampton*, Southampton, P. Cave Publications, 1981.

Mason, C. M. and Witherick, M. E., *Dimensions of Change in a Growth Area: Southampton since 1960*, Aldershot, Gower Publishing, 1982.

Patterson, A., *History of Southampton*, 3 vols, University of Southampton, 1961–75.

Sandell, E., *Southampton Through the Ages: A Short History*, Southampton, Wilson, 1964.

Sandell, E, *Southampton Contrasts*, Southampton, G. F. Wilson, 1977.

Stovold, J., *Bygone Southampton*, Chichester, Phillimore, 1984.

STRATFORD-UPON-AVON

Bearman, R., *Stratford-upon-Avon as it Was*, Nelson, Hendon Publishing, 1979.

Fox, L., *Stratford Past and Present*, London, Oxford University Press, 1975.

Fox, L., *Stratford-upon-Avon*, Norwich, Jarrold, 1975.

Hall, M. and Frankl, E., *Stratford-upon-Avon and the Cotswolds*, Cambridge, Pevensey Press, 1982.

SWANSEA

Balchin, W. C. V., *Swansea and its Region*, Swansea, University College of Swansea, 1971.

Rogers, W. G., *A Pictorial History of Swansea*, Llandysul, Gomer Press, 1981.

WINCHESTER

Bussby, F., *Winchester Cathedral, 1079–1979*, Southampton, Paul Cave, 1979.

Turner, B. C., *Winchester, the Ancient Capital of England*, London, Pitkin, 1972.

Turner, B. C., *Winchester*, Southampton, Paul Cave, 1980.

Williamson, H. R., *Winchester, The Ancient Capital*, London, Muller, 1953.

Wymer, N., *The Story of Winchester*, London, Staples Press, 1955.

YORK

Aylmer, G. E. and Cant, R. E., *History of York Minster*, London, Oxford University Press, 1977.

Beckett, L. and Hornak, A., *York Minster*, London, Sotheby Parke Bernet, 1981.

Broadhead, I., *Walkabout York: A Guided Tour through a Historic City*, Warley, Tetradon Publications, 1980.

Butler, R. M., *Medieval York*, York, Sessions, 1982.

Drake, F., *Eboracum or the History and Antiquities of the City of York*, London, E.P. Publishing, 1978.

Feinstein, C. H. (ed.), *York, 1831–1981: 150 Years of Scientific Endeavour and Social Change*, York, Sessions, 1981.

Harvey, J., *York*, London, Batsford, 1975.

Horton, R. W., *The City of York*, London, Pitkin, 1971.

Hutchinson, J. and Palliser, D. M., *York City Guide*, Edinburgh, Bartholomew, 1980.

Nuttgens, P., *York: The Continuing City*, London, Faber, 1976.

Pocock, M., *York*, Clapham, Dalesman, 1971.

Royal Commission on the Historical Monuments of England, *York: Historic Buildings in the Central Area*, London, HMSO, 1981.

Shannon, J., *York City and Minster*, Jarrold, Norwich, Cotman, 1978.

Willis, R., *York as it Was*, Nelson, Hendon Publishing, 1973.

Willis, R., *York Past and Present*, London, Oxford University Press, 1980.

Willis, R., *Portrait of York*, London, Hale, 1982.

SEE ALSO:

11   Geography
38   Travel and Tourism in Britain

4 COMMONWEALTH AND EMPIRE

Information relating to research on the Commonwealth and Empire is provided in Central Office of Information, *The Commonwealth: A Guide to Material and Information Services*, 1977; Hewitt, A. R., *A Guide to Resources for Commonwealth Studies in London, Oxford and Cambridge*, 1957.

Checklists of bibliographical references can be found in: Flint, J. E., *Books on the British Empire and Commonwealth: A Guide for Students*, 1968; Gipson, L. H., *A Bibliographical Guide to the History of the British Empire, 1748–1776*, 1968; Halstead, J. P. and Porcari, S., *Modern European Imperialism: A Bibliography of Books and Articles, 1815–1972: Vol. 1, General and British Empire*, 1974; Keane, C. (ed.), *The Commonwealth: A Basic Annotated Bibliography*, 1974; Morrell, W. P., *British Overseas Expansion and the History of the Commonwealth: A Select Bibliography*, 1970; National Book League, *Reader's Guide to the Commonwealth*, 1971.

For more recent publications see British Library of Economic and Political Science, *A London Bibliography of the Social Sciences*, annually.

The standard manual for factual information on the Commonwealth is Foreign and Commonwealth Office, *A Year Book of the Commonwealth*, annually. See also, Commonwealth Secretariat, *Commonwealth Organisations*, 1985.

Suggested reading as introductions to the field: Bowle, J., *The Imperial Achievement: The Rise and Transformation of the British Empire*, 1974; Calder, A., *Revolutionary Empire: The Rise of the English-Speaking Empire from the Fifteenth Century to the 1780's*; Central Office of Information, *Britain and the Commonwealth*, 1977; Graham, G. S., *A Concise History of the British Empire*, 1970; Hall, H. D., *Commonwealth: A History of the British Commonwealth of Nations*, 1971; Hussey, W. D., *The British Empire and Commonwealth, 1500–1961*, 1963; Lloyd, T. O., *The British Empire, 1558–1983*, 1984; Mansergh, N., *The Commonwealth Experience*, 2 vols, 1982; Williamson, J. A., *A Short History of British Expansion*, 2 vols, 1964.

The following are comprehensive scholarly studies of the British Empire: Gipson, L. H., *The British Empire before the American Revolution*, 1936–61; Rose, J. H. et al. (eds), *The Cambridge History of the British Empire*, 8 vols, 1929–59.

For analyses of the present-day Commonwealth see Groom, A. J. R. and Taylor, P. (eds), *The Commonwealth in the 1980's*, 1984.

REFERENCE

British Library of Economic and Political Science, *A London Bibliography of the Social Sciences*, London and New York, Mansell, annually.

Central Office of Information, *The Commonwealth: A Guide to Material and Information Services*, London, HMSO, 1977.

Commonwealth Institute, *Annual Report*, London, annually.

Commonwealth Secretariat (publisher), *Commonwealth Organisations*, London, 1985.

Commonwealth Secretariat (publisher), *Commonwealth Factbook: Facts and Figures About Commonwealth*

Countries, London, 1985.

Flint, J. E., *Books on the British Empire and Commonwealth: A Guide for Students*, London, Oxford University Press, 1968.

Foreign and Commonwealth Office, *Year Book of the Commonwealth*, London, HMSO, annually.

Gipson, L. H., *A Bibliographical Guide to the History of the British Empire, 1748–1776*, New York, Knopf, 1968.

Halstead, J. P. and Porcari, S., *Modern European Imperialism: A Bibliography of Books and Articles, 1815–1972: Vol. 1, General and British Empire*, Boston, Mass., Hall, 1974.

Hewitt, A. R. (comp.), *A Guide to Resources for Commonwealth Studies in London, Oxford and Cambridge*, London, Athlone Press, 1957.

Keane, C. (ed.), *The Commonwealth: A Basic Annotated Bibliography*, London, Commonwealth Institute, 1974.

Morrell, W. P., *British Overseas Expansion and the History of the Commonwealth: A Select Bibliography*, London, Historical Association, 1970.

National Book League, *Reader's Guide to the Commonwealth*, London, National Book League, 1971.

GENERAL

Barker, E., *The Ideas and Ideals of the British Empire*, London, Greenwood Press, 1951 (reprint).

Blackburne, K., *Lasting Legacy: A Story of British Colonialism*, London, Johnson Publications, 1976.

Bolton, G., *Britain's Legacy Overseas*, London, Oxford University Press, 1973.

Bowle, J., *The English Experience*, London, Weidenfeld and Nicolson, 1971.

Carrington, C. E., *The British Overseas: Exploits of a Nation of Shopkeepers*, Cambridge, Cambridge University Press, 1968.

Central Office of Information, *Britain and the Process of Decolonisation*, London, HMSO, 1970.

Central Office of Information, *Britain's Associated States and Dependencies*, London, HMSO, 1972.

Dawson, R. M., *The Development of Dominion Status, 1900–1936*, London, Cass, 1965.

Edelstein, M., *Overseas Investment in the Age of High Imperialism*, London, Methuen, 1982.

Griffiths, Sir, P., *Empire into Commonwealth*, London, Benn, 1969.

Gupta, P. S., *Imperialism and the British Labour Movement, 1914–1964*, London, Macmillan, 1975.

Hall, H. P., *A History of England and the Empire Commonwealth*, Chichester, Wiley, 1971.

Hussey, W. D., *The British Empire and Commonwealth, 1500–1961*, Cambridge, Cambridge University Press, 1963.

Hyam, R. and Martin, G., *Reappraisals of British Imperial History*, London, Macmillan, 1975.

Kahler, M., *Decolonisation in Britain and France: The Domestic Consequences of International Relations*, Princeton, University of Princeton Press, 1984.

Knaplund, P., *Commonwealth and Empire, 1901–1955*, London, Greenwood Press, 1956.

Knorr, K., *British Colonial Theories, 1570–1850*, London, Cass, 1963.

Koebner, R. and Schmidt, H. D., *Imperialism: The Story and Significance of a Political Word, 1840–1960*, Cambridge, Cambridge University Press, 1964.

Louis, W. R., *Imperialism at Bay: Britain, the US and the Decolonisation of the British Empire*, Oxford, Clarendon Press, 1977.

Lowe, C. J. (ed.), *The Reluctant Imperialists: British Foreign Policy 1878–1902*, 2 vols, London, Routledge & Kegan Paul, 1967.

Mackenzie, J. M., *Propaganda and*

Empire: The Manipulation of British Public Opinion, 1880–1960, Manchester, Manchester University Press, 1984.

Morrell, W. P., *British Colonial Policy in the Mid-Victorian Age*, London, Oxford University Press, 1969.

Perham, M., *The Colonial Reckoning*, London, Greenwood Press, 1977.

Perry, G. and Mason, N., *Rule Britannia*, London, Times Books, 1974.

Semmel, B., *Imperialism and Social Reform: English Social Imperial Thought, 1895–1914*, London, Allen and Unwin, 1960.

Thornton, A. P., *Doctrines of Imperialism*, New York, Wiley, 1965.

Thornton, A. P., *The Imperial Idea and its Enemies: A Study in British Power*, London, Macmillan, 1985.

Williamson, J. A., *A Short History of British Expansion*, 2 vols, London, Macmillan, 1964.

Winks, R. W. (ed.), *The Historiography of the British Empire Commonwealth: Trends, Interpretations and Resources*, Durham, N. C., Duke University Press, 1966.

Woodcock, G., *Who Killed the British Empire?*, London, Cape, 1974.

COMMONWEALTH

Arnold, G., *Economic Cooperation in the Commonwealth*, Oxford, Pergamon Press, 1967.

Central Office of Information, *Britain and the Commonwealth*, London, HMSO, 1977.

Chadwick, J., *The Unofficial Commonwealth: The Story of the Commonwealth Foundation, 1965–1980*, London, Allen and Unwin, 1983.

Cook, C. and Paxton, J., *Commonwealth Political Facts*, London, Macmillan, 1979.

Cumpston, I. M., *The Growth of the Political Commonwealth, 1880–1932*, London, Arnold, 1973.

Dale, W., *The Modern Commonwealth*, London, Butterworth, 1983.

Dartford, G. P., *The Growth of the British Commonwealth*, 2 parts, London, Longman, 1966.

Darwin, J., *Britain and Decolonisation, 1945–65*, London, Macmillan, 1985.

Groom, A. J. R., and Taylor, P. (eds), *The Commonwealth in the 1980's*, London, Macmillan, 1984.

Harris, P. B., *The Commonwealth*, London, Longman, 1975.

Holland, R. F., *Britain and the Commonwealth Alliance, 1918–1939*, London, Macmillan, 1981.

Jennings, Sir W. I., *The Constitutional Laws of the Commonwealth*, Oxford, Clarendon Press, 1957.

Jennings, Sir W. I., *The British Commonwealth of Nations*, London, Greenwood Press, 1979.

Judd, D. and Slinn, P., *The Evolution of the Modern Commonwealth, 1902–80*, London, Macmillan, 1982.

McIntyre, W. D., *Commonwealth of Nations: Origins and Impact 1869–1971*, Oxford, Oxford University Press, 1978.

Mansergh, N., *The Commonwealth Experience*, 2 vols, London, Macmillan, 1982.

Miller, J. D. M., *Survey of Commonwealth Affairs: Problems of Expansion and Attrition, 1953–1969*, London, Oxford University Press, 1974.

Oppenheimer, H., *The Fading Commonwealth*, Cambridge, Cambridge University Press, 1968.

Rendell, W., *A History of the Commonwealth Development Corporation*, London, Heinemann, 1976.

Walker, P. G., *The Commonwealth*, London, Secker and Warburg, 1965.

Wheare, K. C., *The Constitutional Structure of the Commonwealth*, London, Greenwood Press, 1982.

Wiseman, H. V., *Britain and the Commonwealth*, London, Allen and Unwin, 1965.

EMPIRE

Barclay, G., *The Empire is Marching: A Study of the Military Effort of the British Empire, 1800–1945*, London, Weidenfeld and Nicolson, 1976.

Beloff, M., *Imperial Sunset: Britain's Liberal Empire, 1897–1921*, London, Methuen, 1969.

Bodelsen, C. A. G., *Studies in Mid-Victorian Imperialism*, Copenhagen, Scandinavian University Books, 1960.

Bowle, J., *The Imperial Achievement: The Rise and Transformation of the British Empire*, London, Secker and Warburg, 1974.

Calder, A., *Revolutionary Empire: The Rise of the English-Speaking Empire from the Fifteenth Century to the 1780's*, London, Cape, 1981.

Constantine, S., *The Making of British Colonial Development Policy, 1914–1940*, London, Cass, 1984.

Cross, C., *The Fall of the British Empire, 1918–1968*, Sevenoaks, Hodder and Stoughton, 1968.

Eldridge, C. C., *England's Mission: The Imperial Idea in the Age of Gladstone and Disraeli, 1868–1880*, London, Macmillan, 1973.

Eldridge, C. C., *Victorian Imperialism*, Sevenoaks, Hodder and Stoughton, 1978.

Eldridge, C. C. (ed.), *British Imperialism in the Nineteenth Century*, London, Macmillan, 1984.

Faber, R., *The Vision and the Need: Late Victorian Imperialist Aims*, London, Faber, 1966.

Gallagher, J., *The Decline, Revival and Fall of the British Empire*, Cambridge, Cambridge University Press, 1982.

Gardiner, L. R. and Davidson, J. H., *British Imperialism in the Late Nineteenth Century*, London, Arnold, 1968.

Gipson, L. H., *The British Empire before the American Revolution*, 4 vols, New York, Caldwell, Idaho, Caxton, 1936–61.

Graham, G. S., *A Concise History of the British Empire*, London, Thames and Hudson, 1970.

Harlow, V. T., *The Founding of the Second British Empire, 1763–93*, 2 vols, London, Longman, 1952–64.

Hyam, R. and Martin, G., *Reappraisals in British Imperial History*, London, Macmillan, 1975.

Hyam, R., *Britain's Imperial Century: A Study of Empire and Expansion, 1815–1914*, London, Batsford, 1976.

Knowles, L. C. A. and Knowles, C. M., *The Economic Development of the British Overseas Empire*, 3 vols, London, Routledge & Kegan Paul, 1924–36.

Lloyd, T. O., *The British Empire, 1558–1983*, London, Oxford University Press, 1984.

Louis, W. R., *Imperialism at Bay: The United States and the Decolonisation of the British Empire, 1941–1945*, Oxford, Oxford University Press, 1977.

Martel, G. (ed.), *Studies in British Imperial History*, London, Macmillan, 1985.

Morgan, D. J., *The Official History of Colonial Development*, 5 vols, London, Macmillan, 1980.

Morris, J., *Heaven's Command: An Imperial Progress*, Harmondsworth, Penguin, 1979.

Morris, J., *Pax Britannica: The Climax of an Empire*, Harmondsworth, Penguin, 1979.

Morris, J., *Farewell the Trumpets: An Imperial Retreat*, Harmondsworth, Penguin, 1979.

Porter, B., *The Lion's Share: A Short History of British Imperialism, 1850–1970*, London, Longman, 1984.

Quinn, D. B. and Quinn, A. N., *England's Sea Empire*, London, Allen and Unwin, 1984.

Rich, P. B., *Race and Empire in British Politics*, Cambridge, Cambridge University Press, 1986.

Rose, J. H. et al. (eds), *The Cambridge History of the British Empire*, 8 vols, Cambridge, Cambridge University Press, 1929–59.

Semmel, B., *The Rise of Free Trade Imperialism: Classical Political Economy, the Empire of Free Trade and Imperialism, 1750–1850*, Cambridge, Cambridge University Press, 1970.

Shannon, R., *The Crisis of Imperialism, 1965–1915*, London, Paladin, 1979.

Townsend, P., *The Last Emperor: Decline and Fall of the British Empire*, London, Weidenfeld and Nicolson, 1975.

Ward, J. M., *Colonial Self-Government: The British Experience, 1759–1856*, London, Macmillan, 1976.

Winks, R. W. (ed.), *British Imperialism: Gold, God, Glory*, New York, Holt, Rinehart and Winston, 1963.

Winks, R. W., *Failed Federations: Decolonisation and the British Empire*, Nottingham, University of Nottingham Press, 1970.

SEE ALSO:

10   Foreign Policy
13   History
18   Military
19   Minorities
31   Social and Economic History

5 CUSTOMS, TRADITIONS AND FOLKLORE

For bibliographical references in the general area of folklore and folklore studies see Bonser, W., *A Bibliography of Folklore, 1878–1957*, 1961; Bonser, W., *A Bibliography of Folklore, 1958–1967*, 1969.

The following books are recommended for introductory and general coverage: Alexander, M., *British Folklore and Custom of Rural England*, 1975; Baker, M., *Folklore and Customs of Rural England*, 1974; Hogg, G., *Customs and Traditions of England*, 1971; Hole, C., *British Folk Customs*, 1976; Reader's Digest, *Folklore, Myth and Legends of Britain*, 1977; Smith, D. and Newton, D., *British Customs and Festivals*, 1969; Whitlock, R., *In Search of Lost Gods: A Guide to British Folklore*, 1979.

Information on particular fields can be found in the following:

Ceremonies and Pageants   Milton, R., *The English Ceremonial Book: A History of Orders, Insignia and Ceremonies still in Use in England*, 1972.

Crafts   Jones, J. L., *Crafts from the Countryside*, 1975; Manners, J. E., *Country Crafts Today*, 1974.

Festivals   Trent, C., *The B. P. Book of Festivals and Events in Britain*, 1983.

Folk Customs   Alexander, M., *British Folklore and Customs of Rural England*, 1975; Hole, C., *A Dictionary of British Folk Customs*, 1978.

Folk Tales   Briggs, K. M., *A Dictionary of British Folk Tales in the English Language*, 1971–2.

Legends   Alexander, M., *Enchanted Britain: British Folklore, Myths and Legends*, 1982; Reader's Digest, *Folklore, Myths and Legends of Britain*, 1977.

REFERENCE

Black (publisher), *Titles and Forms of Address: A Guide to their Correct Use*, London, 1981.

Bonser, W., *A Bibliography of Folklore, 1878–1957*, London, Folklore Society, 1961.

Bonser, W., *A Bibliography of Folklore, 1958–67*, London, Folklore Society, 1969.

Cambridge University Press (publisher), *The Cambridge Illustrated Dictionary of British Heritage*, Cambridge, 1986.

Cunnington, C. W. et al., *A Dictionary of English Costume*, London, Black, 1960.

Hole, C., *A Dictionary of British Folk Customs*, London, Paladin, 1978.

Macfadyen, D. and Hole, C., *Folk Customs of Britain: A Gazetteer and Travellers' Companion*, London, Hutchinson, 1983.

Montague-Smith, P. (ed.), *Correct Form*, Debrett's Peerage, Kingston-upon-Thames, 1978.

Trent, C., *The B.P. Book of Festivals and Events in Britain*, London, Phoenix House, 1983.

GENERAL

Ayrton, E., *The Cookery of England*, London, Deutsch, 1975.

Brand, J., *Brand's Popular Antiquities of Great Britain*, New York, Bloom, 1967 (reprint).

Briggs, K. M., *British Folk Tales and Legends: A Sampler*, London, Routledge & Kegan Paul, 1977.

Briggs, K. M., *A Dictionary of British Folk-Tales*, 4 vols, London, Routledge & Kegan Paul, 1985.

Brooke, I., *English Costume*, 7 vols, London, Black, 1935–50.

Brooke, I., *A History of English Costume*, London, Methuen, 1979.

Bushaway, B., *By Rite: Custom, Ceremony and Community in England, 1700–1880*, London, Junction Books, 1983.

Driver, C., *The British at Table, 1940–1980*, London, Chatto and Windus, 1983.

Fearn, J., *Discovering Heraldry*, Aylesbury, Shire Publications, 1980.

Halliwell, J. C., *The Nursery Rhymes of England*, London, Bodley Head, 1970.

Harrowven, J., *The Origins of Rhymes, Songs and Sayings*, London, Kaye and Ward, 1980.

Hogg, G., *Facets of the English Scene*, Newton Abbot, David and Charles, 1973.

Jackson, M., *The English Pub: A Unique Social Phenomenon*, London, Collins, 1976.

Marshall, S., *Everyman's Book of English Folk-Tales*, London, Dent, 1981.

Milton, R., *The English Ceremonial Book: A History of Orders, Insignia and Ceremonies still in Use in England*, Newton Abbot, David and Charles, 1972.

Mossman, K., *The Shell Book of Rural Britain*, Newton Abbot, David and Charles, 1978.

Opie, I. and Opie, P., *The Lore and Language of School Children*, London, Oxford University Press, 1959.

Opie, I. and Opie, P., *Children's Games in Street and Playground*, London, Oxford University Press, 1969.

Opie, I. and Opie, P., *The Oxford Dictionary of Nursery Rhymes*, Oxford, Clarendon Press, 1977.

Paget, J., *The Pageantry of Britain*, London, Michael Joseph, 1979.

Sauvain, P. A., *Britain's Living Heritage*, London, Batsford, 1982.

Senior, M., *Myths of Britain*, London, Orbis Publishing, 1979.

Yarwood, D., *English Costume from the Second Century BC to the Present Day*, London, Batsford, 1973.

FOLKLORE

Alexander, M., *British Folklore and Custom of Rural England*, Newton Abbot, David and Charles, 1975.

Alexander, M., *Enchanted Britain: British Folklore, Myths and Legends*, London, Weidenfeld and Nicolson, 1982.

Bord, C. and Bord, J., *The Secret Country: An Interpretation of the Folklore of Ancient Sites in the British Isles*, London, Paladin, 1978.

E. P. Publishing (publisher), *Folklore and Legends of England*, London, 1972.

Grinsell, L. V., *Folklore of Prehistoric Sites in Britain*, Newton Abbot, David and Charles, 1976.

Grinsell, L. V., *Legends, History and Folklore of Stonehenge*, Newton Abbot, David and Charles, 1976.

Reader's Digest (publisher), *Folklore, Myths and Legends of Britain*, London, 1977.

Rhys, J., *Celtic Folklore*, 2 vols, Hounslow, Wildwood House, 1980.

Whitlock, R., *In Search of Lost Gods: A Guide to British Folklore*, Oxford, Phaidon, 1979.

TRADITIONS

Arnold, J., *The Shell Book of Country Crafts*, London, Black, 1968.

Bradfield, N., *Historical Costumes of England 1066–1968*, London, Harrap, 1985.

Gascoigne, M., *Discovering English Customs and Traditions*, Aylesbury, Shire Publications, 1980.

Gomme, A. B., *Traditional Games of England, Scotland and Ireland*, 2 vols, New York, Dover, 1964.

Hogg, G., *Customs and Traditions of England*, Newton Abbot, David and Charles, 1971.

Hole, C., *Christmas and its Customs*, London, Richard Bell, 1957.

Hole, C., *Easter and its Customs*, London, Richard Bell, 1961.

Hole, C., *English Traditional Customs*, London, Batsford, 1975.

Hole, C., *British Folk Customs*, London, Hutchinson, 1976.

Jenkins, J. G., *Traditional Country Craftsmen*, London, Routledge & Kegan Paul, 1979.

Jones, J. L., *Crafts from the Countryside*, Newton Abbot, David and Charles, 1975.

Knightly, C., *The Customs and Ceremonies of Britain: An Encyclopaedia of Living Traditions*, London, Thames and Hudson, 1986.

Manners, J. E., *Country Crafts Today*, Newton Abbot, David and Charles, 1974.

Mansfield, A., *Ceremonial Costume: Court, Civil and Civic Costume from 1660 to the Present Day*, London, Black, 1980.

Milton, R., *The English Ceremonial Book*, Newton Abbot, David and Charles, 1972.

Paston-Williams, S., *The National Trust Book of Christmas and Festive Days*, Harmondsworth, Penguin, 1983.

Pine, L. G., *Tradition and Custom in Modern Britain*, London, Whiting, 1967.

Rippon, H., *Discovering English Folk Dance*, Aylesbury, Shire Publications, 1981.

Seager, E. (ed.), *The Countryman Book of Village Trades and Crafts*, Newton Abbot, David and Charles, 1978.

Sykes, H., *Once a Year: Some Traditional Customs*, London, Gordon Fraser Gallery, 1977.

Whitlock, R., *A Calendar of Country Customs*, London, Batsford, 1978.

SEE ALSO:

34   Sport and Leisure

6 ECONOMICS AND FINANCE

Checklists of bibliographical references on the British economy are available in Smith, G. M. (ed.), *Britain in Decline? A Select Bibliography*, 1980; Oxford University Press, *A Bibliography for Students of Economics*, 1968. For more recent publications readers should refer to British Library of Economic and Political Science, *A London Bibliography of the Social Sciences*, annually; G. K. Hall (publisher), *Bibliographic Guide to Business and Economics*, annually.

Current information and bibliographical references can be found in the following general surveys and studies of the British economy: Aaronovitch, S., *Political Economy of British Capitalism: A Marxist Analysis*, 1981; Black, N., *Economic Organisation of Modern Britain*, 1979; Cairncross, F. and Keeley, P., *The Guardian Guide to the Economy*, 1981; Cairncross, F. and Keeley, P., *The Guardian Guide to the Economy vol. 3*, 1987; Caves, R. and Krause, L., *Britain's Economic Performance*, 1980; Eatwell, J., *Whatever Happened to Britain? The Economics of Decline*, 1982; Holden, K. et al., *Modelling the U.K. Economy: An Introduction*, 1982; Morris, D. (ed.), *The Economic System in the U.K.*, 1984; Peston, M. H., *The British Economy*, 1982; Prest, A. R. and Coppock, D. J. (eds), *The U.K. Economy: A Manual of Applied Economics*, 1984; National Institute of Economic and Social Research, *The United Kingdom Economy*, 1982.

Readers are directed to the following studies for introductory discussions of specialised areas and problems:

Banking Anderson, B. L. and Cottrell, P. L. (eds), *Money and Banking in England*, 1974; Bank of England, *A Brief Introduction to the Bank of England*, 1980; Central Office of Information, *The British Banking System*, 1970; Hanson, D. G., *Service Banking: A Commentary on Bank Services in the U.K.*, 1979.

Economic and Fiscal Administration Artis, M., *Monetary Control in the United Kingdom*, 1981; Budd, A., *The Politics of Economic Planning*, 1978; Central Office of Information, *The British System of Taxation*, 1977; Gamble, A. and Walkland, S. A., *The British Party System and Economic Policy, 1945–1983*, 1984; Grant, W. and Nath, S., *The Politics of Economic Policy-Making*, 1984; Hare, P. and Kirby, M. (eds), *An Introduction to British Economic Policy*, 1984; Hockley, G. C., *Public Finance*, 1979; Keegan, W. and Pennant-Rea, R., *Who Runs the Economy? Control and Influence in British Economic Policy*, 1979; Wright, M. (ed.), *Public Spending Decisions*, 1980.

Economic Performance Alt, J. E., *The Politics of Economic Decline*, 1979; Bacon, R. and Eltis, W., *Britain's Economic Problem: Too Few Producers*, 1978; Beckerman, W. (ed.), *Slow Growth in Britain: Causes and Consequences*, 1979; Eatwell, J., *Whatever Happened to Britain? The Economics of Decline*, 1982; Gamble, A., *Britain in Decline*, 1981; Pollard, S., *The Wasting of the British Economy: British Policy, 1945 to the Present*, 1982.

Finance and the City Coggan, P., *The Money Machine: How the City Works*, 1986; Committee to Review the Functioning of Financial Institutions, *Report*,

1980; Davies, B., *Business Finance and the City*, 1982; McRae, H. and Cairncross, F., *Capital City: London as a Financial Centre*, 1984; Ritchie, N., *What Goes on in the City?*, 1981; Shaw, E. R., *The London Money Market*, 1981.

REFERENCE

Bannock, G., *The Penguin Dictionary of Economics*, Harmondsworth, Penguin, 1972.

British Library of Economic and Political Science, *A London Bibliography of the Social Sciences*, London and New York, Mansell, annually.

Burgess, N., *How to Find out about Banking and Investment*, Oxford, Pergamon Press, 1969.

Butcher, D., *Official Publications in Britain*, London, Bingley, 1982.

Central Statistical Office, *Economic Trends*, London, HMSO, annually.

Central Statistical Office, *Regional Trends*, London, HMSO, annually.

Central Statistical Office, *Social Trends*, London, HMSO, annually.

Central Statistical Office, *United Kingdom Balance of Payments: The Pink Book*, London, HMSO, annually.

Central Statistical Office, *United Kingdom National Accounts: The Blue Book*, London, HMSO, annually.

Fletcher, J. (ed.), *The Use of Economic Literature*, London, Butterworth, 1971.

Government Statistical Service, *Government Statistics: A Brief Guide to Sources*, London, HMSO, 1977.

Gower Press (publisher), *Who's Who in Finance*, London, 1975.

G. K. Hall (publisher), *Bibliographic Guide to Business and Economics*, Boston, Mass., annually.

Her Majesty's Stationery Office, *Annual Abstract of Statistics*, London, annually.

Her Majesty's Stationery Office, *Guide to Official Statistics*, London, annually.

Her Majesty's Stationery Office, *Inland Revenue Statistics*, London, annually.

London and Cambridge Economic Service, *The British Economy: Key Statistics, 1900–1970*, London, Times Publishing, 1973.

Maltby, A., *Economics and Commerce: The Sources of Information and Their Organisation*, London, Bingley, 1968.

Oxford University Press, *A Bibliography for Students of Economics*, London, 1968.

Parsons, S. A. J., *How to Find out about Economics*, Oxford, Pergamon Press, 1972.

Smith, G. M. (ed.), *Britain in Decline? A Select Bibliography*, Cleveland, Headland Publishing, 1980.

GENERAL

Aaronovitch, S., *Political Economy of British Capitalism: A Marxist Analysis*, Maidenhead, McGraw-Hill, 1981.

Backhouse, R., *Macroeconomics and the British Economy*, Oxford, Blackwell, 1983.

Bain, A. D., *The Economics of the Financial System*, Oxford, Martin Robertson, 1981.

Bellini, J., *Rule Britannia: A Progress Report for Domesday*, London, Cape, 1981.

Britton, A. (ed.), *Employment, Output and Inflation: The National Institute Model of the British Economy*, London, Heinemann, 1983.

Cairncross, A. K., *Sterling in Decline: The Devaluations of 1931, 1949 and 1967*, Oxford, Blackwell, 1983.

Cairncross, F. and Keeley, P., *The Guardian Guide to the Economy*, London, Methuen, 1981.

Cairncross, F. and Keeley, P., *The Guardian Guide to the Economy vol. 3*, London, Methuen, 1987.

Campbell, M., *Capitalism in the U.K.: A Perspective from Marxist Political Economy*, London, Croom Helm, 1981.

Central Statistical Office, *United Kingdom National Accounts: Sources and Methods*, London, HMSO, 1985.

Challen, D. W. et al., *Unemployment and Inflation in the UK*, London, Longman, 1983.

Coghlan, R., *Money, Credit and the Economy*, London, Allen and Unwin, 1981.

Commission of the European Community, *United Kingdom Medium Term Economic Trends and Problems*, Brussels, 1982.

Creedy, J., *The Economics of Unemployment in Britain*, London, Butterworth, 1981.

Davies, B., *The United Kingdom and the World Monetary System*, London, Heinemann, 1979.

Donaldson, P., *Guide to the British Economy*, Harmondsworth, Penguin, 1976.

Donaldson, P., *A Question of Economics*, Harmondsworth, Penguin, 1985.

Ferrier, C. W. and Ferrier, D. G., *UK Money Markets*, London, Butterworth, 1986.

Fine, B. and Harris, L., *The Peculiarities of the British Economy*, London, Central Books, 1983.

Fingleton, E. and Tickell, T., *The Penguin Money Book*, Harmondsworth, Penguin, 1981.

Fothergill, S. and Cudgin, G., *Unequal Growth: Urban and Regional Employment Change, in the U.K.*, London, Heinemann, 1982.

Glyn, A. and Sutcliffe, B., *British Capitalism, Workers and the Profits Squeeze*, Harmondsworth, Penguin, 1972.

Hampden-Turner, C., *Gentlemen and Tradesmen: The Values of Economic Catastrophe*, London, Routledge & Kegan Paul, 1983.

Hannah, L., *The Rise of the Corporate Economy*, London, Methuen, 1983.

Harbury, C. and Lipsey, R. G., *An Introduction to the UK Economy*, London, Pitman, 1983.

Harris, L. and Coakley, J., *The City of Capital*, Oxford, Blackwell, 1983.

Harrod, D., *Making Sense of the Economy*, Oxford, Martin Robertson, 1983.

Hawkins, K., *Unemployment*, Harmondsworth, Penguin, 1984.

Hawkins, K. and McKenzie, G., *The British Economy: What Will Our Children Think?* London, Macmillan, 1982.

Hey, J. D., *Britain in Context*, Oxford, Blackwell, 1979.

Holden, K. et al., *Modelling the U.K. Economy: An Introduction*, Oxford, Martin Robertson, 1982.

Jenkins, C. and Sherman, B., *The Collapse of Work*, London, Eyre Methuen, 1979.

Johnson, R. W., *The Politics of Recession*, London, Macmillan, 1984.

Jones, A., *Britain's Economy: The Roots of Stagnation*, Cambridge, Cambridge University Press, 1985.

Kay, J. A. and King, M. A., *The British Tax System*, London, Oxford University Press, 1983.

Merritt, G., *World Out of Work*, London, Collins, 1982.

Meyer, F. V., *The Functions of Sterling*, London, Croom Helm, 1973.

Meyer, F. V. (ed.), *Prospects for Recovery in the British Economy*, London, Croom Helm, 1985.

Middlemas, K., *Industry, Unions and Government: Twenty-One Years of NEDC*, London, Macmillan, 1984.

Millward, R., *Public Sector Economics*, London, Longman, 1983.

Minford, P., *Unemployment: Cause and Cure*, Oxford, Blackwell, 1986.

Minns, R., *Pension Funds and British Capitalism: The Ownership and Control of Shareholdings*, London, Heinemann, 1980.

Morris, D. (ed.), *The Economic System in the U.K.*, London, Oxford University Press, 1984.

National Institute of Economic and Social Research, *The United Kingdom Economy*, London, Heinemann, 1982.

O'Brien, D. P. and Presley, J. R. (eds), *Pioneers of Modern Economics in Britain*, London, Macmillan, 1981.

Payne, P. F., *British Commerical Institutions*, London, Harrap, 1969.

Peston, M. H., *The British Economy*, Oxford, Philip Allan, 1982.

Prest, A. R., *Public Finance in Theory and Practice*, London, Weidenfeld and Nicolson, 1979.

Prest, A. R. and Coppock, D. J. (eds), *The U. K. Economy: A Manual of Applied Economics*, London, Weidenfeld and Nicolson, 1984.

Rae, W. and Coutts, N., *Contemporary Files Book, 1, The United Kingdom*, London, Heinemann, 1983.

Rees, G., *Britain's Commodity Markets*, London, Elek, 1972.

Rees, G. and Lambert, J., *Cities in Crisis: The Political Economy of British Urban Development*, London, Arnold, 1985.

Richardson, J. and Moon, J., *Unemployment in the UK*, Aldershot, Gower, 1985.

Short, J. R., *The Urban Area: Capital, State and Community in Contemporary Britain*, London, Macmillan, 1984.

Smith, K., *The British Economic Crisis: Its Past and Future*, Harmondsworth, Penguin, 1984.

Smith, T., *The Politics of the Corporate Economy*, Oxford, Martin Robertson, 1979.

Williams, F., *'The Times' on the Economy*, London, Collins, 1984.

Williams, L. J., *Britain and the World Economy, 1918–1968*, London, Fontana, 1971.

ECONOMIC POLICY

Alt, J. E., *The Politics of Economic Decline*, Cambridge, Cambridge University Press, 1979.

Artis, M., *Monetary Control in the United Kingdom*, Oxford, Philip Allan, 1981.

Bain, A. D., *The Economics of the Financial System*, Oxford, Martin Robertson, 1981.

The Bank of England, *Development and Operation of Monetary Policy, 1960–83*, London, Oxford University Press, 1984.

Barnett, J., *Inside the Treasury*, London, Deutsch, 1982.

Beer, S. H., *Treasury Control: The Coordination of Financial and Economic Policy in Great Britain*, London, Greenwood Press, 1982.

Blackaby, F. T. (ed.), *British Economic Policy, 1960–74*, Cambridge, Cambridge University Press, 1978.

Bonnett, K., *Corporatism and the Monetarist Reaction*, London, Macmillan, 1985.

Borooah, V. K. and Van Der Ploeg, F., *Political Aspects of the Economy*, Cambridge, Cambridge University Press, 1983.

Budd, A., *The Politics of Economic Planning*, London, Fontana, 1978.

Burden, T. and Campbell, M., *Capitalism and Public Policy in the UK: A Marxist Approach*, London, Croom Helm, 1985.

Cairncross, F., *Changing Perceptions of British Economic Policy*, London, Methuen, 1981.

Central Office of Information, *The British System of Taxation*, London, HMSO, 1977.

Central Office of Information, *Manpower and Employment in Britain: The Role of Government*, London, HMSO, 1978.

Clark, Sir R., *Public Expenditure Management and Control*, London, Macmillan, 1978.

Colvin, P., *The Economic Ideal in British Government*, Manchester, Manchester University Press, 1985.

Congdon, T., *Monetary Control in Britain*, London, Macmillan, 1982.

Cross, R., *Economic Theory and Policy in the UK: An Outline and Assessment of the Controversies*, Oxford, Martin Robertson, 1982.

Dow, J. C. R., *The Management of the*

British Economy, 1945–60, Cambridge, Cambridge University Press, 1964.

Gamble, A., *Britain in Decline: Economic Policy, Political Strategy and the British State*, London, Macmillan, 1981.

Gamble, A. and Walkland, S. A., *The British Party System and Economic Policy, 1945–83: Studies in Adversary Politics*, London, Oxford University Press, 1984.

Goodhart, C. A. E., *Monetary Theory and Practice: The UK Experience*, London, Macmillan, 1983.

Gowland, D., *Controlling the Money Supply*, London, Croom Helm, 1982.

Grant, W. and Nath, S., *The Politics of Economic Policy-Making*, Oxford, Blackwell, 1984.

Griffiths, B. and Wood, G. E. (eds), *Monetarism in the United Kingdom*, London, Macmillan, 1984.

Hall, M., *Monetary Policy Since 1971: Conduct and Performance*, London, Macmillan, 1983.

Ham, A., *Treasury Rules: Recurrent Themes in British Economic Policy*, London, Quartet, 1985.

Hare, P. and Kirby, M. (eds), *An Introduction to British Economic Policy*, Brighton, Wheatsheaf Books, 1984.

Heald, O., *Public Expenditure*, Oxford, Blackwell, 1983.

Hockley, G. C., *Public Finance*, London, Routledge & Kegan Paul, 1979.

Holmes, N., *Political Pressure and Economic Policy: British Government, 1970–1974*, London, Butterworth, 1982.

Hood, C. and Wright, M. G. (eds), *Big Government in Hard Times*, Oxford, Martin Robertson, 1981.

Jessop, B., *The Political Economy of Post-War Britain*, Oxford, Blackwell, 1984.

Keegan, W., *Mrs Thatcher's Economic Experiment*, London, Allen Lane, 1984.

Keegan, W. and Pennant-Rea, R., *Who Runs the Economy? Control and Influence in British Economic Policy*, London, Maurice Temple Smith, 1979.

Lee, D., *Control of the Economy*, London, Heinemann, 1974.

Leruz, J., *Economic Planning and Politics in Britain*, Oxford, Martin Robertson, 1975.

Llewellyn, D. T. et al., *The Framework of the United Kingdom Monetary Policy*, London, Heinemann, 1982.

Matthews, R. C. O. and Sargent, J. R. (eds), *Contemporary Problems of Economic Policy: Essays from the Clare Group*, London, Methuen, 1984.

Morris, D. (ed.), *The Economic System in the United Kingdom*, London, Oxford University Press, 1984.

Mosley, P., *The Making of Economic Policy: Theory and Evidence from Britain and the U.S. Since 1945*, Brighton, Wheatsheaf, 1984.

Richardson, J. J., *The Policy-Making Process*, London, Routledge & Kegan Paul, 1969.

Robinson, A. and Sandford, C. *Tax Policy-Making in the United Kingdom*, London, Heinemann, 1983.

Sandford, C. T., *National Economic Planning*, London, Heinemann, 1976.

Sandford, C. T., *Economics of Public Finance*, Oxford, Pergamon Press, 1984.

Smith, T. A., *Politics of the Corporate Economy*, Oxford, Martin Robertson, 1979.

Spencer, P. D., *Competition, Innovation and Disequilibrium: Problems of Monetary Management in the UK, 1971–81*, Oxford, Clarendon Press, 1985.

Stewart, M. J., *Politics and Economic Policy in the United Kingdom since 1964*, Oxford, Pergamon Press, 1978.

Thompson, G., *Conservative Economic Policy: 1979–1984*, London, Croom Helm, 1985.

Tomlinson, J., *British Macroeconomic Policy since 1940*, London, Croom Helm, 1985.

Walters, A., *Britain's Economic Renaissance: Margaret Thatcher's Reforms, 1979–1984*, London,

Oxford University Press, 1986.

Williams, R. G., *Comprehensive Aspects of Taxation*, London, Cassell-Collier-Macmillan, 1981.

Willis, J. R. M. and Hardwick, P. J. W., *Tax Expenditure in the United Kingdom*, London, Heinemann, 1978.

Wright, J. F., *Britain in the Age of Economic Management*, London, Oxford University Press, 1979.

Wright, M. (ed.), *Public Spending Decisions*, London, Allen and Unwin, 1980.

Young, H. and Sloman, A., *But Chancellor: An Inquiry into the Treasury*, London, BBC, 1984.

ECONOMIC PERFORMANCE

Aldcroft, D. H. and Feard, P., *Economic Growth in Twentieth Century Britain*, London, Macmillan, 1969.

Bacon, R. and Eltis, W., *Britain's Economic Problem: Too Few Producers*, London, Macmillan, 1978.

Barnett, C., *The Audit of War: The Illusion and Reality of Britain as a Great Nation*, London, Macmillan, 1986.

Beckerman, W. (ed.), *Slow Growth in Britain: Causes and Consequences*, London, Oxford University Press, 1979.

Caves, R. and Krause, L., *Britain's Economic Performance*, Washington D. C., Brookings Institution, 1980.

Creedy, J. (ed.), *The Economics of Unemployment in Britain*, London, Butterworth, 1981.

Davies, J. and Hughes, S., *Investment in the British Economy*, London, Heinemann, 1980.

Eatwell, J., *Whatever Happened to Britain? The Economics of Decline*, London, BBC, 1982.

Economic Intelligence Unit, *The United Kingdom in the 1980's*, London, 1978.

Fine, B. and Harris, L., *The Peculiarities of the British Economy*, London, Lawrence and Wishart, 1984.

Gamble, A., *Britain in Decline: Economic Policy, Political Strategy and the British State*, London, Macmillan, 1981.

Glyn, A. and Harrison, J., *The British Economic Disaster*, London, Pluto Press, 1980.

Matthews, R. C. O. et al., *British Economic Growth, 1956–1973*, Oxford, Oxford University Press, 1982.

Maunder, P. (ed.), *The British Economy in the 1970's*, London, Heinemann, 1980.

National Institute of Economic and Social Research, *The United Kingdom Economy*, London, Heinemann, 1982.

Phillips, G. A. and Maddock, R. T., *The Growth of the British Economy, 1918–1968*, London, Allen and Unwin, 1973.

Pollard, S., *The Wasting of the British Economy: British Policy, 1945 to the Present*, London, Croom Helm, 1982.

Pollard, S., *The Development of the British Economy, 1914–1967*, London, Arnold, 1983.

FINANCIAL INSTITUTIONS

Aaronovitch, S., *Ruling Class: A Study of British Financial Capital*, London, Greenwood Press, 1979.

Anderson, B. L. and Cottrell, P. L. (eds), *Money and Banking in England: The Development of the Banking System, 1694–1914*, Newton Abbot, David and Charles, 1974.

Bank of England, *A Brief Introduction to the Bank of England*, London, 1980.

Bank of England, *How the Bank is Organised*, London, 1982.

Boddy, M., *The Building Societies*, London, Macmillan, 1980.

Briston, R. J., *The Stock Exchange and Investment Analysis*, London, Allen and Unwin, 1975.

Central Office of Information, *The British Banking System*, London, HMSO, 1970.

Central Office of Information, *British Financial Institutions*, London, HMSO, 1970.

Channon, D. F., *British Banking Strategy and the International Challenge*, London, Macmillan, 1979.

Clarke, W. M., *Inside the City*, London, Allen and Unwin, 1979.

Clarke, W. M., *How the City Works: An Introduction*, Oxford, Pergamon, 1985.

Clay, C. J. J. and Wheble, B. S. (eds), *Modern Merchant Banking*, Cambridge, Woodhead-Faulkner, 1976.

Coggan, P., *The Money Machine: How the City Works*, Harmondsworth, Penguin, 1986.

Committee to Review the Functioning of Financial Institutions (Chairman, Sir H. Wilson), *Report and Appendices*, Cmnd. 7937, London, HMSO, 1980.

Davies, B., *Business Finance and the City of London*, London, Heinemann, 1982.

Hanson, D. G., *Service Banking: A Commentary on Bank Services in the U.K.*, London, Institute of Bankers, 1979.

Hobday, P., *Inside the Bank of England*, Hove, Priory Press, 1976.

Jenkins, A., *The Stock Exchange Story*, London, Heinemann, 1973.

Long, J., *Inside the Stock Exchange*, Hove, Priory Press, 1978.

McRae, H. and Cairncross, F., *Capital City: London as a Financial Centre*, London, Methuen, 1984.

Midgley, K. and Burns, R., *The Capital Market: Its Nature and Significance*, London, Macmillan, 1977.

Morgan, E. V. and Thomas, W. A., *The Stock Exchange: Its History and Functions*, London, Elek, 1969.

Nevin, E. T. and Davis, E. W., *The London Clearing Banks*, London, Elek, 1969.

Plender, J. and Wallace, P., *The Square Mile*, London, Century, 1985.

Pringle, R., *Banking in Britain*, London, Methuen, 1975.

Revell, J., *The British Financial System*, London, Macmillan, 1973.

Ritchie, N., *What Goes on in the City*, Cambridge, Woodhead-Faulkner, 1981.

Roseveare, H., *The Treasury: The Evolution of a British Institution*, Harmondsworth, Penguin, 1969.

Shaw, E. R., *The London Money Market*, London, Heinemann, 1981.

Sheppard, D. K., *The Growth and Role of the U.K. Financial Institutions, 1880–1962*, London, Methuen, 1971.

The Stock Exchange, *The Stock Exchange*, London, 1982.

SEE ALSO:

7 EDUCATION

Bibliographical reference guides to education in Britain are provided by: Banks, O. (ed.), *The Sociology of Education: A Bibliography*, 1978; British Library, *British Education Index*, annually; Humby, M., *A Guide to the Literature of Education*, 1975; Marder, J. V., *Bibliographical Aids and Reference Tools for the Literature of Education*, 1981; National Foundation for Educational Research in England and Wales, *Register of Educational Research in the United Kingdom*, 4 vols, 1976–81.

For recent publications see British Library of Economic and Political Science, *A London Bibliography of the Social Sciences*, annually.

For guides and information sources readers are referred to the following: Boehm, K. and Wellings, N. (eds), *The Student Book: The Applicant's Guide to Universities, Polytechnics and U.K. Colleges*, annually; Councils and Education Press, *Education Year Book*, annually; Europa Publications, *The World of Learning*, annually; Dinham, B. and Norton, M., *The Directory of Social Change: Education and Play*, 1977; Izbicki, J., *Daily Telegraph Education A-Z: A Political Guide for Students, Parents and Teachers*, 1978; Longman, *Education Year Book*, annually; Wallis, E., *Where to Look Things Up: A-Z of Sources on All Major Educational Topics*, 1983.

As introductory reading and as outline guides to the field the following can be recommended: Ahier, J. and Flude, M. (eds), *Contemporary Education Policy*, 1982; Central Office of Information, *Education in Britian*, 1981; Department of Education and Science, *The Educational System of England and Wales*, 1982; Dent, H. C., *Education in England and Wales*, 1982; Evans, K., *The Development and Structure of the English School System*, 1985; Simon, B. and Taylor, W. (eds) *Education in the 80's: The Central Issues*, 1981.

REFERENCE

Banks, O. (ed.), *The Sociology of Education· A Bibliography*, London, Frances Pinter, 1978.

Bell, J. and Roderick, G., *Never Too Late to Learn: Complete Guide to Adult Education*, London, Longman, 1982.

Boehm, K and Wellings, N. (eds), *The Student Book: The Applicant's Guide to Universities, Polytechnics and U.K. Colleges*, London, Macmillan, annually.

British Council and The Association of Commonwealth Universities, *Higher Education in the United Kingdom: A Handbook for Students and their Advisers*, London, Longman, biennially.

British Council, *British Educational Reference Books*, London, annually.

British Council, *Annual Report*, London, annually.

British Library, *British Education Index*, London, annually.

British Library of Economic and Political Science, *A London Bibliography of the Social Sciences*, London and New York, Mansell, annually.

Councils and Education Press (publisher), *Education Year Book*, London, annually.

Department of Education and Science, *Annual Report*, London, HMSO, annually.

Department of Education and Science,

Education Statistics for the United Kingdom, London, HMSO.

Dibden, K. and Tomlinson, J., *Information Sources in Education and Work*, London, Butterworth, 1981.

Dinham, B. and Norton, M., *The Directory of Social Change, Vol. 1, Education and Play*, Hounslow, Wildwood House, 1977.

Dixon, D., *Higher Education—Finding Your Way: A Brief Guide for School and College Students*, London, HMSO, 1985.

Eggleston, J. and Roberts, B., *The Companion to Education*, Oxford, Grant McIntyre, 1982.

Europa Publications, (publisher), *The World of Learning*, 2 vols, London, annually.

Heap, B., *The Higher Education Guide*, London, BBC, 1983.

Hills, P. J., *A Dictionary of Education*, London, Routledge & Kegan Paul, 1984.

Humby, M., *A Guide to the Literature of Education*, London, Institute of Education, 1975.

Izbicki, J., *Daily Telegraph Education A-Z: A Political Guide for Students, Parents and Teachers*, London, Collins, 1978.

Longman (publisher), *Education Year Book*, London, annually.

Marder, J. V., *Bibliographical Aids and Reference Tools for the Literature of Education*, University of Southampton, 1981.

National Foundation for Educational Research in England and Wales, *Register of Educational Research in the United Kingdom*, 4 vols, London, 1976–81.

New Opportunity Press (publisher), *Which Degree?* 5 vols, London, 1986.

Pates, A. et al., *The Education Factbook: An A-Z Guide to Education and Training in Britain*, London, Macmillan, 1983.

Payne, V. and Lipschitz, V., *Alternative Prospectus of Universities and Polytechnics*, Hounslow, Wildwood House, 1977.

Regional Advisory Council for Further Education (publisher), *Compendium of Advanced Courses in Further and Higher Education, 1985–6*, London, 1985.

School Government Publishing Co. (publisher), *The Education Authorities Directory and Annual*, London, annually.

Silver, H. and Teague, St J., *The History of British Universities, 1800–1969: A Bibliography*, Guildford, Society for Research into Higher Education, 1970.

Wallis, E. (comp.), *Where to Look Things Up: A-Z of Sources on All Major Educational Topics*, London, Advisory Centre for Education, 1983.

GENERAL

Adams, R. and Chen, D., *The Process of Educational Innovation*, London, Kogan Page, 1981.

Ahier, J. and Flude, M. (eds), *Contemporary Education Policy*, London, Croom Helm, 1982.

Armytage, W. H. G., *Four Hundred Years of English Education*, Cambridge, Cambridge University Press, 1970.

Barnard, H. C., *A History of English Education from 1760*, Sevenoaks, Hodder and Stoughton, 1970.

Baron, S. et al., *Unpopular Education: Schooling and Social Democracy in England since 1944*, Hutchinson, London, 1981.

Bates, A. W., *Broadcasting in Education: An Evaluation*, London Constable, 1984.

Bell, R. et al. (eds), *Education in Great Britain and Ireland: A Sourcebook*, London, Routledge & Kegan Paul, 1973.

Bell, R. and Grant, N., *Patterns of Education in the British Isles*, London, Allen and Unwin, 1978.

Bernstein, B., *Class, Codes and Control*,

3 vols, London, Routledge & Kegan
Paul, 1971–5.

Boyson, R., *The Crisis in Education*,
London, Woburn Press, 1975.

British Council, *Higher Education in the
United Kingdom*, London, biennially.

Central Office of Information, *Schools in
Britain*, London, HMSO, 1978.

Central Office of Information, *Post-
School Education*, London, HMSO,
1981.

Central Office of Information, *Education
in Britain*, London, HMSO, 1984.

Claydon, L., Knight, T. and Rado, M.,
*Curriculum and Culture: Schooling in
a Pluralist Society*, London, Allen and
Unwin, 1978.

Cuff, E. C. and Payne, G. C. F. (eds),
Crisis in the Curriculum, London,
Croom Helm, 1985.

Curtis, S. J., *The History of Education
in Britain*, London, University
Tutorial Press, 1968.

Deem, R., *Women and Schooling*,
London, Routledge & Kegan Paul,
1978.

Dent, H. C., *Education in England and
Wales*, Sevenoaks, Hodder and
Stoughton, 1982.

Department of Education and Science,
*Schools and Working Life: Some
Initiatives*, London, HMSO, 1981.

Department of Education and Science,
School Curriculum, London, HMSO,
1981.

Department of Education and Science,
*The Educational System of England
and Wales*, London, HMSO, 1982.

Department of Education and Science,
*The Department of Education and
Science: A Brief Guide*, London,
HMSO, 1983.

Eggleston, J., *School-Based Curriculum
Development in Britain*, London,
Routledge & Kegan Paul, 1980.

Entwistle, H., *Class, Culture and
Education*, London, Methuen, 1978.

Evans, K., *The Development and
Structure of the English School
System*, Sevenoaks, Hodder and
Stoughton, 1985.

Fenwick, K. and McBride, P., *The
Government of Education in Britain*,
Oxford, Martin Robertson, 1981.

Field, F., *Education and the Urban
Crisis*, London, Routledge & Kegan
Paul, 1977.

Glatter, R., *An Introduction to the
Control of Education in Britain*,
Milton Keynes, Open University Press,
1979.

Gordon, P. and White, J., *Philosophers
as Educational Reformers: The
Influence of Idealism on British
Educational Thought and Practice*,
London, Routledge & Kegan Paul,
1979.

Gower (publisher), *Education: New
Society Social Studies Reader*,
Aldershot, 1986.

Hewton, E., *Education in Recession:
Crisis in County Hall and Classroom*,
London, Allen and Unwin, 1986.

Horton, T. and Raggatt, P. (eds),
*Challenge and Change in the
Curriculum*, London, Hodder and
Stoughton, 1982.

Inglis, F., *The Management of
Ignorance: A Political Theory of the
Curriculum*, Oxford, Blackwell, 1985.

Kogan, M., *Educational Policy Making:
A Study of Interest Groups and
Parliament*, London, Allen and Unwin,
1975.

Kogan, M., *The Politics of Educational
Change*, Manchester, Manchester
University Press, 1978.

Lacey, C., *The Socialization of Teachers*,
London, Methuen, 1977.

Lawson, J. and Silver, H., *A Social
History of Education in England*,
London, Methuen, 1973.

Lawton, D., *Social Class, Language and
Education*, London, Routledge &
Kegan Paul, 1970.

Lawton, D., *Class, Culture and the
Curriculum*, London, Routledge &
Kegan Paul, 1975.

Lawton, D., *Education and Social
Justice*, London, Sage Publications,
1977.

Lawton, D., *The Politics of the School
Curriculum*, London, Routledge &
Kegan Paul, 1980.

Locke, M., *Power and Politics in the
School System: A Guidebook*,

London, Routledge & Kegan Paul, 1974.

Lodge, P. and Blackstone, T., *Educational Policy and Educational Inequality*, Oxford, Martin Robertson, 1982.

Lynch, J., *The Reform of Teacher Education in the United Kingdom*, Guildford, Society for Research into Higher Education, 1979.

McNay, I. and Ozga, J. (eds), *Policy-Making in Education: The Breakdown of Consensus*, Oxford, Pergamon, 1985.

Midwinter, E. C., *Education and the Community*, London, Allen and Unwin, 1975.

Midwinter, E., *Schools in Society: The Evolution of English Education*, London, Batsford, 1980.

Musgrave, P. W., *Society and Education in England Since 1800*, London, Methuen, 1968.

Musgrove, F., *The Family, Education and Society*, London, Routledge & Kegan Paul, 1976.

O'Day, R., *Education and Society, 1500–1800*, London, Longman, 1982.

Peters, R. S., *Education and the Education of Teachers*, London, Routledge & Kegan Paul, 1977.

Pile, W., *The Department of Education and Science*, London, Allen and Unwin, 1979.

Regan, D. E., *Local Government and Education*, London, Allen and Unwin, 1977.

Reid, I., *Sociological Perspectives on School and Education*, London, Open Books, 1978.

Richmond, W. K., *Education in Britain since 1944*, London, Methuen, 1978.

Robinson, M., *Schools and Social Work*, London, Routledge & Kegan Paul, 1978.

Rogers, R., *Crowther to Warnock. A Survey of Government Reports on the Education and Welfare of Children 1959–1980*, London, Heinemann, 1980.

Seaborne, M. and Lowe, R., *The English School: Its Architecture and Organisation, 1870–1970*, 2 vols, London, Routledge & Kegan Paul, 1971–7.

Silver, H., *Education and the Social Condition*, London, Methuen, 1980.

Simon, B. (ed.), *The Radical Tradition of Education in Britain*, London, Lawrence and Wishart, 1972.

Simon, B. and Taylor, W. (eds), *Education in the 80's: The Central Issues*, London, Batsford, 1981.

Simon, J., *The Social Origins of English Education*, London, Routledge & Kegan Paul, 1970.

Smith, W. O. L., *Education in Great Britain*, Oxford, Oxford University Press, 1968.

Wardle, D., *English Popular Education, 1780–1975*, Cambridge, Cambridge University Press, 1976.

Whitehead, D., *The Dissemination of Educational Innovation in Britain*, London, Hodder and Stoughton, 1980.

Whiteside, T., *The Sociology of Educational Innovation*, London, Methuen, 1978.

Willis, P., *School Counterculture*, Aldershot, Gower, 1985.

PRIMARY AND SECONDARY EDUCATION

Banks, O. and Finlayson, D., *Success and Failure in the Secondary Schools*, London, Methuen, 1973.

Bellaby, P., *The Sociology of Comprehensive Schooling*, London, Methuen, 1977.

Benn, C. and Simon, E., *Half-Way There: A Report on the British Comprehensive School Reform*, Harmondsworth, Penguin, 1972.

Berlak, A. and Berlak, H., *Dilemmas of Schooling*, London, Methuen, 1981.

Blyth, W. and Derricot, R., *Social Significance of Middle Schools*, London, Batsford, 1977.

Boyd, J., *Understanding the Primary Curriculum*, London, Hutchinson, 1984.

Corrigan, P., *Schooling the Smash Street Kids*, London, Macmillan, 1979.

Cox, C. B. and Boyson, R., *Black Paper*, London, Dent, 1975.

Cox, C. B. and Boyson, R. (eds), *Black Paper*, London, Temple Smith, 1977.

Cox, C. B. and Dyson, A. E., (eds), *Black Papers on Education*, London, Davis-Poynter, 1971.

Department of Education and Science, *Primary Education in England*, London, HMSO, 1978.

Department of Education and Science, *Aspects of Secondary Education in England*, London, HMSO, 1979.

Department of Education and Science, *The School Curriculum*, London, HMSO, 1981.

Department of Education and Science, *Education 5 to 9*, London, HMSO, 1982.

Department of Education and Science, *The Curriculum from 5 to 16*, London, HMSO, 1985.

Department of Education and Science, *GCSE: A General Introduction*, London, HMSO, 1985.

Eggleston, J., *The Sociology of the School Curriculum*, London, Routledge & Kegan Paul, 1977.

Evans, K., *The Developement and Structure of the English School System*, London, Hodder and Stoughton, 1985.

Fenwick, I. G., *The Comprehensive School, 1944–70*, London, Methuen, 1980.

Fletcher, C. et al., *Schools on Trial: The Trials of Democratic Comprehensives*, Milton Keynes, Open University Press, 1985.

Ford, J., *Social Class and the Comprehensive School*, London, Routledge & Kegan Paul, 1969.

Galton, M. et al., *Inside the Primary Classroom*, London, Routledge & Kegan Paul, 1980.

Hargreaves, D. H., *The Challenge of the Comprehensive School: Culture, Curriculum and Community*, London, Routledge & Kegan Paul, 1982.

Hartley, D., *Understanding the Primary School*, London, Croom Helm, 1986.

Her Majesty's Stationery Office, *9–13 Middle Schools*, London, 1983.

Hyndman, M., *Schools and Schooling in England and Wales: A Documentary History*, London, Harper and Row, 1978.

Jackson, B., *Starting School*, London, Croom Helm, 1980.

Judge, H., *A Generation of Schooling: English Secondary Schools Since 1944*, London, Oxford University Press, 1985.

Locke, M., *Power and Politics in the School Systems: A Guidebook*, London, Routledge & Kegan Paul, 1974.

Macfarlane, N., *Sixth Form Colleges*, London, Heinemann, 1978.

McPherson, A. et al., *Reconstruction of Secondary Education, Theory, Myth and Practice Since the War*, London, Routledge & Kegan Paul, 1983.

Neill, A. S., *Summerhill: A Radical Approach to Education*, Harmondsworth, Penguin, 1970.

Pedley, R., *The Comprehensive School*, Harmondsworth, Penguin, 1978.

Plowden, Lady B., *Children and their Primary Schools: A Report of the Central Advisory Council for Education*, 2 vols, HMSO, 1967.

Rubinstein, D. and Simon, B., *The Evolution of the British Comprehensive School 1926–1972*, London, Routledge & Kegan Paul, 1973.

Sadler, J. E., *Concepts in Primary Education*, London, Allen and Unwin, 1975.

Sharp, R. et al., *Education and Social Control: A Study in Progressive Primary Education*, London, Routledge & Kegan Paul, 1975.

Stewart, J., *The Making of the Primary School*, Milton Keynes, Open University Press, 1986.

Thornbury, R., *The Changing Urban School*, London, Methuen, 1978.

Welton, J., *Comprehensive Education—the Egalitarian Dream*, London, Frances Pinter, 1977.

Whitbread, N., *The Evolution of the Nursery-Infant School*, London, Routledge & Kegan Paul, 1972.

HIGHER AND FURTHER EDUCATION

Ashby, E. and Anderson, M., *The Rise of the Student Estate in Britain*, London, Macmillan, 1970.

Burgess, T., *Education after School*, Harmondsworth, Penguin, 1977.

Burgess, T. and Pratt, J., *Policy and Practice: The Colleges of Advanced Technology*, London, Allen Lane, 1977.

Cantor, M. and Roberts, I. F., *Further Education Today: A Critical Review*, London, Routledge & Kegan Paul, 1983.

Carswell, J., *Government and the Universities in Britain: Programme and Performance, 1960–1980*, Cambridge, Cambridge University Press, 1986.

Central Office of Information, *Britain's Open University*, London, HMSO, 1979.

Department of Education and Science, *A Strategy for Higher Education into the 1990's: The University Grants Committee Advice*, London, HMSO, 1984.

Donaldson, L., *Policy and Polytechnics*, Farnborough, Saxon House, 1975.

Evans, N., *Education Beyond School*, London, Grant McIntyre, 1982.

Ferguson, J., *The Open University from Within*, London, University of London Press, 1975.

Finch, J. and Rustin, M. (eds), *A Degree of Choice: Higher Education and the Right to Learn*, Harmondsworth, Penguin, 1986.

Green, V. H., *The Universities*, Harmondsworth, Penguin, 1969.

Green, V. H., *History of Oxford University*, London, Batsford, 1974.

Halsey, A. H. and Trow, M., *The British Academics*, London, Faber, 1971.

Herriot, P., *Down from the Ivory Tower: Graduates and their Jobs*, Chichester, Wiley, 1984.

Hutchinson, E. E., *Learning Later: Fresh Horizons in English Adult Education*, London, Routledge & Kegan Paul, 1978.

Jarvis, P., *The Sociology of Adult and Continuing Education*, London, Croom Helm, 1985.

Jones, R. K., *The Sociology of Adult Education*, Aldershot, Gower, 1984.

King, R. A., *School and College: Studies of Post-sixteen Education*, London, Routledge & Kegan Paul, 1976.

Layard, R. et al., *The Impact of Robbins: Expansion in Higher Education*, Harmondsworth, Penguin, 1969.

Legge, D., *The Education of Adults in Britain*, Milton Keynes, Open University Press, 1982.

Lynch, J. and Plunkett, D. H., *Teacher Education and Cultural Change*, London, Allen and Unwin, 1973.

Martin, D. A. (ed.), *Anarchy and Culture: The Problem of the Contemporary University*, London, Routledge & Kegan Paul, 1969.

Matterson, A., *Polytechnics and Colleges: Control and Administration in the Public Sector of Higher Education*, London, Longman, 1981.

Moodie, G. L. and Eustace, R., *Power and Authority in British Universities*, London, Allen and Unwin, 1974.

Perry, W., *Open University*, Milton Keynes, Open University Press, 1976.

Robinson, E., *The New Polytechnics—the People's Universities*, London, Cornmarket Press, 1968.

Rudd, E., *The Highest Education: A Study of Graduate Education in Britain*, London, Routledge & Kegan Paul, 1983.

Sanderson, M., *The Universities and British Industry, 1850–1970*, London, Routledge & Kegan Paul, 1972.

Scott, J. H. M., *Dons and Students: British Universities Today*, London, Ward Lock, 1973.

Scott, P., *The Crisis of the University*, London, Croom Helm, 1984.

Shattock, M. (ed.), *The Structure and Governance of Higher Education*, Guildford, Society for Research into Higher Education, 1983.

Startup, R., *The University Teacher and His World*, Aldershot, Gower, 1979.

Stephens, M. and Roderick, G. W. (eds), *Universities for a Changing World*, Newton Abbot, David and Charles, 1975.

Stone, L. (ed.), *Universities in Society, vol. 1, Oxford and Cambridge from the 14th to the Early 19th Century*, London, Oxford University Press, 1975.

Tunstall, J. (ed.), *The Open University Opens*, London, Routledge & Kegan Paul, 1973.

Williams, G. and Blackstone, T., *Response to Adversity: Higher Education in a Harsh Climate*, Guildford, Society for Research into Higher Education, 1983.

PUBLIC SCHOOLS

Bamford, T. W., *The Rise of the Public Schools*, London, Nelson, 1967.

Bishop, T. J. H. and Wilkinson, R., *Winchester and the Public School Elite*, London, Faber, 1967.

Gardner, B., *The Public Schools. An Historical Survey*, London, Hamish Hamilton, 1973.

Gathorne-Hardy, J., *The Public School Phenomenon*, Harmondsworth, Penguin, 1979.

Lambert, R. et al., *New Wine in Old Bottles? Studies in Integration Within the Public Schools*, London, Bell, 1968.

Lambert, R. and Millham, S., *The Hothouse Society*, Harmondsworth, Penguin, 1974.

Leinster-Mackay, D., *The Rise of the English Prep School*, London and Philadelphia, Falmer Press, 1984.

McConnell, J., *English Public Schools*, London, Herbert Press, 1985.

Rae, J., *The Public School Revolution. Britain's Independent Schools 1964–1979*, London, Faber, 1981.

Wakeford, J., *The Cloistered Elite: A Sociological Study of the English Public Boarding School*, London, Macmillan, 1969.

Weinberg, I., *The English Public Schools: The Sociology of Elite Education*, New York, Atherton Press, 1967.

8 ENGLISH LANGUAGE

For extensive bibliographical references to work on English language, language history and linguistics readers should consult: Kinsella, V. (ed.), *Language Teaching and Linguistics*, annually; Martinus Nijhoff (publisher), *Linguistic Bibliography*, annually; Modern Humanities Research Association, *Annual Bibliography of English Language and Literature*, annually; Rice, F. A. and Guss, A. (eds), *Information Sources in Linguistics: A Bibliographical Handbook*, 1965; Wawrzyszko, A. K., *Bibliography of General Linguistics*, 1971; Viereck, W. et al. (comps.), *A Bibliography of Writings on Varieties of English, 1965–1983*, 1984.

Reviews of current publications on English can also be found in English Association, *The Year's Work in English Studies*, annually.

Useful surveys of English, its historical and structural features can be found in: Branford, W., *The Elements of English*, 1967; Burchfield, R., *The English Language*, 1985; Darbyshire, A. E., *A Description of English*, 1967; Francis, W. N., *The English Language, An Introduction*, 1969; Potter, S., *Our Language*, 1969; Smith, L. P., *The English Language*, 1966.

The following can be particularly recommended in their fields:

Dialect   Wakelin, M. F., *English Dialects: An Introduction*, 1977; Wells, J. C., *Accents of English*, 4 vols, 1982.
Dictionaries   Clarendon Press (publisher), *The Shorter Oxford English Dictionary*, 1973; Longman (publisher), *Longman Dictionary of Contemporary English*, 1979.
Discourse Analysis   Brown, G. and Yule, G., *Discourse Analysis*, 1983; Coulthard, M., *An Introduction to Discourse Analysis*, 1977.
English Language Teaching   Dawson, C., *Teaching English as a Foreign Language*, 1985; Harmer, J., *The Practice of English Language Teaching*, 1983.
Grammar   Quirk, R. et al., *A Grammar of Contemporary English*, 1972; Thomson, A. J. and Martinet, A. V., *A Practical English Grammar*, 1980.
History of English   Baugh, A. C., *A History of the English Language*, 1978; Leith, D., *A Social History of English*, 1983.
Linguistics   Brown, K., *Linguistics Today*, 1984; Lyons, J., *Language and Linguistics: An Introduction*, 1981.
Pronunciation   Gimson, A. C., *An Introduction to the Pronunciation of English*, 1980; Jones, D., *The Pronunciation of English*, 1966.
Usage   Partridge, E., *Usage and Abusage: A Guide to Good English*, 1970; Weiner, E. S. C. (ed.), *Oxford Guide to English Usage*, 1984.

REFERENCE

Alston, R. C. (ed.), *A Bibliography of the English Language from the Invention of Printing to the Year 1800*, Leeds, E. J. Arnold, 1965.

British Council, *Index to Twenty-five Years of 'English Language Teaching' 1946–71*, London, 1972.

British Council, *Theses and Dissertations*

Related to the Teaching of English to Speakers of other Languages, deposited with British Universities, 1961–72, London, English Teaching Information Centre, 1973.

British Council, *Index to 'English Language Teaching', 1972–77*, London, 1977.

Centre for Applied Linguistics (publisher), *Language Research in Progress*, Washington, annually.

Crystal, D., *A First Dictionary of Linguistics and Phonetics*, London, Deutsch, 1980.

Ducrot, O. and Todorov, T., *Encyclopedic Dictionary of the Sciences of Language*, trans. C. Porter, Oxford, Blackwell, 1981.

English Association, *The Year's Work in English Studies*, London, Oxford University Press, annually.

Hartmann, R. R. K. and Stork, F. C., *Dictionary of Language and Linguistics*, Barking, Applied Science Publishers, 1972.

Heaton, I. B. and Stocks, J. P., *Overseas Students' Companion to English Studies*, London, Longman, 1979.

Kinsella, V. (ed.), *Language Teaching and Linguistics: Abstracts*, Cambridge, Cambridge University Press, annually.

Martinus Nijhoff (publisher), *Linguistic Bibliography*, The Hague, annually.

Modern Humanities Research Association, *Annual Bibliography of English Language and Literature*, Cambridge, Cambridge University Press, annually.

Partridge, E., *Usage and Abusage: A Guide to Good English*, Harmondsworth, Penguin, 1970.

Percival, A. C., *The English Association Handbook*, London, Library Association, 1977.

Rice, F. A. and Guss, A. (eds), *Information Sources in Linguistics: a Bibliographical Handbook*, Washington, Centre for Applied Linguistics, 1965.

Richards, J. et al., *Longman Dictionary of Applied Linguistics*, London, Longman, 1985.

Treble, H. A. and Vallins, G. H., *An A. B. C. of English Usage*, Oxford, Oxford University Press, 1962.

Viereck, W. et al., (comps.), *A Bibliography of Writings on Varieties of English, 1965–1983*, Amsterdam and Philadelphia, John Benjamin, 1984.

Wawrzyszko, A. K., *Bibliography of General Linguistics, English and American*, Hamden, Connecticut, Archon Books, 1971.

Weiner, E. S. C. (ed.), *Oxford Guide to English Usage*, Oxford, Oxford University Press, 1984.

White, R. V., *The English Teacher's Handbook*, London, Nelson-Harrap, 1982.

GENERAL

Abbott, G. and Wingard, P., *The Teaching of English as an International Language: A Practical Guide*, Glasgow, Collins, 1981.

Adams, V., *An Introduction to Modern English Word Formation*, London, Longman, 1973.

Aitchison, J., *Language Change: Progress or Decay?*, London, Fontana, 1981.

Allen, D., *English Teaching since 1965: How Much Growth?*, London, Heinemann, 1980.

Austin, J. L., *How to Do Things with Words*, Oxford, Clarendon Press, 1962.

Bailey, R. W. and Görlach, M., *English as a World Language*, Cambridge, Cambridge University Press, 1984.

Baker, G. P. and Hacker, P. M. S., *Language, Sense and Nonsense: A Critical Investigation into Modern Theories of Language*, Oxford, Blackwell, 1984.

Barber, C. L., *Linguistic Change in Present-Day English*, Edinburgh, Oliver and Boyd, 1964.

Barnes, D. et al., *Versions of English*,

London, Heinemann, 1984.

Bauer, L., *English Word-Formation*, Cambridge, Cambridge University Press, 1983.

BBC (publisher), *Words: Reflections on the Use of Language*, London, 1976.

Bolinger, D. and Sears, D. A., *Aspects of Language*, New York, Harcourt, Brace Jovanovich, 1981.

Bolton, W. C. and Crystal, D. (eds), *English Language*, 2 vols, Cambridge, Cambridge University Press, 1966–9.

Boulton, M., *The Anatomy of Language*, London, Routledge & Kegan Paul, 1968.

Branford, W., *The Elements of English*, London, Routledge & Kegan Paul, 1967.

Bright, J. and McGregor, G., *Teaching English as a Second Language*, London, Longman, 1970.

British Council, *ELT Documents*, Oxford, Pergamon Press, 1977 (series).

Britton, J. (ed.), *English Teaching: An International Exchange*, London, Heinemann, 1984.

Brook, G. L., *Varieties of English*, London, Deutsch, 1973.

Brook, G. L., *Words in Everyday Life*, London, Macmillan, 1981.

Brown, G., *Listening to Spoken English*, London, Longman, 1977.

Brown, G. and Yule, G., *Discourse Analysis*, Cambridge, Cambridge University Press, 1983.

Brown, K., *Linguistics Today*, London, Fontana, 1984.

Burchfield, R., *The English Language*, London, Oxford University Press, 1985.

Burgess, A., *Language Made Plain*, London, Fontana, 1975.

Byrne, D., *English Teaching Extracts*, London, Longman, 1969.

Byrne, D., *English Teaching Perspectives*, London, Longman, 1980.

Close, R. A., *English as a Foreign Language*, London, Allen and Unwin, 1977.

Collins, V. H., *A Book of English Proverbs, with Origins and Explanations*, London, Longman, 1959.

Cottle, B., *The Plight of English*, Newton Abbot, David and Charles, 1975.

Coulthard, M., *An Introduction to Discourse Analysis*, London, Longman, 1977.

Crystal, D., *Who Cares about English Usage?*, Harmondsworth, Penguin, 1984.

Crystal, D. and Davy, D., *Investigating English Style*, London, Longman, 1973.

Crystal, D. and Davy, D., *Advanced Conversational English*, Longman, 1975.

Cummings, M. and Simmons, R., *The Language of Literature*, Oxford, Pergamon Press, 1983.

Darbyshire, A. E., *A Description of English*, London, Arnold, 1967.

Dawson, C., *Teaching English as a Foreign Language*, London, Nelson-Harrap, 1985.

Downes, W., *Language and Society*, London, Fontana, 1983.

Empson, W., *The Structure of Complex Words*, London, Chatto and Windus, 1969.

Fieldhouse, H., *Everyman's Good English Guide*, London, Dent, 1982.

Foster, B., *The Changing English Language*, London, Macmillan, 1981.

Fowler, H. W. and Fowler, F. G., *The King's English*, Oxford, Clarendon Press, 1973.

Fowler, R. (ed.), *Essays on Style and Language: Linguistic and Critical Approaches to Literary Style*, London, Routledge & Kegan Paul, 1966.

Fowler, R. et al., *Language and Control*, London, Routledge & Kegan Paul, 1979.

Francis, W. N., *The English Language: An Introduction*, London, English Universities Press, 1969.

Freeborn, D., *Varieties of English: An Introduction to Language Studies*, London, Macmillan, 1985.

Fries, C. C., *The Structure of English*, London, Longman, 1964.

Gatherer, W. A., *A Study of English: Learning and Teaching the Language*,

London, Heinemann, 1980.

Goffman, E., *Forms of Talk*, Oxford, Blackwell, 1981.

Gowers, E., *The Complete Plain Words*, revised by S. Greenbaum and J. Whitcut, London, HMSO, 1986.

Greenbaum, S., *The English Language Today: Public Attitudes towards the English Language*, Oxford, Pergamon, 1984.

Halliday, F. E., *The Excellency of the English Tongue*, London, Gollancz, 1975.

Harmer, J., *The Practice of English Language Teaching*, London, Longman, 1983.

Harrison, B., *English as a Second Foreign Language*, London, Arnold, 1973.

Haycraft, J., *An Introduction to English Language Teaching*, London, Longman, 1979.

Heller, L. et al., *The Private Lives of English Words*, London, Routledge & Kegan Paul, 1984.

Holden, S. (ed.), *Second Selection from 'Modern English Teacher'*, 2, London, Longman, 1984.

Hough, G., *Style and Stylistics*, London, Routledge & Kegan Paul, 1969.

Howard, P., *The State of the Language*, London, Hamish Hamilton, 1984.

Jackson, H. B., *Analysing English: An Introduction to Descriptive Linguistics*, Oxford, Pergamon Press, 1982.

Jones, R., *An ABC of English Teaching*, London, Heinemann, 1980.

Jordan, M., *The Rhetoric of Everyday English Texts*, London, Allen and Unwin, 1984.

Jordan, R. R. (ed.), *Case Studies in ELT*, Glasgow, Collins, 1983.

Leech, G. N., *English in Advertising*, London, Longman, 1966.

Leech, G. N., *Principles of Pragmatics*, London, Longman, 1983.

Lyons, J., *An Introduction to Theoretical Linguistics*, Cambridge, Cambridge University Press, 1968.

Lyons, J., *Language and Linguistics: An Introduction*, Cambridge, Cambridge University Press, 1981.

McCrum, R. et al., *The Story of English*, London, BBC, 1986.

McDonough, J., *ESP (English for Specific Purposes) in Perspective: A Practical Guide*, Glasgow, Collins, 1984.

Michaels, L. and Ricks, C. (eds), *The State of the Language*, Berkeley, University of California Press, 1980.

Milroy, J. and Milroy, L., *Authority in Language: A Study of Language Standardisation and Prescription*, London, Routledge & Kegan Paul, 1985.

Moorwood, H. (ed.), *Selections from 'Modern English Teacher'*, 1, London, Longman, 1978.

Nash, W., *The Language of Humour: Style and Technique in Comic Discourse*, London, Longman, 1985.

Ogden, C. K. and Richards, I. A., *The Meaning of Meaning*, London, Routledge & Kegan Paul, 1923.

Potter, S., *Our Language*, Harmondsworth, Penguin, 1969.

Price, G., *The Languages of Britain*, London, Arnold, 1984.

Pugh, A. K. et al (eds), *Language and Language Use*, London, Heinemann, 1980.

Quirk, R., *The Use of English*, London, Longman, 1968.

Quirk, R., *The Linguist and the English Language*, London, Arnold, 1975.

Quirk, R., *Style and Communication in the English Language*, London, Arnold, 1982.

Quirk, R. and Widdowson, H. (eds), *English in the World*, Cambridge, Cambridge University Press, 1985.

Rawson, H., *A Dictionary of Euphemisms and Other Double-Talk*, London, Macdonald, 1981.

Schlauch, M., *The English Language in Modern Times*, London, Oxford University Press, 1960.

Sheard, J. A., *The Words We Use*, London, Deutsch, 1954.

Shores, D. L., *Contemporary English: Change and Variation*, Philadelphia, University of Pennsylvania Press, 1972.

Sinclair, J. M. and Coulthard, M., *Towards an Analysis of Discourse*,

London, Oxford University Press, 1975.

Smith, L. P., *The English Language*, London, Oxford University Press, 1966.

Smith, N. and Wilson, D., *Modern Linguistics: The Results of Chomsky's Revolution*, Harmondsworth, Penguin, 1979.

Strevens, P., *Teaching English as an International Language*, Oxford, Pergamon Press, 1980.

Stubbs, M., *Discourse Analysis*, Oxford, Blackwell, 1983.

Swan, M., *Practical English Usage*, London, Oxford University Press, 1980.

Trudgill, P. and Hannah, J., *International English: A Guide to Varieties of Standard English*, London, Arnold, 1985.

Wade, B. (ed.), *Language Perspectives: Papers from the 'Educational Review'*, London, Heinemann, 1982.

Wardhaugh, R., *How Conversation Works*, Oxford, Blackwell, 1985.

Weiner, E. S. C. and Hawkins, J. M. (eds), *The Oxford Guide to the English Language*, Oxford, Oxford University Press, 1985.

Widdowson, H., *Stylistics and the Teaching of Literature*, London, Longman, 1975.

Wilson, F. P. (ed.), *The Oxford Dictionary of English Proverbs*, Oxford, Oxford University Press, 1970.

Wood, F. T., *Current English Usage*, London, Macmillan, 1981.

Wrenn, C. L., *The English Language*, London, Methuen, 1977.

GRAMMAR

Aarts, F. and Aarts, J., *English Syntactic Structures*, Oxford, Pergamon Press, 1982.

Brown, E. K. and Miller, J. E., *Syntax: A Linguistic Introduction to Sentence Structure*, London, Hutchinson, 1980.

Burton-Roberts, N., *An Introduction to English Syntax*, London, Longman, 1986.

Christophersen, P. and Sandved, A. O., *An Advanced English Grammar*, London, Macmillan, 1969.

Close, R. A., *The New English Grammar*, London, Allen and Unwin, 1964.

Close, R. A., *A Reference Grammar for Students of English*, London, Longman, 1975.

Halliday, M. A. K., *An Introduction to Functional Grammar*, London, Arnold, 1985.

Hornby, A. S., *A Guide to Patterns and Usage in English*, London, Oxford University Press, 1975.

Huddleston, R. D., *Introduction to English Transformational Syntax*, London, Longman, 1976.

Huddleston, R. D., *Introduction to the Grammar of English*, Cambridge, Cambridge University Press, 1984.

Jackson, H. B., *Analysing English*, Oxford, Pergamon, 1982.

Jespersen, O., *Essentials of English Grammar*, London, Allen and Unwin, 1933.

Kruisinga, E., *An English Grammar*, 2 vols, Gröningen, Batavia, 1953–60.

Leech, G., *English Grammar for Today: A New Introduction*, London, Macmillan, 1982.

Leech, G. and Svartik, H., *A Communicative Grammar of English*, London, Longman, 1975.

Matthews, P. H., *Syntax*, Cambridge, Cambridge University Press, 1981.

Neuman, D. M., *English Grammar for Proficiency*, London, Nelson, 1980.

Onions, C. T., *Modern English Syntax*, London, Routledge & Kegan Paul, 1974.

Palmer, F. R., *Grammar*, Harmondsworth, Penguin, 1971.

Palmer, F. R., *The English Verb*, London, Longman, 1974.

Quirk, R. et al., *A Grammar of Contemporary English*, London, Longman, 1972.

Quirk, R. et al., *A Comprehensive*

Grammar of the English Language,
London, Longman, 1985.
Quirk, R. and Greenbaum, S., *A
University Grammar,* London,
Oxford University Press, 1978.
Scheuerweghs, G., *Present-day English
Syntax,* London, Longman, 1959.
Schibsbye, K., *A Modern English
Grammar,* London, Oxford
University Press, 1970.
Scott, F. S. et al., *English Grammar. A
Linguistic Study of its Classes and
Structures,* London, Heinemann,
1970.

Thomson, A. J. and Martinet, A. V., *A
Practical English Grammar,* London,
Oxford University Press, 1980.
Tomori, S. H. O., *Morphology and
Syntax of Present-Day English: An
Introduction,* London, Heinemann,
1977.
Van Ek, J. A. and Robat, N. J., *The
Student's Grammar of English,*
Oxford, Blackwell, 1984.
Zandvoort, R. W., *A Handbook of
English Grammar,* London,
Longman, 1975.

DICTIONARIES

Allen, R. E. (ed.), *The Oxford Dictionary
of Current English,* Oxford, Oxford
University Press, 1985.
Barnhart, C. L. et al., *A Dictionary of
New English, 1963–1972,* London,
Longman, 1973.
Barnhart, C. L. et al., *The Second
Barnhart Dictionary of New English,*
London, Longman, 1982.
Bernstein, T. M., *Bernstein's Reverse
Dictionary,* London, Routledge &
Kegan Paul, 1983.
Bryson, B., *The Penguin Dictionary of
Troublesome Words,*
Harmondsworth, Penguin, 1984.
Courtney, M. R., *Longman Dictionary
of Phrasal Verbs,* London, Longman,
1983.
Cowie, A. P. and Mackin, R., *Oxford
Dictionary of Current Idiomatic
English,* 2 vols, London, Oxford
University Press, 1975–83.
Fowler, H. W., *A Dictionary of Modern
English Usage,* Oxford, Clarendon
Press, 1965.
Funk and Wagnall (publisher), *Funk and
Wagnall's Standard College
Dictionary,* New York, 1978.
Garmonsway, G. N. and Simpson, J.
(eds), *The Penguin English
Dictionary,* Harmondsworth, Penguin,
1970.
Green, J. (comp.), *The Dictionary of
Contemporary Slang,* London, Pan,
1984.

Green, J., *Newspeak: A Dictionary of
Jargon,* London, Routledge & Kegan
Paul, 1985.
Green, J., *The Slang Thesaurus,* London,
Hamish Hamilton, 1986.
Gurnett, J. W. and Kyte, C. H. J. (eds),
Cassell's Dictionary of Abbreviations,
London, Cassell, 1966.
Hayakawa, S. I. and Fletcher, P. J. (eds),
*Cassell's Modern Guide to Synonyms
and Related Words,* London, Cassell,
1971.
Hoad, T. F. (ed.), *The Concise Oxford
Dictionary of English Etymology,*
Oxford, Clarendon Press, 1985.
Hornby, A. S., *The Oxford Student's
Dictionary of Current English,*
London, Oxford University Press,
1981.
Hornby, A. S. et al. (eds), *The Oxford
Advanced Learner's Dictionary of
Current English,* London, Oxford
University Press, 1980.
Hudson, K. (ed.), *Dictionary of Diseased
English,* London, Macmillan, 1980.
Hudson, K. (ed.), *Dictionary of Even
More Diseased English,* London,
Macmillan, 1983.
Kirkpatrick, E. M. (ed.), *Chambers
Twentieth Century Dictionary,*
Edinburgh, Chambers, 1985.
Klein, E., *A Comprehensive
Etymological Dictionary of the
English Language,* Amsterdam,
Elsevier, 1969.

Lee, W. R., *A Study Dictionary of Social English*, Oxford, Pergamon Press, 1983.

Little, W. et al. (eds), *The Shorter Oxford English Dictionary*, Oxford, Oxford University Press, 1944 (1973).

Long, T. H. and Summers, D., *The Longman Dictionary of English Idioms*, London, Longman, 1979.

Longman (publisher), *Longman Dictionary of Contemporary English*, London, 1979.

Longman (publisher), *Longman New Universal Dictionary*, London, 1982.

Longman (publisher), *Longman Dictionary of the English Language*, London, 1984.

McArthur, T. (ed.), *Longman Lexicon of Contemporary English*, London, Longman, 1978.

McArthur, T. and Atkins, B., *Dictionary of English Phrasal Verbs and their Idioms*, Glasgow, Collins, 1974.

McLeod, W. T. (ed.), *The New Collins Thesaurus*, London, Collins, 1984.

McLeod, W. T. and Hanks, P. (eds), *The New Collins Concise Dictionary of the English Language*, London, Collins, 1984.

Murray, J. A. H. et al. (eds), *The Oxford English Dictionary*, 13 vols, Oxford, Clarendon Press, 1933; *Supplements*, R. W. Burchfield (ed.), 4 vols, 1972–86.

Neaman, J. S. and Silver, C. G., *A Dictionary of Euphemisms*, London, Hamilton, 1983.

Onions, C. T. (ed.), *The Oxford Dictionary of English Etymology*, Oxford University Press, 1966.

Oxford University Press (publisher), *The Oxford Dictionary for Writers and Editors*, Oxford, 1981.

Pan (publisher), *Dictionary of Contemporary Slang*, London, 1984.

Partridge, E., *Origins: A Short Etymological Dictionary of Modern English*, London, Routledge & Kegan Paul, 1966.

Partridge, E. (ed.), *A Dictionary of the Underworld, British and American*, London, Routledge & Kegan Paul, 1968.

Partridge, E., *A Dictionary of Clichés*, London, Routledge & Kegan Paul, 1978.

Partridge, E., *A Dictionary of Catch Phrases*, London, Routledge & Kegan Paul, 1983.

Partridge, E., *A Dictionary of Slang and Unconventional English*, edited by P. Beale, London, Routledge & Kegan Paul, 1984.

Partridge, E. and Simpson, J., *The Penguin Dictionary of Historical Slang*, Harmondsworth, Penguin, 1972.

Paxton, J. (ed.), *Dictionary of Abbreviations*, London, Dent, 1981.

Penguin (publisher), *The Penguin Dictionary of English Idioms*, Harmondsworth, 1986.

Penguin (publisher), *The Penguin Reference Dictionary*, Harmondsworth, 1986.

Phythian, B. A., *A Concise Dictionary of English Slang*, London, Hodder and Stoughton, 1976.

Pugh, E., *Pugh's Dictionary of Acronyms and Abbreviations*, London, Bingley, 1981.

Skeat, W. W., *An Etymological English Dictionary*, Oxford, Oxford University Press, 1963.

Skeat, W. W., *Concise Etymological Dictionary*, Oxford, Oxford University Press, 1965.

Strevens, P. and Kay, V., *Beyond the Dictionary in English: A Handbook of Colloquial Usage*, London, Cassell, 1974.

Sykes, J. B. (ed.), *The Concise Oxford Dictionary of Current English*, Oxford, Oxford University Press, 1982.

Urdang, L. and Manser, M. (eds), *Dictionary of Synonyms and Antonyms*, Newton Abbot, David and Charles, 1980.

Wallace, M. J., *Dictionary of English Idioms*, Glasgow, Collins, 1981.

Weekley, E. (ed.), *An Etymological Dictionary of Modern English*, 2 vols, New York, Dover, 1968.

West, M., *A General Service List of English Words*, London, Longman, 1953.

Wilson, F. P., *The Oxford Dictionary of English Proverbs*, Oxford, Clarendon Press, 1970.

Wood, F. T., *English Verbal Idioms*, London, Macmillan, 1966.

Wood, F. T., *English Prepositional Idioms*, London, Macmillan, 1969.

Wood, F. T. (ed.), *Dictionary of English Colloquial Idioms*, London, Macmillan, 1979.

DIALECT AND SOCIOLECT

Barltrop, R. and Wolveridge, J., *The Muvver Tongue*, London, Journeyman Press, 1980.

Brandis, W. and Henderson, D., *Social Class, Language and Communication*, London, Routledge & Kegan Paul, 1970.

Brook, G. L., *Varieties of English*, London, Macmillan, 1973.

Brook, G. L., *English Dialects*, London, Deutsch, 1978.

Chambers, J. K. and Trudgill, P., *Dialectology*, Cambridge, Cambridge University Press, 1980.

Edwards, A. D., *Language in Culture and Class*, London, Heinemann, 1976.

Hudson, K., *The Language of the Teenage Revolution*, London, Macmillan, 1981.

Lawton, D., *Social Class, Language and Education*, London, Routledge & Kegan Paul, 1968.

Lockwood, W. B., *Languages of the British Isles, Past and Present*, London, Deutsch, 1975.

Lodge, K., *Studies in the Phonology of Colloquial English*, London, Croom Helm, 1983.

Matthews, W., *Cockney Past and Present: A Short History of the Dialect of London*, London, Routledge & Kegan Paul, 1972.

Orton, H. et al. (eds), *Survey of English Dialects*, 4 vols, Leeds, E. J. Arnold, 1962–71.

Orton, H. et al. (eds), *The Linguistic Atlas of England*, London, Croom Helm, 1978.

Orton, H. and Wright, N., *A Word Geography of England*, London, Seminar Press, 1974.

Petyt, K. M., *The Study of Dialect: An Introduction to Dialectology*, Oxford, Blackwell, 1984.

Phillips, K. C., *Language and Class in Victorian England*, Oxford, Blackwell, 1984.

Sanderson, S. et al., *The Linguistic Atlas of England*, London, Croom Helm, 1978.

Sutcliffe, D., *British Black English*, Oxford, Blackwell, 1982.

Trudgill, P., *Sociolinguistics: An Introduction*, Harmondsworth, Penguin, 1974.

Trudgill, P., *Accent, Dialect and School*, London, Arnold, 1975.

Trudgill, P. (ed.), *Sociolinguistic Patterns in British English*, London, Arnold, 1979.

Trudgill, P., *On Dialect: Social and Geographical Perspectives*, Oxford, Blackwell, 1984.

Trudgill, P. (ed.), *Language in the British Isles*, Cambridge, Cambridge University Press, 1984.

Trudgill, P. and Hughes, A., *English Accents and Dialects: An Introduction to Social and Regional Varieties of English*, London, Arnold, 1979.

Wakelin, M. F., *Patterns of Folk Speech of the British Isles*, London, Athlone Press, 1972.

Wakelin, M. F., *English Dialects: An Introduction*, London, Athlone, 1977.

Wells, J. C., *Accents of English*, 4 vols, Cambridge, Cambridge University Press, 1982.

Wright, J., *The English Dialect Dictionary*, London, Frowde, 1905, Oxford, Oxford University Press, 1970 (reprint).

Wright, J. (ed.), *The English Dialect Dictionary*, 6 vols, London, Frowde, 1898–1905, Oxford, Oxford University Press, 1970 (reprint).

LANGUAGE HISTORY

Barfield, O., *History in English Words*, London, Faber, 1954.

Baugh, A. C., *A History of the English Language*, London, Routledge & Kegan Paul, 1978.

Blake, N., *The English Language in Medieval Literature*, London, Dent, 1977.

Bloomfield, M. W. and Newmark, L., *Linguistic Introduction to the History of English*, London, Greenwood Press, 1979.

Bourcier, G., *An Introduction to the History of the English Language*, Cheltenham, S. Thornes, 1981.

Bradley, H., *The Making of English*, revised by S. Potter, London, Macmillan, 1968.

Brook, G. L., *English Sound Changes*, Manchester, Manchester University Press, 1957.

Brook, G. L., *A History of the English Language*, London, Deutsch, 1958.

Ekwall, E., *A History of Modern English Sounds and Morphology*, Oxford, Blackwell, 1975.

Foster, B., *The Changing English Language*, London, Macmillan, 1981.

Heller, L. et al., *The Private Lives of English Words*, London, Routledge & Kegan Paul, 1984.

Jespersen, O., *Growth and Structure of the English Language*, Oxford, Blackwell, 1982.

Leith, D., *A Social History of English*, London, Routledge & Kegan Paul, 1983.

McKnight, G., *The Evolution of the English Language: from Chaucer to the Twentieth Century*, New York, Dover, 1968.

McLaughlin, J. C., *Aspects of the History of English*, New York, Holt, Rinehart and Winston, 1970.

Pei, M., *The Story of the English Language*, London, Allen and Unwin, 1968.

Potter, S., *Changing English*, London, Deutsch, 1975.

Pyles, T., *The Origins and Development of the English Language*, New York, Harcourt Brace, 1982.

Scragg, B., *A History of English Spelling*, Manchester, Manchester University Press, 1975.

Shipley, J. T., *The Origins of English Words: A Discursive Dictionary of Indo-European Roots*, Baltimore and London, Johns Hopkins University Press, 1984.

Strang, B. M. H., *A History of English*, London, Methuen, 1974.

Visser, F., *An Historical Syntax of the English Language*, 4 vols, Leiden, Brill, 1963–73.

Williams, J. M., *The Origins of the English Language*, New York, The Free Press, 1975.

Wyld, H., *A History of Modern Colloquial English*, Oxford, Oxford University Press, 1956.

PRONUNCIATION

Chomsky, N. and Halle, M., *The Sound Pattern of English*, New York, Harper and Row, 1968.

Crystal, D., *Prosodic Systems and Intonation in English*, Cambridge, Cambridge University Press, 1969.

Dobson, E. J., *English Pronunciation, 1500–1700*, 2 vols, Oxford, Clarendon Press, 1968.

Fudge, E., *English Word Stress*, London, Allen and Unwin, 1984.

Gimson, A. C., *An Introduction to the Pronunciation of English*, London, Arnold, 1980.

Gimson, A. C. and Ramsaran, S. M., *An English Pronunciation Companion*, Oxford, Oxford University Press, 1984.

Jones, D., *The Pronunciation of English*, Cambridge, Cambridge University Press, 1966.

Jones, D., *An Outline of English*

Phonetics, Cambridge, Cambridge University Press, 1976.

Jones, D., *English Pronouncing Dictionary*, revised by A. C. Gimson, London, Dent, 1984.

Kingdon, R., *The Groundwork of English Stress*, London, Longman, 1958.

Kingdon, R., *The Groundwork of English Intonation*, London, Longman, 1959.

Kurath, H., *A Phonology and Prosody of Modern English*, Ann Arbor, University of Michigan Press, 1964.

Lass, R., *English Phonology and Phonological Theory*, Cambridge, Cambridge University Press, 1976.

O'Connor, J., *Phonetics*, Harmondsworth, Penguin, 1973.

O'Connor, J. D. and Arnold, G. F., *Intonation of Colloquial English*, London, Longman, 1973.

Oxford University Press (publisher), *BBC Pronouncing Dictionary of British Names*, Oxford, 1983.

Poldauf, I. A., *English Word Stress*, Oxford, Pergamon Press, 1983.

9 EUROPE AND BRITAIN

For compilations of bibliographical reference material on Britain and Europe see the following: Cosgrove, C. A., *Reader's Guide to Britain and the European Communities*, 1970; Hennessy, J., *Britain and Europe since 1945: A Bibliographical Guide*, 1973; Jeffries, J., *A Guide to the Official Publications of the European Communities*, 1981; Lodge, J. (ed.), *The European Community: Bibliographical Excursions*, 1984.

Current publications are listed in British Library of Economic and Political Science, *A London Bibliography of the Social Sciences*, annually.

For sources of information on Europe, Britain and the EEC, readers are directed to the following: C. B. D. Research (publisher), *Directory of European Associations*, 2 parts, 1981–4; Council of Europe, *European Yearbook*, annually; Editions Delta, *European Communities Yearbook*, annually; Editions Delta, *European Communities and Other European Organisations Who's Who*, 1982; Mitchell, H. and Birt, P. (comps.), *Who Does What in the Common Market*, 1972; Morris, B. et al., *The European Community: A Practical Guide and Directory for Business, Industry and Trade*, 1982; North Holland Publishing Company, *Guide to EEC Legislation*, 1979; Palmer, D. M. (ed.), *Sources of Information on the European Communities*, 1984; Overton, D., *Common Market Digest: An Information Guide to the European Communities*, 1983; Parker, G. and Parker, B., *A Dictionary of the European Communities*, 1981; Paxton, J., *A Dictionary of the European Economic Communities*, 1982; Struk, K. and Doelken, T. (eds), *Who's Who in European Institutions and Organisations*, 1982.

Outline surveys of the European Community, including the role of Britain within Europe, are provided by: Arbuthnott, H. and Edwards, G., *A Common Man's Guide to the Common Market*, 1979; Evans, D. (ed.), *Britain in the EEC*, 1973: Her Majesty's Stationery Office, *Britain and the European Community*, 1981; Kerr, A. J. C., *The Common Market and How It Works*, 1983; Lewis, D. E. S., *Britain and the European Economic Community*, 1978; Perry, K., *Britain and the Common Market Made Simple*, 1984: Wallace, W. (ed.), *Britain in Europe*, 1980.

Discussion of particular issues is provided by the following:

Economics   Coffey, P. (ed.), *Economic Policies of the Common Market*, 1979; Swann, D., *The Economics of the Common Market*, 1970; Swann, D., *Competition and Industrial Policy in the European Communities*, 1983; Tsoukalis, L., *The Politics and Economics of European Monetary Integration*, 1977: Wallace, H., *Budgetary Politics: The Finances of the European Communities*, 1980.
Government   Butler, D. and Marquand, D., *European Elections and British Politics*, 1981; Cocks, B., *The European Parliament: Structure, Procedure and Practice*, 1973; Gregory, F. C. C., *Dilemmas of Government: Britain and the European Community*, 1983; Jackson, R. and Fitzmaurice, J., *The European Parliament*, 1979; Herman, V. and Van Schendelen, R. (eds), *The European Parliament and National Parliaments*, 1979; Palmer, M., *The European Parliament*, 1981.

Law   Bathurst, M. E. et al. (eds), *Legal Problems of an Enlarged European Community*, 1972; Collins, L., *European Community Law in the United Kingdom*, 1984; Lasok, D. and Bridge, J. W., *An Introduction to the Law and Institutions of the European Communities*, 1982; Parry, A. and Hardy, S., *EEC Law*, 1981; Plender, R., *A Practical Introduction to European Community Laws*, 1980; Rudden, B. and Wyatt, D. (eds), *Basic Community Laws*, 1980; Usher, J., *European Community Law and National Law*, 1981.

REFERENCE

British Library of Economic and Political Science, *A London Bibliography of the Social Sciences*, London and New York, Mansell, annually.

C. B. D. Research Ltd (publisher), *Directory of European Associations*, 2 parts, Beckenham, 1985–6.

Cosgrove, C. A., *Reader's Guide to Britain and the European Communities*, London, PEP, 1970.

Council of Europe, *European Yearbook*, The Hague, Martinus Nijhoff, annually.

Department of Environment, *The European Communities: Sources of Information*, London, HMSO, 1972.

Editions Delta (publisher), *European Communities Yearbook*, Brussels, annually.

Editions Delta (publisher), *European Communities and Other European Organisations Who's Who*, Brussels, 1982.

Hennessy, J., *Britain and Europe since 1945: A Bibliographical Guide*, Brighton, Harvester, 1973.

Hopkins, M. (ed.), *European Communities Information: Its Uses and Users*, London, Mansell, 1984.

Jeffries, J., *A Guide to the Official Publications of the European Communities*, London, Mansell, 1981.

Lodge, J. (ed.), *The European Community: Bibliographical Excursions,* London, Frances Pinter, 1984.

Morris, B. et al., *The European Community: A Practical Guide and Directory for Business, Industry and Trade*, London, Macmillan, 1982.

North Holland Publishing Company (publisher), *Guide to EEC Legislation*, Amsterdam, 1979.

Office for Official Publications of the European Communities (publisher), *General Report on the Activities of the European Communities*, Luxembourg, annually.

Overton, D., *Common Market Digest: An Information Guide to the European Communities*, London, Library Association, 1983.

Palmer, D. M. (ed.), *Sources of Information on the European Communities*, London, Mansell, 1984.

Parker, G. and Parker, B., *A Dictionary of the European Communities*, London, Butterworth, 1981.

Paxton, J., *A Dictionary of the European Economic Communities*, London, Macmillan, 1982.

Simmonds, K. R. (ed.), *Encyclopaedia of European Community Law*, London, Sweet and Maxwell, 1985.

Who's Who, Red Series Verlag (publisher), *Who's Who in European Institutions and Organisations*, West Germany, 1983.

GENERAL

Arbuthnott, H. and Edwards, G., *A Common Man's Guide to the Common Market*, London, Macmillan, 1979.

Bailey, R., *The European Connection: Implications of E.E.C. Membership*, Oxford, Pergamon Press, 1983.

Beesley, M. E. and Hague, D. C., *Britain in the Common Market*, London, Longman, 1973.

Blauvelt, E. and Durlacher, J., *Sources of European Economic Information*,

Aldershot, Gower, 1982.

Bolt, G. J., *Communicating with EEC Markets*, London, Kogan Page, 1973.

Brown, L. N. and Jacobs, F. G., *The Court of Justice of the European Communities*, London, Sweet and Maxwell, 1983.

Butler, D. and Kitzinger, U., *The 1975 Referendum*, London, Macmillan, 1976.

Butler, D. and Marquand, D., *European Elections and British Politics*, London, Longman, 1981.

Campbell, A., *Common Market Law*, 3 vols, London, Longman, 1969–75.

Cocks, Sir B., *The European Parliament: Structure, Procedure and Practice*, London, HMSO, 1973.

Coffey, P. (ed.), *Economic Policies of the Common Market*, London, Macmillan, 1979.

Cohen, C. D. (ed.), *The Common Market—Ten Years After: An Economic Review of British Membership of the EEC, 1973–1983*, Oxford, Allan, 1983.

Collins, D., *The Operation of the European Social Fund*, London, Croom Helm, 1983.

Collins, L., *European Community Law in the United Kingdom*, London, Butterworth, 1984.

Coombes, D., *Westminster to Brussels: The Significance for Parliament of Accession to the European Community*, London, PEP, 1973.

Daltrop, A., *Politics and the European Community*, London, Longman, 1982.

Department of Industry and Trade, *British Business in Europe: Businessmen's Guide to the European Communities*, London, HMSO, 1981.

Drew, J., *Doing Business in the European Community*, London, Butterworth, 1983.

Einzig, P., *The Case against Joining the Common Market*, London, Macmillan, 1971.

El-Agraa, A. M., *Britain within the European Community: The Way Forward*, London, Macmillan, 1983.

Evans, D., *Destiny or Delusion: Britain and the Common Market*, London, Gollancz, 1971.

George, K. D. and Joll, C., *Competition Policy in the U.K. and E.E.C.*, Cambridge, Cambridge University Press, 1975.

George, K. D. and Ward, T. S., *The Structure of Industry in the E.E.C.: An International Comparison*, Cambridge, Cambridge University Press, 1975.

Gregory, F. C. C., *Dilemmas of Government: Britain and the European Community*, Oxford, Martin Robertson, 1983.

Hansard Society, *The British People: Their Voice in Europe*, Aldershot, Teakfield, 1977.

Henig, S., *Power and Decision in Europe*, London, Europotentials Press, 1980.

Her Majesty's Stationery Office, *Treaty Establishing the European Economic Community*, London, 1979.

Her Majesty's Stationery Office, *Treaty of Accession to the European Community and the European Atomic Energy Community*, London, 1979.

Her Majesty's Stationery Office, *Britain and the European Community*, London, 1981.

Herman, V. and Hagger, M., *The Legislation of Direct Elections to the European Parliament*, Aldershot, Gower, 1980.

Herman, V. and Van Schendelen, R. (eds), *The European Parliament and National Parliaments*, Farnborough, Saxon House, 1979.

Hodges, M. and Wallace, W. (eds), *Economic Divergence in the European Community*, London, Allen and Unwin, 1981.

Holland, S., *Uncommon Market*, London, Macmillan, 1980.

Holloway, J., *Social Policy Harmonisation in the European Community*, Aldershot, Gower, 1981.

Hopkins, M., *Policy Formation in the European Communities: A Bibliographical Guide to Community Documentation, 1958–1978*,

London, Mansell, 1981.

Jackson, R. and Fitzmaurice, J., *The European Parliament*, Harmondsworth, Penguin, 1979.

Jenkins, R. (ed.), *Britain and the EEC*, London, Macmillan, 1983.

Joll, J., *Britain and Europe: Pitt to Churchill, 1793–1940*, London, Black, 1961.

Jowell, R. (ed.), *British into Europe*, London, Croom Helm, 1976.

Keeton, G. W. and Frommel, S. N., *British Industry and European Law*, London, Macmillan, 1974.

Kerr, A. J. C., *The Common Market and How it Works*, Oxford, Pergamon, 1983.

King, A., *Britain Says Yes: The 1975 Referendum on the Common Market*, Washington, American Enterprise Institute, 1977.

Kitzinger, U., *The Second Try*, Oxford, Pergamon, 1968.

Kitzinger, U., *Diplomacy and Persuasion: How Britain Joined the Common Market*, London, Thames and Hudson, 1973.

Korah; V., *Competition Law of Britain and the Common Market*, London, Elek, 1975.

Lasok, D. and Bridge, J. W., *An Introduction to the Law and Institutions of the European Communities*, London, Butterworth, 1984.

Lewis, D. E. S., *Britain and the European Economic Community*, London, Heinemann, 1978.

Lieber, R. J., *British Politics and European Unity*, Berkeley, University of California Press, 1970.

Lodge, J. (ed.), *Institutions and Policies of the European Community*, London, Frances Pinter, 1983.

McQueen, M., *Britain, the EEC and the Developing World*, London, Heinemann, 1977.

Marquand, D., *A Parliament for Europe*, London, Cape, 1979.

Marsh, J. S. and Swanney, P. J., *Agriculture and the European Community*, London, Allen and Unwin, 1980.

Mathijsen, P., *A Guide to European Law*, London, Sweet and Maxwell, 1980.

Morris, B. et al., *European Community, The Practical Guide for Business and Government*, London, Macmillan, 1982.

Nairn, T., *The Left against Europe*, Harmondsworth, Penguin, 1973.

Niblock, M., *The E.E.C.: National Parliaments in Community Decision-Making*, London, PEP, 1971.

Noel, E., *The European Community: How it Works*, London, HMSO, 1979.

Palmer, M., *The European Parliament: What it Is—What it Does—How it Works*, Oxford, Pergamon, 1981.

Parry, A. and Hardy, S., *E.E.C. Law*, London, Sweet and Maxwell, 1981.

Perry, K., *Britain and the Common Market Made Simple*, London, Heinemann, 1984.

Plender, R., *A Practical Introduction to European Community Laws*, London, Sweet and Maxwell, 1980.

Robins, L. J., *The Reluctant Party: Labour and the E.E.C., 1961–1975*, London, Hesketh, 1979.

Rogers, S. J. and Davey, B. H., *The Common Agricultural Policy and Britain*, Farnborough, D. C. Heath, 1973.

Rudden, B. and Wyatt, D. (eds), *Basic Community Laws*, Oxford, Clarendon Press, 1980.

Saunders, C., *From Free Trade to Integration in Western Europe*, London, Chatham House, 1975.

Simmonds, K. R. (ed.), *European Community Treaties*, London, Sweet and Maxwell, 1980.

Stuart, Lord M., *The European Communities and the Rule of Law*, London, Stevens, 1977.

Swann, D., *The Economics of the Common Market*, Harmondsworth, Penguin, 1970.

Swann, D., *Competition and Industrial Policy in the European Communities*, London, Methuen, 1983.

Taylor, P., *The Limits of European Integration*, London, Croom Helm, 1983.

Tsoukalis, L., *The Politics and Economics of European Monetary Integration*, London, Allen and Unwin, 1977.

Twitchett, C. C. (ed.), *Harmonisation in the EEC*, London, Macmillan, 1981.

Twitchett, C. and Twitchett, K. J. (eds), *Building Europe: Britain's Partners in the E.E.C.*, London, Europa Publications, 1981.

Twitchett, K. J. (ed.), *European Co-operation Today*, London, Heinemann, 1980.

Uri, P. (ed.), *From Commonwealth to Common Market*, Harmondsworth, Penguin, 1968.

Usher, J., *European Community Law and National Law*, London, Allen and Unwin, 1981.

Wallace, H., *National Governments and the European Communities*, London, Chatham House, 1973.

Wallace, H., *Budgetary Politics: The Finances of the European Communities*, London, Allen and Unwin, 1980.

Wallace, H. et al., *Policy-Making in the European Community*, London, Wiley, 1983.

Wallace, W. (ed.), *Britain in Europe*, London, Heinemann, 1980.

Wallace, W., *Britain's Bilateral Links within Western Europe*, London, Routledge & Kegan Paul, 1984.

Warr, L., *Britain and Europe*, Brighton, Harvester Press, 1980.

Wyatt, D. and Dashwood, A., *The Substantive Law of the E.E.C.*, London, Sweet and Maxwell, 1980.

10 FOREIGN POLICY

Bibliographical guides to publications on British foreign policy are provided in: Aster, S. (ed.), *British Foreign Policy 1918–1945: A Guide to Research and Research Materials*, 1984; Boardman, R., *Britain and the International System, 1945–1973: A Guide to the Literature*, 1974; Her Majesty's Stationery Office, *Documents on British Policy Overseas* (series); Mitchell, C. R. and Groom, A. J. R. (eds), *International Relations Theory: A Bibliography*, 1978; Public Records Office, *The Records of the Foreign Office, 1782–1939*, 1969; Woodward, L. et al., *Documents on British Foreign Policy, 1919–1939*, 1946–.

For current publications see British Library of Economic and Political Science, *A London Bibliography of the Social Sciences*, annually.

Discussions of modern British foreign policy can be found in Barber, J., *Who Makes British Foreign Policy?*, 1976; Boardman, R. and Groom, A. J. R., *The Management of Britain's External Relations*, 1973; Cyr, A., *British Foreign Policy and the Atlantic Area: The Techniques of Accommodation*, 1979; Dilks, D. (ed.), *Retreat from Power: Studies in Britain's Foreign Policy of the Twentieth Century*, 2 vols, 1981; Jenkins, S. and Sloman, A. (eds), *With Respect Ambassador*, 1985; Jones, R., *The Changing Structure of British Foreign Policy*, 1974; Wallace, W., *The Foreign Policy Process in Britain*, 1977.

For historical studies of British foreign policy readers are referred to Bullen, R., *The Foreign Office, 1782–1982*, 1984; Gooch, G. P. and Ward, A. W. (eds), *Cambridge History of British Foreign Policy, 1783–1910*, 3 vols, 1922–3; Medlicott, W. N. (ed.), *From Metternich to Hitler: Aspects of British and Foreign History, 1814–1939*, 1963; Seton-Watson, R. W., *Britain in Europe, 1789–1914: A Survey of Foreign Policy*, 1973; Temperley, H. W. V. and Penson, L. M., *Foundations of British Foreign Policy, 1792–1902*, 1966; Wiener, J. H., *Great Britain: Foreign Policy and the Span of Empire, 1689–1971: A Documentary History*, 4 vols, 1972.

REFERENCE

Aster, S. (ed.), *British Foreign Policy, 1918–1945: A Guide to Research and Research Materials*, Tunbridge Wells, Costello, 1984.

Boardman, R., *Britain and the International System, 1945–1973: A Guide to the Literature*, Halifax, Centre for Foreign Policy Studies, Dalhousie University, 1974.

British Library of Economic and Political Science, *A London Bibliography of the Social Sciences*, London and New York, Mansell, annually.

Foreign and Commonwealth Office, *Select Bibliography on British Aid to Developing Countries*, London, HMSO, 1971.

Foreign and Commonwealth Office, *Catalogue of the Foreign Office Library, 1926–68*, 8 vols, Boston, Mass., G. K. Hall, 1972.

Her Majesty's Stationery Office, *The Diplomatic Service List*, London, annually.

Her Majesty's Stationery Office, *Documents on British Policy Overseas*, London, 1946–, series.

Mitchell, C. R. and Groom, A. J. R.

(eds), *International Relations Theory: A Bibliography*, London, Frances Pinter, 1978.

Parry, C. and Hopkins, C., *An Index of British Treaties, 1101–1968*, London, HMSO, 1970.

Public Records Office, *The Records of the Foreign Office, 1782–1939*, London, HMSO, 1969.

Thomas, D. H. and Case, L. M. (eds), *The New Guide to the Diplomatic Archives of Western Europe*, Philadelphia, University of Pennsylvania, 1975.

GENERAL

Barber, J., *Who Make British Foreign Policy?*, Milton Keynes, Open University Press, 1976.

Barker, E., *The British Between the Superpowers, 1945–50*, London, Macmillan, 1984.

Barnett, C., *The Collapse of British Power*, Gloucester, Alan Sutton, 1984.

Beloff, M., *Foreign Policy and the Democratic Process*, London, Greenwood Press, 1977.

Black, J., *British Foreign Policy in the Age of Walpole*, Edinburgh, Donald, 1985.

Boardman, R. and Groom, A. J. R., *The Management of Britain's External Relations*, London, Macmillan, 1973.

Bourne, K., *The Foreign Policy of Victorian England, 1830–1902*, London, Oxford University Press, 1970.

Burton, J. et al., *Britain between East and West*, Aldershot, Gower Publishing, 1984.

Butler, R. and Pelley, M. E. (eds), *Documents on British Policy Overseas*, London, HMSO, 1984–.

Central Office of Information, *Overseas Aid: A Brief Survey*, HMSO, 1978.

Central Office of Information, *Britain's Overseas Relations*, London, HMSO, 1983.

Connell, J., *The 'Office': A Study of British Foreign Policy and its Makers, 1919–1951*, London, Allan Wingate, 1958.

Crowson, P. S., *Tudor Foreign Policy*, London, Black, 1973.

Cyr, A., *British Foreign Policy and the Atlantic Area: The Techniques of Accommodation*, London, Macmillan, 1979.

Dafter, R. and Davidson, I., *North Sea Oil and Gas and British Foreign Policy*, London, The Royal Institute of International Affairs, 1980.

Darby, P., *British Defence Policy East of Suez, 1947–1968*, London, Oxford University Press, 1973.

Dilks, D. (ed.), *Retreat from Power: Studies in Britain's Foreign Policy of the Twentieth Century*, 2 vols, London, Macmillan, 1981.

Feltham, R. G., *Diplomatic Handbook*, London, Longman, 1970.

Frankel, J., *British Foreign Policy, 1945–1973*, London, Oxford University Press, 1975.

Gooch, G. P. and Masterman, J. H. E., *A Century of British Foreign Policy*, London, Kennikat Press, 1971.

Gooch, G. P. and Ward, A. W. (eds), *Cambridge History of British Foreign Policy, 1783–1910*, 3 vols, Cambridge, Cambridge University Press, 1922–3.

Haigh, A., *Congress of Vienna to Common Market: An Outline of British Foreign Policy, 1815–1972*, London, Harrap, 1973.

Hannah, I. C., *A History of British Foreign Policy*, London, Nicholson and Watson, 1938.

Hayes, P., *Modern British Foreign Policy: The Nineteenth Century, 1814–80*, London, Black, 1973.

Hayes, P., *Modern British Foreign Policy: The Twentieth Century, 1880–1939*, London, Black, 1975.

Heater, D. B., *Britain and the Outside World*, London, Longman, 1976.

Jenkins, S and Sloman, A., *With Respect Ambassador: An Inquiry into the Foreign Office*, London, BBC, 1985.

Jones, P. et al., *British Foreign Secretaries*

since 1945, Newton Abbot, David and Charles, 1977.

Jones, R., *The Nineteenth-Century Foreign Office: An Administrative History*, London, Weidenfeld and Nicolson, 1971.

Jones, R., *The Changing Structure of British Foreign Policy*, London, Longman, 1974.

Kennedy, P. M., *The Realities behind Diplomacy: Background and Influences on British External Policy, 1865–1980*, London, Fontana, 1981.

Leifer, M. (ed.), *Constraints and Adjustments in British Foreign Policy*, London, Allen and Unwin, 1972.

Lowe, C. J. and Dockrill, M. L., *The Mirage of Power: British Foreign Policy*, 3 vols, London, Routledge & Kegan Paul, 1972.

Marcham, A. T., *Foreign Policy*, London, Methuen, 1973.

Medlicott, W. N., *British Foreign Policy since Versailles*, London, Methuen, 1940.

Medlicott, W. N. (ed.), *From Metternich to Hitler: Aspects of British and Foreign History, 1814–1939*, London, Routledge & Kegan Paul, 1963.

Moorhouse, G., *The Diplomats: The Foreign Office Today*, London, Cape, 1977.

Nicolson, H., *Diplomacy*, London, Oxford University Press, 1969.

Northedge, F. S., *British Foreign Policy: The Process of Readjustment, 1945–1961*, London, Bell, 1966.

Northedge, F. S., *Descent from Power: British Foreign Policy, 1945–1973*, London, Allen and Unwin, 1974.

O'Brien, P. J., *Britain's Role in the World*, London, Allen and Unwin, 1975.

Peele, G. and Cooke, C. (eds), *The Politics of Reappraisal, 1918–1939*, London, Macmillan, 1975.

Platt, D. C. M., *Finance, Trade and Politics in British Foreign Policy, 1945–1973*, London, 1975.

Reynolds, P. A., *British Foreign Policy in the Inter-War Years*, London, Longman, 1954.

Rothstein, A., *British Foreign Policy and its Critics, 1830–1950*, London, Lawrence and Wishart, 1969.

Royal Institute of International Affairs, *Survey of International Affairs, 1920–1966*, 44 vols, London, 1925–77.

Royal Institute of International Affairs, *Documents on International Affairs, 1928–1963*, London, 1929–.

Swartz, M., *The Politics of British Foreign Policy in the Era of Disraeli and Gladstone*, London, Macmillan, 1985.

Taylor, A. J. P., *The Troublemakers: Dissent over Foreign Policy, 1792–1939*, Harmondsworth, Penguin, 1957.

Temperley, H. W. V. and Penson, L. M., *Foundations of British Foreign Policy, 1792–1902*, London, Cass, 1966.

Verrier, A., *Through the Looking Glass: British Foreign Policy in an Age of Illusions*, London, Cape, 1983.

Vital, D., *The Making of British Foreign Policy*, London, Allen and Unwin, 1968.

Vivekanandan, B., *The Shrinking Circle: The Commonwealth in British Foreign Policy, 1945–1974*, London, Sangam, 1984.

Wallace, W., *The Foreign Policy Process in Britain*, London, Allen and Unwin, 1977.

Watt, D. C., *Personalities and Policies: Studies in the Formation of British Foreign Policy in the Twentieth Century*, London, Longman, 1965.

Wernham, R. B., *Before the Armada: The Growth of English Foreign Policy, 1485–1588*, London, Cape, 1966.

White, J., *The Politics of Foreign Aid*, London, Bodley Head, 1975.

Wiener, J. H. (comp.), *Great Britain: Foreign Policy and the Span of Empire, 1689–1971: A Documentary History*, 4 vols, New York, Chelsea House, 1972.

Woodward, L., *British Foreign Policy in the Second World War*, 5 vols, London, HMSO, 1970–6.

SEE ALSO:

11 GEOGRAPHY

The following can be recommended for atlas and map references to Great Britain: Automobile Association, *The Complete Atlas of Great Britain*, 1980; Bartholomew, *Road Atlas, Britain*, 1982; Ordnance Survey, *Great Britain, Ordnance Survey Maps*.

Geographical outline surveys of the British Isles are provided by the following: Anderson, J. G. C. and Owen, T. R., *The Structure of the British Isles*, 1980; Beddis, R. A., *The Land and People of Britain*, 1974; Carter, H. et al., *An Advanced Geography of the British Isles*, 1974; Dobson, F. R. and Virgo, H. E., *The Physical and Human Geography of the British Isles*, 1972; Ferriday, A., *The British Isles*, 1971; Graves, N. J. and White, T. J., *Geography of the British Isles*, 1978; Lowry, J. H., *The British Isles: Physical and Regional*, 1973; Stamp, L. D. and Beaver, S. H., *The British Isles: A Geographic and Economic Survey*, 1971; Watson, J. W., et al. (eds), *The British Isles: A Systematic Geography*, 1964.

For introductory reading to particular aspects of British geography readers should consult the following:

Climate   Chandler, T. J. and Gregory, S. (eds), *The Climate of the British Isles*, 1976; Stirling, R., *The Weather of Britain*, 1982.
Economic Geography   Central Office of Information, *Regional Development in Britain*, 1976; Monkhouse, F. J., *The Material Resources of Britain: An Economic Geography of the United Kingdom*, 1971.
Geology   Owen, T. R. (ed.), *United Kingdom: Introduction to General Geology*, 1980; Trueman, A. E., *Geology and Scenery in England and Wales*, 1972.
Social Geography   Dennis, R. and Clout, H., *A Social Geography of England and Wales*, 1980; Short, J. R. and Kirby, A., *The Human Geography of Contemporary Britain*, 1984.
Urban Geography   Champion, T. and Goddard, J. B. (eds), *The Urban and Regional Transformation of Britain*, 1983; Gregory, D., *An Urban Geography of England*, 1984.

REFERENCE

Automobile Association, *AA Book of British Towns*, Drive Publications, 1979.

Automobile Association, *The Complete Atlas of Great Britain*, London, 1980.

Automobile Association, *Great Britain, Road Atlas*, London, 1980.

Barker, M. J. C. (comp.), *Directory of the Environment: Organisations in Britain and Ireland, 1984–5*, London, Routledge & Kegan Paul, 1985.

Bartholomew (publisher), *Gazetteer of the British Isles*, Edinburgh, 1977.

Bartholomew (publisher), *Road Atlas, Britain*, Edinburgh, 1982.

Branson, C. E., *South East England, Reader's Guide*, London, Library Association, 1981.

Brewer, J. G., *The Literature of Geography: A Guide to its Organisation and Use*, London, Bingley, 1978.

Centre for Environmental Studies, *Annual Report*, London, annually.

Clayton, K. M. (ed.), *Bibliography of British Geomorphology*, London, Philip, 1964.

Countryside Commission, *Annual Report*, London, HMSO, annually.

Dolphin, P. et al. (eds), *The London Region: An Annotated Geographical Bibliography*, London, Mansell, 1981.

Elliot, J. D. (ed.), *Northern Ireland, Reader's Guide*, Penzance, Library Association, Public Libraries Group, 1980.

Forestry Commission, *Annual Report*, London, HMSO, annually.

Fothergill, S. and Vincent, J., *The State of the Nation: An Atlas of Britain in the Eighties*, London, Pan, 1985.

George Philips (publisher), *The National Trust Atlas*, London, 1981.

Goddard, S. (ed.), *A Guide to Information Sources in the Geographical Sciences*, London, Croom Helm, 1983.

Hadfield, J. (ed.), *The New Shell Guide to England*, London, Michael Joseph, 1981, revised by A. Brode.

Her Majesty's Stationery Office, *Regional Trends*, London, annually.

Institute of Geological Science, *British Regional Geology*, London, HMSO, series.

Lewis, R. H. (ed.), *Wales, Reader's Guide*, Penzance, Library Association, Public Libraries Group, 1980.

Library Association, *The Environment: A Reader's Guide*, London, 1975.

Lock, C. B. M., *Geography: A Reference Handbook*, London, Bingley, 1968.

Mason, O., *The Gazetteer of England*, Newton Abbot, David and Charles, 1972.

Maxted, I. (comp.), *South West England, Reader's Guide*, Exeter, West Country Studies Library, 1982.

Mullay, S. (ed.), *Scotland, Bibliography, Reader's Guide*, Penzance, Library Association, Public Libraries Group, 1981.

National Conservancy Council, *Handbook*, London, HMSO, annually.

Natural Environment Research Council, *Annual Report*, London, HMSO, annually.

Ordnance Survey, *Great Britain, Ordnance Survey Maps*, Newton Abbot, David and Charles.

Reid, T. D. W. (ed.), *North West England, Reader's Guide*, Penzance, Library Association, Public Libraries Group, 1982.

Ridley, M. (ed.), *North East England, Reader's Guide*, Penzance, Library Association, Public Libraries Group, 1983.

Room, A., *A Concise Dictionary of Modern Place Names in Great Britain and Ireland*, Oxford, Oxford University Press, 1983.

Royal Automobile Club, *Great Britain Road Atlas*, Tonbridge, Map Productions, 1982.

GENERAL

Anderson, J. G. C. and Owen, T. R., *The Structure of the British Isles*, Oxford, Pergamon Press, 1980.

Ardill, J., *The New Citizen's Guide to Town and Country Planning*, London, Town and Country Planning Association, 1974.

Beddis, R. A., *The Land and People of Britain*, Sevenoaks, Hodder and Stoughton, 1974.

Blacksell, M., and Gilg, A. W., *The Countryside: Planning and Change*, London, Allen and Unwin, 1981.

Bowen, D., *Britain's Weather*, Newton Abbot, David and Charles, 1969.

Brooker, R. W., *Assignment Geography: The British Homeland*, London, Harrap, 1969.

Buchanan C., *The State of Britain*, London, Faber, 1972.

Carter, H. et al., *An Advanced Geography of the British Isles*, Amersham, Hulton, 1974.

Central Office of Information, *Town and*

Country Planning in Britain, London, HMSO, 1975.

Chandler, T. J. and Gregory, S. (eds), *The Climate of the British Isles*, London, Longman, 1976.

Clark, R. B., *The Waters of Britain*, London, Oxford University Press, 1984.

Clout, H. D., *Rural Geography: An Introductory Survey*, Oxford, Pergamon, 1972.

Cullingworth, J. B., *Town and Country Planning in Britain*, London, Allen and Unwin, 1985.

Curdall, L., *The British Isles*, London, Evans, 1970.

Curtis, L. F. et al., *Soils of the British Isles*, London, Longman, 1976.

Darby, H. C. (ed.), *A New Historical Geography of England after 1600*, Cambridge, Cambridge University Press, 1978.

Dobson, F. R. and Virgo, H. E., *The Physical and Human Geography of the British Isles*, Sevenoaks, Hodder and Stoughton, 1972.

Dodgshon, R. and Butlin, R. A. (eds), *An Historical Geography of England and Wales*, London, Academic Press, 1978.

Dunning, F. W. et al., *Britain Before Man*, London, HMSO, 1978.

Dury, G. H., *The British Isles*, London, Heinemann, 1978.

Ferriday, A., *The British Isles*, London, Macmillan, 1971.

Freeman, T. W., *Geography and Regional Administration*, London, Hutchinson, 1968.

Geological Sciences Institutue, *Geological Survey of Great Britain*, London, HMSO, 1976.

Geologists' Association, *Guides*, Series, London.

Gilg, A. W., *Countryside Planning: The First Three Decades, 1945–1976*, London, Methuen, 1979.

Goodson, J. B., *The British Isles: A Colour Geography*, London, Nelson, 1976.

Gower (publisher), *Environment: New Society Social Studies Reader*, Aldershot, 1986.

Graves, N. J. and White, T. J., *Geography of the British Isles*, London, Heinemann, 1978.

Hardy, A. V. (ed.), *The British Isles, The Geography of the British Isles Series*, Cambridge, Cambridge University Press, 1981.

House, J. W. (ed.), *The U. K. Space: Resources, Environment and the Future*, London, Weidenfeld and Nicolson, 1977.

Hyams, E., *The Changing Face of Britain*, London, Paladin, 1977.

Johnston, R. J. and Doornkamp, J. C. (ed.), *The Changing Geography of the United Kingdom*, London, Methuen, 1983.

King, W. J., *The Geography of the British Isles*, Macdonald and Evans, Plymouth, 1975.

Kirby, C., *Water in Great Britain*, Harmondsworth, Penguin, 1971.

Kirby, D. A. and Robinson, H., *Geography of Britain: Perspectives and Problems*, Slough, University Tutorial Press, 1981.

Lamb, H. H., *The English Climate*, London, English Universities Press, 1964.

Lowry, J. H., *The British Isles: Physical and Regional*, London, Arnold, 1973.

Manley, G., *Climate and the British Scene*, London, Fontana, 1970.

Marsden, W. E., *Changing Geography of Britain*, Edinburgh, Oliver and Boyd, 1978.

Millward, R. and Robinson, A., *Upland Britain*, Newton Abbot, David and Charles, 1980.

Nixon, W. B., *British Isles*, Slough, University Tutorial Press, 1984.

Owen, T. R., *The Geological Evolution of the British Isles*, Oxford, Pergamon, 1976.

Owen, T. R. (ed.), *United Kingdom: Introduction to General Geology*, London, Institute of Geological Science, 1980.

Parker, D. J. and Penning-Rowsell, E. C., *Water Planning in Britain*, London, Allen & Unwin, 1980.

Preece, D. M. and Wood, H. R. B., *The British Isles*, London, University Tutorial Press, 1977.

Rayner, D., *Stratigraphy of the British Isles*, Cambridge, Cambridge University Press, 1981.

Reed, A. and Hawkes, L. R., *The British Isles through Maps and Diagrams*, Exeter, Wheaton, 1979.

Regional Studies Association, *Report on an Inquiry into Regional Problems of the United Kingdom*, Norwich, Geo Books, 1983.

Renner, J. and Macaulay, J., *Source Book on British Isles Geography*, London, Longman, 1983.

Shave, D. W., *The Homeland: Local Geography and the British Isles*, London, Murray, 1970.

Simmons, W. M., *The British Isles*, Plymouth, Macdonald and Evans, 1980.

Stamp, L. D. and Beaver, S. H., *The British Isles: A Geographic and Economic Survey*, London, Longman, 1971.

Stephenson, K. B., *Geography of the British Isles in Colour*, London, Blandford Press, 1973.

Stirling, R., *The Weather of Britain*, London, Faber, 1982.

Thomas, D. et al., *Advanced Geography of the British Isles*, Amersham, Hulton, 1974.

Tolson, A. R. and Johnstone, M. E., *A Geography of Britain*, London, Oxford University Press, 1976.

Watson, J. W. et al. (eds), *The British Isles: A Systematic Geography*, London, Nelson, 1964.

Waugh, D., *The British Isles*, London, Nelson, 1983.

Williams, H. and Jones, H. P., *The Physical Basis of the British Isles*, London, Macmillan, 1972.

LANDSCAPE

Atterbury, P., *English Rivers and Canals*, London, Weidenfeld and Nicolson, 1983.

Bell, M., *Britain's National Parks*, Newton Abbot, David and Charles, 1975.

Blacksell, M. and Gilg, A. W., *The Countryside: Planning and Change*, London, Allen and Unwin, 1981.

Blunden, J. and Curry, N. (eds), *The Changing Countryside*, London, Croom Helm, 1985.

Blunden, J. and Turner, G., *Critical Countryside*, London, BBC, 1985.

Bush, R., *The National Parks of England*, London, Dent, 1974.

Cheatle, J. R. W., *A Guide to the British Landscape*, London, Collins, 1976.

Coones, P. and Patten, J., *The Penguin Guide to the Landscape of England and Wales*, Harmondsworth, Penguin, 1986.

Freethy, R., *The Making of the British Countryside*, Newton Abbot, David and Charles, 1981.

Gill, C. (ed.), *Countryman's Britain*, Newton Abbot, David and Charles, 1976.

Goudie, A. and Gardner, R., *Discovering Landscape in England and Wales*, London, Allen and Unwin, 1985.

Gray, C., *Countryside in Danger*, London, Macmillan, 1982.

Hinde, T., *Forests of Britain*, London, Gollancz, 1985.

Hoskins, W. G., *The Making of the English Landscape*, Sevenoaks, Hodder and Stoughton, 1977.

Hoskins, W. G., *English Landscapes*, London, BBC, 1977.

James, N. D. G., *A History of English Forestry*, Oxford, Blackwell, 1981.

Morris, M. C., *Britain's Changing Countryside*, London, Oxford University Press, 1971.

Moss, G., *Britain's Wasting Acres: Land Use in a Changing Society*, London, Architectural Press, 1981.

Muir, R., *The Shell Guide to Reading the Landscape*, London, Michael Joseph, 1981.

Muir, R., *Shell Guide to Reading the Celtic Landscapes*, London, Michael Joseph, 1985.

Muir, R. and Duffey, E., *The Shell Countryside Books*, London, Dent, 1984.

Open University, *The Countryside*

Handbook, London, Croom Helm, 1985.

Robinson, A. and Millward, R., *The Shell Book of the British Coast*, Newton Abbot, David and Charles, 1983.

Shepherd, W., *The Living Landscape of Britain*, London, Faber, 1963.

Stamp, L. D., *Britain's Structure and Scenery*, London, Collins, 1974.

Steers, J. A., *The Coastline of England and Wales*, Cambridge, Cambridge University Press, 1964.

Steers, J. A., *Coastal Features of England and Wales*, Cambridge, Oleander Press, 1980.

Tansley, A. G., *The British Islands and their Vegetation*, 2 vols, Cambridge, Cambridge University Press, 1953.

Taylor, C., *Fields in the English Landscape*, London, Dent, 1975.

Trueman, A. E., *Geology and Scenery in England and Wales*, Harmondsworth, Penguin, 1972.

Turner, J., *The Countryside of Britain*, London, Ward Lock, 1977.

Woodell, S. R. J. (ed.), *The English Landscape, Past, Present and Future*, London, Oxford University Press, 1985.

SOCIAL AND ECONOMIC GEOGRAPHY

Barr, J., *Derelict Britain*, Harmondsworth, Penguin, 1969.

Blunden, J., *The Mineral Resources of Britain*, London, Hutchinson, 1975.

Brown, A. J., *The Framework of Regional Economics in the UK*, Cambridge, Cambridge University Press, 1972.

Central Office of Information, *Regional Development in Britain*, HMSO, London, 1976.

Cherry, G. E. (ed.), *Rural Planning Problems*, London, Leonard Hill, 1976.

Chisholm, M., *Resources for Britain's Future*, Harmondsworth, Penguin, 1972.

Chisholm, M. and Manners, G. (eds), *Spatial Policy Problems of the British Economy*, Cambridge, Cambridge University Press, 1971.

Coates, B. E. and Rawston, E. M., *Regional Variations in Britain: Studies in Economic and Social Geography*, London, Batsford, 1971.

Coppock, J. T., *An Agricultural Geography of Great Britain*, London, Bell, 1971.

Coppock, J. T., *An Agricultural Atlas of England and Wales*, London, Faber, 1976.

Cullingworth, J. B., *Town and Country Planning in Britain*, London, Allen and Unwin, 1985.

Dennis, R. and Clout, H., *A Social Geography of England and Wales*, Oxford, Pergamon Press, 1980.

Devereux, M. P., *Industries in Britain*, London, Macmillan, 1974.

Devereux, M. P. and Evans, F. C., *Seaports in Britain*, London, Macmillan, 1976.

Fernie, J., *A Geography of Energy in the United Kingdom*, London, Longman, 1980.

Fothergill, S. and Gudgin, G., *Unequal Growth: Urban and Regional Employment Change in the UK*, London, Heinemann, 1982.

Fullerton, B., *The Development of British Transport Networks*, London, Oxford University Press, 1975.

Healey, M. (ed.), *Urban and Regional Industrial Research: The Changing UK Data Base*, Norwich, Geo Books, 1983.

Hoare, A. G., *The Location of Industry in Britain*, Cambridge, Cambridge University Press, 1983.

Holland, S., *The Regional Problem*, London, Macmillan, 1976.

House, J. W. (ed.), *The UK Space: Resources, Environment and the Future*, London, Weidenfeld and Nicolson, 1977.

Johnson, R., *Farms in Britain*, London, Macmillan, 1971.

Jones, G., *Rural Life: Patterns and Processes*, London, Longman, 1973.

Keeble, D., *Industrial Location and*

Planning in the United Kingdom, London, Methuen, 1976.

Law, C. M., *British Regional Development since World War I*, London, Methuen, 1981.

Maclennan, D. and Parr, J. B., (eds), *Regional Policy: Past Experience and New Directions*, Oxford, Martin Robertson, 1979.

Maltby, D. and White, H. P., *Transport in the United Kingdom*, London, Macmillan, 1982.

Manners, G. et al., *Regional Development in Britain*, Chichester, Wiley, 1980.

Martin, R. and Rowthorn, B., *The Geography of De-Industrialisation*, London, Macmillan, 1985.

Monkhouse, F. J., *The Material Resources of Britain: An Economic Geography of the United Kingdom*, London, Longman, 1971.

Moore, B. et al., *The Effects of Government Regional Economic Policy*, London, HMSO, 1986.

Parson, D. W., *The Political Economy of British Regional Policy*, London, Croom Helm, 1985.

Patmore, J. A., *Land and Leisure in England and Wales*, Newton Abbot, David and Charles, 1970.

Phillips, D. and Williams, A., *Rural Britain: A Social Geography*, Oxford, Blackwell, 1984.

Rees, H., *The Industries of Britain: A Geography of Manufacturing and Power, together with Farming and Fishing*, London, Harrap, 1970.

Regional Studies Association, *Report of an Inquiry into Regional Problems in the United Kingdom*, Norwich, Geo Books, 1983.

Sant, M., *Industrial Movement and Regional Development: The British Case*, Oxford, Pergamon, 1975.

Shirlaw, D. W. G., *An Agricultural Geography of Great Britain*, Oxford, Pergamon, 1971.

Short, J. R. and Kirby, A. (eds), *The Human Geography of Contemporary Britain*, London, Macmillan, 1984.

Smith, W., *An Historical Introduction to the Economic Geography of Great Britain*, London, Bell, 1968.

Starkie, D. N., *Transportation Planning and Public Policy*, Oxford, Pergamon, 1973.

Taylor, C., *Rural Settlements in England*, London, George Philips, 1983.

Taylor, R. et al. (eds), *Britain's Planning Heritage*, London, Croom Helm, 1975.

Warren, K., *The Geography of British Heavy Industry since 1800*, London, Oxford University Press, 1975.

URBAN GEOGRAPHY

Aldridge, M., *The British New Towns: A Programme Without a Policy*, London, Routledge & Kegan Paul, 1979.

Aston, M. and Bond, J., *Landscape of Towns*, London, Dent, 1976.

Cameron, G. C., *The Future of the British Conurbations*, London, Longman, 1980.

Central Office of Information, *The New Towns of Britain*, London, HMSO, 1974.

Champion, T. and Goddard, J. B. (eds), *The Urban and Regional Transformation of Britain*, London, Methuen, 1983.

Cherry, G. E., *Urban Change and Planning: History of Urban Development in Britain since 1756*, Henley-on-Thames, Foulis, 1972.

Cullingworth, J. B., *Town and Country Planning in Britain*, London, Allen and Unwin. 1985.

Evans, H. (ed.), *New Towns: The British Experience*, London, Knight, 1972.

Freeman, T. W., *The Conurbations of Great Britain*, Manchester, Manchester University Press, 1966.

Gregory, D., *An Urban Geography of England*, Cambridge, Cambridge University Press, 1984.

Hall, P. (ed.), *The Inner City in Context*, London, Heinemann, 1981.

Hall, P. et al., *The Containment of*

Urban England, London, Allen and Unwin, 1973.

Lambert, C. and Weir, D. (eds), *Cities in Modern Britain*, London, Fontana, 1975.

Lawless, P., *Britain's Inner Cities*, London, Harper and Row, 1981.

Lawless, P. and Raban, C., *The Contemporary British City*, London, Harper and Row, 1986.

McKay, D. and Cox, A., *The Politics of Urban Change*, London, Croom Helm, 1979.

Nairn, I., *Britain's Changing Towns*, London, BBC, 1967.

Rees, G. and Lambert, J., *Cities in Crisis: The Political Economy of British Urban Development*, London, Arnold, 1985.

Sharp, T., *Town and Townscape*, London, J. Murray, 1968. ·

Short, J. R., *The Urban Area, Capital, State and Community in Contemporary Britain*, London, Macmillan, 1984.

Spence, N. et al., *British Cities: An Analysis of Urban Change*, Oxford, Pergamon, 1982.

Stone, P. A., *Urban Development in Britain*, Cambridge, Cambridge University Press, 1970.

Storm, M., *Urban Growth in Britain*, London, Oxford University Press, 1985.

Thorns, D. C., *Suburbia*, London, Paladin, 1972.

White, B., *The Literature and Study of Urban and Regional Planning*, London, Routledge & Kegan Paul, 1974.

REGIONS

MIDLANDS AND SOUTHERN ENGLAND

Black, H. D., *South West England, the Geography of the British Isles*, Cambridge, Cambridge University Press, 1977.

Dancer, W. S. and Hardy, A. V., *Greater London, the Geography of the British Isles*, Cambridge, Cambridge University Press, 1969.

Ellis, B., *The West Midlands, the Geography of the British Isles*, Cambridge, Cambridge University Press, 1984.

Geological Sciences Institute, *London, and the Thames Valley*, British Regional Geology, London, HMSO, 1960.

Geological Sciences Institute, *East Anglia and the Adjoining Areas*, British Regional Geology, London, HMSO, 1961.

Geological Sciences Institute, *South West England*, British Regional Geology, London, HMSO, 1975.

Greasley, B., *East Anglia, the Geography of the British Isles*, Cambridge, Cambridge University Press, 1987.

Hains, B. and Horton, A., *British Regional Geology: Central England*, London, HMSO, 1969.

Jones, D. K. C., *Southeast and Southern England: The Geomorphology of the British Isles*, London, Methuen, 1981.

Kent, P., *British Regional Geology: Eastern England from the Tees to the Wash*, London, HMSO, 1980.

Martin, J. E., *Greater London: An Industrial Geography*, London, Bell, 1966.

Pritchard, C., *The West Midlands, the Geography of the British Isles*, Cambridge, Cambridge University Press, 1975.

Roberts, B. and Burkhall, S., *The South West, the Geography of the British Isles*, Cambridge, Cambridge University Press, 1987.

Savory, J. H., *South East England, the Geography of the British Isles*, Cambridge, Cambridge University Press, 1972.

Sherlock, R. L., *British Regional Geology: London and Thames*

Valley, London, HMSO, 1976.

Shorter, A. H., *Southwest England, Regions of the British Isles*, London, Nelson, 1969.

Skipp, V., *The Centre of England, Regions of Britain*, London, Methuen, 1979.

Straw, S. and Clayton, K., *Eastern and Central England, the Geomorphology of the British Isles*, London, Methuen, 1976.

Thomas, S., *The South East, the Geography of the British Isles*, Cambridge, Cambridge University Press, 1987.

Tolley, H., *The East Midlands, the Geography of the British Isles*, Cambridge, Cambridge University Press, 1987.

Walker, F., *The Bristol Region*, Regions of the British Isles, London, Nelson, 1972.

Wood, P. A., *The West Midlands*, Newton Abbot, David and Charles, 1976.

NORTHERN ENGLAND

Drury, G. H., *The East Midlands and the Peak, Regions of the British Isles*, London, Nelson, 1963.

Eastwood, T. and Taylor, B. J., et al., *British Regional Geology: Northern England*, London, HMSO, 1979.

Freeman, T. W., *Lancashire, Cheshire and the Isle of Man*, Regions of the British Isles, London, Nelson, 1966.

Geological Sciences Institute, *Northern England*, London, HMSO, 1977.

Geological Sciences Institute, *Eastern England from the Tees to the Wash*, British Regional Geology, London, HMSO, 1981.

House, J., *The North East*, Newton Abbot, David and Charles, 1969.

King, C. A. M., *Northern England, the Geomorphology of the British Isles*, London, Methuen, 1976.

Lewis, P. and Jones, P. N., *The Humberside Region*, Newton Abbot, David and Charles, 1970.

Marsden, W. E., *North West England,*

Geography of the British Isles, Cambridge, Cambridge University Press, 1979.

Millward, R. and Robinson, A., *The Lake District, Regions of Britain*, London, Methuen, 1974.

Raistrick, A., *The Pennine Dales, Regions of Britain*, London, Methuen, 1984.

Sharrod, B., *The North West*, Cambridge, Cambridge University Press, 1984.

Smailes, A. E., *Northern England, Regions of the British Isles*, London, Nelson, 1960.

Smith, D. M., *The North West*, Newton Abbot, David and Charles, 1969.

Tolley, H. and Orrell, K., *Yorkshire and Humberside, the Geography of the British Isles*, Cambridge, Cambridge University Press, 1987.

Waltham, J. E. and Holmes, W. D., *North East England, the Geography of the British Isles*, Cambridge, Cambridge University Press, 1979.

Warn, S. and Warn, C., *The North, the Geography of the British Isles*, Cambridge, Cambridge University Press, 1984.

NORTHERN IRELAND

Allen, F. H. A., *Man and Landscape in Northern Ireland*, London, Academic Press, 1978.

Cruickshank, J. G. and Wilcock, D. N., *Northern Ireland: Environment and Natural Resources*, Belfast, Queen's University, 1982.

Davies, G. L. H. and Stephens, N., *Ireland, the Geomorphology of the British Isles*, London, Methuen, 1978.

Hill, D. A., *Northern Ireland, the Geography of the British Isles*, Cambridge, Cambridge University Press, 1974.

Holland, C. H. (ed.), *The Geology of Ireland*, Edinburgh, Scottish Academic Press, 1981.

Orme, A. R., *Ireland, World's Landscapes*, London, Longman, 1982.

Wilson, H. E., *The Regional Geology of Northern Ireland*, London, HMSO, 1972.

SCOTLAND

Geological Sciences Institute, *Northern Highlands*, British Regional Geology, London, HMSO, 1960.

Geological Sciences Institute, *South of Scotland*, British Regional Geology, London, HMSO, 1972.

Lea, K. J., *A Geography of Scotland*, Newton Abbot, David and Charles, 1977.

McIntosh, I. G. and Marshall, C. B., *The Face of Scotland*, Oxford, Pergamon, 1977.

McWilliam, C., *Scottish Townscape*, London, Collins, 1981.

Millman, R. N., *The Making of the Scottish Landscape*, London, Batsford, 1975.

Muir, R., *Reading the Celtic Landscapes*, London, Michael Joseph, 1985.

O'Dell, A. C. and Walton, K., *The Highlands and Islands of Scotland*, Regions of the British Isles, London, Nelson, 1962.

Parry, M. I. and Slater, T. R. (eds), *The Making of the Scottish Countryside*, London, Croom Helm, 1980.

Sissons, J. B., *The Evolution of Scotland's Scenery*, Edinburgh, Oliver and Boyd, 1967.

Sissons, J. B., *Scotland, the Geomorphology of the British Isles*, London, Methuen, 1976.

Thompson, F., *The Highlands and Islands*, London, Hale, 1973.

White, J. T., *The Scottish Border and Northumberland*, Regions of Britain, London, Methuen, 1973.

Whittow, J. B., *Geology and Scenery in Scotland*, Harmondsworth, Penguin, 1977.

WALES

Bowen, E. G. (ed.), *Wales: A Physical, Historical and Regional Geography*, London, Methuen, 1956.

Emry, F. V., *Wales*, London, Longman, 1969.

Geological Sciences Institute, *North Wales*, British Regional Geology, London, HMSO, 1979.

Geological Sciences Institute, *South Wales*, British Regional Geology, London, HMSO, 1982.

Hammond, R. J. W. (ed.), *Complete Wales*, London, Ward Lock, 1977.

Hughes, M. E. and James, A. J., *Wales: A Physical, Economic and Social Geography*, Sevenoaks, Hodder and Stoughton, 1961.

Humphreys, G., *South Wales*, Newton Abbot, David and Charles, 1972.

Jones, J. L., *A New Geography of Wales*, Wrexham, Hughes, 1969.

Millward, R. and Robinson, A., *Landscapes of North Wales*, Newton Abbot, David and Charles, 1978.

Millward, R. and Robinson, A., *The Welsh Borders*, Regions of Britain, London, Methuen, 1978.

Price, M., *A Modern Geography of Wales*, Llandybie, Davies, 1974.

Sylvester, D., *The Rural Landscape of the Welsh Borderland: A Study in Historical Geography*, London, Macmillan, 1969.

Williams, M., *The Making of the Welsh Landscape*, Sevenoaks, Hodder and Stoughton, 1975.

SEE ALSO:

12 GOVERNMENT AND ADMINISTRATION

For bibliographical guides to earlier literature on government and administration see: Barker, A. (ed.), *Public Participation in Britain: A Classified Bibliography*, 1979; Keary, M. Y. and Howard, B. M., *Civil Service Department, its Organisation and History: A Bibliography*, 1979; Royal Institute of Public Administration, *The Prime Minister and the Cabinet: A Select Bibliography*, 1974; Royal Institute of Public Administration, *Public Administration—General: A Select Bibliography*, 1974; Royal Institute of Public Administration, *Government of the United Kingdom: A Select Bibliography*, 1975.

For recent publications see: British Library of Economic and Political Science, *A London Bibliography of the Social Sciences*, annually.

For information reference on local and central administration see: Boehm, K. and Morris, B., *Who Decides What: The Citizen's Handbook*, 1979; Civil Service Department, *Civil Service Year Book*, annually; Craig, F. W. S. and Craig, E. P. (eds), *The Local Government Companion: Directory of Local Authorities in Great Britain*; Municipal Publications, *The Municipal Yearbook*, annually.

For sources and collections of official government papers and information relating to central and local government readers are directed to the following: British Museum, *State Paper Room, Check List of British Official Serial Publications*, 1967; Butcher, D., *Official Publications in Britain*, 1982; Her Majesty's Stationery Office, *Government Publications: Sectional Lists*, irregular; Her Majesty's Stationery Office, *Government Publications Catalogue*, annually; Her Majesty's Stationery Office, *Catalogues and Indexes of British Government Publications, 1920–1970*, 5 vols, 1975; Pemberton, J. E., *British Official Publications*, 1973; Richard, S. (comp.), *British Government Publications: An Index to Chairmen and Authors, 1800–1982*, 4 vols, 1982–4; Richard, S., *Directory of British Official Publications*, 1984; Sheppard, J. and Foster J., *British Archives: A Guide to Archive Resources in the United Kingdom*, 1984.

The following are recommended as general studies of the field: Barber, M. P., *Public Administration*, 1983; Beloff, M. and Peele, G., *The Government of the United Kingdom: Political Authority in a Changing Society*, 1980; Birch, A. H., *The British System of Government*, 1980; Bromhead, P., *Britain's Developing Constitution*, 1974; Brown, R. G. S. and Steel, D. R., *The Administrative Process in Britain*, 1979; Central Office of Information, *The Central Government of Britain*, 1979; Farnham, D. and McVicar, M., *Public Administration in the United Kingdom: An Introduction*, 1980; Greenwood, J. and Wilson, D., *Public Administration in Britain*, 1984; Hanson, A. H. and Walles, M., *Governing Britain*, 1985; Harvey, J., *How Britain is Governed*, 1975; Jewell, R. E. C., *Outlines of Public Administration*, 1976; Leeds, C., *A Guide to British Government*, 1975; Mackenzie, W. J. M. and Grove, J. W. D., *Central Administration in Britain*, 1976; McLennan, G. et al. (eds), *State and Society in Contemporary Britain: A Critical Introduction*, 1984; Macrae, S. and Pitt, D. C., *Public Administration: An Introduction*, 1980; Mosley, R. K., *Westminster Workshop: A Student's Guide to British Government*, 1979; Padfield, C. F. and Byrne, T., *British Constitution Made Simple*, 1987; Richards, S. G., *Introduction to British Government*, 1978; Sallis, E., *The Machinery of Government: An Introduction to Public Adminis-

tration, 1982; Sampson, A., *The Changing Anatomy of Britain*, 1982; Smith, B. C., *Policy-Making in British Government: An Analysis of Power and Rationality*, 1976; Toch, H., *Essentials of British Constitution and Government*, 1983.

In addition readers are directed to the following as initial reading on particular areas.

Cabinet   Hennessy, P., *Cabinet*, 1986; Rush, M., *The Cabinet and Policy Formation*, 1984.
Civil Service   Central Office of Information, *The British Civil Service*, 1974.
Local Government   Byrne, T., *Local Government in Britain*, 1985.
Prime Minister   Carter, B. E., *The Office of Prime Minister*, 1956; King, A. (ed.), *The British Prime Minister*, 1985.

REFERENCE

Barker, A. (ed.), *Public Participation in Britain: A Classified Bibliography*, London, Bedford Square Press, 1979.

Boehm, K. and Morris, B., *Who Decides What: the Citizen's Handbook*, London, Macmillan, 1979.

British Library of Economic and Political Science, *A London Bibliography of the Social Sciences*, London and New York, Mansell, annually.

Butcher, D., *Official Publications in Britain*, London, Bingley, 1982.

Civil Service Department, *Civil Service Year Book*, London, HMSO, annually.

Craig, F. W. S. and Craig, E. P. (eds), *The Local Government Companion: Directory of Local Authorities in Great Britain*, Chichester, Parliamentary Research Services.

Hazlehurst, C. and Woodland, C., *A Guide to the Papers of British Cabinet Ministers, 1900–1951*, London, Royal Historical Society, 1974.

Her Majesty's Stationery Office (publisher), *Annual Catalogue of Government Publications*, London, annually.

Her Majesty's Stationery Office, *Index to Chairmen of Committees*, London, annually.

Her Majesty's Stationery Office, *Government Publications: Sectional Lists*, London, irregular.

Her Majesty's Stationery Office, *Catalogues and Indexes of British Government Publications*, 1920–1970, 5 vols, Bishop's Stortford, Herts, 1975.

Keary, M. Y. and Howard, B. M., *Civil Service Department, its Organisation and History: A Bibliography*, London, Civil Service Department, 1979.

Labour Party (publisher), *Local Government Handbook*, England and Wales, London, 1977.

Municipal Publications (publisher), *The Municipal Yearbook*, London, annually.

Oyez Longman (publisher), *Directory of Local Authorities*, London, 1985.

Pemberton, J. E., *British Official Publications*, Oxford, Pergamon Press, 1973.

Richard, S. (comp.), *British Government Publications: An Index to Chairmen and Authors, 1800–1982* (4 vols) London, Library Association, 1982–4.

Richard, S., *Directory of British Official Publications*, London, Mansell, 1984.

Royal Commission on Historical Manuscripts, *Papers of British Cabinet Ministers, 1782–1900*, London, HMSO, 1982.

Royal Institute of Public Administration, *The Prime Minister and the Cabinet: A Select Bibliography*, London, RIPA, 1974.

Royal Institute of Public Administration, *Public Administration—General: A Select Bibliography*, London, RIPA, 1974.

Royal Institute of Public Administration,

Government of the United Kingdom: A Select Bibliography, London, RIPA, 1975.

Sheppard, J. and Foster, J., *British Archives: A Guide to Archive Resources in the United Kingdom*, London, Macmillan, 1984.

Snape, W. H., *How to Find out about Local Government*, Oxford, Pergamon, 1969.

GENERAL

Bagehot, W., *The English Constitution*, London, Fontana, 1963.

Barker, A. (ed.), *Quangos in Britain: Government and the Network of Public Policy-Making*, London, Macmillan, 1982.

Birch, A. H., *The British System of Government*, London, Allen and Unwin, 1980.

Bourn, J., *Management in Central and Local Government*, London, Pitman, 1979.

Brennan, T., *Politics and Government in Britain: An Introductory Survey*, Cambridge, Cambridge University Press, 1972.

Bromhead, P., *Britain's Developing Constitution*, London, Allen and Unwin, 1974.

Brown, R. G. S. and Steel, D. R., *The Administrative Process in Britain*, London, Methuen, 1979.

Budd, A., *The Politics of Economic Planning*, London, Fontana, 1978.

Burch, M. and Wood, B., *Public Policy in Britain*, Oxford, Martin Robertson, 1983.

Central Office of Information, *The Central Government of Britain*, London, 1979.

Coombes, D., *Representative Government and Economic Power*, London, Heinemann, 1982.

Delbridge, R. and Smith, M. (eds), *Consuming Secrets: How Official Secrecy Affects Everyday Life in Britain*, London, Burnett, 1982.

Derry, T. K., *The United Kingdom Today: A Survey of British Institutions*, London, Longman, 1970.

Else, P. K. and Marshall, G. P., *The Management of Public Expenditure*, London, Policy Studies Institute, 1979.

Fry, G. K., *The Growth of Government*, London, Cass, 1979.

Garrett, J., *The Management of Government*, Harmondsworth, Penguin, 1972.

Gray, A. and Jenkins, B. (eds), *Policy Analysis and Evaluation in British Government*, London, RIPA, 1983.

Greenwood, J. and Wilson, D., *Public Administration in Britain*, London, Allen and Unwin, 1984.

Gregory, F., *Dilemmas of Government*, Oxford, Martin Robertson, 1983.

Griffith, J. A. G. and Hartley, T. C., *Government and the Law: An Introduction to the Working of the Constitution in Britain*, London, Weidenfeld and Nicolson, 1981.

Hanson, A. H. and Walles, M., *Governing Britain*, London, Fontana, 1985.

Harvey, J., *How Britain is Governed*, London, Macmillan, 1975.

Harvey, J. and Bather, L., *The British Constitution and Politics*, London, Macmillan, 1977.

Heady, B., *British Cabinet Ministers: The Roles of Politicians in Executive Office*, London, Allen and Unwin, 1974.

Heclo, H. and Wildavsky, A., *The Private Government of Public Money*, London, Macmillan, 1981.

Hennessy, P., *The Great and the Good: An Inquiry into the British Establishment*, London, Policy Studies Institute, 1986.

Hogwood, B. W. and Peters, B. G., *The Pathology of Public Policy*, London, Oxford University Press, 1985.

Holland, P., *The Governance of Quangos*, London, Adam Smith Institute, 1981.

Jenkins, W. I., *Policy Analysis: A Political and Organisational Perspective*, Oxford, Martin Robertson, 1978.

Jennings, I., *The British Constitution*, Cambridge, Cambridge University Press, 1966.

Jewell, R. E. C., *The British Constitution*, London, Hodder and Stoughton, 1975.

Jewell, R. E. C., *Outlines of Public Administration*, Croydon, Knight, 1976.

Johnson, N., *In Search of the Constitution*, London, Methuen, 1980.

Keeling, D., *Management in Government*, London, Allen and Unwin, 1977.

King, A., *Why Is Britain Becoming Harder to Govern?*, London, BBC, 1976.

Leeds, C., *A Guide to British Government*, Swanage, Croxton Press, 1975.

Leigh, D., *The Frontier of Secrecy: Closed Government in Britain*, London, Junction Books, 1980.

Levin, P., *Government and the Planning · Process*, London, Allen and Unwin, 1976.

Lord President of the Council, *Devolution within the United Kingdom*, London, HMSO, 1976.

Mackintosh, J., *The Government and Politics of Britain*, London, Hutchinson, 1984.

McLennan, G. et al. (eds), *State and Society in Contemporary Britain: A Critical Introduction*, Cambridge, Polity Press, 1984.

Macrae, S. and Pitt, D. C., *Public Administration: An Introduction*, London, Pitman, 1980.

Marshall, G., *Constitutional Conventions: The Rules and Forms of Political Accountability*, London, Oxford University Press, 1984.

Michael, J., *The Politics of Secrecy: Confidential Government and the Public Right to Know*, Harmondsworth, Penguin, 1982.

Miliband, R., *The State in Capitalist Society*, London, Quartet Books, 1973.

Minogue, M. (ed.), *Documents on Contemporary British Government*, vol. 1, *British Government and Constitutional Change*, Cambridge, Cambridge University Press, 1977.

Minogue, M. (ed.), *Documents on Contemporary British Government*, vol. 2, *Local Government in Britain*, Cambridge, Cambridge University Press, 1977.

Mosley, R. K., *Westminster Workshop: A Student's Guide to British Government*, Oxford, Pergamon, 1979.

Norton, P., *Constitution in Flux*, Oxford, Martin Robertson, 1982.

Ollé, J. G. (ed.), *An Introduction to British Government Publications*, London, Association of Assistant Librarians, 1973.

Padfield, C. F., *British Constitution*, London, Allen and Unwin 1972.

Padfield, C. F. and Byrne, T., *British Constitution Made Simple*, London, Heinemann, 1987.

Parry, G., *British Government*, London, Arnold, 1979.

Phillips, O. H., *Reform of the Constitution*, London, Chatto and Windus, 1970.

Phillips, O. H. and Jackson, P., *Constitutional and Administrative Law*, London, Sweet and Maxwell, 1978.

Randall, F., *British Government and Politics*, Plymouth, Macdonald and Evans, 1984.

Ransom, S. and Walsh, K. (eds), *Between Centre and Locality: The Politics of Public Policy*, London, Allen and Unwin, 1985.

Richards, S. G., *Introduction to British Government*, London, Macmillan, 1978.

Richardson, J. H. and Jordan, G., *Governing under Pressure*, Oxford, Martin Robertson, 1979.

Rose, R., *Understanding the United Kingdom: The Territorial Dimension in Government*, London, Longman, 1982.

Royal Commission on the Constitution, *Report*, Cmnd. 5460, London, HMSO, 1973.

Royal Institute of Public Administration,

Policy and Practice, *The Experience of Government*, London, RIPA, 1981.

Sallis, E., *The Machinery of Government: An Introduction to Public Administration*, Eastbourne, Holt, Rinehart and Winston, 1982.

Sampson, A., *The Changing Anatomy of Britain*, London, Hodder and Stoughton, 1982.

Sedgemore, B., *The Secret Constitution: An Analysis of the Political Establishment*, London, Hodder and Stoughton, 1980.

Shanks, M., *Planning and Politics*, London, Allen and Unwin, 1977.

Sharpe, L. J. and Newton, K., *Does Politics Matter? The Determinants of Public Policy*, Oxford, Clarendon Press, 1984.

Smith, B. C., *Policy-Making in British Government: An Analysis of Power and Rationality*, Oxford, Martin Robertson, 1976.

Smith, G. and Polsby, N. W., *British Government and its Discontents*, London, Harper and Row, 1981.

Smith, S. A. De, *Constitutional and Administrative Law*, edited by H. Street and R. Brazier, Harmondsworth, Penguin, 1985.

Stankiewicz, W. J., *British Government in an Era of Reform*, London, Collier-Macmillan, 1976.

Thornhill, W. (ed.), *The Modernisation of British Government*, London, Pitman, 1975.

Toch, H., *Essentials of British Constitution and Government*, London, Cassell, 1983.

Turner, D. R., *The Shadow Cabinet in British Politics*, London, Routledge & Kegan Paul, 1969.

Turpin, C., *British Government and the Constitution*, London, Weidenfeld and Nicolson, 1986.

Wade, E. C. S. and Phillips, G. C., *Constitutional and Administrative Law*, London, Longman, 1985.

Wade, H. W. R., *Constitutional Fundamentals*, London, Stevens, 1980.

Wass, D., *Government and the Governed: The 1983 Reith Lectures*, London, Routledge & Kegan Paul, 1984.

Wilson, F. M. G. (ed.), *The Organisation of British Central Government*, London, Allen and Unwin, 1968.

Wilson, H., *The Governance of Britain*, London, Sphere, 1977.

Wraith, R. E., *Open Government: The British Interpretation*, London, RIPA, 1977.

Yardley, D. C. M., *Introduction to British Constitutional Law*, London, Butterworth, 1978.

GOVERNMENT AND CABINET

Beloff, M. and Peele, G., *The Government of the United Kingdom: Political Authority in a Changing Society*, London, Weidenfeld and Nicolson, 1980.

Berkeley, H., *The Power of the Prime Minister*, London, Allen and Unwin, 1968.

Blake, R. W. N., *The Office of Prime Minister*, London, British Academy, 1975.

Carter, B. E., *The Office of Prime Minister*, London, Faber, 1956.

Castle, B., *The Castle Diaries, 1964–76*, 2 vols, London, Weidenfeld and Nicolson, 1980–4.

Crossman, R., *The Inside View*, London, Cape, 1972.

Crossman, R. H. S., *The Diaries of a Cabinet Minister*, 3 vols, London, Hamish Hamilton, Cape, 1975–7.

Englefield, D., *Whitehall and Westminster: Government Informs Parliament: The Changing Scene*, London, Longman, 1986.

Headey, B. W., *British Cabinet Ministers: The Roles of Politicians in Executive Office*, London, Allen and Unwin, 1974.

Hellicar, E., *Prime Ministers of Britain*, Newton Abbot, David and Charles, 1978.

Hennessy, P., *Cabinet*, Oxford, Blackwell, 1986.

Herman, V. and Alt, J., *Cabinet Studies: A Reader*, London, Macmillan, 1975.

Jennings, I., *Cabinet Government*, Cambridge, Cambridge University Press, 1969.

King, A. (ed.), *The British Prime Minister*, London, Macmillan, 1985.

Loewenstein, K., *British Cabinet Government*, London, Oxford University Press, 1968.

Mackintosh, J. P., *The British Cabinet*, London, Methuen, 1981.

Mackintosh, J. P. (ed.), *British Prime Ministers in the Twentieth Century*, vol. 1, London, Weidenfeld and Nicolson, 1977.

Mosley, R. K., *The Story of the Cabinet Office*, London, Routledge & Kegan Paul, 1969.

Prophet, J., *The Structure of Government*, London, Longman, 1969.

Punnett, M., *British Government and Politics*, London, Heinemann, 1980.

Rush, M., *The Cabinet and Policy Formation*, London, Longman, 1984.

Walker, P. G., *The Cabinet*, Fontana, London, 1972.

ADMINISTRATION AND CIVIL SERVICE

Barber, M. P., *Public Administration*, Plymouth, Macdonald and Evans, 1983.

Bourn, J., *Management in Central and Local Government*, London, Pitman, 1979.

Brown, R. G. S. and Steel, D. R., *The Administrative Process in Britain*, London, Methuen, 1979.

Cambell, G. A., *The Civil Service in Britain*, London, Duckworth, 1971.

Cartwright, T. J., *Royal Commissions and Departmental Committees in Britain*, London, Hodder and Stoughton, 1975.

Central Office of Information, *The British Civil Service*, London, HMSO, 1974.

Chapman, L., *Your Disobedient Servant*, London, Chatto and Windus, 1978.

Chapman, R., *The Higher Civil Service in Britain*, London, Constable, 1970.

Chapman, R., *Leadership in the British Civil Service*, London, Croom Helm, 1984.

Chapman, R. and Greenway, J. R., *The Dynamics of Administrative Reform*, London, Croom Helm, 1981.

Cohen, E., *The Growth of the British Civil Service, 1780–1939*, London, Cass, 1965.

Cross, J. A., *British Public Administration*, Slough, University Tutorial Press, 1970.

Derbyshire, J. D., *An Introduction to Public Administration: People, Politics, Power*, London, McGraw Hill, 1984.

Drewry, G., *The Civil Service Today*, Oxford, Martin Robertson, 1983.

Farnham, D. and McVicar, M., *Public Administration in the United Kingdom: An Introduction*, London, Cassell, 1980.

Fry, G., *The Administrative Revolution in Whitehall*, London, Croom Helm, 1981.

Fry, G., *The Changing Civil Service*, London, Allen and Unwin, 1985.

Garrett, J., *Managing the Civil Service*, London, Heinemann, 1980.

Jewell, R. E. C., *Outlines of Public Administration*, Croydon, Knight, 1976.

Kellner, P. and Crowther-Hunt, N., *The Civil Servants: An Inquiry into Britain's Ruling Class*, London, Futura, 1981.

Mackenzie, W. J. M. and Grove, J. W. D., *Central Administration in Britain*, London, Greenwood Press, 1976.

Parris, H., *Constitutional Bureaucracy: The Development of British Central Administration since the Eighteenth Century*, London, Allen and Unwin, 1969.

Pitt, D. C. and Smith, B. C., *Government Departments: An Organisational Perspective*, London, Routledge & Kegan Paul, 1981.

Ponting, C., *Whitehall: Tragedy and Farce*, London, Hamish Hamilton, 1986.

Prince, M. J., *Policy Advice and Organisational Survival: Policy Planning and Research Units in British Government*, Aldershot, Gower, 1983.

Rhodes, R. A., *Public Administration and Policy Analysis: Recent Development in Britain and America*, Aldershot, Gower, 1979.

Sallis, E., *The Machinery of Government: An Introduction to Public Administration*, Eastbourne,

Holt, Rinehart and Winston, 1982.

Smith, B. C. and Stanyer, J., *Administering Britain: A Guidebook to Administrative Institutions*, Oxford, Martin Robertson, 1980.

Stacey, R. and Oliver, J., *Public Administration: The Political Environment*, Plymouth, Macdonald and Evans, 1980.

Stanyer, J. and Smith, B. C., *Administering Britain*, London, Fontana, 1976.

Young, H. and Sloman, A., *No, Minister, An Inquiry into the Civil Service*, London, BBC, 1982.

LOCAL GOVERNMENT

Alexander, A., *Local Government in Britain since Reorganisation*, London, Allen and Unwin, 1982.

Alexander, A., *Politics and Local Government in the United Kingdom*, London, Longman, 1982.

Boaden, N. et al., *Public Participation in Local Services*, London, Longman, 1982.

Boddy, M. and Fudge, C. (eds), *Local Socialism*, London, Macmillan, 1984.

Bourn, J., *Management in Central and Local Government*, London, Pitman, 1979.

Brand, J. A., *Local Government Reform in England, 1888–1974*, London, Croom Helm, 1974.

Burgess, T. and Travers, T., *Ten Billion Pounds: Whitehall's Takeover of the Town Halls*, Oxford, Grant McIntyre, 1980.

Byrne, T., *Local Government in Britain*, Harmondsworth, Penguin, 1985.

Central Office of Information, *Local Government in Britain*, London, HMSO, 1980.

Central Policy Review Staff, *Report: Relations Between Central Government and Local Authorities*, London, 1977.

Cockburn, C., *The Local State*, London, Pluto, 1977.

Cowan, M., *Politics and Management in Local Government*, London, RIPA, 1983.

Cross, C. A., *Principles of Local Government Law*, London, Sweet and Maxwell, 1981.

Cross, M. and Mallen, D., *Local Government and Politics*, London, Longman, 1978.

Dearlove, J., *The Politics of Policy in Local Government*, Cambridge, Cambridge University Press, 1973.

Dearlove, J., *The Reorganisation of British Local Government*, Cambridge, Cambridge University Press, 1979.

Elcock, H. and Wheaton, M., *Local Government*, London, Methuen, 1982.

Flynn, N. et al., *Abolition or Reform? The GLC and the Metropolitan County*, London, Allen and Unwin, 1985.

Glasser, R., *Town Hall: Local Government at Work in Britain Today*, London, Century, 1984.

Grant, W., *Independent Local Politics in England and Wales*, Farnborough, Saxon House, 1978.

Griffiths, A., *Local Government Administration*, London, Shaw, 1977.

Gyford, J., *Local Politics in Britain*, London, Croom Helm, 1984.

Hambleton, R., *Policy Planning and Local Government*, London, Hutchinson, 1978.

Hart, Sir W. and Garner, J. F., *Introduction to the Law of Local*

Government and Administration,
London, Butterworth, 1973.

Henney, A., *Inside Local Government*,
London, Sinclair Browne, 1983.

Hepworth, N. P., *The Finance of Local
Government*, London, Allen and
Unwin, 1978.

Her Majesty's Stationery Office, *Local
Government in England and Wales:
A Guide to the New System*, London,
1980.

Hogwood, B. W. and Keating, M. (eds),
Regional Government in England,
London, Oxford University Press,
1982.

Jackson, W. E., *The Structure of Local
Government in England and Wales*,
London, Greenwood Press, 1977.

Jeffries, R., *Tackling the Town Hall: A
Local Authority Handbook*, London,
Routledge & Kegan Paul, 1982.

Jones, G. and Stewart, J., *The Case for
Local Government*, London, Allen
and Unwin, 1983.

Keith-Lucas, B. and Richards, P. G.,
*A History of Local Government in
the Twentieth Century*, London, Allen
and Unwin 1978.

Kogan, M. and Van Der Eyken, W.,
County Hall , Harmondsworth,
Penguin, 1973.

Minogue, M. (ed.), *A Consumer's Guide
to Local Government*, London, 1979.

Newton, K. and Karran, T., *The Politics
of Local Expenditure*, London,
Macmillan, 1985.

Pinkus, C. and Dixson, A., *Solving Local
Government Problems*, London,
Allen and Unwin, 1981.

Poole, K. P., *The Local Government
Service in England and Wales*,
London, Allen and Unwin, 1978.

Prophet, J., *The Councillor*, London,
Shaw, 1979.

Ranson, S. et al. (eds), *Between Centre
and Locality: The Politics of Public
Policy*, London, Allen and Unwin,
1985.

Rhodes, R. A., *Control and Power in
Central-Local Government
Relationships*, Aldershot, Gower,
1981.

Rhodes, R. A., *The National World of
Local Government*, London, Allen
and Unwin, 1986.

Richards, P. G., *The Local Government
System*, London, Allen and Unwin,
1983.

Seeley, I. H., *Local Government
Explained*, London, Macmillan,
1978.

Stanyer, J., *Assessing Local Government*,
Oxford, Martin Robertson, 1985.

Stewart, J., *Local Government: The
Conditions for Local Choice*,
London, Allen and Unwin, 1983.

Walker, D., *Municipal Empire*,
Hounslow, Temple Smith, 1983.

Young, K., *Local Politics and the Rise of
Party*, Leicester, Leicester University
Press, 1975.

Young, K. (ed.), *National Interests and
Local Government*, London,
Heinemann, 1983.

SEE ALSO:

13 HISTORY

Readers are directed to the following reference works for systematic bibliographical coverage of studies in British history: Historical Association, *Annual Bulletin of Historical Literature*, annually; Institute of Historical Research, *Historical Research for University Degrees in the United Kingdom*, University of London, annually; Royal Historical Society, *Annual Bibliography of British and Irish History*, annually.

For bibliographical references on Roman, Celtic and Anglo-Saxon Britain see: Bonser, W., *An Anglo-Saxon and Celtic Bibliography*, 1957; Bonser, W., *A Romano-British Bibliography*, 1965; Rosenthal, J. T., *Anglo-Saxon History: An Annotated Bibliography, 450–1066*, 1985.

For bibliographical references on medieval Britain see: Altschul, M., *Bibliographical Handbook, Anglo-Norman England, 1066–1154*, 1969; Graves, E. B. (ed.), *A Bibliography of English History to 1485*, 1975; Guth, D. J. (ed.), *Bibliographical Handbook, Late Medieval England, 1377–1485*, 1976.

For bibliographical references on Tudor England see: Levine, M., *Bibliographical Handbook, Tudor England, 1485–1603*, 1968; Read, C. (ed.), *Bibliography of British History, Tudor Period, 1485–1603*, 1978.

For bibliographical references on seventeenth-century Britain see: Davies, G. and Keeler, M. F. (eds), *A Bibliography of British History, Stuart Period, 1603–1714*, 1970; Sachse, W. L. *Bibliographical Handbook, Restoration England, 1660–1689*, 1971.

For bibliographical references on eighteenth-century Britain: see Pargellis, S. and Medley, D. J. (eds), *Bibliography of British History, the Eighteenth Century, 1714–1789*, 1977.

For bibliographical references on Victorian Britain see: Altholz, J. L., *Bibliographical Handbook, Victorian England, 1837–1901*, 1970; Brown, L. M. and Christie, I. R. (eds), *A Bibliography of British History, 1789–1851*, 1977; Hanham, H. J. (ed.), *A Bibliography of English History, 1851–1914*, 1976.

For bibliographical references on twentieth-century Britain see: Havighurst, A. F., *Bibliographical Handbook, Modern England, 1901–1970*, 1976; Krikler, B. and Laqueur, W. Z. (eds), *A Reader's Guide to Contemporary History*, 1972; Mowat, C. L., *British History since 1926: A Select Bibliography*, 1960.

Other general reading guides to British history can be found in the following: Christie, I. R., *British History since 1760: A Select Bibliography*, 1970; Fines, J., *The History Student's Guide to the Library*, 1973; Kellaway, W., *Bibliography of Historical Works Issued in the United Kingdom*, 3 vols, 1962–72; Miller, H. and Newman, A., *Early Modern British History, 1485–1760: A Select Bibliography*, 1970: Roach, J. (ed.), *A Bibliography of Modern History*, 1968; Stockham, P. et al., *British Local History: A Select Bibliography*, 1964.

For reference purposes and as general sources of historical information the following may be consulted: Black (publisher), *Who Was Who*, 1967–81; Burston, W. H. et al. (eds), *Handbook for History Teachers*, 1972; Cheney, C. R., *Handbook of Dates for Students of English History*, 1978; Cook, C., *The Longman Handbook of Modern British History*, 1983; Cook, C. and Brendan, K., *British Historical Facts, 1830–1900*,

1975; Cook C. and Stevenson, J., *British Historical Facts, 1760–1830*, 1980; Cook, C. and Wroughton, J. (eds), *English Historical Facts, 1603–88*, 1980: Fines, J., *Who's Who in the Middle Ages*, 1970; Gilbert, M., *British History Atlas*, 1968; Hepworth, P., *How to Find out in History: A Guide to Sources of Information for All*, 1966; Hugget, F. E., *A Dictionary of British History, 1815–1973*, 1975; Kenyon, J. P. (ed.), *A Dictionary of British History*, 1982; Madden, L., *How to Find out about the Victorian Period: A Guide to Sources of Information*, 1970; Palmer, A. W., *A Dictionary of Modern History, 1789–1945*, 1962; Powicke, F. M. and Fryde, E. B., *Handbook of British Chronology*, 1961; Routh, C. R. N. (ed.), *Who's Who in History*, 1960; Steinberg, S. H. and Evans, I. H. (eds), *Steinberg's Dictionary of British History*, 1974.

For general survey accounts of British history readers are directed to the following works: Chrimes, S. B., *English Constitutional History*, 1967; Clark, G., *English History: A Survey*, 1971; Feiling, K., *A History of England*, 1973; Green, J. R., *A Short History of the English People*, 1960; Johnson, P., *The Offshore Islanders: England's People from Roman Occupation to the Present*, 1975; Keir, D. L., *The Constitutional History of Modern Britain since 1485*, 1969; Morgan, K. O. (ed.), *The Oxford Illustrated History of Britain*, 1984; Ridley, J., *The History of England*, 1981; Seaman, L. C. B., *A New History of England, 410–1975*, 1982; Trevelyan, G. M., *A Shortened History of England*, 1970; Woodward, E. L., *A History of England*, 1966.

As introductory reading to particular periods the following can be recommended:

Celtic   Chadwick, N. K. (ed.), *Celt and Saxon*, 1963; Chadwick, N. K., *The Celts*, 1971.

Roman   Richmond, S. I., *Roman Britain*, 1970; Stevens, C. E., *Roman Britain*, 1975.

Anglo-Saxon   Blair, P. H., *An Introduction to Anglo-Saxon England*, 1977; Wilson, D. M., *The Anglo-Saxons*, 1971.

Early Middle Ages   Douglas, D. C., *The Norman Achievement*, 1972; Matthew, D. J. A., *The Norman Conquest*, 1966.

Later Middle Ages   Holmes, G., *The Later Middle Ages*, 1962; Myers, A. R., *England in the Late Middle Ages*, 1953.

Early Tudor   Bindoff, S. T., *Tudor England*, 1969; Elton, G. R., *England Under the Tudors*, 1974; Williams, P., *The Tudor Regime*, 1981.

Elizabethan   Hurstfield, J., *Elizabeth I and the Unity of England*, 1970; Palliser, D. M., *The Age of Elizabeth: England under the Late Tudors, 1547–1603*, 1983; Rowse, A. L., *The Elizabethan Renaissance*, 1971–2.

Early Stuart   Ashley, M., *England in the Seventeenth Century*, 1978; Davies, G., *The Early Stuarts, 1603–60*, 1959; Kenyon, J. P. (ed.), *The Stuarts: A Study in English Kingship*, 1966.

Civil War and Interregnum   Ashley, M., *The English Civil War: A Concise History*, 1975; Parry, R. H. (ed.), *The English Civil War and After, 1642–58*, 1970; Roots, I., *The Great Rebellion, 1642–1660*, 1979.

Late Stuart   Bryant, A., *Restoration England*, 1960; Clark, G., *The Later Stuarts, 1660–1714*, 1956; Jones, J. R., *The Restored Monarchy, 1660–1688*, 1979.

Hanoverian   Cowie, L. W., *Hanoverian England, 1714–1837*, 1967; Plumb, J. H., *England in the Eighteenth Century*, 1969; Speck, W. A., *Stability and Strife: England, 1714–1760*, 1977.

Victorian   Briggs, A., *The Age of Improvement, 1783–1867*, 1979; Thomson, D., *England in the Nineteenth Century*, 1970; Woodward, E. L., *The Age of Reform, 1815–70*, 1962.

Twentieth Century   Beloff, M., *Wars and Welfare: Britain 1914–1945*, 1984; Havighurst, A. F., *Modern England, 1901–1970*, 1976; Lloyd, T. O., *Empire*

to *Welfare State: English History, 1906–1967*, 1979; Thomson, D., *England in the Twentieth Century, 1914–63*, 1970.
Contemporary   Bartlett, C. J., *A History of Postwar Britain, 1945–1974*, 1977; Childs, D., *Britain since 1945: A Political History*, 1984; Sked, A. and Cook, C., *Post-War Britain: A Political History*, 1979.

REFERENCE

A & C Black (publisher), *Who Was Who*, 7 vols, London, 1967–81.
Altholz, J. L., *Bibliographical Handbook. Victorian England, 1837–1901*, Cambridge, Cambridge University Press, 1970.
Altschul, M., *Bibliographical Handbook. Anglo-Norman England, 1066–1154*, Cambridge, Cambridge University Press, 1969.
Bonser, W., *An Anglo-Saxon and Celtic Bibliography*, Oxford, Blackwell, 1957.
Bonser, W., *A Romano-British Bibliography*, Oxford, Blackwell, 1965.
Brooks, G. R., *A Select List of Aids of Use in the Teaching of Recent History*, London, Historical Association, 1971.
Brown, L. M. and Christie, I. R. (eds), *A Bibliography of British History, 1789–1851*, London, Oxford University Press, 1977.
Burston, W. H. et al. (eds), *Handbook for History Teachers*, London, Methuen, 1972.
Cheney, C. R. (ed.), *Handbook of Dates for Students of English History*, London, Royal Historical Society, 1978.
Christie, I. R., *British History since 1760: A Select Bibliography*, London, Historical Association, 1970.
Cook, C. (ed.), *Sources in British Political History, 1900–1951*, London, Macmillan, 1985.
Cook, C. and Keith, B. (eds), *British Historical Facts, 1830–1900*, London, Macmillan, 1975.
Cook, C. and Stevenson, J., *Longman Atlas of Modern British History*, London, Longman, 1978.
Cook, C. and Stevenson, J. (eds), *British Historical Facts, 1760–1830*, London, Macmillan, 1980.
Cook, C. and Stevenson J., *The Longman Handbook of Modern British History, 1714–1980*, London, Longman, 1983.
Cook, C. et al. (eds), *Sources in British Political History, 1900–51*, 5 vols, London, Macmillan, 1975–8.
Cook, C. and Wroughton, J. (eds), *English Historical Facts, 1603–88*, London, Macmillan, 1980.
Davies, G. and Keeler, M. F. (eds), *A Bibliography of British History, Stuart Period, 1603–1714*, Oxford, Oxford University Press, 1970.
Day, A. E., *History: A Reference Handbook*, London, Bingley, 1977.
Elton, G. R., *Modern Historians on British History, 1458–1945: A Critical Bibliography, 1945–1969*, London, Methuen, 1970.
Fakus, M. and Gillingham, J. (eds), *Historical Atlas of Britain*, London, Granada, 1981.
Fines, J., *Who's Who in the Middle Ages*, London, Blond, 1970.
Fines, J., *The History Student's Guide to the Library*, Chichester, Phillimore, 1973.
Gilbert, M., *British History Atlas*, London, Weidenfeld and Nicolson, 1968.
Gilbert, M., *Recent History Atlas, 1860 to 1960*, London, Weidenfeld and Nicolson, 1977.
Graves, E. B. (ed.), *A Bibliography of English History to 1485*, London, Oxford University Press, 1975.
Gross, C., *A Bibliography of English History to 1485 based on the Sources and Literature of English History from the Earliest Times*, edited by E. B. Graves, London, Oxford University Press, 1975.
Guth, D. J. (ed.), *Bibliographical*

Handbook. Late Medieval England, 1377–1485, Cambridge, Cambridge University Press, 1976.

Haigh, C. (ed.), *The Cambridge Historical Encyclopedia of Great Britain and Ireland*, Cambridge, Cambridge University Press, 1985.

Hanham, H. J. (ed.), *A Bibliography of English History, 1851–1914*, London, Oxford University Press, 1976.

Havighurst, A. F., *Bibliographical Handbook, Modern England, 1901–1970*, Cambridge, Cambridge University Press, 1976.

Hepworth, P., *How to find out in History: A Guide to Sources of Information for All*, Oxford, Pergamon, 1966.

Historical Association, *Annual Bulletin of Historical Literature*, London, annually

Historical Manuscripts Commission, *Record Repositories in Great Britain*, London, HMSO, 1973.

Historical Manuscripts Commission, *Papers of British Cabinet Ministers, 1782–1900*, London, HMSO, 1982.

Huggett, F. E., *A Dictionary of British History 1815–1973*, Oxford, Blackwell, 1975.

Institute of Historical Research, *Historical Research for University Degrees in the United Kingdom*, London, University of London, annually.

Kellaway, W., *Bibliography of Historical Works Issued in the United Kingdom, 1957–60*, London, Institute of Historical Research, 1962.

Kellaway, W., *Bibliography of Historical Works Issued in the United Kingdom, 1961–1965*, London, Institute of Historical Research, 1967.

Kellaway, W., *Bibliography of Historical Works Issued in the United Kingdom, 1966–1970*, London, Institute of Historical Research, 1972.

Kenyon, J. P. (ed.), *A Dictionary of British History*, London, Secker and Warburg, 1982.

Krikler, B. and Laqueur, W. Z. (eds), *A Reader's Guide to Contemporary History*, London, Weidenfeld and Nicolson, 1972.

Levine, M., *Bibliographical Handbook: Tudor England, 1485–1603*, Cambridge, Cambridge University Press, 1968.

Macfarlane, A., *A Guide to English Historical Records*, Cambridge, Cambridge University Press, 1983.

Madden, L., *How to Find out about the Victorian Period: A Guide to Sources of Information*, Oxford, Pergamon, 1970.

Miller, H. and Newman, A., *Early Modern British History, 1485–1760: A Select Bibliography*, London, Historical Association, 1970.

Mowat, C. L., *British History since 1926: Helps for Students of History*, London, Historical Association, 1960.

Mullins, E. L. C., *Texts and Calendars: An Analytical Guide to Serial Publications*, 2 vols, London, Royal Historical Society, 1958–83.

Oxford University Press (publisher), *The Concise Dictionary of National Biography*, 2 vols, London, 1906–82.

Palmer, A. W., *A Dictionary of Modern History 1789–1945*, London, Cresset Press, 1962.

Pargellis, S. and Medley, D. J. (eds), *Bibliography of British History: The Eighteenth Century, 1714–1789*, Brighton, Harvester, 1977.

Powicke, F. M. and Fryde, E. B., *Handbook of British Chronology*, London, Royal Historical Society, 1961.

Read, C. (ed.), *Bibliography of British History: Tudor Period, 1485–1603*, Brighton, Harvester, 1978.

Riden, P., *Local History: A Handbook for Beginners*, London, Batsford, 1983.

Roach, J. (ed.), *A Bibliography of Modern History*, Cambridge, Cambridge University Press, 1968.

Rosenthal, J. T., *Anglo-Saxon History: An Annotated Bibliography, 450–1066*, New York, AMS Press, 1985.

Royal Commission of Historical Manuscripts (publisher), *Guides to*

Sources for British History based on the National Register of Archives, 3 vols, London, HMSO, 1983.

Royal Historical Society, *Annual Bibliography of British and Irish History*, Brighton, Harvester Press, annually.

Sachse, W. L., *Bibliographical Handbook: Restoration England, 1660–1689*, Cambridge, Cambridge University Press, 1971.

Steinberg, S. H. and Evans, I. H. (eds), *Steinberg's Dictionary of British History*, London, Arnold, 1974.

GENERAL

Adams, G. B., *A Constitutional History of England*, London, Cape, 1935.

Bowle, J., *The English Experience: A Survey of English History from Early Modern Times*, London, Weidenfeld and Nicolson, 1971.

Bryant, Sir A., *A History of Great Britain and the British People*, 2 vols, London, Collins, 1984–6.

Butler, Sir J. R. M., *A History of England, 1815–1939*, London, Oxford University Press.

Cambridge University Press (publisher), *The New Cambridge Modern History*, 14 vols, Cambridge, Cambridge University Press, 1957–74.

Chrimes, S. B., *English Constitutional History*, London, Oxford University Press, 1967.

Churchill, W. S., *A History of the English Speaking Peoples*, 4 vols, London, Cassell, 1956–8.

Clark, G. N. (ed.), *The Oxford History of England*, 15 vols, Oxford, Clarendon Press, 1936–65.

Clark, G. N., *English History: A Survey*, Oxford, Oxford University Press, 1971.

Feiling, K., *A History of England*, London, Macmillan, 1973.

Green, J. R., *A Short History of the English People*, 2 vols, London, Dent, 1960.

Halliday, F. E., *A Concise History of England from Stonehenge to the Atomic Age*, London, Thames and Hudson, 1980.

Halliday, F. E., *An Illustrated Cultural History of England*, London, Thames and Hudson, 1981.

Hellicar, E., *Prime Ministers of Britain*, Newton Abbot, David and Charles, 1978.

Johnson, P., *The Offshore Islanders: England's People from Roman Occupation to the Present*, Harmondsworth, Penguin, 1975.

Keir, D. L., *The Constitutional History of Modern Britain since 1485*, London, Black, 1969.

Maitland, F. W., *The Constitutional History of England*, Cambridge, Cambridge University Press, 1977 (reprint).

Morgan, K. O. (ed.), *The Oxford Illustrated History of Britain*, London, Oxford University Press, 1984.

Penguin (publisher), *The Pelican History of England*, 9 vols, Harmondsworth, Penguin, 1950–65.

Ridley, J., *The History of England*, London, Routledge & Kegan Paul, 1981.

Seaman, L. C. B., *A New History of England: 410–1975*, London, Macmillan, 1982.

Stubbs, W., *The Constitutional History of England in its Origin and Development*, 3 vols, London, Cass, 1967.

Taylor, A. J. P., *Essays in English History*, Harmondsworth, Penguin, 1976.

Thal, H. Van, *The Prime Ministers*, 2 vols, London, Allen and Unwin, 1978.

Thomson, G. M., *The Prime Minister from Robert Walpole to Margaret Thatcher*, London, Secker and Warburg, 1980.

Toyne, A., *An English-Reader's History of England*, London, Oxford University Press, 1971.

Trevelyan, G. M., *Illustrated History of England*, London, Longman, 1973.

Trevelyan, G. M., *A Shortened History of England*, Harmondsworth, Penguin, 1970.

Webb, R. K., *Modern England from the Eighteenth Century to the Present*, London, Allen and Unwin, 1980.

White, R. J., *A Short History of England*, Cambridge, Cambridge University Press, 1967.

Willson, D. H., *A History of England*, New York, Holt, Rinehart and Winston, 1967.

Woodward, E. L., *A History of England*, London, Methuen, 1966.

ROMAN BRITAIN TO FEUDAL ENGLAND

Arnold, C. J., *Roman Britain to Saxon England*, London, Croom Helm, 1985.

Barlow, F., *The Feudal Kingdom of England: 1042–1216*, London, Longman, 1972.

Barrow, G. W. S., *Feudal Britain: The Completion of the Medieval Kingdom 1066–1314*, London, Arnold, 1965.

Blair, P. H., *Roman Britain and Early England 55BC–871AD*, London, Nelson, 1963.

Blair, P. H., *An Introduction to Anglo-Saxon England*, Cambridge, Cambridge University Press, 1977.

Brown, R. A., *The Normans and the Norman Conquest*, London, Constable, 1973.

Brown, R. A., *The Norman Conquest*, London, Arnold, 1984.

Bryant, Sir A., *The Medieval Foundation*, London, Collins, 1966.

Chadwick, N. K. (ed.), *Celt and Saxon*, Cambridge, Cambridge University Press, 1963.

Chadwick, N. K., *The Celts*, Harmondsworth, Penguin, 1971.

Chancellor, V. E., *Medieval and Tudor Britain*, Harmondsworth, Penguin, 1970.

Chrimes, S. B. et al., *Fifteenth Century England: 1399–1509, Studies in Politics and Society*, Manchester, Manchester University Press, 1972.

Clemoes, P. (ed.), *Anglo-Saxon England*, 10 vols, Cambridge, Cambridge University Press, 1972–82.

Collingwood, R. G. and Myres, J. N. L., *Roman Britain and the English Settlements*, London, Oxford University Press, 1937, Oxford History of England.

Douglas, D. C., *The Norman Fate, 1100–1154*, London, Methuen, 1971.

Douglas, D. C., *The Norman Achievement, 1050–1100*, London, Fontana, 1972.

Fisher, D. J. V., *The Anglo Saxon Age, c.400–1042*, London, Longman, 1973.

Frere, S., *Britannia: A History of Roman Britain*, London, Routledge & Kegan Paul, 1978.

Goodman, A., *The Wars of the Roses: Military Activity and English Society, 1452–97*, London, Routledge & Kegan Paul, 1981.

Green, V. H. H., *The Later Plantagenets: A Survey of English History between 1307 and 1485*, London, Arnold, 1973.

Helm, P. J., *Exploring Roman Britain*, London, Hale, 1975.

Helm, P. J., *Exploring Saxon and Norman England*, London, Hale, 1976.

Hodgkin, R. H., *A History of the Anglo-Saxons*, 2 vols, Oxford, Oxford University Press, 1959.

Holmes, G., *The Later Middle Ages 1272–1483*, Edinburgh, Nelson, 1962.

Ireland, S., *Roman Britain: A Source Book*, London, Croom Helm, 1985.

Jacob, E. F., *The Fifteenth Century, 1399–1485*, London, Oxford University Press, 1961, Oxford History of England.

Johnson, S., *Later Roman Britain*, London, Routledge & Kegan Paul, 1980.

Keen, M. H., *England in the Later Middle Ages: A Political History*, London, Methuen, 1975.

Kirby, D. P., *The Making of Early England*, London, Batsford, 1967.

Laing, L. and Laing, J., *Anglo-Saxon England*, London, Routledge & Kegan Paul, 1979.

Laing, L. and Laing, J., *Celtic Britain*, London, Routledge & Kegan Paul, 1979.

Laing, L. and Laing, J., *The Origins of Britain*, London, Routledge & Kegan Paul, 1980.

Lander, J. R., *The Wars of the Roses* London, Secker and Warburg, 1965.

Lander, J. R., *Conflict and Stability in Fifteenth Century England*, London, Hutchinson, 1977.

Liversidge, J., *Britain in the Roman Empire*, London, Routledge & Kegan Paul, 1970.

Loyn, H. R., *The Governance of Anglo-Saxon England, 500–1087*, London, Arnold, 1984.

Lyon, B. D., *A Constitutional and Legal History of Medieval England*, New York, Harper, 1960.

McKisack, M., *The Fourteenth Century, 1307–1399*, London, Oxford University Press, 1959, Oxford History of England.

Matthew, D. J. A., *The Norman Conquest*, London, Batsford, 1966.

Morris, J., *The Age of Arthur: A History of the British Isles from 350 to 650*, 3 vols, Chichester, Phillimore, 1977.

Myers, A. R., *England in the Late Middle Ages*, Harmondsworth, Penguin, 1953, Pelican History of England.

Poole, A. L., *Medieval England*, Oxford, Oxford University Press, 1958.

Poole, A. L., *From Domesday Book to Magna Carta, 1037–1216*, London, Oxford University Press, 1971, Oxford History of England.

Powicke, M., *The Thirteenth Century, 1216–1307*, London, Oxford University Press, 1962, Oxford History of England.

Powicke, M., *Medieval England 1066–1485*, Oxford, Oxford University Press, 1969.

Prestwich, M., *The Three Edwards: War and State in England 1272–1377*, London, Methuen, 1981.

Renfrew, C. (ed.), *British Prehistory*, London, Duckworth, 1974.

Richmond, I., *Roman Britain*, Harmondsworth, Penguin, 1970, Pelican History of England.

Ross, A., *Pagan Celtic Britain: Studies in Iconography and Tradition*, London, Routledge & Kegan Paul, 1967.

Ross, C., *The Wars of the Roses: A Concise History*, London, Thames and Hudson, 1976.

Rowley, T., *The Norman Heritage, 1066–1200*, London, Routledge & Kegan Paul, 1983.

Salway, S., *Roman Britain*, London, Oxford University Press, 1981, Oxford History of England.

Saul, N., *The Batsford Companion to Medieval England*, London, Batsford. 1983.

Sawyer, P. H., *From Roman Britain to Norman England*, London, Methuen, 1978.

Sayles, G. O., *The Medieval Foundations of England*, London, Methuen, 1966.

Smith, L. M. (ed.), *The Making of Britain: The Dark Ages*, London, Macmillan, 1984.

Smith, L. M. (ed.), *The Making of Britain: The Middle Ages*, London, Macmillan, 1985.

Stenton, D. M., *English Society in the Early Middle Ages*, Harmondsworth, Penguin, 1969, Pelican History of England.

Stenton, F., *Anglo-Saxon England, 556–1087*, London, Oxford University Press, 1971, Oxford History of England.

Thomas, C., *Britain and Ireland in Early Christian Times*, London, Thames and Hudson, 1971.

Thomson, J. A. F., *The Transformation of Medieval England, 1370– 1529*, London, Longman, 1983.

Todd, M., *Roman Britain*, London, Fontana, 1981.

Tuck, A., *Crown and Nobility, 1272–1461, Fontana History of England*, London, Fontana, 1986.

Wacher, J., *The Coming of Rome*, London, Routledge & Kegan Paul, 1979.

Whitelock, D., *The Beginnings of English Society*, Harmondsworth, Penguin, 1971, Pelican History of England.

Wilkinson, B., *The Later Middle Ages in England, 1216–1485*, London, Longman, 1969.

Wilson, D. M., *The Anglo-Saxons*, Harmondsworth, Penguin, 1971.

Wilson, D. M. (ed.), *The Archaeology of Anglo-Saxon England*, London, Methuen, 1976.

Woods, W., *England in the Age of Chaucer*, London, Hart Davis, 1976.

TUDOR TO LATE-STUART BRITAIN

Ashley, M., *England in the Seventeenth Century*, London, Hutchinson, 1978.

Ashley, M., *The English Civil War: A Concise History*, London, Thames and Hudson, 1975.

Ashton, R., *The English Civil War: Conservatism and Revolution, 1603–1649*, London, Weidenfeld and Nicolson, 1978.

Aylmer, G. E., *The Struggle for the Constitution 1603–1689, England in the Seventeenth Century*, London, Blandford Press, 1965.

Aylmer, G. E., *The Interregnum: The Quest for Settlement, 1646–60*, London, Macmillan, 1972.

Bean, J. M. W., *The Decline of English Feudalism 1215–1540*, Manchester, Manchester University Press, 1968.

Bindoff, S. T. (ed.), *Elizabethan Government and Society*, London, Athlone, 1961.

Bindoff, S. T., *Tudor England*, Harmondsworth, Penguin, 1969, Pelican History of England.

Black, J. B., *The Reign of Elizabeth, 1558–1603*, London, Oxford University Press, 1959, Oxford History of England.

Bryant, Sir A., *Restoration England*, London, Collins, 1960.

Clark, G. N., *The Seventeenth Century*, Oxford, Oxford University Press, 1947.

Clark, G. N., *The Later Stuarts, 1660–1714*, London, Oxford University Press, 1956, Oxford History of England.

Clark, P. et al. (eds), *The English Commonwealth, 1547–1640*, Leicester, Leicester University Press, 1979.

Cook, D., *Sixteenth-Century England, 1450–1600, Documents and Debates*, London, Macmillan, 1980.

Coward, B., *The Stuart Age: A History of England 1603–1714*, London, Longman, 1980.

Davies, G., *The Early Stuarts, 1603–1660*, London, Oxford University Press, 1959, Oxford History of England.

Dickens, A. G., *The English Reformation*, London, Fontana, 1967.

Elton, G. R., *The Tudor Revolution in Government*, Cambridge, Cambridge University Press, 1953.

Elton, G. R., *The Tudor Constitution*, Cambridge, Cambridge University Press, 1961.

Elton, G. R., *England under the Tudors*, London, Methuen, 1974.

Elton, G. R., *Reform and Reformation, 1509–58*, London, Arnold, 1977.

Eustace, T., *Statesmen and Politicians of the Stuart Age*, London, Macmillan, 1985.

Fraser, A., *Cromwell: Our Chief of Men*, London, Panther, 1975.

Goodman, A., *A History of England from Edward II to James I*, London, Longman, 1977.

Graves, M. A. R. and Silcock, R. H., *Revolution, Reaction and the Triumph of Conservatism: English History, 1558–1700*, London, Longman, 1984.

Hill, C., *The English Revolution 1640*, London, Lawrence and Wishart, 1955.

Hill, C., *God's Englishman: Oliver Cromwell and the English Revolution*, Harmondsworth, Penguin, 1972.

Hill, C., *Change and Continuity in*

Seventeenth Century England, London, Weidenfeld and Nicolson, 1975.

Hill, C., *A Century of Revolution: 1603–1714*, London, Nelson, 1980.

Holmes, G., *British Politics in the Age of Anne*, London, Macmillan, 1967.

Holmes, G., *Britain after the Glorious Revolution, 1689–1714*, London, Macmillan, 1969.

Hughes, P., *The Reformation in England*, London, Burns and Oates, 1963.

Hurstfield, J., *Elizabeth I and the Unity of England*, London, English Universities Press, 1970.

Hurstfield, J., *Freedom, Corruption and Government in Elizabethan England*, London, Cape, 1973.

Ives, E. W. (ed.), *The English Revolution, 1600–1660*, London, Arnold, 1968.

Jacob, E. F., *The Fifteenth Century, 1399–1485*, Oxford, Oxford University Press, 1961, Oxford History of England.

Jones, J. R., *Britain and Europe in the Seventeenth Century*, London, Arnold, 1966.

Jones, J. R., *The Revolution of 1688 in England*, London, Weidenfeld and Nicolson, 1972.

Jones, J. R., *Country and Court: England 1658–1714*, London, Arnold, 1978.

Jones, J. R. (ed.), *The Restored Monarchy, 1660–1688*, London, Macmillan, 1979.

Kenyon, J. P., *The Stuart Constitution, 1603–88*, Cambridge, Cambridge University Press, 1966.

Kenyon, J. P. (ed.), *The Stuarts: A Study in English Kingship*, London, Severn House, 1976.

Kenyon, J. P., *Stuart England*, Harmondsworth, Penguin, 1985, Pelican History of England.

Lamont, W. and Oldfield, S., *Politics, Religion and Literature in the Seventeenth Century*, London, Dent, 1973.

Lander, J. R., *Politics and Power in England, 1450–1509*, London, Arnold, 1976.

Loades, D. M., *Politics and the Nation,*

1450–1660: Obedience, Resistance and Public Order, London, Fontana, 1974.

MacCaffrey, W., *The Shaping of the Elizabethan Regime*, London, Cape, 1969.

Mackie, J. D., *The Earlier Tudors, 1485–1558*, London, Oxford University Press, 1977, Oxford History of England.

Manning, B. (ed.), *Politics, Religion and the English Civil War*, London, Arnold, 1973.

Manning, B., *The English People and the English Revolution*, Harmondsworth, Penguin, 1978.

Mathew, D., *The Jacobean Age*, London, Kennikat Press, 1973.

Morrill, J. S., *The Revolt of the Provinces: Conservatives and Radicals in the English Civil War*, London, Longman, 1980.

Neale, J. E., *Elizabeth and her Parliaments*, 2 vols, London, Cape, 1953.

Ogg, D., *England in the Reigns of James II and William III*, Oxford, Oxford University Press, 1984.

Ogg, D., *England in the Reign of Charles II*, 2 vols, London, Oxford University Press, 1984.

Palliser, D. M., *The Age of Elizabeth: England under the Late Tudors, 1547–1603*, London, Longman, 1983.

Parry, R. H. (ed.), *The English Civil War and After, 1642–58*, London, Macmillan, 1970.

Patrick, A. J., *The Making of a Nation 1603–1789*, Harmondsworth, Penguin, 1970.

Petrie, C. A., *The Jacobite Movement*, London, Eyre and Spottiswoode, 1959.

Plumb, J. H., *The Growth of Political Stability in England, 1675–1725*, London, Macmillan, 1967.

Richardson, R. C., *The Debate on the English Revolution*, London, Methuen, 1977.

Roots, I., *The Great Rebellion: 1642–1660*, London, Batsford, 1979.

Rowse, A. L., *The Elizabethan Renaissance*, 2 vols, London,

Macmillan, 1971–2.

Rowse, A. L., *The Expansion of Elizabethan England*, London, Macmillan, 1981.

Russell, C. (ed.), *The Origins of the English Civil War*, London, Macmillan, 1973.

Sharp, A., *Political Ideas of the English Civil Wars, 1641–1649*, London, Longman, 1983.

Smith, A. G. R., *The Government of Elizabethan England*, London, Arnold, 1967.

Smith, A. G. R., *The Emergence of a Nation State: The Commonwealth of England, 1529–1660*, London, Longman, 1984.

Stone, L., *The Causes of the English Revolution, 1529–1642*, London, Routledge & Kegan Paul, 1972.

Trevelyan, G. M., *England Under the Stuarts*, London, Methuen, 1966.

Trevelyan, G. M., *The English Revolution: 1688–89*, London, Oxford University Press, 1969.

Wedgwood, C. V., *The King's Peace: 1637–1641*, London, Collins, 1955.

Wedgwood, C. V., *The King's War: 1641–1647*, London, Collins, 1958.

Wedgwood, C. V., *The Trial of Charles I*, London, Collins, 1964.

Wedgwood, C. V., *Oliver Cromwell*, London, Duckworth, 1973.

Wernham, R. B., *Before the Armada*, London, Cape, 1966.

Western, J. R., *Monarchy and Revolution: The English State in the 1680's*, London, Macmillan, 1985.

Williams, P., *The Tudor Regime*, Oxford, Oxford University Press, 1981.

Williamson, J. A., *The Tudor Age: 1485–1603*, London, Longman, 1979.

Woodward, G. W. O., *Reformation and Resurgence: England in the Sixteenth Century*, London, Blandford, 1963.

Woodward, G. W. O. *The Dissolution of the Monasteries*, London, Blandford, 1966.

Woolrych, A. H., *Oliver Cromwell*, Oxford, Oxford University Press, 1966.

Woolrych, A. H., *Commonwealth to Protectorate*, London, Oxford University Press, 1982.

Wroughton, J., *Seventeenth-Century Britain, Documents and Debates*, London, Macmillan, 1980.

HANOVERIAN TO VICTORIAN BRITAIN

Altick, R. D., *Victorian People and Ideas*, London, Norton, 1980.

Ayling, S., *The Elder Pitt, Earl of Chatham*, London, Collins, 1976.

Beales, D., *From Castlereagh to Gladstone, 1815–1885*, London, Nelson, 1969.

Bell, H. C. F., *Lord Palmerston*, 2 vols, London, Cass, 1966.

Bentley, M., *Politics without Democracy, Great Britain, 1815–1914*, Blackwell, Oxford, 1984.

Black, J., *Britain in the Age of Walpole*, London, Macmillan, 1985.

Blake, R., *Disraeli*, London, Eyre and Spottiswoode, 1969.

Briggs, A., *The Age of Improvement 1783–1867*, London, Longman, 1979.

Brown, P. A., *The French Revolution in English History*, London, Cass, 1965.

Brown, R. and Daniels, C., *Nineteenth-Century Britain, Documents and Debates*, London, Macmillan, 1980.

Butler, J. R. M., *The Passing of the Great Reform Bill*, London, Cass, 1964.

Carswell, J., *From Revolution to Revolution in England 1688–1776*, London, Routledge & Kegan Paul, 1973.

Christie, I. R., *Wars and Revolutions: Britain 1760–1815*, London, Arnold, 1982.

Clark, G. S., *Sir Robert Peel and the Conservative Party*, London, Cass, 1964.

Conacher, J. B., *The Emergence of British Parliamentary Democracy in the Nineteenth Century*, London, Wiley, 1971.

Cowie, L. W., *Hanoverian England 1714–1837*, London, Bell, 1967.

Davis, H. W. C., *The Age of Grey and Peel*, London, Oxford University Press, 1965.

Derry, J. W., *Reaction and Reform: England in the Early Nineteenth Century*, London, Blandford, 1963.

Dodd, A. H., *The Growth of Responsible Government from James I to Victoria*, London, Routledge & Kegan Paul, 1956.

Ensor, R. C. K., *England, 1870–1914*, London, Oxford University Press, 1936, Oxford History of England.

Evans, E. J., *The Forging of the Modern State: Early Industrial Britain, 1783–1870*, London, Longman, 1983.

Evans, R. J., *The Victorian Age: 1815–1914*, London, Arnold, 1968.

Feiling, K., *The Second Tory Party 1714–1832*, London, Macmillan, 1951.

Feuchtwanger, E. J., *Disraeli, Democracy and the Tory Party*, Oxford, Clarendon Press, 1968.

Feuchtwanger, E. J., *Gladstone*, London, Allen Lane 1975.

Feuchtwanger, E. J., *Democracy and Empire: Britain, 1865–1914*, London, Arnold, 1985.

Gash, N., *Politics in the Age of Peel*, London, Arnold, 1968.

Gash, N., *Peel*, London, Longman, 1979.

George, D., *England in Transition*, Harmondsworth, Penguin, 1965.

Halévy, E., *A History of the English People in the Nineteenth Century*, 6 vols, London, Benn, 1936.

Hanham, H. J. (ed.), *The Nineteenth Century Constitution, 1815–1914*, Cambridge, Cambridge University Press, 1969.

Harris, R. W., *England in the Eighteenth Century 1689–1793*, London, Blandford, 1963.

Hill, B. W., *The Growth of Parliamentary Parties, 1689–1742*, London, Allen and Unwin, 1977.

Hill, B. W., *British Parliamentary Parties, 1742–1832: From the Fall of Walpole to the First Reform Act*, London, Allen and Unwin, 1985.

Holmes, G. (ed.), *Britain after the Glorious Revolution*, London, Macmillan, 1969.

Holmes, G. S., and Speck, W. A., *Divided Society: Parties and Politics in England, 1694–1716*, London, Arnold, 1967.

Horn, D. B., *Great Britain and Europe in the Eighteenth Century*, London, Oxford University Press, 1967.

Hyam, R., *Britain's Imperial Century, 1815–1914*, London, Batsford, 1976.

Jarrett, D., *Britain, 1688–1815*, London, Longman, 1965.

Jarrett, D., *Pitt the Younger*, London, Weidenfeld and Nicolson, 1974.

Jones, J. R., *Britain and the World, 1648–1815*, London, Fontana, 1980.

Kemp, B., *King and Commons, 1660–1832*, London, Macmillan, 1957.

Kemp, B., *Sir Robert Walpole*, London, Weidenfeld and Nicolson, 1976.

Kitson-Clark, G. S. R., *Peel and the Conservative Party: A Study in Party Politics 1832–1841*, London, Cass, 1964.

Langford, P., *Britain 1688–1815: Foreign Policy in the Eighteenth Century*, London, Black, 1976.

Lenman, B., *The Jacobite Risings in Britain, 1689–1746*, London, Methuen, 1980.

MacDonagh, O., *Early Victorian Government, 1830–1870*, London, Weidenfeld and Nicolson, 1977.

Magnus, P., *Gladstone*, London, Murray, 1954.

Marshall, D., *The Life and Times of Victoria*, London, Weidenfeld and Nicolson, 1972.

Marshall, D., *Eighteenth Century England, 1714–1784*, London, Longman, 1975.

Miller, S. T., *British Political History, 1784–1939*, Plymouth, Macdonald and Evans, 1980.

Namier, L. B., *The Structure of Politics at the Accession of George III*, London, Macmillan, 1957.

Namier, L. B., *England in the Age of the American Revolution*, London, Macmillan, 1961.

Namier, L. B. and Brooke, J., *The House of Commons: 1754–90*, 3 vols, London, HMSO, 1964.

Owen, J. B., *The Eighteenth Century, 1714–1815*, Wokingham, Van Nostrand Reinhold, 1982.

Pares, R., *King George III and the Politicians*, Oxford, Oxford University Press, 1953.

Pearson, H., *Dizzy: The Life and Personality of Benjamin Disraeli*, New York, White Lion, 1974.

Petrie, C., *The Jacobite Movement*, 2 vols, Eyre and Spottiswoode, 1959.

Plumb, J. H., *Sir Robert Walpole*, 2 vols, London, Allen Lane, 1956–60.

Plumb, J. H., *The Growth of Political Stability in England, 1675–1725*, London, Macmillan, 1967.

Plumb, J. H., *England in the Eighteenth Century*, Harmondsworth, Penguin, 1969, Pelican History of England.

Ramsay, A. A. W., *Sir Robert Peel*, London, Constable, 1971.

Read, D., *England, 1868–1914*, London, Longman, 1979.

Reed, M., *The Georgian Triumph, 1700–1830*, London, Routledge & Kegan Paul, 1983.

Ridley, J., *Lord Palmerston*, London, Constable, 1970.

Ritcheson, C. R., *British Politics and the American Revolution*, London, Greenwood Press, 1981.

Royle, E., *Chartism*, London, Longman, 1980.

Rudé, G., *Wilkes and Liberty*, Oxford, Oxford University Press, 1962.

Seaman, L. C. B., *Victorian England: Aspects of English and Imperial History, 1837–1901*, London, Methuen, 1973.

Selley, W. T., *England in the Eighteenth Century*, London, Black, 1962.

Seton-Watson, R. W., *Britain in Europe, 1789–1914*, Cambridge, Cambridge University Press, 1955.

Shannon, R., *The Crisis of Imperialism 1865–1915*, London, Granada, 1974, Paladin History of England.

Smith, F. B., *The Making of the Second Reform Bill*, London, Cambridge University Press, 1966.

Smith, P., *Disraeli, Conservatism and Social Reform*, London, Routledge & Kegan Paul, 1967.

Speck, W. A., *Tory and Whig: The Struggle in the Constituencies*, London, Macmillan, 1970.

Speck, W. A., *Stability and Strife: England 1714–1760*, London, Arnold, 1977.

Sutherland, G. (ed.), *Studies in the Growth of Nineteenth Century Government*, London, Routledge & Kegan Paul, 1972.

Thompson, D., *The Chartists*, London, Maurice Temple Smith, 1983.

Thomson, D., *England in the Nineteenth Century*, Harmondsworth, Penguin, 1970, Pelican History of England.

Trevelyan, G. M., *British History in the Nineteenth Century and After 1782–1919*, Harmondsworth, Penguin, 1971.

Ward, J. T., *Chartism*, London, Batsford, 1973.

Watson, G., *The English Ideology: Studies in the Language of Victorian Politics*, London, Allen Lane, 1978.

Watson, J. S., *The Reign of George III, 1760–1815*, London, Oxford University Press, 1960, Oxford History of England.

Williams, B. and Stuart, C. H., *The Whig Supremacy, 1714–1760*, London, Oxford University Press, 1962, Oxford History of England.

Williams, E. N. (ed.), *The Eighteenth Century Constitution, 1688–1815*, Cambridge, Cambridge University Press, 1960.

Wood, A., *Nineteenth Century Britain, 1815–1914*, London, Longman, 1982.

Woodward, L., *The Age of Reform, 1815–1870*, London, Oxford University Press, 1962, Oxford History of England.

MODERN BRITAIN

Addison, P., *The Road to 1945: British Politics and the Second World War*, London, Quartet, 1975.

Barnett, C., *The Collapse of British Power*, Gloucester, Alan Sutton, 1985.

Bartlett, C. J., *A History of Postwar Britain, 1945–1974*, London, Longman, 1977.

Beloff, M., *Wars and Welfare: Britain 1914–1945*, London, Arnold, 1984.

Blake, R., *The Decline of Power, 1915–1964*, London, Granada, 1985, Paladin History of England.

Boyd, F., *British Politics in Transition: 1945–63*, London, Pall Mall Press, 1964.

Brown, R. and Daniels, C., *Twentieth-Century Britain, Documents and Debates*, London, Macmillan, 1982.

Childs, D., *Britain Since 1945: A Political History*, London, Methuen, 1984.

Churchill, W. S., *The Second World War*, 6 vols, Harmondsworth, Penguin, 1985.

Cook, C. (ed.), *Sources in British Political History, 1900–1951*, 6 vols, London, Macmillan, 1975–84.

Cruttwell, C. R. F., *A History of the Great War, 1914–1918*, Oxford, Clarendon Press, 1936.

Dilks, D. N. (ed.), *Retreat from Power: Studies in Britain's Foreign Policy of the Twentieth Century*, 2 vols, London, Macmillan, 1981.

Edwards, J. R., *British History 1815–1939*, London, Bell, 1970.

Harrison, B., *Peaceable Kingdom: Stability and Change in Modern Britain*, London, Oxford University Press, 1983.

Havighurst, A. F., *Modern England, 1901–1970*, Cambridge, Cambridge University Press, 1976.

Holmes, M., *The Labour Government, 1974–79: Political Aims and Economic Policy*, London, Macmillan, 1985.

James, R. R., *Ambitions and Realities: British Politics 1964–70*, London, Weidenfeld and Nicolson, 1970.

James, R. R., *The British Revolution: British Politics 1880–1939*, London, Methuen, 1978.

Jarman, T. L., *Democracy and World Conflict: A History of Modern Britain*, London, Blandford, 1963.

Lane, P., *British Politics and People, 1760–1980*, London, Heinemann, 1981.

Langan, M. and Schwarz, B. (eds), *Crisis in the British State, 1880–1930*, London, Hutchinson, 1985.

Levin, B., *The Pendulum Years: Britain and the Sixties*, London, Cape, 1970.

Lloyd, T. O., *Empire to Welfare State: English History 1906–1967*, London, Oxford University Press, 1979.

Macfarlane, L. J., *Issues in British Politics since 1945*, London, Longman, 1982.

McKie, D. and Cook, C. (eds), *The Decade of Disillusion: British Politics and the Sixties*, London, Macmillan, 1972.

Medlicott, W. N., *Contemporary England: 1914–64*, London, Longman, 1976.

Miller, S. T., *British Political History: 1784–1939*, Plymouth, Macdonald and Evans, 1980.

Morgan, K. O., *Labour in Power, 1945–1951*, London, Oxford University Press, 1985.

Mowat, C. L., *Britain between the Wars: 1918–40*, London, Methuen, 1968.

Peacock, H. L., *A History of Modern Britain: 1815–1970*, London, Heinemann, 1980.

Pelling, H., *Modern Britain, 1885–1955*, London, Sphere, 1969.

Pelling, H., *Britain and the Second World War*, London, Fontana, 1970.

Pelling, H., *Labour Governments, 1945–1951*, London, Macmillan, 1984.

Porter, B., *Britain, Europe and the World, 1850–1982*, London, Allen and Unwin, 1983.

Proudfoot, M., *British Politics and Government: 1951–1970*, London, Faber, 1974.

Pugh, M., *The Making of Modern British Politics, 1867–1939*, Oxford, Blackwell, 1982.

Reynolds, E. E. and Brasher, N. H., *Britain in the Twentieth Century 1900–1964*, Cambridge, Cambridge University Press, 1960.

Robbins, K., *The Eclipse of a Great Power: Modern Britain 1870–1975*, London, Longman, 1983.

Seaman, L. C. B., *Post-Victorian Britain. 1902–1951*, London, Methuen, 1967.

Sissons, M. and French, P. (eds), *The Age of Austerity 1945–51*, London, Hodder and Stoughton, 1963.

Sked, A. and Cook, C., *Post-War Britain: A Political History*, Harmondsworth, Penguin, 1979.

Stacey, F., *British Government, 1966–1975: Years of Reform*, London, Oxford University Press, 1975.

Taylor, A. J. P., *English History, 1914–1945*, Harmondsworth, Penguin, 1970.

Taylor, A. J. P., *The First World War*, Harmondsworth, Penguin, 1970.

Taylor, A. J. P., *The Origins of the Second World War*, Harmondsworth, Penguin, 1963.

Thomson, D., *England in the 20th Century 1914–63*, Harmondsworth, Penguin, 1970.

Webb, R. K., *Modern England: From the Eighteenth Century to the Present*, London, Allen and Unwin, 1980.

Whitehead, P., *The Writing on the Wall: Britain in the Seventies*, London, Michael Joseph, 1985.

Wilson, H., *The Labour Government, 1964–70*, London, Weidenfeld and Nicolson, 1971.

Wood, A., *Great Britain, 1900–1965*, London, Longman, 1977.

Woodward, E. L., *Great Britain and the War of 1914–1918*, London, Methuen, 1967.

SEE ALSO:

14 INDUSTRY AND COMMERCE

Information relating to research and publications on industry and commerce can be found in the following: American Economic Association, *Index of Economic Articles*, annually; Bolton, K. M., *Sources of Information on Business Organisations in the British Isles*, 1973; Burkett, J., *Industrial and Related Library and Information Services in the United Kingdom*, 1972; Library Association, *Directory of Research Resources in the United Kingdom for Business, Industry and Public Affairs*, 1970; G. K. Hall (publisher), *Bibliographic Guide to Business and Economics*, annually; Bowker (publisher), *Business and Economics Books, 1876–1983*, 4 vols, 1983; Mason, S., *The McGraw-Hill Handbook of British Finance and Trade*, 1983; Martinus Nijhoff (publisher), *Economic Titles and Abstracts*, annually.

Standard business directories containing information on companies, industry and commerce in Great Britain are: Barrow, C., *The Small Business Guide: Sources of Information for New and Small Businesses*, 1982; Bax, A. and Fairfield, S., *The Macmillan Guide to the United Kingdom, 1978–79*, 1978; Dun and Bradstreet (publisher), *Who Owns Whom: United Kingdom and Republic of Ireland*, 1981; Kelly's Directories (publisher), *Kelly's Manufacturers and Merchants Directory*, annually; Kompass (publisher), *Register of British Industry and Commerce;* Millard, P. (comp.), *Trade Associations and Professional Bodies in the United Kingdom*, 1987; Times Books, *1,000 Leading Companies in Britain and Overseas*, annually.

See also Codlin, E. M. (ed.), *Aslib Directory, Vol. 1, Information Sources in Science, Technology and Commerce*, 1982.

For introductory surveys of a general nature readers are referred to: Allen, G. C., *British Industries and their Organisations*, 1970; Allen, G. C., *The Structure of Industry in Britain*, 1970; Allen, G. C., *British Industry and Economic Policy*, 1979; Anthony, V. S., *Britain's Overseas Trade: The Recent History of British Trade*, 1981; Central Office of Information, *The Framework of British Industry*, 1981; Devereux, M. P., *Industries in Britain*, 1974; Devereux, M. P., *Industries in Britain*, 1974; Johnson, P., *British Industry*, 1985; Woolner, A. H., *Modern Industry in Britain*, 1975.

The series by the Central Office of Information, *British Industry Today*, is recommended for introductory reading to particular branches of industry.

For recent publications on the political and economic context readers should refer to British Library of Economic and Political Science, *A London Bibliography of the Social Sciences*, annually.

REFERENCE

American Economic Assocation, *Index of Economic Articles*, Richard D. Irwin Inc., Homewood, Illinois, annually.

Anbar Publications (publisher), *Anbar Management Publications*

Bibliography, London, annually.

Bakewell, K. G. B., *Library and Information Services for Management*, London, Bingley, 1968.

Barrow, C., *The Small Business Guide: Sources of Information for New and*

Small Businesses, London, BBC, 1982.

Bax, A. and Fairfield, S. (comps.), *The Macmillan Guide to the United Kingdom, 1978–79*, London, Macmillan, 1978.

Bowker (publisher), *Business Books and Serials in Print*, London and New York, annually.

Bowker (publisher), *Business and Economics Books, 1876–1983*, 4 vols, New York and London, 1983.

British Institute of Management, *Sources of Management Information*, London, 1975.

British Library of Economic and Political Science, *A London Bibliography of the Social Sciences*, London and New York, Mansell, annually.

Burgess, N., *How to Find out about Banking and Investment*, Oxford, Pergamon, 1970.

Burkett, J., *Industrial and Related Library and Information Services in the United Kingdom*, London, Library Association, 1972.

Business Statistics Office, *Service and Distribution Monitors*, Series, London, HMSO, annually.

Business Statistics Office, *Production Monitors*, Series, London, HMSO, annually.

Codlin, E. M. (ed.), *Aslib Directory, Vol. 1, Information Sources in Science, Technology and Commerce*, London, 1982.

Dare, G. A. and Bakewell, K. G. B., *The Manager's Guide to Getting the Answers*, Library Association, 1983.

Dun and Bradstreet (publisher), *Who Owns Whom: United Kingdom and Republic of Ireland*, 2 vols, London, 1981.

Dun and Bradstreet (publisher), *Key British Enterprises: Top Twenty Thousand British Companies*, 2 vols, London, 1984.

Euromonitor Publications (publisher), *A to Z of United Kingdom Marketing Data*, London, 1982.

Financial Times (publisher), *Financial Times Businessman's Guide to the UK*, London, 1981.

Foster, A. and Smith, G., *The Online Business Sourcebook*, London, Headland Press, 1986.

Gower Press (publisher), *Business Atlas of Great Britain*, Epping, Essex, 1974.

Greener, M., *The Penguin Dictionary of Commerce*, Harmondsworth, Penguin, 1971.

G. K. Hall (publisher), *Bibliographic Guide to Business and Economy*, Boston, Mass., annually.

Jeremy, D. J. (ed.), *Dictionary of Business Biography: A Biographical Dictionary of Business Leaders Active in Britain, 1860–1980*, Sevenoaks, Butterworth, 1984.

Kelly's Directories (publisher), *Kelly's Manufacturers and Merchants Directory*, London, annually.

Kompass (publisher), *Register of British Industry and Commerce*, 1986, 4 vols, Croydon.

Library Association, *Current Technology Index*, London, Library Association, annually; *Directory of Research Resources in the United Kingdom for Business, Industry and Public Affairs*, London, 1970.

Library Association Industrial Group, *Industrial and Commercial Libraries: An Introductory Guide*, London, 1986.

Maltby, A., *Economics and Commerce: The Sources of Information and their Organisation*, London, Bingley, 1968.

Martinus Nijhoff (publisher), *Economic Titles and Abstracts*, The Hague, annually.

Mason, S., *The McGraw-Hill Handbook of British Finance and Trade*, London, McGraw-Hill, 1983.

Millard, P. (comp.), *Trade Associations and Professional Bodies in the United Kingdom*, Oxford, Pergamon, 1987.

Parsons, A. J., *How to Find out about Engineering*, Oxford, Pergamon, 1972.

Segal, A., *A Careers Encyclopedia*, London, Cassell, 1984.

Thomas Skinner (publisher), *The Stock Exchange Official Yearbook*, East Grinstead, annually.

Times Books (publisher), *1,000 Leading Companies in Britain and Overseas*, London, annually.

Vernon, K. D. C. (ed.), *The Use of Management and Business Literature*, London and Boston, Butterworth, 1975.

Wilson (publisher), *Business Periodicals Index*, New York, annually.

GENERAL

Aaronowitch, S. and Sawywer, M. C., *Big Business: Theoretical and Empirical Aspects of Concentration and Mergers in the United Kingdom*, London, Macmillan, 1975.

Abraham, N., *Big Business and Government: The New Disorder*, London, Flame Books, 1979.

Alan Armstrong (publisher), *Inside Information*, London, 1986.

Allen, G. C., *The Structure of Industry in Britain*, London, Macmillan, 1970.

Allen, G. C., *British Industries and their Organisation*, London, Longman, 1970.

Allen, G. C., *British Industry and Economic Policy*, London, Macmillan, 1979.

Allen, R. (ed.), *Exporting to the UK: A Basic Guide for the Developing Country Exporter*, Oxford, Pergamon, 1983.

Anthony, V. S., *Banks and Markets*, London, Heinemann, 1979.

Anthony, V. S., *Britain's Overseas Trade: The Recent History of British Trade*, London, Heinemann, 1981.

Bannock, G., *The Economics of the Small Firm: Return from the Wilderness*, Oxford, Blackwell, 1981.

Blackaby, F. (ed.), *De-industrialisation*, London, Heinemann, 1979.

Blank, S., *Government and Industry in Britain: Federation of British Industries in Politics 1945–65*, Farnborough, Saxon House, 1973.

Bodey, H., *Twenty Centuries of British Industry*, Newton Abbot, David and Charles, 1975.

Branton, N., *Economic Organisation of Modern Britain*, Sevenoaks, Hodder and Stoughton, 1974.

Brown, J. A. C., *The Social Psychology of Industry*, Harmondsworth, Penguin, 1970.

Campbell, M., *Capitalism in the UK*, London, Croom Helm, 1981.

Central Office of Information, *Inland Transport in Britain*, London, HMSO, 1977.

Central Office of Information, *Town Traffic in Britain*, London, HMSO, 1978.

Central Office of Information, *British Industry Today: Organisation and Production*, London, HMSO, 1978.

Central Office of Information, *The Framework of British Industry*, London, HMSO, 1981.

Central Office of Information, *Employment in Britain*, London, HMSO, 1982.

Central Office of Information, *Britain's Invisible Trade*, London, HMSO, 1983.

Channon, D. F., *Strategy and Structure of Management in Private and State Industry*, London, Aims of Industry, 1974.

Channon, D. F., *The Service Industries: Strategy, Structure and Financial Performance*, London, Macmillan, 1978.

Confederation of British Industry, *Industry and the City*, London, CBI, 1977.

Cox, A. (ed.), *The State, Finance and Industry*, Brighton, Wheatsheaf, 1986.

Cronin, J. E., *Industrial Conflict in Modern Britain*, London, Croom Helm, 1979.

Davies, J. R. and Hughes, S., *Investment in the British Economy*, London, Heinemann, 1980.

Department of Industry, *Industrial Movement in the United Kingdom 1966–75*, London, HMSO, 1981.

Dunning, J. H. and Thomas, C. J., *British Industry: Change and Development in the Twentieth Century*, London, Hutchinson, 1961.

Eatwell, J., *Whatever Happened to Britain? The Economics of Decline*,

London, BBC, 1982.

Ganz, G., *Government and Industry: The Provision of Financial Assistance to Industry and its Control*, London, Professional Books, 1977.

George, K. D., *Industrial Organisation: Competition, Growth and Structural Change in Britain*, London, Allen and Unwin, 1981.

Glyn, A. and Harrison, J., *The British Economic Disaster*, London, Pluto, 1980.

Goldsmith, W. and Clutterbuck, D., *The Winning Streak: Britain's Top Companies Reveal their Formulas for Success*, Harmondsworth, Penguin, 1985.

Grant, W., *The Political Economy of Industrial Policy*, London, Butterworth, 1982.

Grant, W. and Marsh, D., *The Confederation of British Industry*, Sevenoaks, Hodder and Stoughton, 1977.

Hansard Society (publisher), *Politics and Industry: The Great Mismatch*, London, 1979.

Hoare, T., *The Location of Industry in Britain*, Cambridge, Cambridge University Press, 1982.

Holland, S., *Capital versus the Regions*, London, Macmillan, 1976.

Hoyes, T. et al., *Planning for Industry*, London, Sweet and Maxwell, 1980.

Ingham, G., *Capitalism Divided? The City and Industry in British Social Development*, London, Macmillan, 1984.

Jamieson, I., *Capitalism and Culture: A Comparative Analysis of British and American Manufacturing Organisations*, Aldershot, Gower Publishing, 1980.

Jervis, F. R., *Bosses in British Industry: Managers and Management from the Industrial Revolution to the Present Day*, London, Routledge & Kegan Paul, 1974.

Johnson, P. S. (ed.), *The Structure of British Industry*, London, Granada, 1980.

Johnson, P., *British Industry: An Economic Introduction*, Oxford,

Blackwell, 1985.

Keeton, G. W. and Frommel, S. N., *British Industry and European Law*, London, Macmillan, 1974.

Kirby, M. W., *The Decline of British Economic Power Since 1870*, London, Allen and Unwin, 1981.

Lee, D., *Regional Planning and the Location of Industry*, London, Heinemann, 1980.

Livingstone, J. M., *Britain and the World Economy*, Harmondsworth, Penguin, 1972.

Luffman, G. A. and Reed, R., *The Strategy and Performance of British Industry, 1970–80*, London, Macmillan, 1985.

Major, R. (ed.), *Britain's Trade and Exchange Rate Policy*, London, Heinemann, 1979.

Mansfield, R. et al., *British Manager in Profile*, London, British Institute of Management, 1981.

Massey, D. and Catalaon, A., *Capital and Land: Landownership by Capital in Great Britain*, London, Arnold, 1978.

Minns, R., *Pension Funds and British Capitalism*, London, Heinemann, 1980.

Morrell, J., *Britain through the 1980's: An Evaluation of Market and Business Prospects*, 2 vols, Aldershot, Gower, 1980.

Musson, A. E., *The Growth of British Industry*, London, Batsford, 1981.

Newbould, G. D. and Luffman, G. A., *Successful Business Policies: An Analysis of the Policies and Performance of the 500 Largest UK Companies*, Aldershot, Gower, 1978.

Northcott, J., *Microelectronics in Industry: Progress and Performance*, London, Policy Studies Institute, 1986.

Packman, R., *A Guide to the Business World*, London, Longman, 1971.

Parker, S. R. et al., *The Sociology of Industry*, London, Allen and Unwin, 1981.

Pavitt, K. (ed.), *Technical Innovation and British Economic Performance*, London, Macmillan, 1980.

Perrott, F. R., *Industry in the Public*

Sector, Aylesbury, Ginn, 1980.

Poole, M. et al., *Managers in Focus: The British Manager in the Early 1980's*, Aldershot, Gower, 1981.

Prais, S. J., *The Evolution of Giant Firms in Britain*, Cambridge, Cambridge University Press, 1976.

Ritchie, N., *What Goes on in the City*, Cambridge, Woodhead Faulkner, 1981.

Robinson, J., *The Risk Takers: Portraits of Money, Ego and Power*, London, Allen and Unwin, 1985.

Roderick, G. and Stephens, M. (eds), *The British Malaise: Industrial Performance, Education and Training in Britain Today*, London, Falmer Press, 1982.

Royal Institute of Public Administration (publisher), *Allies or Adversaries? Perspectives on Government and Industry*, London, 1981.

Scase, R. and Goffee, R., *The Entrepreneurial Middle Class*, London, Croom Helm, 1982.

Scott, J., *Corporations, Classes and Capitalism*, London, Hutchinson, 1979.

Scott, J. and Griff, C., *Directors of Industry: The British Corporate Network, 1904–76*, Cambridge, Polity Press, 1984.

Shaw, E. R., *The London Money Market*, London, Heinemann, 1983.

Sparkes, J. R. and Pass, C. L., *Trade and Growth*, London, Heinemann, 1977.

Taylor, T., *The Financing of Industry and Commerce*, London, Heinemann, 1985.

Thomas, W. A., *The Finance of British Industry, 1918–76*, London,

Methuen, 1978.

Townsend, A. R., *The Impact of Recession on Industry and Employment in the Regions*, London, Croom Helm, 1982.

Tricker, R. I., *Corporate Governance: Practices, Procedures and Powers in British Companies and their Boards of Directors*, Aldershot, Gower, 1984.

Turner, J. (ed.), *Businessmen and Politics: Studies of Business Activity in British Politics, 1900–1945*, London, Heinemann, 1984.

Utton, M. A., *The Political Economy of Big Business*, Oxford, Martin Robertson, 1982.

Watkinson, H. A. Viscount, *Blueprint for Industrial Revival: What has Gone Wrong in Industrial Britain Since the War?*, London, Allen and Unwin, 1976.

Weir, L. (ed.), *Men and Work in Modern Britain*, London, Fontana, 1973.

White, P. R., *Planning for Public Transport*, London, Hutchinson, 1976.

Wiener, M. J., *English Culture and the Decline of the Industrial Spirit 1850–1980*, Cambridge, Cambridge University Press, 1981.

Williams, K. et al., *Why Are the British Bad at Manufacturing?*, London, Routledge & Kegan Paul, 1983.

Williams, T. I. (ed.), *Industrial Research in the United Kingdom: A Guide to Organisations and Programmes*, London, Longman, 1985.

Woolner, A. H., *Modern Industry in Britain*, London, Oxford University Press, 1975.

MANUFACTURING AND OTHER INDUSTRIES

Addy, J., *The Textile Revolution*, London, Longman, 1976.

Beresford, T., *We Plough the Fields: Agriculture in Britain Today*, Harmondsworth, Penguin, 1975.

Blunden, J. R., *The Mineral Resources of Britain: A Study in Exploitation and Planning*, London, Hutchinson, 1975.

Brearley, A., *The Woollen Industry*, Leeds, Wool Industry Research Association, 1977.

Briscoe, L., *The Textile and Clothing Industries of the United Kingdom*, Manchester, Manchester University Press, 1971.

Cambridge Information and Research

Services, *Retail Trade Developments in Great Britain*, Aldershot, Gower, 1982.

Central Office of Information, *British Industry Today: Shipping*, London, HMSO, 1974.

Central Office of Information, *British Industry Today: Ports*, London, HMSO, 1974.

Central Office of Information, *British Industry Today: Motor Vehicles*, London, HMSO, 1975.

Central Office of Information, *Advertising and Public Relations in Britain*, London, HMSO, 1976.

Central Office of Information, *British Industry Today: Electronics*, London, HMSO, 1976.

Central Office of Information, *British Industry Today: Chemicals*, London, HMSO, 1978.

Central Office of Information, *British Industry Today: Manufacturing Industries*, London, HMSO, 1978.

Central Office of Information, *British Industry Today: Textiles and Clothing*, London, HMSO, 1978.

Central Office of Information, *Insurance in Britain*, London, HMSO, 1979.

Central Office of Information, *British Industry Today: Agriculture in Britain*, London, HMSO, 1980.

Central Office of Information, *British Industry Today: Aerospace*, London, HMSO, 1984.

Central Office of Information, *Britain's Manufacturing and Service Industries*, London, HMSO 1985.

Docherty, C., *Steel and Steelworkers: The Sons of Vulcan*, London, Heinemann, 1983.

Fores, M. and Gover, I. (eds), *Manufacturing and Management*, London, HMSO, 1979.

Franklin, P. J. and Woodhead, C., *The United Kingdom Life Assurance Industry*, London, Croom Helm, 1980.

Gale, W. K. V., *The British Iron and Steel Industry: A Technical History*, Newton Abbot, David and Charles, 1970.

Gough, T. J., *The Economics of Building Societies*, London, Macmillan, 1982.

Hamilton, K. and Potter, S., *Losing Track*, London, Routledge & Kegan Paul, 1985.

Hardie, D. W. F. and Pratt, J. D., *A History of the Modern British Chemical Industry*, Oxford, Pergamon, 1966.

Hart, P. E. and Clarke, R., *Concentration in British Industry, 1935–75: A Study of the Growth, Causes and Effects of Concentration in British Manufacturing Industries*, Cambridge, Cambridge University Press, 1980.

Hawkins, K., *Manufacturing in Britain— A Terminal Case?*, Hounslow, Wildwood House, 1985.

Hays, S., *The Engineering Industries*, London, Heinemann, 1972.

Hays, S., *The Chemicals and Allied Industries*, London, Heinemann, 1973.

Hayward, K., *Government and British Civil Aerospace: A Case Study in Post-War Technology Policy*, Manchester, Manchester University Press, 1983.

Heal, D. W., *The Steel Industry in Post-War Britain*, Newton Abbot, David and Charles, 1974.

Hill, B., *Britain's Agricultural Industry*, London, Heinemann, 1975.

Hillebrandt, P. M., *Analysis of the British Construction Industry*, London, Macmillan, 1984.

Hills, J., *Information Technology and Industrial Policy*, London, Croom Helm, 1984.

Hodgson, G., *Lloyds of London: A Reputation at Risk*, Harmondsworth, Penguin, 1985.

Holme, A., *The Motor Vehicle Industry*, London, Ginn, 1977.

Institution of Production Engineers, *Current and Future Trends of Manufacturing Management and Technology in the UK*, London, 1980.

Jenkins, J. G., *The Wool Textile Industry in Great Britain*, London, Routledge & Kegan Paul, 1972.

Livesey, F., *The Distributive Trades*, London, Heinemann, 1979.

Maltby, D. and White, H. P., *Transport in the United Kingdom*, London, Macmillan, 1982.

Moran, M., *The Politics of Banking: The Strange Case of Competition and Credit Control*, London, Macmillan, 1984.

Nevett, T. R., *Advertising in Britain: A History*, London, Heinemann, 1982.

Northcott, J. and Rogers, P., *Microelectronics in Industry*, London, Policy Studies Institute, 1984.

Ovenden, K., *The Politics of Steel*, London, Macmillan, 1978.

Pryke, R. and Dodgson, J., *The Rail Problem*, Oxford, Martin Robertson, 1975.

Silberston, A. et al., *British Manufacturing Investment Overseas*, London, Methuen, 1985.

Smyth, H., *Property Companies and the Construction Industry in Britain*, Cambridge, Cambridge University Press, 1985.

Television History Workshop, *Making Cars*, London, Routledge & Kegan Paul, 1985.

Warren, K., *The British Iron and Steel Sheet Industry since 1840*, London, Bell, 1970.

Whalley, P., *The Social Production of Technical Work: The Case of British Engineers*, London, Macmillan, 1985.

Wilks, S., *Industrial Policy and the Motor Industry*, Manchester, Manchester University Press, 1984.

Williams, K. et al., *Why Are the British Bad at Manufacturing?*, London, Routledge & Kegan Paul, 1983.

Wistrich, E., *The Politics of Transport*, London, Longman, 1983.

Wormwell, P., *Anatomy of Agriculture: A Study of Britain's Greatest Industry*, London, Harrap, 1978.

NATIONALISED INDUSTRIES

Browne, C. (ed.), *Industrial Efficiency and the Role of Government*, London, HMSO, 1977.

Central Office of Information, *Nationalised Industries in Britain*, London, HMSO, 1983.

Chester, N., *The Nationalisation of British Industry 1945–51*, London, HMSO, 1975.

Consumer Council, *Consumers and the Nationalized Industries*, London, HMSO, 1976.

Flegman, V., *Parliament and Nationalised Industries*, Aldershot, Gower, 1985.

McIntosh, R., *A Study of UK Nationalised Industries: Their Role in the Economy and Control in the Future*, London, HMSO, 1977.

Parris, H., *Crisis in the Nationalised Industries*, London, Croom Helm, 1985.

Prosser, T., *Nationalised Industries and Public Control*, Oxford, Blackwell, 1986.

Pryke, R., *The Nationalised Industries: Policies and Performance since 1968*, Oxford, Martin Robertson, 1981.

Redwood, J., *Public Enterprise in Crisis: The Future of the Nationalised Industries*, Oxford, Blackwell, 1980.

Reid, G. L. and Allen, K., *Nationalized Industries*, Harmondsworth, Penguin, 1970.

Smith, J. G. (ed.), *Strategic Planning in Nationalised Industries*, London, Macmillan, 1984.

Steel, D. and Heald, D. (eds), *Privatising Public Enterprises*, London, Royal Institute of Public Administration, 1984.

Thompson, A. W. J. and Hunter, L. C., *The Nationalized Transport Industries*, London, Heinemann, 1973.

Tivey, L., *Nationalisation in British Industry*, London, Cape, 1973.

Welsh, F., *Profit of the State: Nationalised Industries and Public Enterprises*, Hounslow, Maurice Temple Smith, 1982.

ENERGY

Belgrave, R. and Cornell, M. (eds), *Energy Self-Sufficiency for the UK?*, Aldershot, Gower, 1985.

Bending, R. and Eden, R., *UK Energy: Structure, Prospects and Policies*, Cambridge, Cambridge University Press, 1985.

Central Office of Information, *British Industry Today: Energy*, London, HMSO, 1973.

Central Office of Information, *Nuclear Energy in Britain*, London, HMSO, 1980.

Central Office of Information, *Britain's Energy Resources*, London, HMSO, 1982.

Chapman, K., *North Sea Oil and Gas*, Newton Abbot, David and Charles, 1976.

Corti, G. and Frazer, F., *The Nation's Oil: A Story of Control*, London, Graham and Trotman, 1983.

Department of Energy, *Development of the Oil and Gas Resources of the UK*, London, HMSO, 1978.

Ezra, D., *Coal and Energy*, London, Benn, 1980.

Hall, S. G. and Atkinson, F., *Oil and the British Economy*, London, Croom Helm, 1983.

Hall, T., *King Coal: Miners, Coal and Britain's Industrial Future*, Harmondsworth, Penguin, 1981.

Hall, T., *Nuclear Politics: The History of the Nuclear Power in Britain*, Harmondsworth, Penguin, 1986.

Hamilton, A., *North Sea Impact: Off-Shore Oil and the British Economy*, London, International Institute for Economic Research, 1978.

Hannah, L., *Engineers, Managers and Politicians: The Electricity Supply Industry from 1948 to the Present*, London, Macmillan, 1982.

Her Majesty's Stationery Office, *Energy Technologies for the United Kingdom: An Appraisal for Research, Development and Demonstration*, 2 vols, London, HMSO, 1979.

Her Majesty's Stationery Office, *Britain's Energy Resources*, London, 1983.

James, P., *The Future of Coal*, London, Macmillan, 1984.

James, P., *Power Failure: An Anatomy of Britain's Energy*, London, Century, 1985.

Jenkins, M., *British Industry and the North Sea*, London, Macmillan, 1981.

Jones, G., *The State and the Emergence of the British Oil Industry*, London, Macmillan, 1981.

Jones, P. L., *The Economics of Nuclear Power Programmes in the United Kingdom*, London, Macmillan, 1984.

Mackay, D. and Mackay, G. A., *The Political Economy of North Sea Oil*, Edinburgh, Martin Robertson, 1981.

Manners, G., *Coal in Britain*, London, Allen and Unwin, 1981.

Marshall, P. and Belgrave, R., *Oil's Contribution to UK Self Sufficiency*, London, Heinemann, 1984.

Robinson, C. and Morgan, J., *North Sea Oil in the Future: Economic Analysis and Government Policy*, London, Macmillan, 1978.

Royal Commission on Environment Pollution, *Nuclear Power and the Environment*, Cmnd. 6618, London, HMSO, 1976.

Sweet, C., *The Price of Nuclear Power*, London, Heinemann, 1983.

Tempest, P., *Energy Economics in Britain*, London, Graham and Trotman, 1983.

Williams, R., *The Nuclear Power Decisions: British Policies, 1953–78*, London, Croom Helm, 1980.

SEE ALSO:

15 LAW

The following are recommended as bibliographical guides to the literature on the law: Raistrick, D. and Rees, J. (eds), *Lawyers' Law Books: A Practical Index to Legal Literature*, 1985; Chloros, A. G. (ed.), *Bibliographical Guide to the Law of the United Kingdom, the Channel Islands and the Isle of Man*, 1973; Dias, R., *Bibliography of Jurisprudence*, 1979; Jackaman, P. G. (comp.), *Sources of Social and Legal Information: Reader's Guide no. 13*, 1978; Morby, G., *How to Find Out Your Rights: A Guide to Rights Literature and Legal Information*, 1984; Royal Institute of Public Administration, *The Legal System in Britain: A Select Bibliography*, 1974.

As general reference works and as outline guides to aspects of English law readers should consult: 'A Barrister', *Every Man's Own Lawyer*, 1981; Bird, R., *Osborne's Concise Law Dictionary*, 1983; Curzon, L. B., *A Dictionary of Law*, 1983; Jowitt, W. A. and Walshe, C., *The Dictionary of English Law*, 2 vols, 1985; Pritchard, J., *The Penguin Guide to the Law*, 1985; Walker, D. M., *The Oxford Companion to Law*, 1980; Zander, M. (ed.), *Pears Guide to the Law*, 1979.

For outline surveys of law and legal administration in Great Britain see the following: Central Office of Information, *The English Legal System*, 1976; Central Office of Information, *Criminal Justice in Britain*, 1978; Curzon, L. B., *Basic Law*, 1981; Frank, W. F., *General Principles of English Law*, 1976; Geldart, W., *Introduction to English Law*, 1984; Harris, P., *An Introduction to Law*, 1980; James, P. S., *Introduction to English Law*, 1985; Kiralfy, A. K. R., *The English Legal System*, 1984; Metcalfe, O. K., *General Principles of English Law*, 1980; Phillips, O. H., *A First Book of English Law*, 1977; Price, J. P., *The English Legal System*, 1979.

Surveys and introductory treatment of particular areas of law and society can be found in the following:

Civil Rights   Cox, B., *Civil Liberties in Britain*, 1975; Hewitt, P., *Abuse of Power: Civil Liberties in the United Kingdom*, 1981; Street, H., *Freedom, the Individual and the Law*, 1977.

Commercial Law   Arora, A., *Practical Business Law*, 1983; Brown, W. J., *Practical Company Law*, 1984; Goode, R. M., *Commercial Law*, 1982; Lowe, R., *Commercial Law*, 1983; Marsh, S. B. and Soulsby, J., *Business Law*, 1985; Price, T. K., *Practical Business Law*, 1982; Shears, P., *Business Law*, 1982.

Constitutional and Administrative Law   Bradley, A. W., *Wade and Phillips Constitutional and Administrative Law*, 1985; Dalton, P. J. and Dexter, R. S., *Constitutional Law*, 1976; Dicey, A. V. and Wade, E. C. S. (eds), *An Introduction to the Study of the Law of the Constitution*, 1961; Phillips, O. H. and Jackson, P., *Constitutional and Administrative Law*, 1978; Smith, S. A. De, *Constitutional and Administrative Law*, 1981; Yardley, D. C. M., *Introduction to British Constitutional Law*, 1984.

Police and Crime Prevention   Brown, J. and Howes, G. (eds), *The Police and the Community*, 1975; Holdaway, S., *The British Police*, 1979; Leigh, L. H., *Police Powers in England and Wales*, 1985; Varwell, D. W. P., *Police and Public*, 1978; Wegg-Prosser, C., *The Police and the Law*, 1979; Whitaker, B., *The Police in Society*, 1982.

REFERENCE

Berkowitz, D. S. and Thorne, S. E., *English Legal History: A Bibliographical and Reference Manual*, New York, Garland, 1979.

Bird, R., *Osborne's Concise Law Dictionary*, Sweet and Maxwell, 1983.

Butterworth (publisher), London, *Stone's Justices' Manual*, annually.

Carr, A. P. (ed.), *Anthony and Berryman's Magistrate's Court Guide*, London, Butterworth, 1986.

Chloros, A. G. (ed.), *Bibliographical Guide to the Law of the United Kingdom, the Channel Islands and the Isle of Man*, London, Institute of Advanced Legal Studies, 1973.

Clarendon Press (publisher), *A Concise Dictionary of Law*, Oxford, 1983.

Curzon, L. B., *A Dictionary of Law*, Plymouth, Macdonald and Evans, 1983.

Dias, R., *Bibliography of Jurisprudence*, London, Butterworth, 1979.

Harris, B., *The Magistrate's Companion*, Chichester, Barry Rose, 1981.

Hudson, A., *Dictionary of Commercial Law*, London, Butterworth, 1983.

Jackaman, P. G. (comp.), *Sources of Social and Legal Information: Readers' Guide no. 13*, Library Association, Public Libraries Group, 1978.

Jowitt, W. A. and Walshe, C., *The Dictionary of English Law*, 2 vols, London, Sweet and Maxwell, 1985.

Logan, R. G. (ed.), *Information Sources in Law*, London, Butterworth, 1986.

Lord Chancellor's Office, *Legal Aid Handbook*, London, HMSO, 1981.

Martin, E. A. (ed.), *A Concise Dictionary of Law*, Oxford, Oxford University Press, 1983.

Morby, G., *How to Find out Your Rights: A Guide to Rights Literature and Legal Information*, London, Pluto, 1984.

Newington, A. and Willoughby, H. M., *Legal Secretary's Handbook*, London, Oyez Longman, 1982.

Pritchard, J., *The Penguin Guide to the Law*, Harmondsworth, Penguin, 1985.

Raistrick, D. and Rees, J. (eds), *Lawyers' Law Books: A Practical Guide to Legal Literature*, Abingdon, Professional Books, 1985.

Royal Institute of Public Administration, *The Legal System in Britain: A Select Bibliography*, London, RIPA, 1974.

Saunders, J. B. (ed.), *Mozley's and Whiteley's Law Dictionary*, London, Butterworth, 1977.

Stroud, F., *Stroud's Judicial Dictionary of Words and Phrases*, 6 vols, London, Sweet and Maxwell, 1987.

Walker, D. M., *The Oxford Companion to Law*, Oxford, Oxford University Press, 1980.

Way, D., *Student's Guide to Law Libraries*, London, Oyez, 1967.

Zander, M. (ed.), *Pears Guide to the Law*, London, Pelham Books, 1979.

GENERAL

Atiyah, P., *Law and Modern Society*, London, Oxford University Press, 1983.

Aubrey, C., *Who's Watching You?* Harmondsworth, Penguin, 1981.

Babington, A., *The Rule of Law in Britain from the Roman Occupation to the Present Day*, Chichester, Barry Rose, 1978.

Baker, J. H., *Introduction to English Legal History*, London, Butterworth, 1979.

Baker, N. L., *The Law and the Individual*, Plymouth, Macdonald and Evans, 1982.

Barnard, D., *The Civil Court in Action*, London, Butterworth, 1977.

Barnard, D., *The Criminal Court in Action*, London, Butterworth, 1979.

'A Barrister', *Every Man's Own Lawyer*,

London, Macmillan, 1981.

Bowles, Roger A., *Law and the Economy*, Oxford, Martin Robertson, 1982.

Bradley, K. R. and Clark, R. A., *The Legal Framework: Law and the Individual*, Eastbourne, Holt, Rinehart and Winston, 1982.

Central Office of Information, *The English Legal System*, London, HMSO, 1976.

Central Office of Information, *Human Rights in the United Kingdom*, London, HMSO, 1978.

Cook, M., *Courts and You*, London, Oyez Longman, 1976.

Cox, B., *Civil Liberties in Britain*, Harmondsworth, Penguin, 1975.

Curzon, L. B., *English Legal History*, Plymouth, Macdonald and Evans, 1979.

Curzon, L. B., *Basic Law*, Plymouth, Macdonald and Evans, 1981.

Dane, J. and Thomas, P., *How to Use a Law Library*, London, Sweet and Maxwell, 1979.

Denham, P., *A Modern Introduction to Law*, London, Arnold, 1984.

Drewry, G., *Law, Justice and Politics*, London, Longman, 1982.

Edwards, J. Ll. J., *The Attorney General: Politics and the Public Interest*, London, Sweet and Maxwell, 1984.

Farrar, J., *Introduction to Legal Method*, London, Sweet and Maxwell, 1977.

Fitzgerald, M. and Muncie, J., *The System of Justice*, Oxford, Blackwell, 1983.

Frank, W. F., *General Principles of English Law*, London, Harrap, 1976.

Geldart, W., *Introduction to English Law*, London, Oxford University Press, 1984.

Grant, L., *Civil Liberty: National Council of Civil Liberties Guide to Your Rights*, Harmondsworth, Penguin, 1978.

Griffith, J. A. G., *The Politics of the Judiciary*, London, Fontana, 1981.

Hailsham, Lord, *Hamlyn Revisited: The British Legal System Today*, London, Stevens, 1983.

Hale, Sir M., *The History of the Common Law of England*, Chicago and London, University of Chicago Press, 1971.

Harding, A., *A Social History of English Law*, Harmondsworth, Penguin, 1966.

Harris, P., *An Introduction to Law*, London, Weidenfeld and Nicolson, 1980.

Hewitt, P., *Abuse of Power: Civil Liberties in the United Kingdom*, Oxford, Martin Robertson, 1981.

Hodgson, J., *English Legal Heritage*, London, Oyez, 1979.

Holdsworth, W. S., *A History of English Law*, 17 vols, London, Sweet and Maxwell, 1965–72.

Jackson, R. M., *The Machinery of Justice in England*, Cambridge, Cambridge University Press, 1980.

James, P. S., *Introduction to English Law*, London, Butterworth, 1985.

Keeton, G. W. (ed.), *The British Commonwealth: The Development of its Laws and Constitution, Vol. 1, The United Kingdom*, London, Stevens, 1955.

Kiralfy, A. K. R., *The English Legal System*, London, Sweet and Maxwell, 1984.

Manchester, A. H., *A Modern Legal History of England and Wales, 1750–1950*, London, Butterworth, 1980.

Metcalfe, O. K., *General Principles of English Law*, London, Cassell, 1980.

Milsom, S., *Historical Foundations of Common Law*, London, Butterworth, 1981.

Milton, F., *The English Magistracy*, London, Oxford University Press, 1967.

Morrison, F. L., *Courts and the Political Process in England*, London, Sage Publications, 1974.

Newton, C., *General Principles of Law*, London, Sweet and Maxwell, 1977.

Norton, P. (ed.), *Law and Order in British Politics*, Aldershot, Gower, 1984.

Owens, J. L., *The Law Courts*, London, Dent, 1976.

Paterson, A., *The Law Lords*, London, Macmillan, 1982.

105

Phillips, O. H., *A First Book of English Law*, London, Sweet and Maxwell, 1977.

Plucknett, T. F. T., *Concise History of the Common Law*, London, Butterworth, 1975.

Price, J. P., *The English Legal System*, Plymouth, Macdonald and Evans, 1979.

Pritt, D. N., *Law, Class and Society*, 4 vols, London, Lawrence and Wishart, 1970–2.

Radcliffe, G. and Cross, G., *The English Legal System*, London, Butterworth, 1977.

Redmond, P. W. D., *General Principles of English Law*, revised by J. P. Price and I. N. Stevens, Plymouth, Macdonald and Evans, 1979.

Roshier, E. and Teff, H., *Law and Society in England*, London, Tavistock Publications, 1980.

Royal Commission on Legal Services, *Final Report*, 2 vols, Cmnd. 7648, London, HMSO, 1979.

Shetreet, S., *Judges on Trial: A Study of the Appointment and Accountability of the English Judiciary*, Amsterdam, North Holland Publishing, 1976.

Smith, K. and Keenan, D. J., *English Law*, London, Pitman, 1982.

Stevens, R., *Law and Politics: The House of Lords as a Judicial Body 1800–1976*, London, Weidenfeld and Nicolson, 1979.

Street, H., *Freedom, the Individual and the Law*, Harmondsworth, Penguin, 1977.

Van Carnegem, R. C., *The Birth of English Common Law*, Cambridge, Cambridge University Press, 1973.

Walker, R. J. and Walker, M. G., *The English Legal System*, London, Butterworth, 1985.

Wallington, P. (ed.), *Civil Liberties 1984*, Oxford, Martin Robertson, 1984.

Williams, G., *Learning the Law*, London, Stevens, 1982.

Zander, M., *A Bill of Rights*, Chichester, Barry Rose, 1975.

Zander, M., *Legal Services for the Community*, London, M. T. Smith, 1978.

Zander, M., *The Law-Making Process*, London, Weidenfeld and Nicolson, 1985.

CONSTITUTIONAL AND ADMINISTRATIVE LAW

Beatson, J. and Matthews, M., *Administrative Law: Cases and Materials*, London, Oxford University Press, 1983.

Bradley, A. W., *Wade and Phillips' Constitutional and Administrative Law*, London, Longman, 1985.

Cane, P., *An Introduction to Administrative Law*, Oxford, Clarendon Press, 1986.

Craig, P., *Administrative Law*, London, Sweet and Maxwell, 1983.

Dalton, P. J. and Dexter, R. S., *Constitutional Law*, London, Oyez, 1976.

Dicey, A. V. and Wade, E. C. S. (eds), *Introduction to the Study of the Law of the Constitution*, London, Macmillan, 1961.

Eddey, K. J., *The English Legal System*, London, Sweet and Maxwell, 1982.

Garner, J., *Administrative Law*, London, Butterworth, 1985.

Hartley, T. C. and Griffith, J. A. A., *Government and Law*, London, Weidenfeld and Nicolson, 1975.

Marshall, G., *Constitutional Theory*, Oxford, Clarendon Press, 1980.

Phillips, O. H. and Jackson, P., *Constitutional and Administrative Law*, London, Sweet and Maxwell, 1978.

De Smith, S., *Constitutional and Administrative Law*, edited by H. Street and R. Brazier, Harmondsworth, Penguin, 1981.

Turpin, C., *British Government and the Constitution: Law in Context*, London, Weidenfeld and Nicolson, 1985.

Wade, H., *Administrative Law*, London, Oxford University Press, 1982.

Yardley, D. C. M., *Introduction to British Constitutional Law*, London, Butterworth, 1984.

POLICE AND CRIMINAL LAW

Ascoli, D., *The Queen's Peace: The Origins and Development of the Metropolitan Police, 1829–1979*, London, Hamish Hamilton, 1979.

Baxter, J. and Koffman, L., *Police: The Constitution and the Community*, Abingdon, Professional Books, 1985.

Borrell, C. and Cashinella, B., *Crime in Britain Today*, London, Routledge & Kegan Paul, 1975.

Bunyan, T., *The Political Police in Britain*, London, Quartet Books, 1977.

Bunyard, R. S., *Police: Organisation and Command*, Plymouth, Macdonald and Evans, 1978.

Cambell, D., *Police: The Exercise of Power*, Plymouth, Macdonald and Evans, 1978.

Central Office of Information, *The Treatment of Offenders in Britain*, London, HMSO, 1968.

Central Office of Information, *Criminal Justice in Britain*, London, HMSO, 1978.

Critchley, T. A., *A History of the Police in England and Wales*, London, Constable, 1978.

Cross, R. and Jones, P. A., *Introduction to Criminal Law*, London, Butterworth, 1980.

Curzon, L. B., *Criminal Law*, Plymouth, Macdonald and Evans, 1984.

Davidson, R. N., *Crime and Environment*, London, Croom Helm, 1981.

Fitzgerald, M. and Sim, J., *British Prisons*, Oxford, Blackwell, 1982.

Hall Williams, J. E., *Criminology and Criminal Justice*, London, Butterworth, 1982.

Holdaway, S., *The British Police*, London, Arnold, 1979.

Holdaway, S., *Inside the British Police*, Oxford, Blackwell, 1984.

Hough, M. and Mayhew, P., *The British Crime Survey*, London, HMSO, 1983.

Kettle, M. and Hodges, L., *Uprising! The Police, the People and the Riots in Britain's Cities*, London, Pan, 1982.

Leigh, L. H., *Police Powers in England and Wales*, London, Butterworth, 1985.

Mark, F., *Policing a Perplexed Society*, London, Allen and Unwin, 1977.

Reiner, R., *The Politics of the Police*, Brighton, Wheatsheaf, 1985.

Robilliard, S. and McEwan, J., *Police Powers and the Individual*, Oxford, Blackwell, 1986.

Royal Commission on Criminal Procedure, *Investigation and Prosecution of Criminal Offences in England and Wales: Law and Procedure*, Cmnd. 8092–I, London, HMSO, 1981.

Royal Commission on Criminal Procedure, *Report*, Cmnd. 8092, London, HMSO, 1981.

Smith, J. C. and Hogan, B., *Criminal Law*, London, Butterworth, 1983.

Varwell, D. W. P., *Police and Public*, Plymouth, Macdonald and Evans, 1978.

Walker, N., *Crime and Punishment in Britain: An Analysis of the Penal System in Theory, Law and Practice*, Edinburgh, Edinburgh University Press, 1968.

Wegg-Prosser, C., *The Police and the Law*, London, Oyez Longman, 1979.

Whitaker, B., *The Police in Society*, London, Sinclair Browne, 1982.

Williams, G., *Textbook of Criminal Law*, London, Sweet and Maxwell, 1983.

Young, J. and Lee, J., *What is to Be Done about Law and Order?*, Harmondsworth, Penguin, 1984.

COMMERCIAL AND OTHER LAW

Abbott, K. R., *Company Law*, Winchester, D. P. Publications, 1983.

Affley, G., *Business Law*, Plymouth, Macdonald and Evans, 1982.

Anson, W. R. and Guest, A. G., *Principles of the English Law of*

Contract, London, Oxford University Press, 1984.

Arora, A., *Practical Business Law*, Plymouth, Macdonald and Evans, 1983.

Atiyah, P., *Introduction to the Law of Contract*, London, Oxford University Press, 1981.

Blake, A. and Bond, H. J., *Company Law*, London, Financial Training, 1985.

Borrie, G., *Commercial Law*, London, Butterworth, 1980.

Bradley, K. R. and Clark, R. A., *The Legal Environment: Business Law*, Eastbourne, Holt, Rinehart and Winston, 1981.

Bromley, P. M., *Family Law*, London, Butterworth, 1981.

Brown, W. J., *Practical Company Law*, London, Pan, 1984.

Butterworth (publisher), *Butterworth's Company Law Handbook*, London, 1982.

Charlesworth, I., *Mercantile Law*, London, Sweet and Maxwell, 1984.

Cheshire, G. C. and Fifoot, C. H. S., *Law of Contract*, London, Butterworth, 1981.

Cretney, S. M., *Principles of Family Law*, London, Sweet and Maxwell, 1984.

Cross, C. A., *Principles of Local Government Law*, London, Sweet and Maxwell, 1981.

Cross, R. and Wilkins, N., *Outline of the Law of Evidence*, London, Butterworth, 1980.

Curzon, L. B., *Land Law*, Plymouth, Macdonald and Evans, 1982.

Dalton, P. J., *Land Law*, London, Oyez, 1975.

Farrar, H., *Company Law*, London, Cassell, 1985.

Goode, R. M., *Commercial Law*, Harmondsworth, Penguin, 1982.

Guest, A. G. (ed.), *Anson's Law of Contract*, London, Oxford University Press, 1984.

Hampton, C., *Criminal Procedure*, London, Sweet and Maxwell, London, 1982.

Hanbury, H. B. and Maudsley, R. E.,

Modern Equity, London, Sweet and Maxwell, 1981.

Harwood, M., *Modern English Land Law*, London, Sweet and Maxwell, 1982.

Kadar, A. et al., *Business Law Made Simple*, London, Heinemann, 1985.

Lewis, R. (ed.), *Labour Law in Britain*, Oxford, Blackwell, 1985.

Lowe, R., *Commercial Law*, London, Sweet and Maxwell, 1983.

Major, W. R., *The Law of Contract*, Plymouth, 1983.

Marsh, S. B. and Soulsby, J., *Business Law*, Maidenhead, McGraw-Hill, 1985.

Meinhardt, P., *Company Law in Great Britain*, Aldershot, Gower, 1982.

Oliver, M. C., *Company Law*, Plymouth, Macdonald and Evans, 1983.

Palfreman, D., *Law of Banking*, Plymouth, Macdonald and Evans, 1982.

Pearl, D. and Gray, K., *Social Welfare Law*, London, Croom Helm, 1981.

Pennington, R., *Company Law*, London, Butterworth, 1985.

Pettit, P., *Equity and the Law of Trusts*, London, Butterworth, 1984.

Price, T. K., *Practical Business Law*, London, Pan, 1982.

Rawson, D. and Fisher, C. (eds), *Changing Industrial Law*, London, Croom Helm, 1986.

Redmond, P. W. D., *Mercantile Law*, revised by R. G. Lawson, Plymouth, Macdonald and Evans, 1982.

Rideout, R. W., *Principles of Labour Law*, London, Sweet and Maxwell, 1983.

Ruff, A., *Commercial and Industrial Law*, London, Macdonald and Evans, 1984.

Salmond, J. W. and Heuston, R. F. V., *The Law of Torts*, London, Sweet and Maxwell, 1981.

Schmitthoff, C. M., *Commercial Law in a Changing Economic Climate*, London, Sweet and Maxwell, 1981.

Shears, P., *Business Law*, Amersham, Hulton Educational, 1980.

Smith, I. and Ward, J., *Industrial Law*,

London, Butterworth, 1980.

Street, H., *Law of Torts*, London,
Butterworth, 1983.

Treitel, G. H., *Law of Contract*, London,
Stevens, 1979.

Tyas, J. G. M., *Law of Torts*, Plymouth,
Macdonald and Evans, 1982.

SEE ALSO:

12   Government and Administration
24   Parliament

16 LITERATURE

Comprehensive bibliographical coverage of general aspects of English literature can be found in the following: Altick, R. D. (ed.), *A Selective Bibliography for the Study of English and American Literature*, 1979; Bateson, F. W. and Meserole, H. T., *A Guide to English and American Literature*, 1976; Bond, D. F., *A Reference Guide to English Studies*, 1971; Ford, B. (ed.), *A Guide for Readers to the New Pelican Guide to English Literature*, 1984; Howard-Hill, T. H., *Bibliography of British Literary Bibliographies*, 1987; Patterson, M. C., *Literary Research Guide*, 1983; Temple, R. Z. (comp.), *Twentieth Century British Literature: A Reference Guide*, 1968; Watson, G. (ed.) *Concise Cambridge Bibliography of English Literature, 600–1950*, 1965; Watson, G. (ed.), *The New Cambridge Bibliography of English Literature*, 5 vols, 1969–77; Watson, G. (ed.), *The Shorter New Cambridge Bibliography of English Literature*, 1981.

References to current publications on English literature can be found in: English Association, *The Year's Work in English Studies*, annually; Modern Humanities Research Assocation, *Annual Bibliography of English Language and Literature*, annually; Modern Languages Association, *MLA International Bibliography of Books and Articles on the Modern Languages and Literature*, annually.

Readers can locate bibliographical references to the genres, drama, novel and poetry in the works mentioned above, but also in the following:

Drama   Carpenter, C. A. (ed.), *Modern British Drama, Goldentree Bibliographies*, 1979; Conolly, L. W. and Wearing, J. P. (eds), *English Drama and Theatre 1800–1900: A Guide to Information Sources*, 1978; King, K. (ed.), *Twenty Modern British Playwrights: A Bibliography, 1956–76*, 1977; Link, F. M. (ed.), *English Drama, 1660–1800: A Guide to Information Sources*, 1976; Mikhail, E. H. (ed.), *Contemporary British Drama, 1950–1976: An Annotated Critical Bibliography*, 1976; Penninger, F. E. (ed.), *English Drama to 1660 (excluding Shakespeare): A Guide to Information Sources*, 1976; Ribner, I. and Huffman, C. C., *Tudor and Stuart Drama, Goldentree Bibliographies*, 1978; Vinson, J. (ed.), *Contemporary Dramatists*, 1985; Wells, S. (ed.), *English Drama (excluding Shakespeare): Select Bibliographical Guides*, 1975; Weintraub, S. (ed.), *British Dramatists since World War II: A Guide to Information Sources*, 1982; Weintraub, S. (ed.), *Modern British Dramatists, 1900–1945: A Guide to Information Sources*, 2 vols, 1982.

Novel   Beasley, J. C. (ed.), *English Fiction, 1660–1800: A Guide to Information Sources*, 1978; Buckley, J. H., *Victorian Poets and Prose Writers, Goldentree Bibliographies*, 1978; Cassis, A. F. (ed.), *The Twentieth Century English Novel: An Annotated Bibliography of General Criticism*, 1978; Dyson, A. E. (ed.), *The English Novel: Select Bibliographical Guides*, 1974; Heninger, S. K. (ed.), *English Prose, Prose Fiction and Criticism to 1660: A Guide to Information Sources*, 1975; Palmer, H. H. and Dyson, A. E. (comps.), *English Novel Explication: Criticism to 1972*, 1973; Rice, T. J. (ed.), *English Fiction, 1900–1950: A Guide to Information Sources*, 1979; Rosa, A. F. and Escholz,

P. A. (eds), *Contemporary Fiction in America and England, 1950–1970: A Guide to Information Sources,* 1976; Schlueter, P. and Schlueter, J., *English Novel: Twentieth Century Criticism,* 1982; Stanton, R. J., *Bibliography of Modern British Novelists,* 1978; Vinson, J. (ed.), *Contemporary Novelists,* 1982; Watt, I. (comp.), *The British Novel: Scott through Hardy,* 1973; Wiley, P. L. (comp.), *The British Novel: Conrad to the Present,* 1973; Wilson, H. W. and Hoeveler, D. L. (eds), *English Prose and Criticism in the Nineteenth Century: A Guide to Information Sources,* 1979.

Poetry Altieri, C. F. (ed.), *Modern Poetry, Goldentree Bibliographies,* 1979; Anderson, E. A. (ed.), *English Poetry, 1900–1950: A Guide to Information Sources,* 1981; Buckley, J. H., *Victorian Poets and Prose Writers, Goldentree Bibliographies,* 1978; Clines, G. S. and Baker, J. A., *An Index to Criticism of British and American Poetry,* 1973; Dyson, A. E. (ed.), *English Poetry: Select Bibliographical Guides,* 1971; Kuntz, J. M. and Martinez, N. C. (eds), *Poetry Explication: A Checklist of Interpretations since 1925 of British and American Poems Past and Present,* 1980; Regency Press (publisher), *The Bibliography of Contemporary Poets,* 1970; Reiman, D. H. (ed.), *English Romantic Poetry, 1800–1835: A Guide to Information Sources,* 1979; Vinson, J. (ed.), *Contemporary Poets,* 1985.

The following are recommended as standard literary reference manuals: Daiches, D. (ed.), *The Penguin Companion to Literature, vol. I, British and Commonwealth Literature,* 1971; Drabble, M. (ed.), *The Oxford Companion to English Literature,* 1985; Eagles, D., *The Concise Oxford Dictionary of English Literature,* 1970; Gillie, C., *Longman Companion to English Literature,* 1978; Preminger, A. et al. (eds), *Princeton Encyclopedia of Poetry and Poetics,* 1974; Stapleton, M. (ed.), *The Cambridge Guide to English Literature,* 1983.

For general historical surveys of English literature the following can be consulted: Baugh, A. C. et al., *A Literary History of England,* 4 vols, 1968; Blamires, H., *A Short History of English Literature,* 1984; Daiches, D., *A Critical History of English Literature,* 4 vols, 1968; Ford, B. (ed.), *The Pelican Guide to English Literature,* 8 vols, 1969–83; Sampson, G. (ed.), *Concise History of English Literature,* 1970; Ward, A. W. and Waller, A. R. (eds), *The Cambridge History of English Literature,* 15 vols, 1932; Wilson, F. P. and Dobrée, B. (eds), *The Oxford History of English Literature,* 1945–.

REFERENCE

Altick, R. D. (ed.), *A Selective Bibliography for the Study of English and American Literature,* London, Collier-Macmillan, 1979.

Altieri, C. F. (ed.), *Modern Poetry, Goldentree Bibliographies,* Arlington Heights, Ill., AHM, 1979.

Anderson, E. A. (ed.), *English Poetry, 1900–1950: A Guide to Information Sources,* Detroit, Gale, 1981.

Barker, A. E., *Seventeenth Century: Bacon through Marvell, Goldentree Bibliographies,* Arlington Heights, Ill., AHM, 1979.

Bateson, F. W. and Meserole, H. T., *A Guide to English and American Literature,* London, Longman, 1976.

Beale, W. H. (ed.), *Old and Middle English Poetry to 1500: A Guide to Information Sources,* Detroit, Gale, 1976.

Beasley, J. C. (ed.), *English Fiction, 1660–1800: A Guide to Information Sources,* Detroit, Gale, 1978.

Bond, D. F., *The Age of Dryden, Goldentree Bibliographies,* New York, Appleton, 1970.

Bond, D. F., *A Reference Guide to English Studies,* Chicago and London, University of Chicago Press, 1971.

Bond, D. F. (ed.), *Eighteenth Century: Johnson through Burns, Goldentree Bibliographies*, Northbrook, Ill., AHM, 1975.

Browning, D. C., *Everyman's Dictionary of Literary Biography: English and American*, London, Dent, 1969.

Buckley, J. H., *Victorian Poets and Prose Writers, Goldentree Bibliographies*, Arlington Heights, Ill., AHM, 1978.

Carpenter, C. A. (ed.), *Modern British Drama, Goldentree Bibliographies*, Arlington Heights, Ill., AHM, 1979.

Cassis, A. F. (ed.), *The Twentieth Century English Novel: An Annotated Bibliography of General Criticism*, New York, Garland, 1978.

Chandler, G., *How to Find out about Literature*, Oxford, Pergamon, 1968.

Clines, G. S. and Baker, J. A., *An Index to Criticism of British and American Poetry*, Metuchen, N. J., Scarecrow Press, 1973.

Conolly, L. W. and Wearing, J. P. (eds), *English Drama and Theatre, 1800–1900: A Guide to Information Sources*, Detroit, Gale, 1978.

Daiches, D. (ed.), *The Penguin Companion to Literature, I, British and Commonwealth Literature*, Harmondsworth, Penguin, 1971.

Drabble, M. (ed.), *The Oxford Companion to English Literature*, London, Oxford University Press, 1985.

Dyson, A. E. (ed.), *English Poetry: Select Bibliographical Guides*, London, Oxford University Press, 1971.

Dyson, A. E. (ed.), *The English Novel: Select Bibliographical Guides*, London, Oxford University Press, 1974.

Eagle, D., *Concise Oxford Dictionary of English Literature*, London, Oxford University Press, 1970.

English Association, *The Year's Work in English Studies*, London, Oxford University Press, annually.

Ford, B. (ed.), *A Guide for Readers to the New Pelican Guide to English Literature*, Harmondsworth, Penguin, 1984.

Gillie, C., *Longman Companion to English Literature*, London, Longman, 1978.

Heninger, S. K. (ed.), *English Prose, Prose Fiction and Criticism to 1660: A Guide to Information Sources*, Detroit, Gale, 1975.

Howard-Hill, T. H., *British Bibliography and Textual Criticism, 2 vols, A Bibliography*, London, Oxford University Press, 1979.

Howard-Hill, T. H., *British Literary Bibliography and Textual Criticism 1890–1969, An Index*, London, Oxford University Press, 1980.

Howard-Hill, T. H., *Bibliography of British Literary Bibliographies*, Oxford, Clarendon Press, 1987.

King, K. (ed.), *Twenty Modern British Playwrights: A Bibliography, 1956–1976*, New York, Garland, 1977.

Kuntz, J. M. and Martinez, N. C. (eds), *Poetry Explication: A Checklist of Interpretation since 1925 of British and American Poems Past and Present*, Boston, Hall, 1980.

Lievsay, J. L., *The Sixteenth Century: Skelton through Hooker, Goldentree Bibliographies*, New York, Appleton, 1968.

Link, F. M. (ed.), *English Drama, 1660–1800: A Guide to Information Sources*, Detroit, Gale, 1976.

Mikhail, E. H. (ed.), *Contemporary British Drama, 1950–1976: An Annotated Critical Bibliography*, London, Macmillan, 1976.

Mikhail, E. H. (ed.), *English Drama, 1900 1950: A Guide to Information Sources*, Detroit, Gale, 1977.

Modern Humanities Research Association, *Annual Bibliography of English Language and Literature*, Cambridge, Cambridge University Press, annually.

Modern Language Association of America, *MLA Abstracts of Articles in Scholarly Journals*, New York, annually.

Modern Languages Association, *MLA International Bibliography of Books and Articles on the Modern Languages and Literatures*, New York, annually.

Murphy, R. (ed.), *Contemporary Poets of the English Language*, Chicago, London, St James Press, 1970.

Palmer, H. H. and Dyson, A. E. (comps.), *English Novel Explication: Criticism to 1972*, Hamden, Conn., Shoe String, 1973.

Partridge, A. C. A., *A Companion to Old and Middle English Studies*, London, Deutsch, 1982.

Patterson, M. C., *Literary Research Guide*, New York, Modern Language Association of America, 1983.

Penninger, F. E. (ed.), *English Drama to 1660 (excluding Shakespeare): A Guide to Information Sources*, Detroit, Gale, 1976.

Preminger, A. et al. (eds), *Princeton Encyclopedia of Poetry and Poetics*, Princeton, Princeton University Press, 1974.

Regency Press (publisher), *The Bibliography of Contemporary Poets*, London, 1970.

Reiman, D. H. (ed.), *English Romantic Poetry, 1800–1835: A Guide to Information Sources*, Detroit, Gale, 1979.

Ribner, I. and Huffman, C. C., *Tudor and Stuart Drama, Goldentree Bibliographies*, Arlington Heights, Ill, AHM, 1978.

Rice, T. J. (ed.), *English Fiction, 1900–1950: A Guide to Information Sources*, Detroit, Gale, 1979.

Rosa, A. F. and Escholz, P. A. (eds), *Contemporary Fiction in America and England, 1950–1970: A Guide to Information Sources*, Detroit, Gale, 1976.

Schlueter, P. and Schlueter, J., *English Novel: Twentieth Century Criticism*, Vol. 2, Athens, Ohio University Press, 1982.

Spender, S. and Hall, D. (eds), *The Concise Encyclopaedia of English and American Poets and Poetry*, London, Hutchinson, 1970.

Stanton, R. J., *Bibliography of Modern British Novelists*, 2 vols, Troy, New York, Whiston, 1978.

Stapleton, M. (ed.), *The Cambridge Guide to English Literature*, Cambridge, Cambridge University Press, 1983.

Swatridge, C., *British Fiction: A Student's A-Z*, London, Macmillan, 1985.

Temple, R. Z. (comp.), *Twentieth Century British Literature: A Reference Guide*, New York, Ungar, 1968.

Vinson, J. (ed.), *Contemporary Novelists*, London, St James Press, 1982.

Vinson, J. (ed.), *Contemporary Dramatists*, London, St James Press, 1985.

Vinson, J. (ed.), *Contemporary Poets*, London, St James Press, 1985.

Walker, W. S. (comp.), *Twentieth-Century Short Story Explications: Interpretations, 1900–1975, of short fiction since 1800*, London, Bingley, 1977.

Ward, A. C., *Longman Companion to Twentieth Century Literature*, London, Longman, 1981.

Watson, G. (ed.), *The Concise Cambridge Bibliography of English Literature 600–1950*, Cambridge, Cambridge University Press, 1965.

Watson, G. (ed.), *The New Cambridge Bibliography of English Literature*, 5 vols, Cambridge, Cambridge University Press, 1969–77.

Watson, G. (ed.), *The Shorter New Cambridge Bibliography of English Literature*, Cambridge, Cambridge University Press, 1981.

Watt, I. (comp.), *The British Novel: Scott through Hardy*, Northbrook, Ill., AHM, 1973.

Weintraub, S. (ed.), *British Dramatists since World War II: A Guide to Information Sources*, Detroit, Gale, 1982.

Weintraub, S. (ed.), *Modern British Dramatists, 1900–1945: A Guide to Information Sources*, 2 vols, Detroit, Gale, 1982.

Wells, S. (ed.), *English Drama (excluding Shakespeare): Select Bibliographical Guides*, London, Oxford University Press, 1975.

Wiley, P. L., *British Novel: Conrad to*

the Present, Goldentree Bibliographies, Northbrook, Ill., AHM, 1973.
Wilson, H. W. and Hoeveler, D. L. (eds), *English Prose and Criticism in the Nineteenth Century: A Guide to Information Sources*, Detroit, Gale, 1979.

LITERARY HISTORY

GENERAL

Barnard, R., *Short History of English Literature*, Oxford, Blackwell, 1984.
Baugh, A. C. et al., *A Literary History of England*, 4 vols, London, Routledge & Kegan Paul, 1968.
Blamires, H., *A Short History of English Literature*, London, Methuen, 1984.
Bolton, W. F., *A Short History of Literary English*, London, Arnold, 1972.
Chadwick, H. M. and Chadwick, N. K., *The Growth of Literature*, 3 vols, Cambridge, Cambridge University Press, 1968.
Conrad, P., *The Everyman History of English Literature*, London, Dent, 1985.
Daiches, D., *A Critical History of English Literature*, 4 vols, London, Secker and Warburg, 1968.
Ford, B. (ed.), *The Pelican Guide to English Literature*, 8 vols, Harmondsworth, Penguin, 1969–83.
Legouis, E. and Cazamian, L., *A History of English Literature*, London, Dent, 1972.
Mair, G. H., *English Literature, 1450–1900*, London, Oxford University Press, 1969.
Sampson, G. (ed.), *Concise History of English Literature*, Cambridge, Cambridge University Press, 1970.
Scott-Kilvert, I. (ed.), *British Writers*, 6 vols, New York, Scribner's, 1970–84.
Stephen, M., *An Introductory Guide to English Literature*, London, Longman, 1984.
Ward, A. W. and Waller, A. R. (eds), *The Cambridge History of English Literature*, 15 vols, Cambridge, Cambridge University Press, 1932.
Wilson, F. P. and Dobrée, B. (eds), *The Oxford History of English Literature*, Oxford, Clarendon Press, 1945–.
Wimsatt, W. K. and Brooks, C., *Literary Criticism: A Short History*, 4 vols, London, Routledge & Kegan Paul, 1970.

MEDIEVAL PERIOD

Ackerman, R. W., *Backgrounds to Medieval English Literature*, New York, Random House, 1966.
Alexander, M., *Old English Literature*, London, Macmillan, 1983, Macmillan History of Literature.
Bennett, H. S., *Chaucer and the Fifteenth Century*, Oxford, Clarendon Press, 1947, Oxford History of English Literature.
Blake, N., *The English Language in Medieval Literature*, London, Methuen, 1979.
Brewer, D., *English Gothic Literature*, London, Macmillan, 1983, Macmillan History of Literature.
Chambers, E. K., *English Literature at the Close of the Middle Ages*, Oxford, Clarendon Press, 1945, Oxford History of English Literature.
Dunn, C. W. (comp.) and Byrnes, E. T. (ed.), *Middle English Literature*, New York, Harcourt Brace Jovanovich, 1973.
Ford, B. (ed.), *The New Pelican Guide to English Literature 1, Part One, Medieval Literature, Chaucer and the Alliterative Tradition*, Harmondsworth, Penguin, 1982.
Ford, B. (ed.), *The New Pelican Guide to English Literature 1, Part Two, Medieval Literature, The European Inheritance*, Harmondsworth, Penguin, 1983.

Gradon, P., *Form and Style in Early English Literature*, London, Methuen, 1971.

Greenfield, S. B., *A Critical History of Old English Literature*, New York, New York University Press, 1965.

Kane, G., *Middle English Literature*, London, Methuen, 1971.

Legge, M. D., *Anglo-Norman Literature and its Background*, London, Greenwood Press, 1979.

Maclaine, A. H. (ed.), *The Beginnings to 1558*, London, Macmillan, 1980, Great Writers Library.

Medcalfe, S. (ed.), *The Context of English Literature: The Later Middle Ages*, London, Methuen, 1981.

Pope, J. C., *English Literature before the Norman Conquest*, Oxford, Oxford University Press, 1980.

Raw, B. C., *The Art and Background of Old English Poetry*, London, Arnold, 1978.

Wilson, R. M., *Early Middle English Literature*, London, Methuen, 1968.

SIXTEENTH CENTURY

Donno, E. S. (ed.), *The Renaissance (Excluding Drama)*, London, Macmillan, 1983.

Ford, B. (ed.), *The New Pelican Guide to English Literature 2, The Age of Shakespeare*, Harmondsworth, Penguin, 1983.

Kermode, F., *English Renaissance Literature*, Oxford, Blackwell, 1976.

Lewis, C. S., *English Literature in the Sixteenth Century (Excluding Drama)*, Oxford, Clarendon Press, 1973, Oxford History of English Literature.

Pinto, V. De S., *The English Renaissance, 1510–1688*, London, Barrie and Jenkins, 1938.

Roston, M., *Sixteenth Century Literature*, London, Macmillan. 1982, Macmillan History of Literature.

Tillyard, E. M. W., *The Elizabethan World Picture*, Harmondsworth, Penguin, 1972.

SEVENTEENTH CENTURY

Burton, K. M. P., *Restoration Literature*, London, Hutchinson, 1958.

Bush, D., *English Literature in the Earlier Seventeenth Century, 1600–1660*, Oxford, Clarendon Press, 1973, Oxford History of English Literature.

Ford, B. (ed.), *The New Pelican Guide to English Literature, 2, The Age of Shakespeare*, Harmondsworth, Penguin, 1983.

Ford, B. (ed.), *The New Pelican Guide to English Literature, 3, From Donne to Marvell*, Harmondsworth, Penguin, 1983.

Grierson, H. J. C., *Cross Currents in English Literature of the Seventeenth Century*, London, Chatto and Windus, 1969.

King, B., *Seventeenth Century English Literature*, London, Macmillan, 1982, Macmillan History of Literature.

Sutherland, J. R., *English Literature in the Late Seventeenth Century*, Oxford, Clarendon Press, 1969, Oxford History of English Literature.

Wedgwood, C. V., *Seventeenth-Century English Literature*, London, Oxford University Press, 1970.

Willey, B., *The Seventeenth Century Background: Studies in the Thought of the Age in Relation to Poetry and Religion*, London, Routledge & Kegan Paul, 1979.

EIGHTEENTH CENTURY

Dickinson, H. T. (ed.), *Politics and Literature in the Eighteenth Century*, London, Dent, 1974.

Dobrée, B., *English Literature in the Early Eighteenth Century, 1700–1740*, Oxford, Clarendon Press, 1959, Oxford History of English Literature.

Ford, B. (ed.), *The New Pelican Guide to English Literature, 4, From Dryden to Johnson*, Harmondsworth, Penguin, 1982.

Novak, M., *Eighteenth Century English Literature*, London, Macmillan, 1982, Macmillan History of Literature.

Rogers, P. (ed.), *The Context of English Literature, the Eighteenth Century*, London, Methuen, 1978.

Rogers, P. (ed.), *Restoration and 18th Century Prose and Poetry*, London, Macmillan, 1983.

Stephen, L., *English Literature and Society in the Eighteenth Century*, London, Duckworth, 1965.

Tillotson, G. et al., *Eighteenth Century English Literature*, New York, Harcourt Brace Jovanovich, 1969.

Willey, B., *The Eighteenth Century Background: Studies in the Idea of Nature in the Thought of the Period*, London, Chatto and Windus, 1980.

NINETEENTH CENTURY

Bowra, C. M., *The Romantic Imagination*, London, Oxford University Press, 1961.

Buckley, J. H., *The Victorian Temper: A Study in Literary Culture*, Cambridge, Cambridge University Press, 1981.

Chapman, R., *The Victorian Debate: English Literature and Society 1832–1901*, London, Weidenfeld and Nicolson, 1968.

Chesterton, G. K., *The Victorian Age in Literature*, London, Oxford University Press, 1966 (reprint).

Ford, B. (ed.), *The New Pelican Guide to English Literature, 5, From Blake to Byron*, Harmondsworth, Penguin, 1982.

Ford, B. (ed.), *The New Pelican Guide to English Literature, 6, From Dickens to Hardy*, Harmondsworth, Penguin, 1982.

Grierson, H. J. C., *The Background of English Literature: Classical and Romantic*, London, Chatto and Windus, 1970.

Jack, I., *English Literature, 1815–1832*, Oxford, Clarendon Press, 1963, Oxford History of English Literature.

Lerner, L. (ed.), *The Context of English Literature: The Victorians*, London, Methuen, 1981.

Lucas, J. (ed.), *Literature and Politics in the Nineteenth Century*, London, Methuen, 1975.

Muir, K. (ed.), *The Romantic Period excluding the Novel*, London, Macmillan, 1980.

Pollard, A. (ed.), *The Victorian Period excluding the Novel*, London, Macmillan, 1983.

Praz, M., *The Romantic Agony*, London, Oxford University Press, 1970.

Prickett, S. (ed.), *The Context of English Literature: The Romantics*, London, Methuen, 1978.

Renwick, W. L., *English Literature, 1789–1815*, Oxford, Clarendon Press, 1963, Oxford History of English Literature.

Stonyk, M., *Nineteenth Century English Literature*, London, Macmillan, 1983, Macmillan History of Literature.

Sutherland, D., *On Romanticism*, New York, New York University Press, 1971.

Tillotson, G., *A View of Victorian Literature*, Oxford, Clarendon Press, 1978.

Tillotson, G. and Tillotson, K., *Mid-Victorian Studies*, London, Athlone, 1965.

Willey, B., *Nineteenth Century Studies: Coleridge to Matthew Arnold*, Cambridge, Cambridge University Press, 1980.

Willey, B., *More Nineteenth Century Studies: A Group of Honest Doubters*, Cambridge, Cambridge University Press, 1980.

Williams, R., *Culture and Society, 1780–1950*, Harmondsworth, Penguin, 1971.

Wright, A. (ed.), *Victorian Literature*, London, Oxford University Press, 1961.

TWENTIETH CENTURY

Bell, M. (ed.), *The Context of English Literature, 1900–1930*, London,

Methuen, 1980.

Blamires, H., *Twentieth Century English Literature*, London, Macmillan, 1982, Macmillan History of Literature.

Bradbury, M., *The Social Context of Modern English Literature*, Oxford, Blackwell, 1971.

Cox, C. B. and Dyson, A. E. (eds), *The Twentieth Century Mind: History, Ideas and Literature in Britain*, 3 vols, London, Oxford University Press, 1972.

Ford, B. (ed.), *The New Pelican Guide to English Literature, 7, From James to Eliot*, Harmondsworth, Penguin, 1983.

Ford, B. (ed.), *The New Pelican Guide to English Literature, 8, The Present*, Harmondsworth, Penguin, 1983.

Gillie, G., *Movements in English Literature, 1900–1940*, Cambridge, Cambridge University Press, 1975.

Robson, W. W., *Modern English Literature*, London, Oxford University Press, 1970.

Sinfield, A. et al., *The Context of English Literature, Society and Literature 1945–1970*, London, Methuen, 1983.

Stewart, J. I. M., *Eight Modern Writers*, Oxford, Clarendon Press, 1973, Oxford History of English Literature.

GENRES

DRAMA

Barroll, J. L. et al. (eds), *The Revels History of Drama in English, Vol. 3, 1576–1613*, London, Methuen, 1975.

Bentley, G. E., *The Jacobean and Caroline Stage*, 7 vols, Oxford, Oxford University Press, 1941–68.

Bentley, G. E. (ed.), *The Seventeenth Century Stage*, Chicago, University of Chicago Press, 1969.

Bigsby, C. W. E. (ed.), *Contemporary English Drama, Stratford-on-Avon Studies*, London, Arnold, 1981.

Boas, F. S., *An Introduction to Stuart Drama*, London, Oxford University Press, 1946.

Boas, F. S., *Introduction to Tudor Drama*, London, Greenwood Press, 1977.

Boas, F. S., *Introduction to Eighteenth Century Drama, 1700–80*, London, Greenwood Press, 1978.

Booth, M. R. et al. (eds), *The Revels History of Drama in English, Vol. 6, 1750–1880*, London, Methuen, 1975.

Bradbrook, M. C., *English Dramatic Form: A History of its Development*, London, Chatto and Windus, 1970.

Bradbrook, M. C., *The Growth and Structure of Elizabethan Comedy*, Cambridge, Cambridge University Press, 1979.

Bradbrook, M. C., *Themes and Conventions of Elizabethan Tragedy*, Cambridge, Cambridge University Press, 1980.

Brown, J. R., *Modern British Dramatists: A Collection of Critical Essays*, Englewood Cliffs, N. J., Prentice-Hall, 1968.

Brown, J. R., *A Short Guide to Modern British Drama*, London, Heinemann, 1982.

Brown, J. R. and Harris, B. (eds), *Restoration Theatre*, London, Arnold, 1965.

Brown, J. R. and Harris, B. (eds), *Elizabethan Theatre*, London, Arnold, 1966.

Brown, J. R. and Harris, B. (eds), *Jacobean Theatre*, London, Arnold, 1966.

Bull, J., *New British Political Dramtists*, London, Macmillan, 1984.

Cawley, A. C. et al. (eds), *The Revels History of Drama in English, Vol. 1, Medieval Drama*, London, Methuen, 1983.

Chambers, E. K., *The Medieval Stage*, 2 vols, Oxford, Oxford University Press, 1903.

117

Chambers, E. K., *The Elizabethan Stage*, 4 vols, Oxford, Oxford University Press, 1923–51.

Clemen, W. H., *English Tragedy Before Shakespeare: The Development of Dramatic Speech*, London, Methuen, 1961.

Craig, H., *English Religious Drama of the Middle Ages*, London, Greenwood Press, 1978.

Davison, P., *Contemporary Drama and the Popular Dramatic Tradition in England*, London, Macmillan, 1982.

Davison, P., *Popular Appeal in English Drama to 1850*, London, Macmillan, 1982.

Dobrée, B., *Restoration Tragedy, 1660–1720*, Oxford, Clarendon Press, 1929.

Dobrée, B., *Restoration Comedy, 1660–1720*, London, Greenwood Press, 1981 (reprint).

Edwards, P. et al. (eds), *The Revels History of Drama in English, Vol. 4, 1613–1660*, London, Methuen, 1981.

Ellis-Fermor, U. N., *Jacobean Drama*, London, Methuen, 1965.

Esslin, M., *The Theatre of the Absurd*, Harmondsworth, Penguin, 1970.

Goodlad, J. S. R., *A Sociology of Popular Drama*, London, Heinemann, 1971.

Harbage, A., *Annals of English Drama, 975–1700*, London, Methuen, 1964.

Hartnoll, P. (ed.), *The Oxford Companion to the Theatre*, Oxford, Oxford University Press, 1982.

Hayman, R., *British Theatre since 1955: A Reassessment*, London, Oxford University Press, 1979.

Hinchcliffe, A. P., *British Theatre, 1950–70*, Oxford, Blackwell, 1974.

Hudson, L., *The English Stage, 1850–1950*, London, Greenwood Press, 1973.

Hunt, H. et al. (eds), *The Revels History of Drama in English, Vol. 7, 1880 to the Present Day*, London, Methuen, 1978.

Kahrl, S. J., *Traditions of Medieval English Drama*, London, Hutchinson, 1974.

Kerensky, O., *The New British Drama*, London, Hamish Hamilton, 1977.

Kitchen, L., *Drama in the Sixties: Form and Interpretation*, London, Faber, 1966.

Kitchen, L., *Mid-Century Drama*, London, Faber, 1969.

Knights, L. C., *Drama and Society in the Age of Jonson*, Harmondsworth, Penguin, 1962.

Loftis, J., *The Politics of Drama in Augustan England*, Oxford, Clarendon Press, 1963.

Loftis, J. (ed.), *Restoration Drama: Modern Essays in Criticism*, New York, Oxford University Press, 1966.

Loftis, J. et al. (eds), *The Revels History of Drama in English, Vol. 5, 1660–1750*, London, Methuen, 1976.

McAlindon, T., *English Renaissance Tragedy*, London, Macmillan, 1985.

Nicoll, A., *A History of English Drama 1660–1900*, 6 vols, Cambridge, Cambridge University Press, 1952–9.

Nicoll, A., *British Drama*, London, Harrap, 1964.

Nightingale, B., *An Introduction to Fifty Modern British Plays*, London, Heinemann, 1982.

Potter, R., *The English Morality Play: Origins, History and Influence of a Dramatic Tradition*, London, Routledge & Kegan Paul, 1975.

Prosser, E., *Drama and Religion in the English Mystery Plays*, Stanford, Stanford University Press, 1966.

Reynolds, E., *Modern English Drama: A Survey of the Theatre from 1900*, London, Greenwood Press, 1950.

Ribner, I. and Huffman, C. C., *Tudor and Stuart Drama*, New York, AHM, 1979.

Richards, K. and Thomson, P. (eds), *Nineteenth Century Theatre*, London, Methuen, 1971.

Richards, K. and Thomson, P. (eds), *The Eighteenth Century English Stage*, London, Methuen, 1972.

Roger, I., *Radio Drama*, London, Macmillan, 1981.

Rossiter, A. P., *English Drama from Early Times to the Elizabethans*, London, Hutchinson, 1950.

Salgado, G., *English Drama: A Critical Introduction*, London, Arnold, 1980.

Sanders, N. et al. (eds), *The Revels History of Drama in English, Vol. 2, 1500–1576*, London, Methuen, 1980.

Scouten, A. H. (ed.), *The Restoration and Eighteenth Century Drama*, London, Macmillan, 1980.

Self, D., *Television Drama: An Introduction*, London, Macmillan, 1984.

Taylor, J. R., *The Rise and Fall of the Well-Made Play*, London, Methuen, 1967.

Taylor, J. R., *Penguin Dictionary of the Theatre*, Harmondsworth, Penguin, 1970.

Taylor, J. R., *Anger and After: A Guide to the New British Drama*, London, Methuen, 1977.

Taylor, J. R., *The Second Wave: British Drama for the Seventies*, London, Methuen, 1978.

Thompson, J. C., *An Introduction to Fifty British Plays, 1660–1900*, London, Heinemann, 1980.

Traversi, D. (ed.), *Renaissance Drama*, London, Macmillan, 1980.

Trussler, S. (ed.), *Twentieth Century Drama*, London, Macmillan, 1983.

Ure, P., *Elizabethan and Jacobean Drama: Critical Essays*, Liverpool, Liverpool University Press, 1974.

Wells, H. W., *Elizabethan and Jacobean Playwrights*, London, Greenwood Press, 1939.

Wickham, G., *Early English Stages, 1300–1600*, 3 vols, London, Routledge & Kegan Paul, 1963–81.

Wilson, F. P., *English Drama, 1485–1585*, Oxford, Clarendon Press, 1969, Oxford History of English Literature.

Worth, K. J., *Revolutions in Modern English Drama*, London, Bell, 1973.

Young, K., *The Drama of the Medieval Church*, Oxford, Clarendon Press, 1933.

NOVEL

Allen, W., *Tradition and Dream*, Harmondsworth, Penguin, 1965.

Allen, W., *The English Novel*, Harmondsworth, Penguin, 1970.

Allen, W., *The Short Story in English*, London, Oxford University Press, 1982.

Baker, E. A. and Stevenson, L., *The History of the English Novel*, 10 vols, London, Witherby, 1924–39.

Bergonzi, B., *The Situation of the Novel*, London, Routledge & Kegan Paul, 1970.

Boulton, M., *The Anatomy of the Novel*, London, Routledge & Kegan Paul, 1975.

Bradbury, M., *Possibilities: Essays on the State of the Novel*, London, Oxford University Press, 1973.

Bradbury, M. (ed.), *The Novel Today: Contemporary Writers on Modern Fiction*, London, Fontana, 1977.

Bradbury, M. and Palmer, D. (eds), *The Contemporary English Novel*, London, Arnold, 1979.

Burgess, A., *The Novel Now*, London, Faber, 1972.

Cecil, D., *Early Victorian Novelists*, London, Constable, 1964.

Church, R., *The Growth of the English Novel*, London, Methuen, 1961.

Cockshut, A. O. J. (ed.), *The Novel to 1900*, London, Macmillan, 1980.

Crosland, M., *Beyond the Lighthouse: English Women Novelists of the Twentieth Century*, London, Constable, 1981.

Forster, E. M., *Aspects of the Novel*, Harmondsworth, Penguin, 1970.

Friedman, A., *The Turn of the Novel*, New York, Oxford University Press, 1966.

Friedman, A. (ed.), *Forms of Modern British Fiction*, Austin, University of Texas Press, 1975.

Ghent, D. Van, *The English Novel: Form and Function*, New York, Harper and Row, 1968.

Gindin, J., *Post-War British Fiction*, London, Cambridge University Press, 1962.

Green, M., *The English Novel in the Twentieth Century: The Doom of Empire*, London, Routledge & Kegan Paul, 1984.

Haffenden, J., *Novelists in Interview*, London, Methuen, 1985.

Halio, J. L. (ed.), *British Novelists since 1960, Dictionary of Literary Biography*, vol. 14, Detroit, Gale Research, 1983.

Hayman, R., *The Novel Today, 1967–1975*, London, Longman, 1976.

Hazell, S., *The English Novel: Developments in Criticism since Henry James*, London, Macmillan, 1978.

Higdon, D. L., *Shadows of the Past in Contemporary British Fiction*, London, Macmillan, 1984.

Jusserand, J. J., *The English Novel in the Time of Shakespeare*, London, Benn, 1966.

Karl, F. R., *A Reader's Guide to the Contemporary English Novel*, London, Thames and Hudson, 1963.

Karl, F. R., *A Reader's Guide to the Development of the English Novel*, London, Thames and Hudson, 1975.

Karl, F. R. and Magdalaner, M., *A Reader's Guide to Great Twentieth Century Novels*, London, Thames and Hudson, 1960.

Keating, P. J., *The Working Classes in Victorian Fiction*, London, Routledge & Kegan Paul, 1979.

Kettle, A., *An Introduction to the English Novel*, 2 vols, London, Hutchinson, 1967.

Kettle, A. (ed.), *The Nineteenth Century Novel: Critical Essays and Documents*, London, Heinemann, 1981.

Kiely, R., *The Romantic Novel in England*, Cambridge, Mass., Harvard University Press, 1973.

Leech, G. N. and Short, M. H., *Style in Fiction: A Linguistic Introduction to English Fictional Prose*, London, Longman, 1981.

Leavis, F. R., *The Great Tradition*, Harmondsworth, Penguin, 1983.

Leavis, Q. D., *Fiction and the Reading Public*, Harmondsworth, Penguin, 1979.

Lodge, D., *The Language of Fiction*, London, Routledge & Kegan Paul, 1966.

Lodge, D., *The Novel at the Crossroads*, London, Routledge & Kegan Paul, 1971.

Lubbock, P., *The Craft of Fiction*, London, Cape, 1921.

McCullough, B., *Representative English Novelists: Defoe to Conrad*, New York, Books for Libraries Press, 1972.

McEwan, N., *The Survival of the Novel: British Fiction in the Later Twentieth Century*, London, Macmillan, 1981.

McSweeney, K., *Four Contemporary Novelists*, London, Scolar Press, 1983.

Margolies, D., *Novel and Society in Elizabethan England*, London, Croom Helm, 1985.

Marriott, J., *English History in English Fiction*, London, Blackie, 1940.

Milligan, I., *The Novel in English*, London, Macmillan, 1983.

Muir, E., *The Structure of the Novel*, London, Chatto and Windus, 1979.

National Book League, *British and Commonwealth Novels of the Sixties: A Booklist*, London, 1970.

Paulson, N., *Satire and the Novel in Eighteenth Century England*, New Haven, Yale University Press, 1967.

Priestley, J. B., *The English Novel*, London, Nelson, 1935.

Pritchett, V. S., *The Living Novel*, London, Chatto and Windus, 1966.

Sage, L., *Contemporary Women Novelists*, London, Macmillan, 1984.

Salzman, P., *English Prose Fiction, 1558–1700*, Oxford, Clarendon Press, 1984.

Scholes, R., *The Fabulators*, London, Oxford University Press, 1967.

Schorer, M. (ed.), *Modern British Fiction: Essays in Criticism*, New York, Oxford University Press, 1961.

Skilton, D., *Defoe to the Victorians: Two Centuries of the English Novel*, Harmondsworth, Penguin, 1977.

Smith, G., *The Novel and Society: Defoe to George Eliot*, London, Batsford, 1984.

Spearman, D., *The Novel and Society*, London, Routledge & Kegan Paul, 1966.

Spector, R. D. (ed.), *Essays on the*

Eighteenth-Century Novel, Bloomington and London, Indiana University Press, 1965.

Staley, T. F. (ed.), *Twentieth-Century Women Novelists*, London, Macmillan, 1982.

Stevenson, L., *The English Novel: A Panorama*, London, Greenwood Press, 1978.

Stevenson, R., *The British Novel Since the Thirties: An Introduction*, London, Batsford, 1986.

Tillotson, K., *Novels of the 1840's*, London, Oxford University Press, 1954.

Tillyard, E. M. W., *The Epic Strain in the English Novel*, London, Chatto and Windus, 1968.

Tomlinson, T. B., *The English Middle Class Novel*, London, Macmillan, 1976.

Watson, G., *The Story of the Novel*, London, Macmillan, 1979.

Watt, I., *The Rise of the Novel: Studies in Defoe, Richardson and Fielding*, Harmondsworth, Penguin, 1963.

Wheeler, M., *English Fiction and the Victorian Period, 1830–1890*, London, Longman, 1985.

Williams, I., *The Realist Novel in England: A Study in Development*, London, Macmillan, 1974.

Williams, R., *The English Novel from Dickens to Lawrence*, London, Chatto and Windus, 1970.

Woodcock, G. (ed.), *Twentieth Century Fiction*, London, Macmillan, 1983.

Ziegler, H. and Bigsby, C. (eds), *The Radical Imagination and the Liberal Tradition: Interviews with English and American Novelists*, London, Fourth Estate, 1985.

POETRY

Abrams, M. H. (ed.), *English Romantic Poets*, London, Oxford University Press, 1975.

Alpers, P. J. (ed.), *Elizabethan Poetry*, London, Oxford University Press, 1967.

Armstrong, I. (ed.), *The Major Victorian Poets: Reconsiderations*, London, Routledge & Kegan Paul, 1969.

Attridge, D., *The Rhythms of English Poetry*, London, Longman, 1982.

Bateson, F. W., *English Poetry and the English Language*, London, Oxford University Press, 1973.

Bateson, F. W., *English Poetry: A Critical Introduction*, London, Greenwood Press, 1978.

Bayley, J., *The Romantic Survival: A Study in Poetic Evolution*, London, Chatto and Windus, 1969.

Bedient, C., *Eight Contemporary Poets*, London, Oxford University Press, 1976.

Beer, P., *An Introduction to the Metaphysical Poets*, London, Macmillan, 1972.

Bennett, J. A. W., *Poetry of the Passion: Studies in Twelve Centuries of English Verse*, London, Oxford University Press, 1984.

Bodkin, M., *Archetypal Patterns in Poetry*, Oxford, Oxford University Press, 1943.

Booth, M., *British Poetry, 1964–1984: Driving through the Barricades*, London, Routledge & Kegan Paul, 1985.

Boulton, M., *The Anatomy of Poetry*, London, Routledge & Kegan Paul, 1953.

Bush, D., *English Poetry*, London, Methuen, 1965.

Carter, R. (ed.), *Thirties Poets: The Auden Group*, London, Macmillan, 1984.

Caudwell, C., *Illusion and Reality*, London, Lawrence and Wishart, 1946.

Davie, D., *Articulate Energy: An Inquiry into the Syntax of English Poetry*, London, Routledge & Kegan Paul, 1976.

Dodsworth, M. (ed.), *The Survival of Poetry*, London, Faber, 1976.

Eliot, T. S., *On Poetry and Poets*, London, Faber, 1957.

Empson, W., *Seven Versions of Pastoral*, London, Chatto and Windus, 1968.

Empson, W., *Seven Types of Ambiguity: A Study of its Effects in English Verse*, London, Chatto and Windus, 1973.

121

Evans, M., *English Poetry in the Sixteenth Century*, London, Hutchinson, 1967.

Fraser, G. S., *A Short History of English Poetry*, Milton Keynes, Open University Press, 1981.

Fuller, R., *Owls and Artificers: Oxford Lectures on Poetry*, London, Deutsch, 1971.

Graves, R., *Poetic Craft and Principle*, London, Cassell, 1967.

Greenfield, S. B., *The Interpretation of Old English Poems*, London, Routledge & Kegan Paul, 1972.

Grierson, H. J. C. and Smith, J. C., *A Critical History of English Poetry*, London, Athlone, 1983.

Haffenden, J. (ed.), *Viewpoints: Poets in Conversation*, London, Faber, 1981.

Hayter, A., *Opium and the Romantic Imagination*, London, Faber, 1968.

Holbrook, D., *Lost Bearings in English Poetry*, London, Vision, 1977.

Homberger, E., *The Art of the Real: Poetry in England and America since 1939*, London, Dent, 1977.

Hough, G., *The Last Romantics*, London, Duckworth, 1949.

Hough, G., *The Romantic Poets*, London, Hutchinson, 1967.

Hunter, J., *The Metaphysical Poets*, London, Evans, 1965.

Hynes, S., *The Auden Generation: Literature and Politics in the 1930's*, London, Bodley Head, 1976.

Ing, C., *Elizabethan Lyrics*, London, Chatto and Windus, 1968.

Jackson, J. R. De J., *Poetry of the Romantic Period, Routledge History of English Poetry*, London, Routledge & Kegan Paul, 1985.

Johnson, S., *The Lives of the Poets: A Selection*, London, Dent, 1975.

Keast, W. R. (ed.), *Seventeenth-Century English Poetry*, New York, Oxford University Press, 1962.

Kermode, F., *The Romantic Image*, London, Routledge & Kegan Paul, 1957.

King, P. R., *Nine Contemporary Poets: A Critical Introduction*, London, Methuen, 1979.

Knight, G. W., *The Starlit Dome: Studies in the Poetry of Vision*, London, Methuen, 1959.

Leavis, F. R., *Revaluations: Tradition and Development in English Poetry*, London, Chatto and Windus, 1936.

Leavis, F. R., *New Bearings in English Poetry: A Study of the Contemporary Situation*, Harmondsworth, Penguin, 1972.

Leech, G. N., *Linguistic Guide to English Poetry*, London, Longman, 1974.

Leishman, J. B., *The Metaphysical Poets*, Oxford, Clarendon Press, 1934.

Lindop, G. and Schmidt, M., *British Poetry since 1960: A Critical Survey*, Manchester, Carcanet New Press, 1972.

Loomis, R. S., *The Development of the Arthurian Romance*, London, Hutchinson, 1963.

Lucas, F. L., *Ten Victorian Poets*, Cambridge, Cambridge University Press, 1968.

Martin, G. and Furbank, P. M., *Twentieth Century Poetry*, Milton Keynes, Open University Press, 1975.

Maxwell, D. E. S., *Poets of the Thirties*, London, Routledge & Kegan Paul, 1969.

Miles, J., *Eras and Modes in English Poetry*, Westport, Connecticut, Greenwood, 1976.

Muir, E., *The State of Poetry*, London, Hogarth, 1962.

Norbrook, D., *Poetry and Politics in the English Renaissance*, London, Routledge & Kegan Paul, 1984.

Parfitt, G., *English Poetry of the Seventeenth Century*, London, Longman, 1985.

Parry, G., *Seventeenth Century Poetry: The Social Context*, London, Hutchinson, 1985.

Pearsall, D., *Old English and Middle English Poetry, Routledge History of English Poetry*, London, Routledge & Kegan Paul, 1985.

Peterson, D. L., *The English Love Lyric from Wyatt to Donne*, Princeton, Princeton University Press, 1967.

Pinto, V. De S., *The Restoration Court Poets*, London, British Council, 1965.

Pinto, V. De S., *Crisis in English Poetry,*

1880–1940, London, Hutchinson, 1968.

Powell, N., *Carpenters of Light: Some Contemporary British Poets*, Manchester, Carcanet New Press, 1979.

Praz, M., *The Romantic Agony*, London, Oxford University Press, 1970.

Press, J., *A Map of Modern English Verse*, London, Oxford University Press, 1969.

Probyn, C. T., *English Poetry*, London, Longman, 1984.

Read, H., *The True Voice of Feeling: Studies in English Romantic Poetry*, London, Faber, 1968.

Read, H., *Phases of English Poetry*, London, Greenwood Press, 1972.

Rosenthal, M. L., *The Modern Poets: A Critical Introduction*, London, Oxford University Press, 1975.

Rothstein, E., *Restoration and Eighteenth Century Poetry, 1660–1780, Routledge History of English Poetry*, London, Routledge & Kegan Paul, 1985.

Schmidt, M., *An Introduction to Fifty Modern British Poets*, London, Heinemann, 1979.

Schmidt, M., *An Introduction to Fifty British Poets, 1300–1900*, London, Heinemann, 1980.

Sisson, C. H., *English Poetry, 1900–1950: An Assessment*, London, Methuen, 1981.

Smith, S. (ed.), *Twentieth Century Poetry*, London, Macmillan, 1983.

Spearing, A. C., *Criticism and Medieval Poetry*, London, Arnold, 1964.

Spearing, A. C., *Medieval to Renaissance in English Poetry*, Cambridge, Cambridge University Press, 1985.

Speirs, J., *Medieval English Poetry: The Non-Chaucerian Tradition*, London, Faber, 1962.

Stead, C. K., *The New Poetic: Yeats to Eliot*, London, Hutchinson, 1965.

Sutherland, D., *On Romanticism*, New York, New York University Press, 1971.

Sutherland, J. R., *Preface to Eighteenth Century Poetry*, Oxford, Oxford University Press, 1948.

Thurley, G., *The Ironic Harvest: English Poetry in the Twentieth Century*, London, Arnold, 1974.

Thwaite, A., *Poetry Today: A Criticial Guide to British Poetry, 1960–1984*, London, Longman, 1985.

Tillotson, G., *Augustan Poetic Diction*, London, Athlone, 1964.

Tillyard, E. M. W., *Poetry and its Background*, London, Chatto and Windus, 1970.

Tolley, A. T., *The Poetry of the Thirties*, New York, St Martin's Press, 1975.

Tolley, A. T., *The Poetry of the Forties*, Manchester, Manchester University Press, 1986.

Wedgwood, C. V., *Poetry and Politics under the Stuarts*, Cambridge, Cambridge University Press, 1960.

Weston, J. L., *From Ritual to Romance*, New York, Doubleday, 1957.

Williamson, G., *A Reader's Guide to the Metaphysical Poets*, London, Thames and Hudson, 1968.

INDIVIDUAL WRITERS

GEOFFREY CHAUCER

Bowden, M., *A Reader's Guide to Geoffrey Chaucer*, London, Thames and Hudson, 1965.

Brewer, D. S., *Chaucer*, London, Longman, 1973.

Coghill, N., *The Poet Chaucer*, London, Oxford University Press, 1974.

Kean, P., *Chaucer and the Making of English Poetry*, 2 vols, London, Routledge & Kegan Paul, 1972.

Rowland, B. (ed.), *Companion to Chaucer Studies*, London, Oxford University Press, 1968.

WILLIAM LANGLAND

Hussey, S. S. (ed.), *Piers Plowman—Critical Approaches*, London, Methuen, 1969.

Ryan, W. M., *William Langland*, New York, Twayne, 1968.

Salter, E., *Piers Plowman: An Introduction*, Oxford, Blackwell, 1963.

Vasta, E. (ed.), *Interpretations of Piers Plowman*, Notre Dame, University of Notre Dame, 1968.

1550–1660

JOHN DONNE

Gardner, H. (ed.), *Donne: A Collection of Critical Essays*, Englewood Cliffs, N. J., Prentice-Hall, 1962.

Nelley, U., *The Poet Donne: His Dialectical Method*, Cork, Cork University Press, 1969.

Winney, J., *A Preface to John Donne*, London, Longman, 1970.

Zunder, W., *The Poetry of John Donne*, Brighton, Harvester, 1982.

BEN JONSON

Barish, J. A. (ed.), *Ben Jonson: A Collection of Critical Essays*, Englewood Cliffs, N.J., Prentice-Hall, 1963.

Dutton, R., *Ben Jonson: To the First Folio*, Cambridge, Cambridge University Press, 1983.

Partridge, E. B., *The Broken Compass: A Study of the Major Comedies of Ben Jonson*, London, Chatto and Windus, 1964.

Trimpi, H., *Ben Jonson's Poems: A Study of the Plain Style*, Stanford, Stanford University Press, 1962.

CHRISTOPHER MARLOWE

Knoll, R. E., *Chrisopher Marlowe*, New York, Twayne, 1969.

Levin, H., *The Overreacher: A Study of Christopher Marlowe*, Boston, Beacon Press, 1964.

Morris, B. (ed.), *Christopher Marlowe*, London, Benn, 1968.

Steane, J. B., *Marlowe: A Critical Study*, Cambridge, Cambridge University Press, 1964.

JOHN MILTON

Empson, W., *Milton's God*, Cambridge, Cambridge University Press, 1981.

Nicolson, M. H., *John Milton: A Reader's Guide to His Poetry*, London, Thames and Hudson, 1970.

Patrides, C. A. (ed.), *Milton's Epic Poetry*, Harmondsworth, Penguin, 1967.

Tillyard, E. M. W., *Milton*, Harmondsworth, Penguin, 1966.

THOMAS MORE

Chambers, R. W., *The Place of Thomas More in English Literature and History*, New York, Haskell House, 1964.

Kenny, A., *Thomas More*, London, Oxford University Press, 1983.

Nelson, W. (ed.), *Twentieth Century Interpretations of 'Utopia'*, Englewood Cliffs, N.J., Prentice-Hall, 1968.

Reynolds, E. E., *Sir Thomas More*, London, Longman, 1970.

WILLIAM SHAKESPEARE

Alexander, M., *An Introduction to Shakespeare and His Contemporaries*, London, Heinemann, 1979.

Bate, J., *How to Find Out About Shakespeare*, Oxford, Pergamon, 1968.

Bradbrook, M. C., *Shakespeare: The Poet in His World*, London, Methuen, 1980.

Bradley, A. C., *Shakespearean Tragedy*, London, Macmillan, 1905.

Campbell, O. J. and Quinn, E. G., *The Reader's Encyclopedia of Shakespeare*, New York, Crowell, 1966.

Granville-Barker, H., *Prefaces to Shakespeare*, 6 vols, London, Batsford, 1972–4.

Halliday, F. E., *A Shakespeare Companion*, Harmondsworth, Penguin, 1969.

Howard-Hill, T. H. (ed.), *Oxford Shakespeare Concordances*, London, Oxford University Press, 1969–73.

Muir, K. and Schoenbaum, S. (eds), *A New Companion to Shakespeare Studies*, Cambridge, Cambridge University Press, 1971.

Vickers, B. (ed.), *Shakespeare: The Critical Heritage*, 6 vols, London, Routledge & Kegan Paul, 1974.

Wells, S. (ed.), *Shakespeare: A Select Bibliographical Guide*, London, Oxford University Press, 1973.

EDMUND SPENSER

Bayley, P. C., *Edmund Spenser: Prince of Poets*, London, Hutchinson, 1971.

Bayley, P. C. (ed.), *Spenser: The Faerie Queen: A Casebook*, London, Macmillan, 1977.

Nelson, W., *The Poetry of Edmund Spenser*, New York and London, Columbia University Press, 1963.

Watson, E. A. F., *Spenser*, London, Evans, 1967.

1660–1800

JOSEPH ADDISON

Bloom, E. A. and Bloom, L. D., *Joseph Addison's Sociable Animal*, Providence, Brown University Press, 1971.

Elioseff, L. A., *The Cultural Milieu of Addison's Literary Criticism*, Austin, University of Texas Press, 1963.

Humphreys, A. R., *Steele, Addison and Their Periodical Essays*, London, Longman, 1959.

Smithers, P., *The Life of Joseph Addison*, Oxford, Clarendon Press, 1968.

WILLIAM BLAKE

Frye, N., *Fearful Symmetry: A Study of William Blake*, Boston, Beacon, 1965.

Frye, N. (ed.), *Blake: A Collection of Critical Essays*, Englewood Cliffs, N.J., Prentice-Hall, 1966.

Raine, K., *Blake and Tradition*, 2 vols, London, Routledge & Kegan Paul, 1969.

Wilson, M., *The Life of William Blake*, London, Oxford University Press, 1971.

JOHN BUNYAN

Baird, C. W., *John Bunyan: A Study in Narrative Technique*, New York, Kennikat Press, 1977.

Bateson, E. B., *John Bunyan: Allegory and Imagination*, London, Croom Helm, 1984.

Furlong, M., *Puritan's Progress: A Study of John Bunyan*, London, Hodder and Stoughton, 1975.

Sharrock, R. (ed.), *Bunyan—The Pilgrim's Progress: A Casebook*, London, Macmillan, 1976.

DANIEL DEFOE

Earle, P., *The World of Defoe*, London, Weidenfeld and Nicolson, 1976.

Starr, G. A., *Defoe and Spiritual Autobiography*, Princeton, Princeton University Press, 1965.

Sutherland, J. R., *Daniel Defoe: A Critical Study*, Cambridge, Mass., Harvard University Press, 1972.

Zimmerman, E., *Defoe and the Novel*, Berkeley, University of California Press, 1975.

JOHN DRYDEN

Harth, P., *Contexts of Dryden's Thought*, Chicago and London, University of Chicago Press, 1968.

Miner, E., *Dryden's Poetry*, Bloomington and London, Indiana University Press, 1971.

Miner, E. (ed.), *John Dryden*, London, Bell, 1972.

Myers, W., *Dryden*, London, Hutchinson, 1973.

HENRY FIELDING

Alter, R., *Fielding and the Nature of the Novel*, Cambridge, Harvard University Press, 1968.

Paulson, R., *Fielding: A Collection of Critical Essays*, Englewood Cliffs, N.J., Prentice-Hall, 1962.

Rawson, C. J., *Henry Fielding*, London, Routledge & Kegan Paul, 1969.

Wright, A., *Henry Fielding: Mask and Feast*, London, Chatto and Windus, 1968.

SAMUEL JOHNSON

Bate, S. J., *Samuel Johnson*, London, Chatto and Windus, 1978.

Greene, D. J. (ed.), *Samuel Johnson: A Collection of Critical Essays*, Englewood Cliffs, N.J., Prentice-Hall, 1965.

Lane, M., *Samuel Johnson and His World*, London, Hamilton, 1975.

Wain, J., *Samuel Johnson*, London, Macmillan, 1974.

ALEXANDER POPE

Dixon, P. (ed.), *Alexander Pope*, London, Bell, 1972.

Dobrée, B., *Alexander Pope*, Oxford, Oxford University Press, 1963.

Guerinot, J. V. (ed.), *Pope: A Collection of Critical Essays*, Englewood Cliffs, N.J., Prentice-Hall, 1972.

Tillotson, G., *On the Poetry of Pope*, Oxford, Oxford University Press, 1950.

SAMUEL RICHARDSON

Doody, M. A., *A Natural Passion: A Study of the Novels of Samuel Richardson*, Oxford, Clarendon Press, 1974.

Flynn, C. H., *Samuel Richardson: A Man of Letters*, Princeton, Princeton University Press, 1982.

Kearney, A. M., *Samuel Richardson*, London, Routledge & Kegan Paul, 1968.

Kinkead-Weekes, M., *Samuel Richardson: Dramatic Novelist*, London, Methuen, 1973.

TOBIAS SMOLLETT

Bold, A. (ed.), *Smollett: Author of the First Distinction*, London, Vision, 1982.

Boucé, P. G., *The Novels of Smollett*, London, Longman, 1976.

Goldberg, M. A., *Smollett and the Scottish School*, Albuquerque, University of New Mexico Press, 1959.

Grant, D., *Tobias Smollett: A Study in Style*, Manchester, Manchester University Press, 1977.

LAURENCE STERNE

Cash, A. H., *Laurence Sterne: The Early and Middle Years*, London, Methuen, 1975.

Cash, A. H. and Stedmond, J. M. (eds), *The Winged Skull: Papers for the Laurence Sterne Bicentenary Conference*, London, Methuen, 1971.

Moglen, H., *The Philosophical Irony of Laurence Sterne*, Gainesville, University of Florida Press, 1975.

Stedmond, J. M., *The Comic Art of Laurence Sterne*, Toronto, University of Toronto Press, 1967.

JONATHAN SWIFT

Tuveson, E. (ed.), *Swift: A Collection of Critical Essays*, Englewood Cliffs, N. J., Prentice-Hall, 1964.

Vickers, B. (ed.), *The World of Jonathan Swift*, Oxford, Blackwell, 1968.

Ward, D., *Jonathan Swift: An Introductory Essay*, London, Methuen, 1973.

Williams, K., *Jonathan Swift*, London, Routledge & Kegan Paul, 1968.

Nineteenth Century

MATTHEW ARNOLD

Allott, K. (ed.), *Matthew Arnold*, London, Bell, 1975.

Neiman, F., *Matthew Arnold*, New York, Twayne, 1968.

Thorpe, P., *Matthew Arnold*, London, Evans, 1969.

Trilling, L., *Matthew Arnold*, London, Allen and Unwin, 1975.

JANE AUSTEN

Liddell, R., *The Novels of Jane Austen*, London, Allen Lane, 1976.

Pinion, F. B., *A Jane Austen Companion*, London, Macmillan, 1973.

Southam, B. C. (ed.), *Jane Austen: Sense and Sensibility, Pride and Prejudice and Mansfield Park: A Casebook*, London, Macmillan, 1976.

Watt, I. (ed.), *Jane Austen: A Collection of Critical Essays*, Englewood Cliffs, N.J., Prentice-Hall, 1963.

CHARLOTTE BRONTË

Bentley, P., *The Brontës and Their World*, London, Thames and Hudson, 1969.

Gérin, W., *Charlotte Brontë*, Oxford, Oxford University Press, 1967.

Peters, M. C. B., *Charlotte Brontë: Style in the Novel*, Madison, University of Wisconsin Press, 1973.

Pollard, A., *Charlotte Brontë*, London, Routledge & Kegan Paul, 1968.

EMILY BRONTË

Gérin, W., *Emily Brontë: A Biography*, Oxford, Clarendon Press, 1971.

Hewish, J., *Emily Brontë: A Critical and Biographical Study*, London, Macmillan, 1969.

Spark, M. and Stanford, A., *Emily Brontë: Her Life and Work*, London, Owen, 1966.

Stevenson, W. H., *Emily and Anne Brontë*, London, Routledge & Kegan Paul, 1968.

ROBERT BROWNING

Drew, P., *The Poetry of Browning*, London, Methuen, 1970.

Gridley, R. E., *Browning*, London, Routledge & Kegan Paul, 1972.

Halliday, F. E., *Robert Browning: His Life and Work*, London, Jupiter, 1975.

Jack, I., *Browning's Major Poetry*,
Oxford, Oxford University Press, 1973.

LORD BYRON

Blackstone, B., *Byron: A Survey*,
London, Longman, 1975.
Jump, J. D., *Byron*, London,
Routledge & Kegan Paul, 1972.
Marchand, L. A., *Byron's Poetry*,
London, Murray, 1965.
Rutherford, A., *Byron: A Critical Study*,
London, Oliver and Boyd, 1965.

THOMAS CARLYLE

Campbell, I., *Thomas Carlyle*, London,
Hamish Hamilton, 1974.
Fielding, K. J. and Tarr, R. L., *Carlyle
Past and Present*, London, Vision,
1976.
Froude, J., *Thomas Carlyle*, London,
Gregg International, 1970 (reprint).
Neff, E., *Carlyle*, New York, Russell and
Russell, 1960 (reprint).

SAMUEL TAYLOR COLERIDGE

Bate, W. J., *Coleridge*, London,
Weidenfeld and Nicolson, 1968.
Brett, R. L. (ed.), *Samuel Taylor
Coleridge*, London, Bell, 1971.
Hill, J. S., *A Coleridge Companion*,
London, Macmillan, 1984.
Willey, B., *Samuel Taylor Coleridge*,
London, Chatto and Windus, 1972.

CHARLES DICKENS

Collins, P. (ed.), *Dickens: The Critical
Heritage*, London, Routledge &
Kegan Paul, 1971.
Daleski, H. M., *Dickens and the Art of
Analogy*, London, Faber, 1970.
Fido, M., *Charles Dickens*, London,
Routledge & Kegan Paul, 1968.
Hobsbaum, P., *A Reader's Guide to
Charles Dickens*, London, Thames
and Hudson, 1973.

Leavis, F. R. and Leavis, Q. D., *Dickens
the Novelist*, London, Chatto and
Windus, 1970.
Page, N., *A Dickens Companion*,
London, Macmillan, 1984.
Price, M. (ed.), *Dickens: A Collection of
Critical Essays*, Englewood Cliffs,
N.J., Prentice-Hall, 1967.

GEORGE ELIOT

Haight, G. S., *George Eliot*, Oxford,
Oxford University Press, 1968.
Hardy, B., *The Novels of George Eliot*,
London, Athlone, 1981.
Harvey, W. J., *The Art of George Eliot*,
London, Chatto and Windus, 1961.
Pinion, F. B., *A George Eliot
Companion*, London, Macmillan,
1961.

THOMAS HARDY

Draper, R. P. (ed.), *Hardy—The Tragic
Novels: A Casebook*, London,
Macmillan, 1975.
Mahon, M. E., *Thomas Hardy's Novels:
A Study Guide*, London, Heinemann,
1976.
Pinion, F. B., *A Hardy Companion*,
London, Macmillan, 1968.
Wooton, G., *Thomas Hardy: Towards a
Materialist Criticism*, Dublin, Gill and
Macmillan, 1985.

GERARD MANLEY HOPKINS

Bottrall, M. (ed.), *Gerard Manley
Hopkins—Poems: A Casebook*,
London, Macmillan, 1975.
Gardner, W. H., *Gerard Manley
Hopkins*, Oxford, Oxford University
Press, 1950.
Hartman, G. H., *Hopkins: A Collection
of Critical Essays*, Englewood Cliffs,
N. J., Prentice-Hall, 1966.
Sulloway, A. G., *Gerard Manley
Hopkins and The Victorian Temper*,
London, Routledge & Kegan Paul,
1972.

HENRY JAMES

Edel, L., *Henry James*, 5 vols, London, Hart-Davis, 1953–72.

Edel, L. (ed.), *Henry James: A Collection of Critical Essays*, Englewood Cliffs, N.J., Prentice-Hall, 1963.

Powers, L. H. (ed.), *Henry James's Major Novels: Essays in Criticism*, East Lansing, Michigan State University Press, 1973.

Putt, G. S., *A Reader's Guide to Henry James*, London, Thames and Hudson, 1966.

JOHN KEATS

Bate, W. J. (ed.), *Keats: A Collection of Critical Essays*, Englewood Cliffs, N.J., Prentice-Hall, 1964.

Bate, W. J., *John Keats*, London, Oxford University Press, 1967.

Fraser, G. S. (ed.), *John Keats, Odes: A Casebook*, London, Macmillan, 1971.

Jack, I., *Keats and the Mirror of Art*, Oxford, Oxford University Press, 1967.

GEORGE MEREDITH

Bailey, E. J., *The Novels of George Meredith: A Study*, New York, Haskell House, 1971 (reprint).

Beer, G., *Meredith—A Change of Masks: A Study of the Novels*, London, Athlone Press, 1970.

Fletcher, I. (ed.), *Meredith Now: Some Critical Essays*, London, Routledge & Kegan Paul, 1971.

Pritchett, V. S., *George Meredith and English Comedy*, London, Chatto and Windus, 1970.

WALTER SCOTT

Cockshut, A. O. J., *The Achievement of Walter Scott*, London, Collins, 1969.

Devlin, D. D., *Walter Scott: Modern Judgements*, London, Macmillan, 1968.

Mayhead, R., *Walter Scott*, London, Routledge & Kegan Paul, 1968.

Millgate, J., *Walter Scott: The Making of the Novelist*, Edinburgh, Edinburgh University Press, 1985.

PERCY BYSSHE SHELLEY

Foot, P., *Red Shelley*, London, Sidgwick and Jackson, 1980.

Reiman, D. H., *Percy Bysshe Shelley*, New York, Twayne, 1969.

Wasserman, E. R., *Shelley: A Critical Reading*, Baltimore, Johns Hopkins University Press, 1971.

Woodings, R. B. (ed.), *Shelley: Modern Judgements*, London, Macmillan, 1968.

ALFRED TENNYSON

Culler, A. D., *The Poetry of Tennyson*, New Haven and London, Yale University Press, 1977.

Palmer, D. J. (ed.), *Tennyson*, London, Bell, 1973.

Pinion, F. B., *A Tennyson Companion: Life and Works*, London, Macmillan, 1984.

Ricks, C., *Tennyson*, London, Macmillan, 1972.

WILLIAM MAKEPEACE THACKERAY

Loofbourow, J., *Thackeray and the Comedy of Fiction*, Princeton, Princeton University Press, 1964.

McMaster, J., *Thackeray: The Major Novels*, Manchester, Manchester University Press, 1971.

Tillotson, G., *Thackeray the Novelist*, London, Methuen, 1974.

Welsh, A. (ed.), *Thackeray: A Collection of Critical Essays*, Englewood Cliffs, N.J., Prentice-Hall, 1968.

ANTHONY TROLLOPE

Edwards, P. D., *Anthony Trollope*,

London, Routledge & Kegan Paul, 1968.

Edwards, P. D., *Anthony Trollope: His Art and Scope*, Hassocks, Harvester, 1978.

Gerould, W. and Gerould, J. T., *A Guide to Trollope*, Princeton, Princeton University Press, 1975.

Kincaid, J. R., *The Novels of Anthony Trollope*, Oxford, Clarendon Press, 1977.

OSCAR WILDE

Ellmann, R., *Oscar Wilde: Twentieth Century Views*, Englewood Cliffs, N.J., Prentice-Hall, 1969.

Holland, V., *Oscar Wilde and His World*, London, Thames and Hudson, 1979.

Hyde, H. M., *Oscar Wilde*, London, Eyre Methuen, 1976.

Shewan, R., *Oscar Wilde: Art and Egotism*, London, Macmillan, 1977.

WILLIAM WORDSWORTH

Abrams, M. H., *Wordsworth: A Collection of Critical Essays*, Englewood Cliffs, N.J., Prentice-Hall, 1972.

Durrant, G. H., *Wordsworth and the Great System*, Cambridge, Cambridge University Press, 1970.

Hartman, G., *Wordsworth's Poetry, 1787–1814*, New Haven, Yale University Press, 1971.

Pinion, D. H., *A Wordsworth Companion*, London, Macmillan, 1984.

W. B. YEATS

Ellmann, R., *Yeats: The Man and the Masks*, London, Faber, 1961.

Jeffares, A. N., *W. B. Yeats: Man and Poet*, London, Routledge & Kegan Paul, 1962.

Jeffares, A. N., *A New Commentary on the Poems of W. B. Yeats*, London, Macmillan, 1984.

Unterecker, J., *A Reader's Guide to Yeats*, London, Thames and Hudson, 1975.

Twentieth Century

W. H. AUDEN

Fuller, J., *A Reader's Guide to W. H. Auden*, London, Thames and Hudson, 1970.

Spears, M. K., *The Disenchanted Island: The Poetry of W. H. Auden*, London, Oxford University Press, 1963.

Spears, M. K. (ed.), *Auden: A Collection of Critical Essays*, Englewood Cliffs, N.J., Prentice-Hall, 1964.

Wright, G. T., *W. H. Auden*, New York, Twayne, 1969.

SAMUEL BECKETT

Fletcher, B. S. et al., *A Student's Guide to the Plays of Samuel Beckett*, London, Faber, 1978.

Fletcher, J. and Spurling, J., *Beckett: A Study of His Plays*, London, Eyre Methuen, 1972.

Graves, L. and Federman, R. (eds), *Samuel Beckett: The Critical Heritage*, London, Routledge & Kegan Paul, 1979.

Kenner, H., *A Reader's Guide to Samuel Beckett*, London, Thames and Hudson, 1973.

ARNOLD BENNETT

Barker, D., *Writer By Trade: A Portrait of Arnold Bennett*, New York, Atheneum, 1966.

Drabble, M., *Arnold Bennett*, London, Weidenfeld and Nicolson, 1974.

Lucas, J., *Arnold Bennett: A Study of His Fiction*, London, Methuen, 1975.

Wright, W. F., *Arnold Bennett: Romantic Realist*, Lincoln, University of Nebraska Press, 1971.

JOSEPH CONRAD

Hewitt, D., *Conrad: A Reassessment*, London, Bodley Head, 1975.

Karl, F. R., *A Reader's Guide to Joseph Conrad*, London, Thames and Hudson, 1960.

Murdoch, M. (ed.), *Conrad: A Collection of Critical Essays*, Englewood Cliffs, N.J., Prentice-Hall, 1966.

Sherry, N. (ed.), *Conrad: The Critical Heritage*, London, Routledge & Kegan Paul, 1973.

T. S. ELIOT

Grant, M. (ed.), *T. S. Eliot: The Critical Heritage*, 2 vols, London, Routledge & Kegan Paul, 1982.

Kenner, H. (ed.), *T. S. Eliot: A Collection of Critical Essays*, Englewood Cliffs, N.J., Prentice-Hall, 1962.

Southam, B. C., *A Student's Guide to the Selected Poems of T. S. Eliot*, London, Faber, 1981.

Williamson, G., *A Reader's Guide to T. S. Eliot*, New York, Farrar, Strauss and Giroux, 1969.

E. M. FORSTER

Brander, L., *E. M. Forster: A Critical Study*, London, Hart-Davis, 1970.

Gardner, P. (ed.), *E. M. Forster: The Critical Heritage*, London, Routledge & Kegan Paul, 1973.

Rose, M., *E. M. Forster*, London, Evans, 1970.

Scott, P. J. M., *E. M. Forster: Our Permanent Contemporary*, London, Vision, 1984.

JOHN GALSWORTHY

Barker, D., *The Man of Principle: A View of John Galsworthy*, London, Allen and Unwin, 1967.

Holloway, D., *John Galsworthy*, London, Morgan-Grampian, 1968.

Mottram, R. H., *John Galsworthy*, London, Longman, 1953.

JAMES JOYCE

Bolt, S. *A Preface to James Joyce*, London, Longman, 1981.

Ellman, R., *James Joyce*, London, Oxford University Press, 1966.

Golberg, S. L., *James Joyce*, Edinburgh, Oliver and Boyd, 1962.

Hodgart, M., *James Joyce: A Student's Guide*, London, Routledge & Kegan Paul, 1978.

D. H. LAWRENCE

Hobsbaum, P., *A Reader's Guide to D. H. Lawrence*, London, Thames and Hudson, 1981.

Leavis, F. R., *D. H. Lawrence: Novelist*, Harmondsworth, Penguin, 1973.

Pinion, F. B., *D. H. Lawrence*, London, Macmillan, 1978.

Spilka, M. (ed.), *D. H. Lawrence: A Collection of Critical Essays*, Englewood Cliffs, N.J., Prentice-Hall, 1963.

GEORGE ORWELL

Hammond, J. R., *A George Orwell Companion*, London, Macmillan, 1982.

Myers, J., *A Reader's Guide to George Orwell*, London, Thames and Hudson, 1975.

Myers, J. (ed.), *George Orwell: The Critical Heritage*, London, Routledge & Kegan Paul, 1975.

Williams, R., *Orwell*, London, Fontana, 1970.

GEORGE BERNARD SHAW

Bentley, E., *George Bernard Shaw*, London, Hale, 1950.

Evans, T. F. (ed.), *Shaw: The Critical Heritage*, London, Routledge & Kegan Paul, 1984.

Kaufman, R. J. (ed.), *G. B. Shaw: A Collection of Critical Essays*, Englewood Cliffs, N.J., Prentice-Hall, 1965.

Purdom, C. B., *A Guide to the Plays of Bernard Shaw*, London, Methuen, 1963.

H. G. WELLS

Batchelor, J., *H. G. Wells*, Cambridge, Cambridge University Press, 1985.

Hammond, J. R., *An H. G. Wells Companion*, London, Macmillan, 1979.

Haynes, R. D., *H. G. Wells: Discoverer of the Future*, London, Macmillan, 1980.

Parrinder, P. (ed.), *H. G. Wells: The Critical Heritage*, London, Routledge & Kegan Paul, 1972.

VIRGINIA WOOLF

Guiget, J., *Virginia Woolf and Her Works*, London, Hogarth, 1965.

Leaska, M. A., *The Novels of Virginia Woolf*, London, Weidenfeld and Nicolson, 1977.

Majumdar, R. and McLaurin, A. (eds), *Virginia Woolf: The Critical Heritage*, London, Routledge & Kegan Paul, 1975.

Sprague, C. (ed.), *Virginia Woolf; A Collection of Critical Essays*, Englewood Cliffs, N.J., Prentice-Hall, 1971.

Contemporary Writers

DANNIE ABSE

Cohen, J. (ed.), *The Poetry of Dannie Abse: Critical Essays and Reminiscences*, London, Robson, 1983.

KINGSLEY AMIS

Gohn, J. B., *Kingsley Amis: A Checklist*, Kent, USA, Kent State University Press, 1976.

Salwak, D., *Kingsley Amis: A Reference Guide*, Boston, Hall, 1978.

JOHN ARDEN

Gray, F., *John Arden*, London, Macmillan, 1982.

Hayman, R., *John Arden*, London, Heinemann, 1968.

Hunt, A., *Arden: A Study of His Plays*, London, Methuen, 1974.

Trussler, S., *John Arden*, New York, Columbia University Press, 1973.

ALAN AYCKBOURNE

Billington, M., *Alan Ayckbourne*, London, Macmillan, 1983.

Watson, I., *Conversations with Ayckbourne*, London, Macdonald, 1981.

PETER BARNES

Dukore, B. F., *The Theatre of Peter Barnes*, London, Heinemann, 1981.

JOHN BETJEMAN

Standford, D., *John Betjeman: A Study*, Sudbury, Neville Spearman, 1961.

Taylor-Martin, P., *John Betjeman: His Life and Work*, London, Allen Lane, 1983.

ROBERT BOLT

Hayman, R., *Robert Bolt*, London, Heinemann, 1969.

EDWARD BOND

Coult, T., *The Plays of Edward Bond*, London, Methuen, 1979.
Hay, M. and Roberts, P., *Bond: A Study of His Plays*, London, Methuen, 1980.
Hirst, D. L., *Edward Bond*, London, Macmillan, 1985.
Scharine, R., *The Plays of Edward Bond*, Lewisburg, Bucknell University Press, 1977.

JOHN BRAINE

Lee, J. W., *John Braine*, New York, Twayne, 1968.

ANTHONY BURGESS

Aggeler, G., *Anthony Burgess: The Artist as Novelist*, Alabama, University of Alabama Press, 1979.
Coale, S., *Anthony Burgess*, New York, Ungar, 1982.
De Vitis, A. A., *Anthony Burgess*, New York, Twayne, 1972.
Dix, C. M., *Anthony Burgess*, London, Longman, 1971.

JOHN LE CARRÉ

Barley, T., *Taking Sides: The Fiction of John le Carré*, Milton Keynes, Open University Press, 1985.
Homberger, E., *John le Carré*, London, Methuen, 1986.
Monaghan, D., *The Novels of John le Carré*, Oxford, Blackwell, 1985.

MARGARET DRABBLE

Creighton, J. V., *Margaret Drabble*, London, Methuen, 1985.

Myer, V. G., *Margaret Drabble: Puritanism and Permissiveness*, London, Vision Press, 1974.
Rose, E. C., *The Novels of Margaret Drabble: Equivocal Figures*, London, Macmillan, 1980.
Roxman, S., *Guilt and Glory: Studies in Margaret Drabble's Novels, 1963–80*, Stockholm, Almquist and Wiksell, 1984.

LAWRENCE DURRELL

Fraser, G. S., *Lawrence Durrell*, London, Longman, 1970.
Friedman, A. W., *Lawrence Durrell and the Alexandria Quartet*, Norman, University of Oklahoma Press, 1970.
Moore, H. T. (ed.), *The World of Durrell*, Carbondale, Southern Illinois University Press, 1962.
Unterecker, J., *Lawrence Durrell*, New York, Columbia University Press, 1964.

D. J. ENRIGHT

Walsh, W., *D. J. Enright: Poet of Humanism*, Cambridge, Cambridge University Press, 1974.

JOHN FOWLES

Fawkner, H. W., *The Timescapes of John Fowles*, Farleigh Dickinson University Press, 1984.
Loveday, S., *The Romances of John Fowles*, London, Macmillan, 1984.
Olshen, B. N. and Olshen, T. A., *John Fowles: A Reference Guide*, Boston, G. K. Hall, 1980.
Woodcock, B., *Male Mythologies—John Fowles*, Brighton, Harvester, 1984.

ROY FULLER

Austin, A. E., *Roy Fuller*, Boston, Twayne, 1979.

133

WILLIAM GOLDING

Babb, H. S., *The Novels of William Golding*, Columbus, Ohio State University Press, 1970.
Crompton, D., *A View from the Spire: William Golding's Later Novels*, (ed. J. Briggs), Oxford, Blackwell, 1984.
Hodson, L., *William Golding*, Edinburgh, Oliver and Boyd, 1969.
Weekes, M. K. and Gregor, I., *William Golding: A Critical Study*, London, Faber, 1984.

GRAHAM GREENE

Hynes, S. (ed.), *Graham Greene: A Collection of Critical Essays*, Englewood Cliffs, N. J., Prentice-Hall, 1973.
Kulshrestha, J. P., *Graham Greene, the Novelist*, London, Macmillan, 1979.
Pryce-Jones, D., *Graham Greene*, Edinburgh, Oliver and Boyd, 1973.
Spurling, J., *Graham Greene*, London, Methuen, 1983.

TREVOR GRIFFITHS

Poole, M. and Wyver, J., *Powerplays: Trevor Griffiths in Television*, London, BFI, 1982.

SEAMUS HEANEY

Buttel, R., *Heaney*, Lewisburg, Bucknell University Press, 1975.
Curtis, T. (ed.), *The Art of Seamus Heaney*, Ogmore by Sea, Poetry Wales Press, 1985.
Maguire, A., *Notes on Selected Poems of Seamus Heaney*, London, Longman, 1986.
Morrison, B., *Seamus Heaney*, London, Methuen, 1982.

TED HUGHES

Faas, E., *Ted Hughes, the Unaccommodated Universe*, Santa Barbara, Cal., Black Sparrow Press, 1980.
Gifford, T. and Roberts, N., *Ted Hughes: A Critical Study*, London, Faber, 1981.
Sagar, K., *The Art of Ted Hughes*, Cambridge, Cambridge University Press, 1978.
West, T., *Ted Hughes*, London, Methuen, 1985.

PHILIP LARKIN

Bloomfield, B. C., *Philip Larkin, A Bibliography 1933–1976*, London, Faber, 1979.
Brownjohn, A., *Larkin*, London, Longman, 1975.
Motion, A., *Philip Larkin*, London, Methuen, 1982.
Timms, D., *Philip Larkin*, Edinburgh, Oliver and Boyd, 1973.

DORIS LESSING

Pratt, A. and Dembo, L. S. (eds), *Doris Lessing: Critical Studies*, Madison, University of Wisconsin Press, 1974.
Rubenstein, R., *Breaking the Forms of Consciousness: The Novelistic Vision of Doris Lessing*, Urbana, University of Illinois Press, 1979.
Sage, L., *Doris Lessing*, London, Methuen, 1983.
Thorpe, M., *Doris Lessing*, London, Longman, 1973.

HUGH MacDIARMID

Buthlay, K., *Hugh MacDiarmid*, Edinburgh, Oliver and Boyd, 1964.
Gish, N. K., *Hugh MacDiarmid: The Man and His Work*, London, Macmillan, 1984.
Glen, D. (ed.), *Hugh MacDiarmid: A Critical Survey*, Edinburgh, Scottish Academic Press, 1972.
Oxenhorn, H., *Elemental Things: The Poetry of Hugh MacDiarmid*,

Edinburgh, Edinburgh University
Press, 1984.

IRIS MURDOCH

Byatt, A. S., *Iris Murdoch*, London,
Longman, 1976.
Conradi, P. J., *Iris Murdoch: The Saint
and the Artist*, London, Macmillan,
1985.
Dipple, E., *Iris Murdoch: Work For the
Spirit*, London, Methuen, 1982.
Todd, R., *Iris Murdoch*, London,
Methuen, 1984.

JOE ORTON

Charney, M., *Joe Orton*, London,
Macmillan, 1984.
Lahr, J., *Prick up Your Ears: Biography
of Joe Orton*, London, Allen Lane,
1978.

JOHN OSBORNE

Banham, M., *Osborne*, Edinburgh,
Oliver and Boyd, 1969.
Carter, A., *John Osborne*, Edinburgh,
Oliver and Boyd, 1969.
Hayman, R., *John Osborne*, London,
Heinemann, 1968.
Trussler, S., *The Plays of John Osborne:
An Assessment*, London, Gollancz,
1969.

HAROLD PINTER

Almansi, G. and Henderson, S., *Harold
Pinter*, London, Methuen, 1983.
Baker, W. and Tabachnik, S. E., *Harold
Pinter*, Edinburgh, Oliver and Boyd,
1973.
Esslin, M., *Pinter the Playwright*,
London, Methuen, 1982.
Thompson, D. T., *Pinter: The Player's
Playwright*, London, Macmillan,
1985.

PETER SHAFFER

Taylor, J. R., *Peter Shaffer*, London,
Longman, 1974.

ALAN SILLITOE

Atherton, S., *Alan Sillitoe: A Critical
Assessment*, London, W. H. Allen,
1979.
Marland, M. (ed.), *Sillitoe*, London,
Times Newspapers, 1970.
Penner, A. R., *Alan Sillitoe*, New York,
Twayne, 1972.

STEVIE SMITH

Barbera, J. and McBrien, W., *Stevie: A
Biography of Stevie Smith*, London,
Heinemann, 1985.
Rankin, A. C., *The Poetry of Stevie
Smith: 'Little Girl Lost'*, Gerrard's
Cross, Colin Smythe, 1985.

MURIEL SPARK

Bold, A., *Muriel Spark*, London,
Methuen, 1986.
Kemp, P., *Muriel Spark*, London, Elek,
1974.
Stubbs, P., *Muriel Spark*, London,
Longman, 1973.
Whittaker, R., *The Faith and Fiction of
Muriel Spark*, London, Macmillan,
1982.

TOM STOPPARD

Bigsby, C. W. E., *Tom Stoppard*,
London, Longman, 1976.
Brassell, T., *Tom Stoppard: An
Assessment*, London, Macmillan,
1985.
Hayman, R., *Tom Stoppard*, London,
Heinemann, 1982.
Whitaker, T. R., *Tom Stoppard*, London,
Macmillan, 1983.

135

DAVID STOREY

Taylor, J. R., *David Storey*, London, Longman, 1974.

J. R. R. TOLKIEN

Carpenter, H., *J. R. R. Tolkien: A Biography*, London, Allen and Unwin, 1977.

Giddings, R. and Holland, E., *J. R. R. Tolkien: The Shores of Middle-Earth*, London, Fourth Estate, 1981.

Harvey, D., *The Song of Middle-Earth: J. R. R. Tolkien's Themes, Symbols and Myths*, London, Allen and Unwin, 1985.

Isaacs, N. D. and Zimbardo, R. (eds), *Tolkien: New Critical Perspectives*, Lexington, University Press of Kentucky, 1982.

ARNOLD WESKER

Hayman, R., *Arnold Wesker*, London, Heinemann, 1970.

Leeming, G., *Wesker the Playwright*, London, Methuen, 1982.

Leeming, G. (comp.), *Wesker on File*, London, Methuen, 1985.

Leeming, G. and Trussler, S., *The Plays of Arnold Wesker*, London, Gollancz, 1971.

RAYMOND WILLIAMS

Ward, J. P., *Raymond Williams*, Writers of Wales, Cardiff, University of Wales Press, 1981.

SEE ALSO:

35   Theatre

17 MEDIA

For bibliographical coverage of broadcasting in Britain readers are referred to: BBC, *British Broadcasting, 1922–1972: A Select Bibliography*, 1972; Documentation Centre for Mass Communication Research, *Current British Research on Mass Media and Mass Communication: Register of Ongoing and Recently Completed Unpublished Research*, annually. For publications on the press in Britain see Atkinson, F. (comp.), *The English Newspaper since 1900*, 1960. For publications on the cimema see: Ellis, J. C. et al., *The Film Book Bibliography, 1940–1975*, 1979; Gerlach, J. C. and Gerlach, L. (comps.), *The Critical Index: A Bibliography of Articles on Film in English, 1946–73*, 1974.

The following are sources of general information on:

Radio and Television BBC, *BBC Handbook*, annually; British Film Institute, *Film and Television Yearbook*, annually; Carrick Publishing, *Who's Who in Broadcasting*, 1985; Noble, P., *British Film and Television Year Book*, annually; Stenton, Z. (ed.), *The Blue Book of British Broadcasting: A Handbook for Professional Bodies and Students of Broadcasting*, 1984.

Cinema British Film Institute, *Film and Television Yearbook*, annually; Gifford, D., *The British Film Catalogue, 1895–1985*, 1986; Gifford, D., *British Cinema: An Illustrated Guide and Index to 5000 Films*, 1968; Halliwell, L., *The Filmgoer's Companion*, 1984; Halliwell, L., *Halliwell's Film Guide*, 1985; Noble, P. (ed.), *'Screen International' Film and Television Year Book*, annually; Oliver, E. (ed.), *A Researcher's Guide to British Films and Television Collections*, 1981.

Press Atkinson, F. (comp.), *The English Newspaper since 1900: A Bibliography*, 1960; Skinner Directories, *Willing's Press Guide*, annually; Benn Publications (publisher), *Benn's Media Directory incorporating Benn's Press Directory*, Tunbridge Wells, annually.

In their respective fields the following are the most comprehensive surveys:

Broadcasting Briggs, A., *History of Broadcasting in the United Kingdom*, 3 vols, 1961–79; Paulu, B., *Television and Radio in the United Kingdom*, 1981; Sendall, B., *The History of Independent Television in Britain*, 3 vols, 1982–4.

Cinema Armes, R., *A Critical History of the British Cinema*, 1978; Betts, E., *The Film Business: History of the British Cinema, 1896–1972*, 1973; Curran, J. and Porter, V. (eds), *British Cinema History*, 1983; Park, J., *Learning to Dream: The New British Cinema*, 1984; Perry, G., *The Great British Picture Show: From the Nineties to the Seventies*, 1975.

Press Boyce, G. et al. (eds), *Newspaper History from the Seventeenth Century to the Present Day*, 1978; Cranfield, G. A., *The Press and Society: From Caxton to Northcliffe*, 1978; Royal Commission on the Press, *Final Report*, 1977; Smith, A. (ed.), *The British Press since the War*, 1974; Williams, F., *Dangerous Estate: The Anatomy of Newspapers*, 1957.

REFERENCE

Armour, R., *Film: A Reference Guide*, London, Greenwood Press, 1980.

Atkinson, F. (comp.), *The English Newspaper since 1900: A Bibliography*, Library Association, 1960.

Benn Publications (publisher), *Benn's Media Directory, incorporating Benn's Press Directory*, Tunbridge Wells, annually.

British Broadcasting Corporation, *British Broadcasting 1922–1972: A Select Bibliography*, London, BBC, 1972.

British Broadcasting Corporation, *BBC Handbook*, London, BBC Publications, annually.

British Film Institute, *Film and Television Yearbook*, London, annually.

Carrick Publishing (publisher), *Who's Who in Broadcasting*, Ayr, 1985.

Curthoys, A. and Struthers, J. (eds), *Who's Who on Television*, London, Michael Joseph, 1982.

Documentation Centre for Mass Communication Research, *Current British Research on Mass Media and Mass Communication: Register of Ongoing and Recently Completed Unpublished Research*, Leicester, annually.

Ellis, J. C. et al., *The Film Book Bibliography, 1940–1975*, Metuchen, N. J. Scarecrow Press, 1979.

Gerlach, J. C. and Gerlach, L. (comps), *The Critical Index: A Bibliography of Articles on Film in English, 1946–1973, Arranged by Names and Topics*, New York and London, Teachers College Press, 1974.

Gifford, D., *British Cinema: An Illustrated Guide and Index to 5000 Films*, London, Zwemmer, 1968.

Gifford, D., *The British Film Catalogue 1895–1985*, Newton Abbot, David and Charles, 1986.

Gifford, D., *The Illustrated Who's Who in British Films*, London, Batsford, 1978.

Halliwell, L., *The Filmgoer's Companion*, London, Granada, 1984.

Halliwell, L., *Halliwell's Film Guide*, London, Granada, 1985.

Independent Broadcasting Authority, *Annual Report*, London, IBA, annually.

Noble, P. (ed.), *'Screen International' Film and Television Year Book*, London, King, annually.

Oliver, E. (ed.), *A Researchers' Guide to British Films and Television Collections*, London, British Universities Film Council, 1985.

Palmer, S. (ed.), *Who's Who of British Film Actors*, Metuchen, N. J., Scarecrow Press, 1981.

Parish, R., *Film Actor's Guide, Western Europe*, Metuchen, N. J., Scarecrow Press, 1978.

Pedder, E. (ed.), *Who's Who On Television*, London, Michael Joseph, 1985.

Skinner Directories (publisher), *Willing's Press Guide: A Comprehensive Index and Handbook of the Press of the United Kingdom and Great Britain*, London, annually.

Staddon, J. and Holme, P. (comps.), *The Complete Video Movie Guide*, Witham, Galaxy, 1985.

Stenton, Z., (ed.), *The Blue Book of British Broadcasting: A Handbook for Professional Bodies and Students of Broadcasting*, London, Tellex Monitors, 1984.

Wood, L. (comp.), *British Films, 1971–81*, London, BFI, 1984.

GENERAL

Curran, J. and Seaton, J., *Power Without Responsibility: The Press and Broadcasting in Britain*, London, Fontana, 1981.

Downing, J., *The Media Machine*, London, Pluto, 1980.

Eysenk, H. J. and Nias, D. K., *Sex, Violence and the Media*, London,

Paladin, 1980.

Field, M., *The Publishing Industry: Growth Prospects Fade?*, London, Comedia, 1986.

Glasgow Media Group, *Bad News*, London, Routledge & Kegan Paul, 1976.

Glasgow Media Group, *More Bad News*, London, Routledge & Kegan Paul, 1980.

Glasgow University Media Group, *Really Bad News*, London, Routledge & Kegan Paul, 1983.

Gower (publisher), *The Media: New Society Social Studies Reader*, Aldershot, 1985.

Gurevitch, M. et al., *The Media: Contents of Study*, Milton Keynes, Open University Press, 1977.

Hartley, J., *Understanding News*, London, Methuen, 1982.

Hetherington, A., *News, Newspapers and Television*, London, Macmillan, 1985.

Lewis, P. M., *Whose Media? The Annan Report and After*, London, Consumers' Association, 1978.

May, A. and Rowan, K. (eds), *Inside Information: British Government and the Media*, London, Constable, 1982.

Myers, R., *The British Book Trade From Caxton to the Present Day*, Aldershot, Gower, 1975.

Pegg, M., *Broadcasting and Society, 1918–39*, London, Croom Helm, 1983.

Robertson, G. and Nicol, A. G. L., *Media Law*, London, Sage, 1985.

Tunstall, J., *The Media in Britain*, London, Constable, 1983.

Whale, J., *The Politics of the Media*, Manchester, Manchester University Press, 1977.

BROADCASTING

BBC (publisher), *The Task of Broadcasting News*, London, 1976.

BBC (publisher), *The BBC: An Outline of its History, Organisation and Policy*, London, 1982.

BBC (publisher), *Annual Review of BBC Broadcasting Research findings*, London, annually.

Bennett, T. et al., *Popular Television and Film*, London, BFI Publications, 1981.

Brandt, G., *British Television Drama*, Cambridge, Cambridge University Press, 1981.

Bridson, D. G., *Prospero and Ariel: The Rise and Fall of Radio*, London, Gollancz, 1971.

Briggs, A., *History of Broadcasting in the United Kingdom*, 3 vols, London, Oxford University Press, 1961–79.

Briggs, A., *Governing the BBC*, London, BBC, 1979.

Briggs, A., *The BBC: The First Fifty Years*, London, Oxford University Press, 1985.

Briggs, A. and Spicer, J., *The Franchise Affair: Creating Fortunes and Failures in Independent Television*, London, Century, 1986.

Central Office of Information, *Broadcasting in Britain*, London, HMSO, 1981.

Central Office of Information, *Broadcasting in Britain*, London, HMSO, 1982.

Coe, J. and Blanchard, S., *Capital: Local Radio and Private Profit*, London, Comedia Publishing, 1983.

Comedia Publishing Group (publisher), *Radio, Commerce and Democracy: A Critique of British Radio and Strategies for the Future*, London, 1982.

Committee on the Future of Broadcasting, *Report*, Cmnd. 6753, London, HMSO, 1977.

Cox, G., *See it Happen: The Making of ITN*, London, Bodley Head, 1983.

Curran, C., *A Seamless Robe: Broadcasting Philosophy and Practice*, London, Bodley Head, 1979.

Drakakis, J., *Reading Radio*, London, Methuen, 1984.

Drakakis, J. (ed.), *British Radio Drama*, Cambridge, Cambridge University Press, 1981.

Drinkwater, J., *Get it On . . . Radio and Television*, London, Pluto, 1984.

Dunkley, C., *Television Today and Tomorrow: Wall-to-Wall Dallas*, Harmondsworth, Penguin, 1985.

Fiske, J. and Hartley, J., *Reading Television*, London, Methuen, 1978.

Gifford, D., *The Golden Age of Radio*, London, Batsford, 1985.

Goldie, G. W., *Facing the Nation: Television and Politics, 1936–76*, London, Bodley Head, 1977.

Goodhart, G. J. et al., *The Television Audience: Patterns of Viewing*, Farnborough, Saxon House, 1974.

Hall, S., *Reproducing Ideologies*, London, Macmillan, 1984.

Halliwell, L. and Purser, P., *Halliwell's Television Companion*, Glasgow, Collins, 1985.

Halloran, J., *The Effects of Television*, London, Panther, 1970.

Hoggart, R. and Morgan, J., *The Future of Broadcasting*, London, Macmillan, 1982.

Hood, S., *On Television*, London, Pluto, 1983.

Howard, G., *BBC Educational Broadcasting and the Future*, London, BBC, 1981.

Hunt, A., *The Language of Television: Uses and Abuses*, London, Methuen, 1981.

ITV Books (publisher), *25 Years on ITV, 1955–80*, London, 1980.

Lambert, S., *Channel Four: Television with a Difference?*, London, BFI Publications, 1982.

Lewis, P. (ed.), *Radio Drama*, London, Longman, 1981.

Lewis, P. M., *Community TV and Cable in Britain*, London, BFI, 1978.

Lusted, D. and Drummond, P. (eds), *Television and Schooling*, London, BFI, 1985.

Mansell, G., *Let Truth Be Told: 50 Years of BBC External Broadcasting*, London, Weidenfeld and Nicolson, 1982.

Masterman, L., *Teaching about Television*, London, Macmillan, 1980.

Masterman, L. (ed.), *Television*

Mythologies, Stars, Shows and Signs, London, Comedia, 1984.

Morley, D., *Watching Television: Cultural Power and Domestic Leisure*, London, Comedia, 1986.

Munro, C., *Television, Censorship and the Law*, Farnborough, Saxon House, 1979.

Norman, B., *Here's Looking at You: The Story of British Television, 1908–39*, London, BBC, 1984.

Parker, D., *Radio: The Great Years*, Newton Abbot, David and Charles, 1977.

Partridge, S., *Not the BBC/ITA: the Case for Community Radio*, London, Comedia Publishing, 1981.

Paulu, B., *Television and Radio in the United Kingdom*, London and Minneapolis, University of Minnesota Press, 1981.

Pegg, M., *Broadcasting and Society, 1918–1938*, London, Croom Helm, 1983.

Piepe, A. et al., *Television and the Working Class*, Farnborough, Saxon House, 1975.

Pike, F. (ed.), *Ah! Mischief: the Writer and Television*, London, Faber, 1982.

Schlesinger, P., *Putting 'Reality' Together: BBC News*, London, Constable, 1978.

Sendall, B., *The History of Independent Television in Britain*, 3 vols, London, Macmillan, 1982–4.

Shubik, L., *Play for Today: the Evolution of Television Drama*, London, Davis Poynter, 1975.

Smith, A., *The Shadow in the Cave: A Study of the Relationship between the Broadcaster and his Audience and the State*, London, Allen and Unwin, 1973.

Smith, A. (ed.), *British Broadcasting*, Newton Abbot, David and Charles, 1974.

Sutton, S., *The Largest Theatre in the World: Thirty Years of Television Drama*, London, BBC, 1982.

Tinker, J., *The Television Barons*, London, Quartet Books, 1980.

Took, B., *Laughter in the Air: An Informal History of British Radio*

Comedy, London, BBC, 1982.
Tracey, M., *The Production of Political Television*, London, Routledge & Kegan Paul, 1977.
Weddell, E. G. (ed.), *Structures of Broadcasting*, Manchester, Manchester University Press, 1970.
Wenham, E. (ed.), *The Third Age of Broadcasting*, London, Faber, 1982.

Williams, R., *Television: Technology and Cultural Forms*, London, Fontana, 1974.
Windelsham, Lord, *Broadcasting in a Free Society*, Oxford, Blackwell, 1980.
Wyndham-Goldie, G., *Facing the Nation: TV and Politics 1936–76*, London, Bodley Head, 1977.

CINEMA

Adair, G. and Roddick, N., *A Night at the Pictures: Ten Decades of British Film*, London, Columbus Books, 1985.
Armes, R., *A Critical History of the British Cinema*, London, Secker and Warburg, 1978.
Atwell, D., *Cathedrals of the Movies: A History of British Cinemas and Their Audiences*, London, Architectural Press, 1980.
Auty, M. and Roddick, N. (eds), *British Cinema Now*, London, BFI, 1983.
Barnes, J., *The Beginning of Cinema in England*, Newton Abbot, David and Charles, 1976.
Barr, C., *Ealing Studios*, Newton Abbot, David and Charles, 1980.
Betts, E., *The Film Business: History of the British Cinema, 1896–1972*, London, Allen and Unwin, 1973.
Channan, M., *The Dream that Kicks: The Prehistory and the Early History of Cinema in Britain*, London, Routledge & Kegan Paul, 1980.
Comedia Publishing (publisher), *Independent Film: Can It Survive?*, London, 1980.
Cross, R., *The Big Book of British Films*, London, Sidgwick and Jackson, 1984.
Curran, J. and Porter, V. (eds), *British Cinema History*, London, Weidenfeld and Nicolson, 1983.
Dickinson, M. and Street, S., *Cinema and State: The Film Industry and the British Government, 1927–84*, London, BFI, 1985.
Durgnat, R., *A Mirror for England: British Movies from Austerity to Affluence*, London, Faber, 1970.
Gledhill, C. (ed.), *Film Media Studies in Higher Education*, London, BFI, 1981.

Low, R., *The History of the British Film*, 8 vols, London, Allen and Unwin, 1948–86.
Lusted, D. (ed.), *Guide to Film Studies in Secondary and Further Education*, London, BFI, 1983.
Macpherson, D. (ed.), *Traditions of Independence: British Cinema in the Thirties*, London, BFI, 1980.
Manvell, R., *New Cinema in Britain*, London, Studio Vista, 1969.
Park, J., *Learning to Dream: The New British Cinema*, London, Faber, 1984.
Perry, G., *The Great British Picture Show: From the Nineties to the Seventies*, London, Paladin, 1975.
Perry, G., *Movies From the Mansion: A History of Pinewood Studios*, London, Pavilion, 1986.
Perry, G., *Forever Ealing*, London, Michael Joseph, 1985.
Pettigrew, T., *British Film Character Actors*, Newton Abbot, David and Charles, 1985.
Quinlan, D., *British Sound Films: The Studio Years, 1928–1959*, London, Batsford, 1984.
Richards, J., *The Age of the Dream Palace: Cinema and Society in Britain, 1930–1939*, London, Routledge & Kegan Paul, 1984.
Richards, J. and Aldgate, A., *The Best of British: Cinema and Society, 1930–1970*, Oxford, Blackwell, 1983.
Robertson, J., *The British Board of Censors: A History*, London, Croom Helm, 1984.
Sussex, E., *The Rise and Fall of the British Documentary*, Berkeley,

University of California Press, 1976.

Taylor, J. R. (ed.), *Masterworks of the British Cinema*, London, Lorrimer, 1974.

Walker, A., *Hollywood, England: The British Film Industry in the Sixties*, London, Michael Joseph, 1974.

Walker, A., *National Heroes: British Cinema in the Seventies and Eighties*, London, Harrap, 1985.

Walker, J., *The Once and Future Film*, London, Methuen, 1985.

Warren, P., *Elstree: The British Hollywood*, London, Elm Tree, 1984.

Williams, B. (ed.), *Obscenity and Film Censorship: An Abridgement of the Williams Report*, Cambridge, Cambridge University Press, 1983.

Wood, L., *British Film, 1971–1981*, London, BFI, 1984.

PRESS

Arnott-Job, P., *The Magazine and Newspaper Distribution Industry*, London, Comediaa, 1986.

Aspinall, A., *Politics and the Press, 1780–1850*, Hassocks, Harvester, 1973.

Aubrey, C. et al., *Here is the Other News: Challenges to the Local Commercial Press*, London, Comedia, 1980.

Bainbridge, C. (ed.), *One Hundred Years of Journalism: Social Aspects of the Press*, London, Macmillan, 1984.

Berry, D. et al., *Where is the Other News? The News Trade and the Radical Press*, London, Comedia, 1980.

Boyce, G. et al. (eds), *Newspaper History from the Seventeenth Century to the Present Day*, London, Constable, 1978.

Central Office of Information, *The British Press*, London, HMSO, 1976.

Cleverly, G., *The Fleet Street Disaster: British National Newspapers as a Case Study in Mismanagement*, London, Constable, 1976.

Cockerell, M., *Sources Close to the Prime Minister*, London, Macmillan, 1985.

Comedia Publishing Group, *Where is the Other News? The Newstrade and the Radical Press*, London, 1980.

Cranfield, G. A., *The Press and Society: From Caxton to Northcliffe*, London, Longman, 1978.

Curran, J., *The British Press: A Manifesto*, London, Macmillan, 1978.

Gordon, D. and Horsch, F., *Newspaper Money: Fleet Street and the Search for the Affluent Reader*, London, Hutchinson, 1975.

Hattersley, R., *The Press Gang*, London, Robson, 1983.

Jackson, I., *The Provincial Press and the Community*, Manchester, Manchester University Press, 1971.

Jenkins, S., *Newspapers: The Power and the Money*, London, Faber, 1979.

Koss, S., *The Rise and Fall of the Political Press in Britain*, 2 vols, London, Hamish Hamilton, 1981–4.

Lee, A. J., *The Origins of the Popular Press in England, 1855–1914*, London, Croom Helm, 1976.

Lloyd, H., *The Legal Limits of Journalism*, Oxford, Pergamon Press, 1968.

McNae, L. C. J., *Essential Law for Journalists*, London, Lockwood, 1975.

Marshall, A., *Changing the Word: The Printing Industry in Transition*, London, Comedia, 1983.

Morrison, J., *The Media Men*, London, Batsford, 1978.

Murphy, D., *The Silent Watchdog: The Press in Local Politics*, London, Constable, 1976.

Press Council, *Annual Report*, London, annually.

Royal Commission on the Press, *Final Report*, Cmnd. 6810–I, London, HMSO, 1977.

Royal Commission on the Press, *Analysis of Newspaper Content*, by D. McQuail, Cmnd. 6810–4, London, HMSO, 1977.

Smith, A. (ed.), *The British Press since*

the War, Newton Abbot, David and Charles, 1974.

Smith, A. C. H. et al., *Paper Voices: The Popular Press and Social Change*, London, Chatto and Windus, 1975.

Tunstall, J., *The Westminster Lobby Correspondents*, London, Routledge & Kegan Paul, 1970.

Tunstall, J., *Journalists at Work*, London, Constable, 1971.

Whale, J., *Journalism and Government*, London, Macmillan, 1972.

White, C., *Women's Magazines*, London, Michael Joseph, 1970.

White, C., *The Women's Periodical Press in Britain, 1946–1976*, London, HMSO, 1977.

Whitaker, B., *News Ltd. Why You Can't Read all about it*, London, Comedia Publishing, 1981.

Williams, F., *Dangerous Estate: The Anatomy of Newspapers*, London, Longman, 1957.

Woods, O. and Bishop, J., *The Story of the Times*, London, Michael Joseph, 1985.

SEE ALSO:

27   Popular Culture

18 MILITARY

Detailed bibliographical and research references on the military and military policy, including military history, are provided in: Albrecht, U. et al. (eds), *A Short Research Guide on Arms and Armed Forces*, 1981; Bruce, A. P. C., *An Annotated Bibliography of the British Army*, 1975–; Higham, R. (ed.), *A Guide to the Sources of British Military History*, 1972; Ministry of Defence, *Bibliography of the Royal Air Force*, 4 vols, 1977.

For bibliographical guides to disarmament see Burns, R. D., *Arms Control and Disarmament: A Bibliography*, 1978; Lloyd, L. and Sims, N. A., *British Writing on Disarmament from 1914 to 1978: A Bibliography*, 1979.

References to current publications can be found in British Library of Economic and Political Science, *A London Bibliography of the Social Sciences*, annually.

Information on strategic, political, organisational and technical questions concerned with the military can be found in: Goodhart, Rear Admiral N. (ed.), *British Defence Directory*, annually; Royal United Services Institute/Brassey's, *Defence Year Book*, annually; International Institute for Strategic Studies, *The Military Balance*, annually, SIPRI, *Yearbook of World Armaments and Disarmament*, annually; Wilson A., *The Disarmer's Handbook of Military Technology and Organisation*, 1984.

For surveys and discussions of British policy on defence see: Central Office of Information, *Britain and NATO: Thirty Years of Collective Defence*, 1979; Central Office of Information, *Arms Control and Disarmament*, 1978; Her Majesty's Stationery Office, *United Kingdom Defence Programme: The Way Forward*, 1981; Freedman, L., *The Evolution of Nuclear Strategy*, 1981; George, B. and Coughlin, M., *British Defence Policy and Decision-Making*, 1983; Groom, A. J. R., *British Thinking about Nuclear Weapons*, 1974; Greenwood, D. and Drake, J., *The United Kingdom's Current Defence Programme and Budget*, 1980; Simpson, J., *The Independent Nuclear State: The United States, Britain and the Military Atom*, 1983; Smart, I., *The Future of the British Nuclear Deterrent: Technical, Economic, and Strategic Issues*, 1977.

For the debate on nuclear weapons and disarmament readers should also consult: Clarke, M. and Mowlam, M. (eds), *The Debate on Disarmament*, 1982; McMahan, J., *British Nuclear Weapons: For and Against*, 1984; Ryle, M. H., *The Politics of Nuclear Disarmament*, 1984; Thompson, E. P. and Smith, D., *Protest and Survive*, 1980.

Surveys of British military history can be found in the following: Barnett, C., *Britain and her Army, 1509–1970*, 1970; Bartlett, C. J., *The Long Retreat: A Short History of British Defence Policy, 1945–70*, 1972; Fortescue, J. W., *A History of the British Army*, 13 vols, 1899–1930; Haswell, J., *The British Army: A Concise History*, 1975; James, W. M., *A Naval History of Great Britain*, 1971; Lewis, M. A., *The History of the British Navy*, 1959; Warner, O., *The British Navy: A Concise History*, 1975; Young, P., *The British Army, 1642–1970*, 1967.

REFERENCE

Albrecht, U. et al. (eds), *A Short Research Guide on Arms and Insurgency*, London, Croom Helm, 1979.

British Library of Economic and Political Science, *A London Bibliography of the Social Sciences*, London and New York, Mansell, annually.

Bruce, A., *Bibliography of British Military History: From the Roman Invasion to the Restoration*, London, Saur, 1981.

Bruce, A. (ed.), *Bibliography of the British Army, 1660–1914*, London, Saur, 1985.

Burns, R. D., *Arms Control and Disarmament: A Bibliography*, Oxford, Clio Press, 1978.

Dupuy, T. N. and Ropp, T. (eds), *Guide to Research Sources in Military History*, New York, Bowker, 1977.

Enser, A. G. S. (ed.), *A Subject Bibliography of the First World War: Books in English 1914–1978*, Aldershot, Gower, 1979.

Enser, A. G. S. (ed.), *A Subject Bibliography of the Second World War: Books in English 1939–1974*, Aldershot, Gower, 1977.

Enser, A. G. S. (ed.), *A Subject Bibliography of the Second World War: Books in English 1975–1983*, Aldershot, Gower, 1984.

Gander, T., *Encyclopaedia of the Modern British Army*, Cambridge, National and Aviation, 1981.

Gander, T. (ed.), *Encyclopaedia of the Modern Royal Air Force*, Cambridge, Stephens, 1984.

Goodhart, Rear Admiral N. (ed.), *British Defence Directory*, Oxford, Brassey's, annually.

Gordon, C., *The Atlantic Alliance: A Bibliography*, London, Pinter, 1978.

Her Majesty's Stationery Office, *The Second World War: A Guide to Documents in the Public Records Office*, London, 1972.

Higham, R. (ed.), *A Guide to the Sources of British Military History*, London, Routledge & Kegan Paul, 1972.

Lloyd, L. and Sims, N. A., *British Writing on Disarmament from 1914 to 1978: A Bibliography*, London, Pinter, 1979.

Ministry of Defence, *Bibliography of the Royal Air Force*, 4 vols, HMSO, 1977.

Royal United Services Institute and Brassey's, *Defence Year Book*, Oxford, annually.

Scott, B. K. C., *Dictionary of Military Abbreviations*, Hastings, Tamarisk Books, 1982.

SIPRI, *Yearbook of World Armaments and Disarmament*, Stockholm, annually.

Wilson, A., *The Disarmer's Handbook of Military Technology and Organisation*, Harmondsworth, Penguin, 1984.

Windrow, M. and Mason, F. K. (eds), *A Concise Dictionary of Military Biography*, Reading, Osprey, 1975.

GENERAL

Ascoli, D., *A Companion to the British Army, 1660–1983*, London, Harrap, 1983.

Barker, D., *Soldiering On: An Unofficial Portrait of the British Army*, London, Deutsch, 1981.

Barnett, A., *Iron Britannia: Why Parliament Waged its Falklands War*, London, Allison and Busby, 1982.

Barnett, C., *The Collapse of British Power*, London, Methuen, 1972.

Bartlett, C. J., *The Long Retreat: A Short History of British Defence Policy, 1945–70*, London, Macmillan, 1972.

Baylis, J., *British Defence Policy in a Changing World*, London, Croom Helm, 1977.

Baylis, J., *Alternative Approaches to British Defence Policy*, London, Macmillan, 1983.

Baylis, J., *Anglo-American Defence Relations, 1939–1984: The Special*

Relationship, London, Macmillan, 1984.

Baynes, J. C. M., *The Soldier in Modern Society*, London, Eyre and Spottiswoode, 1971.

Beckett, I. and Gooch, J., *Politicans and Defence: Studies in the Formation of British Defence Policy, 1945–1970*, Manchester, Manchester University Press, 1981.

Blaxland, G., *The Regiments Depart: A History of the British Army, 1945–1970*, London, Kimber, 1971.

Burton, J. et al., *Britain Between East and West: A Concerned Independence*, Aldershot, Gower, 1984.

Cable, J., *Britain's Naval Future*, London, Macmillan, 1983.

Calvert, P., *The Falklands Crisis: The Rights and the Wrongs*, London, Pinter, 1982.

Ceadel, M., *Pacifism in Britain, 1914–1945: The Defining of a Faith*, Oxford, Oxford University Press, 1980.

Central Office of Information, *Arms Control and Disarmament*, London, HMSO, 1979.

Central Office of Information, *Britain and NATO: Thirty Years of Collective Defence*, London, HMSO, 1979.

Chalmers, M., *The Cost of Britain's Defence, Peace Studies Papers no. 10*, London, Housmans, 1983.

Chalmers, M., *Paying for Defence: Military Spending and British Decline*, London, Pluto, 1985.

Chant, C. (ed.), *Armed Forces in the UK*, Newton Abbot, David and Charles, 1980.

Chichester, M. and Wilkinson, J., *The Uncertain Ally: British Defence Policy, 1960–1980*, Aldershot, Gower Publishing, 1982.

Coker, C., *A Nation in Retreat? Britain's Defence Commitment*, London, Brasseys, 1986.

Coll, A. R. and Arend, A. C. (eds), *The Falklands War: Lessons For Strategy, Diplomacy and International Law*, London, Allen and Unwin, 1985.

Council for Science and Society, *UK Military R & D: Report of a Working Party*, London, Oxford University Press, 1986.

Darby, P., *British Defence Policy East of Suez, 1947–68*, London, Oxford University Press, 1973.

Freedman, L., *Arms Production in the United Kingdom: Problems and Prospects*, London, Routledge & Kegan Paul, 1978.

George, B. and Coughlin, M., *British Defence Policy and Decision-Making*, Aldershot, Gower, 1983.

Greenwood, D. and Drake, J., *The United Kingdom's Current Defence Programme and Budget*, Aberdeen, Aberdeen University Press, 1980.

Hampshire, A. C., *The Royal Navy since 1945: Its Transition to the Nuclear Age*, London, Kimber, 1975.

Hastings, M. and Jenkins, S., *The Battle for the Falklands*, London, Michael Joseph, 1983.

Her Majesty's Stationery Office, *United Kingdom Defence Programme: The Way Forward*, London, 1981.

Hill, J. R., *The Royal Navy Today and Tomorrow*, Shepperton, Allan, 1981.

Hobkirk, M. D., *The Politics of Defence Budgeting: A Study of Organisation and Resource Allocation in the UK and USA*, London, Macmillan, 1984.

Hooper, A., *The Military and the Media*, Aldershot, Gower, 1982.

Howard, M., *The British Way in Warfare: A Reappraisal*, London, Cape, 1975.

Howard, M. E., *The Continental Commitment: The Dilemma of British Defence Policy in the Era of Two World Wars*, Harmondsworth, Penguin, 1974.

International Institute for Strategic Studies (publisher), *The Military Balance*, London, annually.

International Institute for Strategic Studies (publisher), *Strategic Survey*, London, annually.

Johnson, F. A., *Defence By Ministry: The British Ministry of Defence, 1944–1974*, London, Duckworth, 1980.

Kaldor, M., *The Baroque Arsenal*, London, Deutsch, 1982.

Kaldor, M. et al., *Democratic Socialism and the Cost of Defence: The Report and Papers of the Labour Party Defence Study Group*, London, Labour Party, 1979.

Lane, P., *The Army*, London, Batsford, 1975.

Lider, J., *British Military Thought after World War II*, Aldershot, Gower Publishing, 1985.

Mason, R. A., *The Royal Air Force Today and Tomorrow*, Shepperton, Allan, 1982.

Parker, T., *Soldier, Soldier*, London, Heinemann, 1985.

Rodger, N. A. M., *The Admiralty*, Sudbury, Dalton, 1979.

Roper, J. (ed.), *The Future of British Defence Policy*, Aldershot, Gower, 1985.

Schofield, B. B., *British Sea Power: Naval Policy in the Twentieth Century*, London, Batsford, 1967.

Stanhope, H., *The Soldiers: An Anatomy of the British Army*, London, Hamish Hamilton, 1979.

Taylor, R. and Pritchard, C., *The Protest Makers: The British Nuclear Disarmament Movement of 1958–65, Twenty Years On*, Oxford, Pergamon, 1980.

Wyllie, J. H., *The Influence of British Arms: An Analysis of British Military Intervention since 1956*, London, Allen and Unwin, 1984.

NUCLEAR DETERRENT

Alternative Defence Commission, *Defence without the Bomb: The Report*, London, Taylor and Francis, 1983.

Blakeway, D. and Lloyd-Roberts, S., *Fields of Thunder: Testing Britain's Bomb*, London, Allen and Unwin, 1985.

Buteux, P., *The Politics of Nuclear Consultation in NATO, 1965–1980*, Cambridge, Cambridge University Press, 1983.

Campbell, D., *War Plan UK: The Truth About Civil Defence in Britain*, London, Hutchinson, 1982.

Clarke, M., *The Nuclear Destruction of Britain*, London, Croom Helm, 1982.

Clarke, M. and Mowlam, M. (eds), *The Debate on Disarmament*, London, Routledge & Kegan Paul, 1982.

Dillon, G. M., *Dependence and Deterrence*, Aldershot, Gower, 1983.

Freedman, L., *Britain and Nuclear Weapons*, London, Macmillan, 1980.

Freedman, L., *The Evolution of Nuclear Strategy*, London, Macmillan, 1981.

Gowing, M. and Arnold, L., *Independence and Deterrence: Britain and Atomic Energy, 1945–1951*, 2 vols, London, Macmillan, 1974.

Groom, A. J. R., *British Thinking about Nuclear Weapons*, London, Frances Pinter, 1974.

Kaldor, M. and Smith, D. (eds), *Disarming Europe*, London, Merlin Press, 1982.

Kennard, P. and Sissons, R., *No Nuclear Weapons*, London, Pluto, 1981.

McLean, S. (ed.), *How Nuclear Weapons Decisions Are Made*, London, Macmillan, 1986.

McMahan, J., *British Nuclear Weapons: For and Against*, London, Fourth Estate, 1981.

Malone, P., *The British Nuclear Deterrent: A History*, London, Croom Helm, 1984.

Minnion, J. and Bolsover, P., *The CND Story*, London, Allison and Busby, 1983.

Openshaw, S. et al., *Doomsday: Britain after Nuclear Attack*, Oxford, Blackwell, 1983.

Prins, G. (ed.), *Defend to Death: A Study of the Nuclear Arms Race*, Harmondsworth, Penguin, 1983.

Prins, G. (ed.), *The Choice: Nuclear Weapons versus Security*, London, Chatto and Windus, 1984.

Rumble, G., *The Politics of Nuclear Defence*, Cambridge, Polity Press, 1985.

Ryle, M. H., *The Politics of Nuclear Disarmament*, London, Pluto Press, 1981.

Simpson, J., *The Independent Nuclear State: The United States, Britain and the Military Atom*, London, Macmillan, 1983.

Smart, I., *The Future of the British Nuclear Deterrent: Technical, Economic and Strategic Issues*, London, Routledge & Kegan Paul, 1977.

Smith, D., *The Defence of the Realm in the 1980's*, London, Croom Helm, 1981.

Taylor, R. and Pritchard, G., *The Protest Makers: The British Nuclear Disarmament Movement of 1958–1965 Twenty Years on*, Oxford, Pergamon Press, 1980.

Thompson, E. P. et al., *Britain and the Bomb*, London, New Statesman, 1981.

Thompson, E. P. and Smith, D., *Protest and Survive*, Harmondsworth, Penguin, 1980.

Williams, R., *The Nuclear Power Decisions: British Policies, 1952–1978*, London, Croom Helm, 1980.

Zuckermann, S., *Nuclear Illusion and Reality*, London, Collins, 1982.

MILITARY HISTORY

Barnett, C., *Britain and Her Army, 1509–1970*, London, Allen Lane, 1970.

Beckett, I. F. W. and Simpson, K. (eds), *A Nation in Arms: A Social Study of the British Army in the First World War*, Manchester, Manchester University Press, 1985.

Bond, B., *British Military Policy Between the Two World Wars*, London, Oxford University Press, 1980.

Brereton, J. M., *The British Soldier: A Social History from 1661 to the Present Day*, London, Bodley Head, 1986.

Carver, Lord, *The Seven Ages of the British Army*, London, Weidenfeld and Nicolson, 1984.

Ceadel, M., *Pacifism in Britain, 1914–1945*, London, Oxford University Press, 1980.

Churchill, W. S., *The Second World War*, 6 vols, Cassell, London, 1945–54.

Clark, G., *Britain's Naval Heritage*, London, HMSO, 1981.

Craig, R. S. (ed.), *Maritime History*, 2 vols, Newton Abbot, David and Charles, 1973.

Fortescue, J. W., *A History of the British Army*, 13 vols, London, Macmillan, 1899–1930.

Gooch, J., *The Prospect of War: British Defence Policy, 1847–1942*, London, Cass, 1981.

Harries-Jenkins, G., *The Army in Victorian Society*, London, Routledge & Kegan Paul, 1977.

Hart, B. H. L., *History of the First World War*, London, Pan, 1972.

Hart, B. H. L., *History of the Second World War*, London, Pan, 1973.

Haswell, J., *The British Army: A Concise History*, London, Thames and Hudson, 1975.

James, W. M., *A Naval History of Great Britain*, London, Conway Maritime, 1971.

Kemp, P. K. (ed.), *The History of the Royal Navy*, London, Barker, 1969.

Kennedy, P. M., *The Rise and Fall of British Naval Mastery*, London, Allen Lane, 1976.

Laffin, J., *Tommy Atkins: The Story of the English Soldier*, London, Cassell, 1966.

Lewis, M. A., *The History of the British Navy*, London, Allen and Unwin, 1959.

Luvaas, J., *The Education of an Army: British Military Thought, 1815–1940*, London, Cassell, 1965.

Marcus, G. J., *A Naval History of England*, 2 vols, London, Allen and Unwin, 1961–71.

Marwick, A., *The Deluge: British Society and the First World War*, London, Macmillan, 1973.

Marwick, A., *Home Front: The British and the Second World War*, London, Thames and Hudson, 1978.

Padfield, P., *Rule Britannia: The Victorian and Edwardian Navy*, London, Routledge & Kegan Paul, 1981.

Rothwell, V. H., *British War Aims and Peace Diplomacy, 1914–1918*, Oxford, Oxford University Press, 1971.

Seymour, W., *Battles in Britain and the Political Background*, 2 vols, London, Sidgwick and Jackson, 1979.

Sims, C., *The Royal Air Force: The First Fifty Years*, London, Black, 1968.

Spiers, E. M., *The Army and Society, 1815–1914*, London, Longman, 1980.

Stokesbury, J. L., *Navy and Empire: A Short History of British Sea Power from the Armada to the Falklands*, London, Hale, 1984.

Till, G., *Air Power and the Royal Navy, 1914–45: A Historical Survey*, London, Janes, 1979.

Warner, O., *The British Navy: A Concise History*, London, Thames and Hudson, 1975.

Young, P., *The British Army, 1642–1970*, London, Kimber, 1967.

19 MINORITIES

For bibliographical coverage of minorities in Britain readers should refer to: British Library of Economic and Political Science, *A London Bibliography of the Social Sciences*, annually; Madan, R. (comp.), *Coloured Minorities in Great Britain: A Comprehensive Bibliography, 1970–77*, 1979; Tomlinson, S., *Ethnic Minorities in British Schools: A Review of the Literature, 1960–1982*, 1984.

Outline guides to the situation of ethnic minorities and race relations in Britain are given in the following government publications: Central Office of Information, *Britain's Ethnic Minorities*, 1982; Central Office of Information, *Race Relations in Britain*, 1977.

The following are recommended as introductory reading to the problems of race relations and racial discrimination in Britain: Deakin, N., *Colour, Citizenship and British Society*, 1980; Her Majesty's Stationery Office, *Racial Disadvantage: Fifth Report from the Home Affairs Committee of the House of Commons*, 1981; Pilkington, A., *Race Relations in Britain*, 1984; Runnymede Trust, *Britain's Black Population*, 1980; Smith, D. J., *Facts of Racial Disadvantage*, 1976.

REFERENCE

British Library of Economic and Political Science, *A London Bibliography of the Social Sciences*, London and New York, Mansell, annually.

Cashmore, E. E., *A Dictionary of Race and Ethnic Relations*, London, Routledge & Kegan Paul, 1985.

Commission for Racial Equality, *Annual Report*, London, HMSO, annually.

Commission for Racial Equality, *Ethnic Minorities in Britain: Statistical Background*, London, 1980.

Her Majesty's Stationery Office, *Race Relations Act 1976*, London, 1976.

Her Majesty's Stationery Office, *Immigration Act 1971*, London, 1971.

Institute of Race Relations, *Race Relations Abstracts*, London, irregular.

Madan, R. (comp.), *Coloured Minorities in Great Britain: A Comprehensive Bibliography, 1970–77*, London, Aldwych Press, 1979.

Tomlinson, S., *Ethnic Minorities in British Schools: A Review of the Literature, 1960–82*, Aldershot, Gower, 1984.

GENERAL

Abrahams, Z., *The Jews in England*, London, Mitchell Vallentine, 1984.

Adams, B. et al., *Gypsies and Government Policy in England*, London, Heinemann, 1975.

Banton, M. P., *Racial Minorities*, London, Fontana, 1967.

Batley, R. and Edwards, J., *The Politics of Positive Discrimination*, London, Tavistock, 1978.

Berghahn, M., *German Jewish Refugees in England: The Ambiguities of Assimilation*, London, Macmillan, 1984.

Bowker, G. and Carrier, J. (eds), *Race and Ethnic Relations: Sociological*

Readings, London, Hutchinson, 1976.

Brown, C., *Black and White Britain*, Aldershot, Gower, 1985.

Central Office of Information, *Britain's Ethnic Minorities*, London, HMSO, 1982.

Centre for Contemporary Cultural Studies, *The Empire Strikes Back: Race and Racism in 70's Britain*, London, Hutchinson, 1982.

Choo, N. K., *The Chinese in London*, London, Oxford University Press, 1968.

Cohen, P. and Gardner, C. (eds), *It Ain't Half Racist Mum: Fighting Racism in the Media*, London, Comedia, 1982.

Coleman, D. A. (ed.), *Demography of Immigrants and Minority Groups in the United Kingdom*, London, Academic Press, 1982.

Commission for Racial Equality, *Five Views of Multi-Racial Britain*, London, HMSO, 1978.

Commission for Racial Equality, *Youth in a Multi-Racial Society*, London, HMSO, 1980.

Commission for Racial Equality, *Multi-Racial Britain: The Social Services Response*, London, HMSO, 1982.

Committee of Inquiry into the Education of Children from Minority Groups, *Report*, Cmnd. 1453, London, HMSO, 1985.

Crane, P., *Gays and the Law*, London, Pluto, 1984.

Daniel, W. W., *Racial Discrimination in England*, Harmondsworth, Penguin, 1968.

Deakin, N., *Colour, Citizenship and British Society*, London, Panther, 1980.

Department of Education and Science, *Education For All*, Cmnd 9453, HMSO, 1985.

Field, S., *The Attitudes of Ethnic Minorities*, London, HMSO, 1984.

Fryer, P., *Staying Power: The History of Black People in Britain*, London, Pluto, 1984.

Galloway, B. (ed.), *Prejudice and Pride: Discrimination Against Gay People in Modern Britain*, London, Routledge & Kegan Paul, 1984.

Gould, S. J. and Esh, S. (eds), *Jewish Life in Modern Britain*, London, Routledge & Kegan Paul, 1964.

Gower (publisher), *Race and Riots: New Society Social Studies Reader*, Aldershot, 1985.

Gower (publisher), *Race and Ethnicity: New Society Social Studies Reader*, Aldershot, 1985.

Helweg, A. W., *Sikhs in England: The Development of a Migrant Community*, London, Oxford University Press, 1979.

Her Majesty's Stationery Office, *Racial Discrimination: A Guide to the Race Relations Act 1976*, London, 1977.

Her Majesty's Stationery Office, *Race Relations in Britain*, London, HMSO, 1977.

Her Majesty's Stationery Office, *Racial Disadvantage, Fifth Report from the Home Affairs Committee of the House of Commons*, London. 1981.

Husband, C. (ed.), *White Media and Black Britain*, London, Arrow Books, 1977.

Jackson, J. A., *The Irish in Britain*, London, Routledge & Kegan Paul, 1963.

Jones, C., *Immigration and Social Policy in Britain*, London, Tavistock, 1977.

Khan, V. S. (ed.)., *Minority Families in Britain: Support and Stress*, London, Macmillan, 1979.

Lee, T. R., *Race and Residence: The Concentration and Dispersal of Immigrants in London*, Oxford, Oxford University Press, 1977.

Lipman, V. D., *Social History of the Jews in England 1850–1950*, London, Watts, 1954.

Macdonald, I. A., *Race Relations: The New Law*, London, Butterworth, 1977.

McIntosh, N. and Smith, D. J., *The Extent of Racial Discrimination*, London, PEP, 1974.

Miles, R. and Phizacklea, A. (eds), *Racism and Political Action in Britain*, London, Routledge & Kegan Paul, 1979.

Miles, R. and Phizacklea, A., *White Man's Country: Racism in Britain*,

London, Pluto, 1984.

Milner, D., *Children and Race*, Harmondsworth, Penguin, 1976.

Moore, P., *Racism and Black Resistance in Britain*, London, Pluto, 1975.

Nixon, J., *A Teacher's Guide to Multicultural Education*, Oxford, Blackwell, 1985.

Parekh, B. (ed.), *Colour, Culture and Consciousness—Immigrant Intellectuals in Britain*, London, Allen and Unwin, 1974.

Pilkington, A., *Race Relations in Britain*, Slough, University Tutorial Press, 1984.

Poulter, S., *English Law and Ethnic Minority Customs*, London, Butterworth, 1986.

Ramdin, R., *The Making of the Black Working Class in Britain*, Aldershot, Gower, 1985.

Rigby, A., *Communes in Britain*, London, Routledge & Kegan Paul, 1974.

Roth, C., *A History of the Jews in England*, Oxford, Clarendon Press, 1964.

Runnymede Trust, *Britain's Black Population*, London, Heinemann, 1980.

Sandford, J., *Gypsies*, London, Secker and Warburg, 1973.

Smith, D. J., *Facts of Racial Disadvantage: A National Survey*, London, PEP, 1976.

Smith, D. J., *Racial Disadvantage in Employment*, London, Penguin, 1977.

Tomlinson, S., *Ethnic Minorities in British Schools: A Review of the Literature, 1960–1982*, London, Heinemann, 1984.

Walvin, J., *Passage to Britain: A Nation and Her Immigrants*, Harmondsworth, Penguin, 1984.

Watson, J. L. (ed.), *Between two Cultures: Migrants and Minorities in Britain*, Oxford, Blackwell, 1977.

20 MONARCHY

The following serves as a brief official introduction to the constitutional position of the monarchy in Britain: Central Office of Information, *The Monarchy in Britain*, 1981.

The following studies discuss contemporary issues and constitutional questions relating to the monarchy: Benemy, F. W. G., *The Queen Reigns, She Does Not Rule*, 1963; Duncan, A., *The Reality of Monarchy*, 1976; Howard, P., *The British Monarchy in the Twentieth Century*, 1977; Murray-Brown, J. (ed.), *The Monarchy and its Future*, 1969; Packard, J. M., *A Guide to the British Monarchy Today*, 1981; Petrie, C., *The Modern British Monarchy*, 1961; Thompson, J. A. and Mejia, A., *The Modern British Monarchy*, 1971.

Historical surveys on the English monarchy can be found in: Bryant, Sir A., *A Thousand Years of British Monarchy*, 1975; Fraser, A. (ed.), *The Lives of Kings and Queens of England*, 1975; Hardie, F. M., *The Political Influence of the British Monarchy, 1868–1952*, 1970; Hibbert, C., *The Court of St James's: The Monarch at Work from Victoria to Elizabeth II*, 1979.

REFERENCE

British Library of Economic and Political Science, *A London Bibliography of the Social Sciences*, London and New York, Mansell, annually.

Burke's Peerage (publisher), *Guide to the British Monarchy*, London, 1977.

Hyland, H. S., *King and Parliament: A Selected List of Books*, Cambridge, Cambridge University Press, 1951.

Montgomery-Massingberd, H. (ed.), *Atlas of Royal Britain*, Leicester, Windward, 1984.

Palmer, A. and Palmer, V., *Royal England: A Historical Gazetteer*, London, Methuen, 1983.

Seymour, W., *Sovereign Legacy: An Historical Guide to the British Monarchy*, London, Sidgwick and Jackson, 1979.

GENERAL

Ashe, G., *The Kings and Queens of Early Britain*, London, Methuen, 1982.

Benemy, F. W. G., *The Queen Reigns, She Does not Rule*, London, Harrap, 1963.

Brooke, C., *The Saxon and Norman Kings*, London, Batsford, 1978.

Brooke-Little, J., *Royal Ceremonies of State*, Feltham, Country Life, 1980.

Bryant, A., *A Thousand Years of British Monarchy*, London, Collins, 1975.

Central Office of Information, *The Monarchy in Britain*, London, HMSO, 1981.

Chambers, J., *The Norman Kings*, London, Weidenfeld and Nicolson, 1981.

Clayton, H., *Royal Faces: 900 Years of British Monarchy*, London, HMSO, 1977.

De-La-Noy, M., *The Honours System*, London, Allison and Busby, 1985.

Duncan, A., *The Reality of Monarchy*, London, Heinemann, 1976.

Edgar, D. *Palace*, London, Allen, 1983.
Fisher, G. and Fisher, H., *Monarchy and the Royal Family: A Guide for Everyman*, London, Robert Hale, 1979.
Fraser, A. (ed.), *The Lives of Kings and Queens of England*, London, Weidenfeld and Nicolson, 1975.
Fulford, R., *Hanover to Windsor*, London, Fontana, 1966.
Hamilton, W., *My Queen and I*, London, Quartet, 1975.
Hardie, F. M., *The Political Influence of the British Monarchy, 1868–1952*, London, Batsford, 1970.
Harvey, J., *The Plantagenets*, London, Fontana, 1970.
Hibbert, C., *The Court of Windsor*, London, Allen Lane, 1977.
Hibbert, C., *The Court of St James's: The Monarch at Work from Victoria to Elizabeth II*, London, Weidenfeld and Nicolson, 1979.
Howard, P., *The British Monarchy in the Twentieth Century*, London, Hamish Hamilton, 1977.
Howard, P., *The Changing Monarchy*, London, Hamish Hamilton, 1977.
Hudson, M. E. and Clark, M., *Crown of a Thousand Years*, Sherborne, Alphabooks, 1978.
Keay, D., *Royal Pursuit: The Palace, the Press and the People*, London, Severn House, 1983.
Lofts, N., *Queens of Britain*, London,
Hodder and Stoughton, 1977.
Longford, E., *The Royal House of Windsor*, London, Weidenfeld and Nicolson, 1974.
Morris, C., *The Tudors*, London, Fontana, 1966.
National Portrait Gallery, *Royal Faces: 900 Years of British Monarchy*, London, 1977.
Packard, J. M., *A Guide to the British Monarchy Today*, London, Robson Books, 1981.
Paget, J., *The Pageantry of Britain*, London, Michael Joseph, 1979.
Pinches, J. H. and Pinches, R. V., *The Royal Heraldry of England*, London, Heraldry Today, 1974.
Plumb, J. H., *The First Four Georges*, London, Fontana, 1966.
Thompson, J. A. and Mejia, A., *The Modern British Monarchy*, New York, Eyre and Spottiswoode, 1971.
Walker, J., *The Queen Has Been Pleased: The British Honours System at Work*, London, Secker and Warburg, 1986.
Williams, N., *Royal Homes of the United Kingdom*, Ware, Herts., Omega Books, 1984.
Williamson, D., *Debrett's Kings and Queens of Britain*, Exeter, Webb and Bower, 1986.
Ziegler, P., *Crown and People*, London, Collins, 1978.

INDIVIDUAL KINGS AND QUEENS

EDWARD THE CONFESSOR

Barlow, F. (ed.), *The Life of Edward the Confessor*, London, Nelson, 1962.
Barlow, F., *Edward the Confessor*, London, Methuen, 1979.

WILLIAM I

Ashley, M., *The Life and Times of William I*, London, Weidenfeld and Nicolson, 1973.

Douglas, D. C., *William the Conqueror*, London, Methuen, 1977.
Stenton, F. M., *William the Conqueror and the Rule of the Normans*, London, Cass, 1967.

STEPHEN

Cronne, H. A., *The Reign of Stephen*, London, Weidenfeld and Nicolson, 1970.

Davis, R. H. C., *King Stephen, 1135–1154*, London, Longman, 1967.

HENRY II

Warren, W. L., *Henry II*, London, Methuen, 1973.

RICHARD I

Gillingham, J., *The Life and Times of Richard I*, London, Weidenfeld and Nicolson, 1973.

JOHN

Ashley, M., *The Life and Times of King John*, London, Weidenfeld and Nicolson, 1972.
Warren, W. L., *King John*, London, Methuen, 1978.

HENRY III

Powicke, H., *King Henry III and the Lord Edward*, 2 vols, Oxford, Oxford University Press, 1947.

EDWARD I

Salzman, L. F., *Edward I*, London, Constable, 1968.

EDWARD II

Bingham, C., *The Life and Times of Edward II*, London, Weidenfeld and Nicolson, 1973.

EDWARD III

Packe, M., *King Edward III*, edited by L. C. B. Seaman, London, Routledge & Kegan Paul, 1983.

RICHARD II

Hutchinson, H. F., *The Hollow Crown: A Life of Richard II*, London, Methuen, 1979.

HENRY IV

Kirby, J. L., *Henry IV of England*, London, Constable, 1970.

HENRY V

Earle, P., *The Life and Times of Henry V*, London, Weidenfeld and Nicolson, 1972.
Harriss, G. L. (ed.), *Henry V: The Practice of Kingship*, London, Oxford University Press, 1984.

HENRY VI

Griffiths, R., *The Reign of King Henry VI*, London, Benn, 1981.
Wolffe, B., *Henry VI*, London, Methuen, 1983.

EDWARD IV

Falkus, G., *The Life and Times of Edward IV*, London, Weidenfeld and Nicolson, 1981.
Ross, C., *Edward IV*, London, Methuen, 1975.

RICHARD III

Kendall, M., *Richard III*, London, Allen and Unwin, 1955.
Ross, C., *Richard III*, London, Methuen, 1981.

HENRY VII

Chrimes, S. B., *Henry VII*, London, Methuen, 1977.

Lockyer, R., *Henry VII*, London, Longman, 1968.

Storey, R. L., *The Reign of Henry VII*, London, Blandford Press, 1968.

HENRY VIII

Erickson, C., *Great Harry: Henry VIII*, London, Dent, 1980.

Pollard, A. F., *Henry VIII*, London, Methuen, 1963.

Scarisbrick, J. J., *Henry VIII*, London, Methuen, 1976.

Williams, N., *Henry VIII and his Court*, London, Weidenfeld and Nicolson, 1971.

EDWARD VI

Jordan, W. K., *Edward VI: The Young King*, 2 vols, London, Allen and Unwin, 1969–71.

MARY

Loades, D. M., *The Reign of Mary Tudor*, London, Benn, 1979.

Ridley, J., *The Life and Times of Mary Tudor*, London, Weidenfeld and Nicolson, 1974.

ELIZABETH I

Jenkins, E., *Elizabeth the Great*, London, Gollancz, 1958.

Johnson, P., *Elizabeth I: A Study in Power and Intellect*, London, Weidenfeld and Nicolson, 1974.

Neale, J. E., *Queen Elizabeth I*, London, Panther, 1979.

Smith, L. B., *Elizabeth Tudor: Portrait of a Queen*, London, Hutchinson, 1976.

Williams, N., *The Life and Times of Elizabeth I*, London, Weidenfeld and Nicolson, 1972.

Zamoyska, B., *Queen Elizabeth I*, London, Longman, 1981.

JAMES I

Bingham, C., *James I of England*, London, Weidenfeld and Nicolson, 1981.

Fraser, A., *King James VI of Scotland, I of England*, London, Weidenfeld and Nicolson, 1975.

Mathew, D., *James I*, London, Eyre and Spottiswoode, 1967.

CHARLES I

Bowle, J., *Charles I*, London, Weidenfeld and Nicolson, 1975.

Carlton, C., *Charles I*, London, Ark, 1984.

Falkus, C., *The Life and Times of Charles I*, London, Weidenfeld and Nicolson, 1972.

Hibbert, C., *Charles I*, London, Corgi, 1972.

Watson, D., *The Life and Times of Charles I*, London, Weidenfeld and Nicolson, 1972.

CHARLES II

Ashley, M., *Charles II: The Man and the Statesman*, London, Panther, 1973.

Bryant, Sir A., *King Charles II*, London, Collins, 1960.

Fraser, A.; *King Charles II*, London, Futura, 1981.

Gibson, M., *Charles II*, London, Wayland, 1976.

JAMES II

Ashley, M., *James II*, London, Dent, 1981.

Earle, P., *The Life and Times of James II*, London, Weidenfeld and Nicolson, 1972.

Miller, J., *James II: A Study in Kingship*, London, Wayland, 1978.

WILLIAM AND MARY

Zee, B. Van Der and Zee, H. A. Van Der, *William and Mary*, London, Macmillan, 1973.

ANNE

Curtis, G., *The Life and Times of Queen Anne*, London, Weidenfeld and Nicolson, 1973.

Gregg, E., *Queen Anne*, London, Ark, 1984.

GEORGE I

Beattie, J. M., *The English Court in the Reign of George I*, Cambridge, Cambridge University Press, 1967.

Hatton, R. M., *George I, Elector and King*, London, Thames and Hudson, 1979.

Marlow, J., *The Life and Times of George I*, London, Weidenfeld and Nicolson, 1973.

GEORGE III

Ayling, S., *George III*, London, Collins, 1972.

Brooke, J., *King George III*, London, Constable, 1985.

Clarke, J., *The Life and Times of George III*, London, Weidenfeld and Nicolson, 1972.

Purves, A., *George III*, London, Wayland, 1978.

GEORGE IV

Hibbert, C., *George IV*, Harmondsworth, Penguin, 1976.

Palmer, A., *The Life and Times of George IV*, London, Weidenfeld and Nicolson, 1972.

WILLIAM IV

Ziegler, P., *King William IV*, London, Collins, 1972.

VICTORIA

Duff, D., *Albert and Victoria*, London, Muller, 1972.

Hardie, F., *The Political Influence of Queen Victoria, 1861–1901*, London, Cass, 1963.

Longford, E., *Victoria, R. I.*, London, Weidenfeld and Nicolson, 1971.

Marshall, D., *The Life and Times of Victoria*, London, Weidenfeld and Nicolson, 1972.

Strachey, L., *Queen Victoria*, London, Chatto and Windus, 1969.

Woodham-Smith, C., *Queen Victoria: Her Life and Times*, London, Hamish Hamilton, 1972.

EDWARD VII

Hibbert, C., *Edward VII: A Portrait*, Harmondsworth, Penguin, 1982.

GEORGE V

Judd, D., *The Life and Times of George V*, London, Weidenfeld and Nicolson, 1973.

Nicolson, H., *King George V: His Life and Reign*, London, Constable, 1952.

Rose, K., *King George V*, London, Macmillan, 1984.

EDWARD VIII

Donaldson, F., *Edward VIII*, London, Futura, 1976.

GEORGE VI

Donaldson, F., *King George VI and Queen Elizabeth*, London, Weidenfeld and Nicolson, 1977.

Middlemas, K., *The Life and Times of George VI*, London, Weidenfeld and Nicolson, 1974.

ELIZABETH II

Longford, E., *Elizabeth R.*, London, Weidenfeld and Nicolson, 1983.
Penguin Books (publisher), *The Queen*, Harmondsworth, 1977.

Plumb, J. H. and Weldon, H., *Royal Heritage: The Reign of Elizabeth II*, London, BBC, 1981.

SEE ALSO:

12 Government and Administration
13 History
24 Parliament

21 MUSIC

The standard authority on music for reference purposes is Sadie, S. (ed.), *Grove's Dictionary of Music and Musicians*, 20 vols, 1980. For general reference purposes see also Abraham, G. and Hughes, A. (eds), *The New Oxford History of Music*, 8 vols, 1954–82; Arnold, D. (ed.), *The New Oxford Companion to Music*, 2 vols, 1983; Kennedy, M., *The Oxford Dictionary of Music*, 1985; Slonimsky, N. (ed.), *Baker's Biographical Dictionary of Musicians*, 1985.

Historical surveys of music in Britain can be found in Mackerness, E. D., *A Social History of English Music*, 1964; Walker, E., *A History of Music in England*, 1978; Young, P. M., *A History of British Music*, 1967. Discussions of modern music in Britain are available in: Foreman, L. (ed.), *British Music Now: A Guide to the Work of Younger Composers*, 1975; Routh, F., *Contemporary British Music: The Twenty-five Years from 1945–1970*, 1972.

The following books can be recommended as general introductions to particular areas:

Church Music   Long, K. R., *The Music of the English Church;* 1972; Routley, E., *A Short History of English Church Music*, 1977.
Folk Song   Karpeles, M., *An Introduction to English Folk Song*, 1973; Lloyd, A. L., *Folk Song in England*, 1975.
Jazz   Godbolt, J., *A History of Jazz in Britain, 1919–50*, 1984.
Opera   Dent, E. J., *The Foundations of English Opera*, 1965; White, E. W., *A History of English Opera*, 1983.
Pop Music   Frith, S., *Sound Effects: Youth, Leisure and the Politics of Rock 'n' Roll*, 1983; Chambers, I., *Urban Rhythms: Pop Music and Popular Culture*, 1984.

REFERENCE

Abraham, G. et al. (eds), *The New Oxford History of Music*, 10 vols, London, Oxford University Press, 1954–82.

Arnold, D. (ed.), *The New Oxford Companion to Music*, 2 vols, Oxford, Oxford University Press, 1983.

British Library, *British Catalogue of Music*, London, annually.

Brody, E., *The Music Guide to Great Britain*, London, Hale, 1976.

Davies, J. H., *Musicalia: Sources of Information in Music*, Oxford, Pergamon, 1969.

English Folk and Dance Society, *Folk Directory*, London, 1979.

Jacobs, A. and Barton, M. (eds), *British Music Yearbook*, London, Bowker, annually.

Kennedy, M., *The Oxford Dictionary of Music*, Oxford, Oxford University Press, 1985.

Norris, G., *Musical Gazetteer of Britain*, Newton Abbot, David and Charles, 1981.

Penney, B., *Music in British Libraries*, London, Library Association, 1981.

Rhinegold Publishing (publisher), *British*

Music Education Yearbook, London, annually.

Sadie, S. (ed.), *The New Grove Dictionary of Music and Musicians*, 20 vols, London, Macmillan, 1981.

Sadie, S. and Latham, A. (eds), *The Cambridge Music Guide*, Cambridge, Cambridge University Press, 1985.

Scarecrow Press (publisher), *Annual Index to Popular Music Record Reviews*, Metuchen, New Jersey, annually.

Slonimsky, N. (ed.), *Baker's Biographical Dictionary of Musicians*, London, Oxford University Press, 1985.

Taylor, P., *Popular Music since 1955: A Critical Guide to the Literature*, London, Mansell, 1985.

York, W. (comp.), *Who's Who in Rock Music*, London, Arthur Baker, 1982.

CLASSICAL AND RELIGIOUS MUSIC

Bacharach, A. L., *British Music in our Time*, Harmondsworth, Penguin, 1951.

Blom, E., *Music in England*, London, Penguin, 1947.

Cooper, M. (ed.), *The New Oxford History of Music, Vol. 10, The Modern Age, 1890–1960*, Oxford, Oxford University Press, 1974.

Dent, E. J., *The Foundations of English Opera*, London, Da Capo, 1965.

Dickinson, P. (ed.), *Twenty British Composers*, London, Chester, 1975.

Ehrlich, C., *The Music Profession in Britain Since the Eighteenth Century: A Social History*, Oxford, Clarendon Press, 1985.

Fellowes, E. H., *English Cathedral Music*, London, Greenwood Press, 1981 (reprint).

Fiske, R. (ed.), *The Athlone History of Music in Britain: The Eighteenth Century*, London, Athlone, 1985.

Foreman, L. (ed.), *British Music Now: A Guide to the Work of Younger Composers*, London, Elek, 1975.

Griffiths, P., *New Sounds, New Personalities: British Composers of the 1980's in Conversation*, London, Faber, 1985.

Harrison, F. L., *Music in Medieval Britain*, London, Routledge & Kegan Paul, 1980.

Kerman, J., *Musicology*, London, Fontana, 1985.

Le Huray, P., *Music and the Reformation in England*, Cambridge, Cambridge University Press, 1968.

Long, K. R., *The Music of the English Church*, London, Sevenoaks, Hodder and Stoughton, 1972.

Mackerness, E. D., *A Social History of English Music*, London, Routledge & Kegan Paul, 1964.

Mellers, W., *Music and Society: England and the European Tradition*, London, Dobson, 1964.

Pirie, P. J., *The English Musical Renaissance: Twentieth Century British Composers and Their Works*, London, Gollancz, 1979.

Raynor, H., *Music in England*, London, Hale, 1980.

Routh, F., *Contemporary British Music: The Twenty-five Years from 1945 to 1970*, London, Macdonald, 1972.

Routley, E., *A Short History of English Church Music*, London, Oxford, Mowbray, 1977.

Routley, E., *The English Carol*, London, Greenwood Press, 1981.

Spink, I., *English Song: Dowland to Purcell*, London, Batsford, 1974.

Spink, J. (ed.), *The Athlone History of Music in Britain*, London, Athlone, 1981–.

Stevens, J., *Music and Poetry in the Early Tudor Court*, Cambridge, Cambridge University Press, 1979.

Temperley, N., *The Music of the English Parish Church*, 2 vols, Cambridge, Cambridge University Press, 1979–83.

Temperley, N. (ed.), *The Romantic Age, 1800–1914*, London, Athlone, 1981.

Trend, M., *The Music Makers: The English Musical Renaissance from Edward Elgar to Benjamin Britten*, London, Weidenfeld and Nicolson, 1985.

Walker, E., *A History of Music in England*, London, Da Capo, 1978 (reprint).
White, E. W., *A History of English Opera*, London, Faber, 1983.
White, E., *The Rise of English Opera*, London, Lehmann, 1951.
Wulsten, D. *Tudor Music*, London, Dent, 1985.
Young, P. M., *A History of British Music*, London, Benn, 1967.

FOLK AND TRADITIONAL MUSIC

Harker, D., *Fakesong: The Manufacture of British 'Folksong' 1700 to the Present Day*, Milton Keynes, Open University Press, 1985.
Howes, F., *Folk Music of Britain—and Beyond*, London, Methuen, 1970.
Karpeles, M., *An Introduction to English Folk Song*, Oxford, Oxford University Press, 1973.
Lee, E., *Music of the People: A Study of Popular Music in Great Britain*, London, Barrie and Jenkins, 1970.
Lee, E., *Folksong and Music Hall*, London, Routledge & Kegan Paul, 1982.
Lloyd, A. L., *Folk Song in England*, London, Paladin, 1975.
Nettel, R., *A Social History of Traditional Song*, London, Kelley, 1978.

Palmer, R., *Everyman's Book of English Country Songs*, London, Dent, 1980.
Pearsall, R., *Victorian Popular Music*, Newton Abbot, David and Charles, 1973.
Pearsall, R., *Edwardian Popular Music*, Newton Abbot, David and Charles, 1975.
Pearsall, R., *Popular Music of the Twenties*, Newton Abbot, David and Charles, 1976.
Pollard, M., *Discovering English Folksong*, Aylesbury, Shire Publications, 1984.
Watson, I., *Song and Democratic Culture*, London, Croom Helm, 1983.
Williams, R. V. and Lloyd, A., *Penguin Book of English Folk Songs*, Harmondsworth, Penguin, 1968.

POP MUSIC

Booth, S., *The True Adventures of the Rolling Stones*, London, Heinemann, 1985.
Burchill, J. and Parsons, T., *'The Boy looked at Johnny': The Obituary of Rock and Roll*, London, Pluto, 1978.
Chambers, I., *Urban Rhythms: Pop Music and Popular Culture*, London, Macmillan, 1984.
Cohn, N., *Pop from the Beginning*, London, Weidenfeld and Nicolson, 1969.
Cross, C. et al. (eds), *Encyclopaedia of British Beat Groups and Solo Artists of the Sixties*, London, Omnibus Press, 1981.
Davies, H., *The Beatles*, London, Heinemann, 1968.
Frith, S., *Sound Effects: Youth, Leisure and the Politics of Rock 'n' Roll*, London, Constable, 1983.

Godbolt, J., *A History of Jazz in Britain, 1919–50*, London, Quartet, 1984.
Hardy, P., *The Music Industry*, London, Comedia, 1985.
Jewell, D., *The Popular Voice: A Musical Record of the 60s and 70s*, London, Sphere, 1981.
Kiste, J. Van Der, *Roxeventies: British Popular Music, 1970–9*, Torpoint, Kawabata Press, 1982.
Mellers, W., *The Beatles in Retrospect: Twilight of the Gods*, London, Faber, 1973.
Melly, G., *Revolt into Style: The Pop Arts in Britain*, London, Allen Lane, 1970.
Norman, P., *Shout! The True Story of the Beatles*, London, Hamish Hamilton, 1981.
Norman, P., *The Stones*, London, Elm Tree Books, 1985.

Parnall, H. R., *Pop Music in Britain Today*, London, Harrap, 1981.

Qualen, J., *The Music Industry—The End of Vinyl?*, London, Comedia, 1986.

Rimmer, D., *Like Punk Never Happened*, London, Faber, 1985.

Rogan, J., *The Kinks: The Sound and the Fury*, London, Proteus, 1982.

Rogers, D., *Rock 'n' Roll*, London, Routledge & Kegan Paul, 1982.

Schaffner, N., *The British Invasion: From the First Wave to the New Wave*, New York, McGraw, 1982.

Taylor, P., *Popular Music Since 1955*, London, Mansell, 1985.

Vulliamy, G., *Jazz and Blues*, London, Routledge & Kegan Paul, 1982.

Vulliamy, G. and Lee, E. (eds), *Pop Music in School*, Cambridge, Cambridge University Press, 1980.

Vulliamy, G. and Lee, E., *Popular Music: A Teacher's Guide*, London, Routledge & Kegan Paul, 1982.

Watson, P., *Inside the Pop Scene*, Cheltenham, Thornhill, 1977.

Whitcomb, I., *After the Ball*, Harmondsworth, Penguin, 1973.

Whitcomb, I., *Tin Pan Alley*, London, Wildwood House, 1975.

Whitcomb, I., *Rock Odyssey: A Chronicle of the Sixties*, London, Hutchinson, 1984.

York, P., *Who's Who in Rock Music*, London, Barker, 1982.

INDIVIDUAL COMPOSERS

BENJAMIN BRITTEN

Evans, P., *The Music of Benjamin Britten*, London, Dent, 1979.

Holst, I., *Benjamin Britten*, London, Faber, 1980.

WILLIAM BYRD

Fellowes, E. H., *William Byrd*, Oxford, Oxford University Press, 1948.

PETER MAXWELL DAVIES

Griffiths, P., *Peter Maxwell Davies*, London, Robson Books, 1981.

FREDERICK DELIUS

Jefferson, A., *Delius*, London, Dent, 1972.

Redwood, C. (ed.), *A Delius Companion*, London, John Calder, 1980.

JOHN DOWLAND

Poulton, D., *John Dowland*, London, Faber, 1982.

EDWARD ELGAR

Kennedy, M., *Portrait of Elgar*, London, Oxford University Press, 1969.

Parrott, L., *Elgar*, London, Dent, 1971.

GILBERT AND SULLIVAN

Ayre, L., *The Gilbert and Sullivan Companion*, London, Pan, 1974.

Bailey, L., *Gilbert and Sullivan and their World*, London, Thames and Hudson, 1973.

GEORGE FREDERICK HANDEL

Landon, H. C. R., *Handel and His World*, London, Weidenfeld and Nicolson, 1984.

Young, P. M., *Handel*, London, Dent, 1975.

GUSTAV HOLST

Holst, I., *The Music of Gustav Holst*, Oxford, Oxford University Press, 1969.

HENRY PURCELL

Holst, I., *Henry Purcell, 1659–95: Essays on His Music*, Oxford, Oxford University Press, 1959.
Westrup, J. A., *Purcell*, London, Dent, 1980.

THOMAS TALLIS

Does, P., *Tallis*, Oxford, Oxford University Press, 1976.

MICHAEL TIPPETT

Bowen, M., *Michael Tippett*, London, Robson Books, 1981.

Kemp, I., *Tippet: The Composer and His Music*, London, Eulenburg Books, 1984.

RALPH VAUGHAN WILLIAMS

Day, J., *Vaughan Williams*, London, Dent, 1975.
Kennedy, M. (ed.), *The Works of Ralph Vaughan Williams*, London, Oxford University Press, 1982.

WILLIAM WALTON

Howes, F., *The Music of William Walton*, Oxford, Oxford University Press, 1973.
Tierney, N., *William Walton: His Life and Music*, London, Hale, 1985.

SEE ALSO:

27   Popular Culture

22 NORTHERN IRELAND

For bibliographical reference guides to Ireland, including Northern Ireland, readers should consult: Deutsch, R., *Northern Ireland, 1921–1974: A Select Bibliography*, 1975; Eager, A. (ed.), *A Guide to Irish Bibliographic Material*, 1981; Elliott, J. D., *Northern Ireland, Reader's Guide*, 1980; Johnson, E. M., *Irish History: A Select Bibliography*, 1972; Pollock, L. and McAllister, I., *A Bibliography of United Kingdom Politics: Scotland, Wales and Northern Ireland*, 3 vols, 1980; Shannon, M. O. (comp.), *Modern Ireland: A Bibliography on Politics, Planning, Research and Development*, 1982.

For recent publication see British Library of Economic and Political Science, *A London Bibliography of the Social Sciences*, annually.

The following are authoritative studies of Irish history including the history of Ulster: Beckett, J. C., *The Making of Modern Ireland, 1603–1923*, 1981; Brown, T., *Ireland: A Social and Cultural History*, 1981; Buckland, P., *History of Northern Ireland*, 1981; Curtis, E., *History of Ireland*, 1961; Johnson, P., *Ireland: A History from the Twelfth Century to the Present Day*, 1981; Kee, R., *Ireland: A History*, 1980; Moody, T. W. et al. (eds), *A New History of Ireland*, 8 vols, 1976–83; Norman, E. R., *A History of Modern Ireland*, 1971; Ranelagh, J. O., *A Short History of Ireland*, 1983.

Official reports on the current situation in Northern Ireland are contained in: Central Office of Information, *Northern Ireland*, 1983; Northern Ireland Office, *Government of Northern Ireland: A Society Divided*, 1975.

Readers are referred to the following for critical discussions of the present political and social situation: Arthur, P., *Government and Politics of Northern Ireland*, 1980; Bell, G., *The British in Northern Ireland: A Suitable Case for Withdrawal*, 1984; Darby, J., *Conflict in Northern Ireland*, 1976; Downing, T. (ed.), *The Troubles: The Background to the Question of Northern Ireland*, 1980; Janke, P., *Ulster: A Decade of Violence: Conflict Studies*, 1979; Morgan, A. and Purdie, B. (eds), *Ireland: Divided Nation, Divided Class*, 1980; Rolston, B. and Tomlinson, M., *Between Civil Rights and Civil War*, 1980; Watt, D. (ed.), *The Constitution of Northern Ireland: Problems and Prospects*, 1981.

REFERENCE

British Library of Economic and Political Science, *A London Bibliography of the Social Sciences*, London and New York, Mansell, annually.

Century Services (publisher), *Belfast and Northern Ireland Directory*, Belfast, annually.

Collet, R. J. (ed.), *Northern Ireland Statistics: A Guide to Principal Sources*, Belfast, Queen's University,

Department of Library and Information Studies, 1979.

Compton, P. A. (ed.), *Northern Ireland: A Census Atlas*, Dublin, Gill and Macmillan, 1978.

Deutsch, R. R., *Northern Ireland 1921–1974: A Select Bibliography*, New York and London, Garland, 1975.

Eager, A. (ed.), *A Guide to Irish*

Bibliographic Material, London, Library Association, 1981.

Edwards, R. D., *An Atlas of Irish History*, London, Methuen, 1981.

Elliott, J. D., *Northern Ireland, Reader's Guide no. 24*, Chippenham, Library Association, Public Libraries Group, 1980.

Flackes, W. D., *Northern Ireland: A Political Directory, 1968–83*, London, Ariel Books, 1983.

Her Majesty's Stationery Office, *Northern Ireland Annual Abstract of Statistics*, Belfast, annually.

Her Majesty's Stationery Office, *The Ulster Year Book*, Belfast, annually.

Her Majesty's Stationery Office, *Notes on Northern Ireland*, Belfast, 1978.

Johnson, E. M., *Irish History: A Select Bibliography*, London, Historical Association, 1972.

Killanin, Lord and Duignan, M. V., *Shell Guide to Ireland*, London, Ebury Press, 1967.

Maltby, A., *The Government of Northern Ireland, 1922–1972: A Catalogue and Breviate of Parliamentary Papers*, Dublin, Irish University Press, 1974.

Northern Ireland Information Service, *Government Annual List of Publications*, Belfast, HMSO, annually.

Northern Ireland, Ministry of Finance, *Digest of Statistics*, HMSO, annually.

Pollock, L. and McAllister, I., *A Bibliography of United Kingdom Politics: Scotland, Wales and Northern Ireland*, 3 vols, Glasgow, University of Strathclyde, 1980.

Public Record Office, Northern Ireland, *Sources for the Study of Local History in Northern Ireland*, Belfast, 1969.

Shannon, M. O. (comp.), *Modern Ireland: A Bibliography on Politics, Planning, Research and Development*, London, Library Association, 1981.

GENERAL

Birrell, D. and Murie, A., *Policy and Government in Northern Ireland*, Dublin, Gill and Macmillan, 1980.

Bowen, K., *Protestants in a Catholic State: Ireland's Privileged Minority*, Dublin, Gill and Macmillan, 1983.

Central Office of Information, *Northern Ireland*, London, HMSO, 1983.

Compton, P. A. (ed.), *The Contemporary Population of Northern Ireland and Population-related Issues*, Belfast, Queen's University, Institute of Irish Studies, 1981.

Freeman, T. W., *Ireland: A General and Regional Geography*, London, Methuen, 1969.

Gallagher, S. and Worrall, S., *Christians in Ulster, 1968–1980*, London, Oxford University Press, 1982.

Harbinson, J. F., *The Ulster Unionist Party, 1882–1973: Its Development and Organisation*, Belfast, Blackstaff Press, 1973.

Harvey, S. and Rea, D., *The Northern Ireland Economy with Particular Reference to Industrial Development*, Ulster Polytechnic, Newtownabbey, Co. Antrim, 1983.

Her Majesty's Stationery Office, *Economic and Social Progress in Northern Ireland: Review and Prospects*, Belfast, 1979.

Her Majesty's Stationery Office, *Industrial Development in Northern Ireland: A Framework for Action*, Belfast, 1983.

Hill, D. A., *Northern Ireland*, Cambridge, Cambridge University Press, 1974.

Longford, Lord and McHardy, A., *Ulster*, London, Weidenfeld and Nicolson, 1981.

Maltby, A. (ed.), *The Government of Northern Ireland*, Dublin, Irish University Press, 1974.

Murphy, D., *A Place Apart*, Harmondsworth, Penguin, 1979.

O'Brien, C. C., *Neighbours*, London, Faber, 1980.

O'Faolain, S., *The Irish*, Harmondsworth, Penguin, 1969.

Oliver, J., *Ulster Today and Tomorrow*,

London, PEP, 1978.

Quigley, W. G. H., *Economic and Industrial Strategy for Northern Ireland*, Belfast, HMSO, 1976.

Rose, R. and McAllister, I., *United*

Kingdom Facts, London, Macmillan, 1982.

Whittow, J. B., *Geology and Scenery in Ireland*, Harmondsworth, Penguin, 1978.

POLITICAL SITUATION

Alexander, Y., *Terrorism in Ireland*, London, Croom Helm, 1983.

Arthur, P., *Government and Politics of Northern Ireland*, London, Longman, 1980.

Bell, G., *The British in Northern Ireland: A Suitable Case for Withdrawal*, London, Pluto, 1984.

Bew, P. et al., *The State in Northern Ireland, 1921–1972: Political Forms and Social Classes*, Manchester, Manchester University Press, 1980.

Bew, P. and Patterson, H., *The British State and the Ulster Crisis: From Wilson to Thatcher*, London, Verso, 1985.

Birrell, D. and Murie, A., *Policy and Government in Northern Ireland: Lessons of Devolution*, Dublin, Gill and Macmillan, 1980.

Boal, F. W. et al. (eds), *Integration and Division: Geographical Perspectives on the Northern Ireland Problem*, London, Academic Press, 1982.

Boyce, D. G., *Nationalism in Ireland*, London, Croom Helm, 1982.

Burton, F., *The Politics of Legitimacy: Struggles in a Belfast Community*, London, Routledge & Kegan Paul, 1978.

Coogan, T. P., *The IRA*, London, Fontana, 1980.

Darby, J., *Conflict in Northern Ireland*, Dublin, Gill and Macmillan, 1976.

Darby, J. (ed.), *Northern Ireland: The Background to the Conflict*, Belfast, Appletree Press, 1983.

Downing, T. (ed.), *The Troubles: The Background to the Question of Northern Ireland*, London, Macdonald Futura, 1980.

Farrell, M., *Northern Ireland: The Orange State*, London, Pluto, 1982.

Galliher, J. F. and DeGregory, J. L., *Violence in Northern Ireland:*

Understanding Protestant Perspectives, Dublin, Gill and Macmillan, 1985.

Gibbon, P., *The Origins of Ulster Unionism*, Manchester, Manchester University Press, 1975.

Hamill, D., *Pig in the Middle: The Army in Northern Ireland, 1969–1984*, London, Methuen, 1985.

Heskin, K., *Northern Ireland: A Psychological Analysis*, Dublin, Gill and Macmillan, 1980.

Hickey, J., *Religion and the Northern Ireland Problem*, Dublin, Gill and Macmillan, 1984.

Janke, P., *Ulster: A Decade of Violence: Conflict Studies*, London, Institute of Conflict Studies, 1979.

Kelley, K., *The Longest War: Northern Ireland and the IRA*, London, Zed Press, 1982.

McAllister, I., *The Northern Ireland Social Democratic and Labour Party: Political Opposition in a Divided Society*, London, Macmillan, 1977.

Magee, J. (ed.), *Northern Ireland: Crisis and Conflict*, London, Routledge & Kegan Paul, 1974.

Moody, T. W., *The Ulster Question 1603–1973*, Cork, Mercier Press, 1974.

Morgan, A., and Purdie, B. (eds), *Ireland: Divided Nation, Divided Class*, London, Ink Links, 1980.

Moxon-Browne, E., *Nation, Class and Creed in Northern Ireland*, Aldershot, Gower Publishing, 1983.

Nelson, S., *Ulster's Uncertain Defenders: Loyalists and the Northern Ireland Conflict*, Belfast, Appletree Press, 1985.

Northern Ireland Office, *Government of Northern Ireland: A Society Divided*, Belfast, 1975.

O'Dowd, L., *Northern Ireland: Between*

Civil Rights and Civil War, London, CSE Books, 1980.

Palley, C., *The Evolution, Disintegration and Possible Reconstruction of the Northern Ireland Constitution*, Chichester, Barry Rose, 1972.

Probert, B., *Beyond Orange and Green: The Political Economy of the Northern Ireland Crisis*, London, Zed Press, 1978.

Rees, M., *Northern Ireland: A Personal Perspective*, London, Methuen, 1985.

Rose, R., *Northern Ireland: A Time of Choice*, London, Macmillan, 1976.

Sheane, M. S., *Ulster and its Future After the Troubles*, Stockport, Highfield Press, 1977.

Stewart, A. T. Q., *The Narrow Ground: Aspects of Ulster*, London, Faber, 1977.

Wallace, M., *British Government in Northern Ireland: From Devolution to Direct Rule*, Newton Abbot, David and Charles, 1982.

Watt, D. (ed.), *The Constitution of Northern Ireland: Problems and Prospects*, London, Heinemann, 1981.

Younger, C., *Ireland's Civil War*, London, Fontana, 1986.

HISTORY

Beckett, J. C., *A Short History of Ireland*, London, Hutchinson, 1979.

Beckett, J. C., *The Making of Modern Ireland, 1603–1923*, London, Faber, 1981.

Brown, T., *Ireland: A Social and Cultural History*, London, Fontana, 1981.

Buckland, P., *History of Northern Ireland*, Dublin, Gill and Macmillan, 1981.

Canning, P., *British Policy towards Ireland, 1921–1941*, London, Oxford University Press, 1985.

Cullen, L. M., *The Emergence of Modern Ireland*, London, Batsford, 1976.

Cullen, L. M., *An Economic History of Ireland since 1660*, London, Batsford, 1976.

Falls, C., *The Birth of Ulster*, London, Methuen, 1973.

Gibbon, P., *The Origins of Ulster Unionism*, Manchester, Manchester University Press, 1975.

Johnson, P., *Ireland: A History from the Twelfth Century to the Present Day*, London, Panther, 1981.

Kee, R., *Ireland: A History*, London, Weidenfeld and Nicolson, 1980.

Kennedy, L. and Ollershaw, P. (eds), *An Economic History of Ulster*, Manchester, Manchester University Press, 1985.

Macdonagh, O., *Ireland: The Union and its Aftermath*, London, Allen and Unwin, 1977.

Mansergh, N. S., *The Irish Question, 1840–1921*, London, Allen and Unwin, 1975.

Moody, T. W., Martin, F. X. and Byrne, F. J. (eds), *A New History of Ireland*, 8 vols, Oxford, Oxford University Press, 1976–83.

Norman, E. R., *A History of Modern Ireland*, Harmondsworth. Penguin, 1971.

O'Farrell, P., *England and Ireland since 1800*, London, Oxford University Press, 1975.

O'Farrell, P., *Ireland's English Question: Anglo-Irish Relations 1534–1970*, New York, Schocken, 1976.

Ranelagh, J. O., *A Short History of Ireland*, Cambridge, Cambridge University Press, 1983.

Sheane, M. S., *Ulster and the British Connection*, Stockport, Highfield Press, 1979.

Sheane, M. S., *Ulster and the Lords of the North*, Stockport, Highfield Press, 1980.

Sheane, M. S., *Ulster and the Middle Ages*, Stockport, Highfield Press, 1982.

CULTURE

Catto, M., *Art in Ulster*, vol. 2, Belfast, Blackstaff Press, 1977.

Dixon, H., *Introduction to Ulster Architecture*, Belfast, Ulster Architectural Society, 1975.

Foster, J. C., *Ulster Folklore*, Dublin, Carter, 1951.

Foster, J. W., *Themes and Forces in Ulster Fiction*, Dublin, Gill and Macmillan, 1974.

Gailey, A., *Ulster Folk Ways*, Dublin, Eason, 1978.

Hewitt, J., *Art in Ulster*, Vol. 1, Belfast, Blackstaff Press, 1977.

St Clair, S., *Folklore of the Ulster People*, Cork, Mercier Press, 1972.

SEE ALSO:

23 PAINTING AND SCULPTURE

Detailed information and guides to artists and painters can be found in the following general reference works: Art Trade Press (publisher), *Who's Who in Art*, 1984; Bindman, D. (ed.), *Thames and Hudson Encyclopaedia of British Art*, 1985; Brook-Hart, D., *Twentieth Century British Marine Painters*, 1981; Dolman, B. (ed.), *Dictionary of Contemporary British Artists*, 1981; Jacobs, M. and Warner, M., *The Phaidon Companion to Art and Artists in the British Isles*, 1980; Johnson, J., *The Dictionary of British Artists, 1880–1940*, 1976; Mallalieu, H. L. (ed.), *Dictionary of British Watercolour Artists up to 1920*, 1976; Ormond, R. L. and Rogers, M. (eds), *Dictionary of British Portraiture*, 1979–81; Osborne, H., *Oxford Companion to Art*, 1970; Osborne, H., *Oxford Companion to Twentieth Century Art*, 1985; Waters, G. M., *Dictionary of British Artists Working 1900–1950*, 1975.

The following are suitable as introductory surveys of British art history: Gaunt, W., *A Concise History of English Painting*, 1964; Halliday, F. E., *An Illustrated Cultural History of England*, 1981; Pevsner, N., *The Englishness of English Art*, 1964; Sunderland, J., *Painting in Britain, 1515–1975*, 1976; Waterhouse, E. K., *Painting in Britain, 1530–1790*, 1978; Wilenski, R. H., *An Outline of English Painting*, 1969; Wilson, S., *Holbein to Hockney: History of British Art*, 1983.

Scholarly guides to British art history are provided in Boase, T. S. R. (ed.), *The Oxford History of English Art*, 11 vols, 1949–79.

Detailed guides to collections of art and painting in Great Britain can be found in: Abse, J., *The Art Galleries of Britain and Ireland: A Guide to their Collections*, 1985; Gordon, C., *Where Is It? British Paintings—Hogarth to Turner*, 1981; Copplestone, T., *Art Treasures in the British Isles*, 1969; Potterton, H., *A Guide to the National Gallery*, 1977; Tate Gallery, *The Tate Gallery Collections: British Painting, Modern Painting and Sculpture*, 1973.

REFERENCE

Abse, J., *The Art Galleries of Britain and Ireland: A Guide to their Collections*, London, Robson, 1985.

Art Trade Press (publisher), *Who's Who in Art*, 1984.

Bindman, D. (ed.), *Thames and Hudson Encyclopaedia of British Art*, London, Thames and Hudson, 1986.

Boase, T. S. R. (ed.), *The Oxford History of English Art*, 11 vols, Oxford, Oxford University Press, 1949–79.

Brook-Hart, D., *Twentieth Century British Marine Painters*, Woodbridge, Antique Collectors Club, 1981.

Carrick, N., *How to Find out about the Arts: A Guide to Sources of Information*, Oxford, Pergamon, 1965.

Chadwyck-Healey (publisher), *Bibliography of Museum and Art Gallery Publications and Audiovisual Aids in Great Britain and Ireland*, Cambridge, 1980.

Dolman, B. (ed.), *Dictionary of Contemporary British Artists*, Woodbridge, Antique Collectors Club, 1981.

Emanuel, E. et al. (eds), *Contemporary Artists*, London, St James Press, 1983.

Gordon, C., *Where Is It? British*

Paintings—Hogarth to Turner, London, Warne, 1981.

Gordon, C., *Where Is It? British Paintings of the Nineteenth Century*, London, Warne, 1981.

Grant, M. H., *Dictionary of British Landscape Painters From 16th to Early 20th Century*, London, Black, 1952.

Gunnis, R., *A Dictionary of British Sculptures, 1660–1851*, London, Abbey Library, 1968.

Hendy, P., *The National Gallery*, London, National Gallery, 1960.

Jacobs, M. and Warner, M., *The Phaidon Companion to Art and Artists in the British Isles*, Oxford, Phaidon, 1980.

Johnson, J., *The Dictionary of British Artists, 1880–1940*, Woodbridge, Antique Collectors Club, 1976.

Lewis, F., *Dictionary of British Historical Painters*, London, Black, 1979.

Mallalieu, J. (ed.), *The Dictionary of British Watercolour Artists up to 1920*, Woodbridge, Antique Collectors Club, 1976.

Ormond, R. L. and Rogers, M. (eds), *Dictionary of British Portraiture*, 4 vols, Batsford, 1979–81.

Osborne, H., *Oxford Companion to Twentieth Century Art*, Oxford, Oxford University Press, 1985.

Osborne, H. (ed.), *The Oxford Companion to Art*, Oxford, Oxford University Press, 1970.

Pavière, S. H., *Dictionary of British Sporting Painters*, London, Black, 1979.

Potterton, H., *A Guide to the National Gallery*, London, Thames and Hudson, 1977.

Tate Gallery, *The Tate Gallery Collections: British Painting, Modern Painting and Sculpture*, London, 1973.

Waters, G. M., *Dictionary of British Artists Working 1900–1950*, Eastbourne, Fine Art Publications, 1975.

Wilson, A., *Dictionary of British Marine Painters*, London, Black, 1979.

Wood, C., *Dictionary of Victorian Painters*, Woodbridge, Antique Collectors Club, 1971.

GENERAL

Ayres, J., *British Folk Art*, London, Barrie and Jenkins, 1976.

Ayres, J., *English Naive Painting, 1750–1900*, London, Thames and Hudson, 1980.

Backhouse, J. et al. (eds), *The Golden Age of Anglo-Saxon Art*, London, British Museum Publications, 1984.

Boase, T. S. R., *The Oxford History of Art, vol. 3, English Art, 1100–1216*, Oxford, Clarendon Press, 1953.

Boase, T. S. R., *The Oxford History of English Art, vol. 10, English Art, 1800–1870*, Oxford, Clarendon Press, 1959.

Brieger, P., *The Oxford History of English Art, vol. 4, English Art, 1216–1307*, Oxford, Clarendon Press, 1957.

British Museum, *British Landscape Watercolours, 1460–1860*, London, 1985.

Burke, J. T. A., *The Oxford History of English Art, vol. 9, English Art, 1714–1800*, Oxford, Clarendon Press, 1976.

Edwards, R. and Ramsey, L. G. G. (eds), *The Connoisseur Period Guides to the Houses, Decoration, Furnishing and Chattels of the Classic Period*, 5 vols, London, Connoisseur, 1956–71.

Evans, J., *The Oxford History of English Art, vol. 5, English Art, 1307–1461*, Oxford, Clarendon Press, 1949.

Farr, D., *Oxford History of English Art, vol. 11, English Art, 1870–1940*, Oxford, Clarendon Press, 1984.

Gardner, A., *English Medieval Sculpture*, Cambridge, Cambridge University Press, 1951.

Gaunt, W., *A Concise History of English Painting*, London, Thames and Hudson, 1964.

Gaunt, W., *The Great Century of British*

Painting: Hogarth to Turner, Oxford, Phaidon, 1971.

Gaunt, W., *The Restless Century: Painting in Britain 1800–1900*, Oxford, Phaidon, 1978.

George, M. D., *English Political Caricature*, Oxford, Oxford University Press, 1959.

Gibson, R. and Roberts, K., *British Portrait Painters*, Oxford, Phaidon, 1971.

Gordon, C., *British Paintings of the 19th Century*, London, Warne, 1981.

Halliday, F. E., *An Illustrated Cultural History of England*, London, Thames and Hudson, 1981.

Hardie, M., *Water-Colour Painting in Britain*, 3 vols, London, Batsford, 1966–9.

Harrison, C., *English Art and Modernism*, 1900–1939, London, Allen Lane, 1981.

Herrmann, L., *British Landscape Painting of the Eighteenth Century*, London, Faber, 1973.

Irwin, D., *English Neoclassical Art*, London, Faber, 1966.

Jung, K. K., *National Portrait Gallery: Complete Illustrated Catalogue*, London, 1981.

Kendrick, T., *Anglo-Saxon Art to AD 900*, London, Methuen, 1970.

Klingender, F. D., *Art and the Industrial Revolution*, London, Paladin, 1972.

Lister, R., *British Romantic Art*, London, Bell, 1973.

Lister, R. and Williams, S., *Twentieth Century British Naive and Primitive Artists*, London, Astragal Books, 1977.

Marks, R. and Morgan, N., *The Golden Age of English Manuscript Painting, 1200–1500*, London, Chatto and Windus, 1981.

Mayoux, J. J., *English Painting From Hogarth to the Pre-Raphaelites*, London, Macmillan, 1975.

Mercer, E. B., *The Oxford History of English Art, vol. 7, English Art, 1553–1625*, Oxford, Clarendon Press, 1962.

Nairne, S. and Serota, N. (eds), *British Sculpture in the Twentieth Century*, London, Whitechapel, 1981.

Naylor, G., *The Arts and Crafts Movement*, London, Studio Vista, 1971.

Parry, C. (ed.), *Contemporary British Artists*, London, Bergstrom and Boyle, 1979.

Pevsner, N., *The Englishness of English Art*, Harmondsworth, Penguin, 1964.

Redgrave, R. and Redgrave, S., *A Century of British Painters*, Oxford, Phaidon, 1981.

Rawley, T., *British Painting*, Oxford, Phaidon, 1975.

Read, B., *Victorian Sculpture*, New Haven, Yale University Press, 1984.

Rickert, M., *Painting in Britain: The Middle Ages*, Harmondsworth, Pelican, 1965.

Ross, A., *Pagan Celtic Britain: Studies in Iconography and Tradition*, London, Routledge & Kegan Paul, 1967.

Rothenstein, J., *An Introduction to English Painting*, London, Cassell, 1965.

Rothenstein, J., *Modern English Painters*, 3 vols, London, Macdonald, 1974–6.

Shone, R., *The Century of Change: British Painting since 1900*, Oxford, Phaidon, 1977.

Solomon, R., Guggenheim Foundation (publisher), *British Art Now: An American Perspective*, New York, 1979.

Spalding, F., *British Art Since 1900*, London, Thames and Hudson, 1986.

Stone, L., *Sculpture in Britain, Pelican History of Art*, Harmondsworth, Penguin, 1973.

Strachan, W. J., *Open Air Sculpture in Britain: A Comprehensive Guide*, London, Zwemmer, 1984.

Sunderland, J., *Painting in Britain, 1515–1975*, Oxford, Phaidon, 1976.

Talbot-Rice, D., *The Oxford History of English Art, vol. 2, English Art, 871–1100*, Oxford, Clarendon Press, 1952.

Trustees of the Tate Gallery, *Henry Moore to Gilbert and George: Modern British Art from the Tate Gallery*, London, Tate Gallery, 1973.

Waterhouse, E. K., *Painting in Britain 1530–1790*, Harmondsworth, Penguin, 1978.

Whinney, M., *Sculpture in Britain, 1530–1830*, Harmondsworth, Penguin, 1970.

Whinney, M., *English Sculpture, 1720–1830*, Harmondsworth, Penguin, 1971.

Whinney, M. and Millar, O., *The Oxford History of English Art, vol. 8, English Art, 1625–1714*, Oxford, Clarendon Press, 1957.

Wilenski, R. H., *An Outline of English Painting*, London, Faber, 1969.

Wilson, D. M., *Anglo-Saxon Art from the Seventh Century to the Norman Conquest*, London, Thames and Hudson, 1984.

Wilson, S., *Holbein to Hockney: History of British Art*, London, Bodley Head, 1983.

Zarnecki, G. et al. (eds), *English Romanesque Art, 1066–1200*, London, Weidenfeld and Nicolson, 1984.

INDIVIDUAL ARTISTS AND MOVEMENTS

FRANCIS BACON

Ades, D. and Forge, A., *Francis Bacon*, London, Thames and Hudson, 1985.

Trucchi, L., *Francis Bacon*, London, Thames and Hudson, 1975.

AUBREY BEARDSLEY

Brophy, B., *Beardsley and his World*, London, Thames and Hudson, 1976.

Reade, B., *Beardsley*, London, Studio Vista, 1967.

WILLIAM BLAKE

Blunt, A., *The Art of William Blake*, London, Oxford University Press, 1959.

Todd, R., *William Blake, The Artist*, London, Studio Vista, 1971.

ANTHONY CARO

Rubin, W., *Anthony Caro*, London, New York, Museum of Modern Art, 1975.

JOHN CONSTABLE

Sunderland, J., *Constable*, Oxford, Phaidon, 1981.

Walker, J., *Constable*, London, Thames and Hudson, 1979.

THOMAS GAINSBOROUGH

Hayes, J., *Gainsborough: Painting and Drawings*, Oxford, Phaidon, 1978.

Lindsay, J., *Thomas Gainsborough*, London, Granada, 1981.

ERIC GILL

Gill, E. R. (ed.), *Bibliography of Eric Gill*, Folkestone, Dawsons of Pall Mall, 1974.

Yorke, M., *Eric Gill: Man of Flesh and Spirit*, London, Constable, 1982.

BARBARA HEPWORTH

Browness, A. (ed.), *Barbara Hepworth: Complete Sculpture*, London, Lund Humphries, 1971.

DAVID HOCKNEY

Livingstone, M., *David Hockney*, London, Thames and Hudson, 1981.

Stangos, N. (ed.), *David Hockney*, Thames and Hudson, 1969.

WILLIAM HOGARTH

Lindsay, J., *Hogarth: His Art and his World*, London, Hart-Davies, 1977.
Paulson, R., *The Art of Hogarth*, Oxford, Phaidon, 1979.

AUGUSTUS JOHN

Holroyd, M., *Augustus John: A Biography*, 2 vols, London, 1974–5.
Holroyd, M. and Easton, M., *The Art of Augustus John*, London, Secker and Warburg, 1974.

L. S. LOWRY

Levy, M., *The Painting of L. S. Lowry*, London, Jupiter, 1975.
Rhodes, S., *A Private View of L. S. Lowry*, London, Collins, 1979.

HENRY MOORE

Read, Sir H., *Henry Moore: A Study of his Life and Work*, London, Thames and Hudson, 1965.
Russell, J., *Henry Moore*, Harmondsworth, Penguin, 1973.

PAUL NASH

Eates, M., *Paul Nash: The Maestro of the Image, 1889–1946*, London, Murray, 1973.

BEN NICHOLSON

Read, H. (ed.), *Ben Nicholson: Paintings, Reliefs and Drawings*, London, Lund Humphries, 1948.
Russell, J. (ed.), *Ben Nicholson: Drawings, Paintings and Reliefs*, London, Thames and Hudson, 1969.

POP ART

Finch, C., *Pop Art: Object and Image*, Studio Vista, 1968.
Mabey, R., *The Pop Process*, London, Hutchinson, 1969.

PRE-RAPHAELITES

Hunt, J. D., *The Pre-Raphaelite Imagination, 1848–1900*, London, Routledge & Kegan Paul, 1968.
Nicoll, J., *The Pre-Raphaelites*, London, Studio Vista, 1970.

JOSHUA REYNOLDS

Waterhouse, E. K., *Reynolds*, Oxford, Phaidon, 1973.

WALTER SICKERT

Baron, W., *Sickert*, Oxford, Phaidon, 1973.
Sutton, D., *Walter Sickert*, London, Michael Joseph, 1976.

GRAHAM SUTHERLAND

Hayes, J., *The Art of Graham Sutherland*, Oxford, Phaidon, 1982.

J. M. W. TURNER

Gaunt, W., *Turner*, Oxford, Phaidon, 1981.
Lindsay, J., *Turner*, London, Panther, 1973.

VORTICISM

Cork, R., *Vorticism and Abstract Art in the First Machine Age*, 2 vols, London, Gordon Fraser, 1976.
Wees, W. C., *Vorticism and the English Avant-Garde*, Manchester, Manchester University Press, 1972.

24 PARLIAMENT

General and detailed bibliographical references to the British Parliament can be found in Bond, M., *Guide to the Records of Parliament*, 1971; Goehlert, R. and Fenton, M. S., *The Parliament of Great Britain: A Bibliography*, 1983; Royal Institute of Public Administration, *The British Parliament: A Select Bibliography*, 1974.

For current publications on British politics relating to Parliament see British Library of Economic and Political Science, *A London Bibliography of the Social Sciences*, annually.

Information on all major aspects of Parliament, the Commons, the Lords and Parliamentary procedure can be found in the following reference works and handbooks: Hawtrey, S. C. and Barclay, H. M., *Abraham and Hawtrey's Parliamentary Dictionary*, 1970; Kerswill, A. S., *Vacher's Parliamentary Companion*, annually; Laundy, P. and Wilding, N., *An Encyclopaedia of Parliament*, 1975; Lucioni, J. (ed.), *The Times Guide to the House of Commons*, 1984; Smith, J. B. (ed.), *Dod's Parliamentary Companion*, 1985; Thomas, M. (ed.), *The BBC Guide to Parliament*, 1983.

Transcripts of Parliamentary debate are published in Her Majesty's Stationery Office, *Hansard's Parliamentary Debates*.

For an introduction to the role and work of Parliament readers are directed to: Butt, R., *The Power of Parliament*, 1967; Campion, G. F. M., *An Introduction to the Procedure of the House of Commons*, 1958; Central Office of Information, *Parliamentary Elections in Britain*, 1978; Central Office of Information, *The British Parliament*, 1984; May, T. E., *Parliamentary Practice*, 1983; Norton, P., *The Commons in Perspective*, 1981; Robert, H. M., *Parliamentary Practice: An Introduction to Parliamentary Law*, 1975; Rush, M., *Parliamentary Government in Britain*, 1981; Taylor, E., *The House of Commons at Work*, 1979; Walkland, S. A. and Ryle, M. (eds), *The Commons Today*, 1981.

The following are additionally suggested as introductory reading to particular areas:

Backbenchers   Judge, D., *Backbench Specialisation in the House of Commons*, 1981.
House of Lords   Massereene and Ferrard, J. S., Lord, *The Lords*, 1973.
Parliamentary Commissioner   Gregory, R. and Hutchesson, P., *The Parliamentary Ombudsman*, 1975.
Select Committees   Englefield, D., *The Commons Select Committees: Catalysts for Progress?*, 1984.

REFERENCE

Bond, M., *Guide to the Records of Parliament*, London, HMSO, 1971.
British Library of Economic and Political Science, *A London Bibliography of the Social Sciences*, London and New York, Mansell, annually.
Cobb, H. S., *A Handlist of Articles in Periodicals and Other Serial*

Publications Relating to the History of Parliament, London, House of Lords Record Office, 1973.

Craig, F. W. S., *British Electoral Facts, 1832–1980*, Chichester, Parliamentary Research Services, 1981.

Englefield, D., *Parliament and Information: The Westminster Scene*, London, Library Association, 1981.

Ford, P. and Ford, G., *Breviate of Parliamentary Papers, 1917–1939*, Oxford, Blackwell, 1951.

Ford, P. and Ford, G., *Hansard's Catalogue and Breviate of Parliamentary Papers, 1696–1934*, Oxford, Blackwell, 1953.

Ford, P. and Ford, G., *Select List of British Parliamentary Papers, 1833–1899*, Oxford, Blackwell, 1953.

Ford, P. and Ford, G., *Breviate of Parliamentary Papers, 1900–1916*, Oxford, Blackwell, 1957.

Ford, P. and Ford, G., *Breviate of Parliamentary Papers, 1940–1954*, Oxford, Blackwell, 1961.

Ford, P. and Ford, G., *Select List of British Parliamentary Papers, 1833–1899*, Shannon, Irish University Press, 1970.

Ford, P. and Ford, G., *A Guide to Parliamentary Papers: What They Are, How to Find Them, How to Use Them*, Shannon, Irish University Press, 1972.

Ford, P. and Marshallsay, D., *Select List of British Parliamentary Papers, 1955–1964*, Shannon, Irish University Press, 1970.

Goehlert, R. and Fenton, M. S., *The Parliament of Great Britain: A Bibliography*, San Diego, CA, Lexington Books, 1983.

Hawtrey, S. C. and Barclay, H. M., *Abraham and Hawtrey's Parliamentary Dictionary*, London, Butterworth, 1970.

Her Majesty's Stationery Office, *Hansard's Parliamentary Debates: House of Commons*, London.

House of Commons, *General Index to the Bills, Reports and Papers Printed by Order of the House of Commons, 1900–1948/9*, London, HMSO, 1960.

House of Commons, *General Alphabetical Index to the Bills, Reports and Papers Printed by Order of the House of Commons, 1950–1959*, London, HMSO, 1963.

Hulke, M. (ed.), *Cassell's Parliamentary Directory*, London, Cassell, 1975.

Irish Academic Press (publisher), *British Parliamentary Papers, 1800–1900*, Series, Dublin, 1972.

Kerswill, A. S. (publisher), *Vacher's Parliamentary Companion*, London, annually.

Lucioni, J. (ed.), *The Times Guide to the House of Commons*, London, Times Books, 1984.

Menhennet, D., *The Journal of the House of Commons: A Bibliographical and Historical Guide*, London, HMSO, 1971.

Mitchell, H. and Birt, P. (eds), *Who Does What in Parliament*, London, Westminster Bookstall, 1976.

Palmer, J., *Government and Parliament in Britain: A Bibliography*, London, Hansard Society, 1964.

Parliamentary Research Services (publisher), *The BBC/ITN Guide to the New Parliamentary Constituencies*, London, 1983.

Royal Institute of Public Administration, *The British Parliament: A Select Bibliography*, London, RIPA, 1974.

Rodgers, F., *Serial Publications in the British Parliamentary Papers, 1900–1968*, London, Library Association, 1971.

Smith, J. B. (ed), *Dod's Parliamentary Companion*, Herstmonceux, Dod, 1982.

Stenton, M. and Lees, S. (eds), *Who's Who of British Members of Parliament*, 4 vols, Brighton, Harvester, 1976–81.

Thomas, M. (ed.), *The BBC Guide to Parliament*, London, BBC, 1983.

Wilding, N. and Laundy, P., *An Encyclopaedia of Parliament*, London, Cassell, 1975.

GENERAL

Bailey, S. D., *British Parliamentary Democracy*, London, Greenwood Press, 1978.

Barker, R. and Rush, M., *The Member of Parliament and His Information*, London, Allen and Unwin, 1970.

Blom-Cooper, L. and Drewry, D., *Final Appeal: A Study of the House of Lords in Its Judicial Capacity*, London, Oxford University Press, 1972.

Bradshaw, K. and Pring, D., *Parliament and Congress*, London, Quartet Books, 1982.

Butler, D., *Governing without a Majority: Dilemmas for Hung Parliaments in Britain*, London, Collins, 1984.

Butt, R., *The Power of Parliament*, London, Constable, 1967.

Central Office of Information, *Parliamentary Elections in Britain*, London, HMSO, 1983.

Central Office of Information, *The British Parliament*, London, HMSO, 1984.

Coombes, D. and Walkland, S. A. (eds), *Parliament and Economic Affairs*, Policy Studies Institute, London, 1980.

Cormack, P., *Westminster: Palace and Parliament*, London, Warne, 1981.

Crewe, I. and Fox, A., *British Parliamentary Constituencies*, London, Faber, 1984.

Crick, B. R., *The Reform of Parliament*, London, Weidenfeld and Nicolson, 1970.

Derry, T. K., *The United Kingdom Today*, London, Longman, 1970.

Drewry, G. (ed.), *The New Select Committees: A Study of the 1979 Reforms*, London, Oxford University Press, 1985.

Englefield, D., *The Commons Select Committees: Catalysts for Progress?*, London, Longman, 1984.

Finer, S., *Anonymous Empire: A Study of the Lobby in Great Britain*, London, Pall Mall, 1966.

Gregory, R. and Hutchesson, P., *The Parliamentary Ombudsman*, London, Allen and Unwin, 1975.

Griffiths, J. A. G., *Parliamentary Scrutiny of Government Bills*, London, Allen and Unwin, 1974.

Hanson, A. H. and Wiseman, H. V., *Parliament at Work*, London, Greenwood Press, 1976.

Hartley, T. C. and Griffith, J. A. G., *Government and Law: An Introduction to the Working of the Constitution in Britain*, London, Weidenfeld and Nicolson, 1981.

Her Majesty's Stationery Office, *Questions in the House of Commons*, London, 1979.

Her Majesty's Stationery Office, *Standing Orders of the House of Commons*, London, 1980.

Her Majesty's Stationery Office, *The Select Committee System: First Report of the House of Commons Liaison Committee, 1982–83*, London, 1983.

Hollis, C., *Parliament and its Sovereignty*, London, Hollis and Carter, 1973.

Jennings, I., *The Law and the Constitution*, London, University of London Press, 1959.

Jennings, I., *Parliament*, Cambridge, Cambridge University Press, 1969.

Johnson, N., *Parliament and Administration*, London, Allen and Unwin, 1966.

Judge, D., *Backbench Specialisation in the House of Commons*, London, Heinemann, 1981.

Judge, D. (ed.), *The Politics of Parliamentary Reform*, London, Heinemann, 1983.

Leonard, R. and Valentine, H., *The Backbencher and Parliament*, London, Macmillan, 1972.

Liversidge, D., *The House of Commons*, London, Watts, 1974.

Liversidge, D., *The House of Lords*, London, Watts, 1976.

Mackintosh, J. P. (ed.), *People and Parliament*, Farnborough, Saxon House, 1978.

Margach, J., *How Parliament Works*,

London, Stacey, 1972.

Marsden, P., *The Officers of the Commons 1363–1978*, London, HMSO, 1979.

Marshall, E., *Parliament and the Public*, London, Macmillan, 1984.

Massereene and Ferrard, J. S., Lord, *The Lords*, London, Frewin, 1973.

May, T. E., Sir, *Parliamentary Practice*, London, Butterworth, 1983.

Mellors, C., *The British M.P.: A Socio-Economic Study of the House of Commons*, Aldershot, Gower, 1978.

Morgan, J., *The House of Lords and the Labour Government, 1964–70*, Oxford, Oxford University Press, 1975.

Morris, A. (ed.), *The Growth of Parliamentary Scrutiny by Committee: A Symposium*, Oxford, Pergamon, 1970.

Mosely, R. K., *Westminster Workshop*, Oxford, Pergamon, 1969.

Norton, P., *The Commons in Perspective*, Oxford, Martin Robertson, 1981.

Paterson, A., *The Law Lords*, London, Macmillan, 1982.

Punnett, R. M., *Front Bench Opposition: The Role of the Leader of the Opposition, the Shadow Cabinet and Shadow Government in British Politics*, London, Heinemann, 1973.

Raison, T., *Power and Parliament*, Oxford, Blackwell, 1980.

Rhodes, G., *Committees of Inquiry*, London, Allen and Unwin, 1975.

Richards, P. G., *The Backbenchers*, London, Faber, 1972.

Robert, H. M., *Parliamentary Practice: An Introductiom to Parliamentary Law*, London, Halsted, 1975.

Robinson, A., *Parliament and Public Spending*, London, Heinemann, 1978.

Royal Institute of Public Administration, *Parliament and the Executive*, London, RIPA, 1982.

Rush, M., *Parliament and the Public*, London, Longman, 1978.

Rush, M., *Parliamentary Government in Britain*, London, Pitman, 1981.

Stacey, F., *The British Ombudsman*, Oxford, Oxford University Press, 1971.

Taylor, E., *The House of Commons at Work*, London, Macmillan, 1979.

Vallance, E., *Women in the House: A Study of Women Members of Parliament*, London, Athlone, 1979.

Walkland, S. A. (ed.), *The House of Commons in the Twentieth Century*, Oxford, Clarendon Press, 1979.

Walkland, S. A. and Ryle, M. (eds), *The Commons Today*, Glasgow, Fontana, 1981.

Weston, C. C., *English Constitutional Theory and the House of Lords*, London, Routledge & Kegan Paul, 1965.

Winchester, S., *Their Noble Lordships: The Hereditary Peerage Today*, London, Faber, 1981.

HISTORY

Bromhead, P., *The House of Lords and Contemporary Politics, 1911–57*, London, Routledge & Kegan Paul, 1958.

Cannon, J., *Parliamentary Reform, 1640–1832*, Cambridge, Cambridge University Press, 1973.

Cobbett, H. W. (ed.), *The Parliamentary History of England from the Earliest Period to the Year 1803*, 36 vols, London, New York, Johnson Reprint Corporation, 1806–1820.

Conacher, J. B. (ed.), *The Emergence of*

British Parliamentary Democracy in the Nineteenth Century, Chichester, Wiley, 1971.

Cruikshanks, E. (ed.), *Parliamentary History*, Gloucester, A. Sutton, 1983.

Davies, R. G. and Denton, J. H. (eds), *English Parliament in the Middle Ages*, Manchester, Manchester University Press, 1981.

Fryde, E. E. and Miller, E. (eds), *Historical Studies of the English Parliament*, 2 vols, Cambridge, Cambridge University Press, 1970.

History of Parliament Trust, *House of Commons, 1558–1603*, 3 vols, London, HMSO, 1982.

History of Parliament Trust, *House of Commons, 1715–54*, 2 vols, London, HMSO, 1970.

History of Parliament Trust, *House of Commons, 1754–90*, 3 vols, London, HMSO, 1963.

Jones, C., *The Great Palace: The Story of Parliament*, London, BBC, 1983.

Norton, P., *Dissension in the House of Commons, 1945–74*, London, Macmillan, 1975.

Norton, P., *Dissension in the House of Commons, 1974–1979*, Oxford, Oxford University Press, 1980.

Parliamentary History Yearbook Trust, *Parliamentary History: A Yearbook*, Gloucester, Alan Sutton, annually.

Spufford, P., *The Origins of the English Parliament*, London, Longman, 1967.

Stevens, R., *Law and Politics: The House of Lords as a Judicial Body, 1800–1976*, London, Weidenfeld and Nicolson, 1979.

SEE ALSO:

25 POLITICAL PARTIES

For current bibliographical references to publications on British politics and political parties readers should consult: British Library of Economic and Political Science, *A London Bibliography of the Social Sciences*, annually.

Earlier reading lists on politics and parties can be found in: Bogdanor, V. (ed.), *A Bibliography for Students of Politics*, 1971; Labour Party, *Labour Party Bibliography*, 1967; Royal Institute of Public Administration, *Politics, Political Parties and Elections in the United Kingdom: A Select Bibliography*, 1975.

The following studies can be recommended as introductory general reading to British political parties: Ball, A., *British Political Parties: The Emergence of a Modern Party System*, 1981; Beattie, A. J. (comp.), *English Party Politics*, 2 vols, 1970; Central Office of Information, *The Organisation of Political Parties in Britain*, 1983; Ingle, S., *British Political Parties*, 1986; Lees, J. D. and Kimber, T. (eds), *Political Parties in Modern Britain: An Organisational and Functional Guide*, 1972; Finer, S. E., *The British Party System*, 1985; Roberts, G. K., *Political Parties and Pressure Groups in Britain*, 1970.

For suggested introductory reading on the individual political parties see the following:

Conservative Party   Blake, R., *The Conservative Party, from Peel to Thatcher*, 1985; Lane, P., *The Conservative Party*, 1974; Lindsay, T. F. and Harrington, M., *The Conservative Party, 1918–1978*, 1978.

Labour Party   Cook, C. and Taylor, I. (eds), *The Labour Party: An Introduction to its History, Structure and Politics*, 1980; Pelling, H., *A Short History of the Labour Party*, 1982.

Liberal Party   Cook, C., *A Short History of the Liberal Party, 1900–1983*, 1984; Douglas, R., *The History of the Liberal Party, 1895–1970*, 1974.

Social Democratic Party   Stephenson, H., *Claret and Chips: The Rise of the SDP*, 1982; Tracey, N., *The Origins of the Social Democratic Party*, 1983.

REFERENCE

Bogdanor, V. (ed.), *A Bibliography for Students of Politics*, London, Oxford University Press, 1971.

British Library of Economic and Political Science, *A London Bibliography of the Social Sciences*, London and New York, Mansell, annually.

Labour Party, *Labour Party Bibliography*, London, 1967.

Rees, P. (ed.), *Fascism in Britain: An Annotated Bibliography*, Brighton, Harvester, 1979.

Royal Institute of Public Administration (publisher), *Politics, Political Parties and Elections in the United Kingdom: A Select Bibliography*, London, 1975.

Smith, H. (comp.), *The British Labour Movement to 1970: A Bibliography*, London, Mansell, 1981.

Spiers, J. (ed.), *The Left in Britain: A Checklist and Guide*, Brighton, Harvester Press, 1976.

GENERAL

Ball, A., *British Political Parties: The Emergence of a Modern Party System*, London, Macmillan, 1981.

Beattie, A. J. (comp.), *English Party Politics*, 2 vols, London, Weidenfeld and Nicolson, 1970.

Bogdanor, V., *People and the Party System: Referendum and Electoral Reform in British Politics*, Cambridge, Cambridge University Press, 1981.

Bogdanor, V., *Multi-Party Politics and the Constitution*, Cambridge, Cambridge University Press, 1983.

Bogdanor, V. (ed.), *Parties and Democracy in Britain and America*, New York, Praeger, 1984.

Bulmer-Thomas, I., *The Growth of the British Party System*, 2 vols, New York, Humanities Press, 1966.

Butler, D. and Jowett, P., *Party Strategies in Britain*, London, Macmillan, 1985.

Central Office of Information, *The Organisation of Political Parties in Britain*, London, HMSO, 1983.

Coxall, W. N., *Parties and Pressure Groups*, London, Longman, 1980.

Craig, F. W. S., *British General Election Manifestoes, 1900–1974*, London, Macmillan, 1975.

Finer, S. E., *The Changing British Party System, 1945–79*, Washington D. C., American Enterprise Institute, 1980.

Finer, S. E., *The British Party System*, London, Frances Pinter, 1985.

Gyford, J., and James, M., *National Parties and Local Politics*, London, Allen and Unwin, 1983.

Hill, B. W., *The Growth of Parliamentary Parties, 1689–1742*, London, Allen and Unwin, 1976.

Hill, B. W., *British Parliamentary Parties, 1742–1832, From the Fall of Walpole to the First Reform Act*, London, Allen and Unwin, 1985.

Ingle, S., *British Political Parties*, Oxford, Blackwell, 1986.

Lane, P., *Political Parties*, London, Batsford, 1972.

Lees, J. D. and Kimber, R. (eds), *Political Parties in Modern Britain: An Organisational and Functional Guide*, London, Routledge & Kegan Paul, 1972.

O'Gorman, F., *The Emergence of the British Two-Party System, 1760–1832*, London, Arnold, 1982.

Roberts, G. K., *Political Parties and Pressure Groups in Britain*, London, Weidenfeld and Nicolson, 1970.

Rose, R., *The Problem of Party Government*, London, Macmillan, 1974.

Rose, R., *Do Parties Make a Difference?*, London, Macmillan, 1984.

Wilson, D. J., *Power and Party Bureaucracy in Britain: Regional Organisation in the Conservative and Labour Parties*, Farnborough, Saxon House, 1975.

CONSERVATIVE PARTY

Behrens, R., *Conservative Party from Heath to Thatcher, Policies and Politics 1974–79*, Farnborough, Saxon House, 1980.

Bell, D. S., (ed.), *The Conservative Government 1979–84: An Interim Report*, London, Croom Helm, 1985.

Blake, R., *The Conservative Party from Peel to Thatcher*, London, Methuen, 1985.

Block, G. D. M., *A Source Book of Conservatism*, London, Conservative Political Centre, 1964.

Buck, P. W. (ed.), *How Conservatives Think*, Harmondsworth, Penguin, 1975.

Butler, Lord et al., *The Conservatives: A History from their Origins to 1965*, London, Allen and Unwin, 1977.

Cosgrave, P., *Thatcher: The First Term*, London, Bodley Head, 1985.

Feiling, K., *A History of the Tory Party, 1640–1714*, London, Oxford University Press, 1951.

Feiling, K., *The Second Tory Party, 1714–1832*, London, Oxford

University Press, 1951.

Fisher, N., *The Tory Leaders: Their Struggle for Power*, London, Weidenfeld and Nicolson, 1977.

Gamble, A., *The Conservative Nation*, London, Routledge & Kegan Paul, 1975.

Gash, N., *The Conservatives: A History of their Origins to 1965*, London, Allen and Unwin, 1977.

Hall, S. and Jacques, M. (eds), *The Politics of Thatcherism*, London, Lawrence and Wishart, 1983.

Harris, N., *Competition and the Corporate Society: British Conservatives, the State and Industry 1945–64*, London, Methuen, 1972.

Holmes, M., *The First Thatcher Government, 1979–1983*, Brighton, Wheatsheaf, 1985.

Jones, M., *Thatcher's Kingdom: A View of Britain in the Eighties*, London, Collins, 1985.

Lane, P., *The Conservative Party*, London, Batsford, 1974.

Layton-Henry, Z. (ed.), *Conservative Party Politics*, London, Macmillan, 1980.

Lindsay, T. F. and Harrington, M., *The Conservative Party 1918–1978*, London, Macmillan, 1979.

McDowell, R. B., *British Conservatism 1832–1914*, London, Faber, 1959.

McKenzie, R. and Silver, J., *Angels in Marble: Working Class Conservatives in Urban England*, London, Heinemann, 1968.

Nugent, N. and King, R. (eds), *British Right: Conservative and Right Wing Politics for Britain*, Farnborough, Saxon House, 1977.

Ramsden, J., *The Making of Conservative Party Policy: The Conservative Research Department since 1929*, London, Longman, 1980.

Riddell, P., *The Thatcher Government*, Oxford, Blackwell, 1985.

Ross, J., *Thatcher and Friends: The Anatomy of the Tory Party*, London, Pluto, 1983.

Russel, T., *The Tory Party*, Harmondsworth, Penguin, 1978.

Stewart, R., *The Foundation of the Conservative Party, 1830–1867*, London, Longman, 1978.

Thompson, G., *Conservative Economic Policy: 1979–1984*, London, Croom Helm, 1986.

Walters, A. A., *Britain's Economic Renaissance: Margaret Thatcher's Reforms, 1979–84*, London, Oxford University Press, 1986.

White, R. J. (ed.), *The Conservative Tradition*, London, Black, 1964.

Young, H. and Sloman, A., *The Thatcher Phenomenon*, London, BBC, 1986.

LABOUR PARTY

Adelman, P., *The Rise of the Labour Party 1880–1945*, London, Longman, 1972.

Bealey, F. (ed.), *The Social and Political Thought of the British Labour Party*, London, Weidenfeld and Nicolson, 1970.

Burnell, J. B. (ed.), *Democracy and Accountability in the Labour Party*, Nottingham, Spokeman Books, 1980.

Coates, D., *The Labour Party and the Struggle for Socialism*, Cambridge, Cambridge University Press, 1975.

Coates, D., *Labour Power: A Study of the Labour Government 1974–79*, London, Longman, 1980.

Cole, G. D. H., *A History of the Labour Party from 1914*, London, Routledge & Kegan Paul, 1948.

Cole, G. D. H., *A History of Socialist Thought*, 5 vols, London, Macmillan, 1953–60.

Cole, G. D. H., *The Story of Fabian Socialism*, London, Heinemann, 1961.

Cook, C. and Taylor, I. (eds), *The Labour Party: An Introduction to its History, Structure and Politics*, London, Longman, 1980.

Cronin, J., *Labour and Society in Britain 1918–1979*, London, Batsford, 1984.

Drucker, H. M., *Doctrine and Ethos in the Labour Party*, London, Allen and Unwin, 1979.

Foote, G., *The Labour Party's Political Thought: A History*, London, Croom Helm, 1985.

Forester, T., *The Labour Party and the Working Class*, London, Heinemann, 1976.

Hindess, B., *The Decline of Working Class Politics*, London, Paladin, 1972.

Hinton, J., *Labour and Socialism: A History of the British Labour Movement, 1867–1974*, Brighton, Wheatsheaf, 1984.

Hodgson, G., *Labour At The Crossroads*, Oxford, Martin Robertson, 1981.

Holland, S., *The Socialist Challenge*, London, Quartet Books, 1976.

Howell, D., *British Social Democracy*, London, Croom Helm, 1980.

Jones, B. and Keating, M., *Labour and the British State*, Oxford, Clarendon Press, 1985.

Kavanagh, D. (ed.), *The Politics of the Labour Party*, London, Allen and Unwin, 1982.

Kogan, D. and Kogan, M., *The Battle for the Labour Party*, London, Kogan Page, 1983.

Lane, P., *The Labour Party*, London,

Batsford, 1974.

Miliband, R., *Parliamentary Socialism: A Study in the Politics of Labour*, London, Merlin, 1973.

Minkin, L., *The Labour Party Conference*, Manchester, Manchester University Press, 1978.

Moore, R., *The Emergence of the Labour Party, 1880–1924*, London, Hodder and Stoughton, 1978.

Pelling, H., *The Origins of the Labour Party, 1880–1900*, London, Oxford University Press, 1966.

Pelling, H., *A Short History of the Labour Party*, London, Macmillan, 1982.

Stewart, M., *Protest or Power: A Study of the Labour Party*, London, Allen and Unwin, 1974.

Warde, A., *Labour Party Strategy Since the Second World War*, Manchester, Manchester University Press, 1982.

Wright, A. H., *British Socialism, 1884–1964*, London, Longman, 1983.

Zentner, P., *Social Democracy in Britain: Must Labour Lose?*, London, Martin, 1982.

LIBERAL PARTY

Barker, M., *Gladstone and Radicalism: The Reconstruction of Liberal Policy in Britain 1885–94*, Hassocks, Harvester, 1975.

Bogdanor, V. (ed.), *Liberal Party Politics*, London, Oxford University Press, 1983.

Bullock, A. and Shock, M. (eds), *The Liberal Tradition*, Oxford, Oxford University Press, 1956.

Cook, C., *A Short History of the Liberal Party 1900–1983*, London, Macmillan, 1984.

Cyr, A., *Liberal Party Politics in Britain*, London, John Calder, 1977.

Dangerfield, G., *The Strange Death of Liberal England*, London, Paladin, 1970.

Douglas, R., *The History of the Liberal Party 1895–1970*, London, Sidgwick and Jackson, 1971.

Lane, P., *The Liberal Party*, London, Batsford, 1974.

McCallum, R. B., *The Liberal Party from Earl Grey to Asquith*, London, Gollancz, 1963.

Rasmussen, J., *The Liberal Party*, London, Constable, 1965.

Vincent, J., *The Formation of the Liberal Party 1857–68*, Hassocks, Harvester, 1980.

SOCIAL DEMOCRATIC PARTY

Bradley, I., *Breaking the Mould? The Birth and Prospects of the Social Democratic Party*, Oxford, Martin Robertson, 1981.

Josephs, J., *Inside the Alliance: An Inside Account of the Development and Prospects of the Social Democratic Party and Liberal Alliance*, London, Martin, 1983.

Stephenson, H., *Claret and Chips: The Rise of the SDP*, London, Michael Joseph, 1982.

Tracey, N., *The Origins of the Social Democratic Party*, London, Croom Helm, 1983.

REVOLUTIONARY LEFT

Baker, B., *The Far Left*, London, Weidenfeld and Nicolson, 1981.

Barltrop, R., *The Monument: The Story of the Socialist Party of Great Britain*, London, Pluto Press, 1976.

Branson, N., *A History of the Communist Party of Great Britain: Class-against-Class, Anti-Fascism and Imperialist War, 1927–1941*, London, Lawrence and Wishart, 1984.

Callaghan, J., *British Trotskyism: Theory and Practice*, Oxford, Blackwell, 1984.

Crick, M., *Militant*, London, Faber, 1984.

Dewar, H., *Communist Politics in Britain*, London, Pluto, 1976.

Kendall, W., *The Revolutionary Movement in Britain, 1900–1921: The Origins of British Communism*, London, Weidenfeld and Nicolson, 1969.

Klugmann, J., *History of the Communist Party of Great Britain*, 3 vols, London, Lawrence and Wishart, 1968–75.

Newton, K., *The Sociology of British Communism*, London, Allen Lane, 1970.

Pelling, H., *The British Communist Party*, London, Black, 1975.

Quail, J., *The Slow Burning Fuse: The Lost History of the British Anarchists*, London, Paladin, 1978.

Widgery, D., *The Left in Britain 1956–68*, Harmondsworth, Penguin, 1976.

EXTREME RIGHT

Benewick, R., *The Fascist Movement in Britain*, London, Allen Lane, 1973.

Cross, C., *The Fascists in Britain*, London, Barrie and Rockliffe, 1961.

Fielding, N., *The National Front*, London, Routledge & Kegan Paul, 1981.

Lunn, K. and Thurlow, R., *British Fascism*, London, Croom Helm, 1980.

Taylor, S., *The National Front in English Politics*, London, Macmillan, 1982.

Walker, M., *The National Front*, London, Fontana, 1978.

SEE ALSO:

26 POLITICS

For current bibliographical references to publications on politics readers should consult: British Library of Economic and Political Science, *A London Bibliography of the Social Sciences*, annually.

References to earlier publications on politics can be found in Bogdanor, V. (ed.), *A Bibliography for Students of Politics*, 1971; Goehlert, R., *Resources for the Study of British Politics*, 1979; Macdonald, K. I., *The Essex Reference Index: British Journals on Politics and Sociology 1850–1973*, 1975; Royal Institute of Public Administration, *Politics, Political Parties and Elections in the United Kingdom: A Select Bibliography*, 1975.

The following also contain bibliographical references and guides to sources of information: Brennan, T., *Political Studies: A Handbook for Teachers*, 1975; Mardall, B., *How to Find out in Politics and Government*, 1976.

Useful general studies of political life and institutions in Britain can be found in: Berrington, H. (ed.), *Change in British Politics*, 1984; Birch, A. H., *Political Integration and Disintegration in the British Isles*, 1980; Budge, I. et al., *The New British Political System*, 1983; Dearlove, J. and Saunders, P., *Introduction to British Politics: Analysing Capitalist Democracy*, 1984; Drucker, H. et al. (eds), *Developments in British Politics*, 1984; Hall, S. et al. (eds), *State and Society in Contemporary Britain*, 1984; Jones, B. and Kavanagh, D. (eds), *British Politics Today: A Student's Guide*, 1979; Leys, C., *Politics in Britain: An Introduction*, 1983; Mackintosh, J. P., *The Government and Politics of Britain*, 1984; Miliband, R., *Capitalist Democracy in Britain*, 1984; Rose, R., *Politics in England: An Interpretation for the 1980's*, 1980; Sampson, A., *The Changing Anatomy of Britain*, 1982.

The following provide useful coverage of elections and electoral politics in Britain: Alderman, G., *British Elections: Myth and Reality*, 1978; Butler, D. E., *The Electoral System in Britain since 1918*, 1963; Central Office of Information, *Parliamentary Elections in Britain*, 1978: Pulzer, P. G., *Political Representation and Elections in Britain*, 1975; McAllister, I. and Rose, P., *The Nationwide Competition for Votes*, 1984.

REFERENCE

Bogdanor, V. (ed.), *A Bibliography for Students of Politics*, London, Oxford University Press, 1971.

Butcher, D., *Official Publications in Britain*, London, Bingley, 1982.

Cook, C. and Weeks, J. (eds), *Sources in British Political History, 1900–1951*, 5 vols, London, Macmillan, 1975–8.

Goehlert, R., *Resources for the Study of British Politics*, Monticello, Ill., Vance Bibliographies, 1979.

Kinnear, M., *The British Voter: An Atlas and Survey since 1885*, London, Batsford, 1981.

Macdonald, K. I., *The Essex Reference Index: British Journals on Politics and Sociology, 1850–1973*, London, Macmillan, 1975.

Mardall, B., *How to Find out in Politics and Government*, London, LLRS Publications, 1977.

Royal Institute of Public Administration

(publisher), *Politics, Political Parties and Elections in the United Kingdom: A Select Bibliography*, London, 1975.

Shipley, P. (ed.), *The Guardian Directory of Pressure Groups and Representative Associations*, London, Wilton House, 1976.

Social Science Research Council, *Political Science Theses*, London, annually.

Waller, R., *The Almanac of British Politics*, London, Croom Helm, 1983.

Waller, R., *The Atlas of British Politics*, London, Croom Helm, 1985.

GENERAL

Alderman, G., *British Elections: Myth and Reality*, London, Batsford, 1978.

Alderman, G., *Pressure Groups and Government in Great Britain*, London, Longman, 1984.

Alderson, S., *Yea or Nay? Referenda in the United Kingdom*, London, Cassell, 1975.

Ashford, D. E., *Policy and Politics in Britain: The Limits of Consensus*, Oxford, Blackwell, 1981.

Bailey, S. D., *British Parliamentary Democracy*, London, Greenwood Press, 1978.

Barker, R., *Political Ideas in Modern Britain*, London, Methuen, 1978.

Beer, S. H., *Britain against Itself: Political Contradictions of Collectivism*, London, Norton, 1982.

Beer, S. H., *Modern British Politics: A Study of Parties and Pressure Groups*, London, Faber, 1982.

Bentley, M. and Stevenson, J. (eds), *High and Low Politics in Modern Britain*, London, Oxford University Press, 1983.

Berrington, H. (ed.), *Change in British Politics*, London, Cass, 1984.

Birch, A. H., *Political Integration and Disintegration in the British Isles*, London, Allen and Unwin, 1980.

Bogdanor, V., *The People and the Party System: The Referendum and Electoral Reform in British Politics*, Cambridge, Cambridge University Press, 1981.

Bogdanor, V., *Multi-Party Politics and the Constitution*, Cambridge, Cambridge University Press, 1983.

Bogdanor, V., *What is Proportional Representation? A Guide to the Issues*, Oxford, Martin Robertson, 1983.

Borthwick, R. L. and Spence, J. E. (eds), *British Politics in Perspective*, Leicester, Leicester University Press, 1984.

Brennan, T., *Political Studies: A Handbook for Teachers*, London, Longman, 1975.

Budge, I. et al., *The New British Political System*, London, Longman, 1983.

Budge, I. and Farlie, D. J., *Voting and Party Competition*, Chichester, Wiley, 1977.

Bulmer-Thomas, I., *The Growth of the British Party System*, 2 vols, London, Baker, 1965.

Burch, M. and Wood, B., *Public Policy in Britain*, Oxford, Martin Robertson, 1983.

Butler, D. E., *The Electoral System in Britain since 1918*, London, Oxford University Press, 1963.

Butler, D. E. and Butler, G., *British Political Facts, 1900–1985*, London, Macmillan, 1986.

Butler, D. E. and Jowett, P., *Party Strategies in Britain: A Study of the 1984 European Elections*, London, Macmillan, 1985.

Butler, D. E. and Stokes, D., *Political Change in Britain*, London, Macmillan, 1975.

Central Office of Information, *Parliamentary Elections in Britain*, London, HMSO, 1978.

Coates, D., *British Politics*, London, Hutchinson, 1984.

Coates, D. et al. (eds), *A Socialist Anatomy of Britain*, Cambridge, Polity Press, 1985.

Cook, C. and Ramsden, J. A. (eds), *By-Elections in British Politics*, London, Macmillan, 1973.

Craig, F. W. S. (ed.), *British General*

Election Manifestoes 1900–1974, London, Macmillan, 1975.

Cronin, J. E. and Schneer, J., *Social Conflict and the Political Order in Modern Britain*, London, Croom Helm, 1982.

Dahrendorf, R., *On Britain*, London, BBC, 1983.

Dearlove, J. and Saunders, P., *Introduction to British Politics: Analysing Capitalist Democracy*, Cambridge, Polity Press, 1984.

Doig, A., *Corruption and Misconduct in Contemporary British Politics*, Harmondsworth, Penguin, 1983.

Drucker, H., *The Politics of Nationalism and Devolution*, London, Longman, 1980.

Drucker, H. et al. (eds), *Developments in British Politics*, London, Macmillan, 1984.

Dunleavy, P. and Husbands, C. T., *British Democracy at the Crossroads: Voting and Party Competition in the 1980s*, London, Allen and Unwin, 1985.

Finer, S. E. (ed.), *Adversary Politics and Electoral Reform*, London, Wigram, 1975.

Forman, F. N., *Mastering British Politics*, London, Macmillan, 1985.

Franklin, M. N., *The Decline of Class Voting in Britain*, London, Oxford University Press, 1985.

Gamble, A. and Walkland, S. A., *The British Party System and Economic Policy, 1945–83: Studies in Adversary Politics*, Oxford, Clarendon Press, 1984.

Greenleaf, W. H., *The British Political Tradition, Vol. I. The Rise of Collectivism*, London, Methuen, 1983.

Greenleaf, W. H., *The British Political Tradition, Vol. II. The Ideological Heritage*, London, Methuen, 1983.

Gyford, J., *Local Politics in Britain*, London, Croom Helm 1983.

Hailsham, Lord, *The Dilemma of Democracy*, London, Collins, 1978.

Hall, S. et al. (eds), *State and Society in Contemporary Britain*, Cambridge, Polity Press, 1984.

Harvey, J. and Bather, L., *The British Constitution*, London, Macmillan, 1972.

Heald, G. and Wybrow, R. J., *The Gallup Survey of Britain*, London, Croom Helm, annually.

Heath, A. et al., *How Britain Votes*, Oxford, Pergamon, 1985.

Himmelweit, H. T. et al., *How Voters Decide*, London, Academic Press, 1981.

Jackson, R. J., *Rebels and Whips: An Analysis of Dissension, Discipline and Cohesion in British Political Parties*, London, Macmillan, 1968.

James, R. R., *British Revolution, British Politics*, 2 vols, London, Hamish Hamilton, 1976–7.

Jennings, I., *Party Politics*, 3 vols, Cambridge, Cambridge University Press, 1962.

Jessop, B., *Traditionalism, Conservatism and British Political Culture*, London, Allen and Unwin, 1974.

Jewell, R. E. C., *The British Constitution*, London, Hodder and Stoughton, 1975.

Johnston, R. J., *Who Votes Where? The Geography of the 1983 General Election in England*, London, Croom Helm, 1985.

Jones, B. (ed.), *Political Issues in Britain Today*, Manchester, Manchester University Press, 1985.

Jones, B. and Kavanagh, D. (eds), *British Politics Today: A Student's Guide*, Manchester, Manchester University Press, 1979.

Jones, G. A., *The Political Structure*, London, Longman, 1969.

Jowell, R. and Airey, C. (eds), *British Social Attitudes*, Aldershot, Gower, 1984–.

Kavanagh, D., *British Politics: Continuities and Change*, London, Oxford University Press, 1985.

Kavanagh, D. and Rose, R. (eds), *New Trends in British Politics*, London, Sage, 1977.

Kimber, R. and Richardson, J. J. (eds), *Pressure Groups in Britain*, London, Everyman, 1974.

Koss, S., *Nonconformity in Modern*

British Politics, London, Batsford, 1975.

Lakeman, E., *Power to Elect: The Case for Proportional Representation*, London, Heinemann, 1984.

Leeds, C., *Politics in Action: Contemporary Sources for Students of Politics and Government*, Cheltenham, Thornes, 1986.

Leys, C., *Politics in Britain: An Introduction*, London, Heinemann, 1983.

McAllister, I. and Rose, P., *The Nationwide Competition for Votes*, London, Frances Pinter, 1984.

McBriar, A. M., *Fabian Socialism and English Politics*, Cambridge, Cambridge University Press, 1966.

Macfarlane, L. J., *Issues in British Politics since 1945*, London, Longman, 1982.

Mackintosh, J. P., *The Government and Politics of Britain*, London, Hutchinson, 1984.

Madgwick, P. J., *Introduction to British Politics*, London, Hutchinson, 1984.

Madgwick, P. and Rose, R., *The Territorial Dimension in United Kingdom Politics*, London, Macmillan, 1982.

Marsh, A., *Protest and Political Consciousness*, London, Sage, 1977.

Marsh, D. (ed.), *Pressure Politics: Interest Groups in Britain*, London, Fourth Estate, 1985.

Middlemass, K., *Politics in Industrial Society: The Experience of the British System since 1911*, London, Deutsch, 1980.

Miliband, R., *Capitalist Democracy in Britain*, London, Oxford University Press, 1984.

Miller, W., *Electoral Dynamics in Britain since 1918*, London, Macmillan, 1977.

Miller, W., *The End of British Politics? Scots and English Political Behaviour in the Seventies*, London, Oxford University Press, 1981.

Moran, M., *Politics and Society in Modern Britain: An Introduction*, London, Macmillan, 1985.

Nairn, T., *The Break-Up of Britain*, London, Verso, 1982.

Norton, P., *The British Polity*, London, Longman, 1984.

Penniman, H. (ed.), *Britain at the Polls*, Washington D.C., American Enterprise Institute, 1981.

Pinto-Duschinsky, V. H. M., *British Political Finance, 1830–1980*. Washington D. C., American Enterprise Institute, 1981.

Proudfoot, M., *British Politics and Government 1951–1970*, London, Faber, 1974.

Pugh, M., *The Making of Modern British Politics, 1867–1939*, Oxford, Blackwell, 1982.

Ranney, A. (ed.), *Britain at the Polls 1983: A Study of the General Election*, London, Duke University Press, 1985.

Robertson, D., *Class and the British Electorate*, Oxford, Blackwell, 1984.

Robins, L. (ed.), *Topics in British Politics*, London, The Politics Association, 1982.

Rose, R., *The Problem of Party Government*, London, Macmillan, 1974.

Rose, R., *Politics in England: Persistence and Change*, London, Faber, 1985.

Rose, R., *Politics in England: An Interpretation for the 1980's*, London, Faber, 1980.

Sampson, A., *The Changing Anatomy of Britain*, Sevenoaks, Hodder and Stoughton, 1982.

Särlvik, B. and Crewe, I., *Decade of Dealignment: the Conservative Victory of 1979 and Electoral Trends in the 1970's*, Cambridge, Cambridge University Press, 1983.

Saunders, P., *Urban Politics*, London, Hutchinson, 1979.

Studlar, D. T. and Waltman, J. L. (eds), *Dilemmas of Change in British Politics*, London, Macmillan, 1984.

Taylor, P. J. and Johnston, R. J., *Geography of Elections*, Harmondsworth, Penguin, 1979.

Wooton, G., *Pressure Politics and Contemporary Britain*, San Diego, CA, Lexington Books, 1978.

SEE ALSO:

27 POPULAR CULTURE

The following books are particularly recommended as useful studies in their respective fields:

Advertising   Williamson, J., *Decoding Advertisements*, 1978.
Children's Literature   Carpenter, H. and Pritchard, M., *The Oxford Companion to Children's Literature*, 1984.
Fashion   Hebdige, D., *Subculture: The Meaning of Style*, 1979.
Humour and Satire   Wilmut, R., *From Fringe to Flying Circus*, 1982.
Popular Literature   Sutherland, J., *Bestsellers: Popular Fiction in the 1970's*, 1981.
Pop Music   Frith, S., *Sound Effects: Youth, Leisure and the Politics of Rock 'n' Roll*, 1983.
Women's Magazines   Ferguson, M., *Forever Feminine: The Sociology of Women's Magazines*, 1983.
Youth Culture   Brake, M., *The Sociology of Youth Culture and Youth Subcultures: Sex, Drugs and Rock 'n' Roll*, 1980.

GENERAL

Barker, M., *A Haunt of Fears: The Strange History of the British Horror Comics Campaign*, London, Pluto, 1984.

Bisgby, C. W. E. (ed.), *Approaches to Popular Culture*, London, Arnold, 1976.

Brake, M., *The Sociology of Youth Culture and Youth Subcultures: Sex, Drugs and Rock 'n' Roll?*, London, Routledge & Kegan Paul, 1980.

Busby, R., *British Music Hall: An Illustrated Who's Who from 1850 to the Present Day*, London, Elek, 1976.

Clarke, J. and Jefferson, T., *Culture and Sub-Culture: The Politics of Popular Culture*, Birmingham, Centre for Contemporary Cultural Studies, 1973.

Cohen, S., *Folk Devils and Moral Panics: The Creation of the Mods and Rockers*, London, MacGibbon & Kee, 1972.

Davis, H. and Walton, P., *Language, Image, Media*, Oxford, Blackwell, 1983.

Everett, P. *You'll Never Be Sixteen Again: An Illustrated History Of The British Teenager*, London, BBC, 1986.

Frith, S., *Sound Effects: Youth, Leisure and the Politics of Rock 'n' Roll*, London, Constable, 1983.

Gifford, D. (ed.), *British Comic Catalogue, 1874–1974*, London, Mansell, 1975.

Golby, J. M. and Purdue, A. W., *The Civilisation of the Crowd: Popular Culture in England, 1750–1900*, London, Batsford, 1984.

Hall, S. and Jefferson, T. (eds), *Resistance through Rituals*, London, Hutchinson, 1976.

Hall, S. et al. (eds), *Culture, Media and Language*, London, Hutchinson, 1980.

Harker, D., *One for the Money: Politics and Popular Song*, London, Hutchinson, 1980.

Hebdige, D., *Subculture: The Meaning of Style*, London, Methuen, 1979.

Hoggart, R., *The Uses of Literacy*, Harmondsworth, Penguin, 1984.

Hudson, K., *Dictionary of the Teenage Revolution and its Aftermath*, London, Macmillan, 1983.

Jasper, T. (comp.), *The Top Twenty Book: The Official British Record Charts 1955–1983*, Poole, Blandford, 1983.

Jones, B., *The Politics of Popular Culture*, Birmingham, Centre for Contemporary Cultural Studies, 1974.

Jones, J. P., *Gambling Yesterday and Today: A Complete History*, Newton Abbot, David and Charles, 1973.

Laing, D., *One Chord Wonders: Power and Meaning in Punk Rock*, Milton Keynes, Open University Press, 1985.

Melly, G., *Revolt into Style: Pop Arts in Britain*, London, Allen Lane, 1970.

Morley, D. and Warpole, K. (eds), *Republic of Letters: Working Class Writing and Local Publishing*, London, Comedia, 1982.

Mungham, G. and Pearson, G. (eds), *Working-Class Youth Culture*, London, Routledge & Kegan Paul, 1976.

Murdock, G., *Culture, Class and Schooling: The Impact of Pop*, London, Constable, 1974.

Myers, K., *Understains: The Sense and Seduction of Advertising*, London, Comedia, 1986.

Nuttall, J., *Bomb Culture*, London, Paladin, 1970.

Reay, B. (ed.), *Popular Culture in Seventeenth Century England*, London, Croom Helm, 1985.

Smith, M. and Miles, P., *Cinema, Literature and Society: Elite and Mass Culture in Interwar Britain*, London, Croom Helm, 1985.

Steward, S. and Garrett, S., *Signed, Sealed and Delivered: True Life Stories of Women in Pop*, London, Pluto, 1984.

Thompson, D. (ed.), *Discrimination and Popular Culture*, Harmondsworth, Penguin, 1974.

Waites, B. et al. (eds), *Pop Culture, Past and Present*, London, Croom Helm, 1982.

Williamson, J., *Decoding Advertisements*, London, Marion Boyars, 1978.

Williamson, J., *Consuming Passions: The Dynamics of Popular Culture*, London, Marion Boyars, 1986.

Willis, P., *Profane Culture*, London, Routledge & Kegan Paul, 1978.

Wilmut, R., *From Fringe to Flying Circus*, London, Methuen, 1982.

Wilson, B., *The Youth Culture and the Universities*, London, Faber, 1970.

Yeo, E. and Yeo, S., *Popular Culture and Class Conflict 1590–1914: Explorations in the History of Labour and Leisure*, Hassocks, Harvester, 1981.

York, P., *Style Wars*, London, Sidgwick and Jackson, 1980.

FICTION

Alderson, C., *Magazines Teenagers Read*, Oxford, Pergamon Press, 1968.

Altick, R. D., *The English Common Reader: A Social History of the Mass Reading Public, 1800–1900*, Chicago, University of Chicago Press, 1957.

Cadogan, M. and Craig, P., *You're a Brick, Angela: A New Look at Girls' Fiction, 1840–1975*, London, Gollancz, 1976.

Carpenter, H. and Pritchard, M., *The Oxford Companion to Children's Literature*, Oxford, Oxford University Press, 1984.

Dalziel, M., *Popular Fiction a Hundred Years Ago*, London, Cohen and West, 1957.

Dixon, B., *Catching Them Young, Vol. 1, Sex, Race and Class in Children's Fiction*, London, Pluto, 1977.

Dixon, B., *Catching Them Young,*

Vol. 2, Political Ideas in Children's Fiction, London, Pluto, 1977.

Ferguson, M., *Forever Feminine. The Sociology of Women's Magazines*, London, Heinemann, 1983.

James, L., *Fiction for the Working Man*, Harmondsworth, Penguin, 1974.

Klaus, H. G., *The Literature of Labour: 200 Years of Working Class Writing*, Brighton, Harvester Press, 1985.

Knight, S., *Form and Ideology in Crime Fiction*, London, Macmillan, 1980.

Leeson, R., *Reading and Righting*, London, Collins, 1985.

Neuburg, V. E. (ed.), *Popular Literature: A History and Guide*, Harmondsworth, Penguin, 1977.

Neuburg, V. E. (ed.), *The Batsford Companion to Popular Literature*, London, Batsford, 1982.

Palmer, J., *Thrillers: Genesis and Structure of a Popular Genre*, London, Arnold, 1978.

Pawling, C. (ed.), *Popular Fiction and Social Change*, London, Macmillan, 1984.

Sauerberg, L. O., *The Secret Agent in Fiction*, London, Macmillan, 1984.

Sutherland, J., *Fiction and the Fiction Industry*, London, Athlone, 1978.

Sutherland, J., *Bestsellers: Popular Fiction in the 1970's*, London, Routledge & Kegan Paul, 1981.

Symons, J., *Bloody Murder: From the Detective Story to the Crime Novel*, London, Viking, 1985.

Warpole, K., *Dockers and Detectives: Popular Reading, Popular Writing*, London, Verso, 1983.

Warpole, K., *Reading by Numbers: Contemporary Publishing and Popular Fiction*, London, Marion Boyars, 1984.

SEE ALSO:

17 Media
21 Music
34 Sport and Leisure

28 RELIGION

For access to general information and research sources on religion and religious practice in Britain today see Brierly, P. (ed.), *U.K. Christian Handbook*, 1984.

For research guides to religious history readers are directed to Chadwick, O., *The History of the Church: A Select Bibliography*, 1966; Institute of Religion and Theology of Great Britain and Ireland, *Current Research*, annually.

Outline surveys of religion in Great Britain are provided in: Bowker, J., *Worlds of Faith: Religious Belief and Practice in Britain Today*, 1983; Hick, J., *God Has Many Names: Britain's New Religious Pluralism*, 1980; Jenkins, D., *The British, Their Identity and Their Religion*, 1975.

Comprehensive studies of theology and religious practice are: Davies, H., *Worship and Theology in England*, 5 vols, 1961–75. For historical surveys see Dickinson, J. C. (ed.), *An Ecclesiastical History of England*, 4 vols, 1961–1979; Moorman, J. R. H., *A History of the Church in England*, 1973; Norman, E. R., *Church and Society in England, 1770–1970*, 1976; Stephens, W. P. and Hunt, W. (eds), *A History of the English Church*, 8 vols, 1899–1910.

The following are recommended as introductory reading to particular areas:

Catholicism   Norman, E., *Roman Catholicism in England*, 1985; Reynolds. E. E., *The Roman Catholic Church in England and Wales: A Short History*, 1973.

Church of England   Balleine, G. R. and Davies, C., *A Popular History of the Church of England*, 1976; Welsby, P. A., *A History of the Church of England, 1945–80*, 1984.

Methodism   Davies, R., *Methodism*, 1976; Davies, R. and Rupp, G. (eds), *A History of the Methodist Church in Great Britain*, 1965–.

Quakers   Braithwaite, W. C., *The Beginnings of Quakerism*, 1974.

Reformation   Dickens, A. G., *The English Reformation*, 1967; Powicke, F. M., *The Reformation in England*, 1961.

REFERENCE

Associated Catholic Newspapers, *The Catholic Directory of England and Wales*, London, annually.

Baptist Union of Great Britain and Ireland, *The Baptist Union Directory*, London, annually.

Brierly, P. (ed.), *U. K. Christian Handbook*, London, Evangelical Alliance, 1984.

Chadwick, O., *The History of the Church: A Select Bibliography*, London, Historical Association, 1966.

Church Information Office, *The Church of England Yearbook*, London, annually.

Church of Scotland, *The Church of Scotland Yearbook*, Edinburgh, annually.

Congregational Union, *The Congregational Year Book*, London, annually.

Cross, F. L. and Livingstone, E. A., *The*

Oxford Dictionary of the Christian Church, London, Oxford University Press, 1974.

Institute of Religion and Theology of Great Britain and Ireland, *Current Research*, Newport, Salop., annually.

Ollard, S. L. et al. (eds), *A Dictionary of English Church History*, Oxford,

Mowbray, 1948.

Oxford University Press (publisher), *Crockford's Clerical Directory*, London, annually.

Publishing Office of the Presbyterian Church, *The Official Handbook of the Presbyterian Church of England*, London, annually.

GENERAL

Barley, M. W. and Hanson, R. P. C. (eds), *Christianity in Britain, 300–700*, Leicester, Leicester University Press, 1968.

Bowker, J., *Worlds of Faith: Religious Belief and Practice in Britain Today*, London, Ariel, 1983.

Buckley, G. T., *Atheism in the English Renaissance*, Chicago, University of Chicago Press, 1986.

Budd, S., *Varieties of Unbelief: Atheists and Agnostics in English Society, 1850–1960*, London, Heinemann, 1977.

Campbell, C., *Towards a Sociology of Irreligion*, London, Macmillan, 1971.

Chadwick, O. (ed.), *The Pelican History of the Church*, 6 vols, Harmondsworth, Penguin, 1964–72.

Chadwick, O., *The Victorian Church*, 2 vols, London, Black, 1971–2.

Church Information Office, *Church and State*, London, 1970.

Collinson, P., *The Elizabethan Puritan Movement*, London, Cape, 1967.

Cornwell, P., *The Church and the Nations: The Case for Disestablishment*, Oxford, Blackwell, 1983.

Coulton, G. G., *Five Centuries of Religion*, 4 vols, Woodbridge, Suffolk, Boydell Press, 1980.

Cowherd, R. G., *The Politics of English Dissent*, London, Epworth Press, 1959.

Cowling, M., *Religion and Public Doctrine in Modern England*, 2 vols, Cambridge, Cambridge University Press. 1980.

Cragg, G. R., *The Church and the Age of Reason, 1648–1789*, Harmondsworth, Penguin, 1970.

Cross, C., *Church and People, 1450–1660, The Triumph of the Laity in the English Church*, London, Fontana, 1976.

Currie, R., *Church and Churchgoers: Patterns of Church Growth in the British Isles since 1700*, Oxford, Oxford University Press, 1978.

Davies, H., *Worship and Theology in England*, 5 vols, Princeton, Princeton University Press, 1961–75.

Dickens, A. G., *The English Reformation*, London, Fontana, 1967.

Dickinson, J. C. (ed.), *An Ecclesiastical History of England*, 4 vols, London, Black, 1961–79.

Edwards, D. L., *Christian England: Its Story to the Reformation*, 3 vols, Glasgow, Collins, 1981–4.

Gay, J. D., *The Geography of Religion in England*, London, Duckworth, 1971.

George, C. H. and George, K., *The Protestant Mind of the English Reformation, 1570–1640*, London, Princeton, Princeton University Press, 1961.

Gilbert, A. D., *Religion and Society in Industrial England: Church, Chapel and Social Change, 1740–1914*, London, Longman, 1976.

Gilbert, A. D., *The Making of Post-Christian Britain: The History of the Secularisation of Modern Society*, London, Longman 1980.

Hammond, G., *The Making of the English Bible*, Manchester, Carcanet, 1982.

Heal, F. and O'Day, R., *Church and Society in England: Henry VIII to James I*, London, Macmillan, 1977.

Hick, J., *God Has Many Names: Britain's New Religious Pluralism*, London, Macmillan, 1980.

Hill, C., *Society and Puritanism in Pre-Revolutionary England*, London, Panther, 1969.

Hill, C., *The World Turned Upside Down*, Harmondsworth, Penguin, 1975.

Hughes, P., *The Reformation in England*, 3vols, London, Hollis and Carter, 1951–4.

Hunter, A. G., *Christianity and Other Faiths in Britain*, London, SCM Press, 1985.

Independent Television Authority (publisher), *Religion in Britain and Northern Ireland*, London, 1970.

Jenkins, D., *The British, their Identity and their Religion*, London, S.C.M. Press, 1975.

Jordan, W. K., *The Development of Religious Toleration in England*, 4 vols, London, Allen and Unwin, 1932–40.

Knowles, D., *The Monastic Order in England: A History of its Development from the Times of St Dunstan to the Fourth Lateran Council*, Cambridge, Cambridge University Press, 1963.

Knowles, D., *The Religious Orders in England*, 3vols, Cambridge, Cambridge University Press, 1948–79.

Knowles, D. and Hadcock, R. N., *Medieval Religious Houses: England and Wales*, London, Longman, 1971.

Koss, S., *Nonconformity in Modern British Politics*, London, Batsford, 1975.

Laqueur, T., *Religion and Respectability: Sunday Schools and Working Class Culture, 1780–1850*, New Haven, Yale University Press, 1976.

Lawrence, C. H. (ed.), *The English Church and the Papacy in the Middle Ages*, London, Burns and Oates, 1965.

Macfarlane, K. B., *Wycliffe and the Beginnings of English Nonconformity*, Harmondsworth, Penguin, 1972.

McGregor, J. F. and Reay, B. (ed.), *Radical Religion in the English Revolution*, London, Oxford University Press, 1984.

Manwaring, R., *From Controversy to Co-existence: Evangelicals in the Church of England, 1914–1980*, Cambridge, Cambridge University Press, 1985.

Martin, D., *A Sociology of English Religion*, London, Heinemann, 1967.

Moorman, J. R. H., *A History of the Church in England*, London, Black, 1973.

Morton, A. L., *The World of the Ranters, Religious Radicalism in the English Revolution*, London, Lawrence and Wishart, 1979.

Nicholls, D., *Church and State in Britain since 1820*, London, Routledge & Kegan Paul, 1967.

Norman, E. R., *Church and Society in England 1770–1970, A Historical Survey*, London, Oxford University Press, 1976.

O'Day, R., *The English Clergy*, Leicester, Leicester University Press, 1979.

Pailin, D., *Attitudes to other Religions: Comparative Religion in Seventeenth and Eighteenth Century Britain*, Manchester, Manchester University Press, 1984.

Pawley, B. and Pawley, M., *Rome and Canterbury through Four Centuries: A Study of the Relations between the Church of Rome and the Anglican Churches 1530–1973*, Oxford, Mowbray, 1981.

Powicke, F. M., *The Reformation in England*, Oxford, Oxford University Press, 1961.

Powicke, F. M., *The Christian Life in the Middle Ages*, London, Greenwood Press, 1973.

Reardon, B. M. G., *Religious Thought in the Victorian Age*, London, Longman, 1980.

Rupp, G., *Religion in England, 1688–1971*, Oxford, Clarendon Press, 1986.

Spinks, G. S., *Religion in Britain since 1900*, London, Datters, 1962.

Stephens, W. P. and Hunt, W. (eds), *A History of the English Church*, 8 vols, London, Macmillan, 1899–1910.

Tawney, R. H., *Religion and the Rise of Capitalism*, Harmondsworth, Penguin, 1969.

Towler, R., *The Need for Certainty: A Sociological Study of Conventional Religion*, London, Routledge & Kegan Paul, 1985.

Ward, W. R., *Religion and Society in England, 1790–1850*, London, Batsford, 1972.

Youings, J., *The Dissolution of the Monasteries*, London, Allen and Unwin, 1972.

CHURCH OF ENGLAND

Armstrong, A., *The Church of England, the Methodists and Society, 1700–1850*, London, University of London Press, 1972.

Balleine, G. R. and Davies, C., *A Popular History of the Church of England*, London, Vine Books, 1976.

Cuming, G., *A History of Anglican Liturgy*, London, Macmillan, 1982.

Davies, R. E., *The Church of England Observed*, London, S.C.M. Press, 1984.

Dixon, R. W., *A History of the Church of England from the Abolition of the Roman Jurisdiction*, 6 vols,

Amersham, Farnborough, Gregg International, 1971.

Holloway, R.(ed.), *Anglican Tradition*, Oxford, Mowbray, 1984.

Kilminster, A. (ed.), *When Will Ye Be Wise? The State and the Church of England*, London, Blond and Briggs, 1983.

Moorman, J. R. H., *The Anglican Spiritual Tradition*, London, Darton, Longman and Todd, 1983.

Welsby, P. A., *A History of the Church of England, 1945–80*, London, Oxford University Press, 1984.

CATHOLIC CHURCH

Bossy, J., *The English Catholic Community, 1570–1850*, London, Darton, Longman and Todd, 1975.

Edwards, F., *The Jesuits in England: From 1580 to the Present Day*, Tunbridge Wells, Burns and Oates, 1985.

Hickey, J., *Urban Catholics in England and Wales from 1829 to the Present Day*, London, Chapman, 1967.

Leys, M. D. R., *Catholics in England 1559–1829. A Social History*, London, Longman, 1961.

Norman, E., *The English Catholic Church in the Nineteenth Century*,

Oxford, Clarendon Press, 1984.

Norman, E., *Roman Catholicism in England: From the Elizabethan Settlement to the Second Vatican Council*, London, Oxford University Press, 1985.

Reynolds, E. E., *The Roman Catholic Church in England and Wales: A Short History*, Wheathampstead, A. Clarke Books, 1973.

Watkin, E. I., *Roman Catholicism in England from the Reformation to 1950*, London, Oxford University Press, 1957.

METHODISTS AND OTHER CHURCHES

Armstrong, A., *The Church of England, the Methodists and Society, 1700–1850*, London, University of London Press, 1973.

Baker, F., *John Wesley and the Church of England*, London, Epworth, 1970.

Bebb, E. D., *Nonconformity and Social*

Economic Life, 1660–1800, London, Epworth, 1935.

Bolam, C. G. et al., *The English Presbyterians: From Elizabethan Puritanism to Modern Unitarianism*, London, Allen and Unwin, 1968.

Braithwaite, W. C., *The Beginnings of*

Quakerism, York, Sessions, 1974.

Braithwaite, W. C., *The Second Period of Quakerism*, York, Sessions, 1974.

Briggs, J. H. Y. and Sellars, I. (eds), *Victorian Nonconformity*, London, Arnold, 1973.

Clark, H. W., *History of English Nonconformity*, 2 vols, London, Chapman and Hall, 1911–13.

Davies, R., *Methodism*, London, Epworth Press, 1976.

Davies, R. and Rupp, G. (eds), *A History of the Methodist Church in Great Britain*, London, Epworth Press, 1965–.

Hempton, D., *Methodism and Politics in British Society, 1750–1850*, London, Hutchinson, 1984.

Jones, R. T., *Congregationalism in England, 1662–1962*, London, Independent Press, 1962.

McFarlane, J. B., *John Wycliffe and the Beginnings of English Nonconformity*, London, English Universities Press, 1970.

Pudney, J., *John Wesley and his World*, London, Thames and Hudson, 1979.

Reay, B., *The Quakers and the English Revolution*, Hounslow, Maurice Temple Smith, 1985.

Semmel, P., *The Methodist Revolution*, London, Heinemann, 1974.

Thompson, D. M. (ed.), *Nonconformity in the Nineteenth Century*, London, Routledge & Kegan Paul, 1972.

Underwood, A. C., *A History of the English Baptists*, London, Baptist Union, 1947.

Vann, R. T., *The Social Development of English Quakerism, 1655–1755*, Harvard, Harvard University Press, 1970.

Vipoint, E., *The Story of Quakerism*, London, Quaker Home Service, 1977.

Wilson, B. R., *Sects and Society: A Sociological Study of Three Religious Groups in Britain*, London, Greenwood Press, 1978.

29 SCIENCE AND TECHNOLOGY

For detailed information on sources of information on science, technology and medicine see: Burkett, J. (ed.), *Directory of Scientific Directories*, 1984; British Council, *British Scientific Documentary Services*, 1974; British Library, *Current Research in Britain: Physical Sciences*, Boston Spa, annually; British Library, *Current Research in Britain: Biological Sciences*, Boston Spa, annually; Cabinet Office, *Government Research and Development: A Guide to Sources of Information*, 1979; Codlin, E. M. (ed.), *ASLIB Directory, vol. 1, Information Sources in Science, Technology and Commerce*, 1982; Codlin, E. M. (ed.), *ASLIB Directory, vol. 2, Information Sources in the Social Sciences, Medicine and the Humanities*, 1984; Grogan, D., *Science and Technology: An Introduction to the Literature*, 1982; Henwood, F. (comp.), *Science, Technology and Innovation: A Research Bibliography*, 1983; Lambert. J. and Lambert, P.A., *How to Find Information in Science and Technology*, London, Library Association, 1986; Science Research Council, *Annual Report*, annually; Walford, A. J. (ed.), *Guide to Reference Material, vol. 1, Science and Technology*, 1980.

For outline surveys on British work in science and technology, past and present, see Cabinet Office, *Annual Review of Government Funded R. & D.*, annually; Central Office of Information, *British Inventions: A Study of Discovery and Development*, 1975; Central Office of Information, *British Achievements in Science and Technology*, 1981; Central Office of Information, *Some British Records and Achievements in Science, Industry and Technology*, 1965; Central Office of Information, *The Promotion of the Sciences in Britain*, 1978; Royal Society (publisher), *Highlights of British Science*, 1978; Science and Engineering Research Council, *Annual Report*, annually.

The following provide useful reading on current science policy in Britain: Dalyell, T. A., *A Science Policy for Britain*, 1983; Goldsmith, M. (ed.), *U. K. Science Policy*, 1984; Harvey, A. P., *Science and Technology in the U. K.*, 1984; Gibbons, M. and Gummett, P. (eds), *Science and Technology Policy in the 1980's and Beyond*, 1984.

Bibliographical information on the history of science is provided by: Davies, G. R. C. (ed.), *Guides to Sources for British History, vol. 2: Papers of British Scientists, 1600–1940*, 1982; Neu, J. (ed.), *ISIS Cumulative Bibliography 1966–1975: A Bibliography of the History of Science Formed from ISIS Critical Bibliographies 91–100*, 1980–; Rider, K. J., *History of Science and Technology: A Select Bibliography for Students*, 1970; Whitrow, M. (ed.), *ISIS Cumulative Bibliography: A Bibliography of the History of Science Formed from ISIS Critical Bibliographies 1–90, 1913–65*, 1971–82.

REFERENCE

Bott, S. (ed.), *Who's Who of British Scientists*, Surbiton, Simon Books, 1980.

Bowker (publisher), *Scientific and Technical Books and Serials in Print*, 3 vols, London, 1985.

British Council, *British Scientific Documentary Services*, London, 1974.

British Council, *British Scientific and Technical Reference Books*, London, 1975.

British Library, *Current Research in Britain: Physical Sciences,* Boston Spa, annually.

British Library, *Current Research in Britain: Biological Sciences,* Boston Spa, annually.

Burkett, J. (ed.), *Directory of Scientific Directories,* London, Longman, 1984.

Bynum, W. F. et al., *Dictionary of the History of Science,* London, Macmillan, 1981.

Cabinet Office, *Annual Review of Government Funded R. & D.,* London, HMSO, annually.

Cabinet Office, *Government Research and Development: A Guide to Sources of Information,* London, HMSO, 1979.

Codlin, E. M. (ed.), *ASLIB Directory, vol. 1, Information Sources in Science, Technology and Commerce,* London, 1982.

Codlin, E. M. (ed.), *ASLIB Directory, vol. 2, Information Sources in the Social Sciences, Medicine and the Humanities,* London, 1984.

Commission of the European Community, *Inventory of the Major Research Facilities in the European Community,* 2 vols, Munich, 1977.

Corsi, P. and Weindling, P. (eds), *Information Sources in the History of Science and Medicine,* London, Butterworth, 1982.

Data Research Group (publisher), *Research Establishments in the United Kingdom,* Great Missenden, 1981.

Davies, G. R. C. (ed.), *Guides to Sources for British History, vol. 2, Papers of British Scientists, 1600–1940,* London, HMSO, 1982.

Ferguson, E. S., *A Bibliography of the History of Technology,* Cambridge, Mass., M. I. T. Press, 1969.

Grogan, D., *Science and Technology: An Introduction to the Literature,* London, Bingley, 1982.

Hanson, C. W., *Introduction to Science Information Work,* London, Aslib, 1971.

Henwood, F. (comp.), *Science, Technology and Innovation: A Research Bibliography,* Brighton, Wheatsheaf, 1983.

Houghton, B., *Technical Information Sources,* Nijmegen, SIS Books, 1974.

Lambert, J., *Scientific and Technical Journals,* London, Bingley, 1985.

Lambert, J. and Lambert, P.A., *How to Find Information in Science and Technology,* London, Library Association, 1986.

Lasworth, E. J., *Reference Sources in Science and Technology,* Metuchen, New Jersey, Scarecrow Press, 1972.

Neu, J. (ed.), *ISIS Cumulative Bibliography 1966–1975: A Bibliography of the History of Science Formed from ISIS Critical Bibliographies 91–100, indexing Literature Published from 1965 through 1974,* London, Mansell, 1980–.

Parker, C. C. and Turley, R. V., *Information Sources in Science and Technology,* London, Butterworth, 1975.

Rider, K. J., *History of Science and Technology: A Select Bibliography for Students,* London, Library Association, 1970.

Roberts, S. A. et al. (eds), *Research Libraries and Collections in the U. K.,* London, Bingley, 1978.

Science and Engineering Research Council, *Annual Report,* London, annually.

Science Research Council, *Annual Report,* London, annually.

Walford, A. J. (ed.), *Guide to Reference Material, Vol. 1, Science and Technology,* London, Library Association, 1980.

Williams, T. I. (ed.), *A Biographical Dictionary of Scientists,* London, Black, 1982.

Whitrow, M. (ed.), *ISIS Cumulative Bibliography: A Bibliography of the History of Science Formed from ISIS Critical Bibliographies 1–90, 1913–65,* 5 vols, London, Mansell, 1971–82.

GENERAL

Advisory Board for the Research Councils, *A Study of Commissioned Research*, London, Department of Education and Science, 1983.

Armstrong, D., *Political Anatomy of the Body: Medical Knowledge in Britain in the Twentieth Century*, Cambridge, Cambridge University Press, 1983.

British Council, *Government Organisation of Science and Technology in Britain*, London, 1976.

Cabinet Office, *Industrial Innovation*, London, HMSO, 1979.

Cabinet Office, *Technological Change: Threats and Opportunities for the United Kingdom*, London, HMSO, 1980.

Cardwell, D. S. L., *The Organisation of Science in England*, London, Heinemann, 1972.

Central Advisory Council for Science and Technology, *Technological Innovation in Britain*, London, 1968.

Central Office of Information, *Some British Records and Achievements in Science, Industry and Technology*, London, HMSO, 1965.

Central Office of Information, *British Inventions: A Study of Discovery and Development*, London, HMSO, 1975.

Central Office of Information, *Nuclear Energy in Britain*, London, HMSO, 1975.

Central Office of Information, *Britain and International Scientific Cooperation*, London, HMSO, 1978.

Central Office of Information, *British Achievements in Science and Technology*, London, HMSO, 1981.

Central Office of Information, *The Promotion of the Sciences in Britain*, London, HMSO, 1978.

Dalyell, T. A., *A Science Policy for Britain*, London, Longman, 1983.

Fishlock, D., *The Business of Science: The Risks and Rewards of Research and Development*, London, Associated Business Programmes, 1975.

Gerstenfeld, A., *Technological Innovation: Government-Industry Cooperation*, Chichester, Wiley, 1979.

Gibbons M. and Gummett, P. (eds), *Science and Technology Policy in the 1980's and Beyond*, London, Longman, 1984.

Goldsmith, M., *United Kingdom Science Policy: A Critical Review of Policies for Publicly Funded Research*, London, Longman, 1984.

Goldsmith, M. (ed.), *UK Science Policy*, London, Longman, 1984.

Gummett, P., *Scientists in Whitehall*, Manchester, Manchester University Press, 1980.

Harvey, A. P., *Science and Technology in the U. K.*, London, Longman, 1984.

Hodgson, F., *Industrial Research in the United Kingdom*, London, Longman, 1980.

Holloway, H. L. et al., *Information Technology: UK Government Policy Decision Making*, Amsterdam, Elsevier, 1984.

Johnson, P. S., *The Economics of Invention, Innovation and Research and Development*, Oxford, Martin Robertson, 1975.

Mansfield, E., *Industrial Research and Technological Innovation*, London, Longman, 1969.

Norris, K. and Vaizey, J. E., *The Economics of Research and Technology*, London, Allen and Unwin, 1973.

Northcott, J. and Rogers, P., *Microelectronics in British Industry: The Pattern of Change*, London, Policy Studies Institute, 1984.

Pavitt, K. (ed.), *Technical Innovation and British Economic Performance*, London, Macmillan, 1980.

Pile, W., *The Department of Education and Science*, London, Allen and Unwin, 1979.

Poole, J. B. and Andrews, K. (eds), *The Government of Science in Britain*, London, Weidenfeld and Nicolson, 1972.

Ronayne, J., *Science in Government*, London, Arnold, 1984.

Sanderson, M., *The Universities and

British Industry 1850–1970, London, Routledge & Kegan Paul, 1972.

Select Committee on Science and Technology, *Scientific Research in British Universities*, London, HMSO, 1976.

Stoneman, P., *Technological Diffusion and the Computer Revolution: The UK Experience*, Cambridge,

Cambridge University Press, 1976.

Varcoe, I., *Organising for Science in Britain: A Case-Study*, Oxford, Oxford University Press, 1974.

Zuckerman, S., *Beyond the Ivory Tower: Functions of Public and Private Science*, London, Weidenfeld and Nicolson, 1970.

HISTORY

Argles, M., *South Kensington to Robbins: An Account of English Technical and Scientific Education since 1851*, London, Longman, 1964.

Bernal, J. D., *Science and Industry in the Nineteenth Century*, London, Routledge & Kegan Paul, 1953.

Derry, T. K. and Williams, T. I., *A Short History of Technology from Earliest Times to 1900*, London, Oxford University Press, 1970.

Habakkuk, H. J., *British and American Technology in the Nineteenth Century*, Cambridge, Cambridge University Press, 1967.

Hartley, H. (ed.), *The Royal Society: Its Origins and Founders*, London, Royal Society, 1960.

Inkster, I. and Morrell, J. (eds), *Metropolis and Province: Science in British Culture, 1780–1850*, London, Hutchinson, 1983.

Lyons, H. G., *The Royal Society, 1660–1940*, London, Greenwood Press, 1944 (reprint).

Maclcod, R. and Collins, R. (cds), *The Parliament of Science: The British Association for the Advancement of Science, 1831–1981*, Northwood, Science Reviews, 1981.

Mason, S. F., *A History of the Sciences*, London, Collier-Macmillan, 1962.

Mathias, P. (ed.), *Science and Society, 1600–1900*, Cambridge, Cambridge University Press, 1972.

Morrell, J. and Thackray, A., *Gentlemen of Science: Early Years of the British Association for the Advancement of Science*, London, Oxford University Press, 1983.

Purver, M., *The Royal Society: Concept and Creation*, London, Routledge & Kegan Paul, 1967.

Royal Society (publisher), *Highlights of British Science*, London, 1978.

Russell, C. A., *Science and Social Change, 1700–1900*, London, Macmillan, 1983.

Singer, C. et al. (eds), *A History of Technology*, 7 vols, Oxford, Oxford University Press, 1954–79.

Stimson, D., *Scientists and Amateurs: A History of the Royal Society*, London, Greenwood Press, 1948 (reprint).

SEE ALSO:

14 Industry and Commerce

30 SCOTLAND

Bibliographical references to publications on Scotland can be found in Grant, E. G. (comp.), *Scotland: World Bibliographical Series*, 1982; Hancock, P. D. (ed.), *A Bibliography of Works Relating to Scotland, 1916–1950*, 1960; Lloyd, D. M. (ed.), *Reader's Guide to Scotland: A Bibliography*, 1968; Mullay, S., *Scotland, Reader's Guide*, 1981; Pollock, L. and McAllister, I. *A Bibliography of United Kingdom Politics: Scotland, Wales and Northern Ireland*, 3 vols, 1980.

For current publications on Scotland consult: National Library of Scotland, *Bibliography of Scotland*, annually.

The following are recommended as reading in their respective fields:

Economy Hodgson, A. (ed.), *Scotland in the 1980's*, 1976; Johnston, T. L. et al., *Structure and Growth of the Scottish Economy*, 1975; Murray, G. T., *Scotland, The New Future*, 1973.

Geography see pages 64–70.

Government and Politics Drucker, H. M., *The Politics of Nationalism and Devolution*, 1980; Keating, M. and Midwinter, A., *The Government of Scotland*, 1983: Kellas, J. G., *The Scottish Political System*, 1984; MacCormick, N. (ed.), *The Scottish Debate*, 1970; Mercer, J., *Scotland: The Devolution of Power*, 1978; Scottish Information Office, *Government in Scotland: A Guide to the Differences from England*, 1974; Miller, W. L., *The End of British Politics: Scots and English Political Behaviour in the Seventies*, 1981.

History Donaldson, G., *Scotland: The Shaping of a Nation*, 1980; Fry, P. and Fry, F., *History of Scotland*, 1985; Lenman, B., *An Economic History of Modern Scotland, 1660–1976*, 1977; Mackie, J. D., *A History of Scotland*, 1978; Maclean, F., *A Concise History of Scotland*, 1970; Wormald, J. et al. (eds), *The New History of Scotland*, 1981–.

Literature Royle, T., *The Macmillan Companion to Scottish Literature*, 1983; Speirs, J., *The Scots Literary Tradition*, 1962; Watson, R., *The Literature of Scotland*, 1984; Wittig, K., *The Scottish Tradition in Literature*, 1978.

Travel and Tourism see pages 249–264.

REFERENCE

Aberdeen University Press, *The Concise Scots Dictionary*, Aberdeen, 1985.

Bryan, G. (comp.), *Scottish Nationalism and Cultural Identity in the Twentieth Century: An Annotated Bibliography of Secondary Sources*, London, Greenwood Press, 1984.

Countryside Commission for Scotland, *Annual Report*, Edinburgh, HMSO, annually.

Craigie, W. A. and Atiken, A. J. (eds), *A Dictionary of the Older Scottish Tongue: From the Twelfth Century to the End of the Seventeenth*, London, Oxford University Press, 1937.

Daiches, D. (ed.), *A Companion to Scottish Culture*, London, Arnold, 1981.

Donaldson, G. and Morpeth, R. S., *Who's Who in Scottish History*,

Oxford, Blackwell, 1973.

Drucker, H. M. and Drucker, N. L., *Scottish Government Yearbook*, Edinburgh, Paul Harris, annually.

Fraser, K. C., *A Bibliography of the Scottish National Movement, 1844–1973*, Dollar, D. S. Mack, 1976.

Grant, E. G. (comp.), *Scotland: World Bibliographical Series*, Vol. 34, Oxford, Santa Barbara, Clio Press, 1982.

Grant, W. and Murison, D. D., *The Scottish National Dictionary*, 10 vols, Edinburgh, Scottish National Dictionary Association, 1929–76.

Hancock, P. D. (ed.), *A Bibliography of Works Relating to Scotland, 1916–1950*, Edinburgh, Edinburgh University Press, 1960.

Her Majesty's Stationery Office, *Scottish Abstract of Statistics*, Edinburgh, annually.

Johnston, J. B., *The Place-Names of Scotland*, East Ardsley, S. R.

Publishers, 1970.

Lloyd, D. M. (ed.), *Reader's Guide to Scotland: A Bibliography*, London, National Book League, 1968.

Mullay, S., *Scotland, Reader's Guide no. 28*, London, Library Association, Public Libararies Group, 1981.

National Library of Scotland, *Bibliography of Scotland*, Edinburgh, HMSO, annually.

Pollock, L. and McAllister, I., *A Bibliography of United Kingdom Politics: Scotland, Wales and Northern Ireland*, 3 vols, Glasgow, University of Strathclyde, 1980.

Rose, R. and McAllister, I., *United Kingdom Facts*, London, Macmillan, 1982.

Scottish Office, *Scottish Abstract of Statistics*, Edinburgh, HMSO, annually.

Warrack, A., *Chambers Scots Dictionary*, Edinburgh, Chambers, 1985.

GENERAL

Aitken, A. J. and McArthur, T., *Languages of Scotland*, Edinburgh, Chambers, 1979.

Bryan, G. (comp.), *Scottish Nationalism and Cultural Identity in the Twentieth Century*, London, Greenwood Press, 1984.

Central Office of Information, *Scotland*, London, HMSO, 1974.

Clapperton, C. M. (ed.), *Scotland: A New Study*, Newton Abbot, David and Charles, 1983.

Credland, G. D. and Murray, G. T., *Scotland: A New Look*, London, Scottish Television, 1969.

Dickson, T. (ed.), *Capital and Class in Scotland*, Edinburgh, John Donald, 1982.

Highet, J., *The Scottish Churches*, London, Skeffington, 1960.

Hodgson, A. (ed.), *Scotland in the 1980's*, London, Henley Centre for Forecasting, 1976.

Hood, N. and Young, S. (eds), *Industrial Policy and the Scottish Economy*, Edinburgh, Edinburgh University

Press, 1984.

Hunter, S. L., *The Scottish Educational System*, Oxford, Pergamon, 1972.

Hutcheson, M. A. and Hogg, A., *Scotland and Oil*, Edinburgh, Oliver and Boyd, 1975.

Ingham, K. and Love, J. (eds), *Understanding the Scottish Economy*, Oxford, Blackwell, 1983.

Johnston, T. I., Buxton, N. K. and Mair, D., *Structure and Growth of the Scottish Economy*, Plymouth, Macdonald and Evans, 1975.

Kellas, J., *Modern Scotland: The Nation Since 1870*, London, Allen and Unwin, 1980.

McEwen, J., *Who Owns Scotland? A Study in Land Ownership*, Edinburgh, Polygon Books, 1977.

McIntosh, L. G. and Marshall, C. B., *The Face of Scotland*, Oxford, Pergamon Press, 1966.

Mackay, D. I., *Scotland: The Framework for Change*, Edinburgh, Paul Harris, 1979.

Maclean, C. (ed.), *The Crown and the*

Thistle: The Nature of Nationhood, Edinburgh, Scottish Academic Press, 1979.

Macmillan, J., *The Anatomy of Scotland*, London, Frewin, 1969.

Mitchison, R., *Life in Scotland*, London, Batsford, 1978.

Murray, G. T., *Scotland: The New Future*, Glasgow, Blackie, 1973.

Parsler, R. (ed.), *Capitalism, Class and Politics in Scotland*, Aldershot, Gower, 1980.

Prebble, J., *John Prebble's Scotland*, London, Secker and Warburg, 1984.

Saville, R., *The Economic Development of Modern Scotland, 1950–80*, Edinburgh, John Donald, 1985.

Speitel, H. et al. (eds), *The Linguistic Atlas of Scotland*, 3 vols, London, Croom Helm, 1975–86.

Turnock, D., *The New Scotland*, Newton Abbot, David and Charles, 1979.

Underwood, R. (ed.), *The Future of Scotland*, London, Croom Helm, 1977.

Wilson, N. (ed.), *Scotland and the Scots*, Edinburgh, Ramsay Head Press, 1977.

Withers, C. W. J., *Gaelic in Scotland, 1698–1981: The Geographical History of a Language*, Edinburgh, Donald, 1983.

HISTORY

Adams, I., *The Making of Urban Scotland*, London, Croom Helm, 1978.

Barrow, G. W. S., *The New History of Scotland, Vol. 2, Kingship and Unity: Scotland 1000–1306*, London, Arnold, 1981.

Blackwell (publisher), *The Companion To Gaelic Scotland*, Oxford, 1984.

Brander, M., *The Making of the Highlands*, London, Constable, 1980.

Burleigh, J. H. S., *A Church History of Scotland*, London, Oxford University Press, 1960.

Campbell, R. H., *Scotland since 1707: The Rise of an Industrial Society*, Oxford, Blackwell, 1965.

Campbell, R. H. and Dow, J. B. A., *Source Book of Scottish Economic and Social History*, Oxford, Blackwell, 1968.

Checkland, S. and Checkland, O., *New History of Scotland, Vol. 7, Industry and Ethos: Scotland 1832–1914*, London, Arnold, 1984.

Dickson, T. (ed.), *Scottish Capitalism: Class, State and Nation from before the Union to the Present*, London, Lawrence and Wishart, 1980.

Donaldson, G., *The Scottish Reformation*, Cambridge, Cambridge University Press, 1972.

Donaldson, G., *Scotland, Church and Nation Through Sixteen Centuries*, London, Chatto and Windus, 1972.

Donaldson, G., *Scottish Kings*, London, Batsford, 1977.

Donaldson, G., *The Edinburgh History of Scotland, Vol. III, Scotland: James V to James VII*, Edinburgh, Oliver and Boyd, 1978.

Donaldson, G., *Scotland: The Shaping of a Nation*, Newton Abbot, David and Charles, 1980.

Duncan, A. A. M., *The Edinburgh History of Scotland, Vol. I, Scotland: The Making of the Kingdom*, Edinburgh, Oliver and Boyd, 1978.

Ferguson, W., *The Edinburgh History of Scotland, Vol. IV, Scotland: 1689 to the Present*, Edinburgh, Oliver and Boyd, 1978.

Fry, P. and Fry, F., *History of Scotland*, London, Routledge & Kegan Paul, 1985.

Glover, J. R., *The Story of Scotland*, London, Faber, 1977.

Gordon, G. and Dicks, B., *Scottish Urban History*, Aberdeen, Aberdeen University Press, 1982.

Grant, A., *The New History of Scotland, Vol. 3, Independence and Nationhood: Scotland, 1306–1469*, London, Arnold, 1982.

Grant, I F., *The Economic History of Scotland*, London, Greenwood Press,

1934, (reprint).

Harvie, C., *Scotland and Nationalism: Scottish Society and Politics, 1707–1977*, London, Allen and Unwin, 1977.

Harvie, C., *The New History of Scotland, Vol. 8, No Gods and Precious Few Heroes: Scotland, 1914–1980*, London, Arnold, 1981.

Lenman, B., *An Economic History of Modern Scotland 1660–1976*, London, Batsford, 1977.

Lenman, B., *The New History of Scotland, Vol. 6, Integration, Enlightenment and Industrialisation, Scotland, 1746–1832*, London, Arnold, 1981.

Lythe, S. G. E. and Butt, J., *An Economic History of Scotland 1100–1939*, Glasgow, Blackie, 1975.

Mackie, J. D., *A History of Scotland*, Harmondsworth, Penguin, 1978.

Maclean, F., *A Concise History of Scotland*, London, Thames and Hudson, 1970.

Mitchison, R., *A History of Scotland*, London, Methuen, 1970.

Mitchison, R., *The New History of Scotland, Vol. 5, Union of the Crowns and Union of the Kingdoms*, London, Arnold, 1982.

Nicholson, R., *The Edinburgh History of Scotland, Vol. II, Scotland: The Later Middle Ages*, Edinburgh, Oliver and Boyd, 1978.

Orel, H. et al. (eds), *Scottish World: Culture and History*, London, Thames and Hudson, 1981.

Prebble, J., *Culloden*, Harmondsworth, Penguin, 1970.

Prebble, J., *Glencoe: The Story of the Massacre*, Harmondsworth, Penguin, 1969.

Prebble, J., *The Highland Clearances*, Harmondsworth, Penguin, 1969.

Richards, E., *A History of the Highland Clearances*, 2 vols, London, Croom Helm, 1982–5.

Ritchie, G. and Ritchie, A., *Scotland: Archaeology and Early History*, London, Thames and Hudson, 1975.

Smout, T. C., *A History of the Scottish People 1560–1830*, London, Fontana, 1972.

Smout, T. C., *A Century of the Scottish People, 1830–1950*, London, Collins, 1986.

Smyth, A. P., *The New History of Scotland, Vol. 1, Dark Age Scotland*, London, Arnold, 1982.

Steel, T., *Scotland's Story*, Glasgow, Collins, 1984.

Turnock, D., *Historical Geography of Scotland since 1707*, Cambridge, Cambridge University Press, 1982.

Wormald, J., *The New History of Scotland, Vol. 4, Court, Kirk and Community: Scotland, 1470–1625*, London, Arnold, 1981.

GOVERNMENT AND POLITICS

Bogdanor, V., *Devolution*, Oxford, Oxford University Press, 1979.

Brand, J., *The National Movement in Scotland*, London, Routledge & Kegan Paul, 1978.

Central Office of Information, *Devolution: The New Assembly for Scotland and Wales*, London, HMSO, 1976.

Coull, J. W. and Merry, E. W., *Principles and Practice of Scots Law*, London, Butterworth, 1971.

Dalyell, T., *Devolution: The End of Britain?*, London, Cape, 1977.

Drucker, H. M., *The Politics of Nationalism and Devolution*, London, Longman, 1980.

Edwards, O. D. et al., *Celtic Nationalism*, London, Routledge & Kegan Paul, 1968.

Hanham, H. J., *Scottish Nationalism*, London, Faber, 1969.

Harvie, C., *Scotland and Nationalism: Scottish Society and Politics 1707–1977*, London, Allen and Unwin, 1977.

Hechter, M., *Internal Colonialism: The Celtic Fringe in British National Development 1536–1966*, London, Routledge & Kegan Paul, 1975.

Her Majesty's Stationery Office, *The Legal System of Scotland*, Edinburgh, 1981.

Keating, M. and Bleinman, D., *Labour and Scottish Nationalism*, London, Macmillan, 1979.

Keating, M. and Midwinter, A., *The Government of Scotland*, Edinburgh, Mainstream, 1983.

Keith, R. and Clark, G., *A Guide to Scots Law*, Stirling, Johnston and Bacon, 1978.

Kellas, J., *The Scottish Political System*, Cambridge, Cambridge University Press, 1984.

MacCormick, N. (ed.), *The Scottish Debate: Essays on Scottish Nationalism*, London, Oxford University Press, 1970.

Mackintosh, J. P., *On Scotland*, London, Longman, 1982.

Macneill, D. H., *The Historical Scottish Constitution*, Edinburgh, Albyn Press, 1972.

Mercer, J., *Scotland: The Devolution of Power*, London, Calder, 1978.

Miller, W. L., *The End of British Politics: Scots and English Political Behaviour in the Seventies*, London, Oxford University Press, 1981.

Parsler, R. (ed.), *Capitalism, Class and Politics in Scotland*, Aldershot, Gower, 1980.

Scottish Information Office, *Government in Scotland: A Guide to the Differences from England*, Edinburgh, HMSO, 1974.

Walker, D. M., *The Scottish Legal System: An Introduction to the Study of Scots Law*, Edinburgh, Green, 1978.

Webb, K., *The Growth of Nationalism in Scotland*, Glasgow, Molendinar Press, 1978.

CULTURE AND TRADITIONS

Bold, A., *Modern Scottish Literature*, London, Longman, 1983.

Chitnis, A., *The Scottish Enlightenment*, London, Croom Helm, 1976.

Collinson, F., *The Traditional and National Music of Scotland*, London, Routledge & Kegan Paul, 1978.

Craig, D., *Scottish Literature and the Scottish People, 1680–1830*, London, Chatto and Windus, 1961.

Dunbar, J. J., *Highland Costume*, Edinburgh, Blackwood, 1977.

Elliott, K. and Rimmer, F., *A History of Scottish Music*, London, BBC, 1973.

Farmer, H. G., *A History of Music in Scotland*, London, Hinrichsen, 1947.

Grimble, I., *Scottish Clans and Tartans*, London, Hamlyn, 1977.

Hendry, I. and Stephen, G., *Scotscape: Lore, Legends and Customs of Scotland*, Edinburgh, Oliver and Boyd, 1978.

Humes, W. M. and Paterson, H. M. (eds), *Scottish Culture and Scottish Education, 1800–1900*, Edinburgh, Donald, 1983.

Innes, of Learney, Sir T., *The Tartans of the Clans and Families of Scotland*, Edinburgh, Johnston and Bacon, 1971.

Lindsay, M., *History of Scottish Literature*, London, Hale, 1977.

McClure, J. D. et al. (eds), *The Scots Language: Planning for Modern Use*, Edinburgh, Ramsay Head, 1980.

McNeill, F. M., *The Silver Bough: A Four-Volume Study of the National and Local Festivals of Scotland*, Glasgow, McLellan, 1957.

Munro, R. W., *Highland Clans and Tartans*, London, Octopus, 1977.

Petzsch, H., *Architecture in Scotland*, London, Longman, 1971.

Robinson, D. S., *The Story of Scottish Philosophy*, London, Greenwood Press, 1979.

Ross, A., *The Folklore of the Scottish Highlands*, London, Batsford, 1976.

Royle, T., *The Macmillan Companion to Scottish Literature*, London, Macmillan, 1983.

Scarlett, J., *Scotland's Clans and Tartans*, London, Lutterworth, 1975.

Speirs, J., *The Scots Literary Tradition*, London, Faber, 1962.

Watson, R., *The Literature of Scotland*,

London, Macmillan, 1984, Macmillan History of Literature.

Withers, C. W. J., *Gaelic in Scotland, 1698–1981: The Geographical History of a Language*, Edinburgh, Donald, 1983.

Wittig, K., *The Scottish Tradition in Literature*, Edinburgh, Mercat Press, 1978.

SEE ALSO:

3   Cities
11   Geography
38   Travel and Tourism in Britain

31 SOCIAL AND ECONOMIC HISTORY

For bibliographical references to works on British social and economic history readers should consult the general history bibliography on pages 81–94 See also: Chaloner, W. H. and Richardson, R. S., *British Economic and Social History: A Bibliographical Guide*, 1984; Kuhlicke, F. W. and Emmison, F. G. (eds), *English Local History Handlist: A Select Bibliography and List of Sources for the Study of Local History and Antiquities*, 1969.

For general reference purposes see the general history reference works listed on pages 81–5. See also Cowie, L. W., *A Dictionary of British Social History*, 1973; Richardson, J., *The Local Historian's Encyclopaedia*, 1975.

As introductions to the field see: Briggs, M. and Jordan, P., *Economic History of England*, 1967; Chappell, D. J., *An Economic History of England*, 1980; Cheyney, E. P., *An Introduction to the Industrial and Social History of England*, 1969.

More detailed surveys are: Briggs, A., *Social History of England*, 1985; Clapham, J. H., *An Economic History of Modern Britain*, 3 vols, 1950–1; Cole, G. D. H. and Postgate, R., *The Common People, 1746–1946*, 1961; Deane, P., *The First Industrial Revolution*, 1980; Flinn, M. W., *An Economic and Social History of Britain since 1700*, 1975; Gregg, P., *A Social and Economic History of Britain, 1700–1965*, 1977; Harrison, J. F. C., *The Common People: A History from the Norman Conquest to the Present*, 1984; Hill, C. P., *British Economic and Social History, 1700–1982*, 1985; Lane, P., *British Social and Economic History from 1760 to the Present Day*, 1979; Lipson, E., *The Economic History of England*, 3 vols, 1956–9; Morton, A. L., *A People's History of England*, 1971; Redford, A., *The Economic History of England*, 1961; Trevelyan, G. M., *English Social History: A Survey of Six Centuries, Chaucer to Queen Victoria*, 1970.

The following can be recommended as introductory reading to particular periods:

Roman Britain   Birley, A., *Life in Roman Britain*, 1976; Collingwood, R. G. and Myres, J. N. L., *Roman Britain and the English Settlements*, 1937.
Norman England   Lane, P., *Norman England*, 1980; Platt, C., *Medieval England: A Social History and Archaeology from the Conquest to AD 1600*, 1978.
Tudor England   Elton, G. R., *England and the Tudors*, 1974; Rowse, A. L., *The Expansion of Elizabethan England*, 1981; Williams, P., *Life in Tudor England*, 1964; Youings, J., *Sixteenth Century England*, 1984.
Seventeenth-Century Britain   Ashley, M., *Life in Stuart England*, 1964; O'Day, R., *Economy and Community: Economic and Social History of Pre-industrial England, 1550–1700*, 1975; Wilson, C., *England's Apprenticeship, 1603–1763*, 1984.
Eighteenth-Century Britain   Ashton, T. S., *An Economic History of England: The Eighteenth Century*, 1955; Marshall, D., *Eighteenth Century England*, 1975; Porter, R., *English Society in the Eighteenth Century*, 1982.
Nineteenth-Century Britain   Hobsbawm, E. J., *The Age of Capital, 1848–1875*, 1977; Perkin, H., *The Origins of Modern English Society, 1780–1880*, 1985; Young, G. B., *The Making of Victorian England*, 1962.

Twentieth-Century Britain   Gilbert, B. B., *Britain since 1918*, 1980; Johnson. W. et al., *A Short Economic and Social History of Twentieth Century Britain*, 1967; Marwick, A., *The Explosion of British Society 1914–1970*, 1971; Wood, A., *Great Britain, 1900–65*, 1978.

REFERENCE

Bellamy, J. M. and Saville, J. (eds), *Dictionary of Labour Biography*, 7 vols, London, Macmillan, 1972–84.

Chaloner, W. H. and Richardson, R. S., *British Economic and Social History: A Bibliographical Guide*, Manchester, Manchester University Press, 1984.

Cowie, L. W., *A Dictionary of British Social History*, London, Bell, 1973.

Darby, H. C. (ed.), *A New Historical Geography of England after 1600*, Cambridge University Press, 1976.

Emmison, F. G., *Archives and Local History*, Chichester, Phillimore, 1978.

Gilbert, V. F., *Labour and Social History Theses: American, British and Irish University Theses and Dissertations in the Field of British and Irish Labour History Presented Between 1900 and 1978*, London, Mansell, 1982.

Her Majesty's Stationery Office, *Record Repositories in Great Britain*, London, 1979.

Hoskins, W. G., *Local History in England*, London, Longman, 1973.

Kuhlicke, F. W. and Emmison, F. G. (eds), *English Local History Handlist: A Select Bibliography and List of Sources for the Study of Local History and Antiquities*, London, Historical Association, 1969.

London and Cambridge Economic Service, *The British Economy: Key Statistics, 1900–1970*, London, 1973.

Richardson, J., *The Local Historian's Encyclopaedia*, New Barnet, Historical Publications, 1975.

Riden, P., *Local History: A Handbook for Beginners*, London, Batsford, 1983.

Stephens, W. B., *Sources for English Local History*, Cambridge, Cambridge University Press, 1981.

Stockham, P. et al., *British Local History: A Select Bibliography*, London, 1964.

GENERAL

Alderman, G., *Modern Britain 1700–1983: A Domestic History*, London, Croom Helm, 1986.

Ashley, M., *The People of England: A Short Economic and Social History*, London, Macmillan, 1984.

Ashworth, W., *An Economic History of England 1870–1939*, London, Methuen, 1960.

Bagwell, P. S., *The Transport Revolution from 1770*, London, Batsford, 1974.

Barker, T. (ed.), *The Long March of Everyman*, Harmondsworth, Penguin, 1978.

Barker, T. (ed.), *Population and Society in Britain, 1850–1980*, London, Batsford, 1982.

Barker, T. C., *Road Transport in Britain* since 1700, London, Macmillan, 1985.

Bédarida, F., *A Social History of England, 1851–1975*, London, Methuen, 1979.

Bodley, H., *Twenty Centuries of British Industry*, Newton Abbot, David and Charles, 1975.

Briggs, A., *A Social History of England*, Harmondsworth, Penguin, 1985.

Briggs, M. and Jordan, P., *Economic History of England*, London, University Tutorial Press, 1967.

Capie, F. and Webber, A., *A Monetary History of the United Kingdom, 1870–1939*, London, Allen and Unwin, 1985–.

Chappell, D. J., *An Economic History of*

England, Plymouth, Macdonald and Evans, 1980.

Checkland S., *British Public Policy 1776–1939: An Economic, Social and Political Perspective*, Cambridge, Cambridge University Press, 1983.

Cheyney, E. P., *An Introduction to the Industrial and Social History of England*, New York, AMS Press, 1969.

Clapham, J. H. *An Economic History of Modern Britain*, 3 vols, Cambridge, Cambridge University Press, 1950–1.

Clapham, J. H., *A Concise Economic History of Britain from Earliest Times to 1750*, Cambridge, Cambridge University Press, 1949.

Clark, J. C. D., *English Society, 1688–1982*, Cambridge, Cambridge University Press, 1986.

Clark, P A. and Slack, P., *English Towns in Transition*, London, Oxford University Press, 1976.

Cole, G. D. H. and Postgate, R., *The Common People, 1746–1946*, London, Methuen, 1961.

Coleman, D. C., *The Economy of England, 1450–1750*, London, Oxford University Press, 1977.

Cossons, N., *BP Book of Industrial Archaeology*, Newton Abbot, David and Charles, 1975.

Cunningham, W., *The Growth of English Industry and Commerce*, 2 vols, London, Cass, 1968 (reprint).

Deane, P., *The First Industrial Revolution*, Cambridge, Cambridge University Press, 1980.

Deane, P. and Cole, W. A., *British Economic Growth 1688–1959: Trends and Structures*, Cambridge, Cambridge University Press, 1967.

Derry, T. K. and Jarman, M. A., *Modern Britain: Life and Work through Two Centuries of Change*, London, Murray, 1979.

Dickson, P. G., *The Financial Revolution in England: A Study in the Development of Public Credit, 1688–1956*, London, Macmillan, 1967.

Feaveryear, A. E., *The Pound Sterling: A History of English Money*, Oxford,

Oxford University Press, 1963.

Finberg, H. P. R. and Thirsk, J. (eds), *The Agrarian History of England and Wales*, Cambridge, Cambridge University Press, 1967–.

Flinn, M. W., *An Economic and Social History of Britain since 1700*, London, Macmillan, 1975.

Floud, R. and McClosky, D. (eds), *The Economic History of Britain since 1700*, 2 vols, Cambridge, Cambridge University Press, 1981.

Gregg, P., *Black Death to Industrial Revolution: A Social and Economic History of Britain*, London, Harrap, 1977.

Harrison, J. F. C., *The Common People: A History From the Norman Conquest to the Present*, London, Croom Helm, 1984.

Hill, C. P., *British Economic and Social History, 1700–1982*, London, Arnold, 1985.

Hobsbawm, E. J., *Labouring Men. Studies in the History of Labour*, London, Weidenfeld and Nicolson, 1964.

Hobsbawm, E. J., *Pelican Economic History of Britain, 1750 to the Present Day*, Harmondsworth, Penguin, 1969.

Hoffmann, W., *The Structure of British Industry, 1700–1950*, Oxford, Blackwell, 1955.

Jones, E., *Accountancy and the British Economy, 1840–1980*, London, Batsford, 1981.

Landes, D. S., *The Unbound Prometheus: Technological Change and Industrial Development in Western Europe since 1750*, Cambridge, Cambridge University Press, 1969.

Lane, P., *Documents on British Economic and Social History*, 3 vols, London, Macmillan, 1968–9.

Lane, P., *British Social and Economic History from 1760 to the Present Day*, Oxford, Oxford University Press, 1979.

Mathias, P., *The First Industrial Nation: An Economic History of Britain since 1750*, London, Methuen, 1983.

Minchinton, W., *A Guide to the Industrial Archaeology Sites in Britain*, London, Granada, 1984.

Mitchell, R. J. and Leys, M D. R., *A History of the English People*, London, Pan, 1967.

Mitchison, R., *British Population Change since 1860*, London, Macmillan, 1977.

Mokyr, J. (ed.), *The Economics of the Industrial Revolution*, London, Allen and Unwin, 1985.

Morton, A. L., *A People's History of England*, London, Lawrence and Wishart, 1971.

Murphy, B. D., *A History of the British Economy 1086–1970*, London, Longman, 1973.

Musson, A. E., *The Growth of British Industry*, London, Batsford, 1978.

Perkin, H., *The Origins of Modern English Society*, London, Routledge & Kegan Paul, 1969.

Pollard, S. and Crossley, D. W., *The Wealth of Britain 1085–1966*, London, Batsford, 1968.

Quennell, M. and Quennell, C. H. B., *A History of Everyday Things in England*, 6 vols, London, Batsford, 1957–68.

Ryder, J. and Silver, H., *Modern English Society: History and Structure, 1850–1970*, London, Methuen, 1977.

Schubert, H., *History of the British Iron and Steel Industry*, London, Routledge & Kegan Paul, 1957.

Smith, L. (ed.), *The Making of Britain*, 4 vols, London, Macmillan, 1985–6.

Snell, K. D. M., *Annals of the Labouring Poor: Social Change and Agrarian England, 1660–1900*, Cambridge, Cambridge University Press, 1985.

Taylor, C., *Village and Farmstead: A History of Rural Settlement in England*, London, George Philip, 1983.

Thirsk, J. (ed.), *The Agrarian History of England and Wales*, 4 vols, Cambridge, Cambridge University Press, 1967–.

Treble, J. H., *Urban Poverty in Britain, 1830–1960*, London, Batsford, 1979.

Trevelyan, G. M., *English Social History: A Survey of Six Centuries, Chaucer to Queen Victoria*, Hardmondsworth, Penguin, 1970.

Trevelyan, G. M., *A Shortened History of England*, Harmondsworth, Penguin, 1970.

Trevelyan, G. M., *Illustrated History of England*, London, Longman, 1973.

Walker, J., *British Economic and Social History 1700–1980*, Plymouth, Macdonald and Evans, 1982.

Ward, J. T., *The Factory System*, 2 vols, Newton Abbot, David and Charles, 1970.

Wiener, J. H. (ed.), *Great Britain: The Lion at Home: A Documentary History of Domestic Policy, 1689–1973*, New York and London, Chelsea House, 1974.

Wrigley, E. A. and Schofield, R. S., *The Population History of England, 1541–1871: A Reconstruction*, London, Arnold, 1981.

ROMAN TO ANGLO-SAXON BRITAIN

Alcock, L., *Arthur's Britain: History and Archaeology*, Harmondsworth, Penguin, 1973.

Arnold, C. J., *Roman Britain to Saxon England: An Archaeological Study*, London, Croom Helm, 1984.

Birley, A., *Life in Roman Britain*, London, Batsford, 1976.

Blair, P. H., *An Introduction to Anglo-Saxon England*, Cambridge, Cambridge University Press, 1977.

Campbell, J. (ed.), *The Anglo-Saxons*, Oxford, Phaidon 1982.

Collingwood, R. G. and Myres, J. N. L., *Roman Britain and the English Settlements*, Oxford, 1937, Oxford History of England.

Evison, V. (ed.), *Angles, Saxons and Jutes*, Oxford, Oxford University Press, 1981.

Finberg, H. P. R., *The Formation of England, 550–1042*, London, Paladin, 1976.

Fisher, D. J. V., *The Anglo-Saxon Age,*

c. 400–1042, London, Longman, 1973.

Hallam, H. E., *Rural England, 1066–1272*, London, Fontana, 1981.

Hawkes, J., *The Shell Guide to British Archaeology*, London, Michael Joseph, 1985.

Hill, D., *An Atlas of Anglo-Saxon England*, Oxford, Blackwell, 1981.

Laing, L., *Celtic Britain: Britain before the Conquest*, London, Routledge & Kegan Paul, 1979.

Laing, L. and Laing, J., *Anglo-Saxon England*, London, Routledge & Kegan Paul, 1979.

Lane, P., *Roman Britain*, London, Batsford, 1980.

Loyn, H. R., *Norman Britain*, London, Lutterworth, 1966.

Loyn, H. R., *Anglo-Saxon England and the Norman Conquest*, Longman, 1970.

Powell, T. G. E., *The Celts*, London, Thames and Hudson, 1979.

Sawyer, P. H., *The Age of the Vikings*, London, Arnold, 1975.

Sawyer, P. H., *From Roman Britain to Norman England*, London, Methuen, 1978.

Stenton, F. M., *Anglo-Saxon England*, Oxford, Oxford University Press, 1971.

Tomkieff, O. G., *Life in Norman England*, London, Batsford, 1966.

Wacher, J. S., *The Towns of Roman Britain*, London, Batsford, 1975.

Wilson, D. M., *The Anglo-Saxons*, Harmondsworth, Penguin, 1970.

MEDIEVAL, TUDOR AND STUART BRITAIN

Baker, T., *The Normans*, London, Cassell, 1966.

Barlow, F., *William I and the Norman Conquest*, London, Collier-Macmillan, 1967.

Barlow, F., *The Feudal Kingdom of England, 1042–1216*, London, Longman, 1972.

Barrow, G. W. S., *Feudal Britain: The Completion of the Medieval Kingdoms, 1066–1314*, London, Arnold, 1956.

Bean, J. M. W., *The Decline of English Feudalism, 1215–1540*, Manchester, Manchester University Press, 1968.

Bolton, J. L., *The Medieval English Economy, 1150–1500*, London, Dent, 1980.

Brewer, D. S., *Chaucer in His Time*, London, Greenwood Press, 1977.

Bridbury, A. R., *Economic Growth: England in the Later Middle Ages*, Brighton, Harvester, 1975.

Byrne, M. S., *Elizabethan Life in Town and Country*, London, Methuen, 1961.

Chancellor, V. E., *Medieval and Tudor Britain*, Harmondsworth, Penguin, 1970.

Chibnall, M., *Anglo-Norman England 1066–1166*, Oxford, Blackwell, 1985.

Clark, G. N., *The Wealth of England from 1496 to 1760*, London, Oxford University Press, 1946.

Coleman, D. C., *Industry in Tudor and Stuart England*, London, Macmillan, 1975.

Coulton, G. G., *Life in the Middle Ages*, 2 vols, Cambridge, Cambridge University Press, 1967.

Davies, C. S. L., *Peace, Print and Protestantism, 1450–1558*, London, Paladin, 1976.

Dodd, A. H., *Elizabethan England*, London, Batsford, 1974.

Douglas, D. C., *William the Conqueror: The Norman Impact upon England*, Methuen, 1977.

Du Boulay, F. R. H., *An Age of Ambition: English Society in the Late Middle Ages*, London, Nelson, 1970.

Elton, G. R., *England and the Tudors*, London, Methuen, 1974.

Gould, J. D., *The Great Debasement: Currency and the Economy in Mid-Tudor England*, Oxford, Oxford University Press, 1970.

Hilton, R., *Bond Men Made Free: Medieval Peasant Movements and the*

English Rising of 1381, London, Temple Smith, 1973.

Hilton, R., *The English Peasantry in the Later Middle Ages*, Oxford, Clarendon Press, 1975.

Hoskins, W. G., *The Age of Plunder: The England of Henry VIII, 1500–1547*, London, Longman, 1976.

Hurstfield, J. and Smith, A. G. R., *Elizabethan People: State and Society*, London, Oxford University Press, 1972.

Hyams, P., *Kings, Lords and Peasants in Medieval England*, London, Oxford University Press, 1980.

Jack, S. M., *Trade and Industry in Tudor and Stuart England*, London, Allen and Unwin, 1977.

Jones, W. R. D., *The Tudor Commonwealth, 1529–1559*, London, Athlone, 1970.

Jusserand, J. J., *Wayfaring Life in the Middle Ages*, London, Chivers, 1970.

Kendall, P. M., *The Yorkist Age: Daily Life during the Wars of the Roses*, London, Allen and Unwin, 1980.

King, E., *England 1175–1425*, London, Routledge & Kegan Paul, 1979.

Lander, J. R., *Conflict and Stability in Fifteenth Century England*, London, Hutchinson, 1977.

Lane, P., *Tudor England*, London, Batsford, 1977.

Lane, P., *Norman England*, London, Batsford, 1980.

Lane, P., *Elizabethan England*, London, Batsford, 1981.

Mackie, J. D., *The Earlier Tudors, 1485–1588*, Oxford, Oxford University Press, 1952.

Miller, E. and Hatcher, J., *Medieval England: Rural Society and Economic Change 1086–1345*, London, Longman, 1978.

Myers, A. R., *England in the Late Middle Ages, 1307–1536*, Harmondsworth, Penguin, 1963, Pelican History of England,

Palliser, D. M., *The Age of Elizabeth*, London, Longman, 1983.

Platt, C., *Medieval England: A Social History and Archaeology from the Conquest to AD 1600*, London, Routledge & Kegan Paul, 1978.

Postan, M. M., *The Medieval Economy and Society: An Economic History of Britain 1100–1500*, Harmondsworth, Penguin, 1975.

Power, E., *The Wool Trade in English Medieval History*, Oxford, Oxford University Press, 1941.

Ramsey, P., *Tudor Economic Problems*, London, Gollancz, 1965.

Reynolds, S., *An Introduction to the History of English Medieval Towns*, London, Oxford University Press, 1982.

Rowley, T., *The Norman Heritage 1066–1200*, London, Routledge & Kegan Paul, 1983.

Rowse, A. L., *The England of Elizabeth: The Structure of Society*, London, Macmillan, 1981.

Rowse, A. L., *The Expansion of Elizabethan England*, London, Macmillan, 1981.

Salzman, L. F., *English Life in the Middle Ages*, Oxford, Oxford University Press, 1926.

Salzman, L. F., *English Industries of the Middle Ages*, London, Pordes, 1964.

Salzman, L. F., *English Trade in the Middle Ages*, London, Pordes, 1964.

Sayles, G. O., *The Medieval Foundations of England*, London, Methuen, 1966.

Southern, R. W., *The Making of the Middle Ages*, London, Hutchinson, 1967.

Stenton, D. M., *English Society in the Early Middle Ages, 1066–1307*, Harmondsworth, Penguin, 1969, Pelican History of England.

Thomson, J. A. F., *The Transformation of Medieval England, 1370–1529*, London, Longman, 1983.

Wilkinson, B., *The Later Middle Ages in England, 1216–1485*, London, Longman, 1977.

Youings, J., *Sixteenth Century England*, Harmondsworth, Penguin, 1984, Pelican Social History of Britain.

SEVENTEENTH AND EIGHTEENTH CENTURIES

Ashley, M., *Life in Stuart England*, London, Batsford, 1964.

Ashley, M., *England in the Seventeenth Century*, Harmondsworth, Penguin, 1970, Pelican History of England.

Ashton, T. S., *An Economic History of England in the Eighteenth Century*, London, Methuen, 1955.

Ashton, T. S., *The Industrial Revolution, 1760–1830*, London, Oxford University Press, 1969.

Berg, M., *The Age of Manufacture: Industry, Innovation and Work in Britain, 1700–1820*, London, Fontana, 1985.

Chambers, J. D., *Population, Economy and Society in Pre-Industrial England*, London, Oxford University Press, 1972.

Clark, P. (ed.), *The Transformation of English Provincial Towns, 1600–1800*, London, Hutchinson, 1984.

Clarkson, L., *The Pre-Industrial Economy in England, 1500–1750*, London, Batsford, 1974.

Clarkson, L., *An Economic History of England, 1500–1800*, London, Methuen, 1984.

Clay, C., *Economic Expansion and Social Change, England 1500–1700*, 2 vols, Cambridge, Cambridge University Press, 1985.

Davis, R., *English Overseas Trade, 1500–1700*, London, Macmillan, 1973.

Deane, P., *The First Industrial Revolution*, Cambridge, Cambridge University Press, 1980.

Dobb, M. H., *Studies in the Development of Capitalism*, London, Routledge & Kegan Paul, 1946.

Flinn, M. W., *The Origins of the Industrial Revolution*, London, Longman, 1966.

Flinn, M. W., *British Population Growth, 1700–1850* London, Macmillan, 1970.

Floud, R. and McClosky, D. (eds), *The Economic History of Britain since 1700, Vol. 1, 1700–1860*, Cambridge, Cambridge University Press, 1981.

George, M. D., *London Life in the Eighteenth Century*, Harmondsworth, Penguin, 1966.

Hammond, J. L. and Hammond, B., *The Village Labourer 1760–1831*, Harmondsworth, Penguin, 1976.

Hill, C., *The English Revolution, 1640*, London, Lawrence and Wishart, 1955.

Hill, C., *Society and Puritanism in Pre-Revolutionary England*, London, Secker and Warburg, 1964.

Hill, C., *Pelican Economic History of Britain, Vol. 2, 1530–1780, Reformation to Industrial Revolution 1530–1780*, Harmondsworth, Penguin, 1969.

Hill, C., *Change and Continuity in Seventeenth Century England*, London, Weidenfeld and Nicolson, 1975.

Holmes, G., *The Making of a Great Power: Pre-Industrial Britain, 1660–1783*, London, Longman, 1985.

Ives, E. W. (ed.), *The English Revolution, 1600–1660*, London, Arnold, 1968.

Jack, S. M., *Economic Revolution in Britain, 1760–1830*, London, Warne, 1968.

Jack, S. M., *Trade and Industry in Tudor and Stuart England*, London, Allen and Unwin, 1977.

Jarrett, D., *Britain, 1688–1815*, London, Longman, 1965,

Jarrett, D., *England in the Age of Hogarth*, London, Paladin, 1976.

Jones, E. L., *Agriculture and the Industrial Revolution*, Oxford, Blackwell, 1975.

Jones, E. L. (ed.), *Agriculture and Economic Growth in England 1650–1815*, New York, London, Methuen, 1967.

Jones, J. R., *Country and Court: England 1658–1714*, London, Arnold, 1978.

Lane, P., *The Stuart Age*, London, Batsford, 1977.

Lane, P., *Georgian England*, London, Batsford, 1981.

Laslett, P., *The World We Have Lost*, London, Methuen, 1971.

Marshall, D., *Eighteenth Century England*, London, Longman, 1975.

Marshall, D., *English People in the Eighteenth Century*, London, Greenwood Press, 1980.

Mathew, D., *The Social Structure in Caroline England*, Oxford, Clarendon Press, 1948.

Mathew, D., *The Age of Charles I*, London, Eyre and Spottiswoode, 1951.

Mathew, D., *The Jacobean Age*, London, Kennikat Press, 1973.

Minchinton, W. E. (ed.), *The Growth of English Overseas Trade in the Seventeenth and Eighteenth Centuries*, London, Methuen, 1969.

Mingay, G. E., *English Landed Society in the Eighteenth Century*, London, Routledge & Kegan Paul, 1963.

Morrill, J. S., *Seventeenth-Century Britain, 1603–1714*, Folkestone, Dawson, 1880.

Neale, R. S., *Class in English History, 1680–1850*, Oxford, Blackwell, 1982.

O'Day, R., *Economy and Community: Economic and Social History of Pre-Industrial England, 1550–1700*, London, Black, 1975.

Pawson, E., *The Early Industrial Revolution: Britain in the 18th Century*, London, Batsford, 1979.

Porter, R., *English Society in the Eighteenth Century*, Harmondsworth, Penguin, 1982, Pelican Social History of Britain.

Stevenson, J., *Popular Disturbances in England 1700–1870*, London, Longman, 1979.

Stone, L., *The Family, Sex and Marriage in England, 1500–1800*, Harmondsworth, Penguin, 1982.

Supple, B. E., *Commercial Crisis and Change in England, 1600–1642*, Cambridge, Cambridge University Press, 1959.

Tawney, R. H., *Religion and the Rise of Capitalism*, Harmondsworth, Penguin, 1969.

Trevelyan, G. M., *England under the Stuarts*, London, Methuen, 1965.

Turberville, A. S., *English Men and Manners in the Eighteenth Century*, Oxford, Oxford University Press, 1957.

Williams, E. N., *Life in Georgian England*, London, Batsford, 1967.

Wilson, C., *England's Apprenticeship, 1603–1763*, London, Longman, 1984.

Wrightson, K., *English Society, 1580–1680*, London, Hutchinson, 1982.

Wrigley, E. A. and Schofield, R. S., *The Population History of England, 1541–1871: A Reconstruction*, London, Arnold, 1981.

NINETEENTH CENTURY

Aldcroft, D. H. and Richardson, H. W., *The British Economy 1870–1939*, London, Macmillan, 1969.

Best, G. F. A., *Mid-Victorian Britain, 1851–75*, London, Fontana, 1979.

Black, E. C. (ed.), *Victorian Culture and Society*, London, Macmillan, 1974.

Briggs, A., *Victorian Cities*, Harmondsworth, Penguin, 1968.

Briggs, A., *The Age of Improvement, 1780–1867*, London, Longman, 1979.

Briggs, A. (ed.), *Chartist Studies*, London, Macmillan, 1970.

Butt, J. and Clarke, I. F. (eds), *The Victorians and Social Protest*, Newton Abbot, David and Charles, 1973.

Chambers, J. D., *Workshop of the World: British Economic History from 1820 to 1880*, Oxford, Oxford University Press, 1968.

Chambers, J. D. and Mingay, G. F., *The Agricultural Revolution, 1750–1880*, London, Batsford, 1966.

Checkland, S. G., *The Rise of Industrial Society in England, 1815–1885*, London, Longman, 1984.

Clark, K., *The Making of Victorian England*, London, Methuen, 1966.

Clark, K., *An Expanding Society: Britain, 1830–1900*, Cambridge,

Cambridge University Press, 1967.

Corfield, P. J., *The Impact of English Towns, 1700–1800*, London, Oxford University Press, 1982.

Cornish, W. R. (ed.), *Crime and Law in 19th Century Britain*, Dublin, Irish University Press, 1977.

Cottrell, P. L., *Industrial Finance, 1830–1914: The Finance and Organisation of English Manufacturing Industry*, London, Methuen, 1980.

Court, W. H. B., *British Economic History, 1870–1914*, Cambridge, Cambridge University Press, 1965.

Crafts, N. F. R., *British Economic Growth During the Industrial Revolution*, Oxford, Clarendon Press, 1985.

Crouzet, F., *The Victorian Economy*, London, Methuen, 1982.

Davis, R., *The Industrial Revolution and British Overseas Trade*, Leicester, Leicester University Press, 1979.

Deane, P., *The First Industrial Revolution*, Cambridge, Cambridge University Press, 1980.

Dennis, R. J., *English Industrial Cities of the Nineteenth Century: A Social Geography*, Cambridge, Cambridge University Press, 1984.

Emsley, C., *British Society and the French Wars, 1793–1815*, London, Macmillan, 1979.

Ensor, R. C. K., *England 1870–1914*, Oxford, Oxford University Press, 1936.

Evans, E. J., *The Forging of the Modern State: Early Industrial Britain, 1783–1870*, London, Longman, 1983.

Foster, J., *Class Struggle and the Industrial Revolution*, London, Methuen, 1977.

Gash, N., *Aristocracy and People: Britain 1815–1865*, London, Arnold, 1979.

Gayer, A. D. et al., *The Growth and Fluctuation of the British Economy, 1790–1850*, Hassocks, Harvester, 1975.

Halévy, E., *A History of the English People in the Nineteenth Century*, 6 vols, London, Benn, 1961.

Harrison, J. F. C., *The Early Victorians*, London, Weidenfeld and Nicolson, 1971.

Hartwell, R. M. (ed.), *The Causes of the Industrial Revolution in England*, London, Methuen, 1967.

Harvey, A. D., *Britain in the Early 19th Century*, London, Batsford, 1978.

Henriques, U. R. Q., *Before the Welfare State: Social Administration in Early Industrial Britain*, London, Longman, 1979.

Hobsbawm, E. J., *The Age of Capital, 1848–1875*, London, Sphere, 1977.

Hopkins, E., *Social History of the English Working Classes, 1815–1945*, London, Arnold, 1979.

Horn, P., *The Rural World, 1780–1850*, London, Hutchinson, 1980.

Jones, D., *Chartism and the Chartists*, London, Allen Lane, 1975.

Knowles, L. C. A., *Industrial and Commercial Revolutions in Great Britain during the Nineteenth Century*, London, Routledge & Kegan Paul, 1967.

Lane, P., *The Industrial Revolution: Birth of the Modern Age*, London, Weidenfeld and Nicolson, 1978.

McCord, N., *The Anti-Corn Law League, 1838–1846*, London, Allen and Unwin, 1958.

Marshall, D., *Industrial England, 1776–1851*, London, Routledge & Kegan Paul, 1982.

Mathias, P., *The First Industrial Nation: An Economic History of Britain, 1700–1914*, Methuen, 1983.

Pelling, H., *Popular Politics and Society in Late Victorian Britain*, London, Macmillan, 1968.

Perkin, H., *The Origins of Modern English Society, 1780–1880*, London, Ark, 1985.

Platt, D. C. M., *Finance, Trade and Politics in British Foreign Policy 1815–1914*, London, Oxford University Press, 1967.

Read, D., *England, 1868–1914: The Age of Urban Democracy*, London, Longman, 1979.

Reeve, R. M., *The Industrial Revolution 1750–1850*, London, University of

London Press, 1971.

Richardson, J., *The Regency*, London, Collins, 1973.

Roach, J., *Social Reform in England*, London, Batsford, 1978.

Roebuck, J., *The Making of Modern English Society from 1850*, London, Routledge & Kegan Paul, 1973.

Rose, M. E., *The Relief of Poverty, 1834–1914*, London, Macmillan, 1972.

Rostow, W., *British Economy of the Nineteenth Century*, London, Greenwood Press, 1982.

Seaman, L. C. B., *Life in Victorian London*, London, Batsford, 1973.

Semmel, B., *The Rise of Free Trade Imperialism*, Cambridge, Cambridge University Press, 1970.

Smith, D., *Conflict and Compromise: Class Formation in English Society, 1830–1914*, London, Routledge & Kegan Paul, 1982.

Stevenson, J., *Popular Disturbance in England, 1700–1870*, London, Longman, 1979.

Taylor, A. J., *Laissez-Faire and State Intervention in Nineteenth Century Britain*, London, Macmillan, 1972.

Taylor, A. J., *The Standard of Living in Britain in the Industrial Revolution*, London, Methuen, 1975.

Thomis, M. and Holt, P., *Threats of Revolution in Britain 1789–1848*, London, Macmillan, 1977.

Thompson, A., *The Dynamics of the Industrial Revolution*, London, Arnold, 1973.

Thompson, E. P., *The Making of the English Working Class*, Harmondsworth, Penguin, 1970.

Thompson, F. M. L., *English Landed Society in the Nineteenth Century*, London, Routledge & Kegan Paul, 1971.

Tunzelmann, G. N. Von, *The Standard of Living in the English Industrial Revolution*, Oxford, Clarendon Press, 1985.

Waller, P. J., *Town, City and Nation: England, 1850–1914*, Oxford, Oxford University Press, 1983.

Ward, J. T., *Chartism*, London, Batsford, 1973.

Ward, J. T., *The Age of Change, 1770–1870: Documents in Social History*, London, Black, 1975.

White, R. J., *Life in Regency England*, London, Batsford, 1963.

White, R. J., *Waterloo to Peterloo*, Harmondsworth, Penguin, 1968.

Williams, J. B., *British Commercial Policy and Trade Expansion, 1750–1850*, Oxford, Oxford University Press, 1972.

Wood, A., *Nineteenth Century Britain, 1815–1914*, London, Longman, 1982.

Woodward, E. L., *The Age of Reform, 1815–1870*, London, Oxford University Press, 1962.

Young, G. M., *Victorian England: Portrait of an Age*, London, Oxford University Press, 1977.

TWENTIETH CENTURY

Aldcroft, D. H., *British Transport Since 1914: An Economic History*, Newton Abbot, David and Charles, 1975.

Aldcroft, D. H., *The British Economy Between the Wars*, Oxford, Philip Allan, 1983.

Aldcroft, D. H., *The British Economy, vol. 1, The Years of Turmoil, 1920–1951*, Brighton, Wheatsheaf, 1986.

Alford, B. W. E., *Depression and Recovery? British Economic Growth, 1918–1939*, London, Macmillan, 1972.

Ashworth, W., *An Economic History of England, 1870–1939*, London, Methuen, 1972.

Barker, T. and Drake, M. (eds), *Population and Society in Britain, 1850–1980*, London, Batsford, 1982.

Bédarida, F., *A Social History of England, 1851–1975*, London, Methuen, 1979.

Beloff, M., *Wars and Welfare: Britain*

1914–1945, London, Arnold, 1984.

Blythe, R., *The Age of Illusion: Glimpses of Britain Between the Wars, 1918–1940*, London, Oxford University Press, 1983.

Bogdanor, V. and Skidelsky, R. (eds), *The Age of Affluence, 1951–1964*, London, Macmillan, 1970.

Booker, C., *The Neophiliacs: A Study of the Revolution in English Life in the Fifties and Sixties*, London, Fontana, 1969.

Booker, C., *The Seventies*, London, Harmondsworth, Penguin, 1980.

Booth, A. and Pack, M., *Employment, Capital and Economic Policy: Great Britain, 1918–1939*, Oxford, Blackwell, 1985.

Borer, M. C., *Britain – Twentieth Century: The Story of Social Conditions*, London, Warne, 1961.

Branson, N. and Heinemann, M., *Britain in the Nineteen-Thirties*, London, Weidenfeld and Nicolson, 1971.

Breach, R. W. and Hartwell, R. M. (eds), *British Economy, 1870–1970: Documents, Descriptions, Statistics*, London, Oxford University Press, 1972.

Broadberry, S., *The British Economy Between the Wars: A Microeconomic Survey*, Oxford, Blackwell, 1986.

Burnet, A. and Landels, W., *The Time of Our Lives: A Pictorial History of Britain since 1945*, London, Elm Tree Books, 1981.

Calvocoressi, P., *The British Experience, 1945–1975*, Harmondsworth, Penguin, 1979.

Capie, F. and Webber, A., *A Monetary History of the United Kingdom, 1870–1982*, London, Allen and Unwin, 1985–.

Cecil, R., *Life in Edwardian England*, London, Batsford, 1969.

Constantine, S., *Social Conditions in Britain, 1918–1939*, London, Methuen, 1983.

Cronin, J. E. and Schneer, J. (eds), *Social Conflict and the Political Order in Modern Britain*, London, Croom Helm, 1982.

Cronin, J. E., *Labour and Society in Britain, 1918–79*, London, Batsford, 1984.

Derry, T. K. and Jarman, M. A., *Modern Britain: Life and Work through Two Centuries of Change*, London, Murray, 1979.

Fraser, D., *The Evolution of the British Welfare State: A History of Social Policy since the Industrial Revolution*, London, Macmillan, 1973.

Fullerton, B., *Development of British Transport Networks*, London, Oxford University Press, 1984.

Gilbert, B. B., *Britain since 1918*, London, Batsford, 1980.

Gloversmith, F. (ed.), *Class, Culture and Social Change: A New View of the 1930's*, Brighton, Harvester, 1980.

Glynn, S. and Oxborrow, J., *Inter-War Britain: A Social and Economic History*, London, Allen and Unwin, 1976.

Graves, R. and Hodges, A., *The Long Week-end: A Social History of Great Britain, 1918–1939*, London, Faber, 1940.

Gregg, P., *A Social and Economic History of Britain: 1760–1970*, London, Harrap, 1972.

Halsey, A. H. (ed.), *Trends in British Society since 1900: A Guide to the Changing Social Structure of Britain*, London, Macmillan, 1972.

Halsey, A. H., *Change in British Society*, London, Oxford University Press, 1986.

Hopkins, H., *The New Look: A Social History of the Forties and Fifties in Britain*, London, Secker and Warburg, 1963.

Johnson, W. et al., *A Short Economic and Social History of Twentieth Century Britain*, London, Allen and Unwin, 1967.

Jones, G. P. and Pool, A. G., *Economic Development in Britain, 1840–1940*, London, Duckworth, 1966.

Kirby, M. W., *The Decline of British Economic Power, since 1870*, London, Allen and Unwin, 1981.

McKie, D. and Cook, C., *The Decade of Disillusion: Britain in the Sixties*, London, Macmillan, 1972.

217

Marsh, D. C., *The Changing Social Structure of England and Wales, 1871–1961*, London, Routledge & Kegan Paul, 1977.

Marwick, A., *Britain in the Century of Total War: Peace and Social Change, 1900–1967*, London, Bodley Head, 1968.

Marwick, A., *The Explosion of British Society 1914–1970*, London, Macmillan, 1971.

Marwick, A., *British Society since 1945*, Harmondsworth, Penguin, 1982, Pelican Social History of Britain.

Medlicott, W. N., *Contemporary Britain, 1914–74*, London, Longman, 1976.

Milward, A. S., *The Economic Effects of the Two World Wars on Britain*, London, Macmillan, 1984.

Montgomery, J., *The Fifties*, London, Allen and Unwin, 1965.

Mowat, C. L., *Britain between the Wars, 1918–1940*, London, Methuen, 1968.

Nowell-Smith, S. (ed.), *Edwardian England, 1901–1914*, London, Oxford University Press, 1964.

Pagnamenta, P. and Overy, R., *All Our Working Lives*, London, BBC, 1984.

Pelling, H., *Modern Britain, 1885–1955*, Edinburgh, Nelson, 1960.

Phillips, G., *The General Strike*, London, Weidenfeld and Nicolson, 1976.

Pollard, S., *The Development of the British Economy, 1914–1967*, London, Arnold, 1973.

Pope, R. and Hoyle, B. (eds), *British Economic Performance 1880–1980: A Collection of Historical Sources*, London, Croom Helm, 1985.

Priestley, J. B., *The Edwardians*, London, Heinemann, 1970.

Read, D., *Edwardian England, 1901–15*, London, Harrap, 1972.

Read, D. (ed.), *Edwardian England: Reassessments*, London Croom Helm, 1982.

Reynolds, E. E. and Brasher, N. H., *Britain in the Twentieth Century 1900–64*, Cambridge, Cambridge University Press, 1967.

Roebuck, J., *The Making of Modern English Society from 1850*, London,

Routledge & Kegan Paul, 1982.

Ryder, J. and Silver, H., *Modern English Society: History and Structure*, London, Methuen, 1985.

Sayers, R. S., *A History of Economic Change in England, 1880–1939*, Oxford, Oxford University Press, 1967.

Seaman, L. C. B., *Post-Victorian Britain, 1902–51*, London, Methuen, 1967.

Seaman, L. C. B., *Life in Britain between the Wars*, London, Batsford, 1970.

Shrapnel, N., *The Seventies: Britain's Inward March*, London, Constable, 1980.

Smith, S. N., *Edwardian England, 1901–1914*, London, Oxford University Press, 1964.

Stafford, G. B., *End of Economic Growth? Growth and Decline in the UK since 1945*, Oxford, Robertson, 1981.

Stevenson, J., *British Society, 1914–45*, Harmondsworth, Penguin, 1984, Pelican Social History of Britain.

Stevenson, J. (ed.), *Social Conditions in Britain between the Wars*, Harmondsworth, Penguin, 1977.

Stevenson, J. and Cook, C., *The Slump: Society and Politics During the Depression*, London, Cape, 1978.

Thomas, W. A., *The Finance of British Industry, 1918–1976*, London, Methuen, 1978.

Thompson, P., *The Edwardians: The Remaking of British Society*, London, Paladin, 1977.

Tomlinson, J., *Problems of British Economic Policy, 1870–1945*, London, Methuen, 1981.

Tranter, N. L., *Population since the Industrial Revolution: the English Experience*, London, Croom Helm, 1973.

Whitehead, P., *The Writing on the Wall: Britain in the Seventies*, London, Michael Joseph, 1986.

Wood, A., *Great Britain, 1900–65*, London, Longman, 1978.

Wright, J., *Britain in the Age of Economic Management: An Economic History since 1939*, London, Oxford University Press, 1979.

SEE ALSO:

32 SOCIAL POLICY AND SOCIAL SERVICES

Bibliographical guides to publications on British society and social policy are contained in the following: Blackstone, T., *Social Policy and Administration in Britain: A Bibliography*, 1975; Royal Institute of Public Administration, *Welfare Services in Britain: A Select Bibliography*, 1975; Westergaard, J. et al., *Modern British Society: A Bibliography*, 1977; Williams, G., *Poverty in the UK: A Classified Bibliography*, 1980.

For recent publications see British Library of Economic and Political Science, *A London Bibliography of the Social Sciences*, annually; British Library, *Current Research in Britain: Social Sciences,* Boston Spa, annually.

For further information on society, social research and social policy the following can be referred to: Brittain, J. M. and Roberts, S. A., *Inventory of Information Resources in the Social Sciences*, 1975; Councils and Education Press (publisher), *Social Services Year Book*, annually; Edwards, B., *Sources of Social Statistics*, 1974; Jackaman, P. G., *Sources of Social and Legal Information*, 1978; National Council of Voluntary Organisations, *Voluntary Organisations: An NCVO Directory*; Routledge & Kegan Paul (publisher), *The Year Book of Social Policy in Britain*, annually; Social Science Research Council, *Research Supported by the Social Science Research Council*, annually.

Statistical data on British society can be located in: Central Statistical Office, *Great Britain: Guide to Official Statistics*, annually; Department of Health and Social Security, *Health and Personal Social Service Statistics for England*, annually; Her Majesty's Stationery Office, *Social Trends*, London, annually.

The following provide useful general surveys of the field of social policy and social administration: Baugh, W. E., *Introduction to the Social Services*, 1983; Brown, M., *Introduction to Social Administration in Britain*, 1983; Byrne, T. and Padfield, C. F., *Social Services Made Simple*, 1983; Central Office of Information, *Social Services in Britain*, 1976; Central Office of Information, *Social Welfare in Britain*, 1981; Hill, M. J., *Understanding Social Policy*, 1983; Marsh, D. C., *Introducing Social Policy*, 1979; Randall, F., *British Social Services*, 1981, Preston, B. (ed.), *Guide to the Social Services*, 1983; Wilmott, P., *Consumer's Guide to the British Social Services*, 1978.

As reading to particular areas the following are recommended:

Housing   Burke, G., *Housing and Social Justice*, 1981; Dunleavy, P., *The Politics of Mass Housing in Britain, 1945–1975*, 1982; Lansley, S., *Housing and Public Policy*, 1979, Merrett, S., *State Housing Policy in Britain*, 1979.

National Health   Central Office of Information, *Health Services in Britain*, 1974; Butler, J. R. and Vaile, M. S. B., *Health and Health Services: An Introduction to Health Care in Britain*, 1984; Ham, C., *Health Policy in Britain*, 1982; Klein, R., *The Politics of the National Health Service*, 1983; Thornhurst, C., *It Makes You Sick: The Politics of the NHS*, 1984; Vaizey, J., *National Health*, 1984.

Poverty   Berthoud, R. and Brown, J. C., *Poverty and the Development of Anti-Poverty Policy in the United Kingdom*, 1981; Mack, J. and Lansley, S., *Poor Britain*, 1985.

Social Security   Central Office of Information, *Social Security in Britain*, 1977; Dilnot, A. W. et al., *The Reform of Social Security*, 1984.
Social Work   Barclay, P. et al., *Social Workers: Their Role and Tasks*, 1982; Byrne, T. and Padfield, C. F., *Social Services Made Simple*, 1983; Jones, C., *State Social Work and the Working Class*, 1983; Young, P., *Mastering Social Work*, 1985.

REFERENCE

Blackstone, T., *Social Policy and Administration in Britain: A Bibliography*, London, Frances Pinter, 1975.

British Library, *Current Research in Britain: Social Sciences*, Boston Spa annually.

British Library of Economic and Political Science, *A London Bibliography of the Social Sciences*, London and New York, Mansell, annually.

Brittain, J. M. and Roberts, S. A., *Inventory of Information Resources in the Social Sciences*, Farnborough, Saxon House, 1975.

Butcher, D., *Official Publications in Britain*, London, Bingley, 1982.

Central Statistical Office, *Great Britain: Guide to Official Statistics*, London, HMSO, annually.

Central Statistical Office, *Regional Trends*, London, HMSO, annually.

Central Statistical Office, *Social Trends*, London, HMSO, annually.

Comfort, A. C. and Loveless, C. (eds), *Guide to Government Data: A Survey of Unpublished Social Science Material in Libraries of Governments in London*, London, Macmillan, 1974.

Councils and Education Press (publisher), *Social Services Year Book*, London, annually.

Department of Health and Social Security, *Health and Personal Social Service Statistics for England*, London, annually.

Edwards, B., *Sources of Social Statistics*, London, Heinemann, 1974.

Her Majesty's Stationery Office, *People in Britain: A Census Atlas*, London, 1980.

International Committee for Social Science Information and Documentation, *International Bibliography of the Social Sciences: Political Science*, London, 1981.

Jackaman, P. G., *Sources of Social and Legal Information*, London, Library Association, 1978.

Lynes, T., *The Penguin Guide to Supplementary Benefits*, Harmondsworth, Penguin, 1985.

Maunder, W. F. (ed.), *Reviews of United Kingdom Statistical Sources*, 15 vols, Oxford, Pergamon Press, 1974–81.

Morby, G., *Know How to Find out Your Rights*, London, Pluto Press, 1982.

National Council for Voluntary Organisations, *Voluntary Organisations: An NCVO Directory*, London, Bedford Square Press, annually.

Pickett, K. G., *Sources of Official Data*, London, Longman, 1974.

Preston, B., *A Guide to the Social Services*, London, Family Welfare Association, 1983.

Richard, S., *British Government Publications: An Index to Chairmen and Authors*, 4 vols, London, Library Association, 1982–4.

Roberts, N., *The Use of Social Sciences Literature*, London, Butterworth, 1977.

Routledge & Kegan Paul (publisher), *The Year Book of Social Policy in Britain*, London, annually.

Royal Institute of Public Administration, *Welfare Services in Britain: A Select Bibliography*, London, RIPA, 1975.

Sillitoe, A. F., *Britain in Figures: A Handbook of Social Statistics*, Harmondsworth, Penguin, 1973.

Social Science Research Council, *Research Supported by the Social Science Research Council*, London, annually.

Stewart, G., *Personal Social Services*

Bibliography, London, Library
Association, 1980.
Westergaard, J. et al., *Modern British
Society: A Bibliography*, London,
Frances Pinter, 1977.
Williams, G., *Poverty and Policy in the
UK, A Classified Bibliography*,
London, Policy Studies Institute, 1980.

SOCIAL POLICY

Abrams, P., *Practice and Progress:
British Sociology 1950–1980*,
London, Allen and Unwin, 1981.
Allsop, J., *Health Policy and the
National Health Service*, London,
Longman, 1984.
Balchin, P. N., *Housing Policy: An
Introduction*, London, Croom Helm,
1984.
Banting, K., *Poverty, Politics and Policy*,
London, Macmillan, 1979.
Barker, P. (ed.), *Founders of the Welfare
State*, Aldershot, Gower, 1985.
Berthoud, R. and Brown, J. C., *Poverty
and the Development of Anti-Poverty
Policy in the UK*, Aldershot, Gower,
1981.
Booth, T. A. (ed.), *Planning for Welfare:
Social Policy and the Expenditure
Process*, Oxford, Blackwell, 1979.
Brown, M., *Introduction to Social
Administration in Britain*, London,
Hutchinson, 1983.
Brown, M. and Madge, N., *Despite the
Welfare State*, London, Heinemann,
1982.
Burke, G., *Housing and Social Justice*,
London, Longman, 1981.
Cawson, A., *Corporatism and Welfare*,
London, Heinemann, 1982.
Chesterman, M., *Charities, Trusts and
Social Welfare*, London, Weidenfeld
and Nicolson, 1979.
Cooper, J. D., *The Creation of the British
Personal Social Services, 1962–74*,
London, Heinemann, 1983.
Dilnot, A. W. et al., *The Reform of Social
Security*, Oxford, Clarendon Press,
1984.
Donnison, D. et al., *Social Policy and
Administration Revisited*, London,
Allen and Unwin, 1976.
Donnison, D. and Ungerson, C., *Housing
Policy*, Harmondsworth, Penguin,
1982.
Dunleavy, P., *The Politics of Mass

Housing in Britain, 1945–1975,
Oxford, Clarendon Press, 1982.
Eisenstadt, S. N. and Ahimer, O. (eds),
The Welfare State and its Aftermath,
London, Croom Helm, 1985.
Eldridge, J., *Recent British Sociology: A
Critical Essay and Bibliography*,
London, Macmillan, 1981.
Ermish, J. F., *The Political Economy of
Demographic Change: Causes and
Implications of Population Trends in
Great Britain*, London, Heinemann,
1983.
George, V. and Wilding, P., *Ideology and
Social Welfare*, London, Routledge &
Kegan Paul, 1976.
George, V. and Wilding, P., *The Impact
of Social Policy*, London,
Routledge & Kegan Paul, 1984.
Glennerster, H. (ed.), *The Future of the
Welfare State*, London, Heinemann,
1983.
Glennerster, H., *Paying For Welfare*,
Oxford, Blackwell, 1985.
Gough, I., *The Political Economy of the
Welfare State*, London, Macmillan,
1979.
Gower (publisher), *The Growth of the
Social Services; New Society Social
Studies Reader*, Aldershot, 1986.
Gower (publisher), *New Directions in
Social Policy; New Society Social
Studies Reader*, Aldershot, 1985.
Gower (publisher), *The Origins of the
Social Services; New Society Social
Studies Reader*, Aldershot, 1985.
Hadley, R. and Hatch, S., *Social Welfare
and the Future of the State*, London,
Allen and Unwin, 1981.
Hall, P. et al., *Change, Choice and
Conflict in Social Policy*, London,
Heinemann, 1975.
Halsey, A H. (ed.), *Trends in British
Society since 1900*, London,
Macmillan, 1972.
Halsey, A. H., *Change in British Society*,

London, Oxford University Press, 1981.

Ham, C., *Health Policy in Britain: The Organisation and Politics of the NHS*, London, Macmillan, 1982.

Harrison, P., *Inside the Inner City*, Harmondsworth, Penguin, 1985.

Hay, J. R. (ed.), *The Development of the British Welfare State, 1880–1975*, London, Arnold, 1978.

Her Majesty's Stationery Office, *Demographic Review: A Report on Population in Great Britain*, London, 1977.

Her Majesty's Stationery Office, *General Household Survey*, London, 1983.

Hill, M. J., *Understanding Social Policy*, Oxford, Blackwell, 1983.

Hill, M. J. and Bramley, G., *Analysing Social Policy*, Oxford, Blackwell, 1986.

Jones, K. et al., *Issues in Social Policy*, London, Routledge & Kegan Paul, 1978.

Jordan, B., *Freedom and the Welfare State*, London, Routledge & Kegan Paul, 1976.

Klein, R., *The Politics of the National Health Service*, London, Longman, 1983.

Lansley, S., *Housing and Public Policy*, London, Croom Helm, 1979.

Le Grand, J. and Robinson, R. (eds), *Privatization and the Welfare State*, London, Allen and Unwin, 1984.

Levitt, R., *Implementing Public Policy*, London, Croom Helm, 1980.

Loney, M. et al (eds), *Social Policy and Social Welfare*, Milton Keynes, Open University Press, 1983.

Mack, J. and Lansley, S., *Poor Britain*, London, Allen and Unwin, 1985.

Malpass, P. and Murie, A., *Housing Policy and Practice*, London, Macmillan, 1982.

Marsh, D. C. *Introducing Social Policy*, London, Routledge & Kegan Paul, 1979.

Marsh, D. C., *The Welfare State*, London, Longman, 1980.

Merrett, S., *State Housing Policy in Britain*, London, Routledge & Kegan Paul, 1979.

Mishra, R., *Society and Social Policy*, London, Macmillan, 1981.

Mitchell, J., *What is to Be Done about Illness and Health?*, Harmondsworth, Penguin, 1984.

Newby, H., *Green and Pleasant Land? Social Change in Rural England*, Penguin, 1980.

Newson, T. and Potter, P., *Housing Policy in Britain: An Information Sourcebook*, London, Mansell, 1985.

Robson, W. A., *Welfare State and Welfare Society: Illusion and Reality*, London, Allen and Unwin, 1976.

Sandford, C. et al., *Taxation and Social Policy*, London, Heinemann, 1981.

Scoffham, E. R., *The Shape of British Housing*, London, George Godwin, 1984.

Shragge, E., *Pensions Policy in Britain: A Socialist Analysis*, London, Routledge & Kegan Paul, 1984.

Taylor-Gooby, P., *Public Opinion, Ideology and State Welfare*, London, Routledge & Kegan Paul, 1985.

Thane, P. (ed.), *The Origins of British Social Policy*, London, Longman, 1978.

Thomas, P., *The Aims and Outcomes of Social Policy Research*, London, Croom Helm, 1985.

Thornhurst, C., *It Makes You Sick: The Politics of the NHS*, London, Pluto, 1984.

Townsend, P., *Sociology and Social Policy*, Harmondsworth, Penguin, 1976.

Walker, A., *Social Planning and Social Policy*, Oxford, Martin Robertson, 1981.

Walker, A. (ed.), *Public Expenditure and Social Policy*, London, Heinemann, 1982.

Watkin, B., *Documents on Health and Social Services 1834 to the Present Day*, London, Methuen, 1975.

SOCIAL SERVICES

Bailey, R. and Brake, M., *Radical Social Work*, London, Arnold, 1975.

Barclay, P. et al., *Social Workers: Their Role and Tasks*, London, Bedford Square Press, 1982.

Baugh, W. E., *Introduction to the Social Services*, London, Macmillan, 1983.

Bolger, A. W., *Counselling in Britain: A Reader*, London, Batsford, 1982.

Bruce, M., *The Coming of the Welfare State*, London, Batsford, 1971.

Butler, J. R. and Vaile, M. S. B., *Health and Health Services: An Introduction to Health Care in Britain*, London, Routledge & Kegan Paul, 1984.

Butterworth, E. and Holman, R. (eds), *Social Welfare in Modern Britain*, London, Fontana, 1975.

Byrne, T. and Padfield, C. F., *Social Services Made Simple*, London, Heinemann, 1983.

Central Office of Information, *Health Services in Britain*, London, HMSO, 1974.

Central Office of Information, *Social Services in Britain*, London, HMSO, 1976.

Central Office of Information, *Social Security in Britain*, London, HMSO, 1977.

Central Office of Information, *Care of the Elderly in Britain*, London, HMSO, 1977.

Central Office of Information, *Social Welfare in Britain*, London, HMSO, 1981.

Central Office of Information, *Elderly People in the Community*, London, HMSO, 1983.

Central Office of Information, *Social Services: Care of Mentally Handicapped People*, London, HMSO, 1983.

Chaplin, N. W. (ed.), *Health Care in the United Kingdom: Its Organization and Management*, London, Kluwer, 1982.

Cherns, A., *Using the Social Services*, London, Routledge & Kegan Paul, 1979.

Department of Health and Social Security, *The Health Service in England*, Annual Report, London, HMSO, annually.

Department of Health and Social Security, *Supplementary Benefits Handbook*, London, HMSO, 1983.

Fraser, D., *The Evolution of the Welfare State: A History of Social Policy since the Industrial Revolution*, London, Macmillan, 1984.

Gower (publisher), *Medicine and Health: New Society Social Studies Reader*, Aldershot, 1985.

Hall, M. P., *The Social Services in England and Wales*, London, Routledge & Kegan Paul, 1983.

Her Majesty's Stationery Office, *National Dwelling and Housing Survey*, London, 1979.

Jacques, E. (ed.), *Health Services*, London, Heinemann, 1978.

Jones, C., *State Social Work and the Working Class*, London, Macmillan, 1983.

Levitt, R. and Wall, A., *The Reorganised National Health Service*, London, Croom Helm, London, 1985.

Lister, R., *Welfare Benefits*, London, Sweet and Maxwell, 1981.

Marsh, D. C., *The Welfare State*, London, Longman, 1980.

Merrett, S., *State Housing in Britain*, London, Routledge & Kegan Paul, 1979.

Oswin, M., *Holes in the Welfare Net*, London, Bedford Square Press, 1978.

Preston, B. (ed.), *Guide to the Social Services*, London, Family Welfare Association, 1983.

Randall, F., *British Social Services*, Plymouth, Macdonald and Evans, 1981.

Robinson, D., *Patients, Practitioners and Medical Care*, London, Heinemann, 1978.

Royal Commission on the National Health Service, *Report*, Cmnd. 7615, London, HMSO, 1979.

Sainsbury, E., *The Personal Social Services and Social Work*, London, Pitman, 1977.

Topliss, E., *Provision for the Disabled*, Oxford, Blackwell, 1975.

Townsend, P. and Davidson, N., *Inequalities in Health: The Black Report*, Harmondsworth, Penguin, 1982.

Vaizey, J., *National Health*, Oxford, Blackwell, 1984.

Willcocks, A. J., *The Creation of the National Health Service*, London, Routledge & Kegan Paul, 1967.

Wilmott, P., *Consumer's Guide to the British Social Services*, Harmondsworth, Penguin, 1978.

Young, P., *Mastering Social Work*, London, Macmillan, 1985.

Younghusband, E., *Social Work in Britain, 1950–1975*, London, Allen and Unwin, 1978,

SEE ALSO:

33 SOCIAL STRUCTURE AND CLASS

For bibliographical references to writing on social structure in Britain readers are directed to the relevant sections of Westergaard, J. et al. (eds), *Modern British Society: A Bibliography*, 1977.

Current work and writings are listed in British Library of Economic and Political Science, *A London Bibliography of the Social Sciences*, annually; British Library, *Current Research in Britain: Social Sciences*, Boston Spa, annually

The following are recommended as comprehensive studies of social structure, wealth and class in Britain: Goldthorpe, J. H. et al., *Social Mobility and Class Structure in Modern Britain*, 1980; Kelsall, R. K., *The Social Structure of Modern Britain*, 1979; Noble, T., *Structure and Change in Modern Britain*, 1981; Reid, I., *Social Class Differences in Britain*, 1981; Richardson, C. J., *Contemporary Social Mobility*, 1977; Westergaard, J. H. and Resler, H., *Class in a Capitalist Society*, 1975.

Recommended reading on particular aspects of the field:

Education   Boudon, R., *Education, Opportunity and Social Inequality*, 1974; Halsey, A. H. et al., *Origins and Destinations: Family, Class and Education in Modern Britain*, 1980; Craft, M. (ed.), *Family, Class and Education*, 1970; Morris, V. and Verry, D., *Education, Equality and Income Distribution*, 1977.

Occupation   Abrams, P. and Brown, R. (eds), *UK Society: Work, Urbanism and Inequality*, 1984; Coxon, A. P. M. and Jones, C. L., *Class and Hierarchy: The Social Meaning of Occupations*, 1979; Stewart, A. et al., *Social Stratification and Occupational Structure*, 1980.

Wealth   Atkinson, A. B., *Wealth, Income and Inequality*, 1981; Field, F., *The Wealth Report*, 1979; Field, F., *The Wealth Report 2*, 1983; Harbury, C. D. and Hitchens, D. M., *Inheritance and Wealth Inequality in Britain*, 1979.

GENERAL

Abercrombie, N. et al., *Contemporary British Society*, Cambridge, Polity, 1987.

Abrams, P. and Brown, R. (eds), *UK Society: Work, Urbanism and Inequality*, London, Weidenfeld and Nicolson, 1984.

Atkinson, A. B., *Unequal Shares: Wealth in Britain*, Harmondsworth, Penguin, 1974.

Atkinson, A. B., *The Economics of Inequality*, London, Oxford University Press, 1975.

Atkinson, A. B., *The Distribution of Personal Wealth in Britain*, Cambridge, Cambridge University Press, 1978.

Atkinson, A. B., *Wealth, Income and Inequality*, London, Oxford University Press, 1981.

Butterworth, E. and Weir, D. (eds), *The New Sociology of Modern Britain: An Introductory Reader*, London, Fontana, 1984.

Cole, G. D. H., *Studies in Class Structure*, London, Routledge & Kegan Paul, 1968.

Cottrell, A., *Social Classes in Marxist*

Theory and in Post-War Britain, London, Routledge & Kegan Paul, 1984.

Coxon, A. P. M. and Jones, C. L., *Class and Hierarchy: The Social Meaning of Occupations*, London, Macmillan, 1979.

Davis, H. H., *Beyond Class Images: Explorations in the Structure of Social Consciousness*, London, Croom Helm, 1979.

Eagleton, M. and Pierce, D., *Attitudes to Class in the English Novel*, London, Thames and Hudson, 1980.

Franklin, M. N., *The Decline of Class Voting in Britain*, Oxford, Clarendon, 1985.

Furbank, P. N., *Unholy Pleasure: The Idea of Class*, London, Oxford University Press, 1985.

Gallie, D., *Social Inequality and Class Radicalism: France and Britain*, Cambridge, Cambridge University Press, 1983.

Goldthorpe, J. H. and Hope, K., *Social Grading of Occupations: A New Approach and Scale*, Oxford, Clarendon Press, 1974.

Goldthorpe, J. H. et al., *Social Mobility and Class Structure in Modern Britain*, Oxford, Oxford University Press, 1980.

Gower (publisher), *The New Classes: New Society Social Studies Reader*, Aldershot, 1985.

Halsey, A. H., *Change in British Society*, London, Oxford University Press, 1981.

Halsey, A. H. et al., *Origins and Destinations: Family, Class and Education in Modern Britain*, Oxford, Oxford University Press, 1980.

Harbury, C. D. and Hitchens, D. M., *Inheritance and Wealth Inequality in Britain*, London, Allen and Unwin, 1979.

Hawkins, K., *Unemployment*, Harmondsworth, Penguin, 1979.

Her Majesty's Stationery Office, *Report of the Royal Commission on the Distribution of Income and Wealth*, 4 vols, Cmnd. 6171, 6122, 6383, 6626, London, 1975–6.

Her Majesty's Stationery Office, *Social Trends*, London, annually.

Johns, E. A., *The Social Structure of Modern Britain*, Oxford, Pergamon, 1979.

Kelsall, R. K., *The Social Structure of Modern Britain: Population*, London, Longman, 1979.

Littler, C. R. and Salaman, G., *Class at Work: The Design, Allocation and Control of Jobs*, London, Batsford, 1984.

Marsh, D. C., *The Changing Social Structure of England and Wales, 1871–1961*, London, Routledge & Kegan Paul, 1977.

Morris, V. and Verry, D., *Education, Equality and Income Distribution*, Milton Keynes, Open University Press, 1977.

Noble, T., *Structure and Change in Modern Britain*, London, Batsford, 1981.

Osman, T., *The Facts of Everyday Life*, London, Faber, 1985.

Parkin, F. (ed.), *The Social Analysis of Class Structure*, London, Tavistock, 1974.

Pollard, S. and Crossley, D. W., *The Wealth of England, 1085–1966*, London, Batsford, 1968.

Reid, I., *Social Class Differences in Britain: A Sourcebook*, London, Grant McIntyre, 1981.

Richardson, C. J., *Contemporary Social Mobility*, London, Frances Pinter, 1977.

Robbins, D. et al. (eds), *Rethinking Social Inequality*, Aldershot, Gower, 1982.

Robertson, D., *Class and the British Electorate*, Oxford, Blackwell, 1984.

Routh, G., *Occupation and Pay in Great Britain, 1900–1979*, London, Macmillan, 1980.

Seabrook, J., *Unemployment in the Eighties*, London, Quartet Books, 1982.

Sinfield, A., *What Unemployment Means*, Oxford, Martin Robertson, 1981.

Stewart, A. et al., *Social Stratification and Occupational Structure*, London,

227

Macmillan, 1980.

Stewart, A. (ed.), *Contemporary Britain*, London, Routledge & Kegan Paul, 1983.

Wedderburn, D. (ed.), *Poverty, Inequality and Class Structure*, Cambridge, Cambridge University

Press, 1974.

Westergaard, J. H. and Resler, H., *Class in a Capitalist Society: A Study of Contemporary Britain*, London, Heinemann, 1975.

Williams, R. M., *British Population*, London, Heinemann, 1978.

ELITES

Beckett, J. V., *The Aristocracy in England, 1660–1915*, Oxford, Blackwell, 1986.

Bence-Jones, M. and Montgomery-Massingberd, H., *The British Aristocracy*, London, Constable, 1979.

Cannadine, D., *Lords and Landlords: The Aristocracy and the Towns, 1774–1967*, Leicester, Leicester University Press, 1980.

Davidoff, L., *The Best Circles: Society, Etiquette and the Season*, London, Croom Helm, 1973.

Fidler, J., *The British Business Elite: Its Attitudes to Class, Status and Power*, London, Routledge & Kegan Paul, 1981.

Guttsman, W. L. (ed.), *The English Ruling Class*, London, Weidenfeld and Nicolson, 1969.

Harbury, C. D. and Hitchens, D., *Inheritance and Wealth Inequality in Britain*, London, Allen and Unwin, 1980.

Lane, P., *The Upper Class*, London, Batsford, 1972.

Lukes, S., *Power: A Radical View*, London, Macmillan, 1975.

Mason, P., *The English Gentleman: The Rise and Fall of an Ideal*, London, Deutsch, 1982.

Mingay, G. E., *The Gentry: The Rise and Fall of a Ruling Class*, London, Longman, 1976.

Rubinstein, W. D., *Men of Property: The Very Wealthy in Britain since the Industrial Revolution*, London, Croom Helm, 1981.

Scott, J., *The Upper Classes: Property and Privilege in Britain*, London, Macmillan, 1982.

Stanworth, P. and Giddens, A. (eds), *Elites and Power in British Society*, Cambridge, Cambridge University Press, 1974.

Urry, J. and Wakeford, J. (eds), *Power in Britain*, London, Heinemann, 1973.

Winchester, S., *Their Noble Lordships: The Hereditary Peerage Today*, London, Faber, 1981.

Yass, M., *The English Aristocracy*, London, Wayland, 1974.

MIDDLE CLASS

Bell, C. R., *Middle Class Families: Social and Geographical Mobility*, London, Routledge & Kegan Paul, 1969.

Bradley, I., *The English Middle Classes are Alive and Kicking*, London, Collins, 1982.

Crossick, G., *The Lower Middle Class in Britain*, London, Croom Helm, 1979.

Deverson, J. and Lindsay, K., *Voices from the Middle Class*, London, Hutchinson, 1975.

King, R. and Nugent, N. (eds), *Respectable Rebels: Middle Class*

Campaigns in Britain in the 1970's, London, Hodder and Stoughton, 1979.

King, R. and Raynor, J., *The Middle Class*, London, Longman, 1981.

Parkin, F., *Middle Class Radicalism*, Manchester, Manchester University Press, 1968.

Raynor, J., *The Middle Class*, London, Longman, 1969.

Scase, R., *The Entrepreneurial Middle Class*, London, Croom Helm, 1982.

WORKING CLASS

Baumann, Z., *Between Class and Elite: The Evolution of the British Labour Movement*, Manchester, Manchester University Press, 1972.

Blackburn, R. M. and Mann, M., *The Working Class in the Labour Market*, London, Macmillan, 1979.

Blackwell, T. and Seabrook, J., *A World Still to Win: The Reconstruction of the Post-War Working Class*, London, Faber, 1985.

Briggs, A. and Saville, J. (eds), *Essays in Labour History, 1918–1939*, London, Croom Helm, 1977.

Broom, L. et al., *The Inheritance of Inequality*, London, Routledge & Kegan Paul, 1980.

Bulmer, M. (ed.), *Working Class Images of Society*, London, Routledge & Kegan Paul, 1975.

Burnett, J. (ed.), *Useful Toil: Autobiographies of Working People from the 1820's to the 1920's*, London, Allen Lane, 1974.

Campbell, B., *Wigan Pier Revisited: Poverty and Politics in the 1980's*, London, Virago, 1984.

Coates, K. and Silburn, R., *Poverty: The Forgotten Englishman*, Harmondsworth, Penguin, 1981.

Cole, G. D. H. and Filson, A. (eds.), *British Working Class Movements*, London, Macmillan, 1965.

Cole, G. D. H. and Filson, A. W., *British Working Class Movements*, London, Macmillan, 1968.

Fagin, L. and Little, M., *The Forsaken Families: The Effects of Unemployment on Contemporary British Life*, Harmondsworth, Penguin, 1984.

Field, F., *Britain's Conscript Army: A Study of Britain's Unemployed*, London, Routledge & Kegan Paul, 1977.

Gallie, D., *In Search of the New Working Class*, Cambridge, Cambridge University Press, 1978.

Gower (publisher), *How the Poorest Live: New Society Social Studies Reader*, Aldershot, 1986.

Gower (publisher), *Unemployment and the Black Economy: New Society Social Studies Reader*, Aldershot, 1985.

Harrison, P., *Inside the Inner City: Life under the Cutting Edge*, Harmondsworth, Penguin, 1985.

Hasbach, W., *History of the English Agricultural Labourer*, London, Cass, 1966.

Hobsbawm, E. J., *Labouring Men*, London, Weidenfeld and Nicolson, 1964.

Holman, B., *Poverty: Explanations of Social Deprivation*, Oxford, Martin Robertson, 1978.

Hopkins, E., *A Social History of the English Working Classes, 1815–1945*, London, Arnold, 1979.

Hunt, E. H., *British Labour History, 1815–1914*, London, Weidenfeld and Nicolson, 1981.

Hyman, R. and Price, R. (eds), *The New Working Class? White Collar Workers and their Organisations*, London, Macmillan, 1983.

Jones, G. S., *Languages of Class: Studies in English Working Class History, 1832–1982*, Cambridge, Cambridge University Press, 1983.

Lansley, S. and Mack, J., *Poor Britain*, Oxford, Blackwell, 1984.

More, C., *Skill and the English Working Class*, London, Croom Helm, 1982.

Parker, T., *The People of Providence: Interviews from an Urban Housing Estate*, Harmondsworth, Penguin, 1985.

Price, R., *Labour in British Society: An Interpretative History*, London, Croom Helm, 1985.

Roberts, K., *The Working Classes*, London, Longman, 1978.

Royal Commission on the Distribution of Income and Wealth, *Causes of Poverty*, Cmnd. 7175, London, HMSO, 1978.

Rutter, M. and Madge, N., *Cycles of Disadvantage*, London, Heinemann, 1976.

Saville, J., *Working Conditions in the*

229

Victorian Age, London, Gregg, 1973.

Seabrook, J., *Landscapes of Poverty*, Oxford, Blackwell, 1985.

Sen, A., *Poverty and Families*, London, Oxford University Press, 1981.

Taylor, R., *Workers and the New Depression*, London, Macmillan, 1982.

Tholfsen, T., *Working Class Radicalism in Mid-Victorian England*, London, Croom Helm, 1976.

Webb, R. K., *The British Working Class Reader, 1790–1848*, London, George Allen, 1955.

Willis, P., *Learning to Labour: How Working Class Kids Get Working Class Jobs*, Aldershot, Gower, 1977.

Winter, J. (ed.), *The Working Class in Modern British History*, Cambridge, Cambridge University Press, 1983.

SEE ALSO:

34 SPORT AND LEISURE

Studies of the social aspects of sport and leisure in Britain are provided in: Brailsford, D., *Sport and Society*, 1969; Central Office of Information, *Planning for Leisure*, 1969; Central Office of Information, *Sport and Recreation in Britain*, 1976; Dunning, E. (ed.), *The Sociology of Sport*, 1972; Harris, H. A., *Sport in Britain: Its Origins and Development*, 1975; Parker, S., *The Sociology of Leisure*, 1976; Roberts, K., *Contemporary Society and the Growth of Leisure*, 1979; Smith, M. et al. (eds), *Leisure and Society in Britain*, 1973; Walvin, J., *Leisure and Society, 1830–1950*, 1978; Whannel, G., *Blowing the Whistle: The Politics of Sport*, 1983.

REFERENCE

Arlott, J. (ed.), *The Oxford Companion to Sports and Games*, Oxford, Oxford University Press, 1975.

Brander, M., *A Dictionary of Sporting Terms*, London, Black, 1968.

Cuddon, J. A., *The Macmillan Dictionary of Sport and Games*, London, Macmillan, 1980.

Greenaway, L. (ed.), *Sport in Education and Recreation*, London, National Book League, 1970.

Kaye and Ward (publisher), *Official Rules of Sports and Games*, London, 1980.

Lawn Tennis Association, *The Official Yearbook*, London, annually.

Macdonald (publisher), *Wisden Cricketers' Almanack*, London, annually.

Oliver, K. (ed.), *Ruff's Guide to the Turf*, London, Sporting Life, annually.

Padwick, E. W., *A Bibliography of Cricket*, London, Library Association, 1984.

Pelham Books (publisher), *Benson and Hedges Cricket Year*, London, annually.

Pelham Books (publisher), *Football Association Yearbook*, London, annually.

GENERAL

Armitage, J., *Man at Play: Nine Centuries of Pleasure Making*, London, Warne, 1977.

Brailsford, D., *Sport and Society*, London, Routledge & Kegan Paul, 1969.

Central Office of Information, *Planning for Leisure*, London, HMSO, 1969.

Central Office of Information, *Sport in Britain*, London, HMSO, 1972.

Central Office of Information, *Sport and Recreation in Britain*, London, HMSO, 1976.

Clarke, J. and Critcher, C., *The Devil Makes Work: Leisure in Capitalist Society*, London, Macmillan, 1984.

Dunning, E. (ed.), *The Sociology of Sport*, London, Cass, 1971.

Euromonitor Publications (publisher), *The United Kingdom Leisure Market*, London, 1980.

Gower (publisher), *Leisure Studies: New Society Social Studies Reader*, Aldershot, 1985.

Gratton, C. and Taylor, P., *Sport and Recreation: An Economic Analysis*, London, Spon, 1985.

Harris, H. A., *Sport in Britain: Its*

Origins and Development, London, Paul, Trench, Trubner, 1975.

Malcolmson, R. W., *Popular Recreations in English Society*, Cambridge, Cambridge University Press, 1973.

Parker, S., *The Sociology of Leisure*, London, Allen and Unwin, 1976.

Roberts, K., *Contemporary Society and the Growth of Leisure*, London, Longman, 1979.

Roberts, K., *Youth and Leisure*, London, Allen and Unwin, 1985.

Smith, M. et al. (eds), *Leisure and Society in Britain*, London, Allen Lane, 1973.

Walton, J. K. and Walvin, J. (eds), *Leisure in Britain, 1780–1939*, Manchester, Manchester University Press, 1983.

Walvin, J., *Leisure and Society, 1830–1950*, London, Longman, 1978.

Whannel, G., *Blowing the Whistle: The Politics of Sport*, London, Pluto, 1983.

FOOTBALL

Barrett, N. (ed.), *Encyclopaedia of Association Football*, Bristol, Purnell Books, 1978.

Centre for Contemporary Cultural Studies (publisher), *Football Hooliganism*, Birmingham, 1973.

Critcher, C., *Football since the War: A Study in Social Change and Popular Culture*, Birmingham, Centre for Contemporary Cultural Studies, 1973.

Dunk, P., *Rothman's Football Yearbook*, London, Macdonald, annually.

Golesworthy, M., *Encyclopaedia of Association Football*, London, Hale, 1976.

Keeton, G. W., *The Football Revolution: A Study of the Changing Pattern of Association Football*, Newton Abbot, David and Charles, 1972.

Morris, D. *The Soccer Tribe*, London, Cape, 1981.

Soar, P. and Tyler, M., *Encyclopaedia of British Football*, London, Collins, 1984.

Sunday Telegraph (publisher), *Canon Football Year Book*, London, annually.

Wagg, S., *The Football World: A Contemporary Social History*, Brighton, Harvester, 1984.

Walvin, J., *The People's Game: A Social History of British Football*, London, Allen Lane, 1975.

Young, P., *A History of British Football*, London, Arrow, 1974.

CRICKET

Bailey, T., *A History of Cricket*, London, Allen and Unwin, 1979.

Brodribb, G., *Next Man In: A Survey of Cricket Laws and Customs*, London, Pelham, 1985.

Down, M., *Is It Cricket? Power, Money and Politics in Cricket since 1945*, London, Queen Anne Press, 1985.

Frindall, B. (ed.), *The Wisden Book of Test Cricket, 1876–77 to 1977–78*, London, Macdonald & Jane's, 1980.

Frith, D., *England versus Australia: A Pictorial History of the Test Matches since 1877*, Guildford, Lutterworth Press, 1981.

Golesworthy, M., *Encyclopaedia of Cricket*, London, Hale, 1977.

Martin-Jenkins, C., *The Wisden Book of County Cricket*, London, Macdonald Futura, 1981.

Moorhouse, G., *Lord's*, Sevenoaks, Hodder and Stoughton, 1983.

Ross, A. (ed.), *Cricketer's Companion*, Harmondsworth, Penguin, 1981.

Sheppard, J. (ed.), *Cricket: More than a Game*, London, Angus and Robertson, 1975.

Sproat, I., *The Cricketer's Who's Who*, London, Who's Who Ltd, 1983.

Tyler, M. and Frith, D. (eds), *The Illustrated History of Test Cricket*, London, Marshall Cavendish, 1979.

OTHER SPORTS

Butler, F., *A History of Boxing in Britain*, London, Arthur Barker, 1972.

Campbell, B., *Horse Racing in Britain*, London, Michael Joseph, 1977.

Carr, R., *English Fox-Hunting: A History*, London, Weidenfeld and Nicolson, 1976.

Cousins, G., *Golf in Britain: A Social History from the Beginning to the Present Day*, London, Routledge & Kegan Paul, 1975.

De Moubray, J., *Horseracing and Racing Society*, London, Sidgwick and Jackson, 1985.

Dodd, C., *The Oxford and Cambridge Boat Race*, London, Stanley Paul, 1983.

Gill, J., *Racecourses of Great Britain*, London, Barrie and Jenkins, 1975.

Golesworthy, M., *Encyclopaedia of Rugby Union Football*, London, Hale, 1976.

Golesworthy, M., *Encyclopaedia of Boxing*, London, Hale, 1979.

Griffiths, J. (ed.), *The Book of English International Rugby 1871–1982*, London, Collins, 1982.

Jones, D., *Rock Climbing in Britain*, London, Collins, 1984.

Longrigg, R., *The History of Horseracing*, London, Macmillan, 1972.

Longrigg, R., *The Turf: Three Centuries of Horse Racing*, London, Methuen, 1975.

Longrigg, R., *The History of Foxhunting*, London, Macmillan, 1975.

Lovesey, P., *The Official Centenary History of the Amateur Athletic Association*, Enfield, Guinness Superlatives, 1979.

Macklin, K., *The History of Rugby League Football*, London, Stanley Parker, 1974.

Mitchell, B. (ed.), *The Rugby Annual*, London, Pelham, annually.

Mortimer, R., *The Flat: Flat Racing In Britain since 1939*, London, Allen and Unwin, 1979.

Mortimer, R., *The Epsom Derby*, London, Michael Joseph, 1984.

Rea, C., *Rugby: A History of Rugby Union Football*, London, Hamlyn, 1978.

Seth-Smith, M. (ed.), *A History of Flat Racing*, London, New English Library, 1978.

Titley, U. A. and McWhirter, R., *The Centenary History of the Rugby Football Union*, London, Rugby Football Union, 1971.

SEE ALSO:

35 THEATRE

For reference guides to literature on the theatre see: Cheshire, D., *Theatre: History, Criticism and Reference*, 1967; Clunes, A., *British Theatre History*, 1955; Howard, D., *London Theatres and Music Halls, 1850–1950: A Bibliography*, 1970; Howard, D. (ed.), *Directory of Theatre Research Resources in Greater London*, 1974; Loewenberg, A. (ed.), *The Theatre of the British Isles, Excluding London: A Bibliography*, 1950; Mikhail, E. H., *Contemporary British Drama, 1950–1976: An Annotated Bibliography*, 1976; Stratman, C. J., *Britain's Theatrical Periodicals, 1720–1967: A Bibliography*, 1972; Vinson, J. (ed.), *Contemporary Dramatists*, 1985.

For general reference manuals on theatre and theatre production consult: Cooper, D. (ed.), *Theatre Year*, annually; Itzin, C. (ed.), *British Alternative Theatre Directory*, 1982; Itzin, C., *Directory of Playwrights, Directors, Designers*, 1983; Roberts, P., *Theatre in Britain: A Playgoer's Guide*, 1975; Vance-Offord (publisher), *British Theatre Directory*, annually.

Historical surveys of theatre and drama in Britain are contained in the following: Craik, T. W. and Potter, L.(eds), *The Revels History of Drama in English*, 8 vols. 1975–83. Leacroft, R., *The Development of the English Playhouse*, 1973; Nicoll, A., *English Theatre: A Short History*, 1936; Southern, R., *The Seven Ages of the Theatre*, 1967.

The following are recommended as surveys of modern and contemporary theatre in Britain: Ansorge, P., *Disrupting the Spectacle: Five Years of Experimental and Fringe Theatre in Britain*, 1975; Barker, C., *British Alternative Theatre*, 1984; Barnes, P., *A Companion to Post-War British Theatre*, 1986; Elsom, J., *Post-War British Theatre*, 1979; Hayman, R., *The Set-Up: An Anatomy of English Theatre Today*, 1974; Hayman, R., *British Theatre since 1955: A Reassessment*, 1979; Itzin, C., *Stages in the Revolution: Political Theatre in Britain since 1968*, 1980; Taylor, J. R., *Anger and After*, 1977; Taylor, J. R., *The Second Wave*, 1978.

Useful studies of acting and actors are provided in: Billington, M., *The Modern Actor*, 1973; Forbes, B., *That Despicable Race: A History of the British Acting Tradition*, 1980; Sanderson, M., *From Irving to Olivier: A Social History of the Acting Profession in England, 1890–1980*, 1984.

REFERENCE

Arts Council, *Annual Report*, London, annually.

Cheshire, D., *Theatre: History, Criticism and Reference*, London, Bingley, 1967.

Clunes, A., *British Theatre History*, London, National Book League, 1955.

Cooper, D. (ed.), *Theatre Year*, London, annually.

Howard, D., *London Theatres and Music Halls, 1850–1950: A Bibliography*, London, Library Association, 1970.

Howard, D. (ed.), *Directory of Theatre Research Resources in Greater London*, London, British Theatre Institute, 1974.

Itzin, C. (ed.), *Directory of Playwrights, Directors, Designers*, Eastbourne, Offord, 1982.

Itzin, C. (ed.), *British Alternative Theatre Directory, 1983–4*, Eastbourne, Offord, 1983.

Loewenberg, A. (ed.), *The Theatre of the British Isles, Excluding London: A Bibliography*, London, Society for Theatre Research, 1950.

London Theatre Record (publisher), *London Theatre Index*, Twickenham, annually.

Mikhail, E. H., *Contemporary British Drama, 1950–1976: An Annotated Bibliography*, London, Macmillan, 1976.

Pitman (publisher), *Who's Who in the Theatre: A Biographical Record*, London, 1977.

Roberts, P., *Theatre in Britain: A Playgoer's Guide*, London, Pitman, 1975.

Stratman, C. J., *Britain's Theatrical Periodicals, 1720–1967: A Bibliography*, New York, New York Public Libraries, 1972.

Vance-Offord (publisher), *British Theatre Directory*, Eastbourne, annually.

Vinson, J. (ed.), *Contemporary Dramatists*, London, Macmillan, 1985.

Wearing, J. (ed.), *British and American Theatrical Biography*, Metuchen, N. J., Scarecrow Press, 1979.

THEATRE HISTORY

Bentley, G. E., *The Jacobean and Caroline Stage*, 7 vols, Oxford, Clarendon Press, 1941–68.

Bristol, M., *Carnival and Theatre*, London, Methuen, 1985.

Chambers, E. K., *The Medieval Stage*, 2 vols, Oxford, Clarendon Press, 1903.

Chambers, E. K., *The Elizabethan Stage*, 4 vols, Oxford, Oxford University Press, 1923.

Cheshire, D. F., *Music Hall in Britain*, Newton Abbot, David and Charles, 1974.

Craik, T. W. and Potter, L. (eds), *The Revels History of Drama in English*, 8 vols., London, Methuen, 1975–83.

Donohue, J., *Theatre in the Age of Kean*, Oxford, Blackwell, 1979.

Edwards, F., *Ritual and Drama, The Medieval Theatre*, Guildford and London, Lutterworth, 1976.

Forbes, B., *That Despicable Race: A History of the British Acting Tradition*, London, Elm Tree Books, 1980.

Frow, G., *'Oh Yes It Is!': A History of Pantomime*, London, BBC, 1985.

Gurr, A., *The Shakespearean Stage 1574–1642*, Cambridge, Cambridge University Press, 1980.

Hattaway, M., *Elizabethan Popular Theatre*, London, Routledge & Kegan Paul, 1985.

Hewison, R., *Footlights! A Hundred Years of Cambridge Comedy*, London, Methuen, 1983.

Hodges, C. W., *Shakespeare and the Players*, London, Bell, 1970.

Hodges, C. W., *Shakespeare's Theatre*, Oxford, Oxford University Press, 1980.

Hudson, L. A., *The English Stage, 1850–1950*, London, Greenwood Press, 1951.

Hughes, L., *A Century of English Farce*, London, Greenwood Press, 1956.

Leacroft, R., *The Development of the English Playhouse*, London, Eyre Methuen, 1973.

Leyson, P., *London Theatres: A Short History and Guide*, London, Apollo Publications, 1970.

Mander, R. and Mitchenson, J., *The Theatres of London*, London, New English Library, 1975.

Mander, R. and Mitchenson, J., *British Music Hall*, London, Gentry Books, 1975.

Nelson, A. H., *The Medieval English Stage*, Chicago, University of Chicago Press, 1974.

Nicoll, A., *English Theatre: A Short*

History, London, Greenwood Press, 1936.

Nicoll, A., *Garrick Stage: Theatre and Audience in the Eighteenth Century*, Manchester, Manchester University Press, 1982.

Price, C., *Theatre in the Age of Garrick*, Oxford, Blackwell, 1973.

Reynolds, E. R., *Modern English Drama: A Survey of the Theatre from 1900*, London, Greenwood Press, 1950.

Rowell, G., *The Victorian Theatre, 1792–1914: A Survey*, Cambridge, Cambridge University Press, 1969.

Rowell, G. and Jackson, A., *The Repertory Movement: A History of Regional Theatre in Britain*, Cambridge, Cambridge University Press, 1984.

Sanderson, M., *From Irving to Olivier: A Social History of the Acting Profession in England, 1890–1980*, London, Athlone, 1984.

Southern, R., *The Seven Ages of the Theatre*, London, Faber, 1968.

Summers, M., *The Restoration Theatre*, London, Cass, 1967.

Trewin, J. C., *The Edwardian Theatre*, Oxford, Blackwell, 1978.

Wickham, G., *Early English Stages, 1300–1660: A History of the Development of Dramatic Spectacle and Stage Convention in England*, 3 vols, London, Routledge & Kegan Paul, 1963–81.

Wilmut, R., *Kindly Leave the Stage: The Story of Variety, 1919–1960*, London, Methuen, 1985.

CONTEMPORARY THEATRE

Addenbrooke, D., *The Royal Shakespeare Company: The Peter Hall Years*, London, Kimber, 1974.

Ansorge, P., *Disrupting the Spectacle: Five Years of Experimental and Fringe Theatre in Britain*, London, Pitman, 1975.

Arden, J., *To the Present Pretence*, London, Methuen, 1977.

Barker, C., *British Alternative Theatre*, London, Macmillan, 1984.

Barnes, P., *A Companion to Post-War British Theatre*, London, Croom Helm, 1986.

Beaumann, S., *The Royal Shakespeare Company: A History of Ten Decades*, London, Oxford University Press, 1982.

Billington, M., *The Modern Actor*, London, Hamish Hamilton, 1973.

Browne, T. W., *Playwright's Theatre: The English Stage Company at the Royal Court Theatre*, London, Pitman, 1975.

Burton, H. (ed.), *Acting in the Sixties*, London, BBC, 1970.

Chambers, C., *Other Spaces: New Theatre and the R. S. C.*, London, Methuen, 1980.

Cole, T. and Chinoy, H. K. (eds), *Directors on Directing: The*

Emergence of the Modern Theatre, London, P. Owen, 1970.

Cook, J., *Director's Theatre*, London, Harrap, 1974.

Cook, J., *The National Theatre*, London, Harrap, 1976.

Cottrell, J., *Laurence Olivier*, London, Hodder and Stoughton, 1977.

Davison, P., *Contemporary Drama and the Popular Dramatic Tradition in England*, London, Macmillan, 1982.

Elms, S. (ed.), *The London Theatre Scene*, Chislehurst, Frank Cook, 1979.

Elsom, J., *Post-War British Theatre*, London, Routledge & Kegan Paul, 1979.

Elsom, J., *Post-War British Theatre Criticism*, London, Routledge & Kegan Paul, 1981.

Elsom, J. and Tomlin, N., *The History of the National Theatre*, London, Cape, 1980.

Evans, G. and Evans, B. (eds), *Plays in Review: British Drama and the Critics, 1956–1980*, London, Batsford, 1985.

Findlater, R., *Banned! A Review of Theatrical Censorship in Britain*, London, MacGibbon and Kee, 1967.

Findlater, R. et al., *The Complete Guide*

to *Britain's National Theatre*,
London, Heinemann, 1977.

Findlater, R. (ed.), *At the Royal Court:
25 Years of the English Stage
Company*, Ambergate, Ambergate
Lane Press, 1981.

Gooch, S., *All Together Now:
Community Theatre - An Alternative
View*, London, Methuen, 1984.

Goorney, H., *The Theatre Workshop
Story*, London, Methuen, 1981.

Hayman, R., *Techniques of Acting*,
London, Methuen, 1969.

Hayman, R., *Sir John Gielgud*, London,
Heinemann, 1971.

Hayman, R., *The Set-Up: An Anatomy
of English Theatre Today*, London,
Eyre Methuen, 1974.

Hayman, R., *British Theatre since 1955:
A Reassessment*, London, Oxford
University Press, 1979.

Hinchcliffe, A. P., *British Theatre,
1950–1970*, Oxford, Blackwell,
1974.

Hobson, H., *Theatre in Britain: A
Personal View*, Oxford, Phaidon,
1984.

Holden, M., *The Stage Guide: Technical
Information on British Theatres*,
London, Carson and Comerford,
1971.

Kerensky, O., *The New British Drama*,
London, Hamish Hamilton, 1977.

Kershaw, J., *The Present Stage: New
Directions in Theatre Today*, London,
Collins, 1966.

Keyssar, H., *Feminist Theatre: An
Introduction to Plays of
Contemporary British and American
Women*, London, Macmillan, 1984.

Itzin, C., *Stages in the Revolution:
Political Theatre in Britain since
1968*, London, Methuen, 1980.

Lambert, J. W., *Drama in Britain
1964–73*, London, Longman, 1974.

McGrath, J., *A Good Night Out:
Popular Theatre - Audience, Class
and Form*, London, Methuen, 1981.

Marowitz, C. (ed.), *Theatre Voices of the
Fifties and Sixties*, London, Methuen,
1981.

Marowitz, C. and Trussler, S. (eds),
*Theatre at Work: Playwrights and
Productions in the Modern British
Theatre*, London, Methuen, 1967.

Monahan, J., *British Ballet Today*,
London, Davis Poynter, 1980.

Pick, J., *The West End: Mismanagement
and Snobbery*, Eastbourne, Offord,
1983.

Pick, J., *The Theatre Industry: Profit,
Subsidy and the Search for New
Audiences*, London, Comedia, 1986.

Taylor, J. R., *Anger and After: A Guide
to the Post-Osborne British Drama*,
London, Methuen, 1977.

Taylor, J. R., *The Second Wave: British
Drama of the Sixties*, London,
Methuen, 1978.

Trussler, S. (ed.), *New Theatre Voices of
the Seventies*, London, Methuen,
1981.

Tynan, K., *A View of the English Stage,
1944–63*, London, Methuen, 1984.

SEE ALSO:

16   Literature

36 THOUGHT AND PHILOSOPHY

Research and bibliographical reference guides on thought and philosophy are available in the following: Borchardt, D. H., *How to Find Out in Philosophy and Psychology*, 1968; Bowling Green University, *The Philosopher's Index: An International Index to Philosophical Periodicals*, annually; De George, R. T., *A Guide to Philosophical Bibliography and Research*, 1971; Guerry, H. (ed.), *A Bibliography of Philosophical Bibliographies*, 1977; Leicester University Press (publisher), *Philosophical Books*, annually; Library Association, *Readers' Guide to Books on Philosophy*, 1974.

For individual British thinkers and philosophical movements reference should be made to the following handbooks and historical surveys: Burr, J. R. (ed.), *Handbook of World Philosophy: Contemporary Developments since 1945*, 1980; Copleston, F. C., *A History of Philosophy*, 9 vols, 1947–75; Edwards, P. (ed.), *The Encyclopaedia of Philosophy*, 4 vols, 1973; Flew, A., *Dictionary of Philosophy*, 1979; Russell, B., *A History of Western Philosophy*, 1961; Wiener, P. (ed.), *Dictionary of the History of Ideas: Studies of Selected Pivotal Ideas*, 1973.

For critical surveys and discussions of modern British thought see: Barker, R., *Political Ideas in Modern Britain*, 1978; Lewis, H. D. (ed.), *Contemporary British Philosophy: Personal Statements*, 1976; Mace, C. A., *British Philosophy in the Mid-Century*, 1957; Magee, B., *Modern British Philosophy*, 1971; Shanker, S. (ed.) *Philosophy in Britain Today*, 1986.

Recommended as surveys of political thought in Britain are: Barker, R., *Political Ideas in Modern Britain*, 1978; Brinton, C., *English Political Thought in the Nineteenth Century*, 1933; Davidson, W. L., *Political Thought in England: The Utilitarians from Bentham to Mill*, 1957; Gooch, G. P., *Political Thought in England: Bacon to Halifax*, 1960; Laski, H. J., *Political Thought in England: Locke to Bentham*, 1961; Morris, C., *Political Thought in England: Tyndale to Hooker*, 1953.

REFERENCE

Baylen, J. O. and Gossman, N. J. (eds), *Biographical Dictionary of Modern British Radicals, Vol. 2, 1830–1870*, Brighton, Harvester, 1984.

Borchardt, D. H., *How to Find Out in Philosophy and Psychology*, Oxford, Pergamon Press, 1968.

Bowling Green University, *The Philosopher's Index: An International Index to Philosophical Periodicals*, Bowling Green, Ohio, annually.

Bullock, A. and Stallybrass, O. (eds), *The Fontana Dictionary of Modern Thought*, London, Fontana, 1977.

Bullock, A. and Woodings, R. B. (eds), *The Fontana Biographical Companion to Modern Thought*, London, Fontana, 1983.

Burr, J. R. (ed.), *Handbook of World Philosophy: Contemporary Developments since 1945*, London, Aldwych Press, 1980.

Edwards, P. (ed.), *The Encyclopedia of Philosophy*, 4 vols, New York, London, Collier-Macmillan, 1973.

Flew, A. (ed.), *Dictionary of Philosophy*, London, Macmillan, 1979.

George, R. T. De, *A Guide to*

Philosophical Bibliography and Research, New York, Appleton-Century-Crofts, 1971.

George, R. T. De, *The Philosopher's Guide*, University Press of Kansas, Lawrence, Kansas, 1980.

Guerry, H. (ed.), *A Bibliography of Philosophical Bibliographies*, Westport, Connecticut, Greenwood Press, 1977.

Leicester University Press (publisher), *Philosophical Books*, Leicester, annually.

Library Association, *Readers' Guide to Books on Philosophy*, London, 1974.

Scruton, R., *A Dictionary of Political Thought*, London, Pan, 1983.

Urmson, J. O. (ed.), *The Concise Encyclopaedia of Western Philosophy and Philosophers*, London, Hutchinson, 1960.

Wiener, P. (ed.), *Dictionary of the History of Ideas: Studies of Selected Pivotal Ideas*, 5 vols, New York, Scribner, 1973.

Williams, R., *Keywords*, London, Fontana, 1976.

GENERAL

Benn, A. W., *A History of English Rationalism in the Nineteenth Century*, 2 vols, Longman, 1906.

Carré, M. H., *Phases of Thought in England*, Oxford, Clarendon Press, 1949.

Clubbe, J. and Lovell, E. J., *English Romanticism: The Grounds of Belief*, London, Macmillan, 1983.

Copleston, F. C., *A History of Philosophy*, 9 vols, London, Burns and Oates, 1947–75.

Cosslett, T., *Science and Religion in the Nineteenth Century*, Cambridge, Cambridge University Press, 1984.

Cowley, G. F., *A Critique of English Empiricism*, London, Macmillan, 1968.

Cox, C. B. and Dyson, A. E. (eds), *The Twentieth Century Mind: History, Ideas and Literature in Britain*, 3 vols, London, Oxford University Press, 1972.

Cragg, G. R., *Reason and Authority in the Eighteenth Century*, Cambridge, Cambridge University Press, 1964.

Craig, H., *The Enchanted Glass: The Elizabethan Mind in Literature*, Oxford, Blackwell, 1950.

Dampier, Sir W. C., *A History of Science and its Relations with Philosophy and Religion*, Cambridge, Cambridge University Press, 1942.

Davies, H. S. and Watson, G., *The English Mind: Studies in the English Moralists*, Cambridge, Cambridge University Press, 1964.

Dowling, M., *Humanism in the Age of Henry VIII*, London, Croom Helm, 1985.

Grave, S. A., *The Scottish Philosophy of Common Sense*, Oxford, Clarendon Press, 1960.

Halévy, E., *The Growth of Philosophic Radicalism*, London, Faber, 1972.

Hazard, P., *European Thought in the Eighteenth Century*, Harmondsworth, Penguin, 1965.

Heyck, T. W., *The Transformation of Intellectual Life in Victorian England*, London, Croom Helm, 1983.

Hill, C., *The Intellectual Origins of the English Revolution*, London, Oxford University Press, 1980.

Hill, C., *Some Intellectual Consequences of the English Revolution*, London, Weidenfeld and Nicolson, 1980.

Himmelfarb, G., *Victorian Minds*, London, Weidenfeld and Nicolson, 1968.

Houghton, W. E., *The Victorian Frame of Mind, 1830–1970*, New Haven, Yale University Press, 1957.

Inglis, F., *Radical Earnestness: English Social Theory, 1880–1980*, Oxford, Martin Robertson, 1982.

Jones, G., *Social Darwinism and English Thought: The Interaction between Biological and Social Theory*, Brighton, Harvester, 1980.

239

Knowles, D., *The English Mystical Tradition*, London, Burns and Oates, 1961.

Korshin, P. J., *Studies in Change and Revolution: Aspects of English Intellectual History, 1640–1800*, London, Scolar Press, 1972.

Lewis, H. D. (ed.), *Contemporary British Philosophy*, London, Allen and Unwin, 1976.

Lovejoy, A. O., *The Great Chain of Being*, Cambridge, Mass., Harvard University Press, 1936.

Mace, C. A. (ed.), *British Philosophy in Mid-Century*, London, Allen and Unwin, 1957.

Macfarlane, A., *Origins of English Individualism: Family, Property and Social Transition*, Oxford, Blackwell, 1978.

Macpherson, C. B., *The Political Theory of Possessive Individualism*, Oxford, Oxford University Press, 1962.

Magee, B., *Modern British Philosophy*, London, Secker and Warburg, 1971.

McGregor, J. F. and Reay, B. (eds), *Radical Religion in the English Revolution*, Oxford, Clarendon Press, 1984.

McLean, A., *Humanism and the Rise of Science in Tudor England*, London, Heinemann, 1972.

Martindale, J. (ed.), *English Humanism: Wyatt to Cowley*, London, Croom Helm, 1985.

Metz, R., *A Hundred Years of British Philosophy*, London, Allen and Unwin, 1938.

Morton, A. L., *English Utopia*, London, Lawrence and Wishart, 1969.

Mundle, C. W. K., *A Critique of Linguistic Philosophy*, London, Oxford University Press, 1970.

Nugent, E. M. (ed.), *The Thought and Culture of the English Renaissance*, Cambridge, Cambridge University Press, 1956.

Passmore, J. A., *A Hundred Years of Philosophy*, Harmondsworth, Penguin, 1970.

Patrides, C. A., *The Cambridge Platonists*, Cambridge, Cambridge University Press, 1980.

Paul, L., *The English Philosophers*, London, Faber, 1953.

Plamenatz, J., *English Utilitarianism*, Oxford, Blackwell, 1949.

Quinton, A., *The Politics of Imperfection: The Religious and Secular Traditions of Conservative Thought in England from Hooker to Oakshott*, London, Faber, 1978.

Raphael, D. D. (ed.), *British Moralists, 1650–1800*, 2 vols, Oxford, Clarendon Press, 1969.

Rosenbaum, S. P. (ed.), *English Literature and British Philosophy*, Chicago and London, University of Chicago Press, 1971.

Russell, B., *History of Western Philosophy*, London, Allen and Unwin, 1961.

Shanker, S. (ed.), *Philosophy in Britain Today*, London, Croom Helm, 1986.

Shapiro, B. J., *Probability and Certainty in Seventeenth Century England: A Study of the Relationships between Natural Science, Religion, History, Law and Literature*, Princeton, Princeton University Press, 1983.

Skilton, D., *Reform and Intellectual Debate in Victorian England*, London, Croom Helm, 1986.

Somervell, D. C., *English Thought in the Nineteenth Century*, London, Methuen, 1963.

Sorley, W. R., *A History of British Philosophy to 1900*, Cambridge, Cambridge University Press, 1965.

Stephen, L., *The English Utilitarians*, London, Duckworth, 1950.

Stephen, L., *A History of English Thought in the Eighteenth Century*, 2 vols, New York, Harcourt Brace, 1971.

Stephen, L., *Selected Writings in British Intellectual History*, edited by N. Annan, Chicago, University of Chicago Press, 1979.

Thomas, K., *Man and the Natural World: Changing Attitudes in England, 1500–1800*, London, Allen Lane, 1984.

Tillyard, E. M. W., *The Elizabethan World Picture*, Harmondsworth, Penguin, 1972.

Vaughan, C. E., *Studies in the History of Political Philosophy before and after Rousseau*, 2 vols, Manchester, Manchester University Press, 1925.

Warnock, G. J., *Contemporary Moral Philosophy*, London, Macmillan, 1967.

Warnock, G. J., *English Philosophy since 1900*, London, Oxford University Press, 1969.

Webster, C., *The Great Instauration, 1626–60*, London, Duckworth, 1975.

Webster, C. (ed.), *The Intellectual Revolution of the Seventeenth Century*, London, Routledge & Kegan Paul, 1974.

Wedberg, A., *A History of Philosophy*, 3 vols, London, Oxford University Press, 1982–4.

Willey, B., *Nineteenth Century Studies*, Cambridge, Cambridge University Press, 1980.

Willey, B., *The Eighteenth Century Background*, London, 1940, Chatto and Windus, 1949.

Willey, B., *The Seventeenth Century Background*, London, Routledge & Kegan Paul, 1979.

Willey, B., *More Nineteenth Century Studies: A Group of Honest Doubters*, Cambridge, Cambridge University Press, 1980.

Williams, R., *The Long Revolution*, Harmondsworth, Penguin, 1965.

Yolton, J. W., *Thinking Matter: Materialism in Eighteenth-Century Britain*, Oxford, Blackwell, 1984.

POLITICAL THOUGHT

Allen, J. W., *English Political Thought, 1603–1694*, London, Methuen, 1938.

Barker, E., *Political Thought in England, 1848–1914*, London, Greenwood Press, 1980 (reprint).

Barker, R., *Political Ideas in Modern Britain*, London, Methuen, 1978.

Beer, M., *A History of British Socialism*, Nottingham, Spokesman, 1985.

Brinton, C., *English Political Thought in the Nineteenth Century*, London, Benn, 1933.

Brinton, C., *The Political Ideas of the English Romanticists*, London, Oxford University Press, 1966.

Cole, G. D. H., *A History of Socialist Thought*, 7 vols, London, Macmillan, 1953–60.

Davidson, W. L., *Political Thought in England: The Utilitarians from Bentham to Mill*, London, Oxford University Press, 1957.

Derry, J. W., *The Radical Tradition: Tom Paine to Lloyd George*, London, Macmillan, 1967.

Dickinson, H. T., *Liberty and Property: Political Ideology in Eighteenth-Century Britain*, London, Weidenfeld and Nicolson, 1977.

Dickinson, H. T., *British Radicalism and the French Revolution, 1789–1815*, Oxford, Blackwell, 1985.

Dow, P. D., *Radicalism in the English Revolution 1640–1660*, Oxford, Blackwell, 1985.

Eccleshall, R. et al., *Political Ideologies: An Introduction*, London, Hutchinson, 1985.

Eccleshall, P., *British Liberalism: Liberal Thought from the 1640's to the 1980's*, London, Longman, 1986.

Gooch, G. P., *Political Thought in England: Bacon to Halifax*, London, Oxford University Press, 1960.

Gooch, G. P. and Laski, H. J., *The History of English Democratic Ideas in the Seventeenth Century*, Cambridge, Cambridge University Press, 1927.

Greenleaf, W. H., *Order, Empiricism and Politics: Two Traditions of English Political Thought, 1500–1700*, London, Greenwood Press, 1980 (reprint).

Harrison, W., *Conflict and Compromise: A History of British Political Thought*, London, Collier-Macmillan, 1965.

Harrison, W. (ed.), *Sources in British Political Thought, 1534–1900*, New York, Free Press, 1965.

Hearnshaw, F. J. C., *Social and Political*

Ideas of Some Representative Thinkers of the Augustan Age, 1650–1750, London, Greenwood Press, 1983 (reprint).

Hearnshaw, F. J. C., *Social and Political Ideas of Some Representative Thinkers of the Age of Reaction and Reconstruction, 1815–65*, London, Greenwood Press, 1983 (reprint).

Hearnshaw, F. J. C., *Social and Political Ideas of Some Representative Thinkers of the Victorian Age*, London, Greenwood Press, 1983 (reprint).

Hill, C. *The World Turned Upside Down: Radical Ideas during the English Revolution*, Harmondsworth, Penguin, 1975.

Laski, H. J., *Political Thought in England: Locke to Bentham*, London, Oxford University Press, 1961.

Maccoby, S., *English Radicalism, 1832–1914*, 3 vols, London, Allen and Unwin, 1935–53.

Maccoby, S., *English Radicalism, 1786–1832: From Paine to Cobbett*, London, Allen and Unwin, 1955.

Maccoby, S. (ed.), *The English Radical Tradition, 1763–1914*, London, Black, 1966.

Mendilow, J., *The Romantic Tradition in British Political Thought*, London, Croom Helm, 1985.

Morris, C., *Political Thought in England: Tyndale to Hooker*, London, Oxford University Press, 1953.

Murray, R. H., *Studies in the English Social and Political Thinkers of the Nineteenth Century*, 2 vols, London, Gregg, 1929 (reprint).

Pugh, P., *Educate, Agitate, Organize: 100 Years of Fabian Socialism*, London, Methuen, 1984.

Quinton, A. (ed.), *Political Philosophy*, London, Oxford University Press, 1967.

Ree, J., *Proletarian Philosophies: Problems in Socialist Culture in Britain, 1900–1940*, London, Oxford University Press, 1984.

Wright, A. W., *British Socialism: Socialist Thought from the 1880's to the 1960's*, London, Longman, 1983.

Zagorin, P., *A History of Political Thought in the English Revolution*, London, Routledge & Kegan Paul, 1954.

INDIVIDUAL THINKERS

MATTHEW ARNOLD

Chambers, E. K., *Matthew Arnold: A Study*, London, Oxford, Clarendon Press, 1947.

Trilling, L., *Matthew Arnold*, London, Allen and Unwin, 1939.

A. J. AYER

Foster, J., *Ayer*, London, Routledge & Kegan Paul, 1985.

FRANCIS BACON

Farrington, B., *Francis Bacon: Philosopher of Industrial Science*, London, Macmillan, 1973.

Quinton, A., *Francis Bacon*, London, Oxford University Press, 1980.

ROGER BACON

Easton, S. C., *Roger Bacon and His Search for a Universal Science*, Oxford, Blackwell, 1952.

JEREMY BENTHAM

Everett, C. W., *Jeremy Bentham*, London, Weidenfeld and Nicolson, 1966.

Harrison, R., *Bentham*, London, Routledge & Kegan Paul, 1985.

GEORGE BERKELEY

Urmson, J. O., *Berkeley*, London,
  Oxford University Press, 1982.
Warnock, G. J., *Berkeley*, London,
  Oxford University Press, 1982.

F. H. BRADLEY

Manser, A. (ed.), *The Philosophy of
  F. H. Bradley*, Oxford, Clarendon
  Press, 1984.
Wollheim, R., *F. H. Bradley*,
  Harmondsworth, Penguin, 1969.

EDMUND BURKE

Cone, C. B., *Burke and the Nature of
  Politics*, 2 vols, Lexington, University
  of Kentucky Press, 1957–64.
Macpherson, C. B., *Burke*, London,
  Oxford University Press, 1980.

THOMAS CARLYLE

Quesne, A. L. Le, *Carlyle*, London,
  Oxford University Press, 1982.
Rosenberg, J. D., *Carlyle and the Burden
  of History*, Oxford, Clarendon Press,
  1985.

R. G. COLLINGWOOD

Donagan, A., *The Later Philosophy of
  R. G. Collingwood*, Oxford,
  Clarendon, 1962.
Rubinoff, L., *Collingwood and the
  Reform of Metaphysics*, Toronto and
  Buffalo, University of Toronto Press,
  1970.

CHARLES DARWIN

Himmelfarb, G., *Darwin and the
  Darwinian Revolution*, London,
  Chatto and Windus, 1959.
Howard, J., *Darwin*, London, Oxford
  University Press, 1982.

WILLIAM GODWIN

Locke, D., *A Fantasy of Reason: The Life
  and Thought of William Godwin*,
  London, Routledge & Kegan Paul,
  1980.
Ryan, A., *Godwin*, London, Oxford
  University Press, 1985.

THOMAS HOBBES

Gauthier, D. P., *The Logic of Leviathan:
  The Moral and Political Theory of
  Thomas Hobbes*, London, Oxford
  University Press, 1979.
Peters, R., *Hobbes*, Harmondsworth,
  Penguin, 1967.

DAVID HUME

Ayer, A. J., *Hume*, London, Oxford
  University Press, 1980.
Stroud, B., *Hume*, London, Routledge &
  Kegan Paul, 1977.

J. M. KEYNES

Moggridge, D. E., *Keynes*, London,
  Macmillan, 1976.
Wood, J. C. (ed.), *John Maynard Keynes,
  Critical Assessments*, 4 vols, London,
  Croom Helm, 1984.

R. D. LAING

Collier, A., *R. D. Laing: The Philosophy
  and Politics of Psychotherapy*,
  Brighton, Harvester, 1985.
Friedenberg, *R. D. Laing*, London,
  Woburn Press, 1974.

JOHN LOCKE

Cranston, M., *Locke*, London,
  Longman, 1957.
Dunn, J., *Locke*, London, Oxford
  University Press, 1984.

THOMAS MACAULAY

Clive, J., *Thomas Babington Macaulay: The Shaping of the Historian*, London, Secker and Warburg, 1973.
Potter, G. R., *Macaulay*, London, Longman, 1959.

T. R. MALTHUS

Glass, D. V. (ed.), *Introduction to Malthus*, London, Watts, 1953.
Turner, M., *Malthus and His Times*, London, Macmillan, 1985.

J. S. MILL

McClosky, H. J., *John Stuart Mill: A Critical Study*, London, Macmillan, 1971.
Ryan, A., *J. S. Mill*, London, Routledge & Kegan Paul, 1975.

G. E. MOORE

Levy, P., *G. E. Moore and the Cambridge Apostles*, London, Oxford University Press, 1981.
Schilp, P. A. (ed.), *The Philosophy of G. E. Moore*, Evanston and Chicago, Northwestern University Press, 1952.

THOMAS MORE

Chambers, R. W., *Thomas More*, Brighton, Harvester, 1982.
Kenny, A., *Thomas More*, London, Oxford University Press, 1983.

ISAAC NEWTON

Manual, F. E., *A Portrait of Sir Isaac Newton*, Cambridge, Mass., Harvard University Press, 1968.
More, L. T., *Isaac Newton: A Biography*, New York and London, Scribner, 1934.

THOMAS PAINE

Powell, D., *Tom Paine: The Greatest Exile*, London, Croom Helm, 1985.
Williamson, A., *Tom Paine: His Life, Work and Times*, London, Allen and Unwin, 1973.

KARL POPPER

Burke, T. E., *The Philosophy of Popper*, Manchester, Manchester University Press, 1983.
Magee, B., *Popper*, London, Fontana, 1973.

DAVID RICARDO

Blaug, M., *Ricardian Economics: A Historical Study*, New Haven, Yale University Press, 1958.
Wood, J. C. (ed.), *David Ricardo: Critical Assessments*, 4 vols, London, Croom Helm, 1985.

JOHN RUSKIN

Bell, Q., *Ruskin*, London, Hogarth, 1978.
Landow, G. P., *Ruskin*, London, Oxford University Press, 1985.

BERTRAND RUSSELL

Kilminster, C. W., *Russell*, Brighton, Harvester, 1984.
Pears, D. F., *Bertrand Russell and the British Tradition of Philosophy*, London, Fontana, 1968.

GILBERT RYLE

Lyons, W., *Gilbert Ryle*, Brighton, Harvester, 1980.
Wood, O. P. and Pitcher, G. (eds), *Ryle: A Collection of Critical Essays*, London, Macmillan, 1970.

ADAM SMITH

Raphael, D. D., *Adam Smith*, London, Oxford University Press, 1985.

Wood, J. C. (ed.), *Adam Smith: Critical Assessments*, 4 vols, London, Croom Helm, 1984.

SEE ALSO:

28   Religion

LUDWIG WITTGENSTEIN

Kenny, A., *Wittgenstein*, London, Allen Lane, 1973.

Pears, D. F., *Ludwig Wittgenstein*, London, Fontana, 1971.

37 TRADE UNIONS AND INDUSTRIAL RELATIONS

For bibliographical guides to publications on industrial relations, trades unions and trades union history see: Bain, G. S. and Bennett, J. D. (eds), *A Bibliography of British Industrial Relations, 1971–79*, 1985; Bain, G. S. and Woolven, G. B., *A Bibliography of British Industrial Relations*, 1979; Frow, R. et al., *History of British Trade Unionism: A Select Bibliography*, 1969.

For current publications see British Library of Economic and Political Science, *A London Bibliography of the Social Sciences*, annually.

General and detailed information relating to British trades unions can be found in the following reference works: Eaton, J. and Gill, C., *The Trade Union Directory*, 1981; Jones, J. and Morris, M., *A-Z of Trade Unionism and Industrial Relations*, 1982; Marsh, A. I. (ed.), *A Concise Encyclopaedia of Industrial Relations*, 1978; Marsh, A. I., *Trade Union Handbook*, 1985.

The following works provide detailed discussions of matters relating to trades unions and industrial relations in Britain today: Arnold, G., *The Unions*, 1981; Bain, G. S. and Bennett, J. D., *Industrial Relations in Britain*, 1983; Brewster, C., *Understanding Industrial Relations*, 1984; Brown, W. (ed.), *The Changing Contours of British Industrial Relations*, 1981; Clegg, H. A., *The Changing System of Industrial Relations in Britain*, 1979; Hawkins, K., *Trade Unions*, 1981; Taylor, R., *The Fifth Estate: Britain's Unions in the Modern World*, 1980; Williamson, H., *The Trade Unions*, 1981.

Surveys of trades union history are given in Baker, C. and Caldwell, P., *Unions and Change since 1945*, 1981; Clegg, H. A. et al., *A History of British Trade Unions since 1889*, 1964–; Pelling, H., *History of British Trade Unionism*, 1976.

REFERENCE

ACAS, *Industrial Relations Handbook*, London, HMSO, 1980.

Bain, G. S. and Bennett, J. D. (eds), *A Bibliography of British Industrial Relations, 1971–79*, Cambridge, Cambridge University Press, 1985.

Bain, G. S. and Woolven, G. B., (eds), *A Bibliography of British Industrial Relations*, Cambridge, Cambridge University Press, 1979.

Bellamy, J. M. and Saville, J., *Dictionary of Labour Biography*, 7 vols, London, Macmillan, 1972–84.

British Library of Economic and Political Science, *A London Bibliography of the Social Sciences*, London and New York, Mansell, annually.

Eaton, J. and Gill, C., *The Trade Union Directory*, London, Pluto Press, 1981.

Frow, R. et al., *The History of British Trade Unionism: A Select Bibliography*, London, Historical Association, 1969.

Jones, J. and Morris, M., *A-Z of Trade Unionism and Industrial Relations*, London, Heinemann, 1982.

Marsh, A. I. (ed.), *A Concise Encyclopaedia of Industrial Relations*, Aldershot, Gower Publishing, 1978.

Marsh, A. I., *Trade Union Handbook*, Aldershot, Gower Publishing, 1985.

GENERAL

Arnold, G., *The Unions*, London, Hamish Hamilton, 1981.

Baker, C. and Caldwell, P., *Unions and Change since 1945*, London, Pan, 1981.

Banks, J. A., *Trade Unionism*, London, Collier-Macmillan, 1974.

Batstone, E. and Gourlay, S., *Unions, Unemployment and Innovation*, Oxford, Blackwell, 1986.

Benyon, H. (ed.), *Digging Deeper: Issue in the Miners' Strike*, London, Verso, 1985.

Boraston, I. et al., *Workplace and Union*, London, Heinemann, 1975.

Brannen, P., *The Worker Directors*, London, Hutchinson, 1976.

Brewster, C., *Understanding Industrial Relations*, London, Pan, 1984.

Brown, H. P., *The Origin of Trade Union Power*, Oxford, Oxford University Press, 1983.

Brown, W. (ed.), *The Changing Contours of British Industrial Relations: A Survey of Manufacturing Industry*, Oxford, Blackwell, 1981.

Burgess, K., *The Origins of British Industrial Relations*, London, Croom Helm, 1975.

Clegg, H. A. et al., *A History of British Trade Unions since 1889*, London, Oxford University Press, 1964–.

Clegg, H. A., *The Changing System of Industrial Relations in Britain*, Oxford, Blackwell, 1979.

Coates, K. and Topham, T., *Trade Unions and Politics*, Oxford, Blackwell, 1985.

Committee of Inquiry on Industrial Democracy, *Report*, Cmnd. 6706, London, HMSO, 1977.

Crouch, C., *The Politics of Industrial Relations*, London, Fontana, 1975.

Daniel, B. and Millward, N., *Workplace Industrial Relations in Britain*, London, Policy Studies Institute, 1983.

Dorfman, G., *British Trade Unions Against the Trades Union Congress*, London, Macmillan, 1983.

Dunn, S. and Gennard, J., *The Closed Shop in British Industry*, London, Macmillan, 1984.

Elliott, J., *Conflict or Cooperation? The Growth of Industrial Democracy*, London, Kogan Page, 1978.

Fairbrother, P., *All Those in Favour: The Politics of Union Democracy*, London, Pluto Press, 1984.

Fosh, P. and Littler, C. R. (eds), *Industrial Relations and the Law in the 1980's*, Aldershot, Gower, 1985.

Fox, A., *History and Heritage: The Social Origins of the British Industrial Relations System*, London, Allen and Unwin, 1985.

Hawkins, K., *Trade Unions*, London, Hutchinson, 1981.

Hutt, A., *British Trade Unionism*, London, Lawrence and Wishart, 1975.

Hyman, R., *Industrial Relations: A Marxist Introduction*, London, Macmillan, 1975.

Hyman, R. and Brough, I., *Social Values and Industrial Relations*, Oxford, Blackwell, 1985.

Jackson, M. P., *Industrial Relations*, London, Croom Helm, 1983.

Jenkins, C. and Sherman, B. D., *Collective Bargaining*, London, Routledge & Kegan Paul, 1977.

Jenkins, C. and Sherman, B., *White Collar Unionism*, London, Routledge & Kegan Paul, 1979.

Lovell, J. and Roberts, B. C., *A Short History of the TUC*, London, Macmillan, 1968.

McCarthy, W. E. J. (ed.), *Trade Unions*, Harmondsworth, Penguin, 1985.

Marsh, A. and Ryan, V., *Historical Directory of Trade Unions*, 4 vols, Aldershot, Gower, 1980–4.

Martin, R. M., *TUC: The Growth of a Pressure Group*, London, Oxford University Press, 1980.

Morton, A. L. and Tate, G., *The British Labour Movement, 1770–1920*, London, Lawrence and Wishart, 1980 (reprint).

Palmer, G., *British Industrial Relations*, London, Allen and Unwin, 1983.

Pelling, H., *History of British Trade*

Unionism, London, Macmillan, 1976.

Pimlott, B. and Cook, C., *Trade Unions in British Politics*, London, Longman, 1982.

Simpson, B., *Labour: The Unions and the Party: A Study of the Trade Unions and the British Labour Movement*, London, Allen and Unwin, 1973.

Strinati, D., *Capitalism, the State and Industrial Relations*, London, Croom Helm, 1983.

Taylor, R., *The Fifth Estate: Britain's Unions in the Modern World*, London, Pan Books, 1980.

Undy, R. et al., *Change in Trade Unions: The Development of U. K. Unions since 1960*, London, Hutchinson, 1984.

Williamson, H., *The Trade Unions*, London, Heinemann, 1981.

Wright, M., *Labour Law*, Plymouth, Macdonald and Evans, 1981.

SEE ALSO:

14   Industry and Commerce
25   Political Parties
31   Social and Economic History

38 TRAVEL AND TOURISM IN BRITAIN

The following books are recommended as comprehensive travel and tourist guides:

Britain and England   Automobile Association, *Illustrated Guide to Britain*, 1977; Automobile Association, *Second Touring Guide to Britain*, 1985; Fedden, R. and Joekes, R. (comps. and eds), *The National Trust Guide*, 1984; Rossiter, S., *England, Blue Guide*, 1980; Speaight, G., *The New Shell Guide to Britain*, 1985.

Scotland   Automobile Association, *Scotland: Where to Go, What to Do*, 1982; Automobile Association, *Touring Guide to Scotland*, 1978; Hammond, R. J. W., *Complete Scotland*, 1980; Maclaren, M. and McNie, D. L., *The New Shell Guide to Scotland*, 1977; Prentice, R. (ed.), *The National Trust for Scotland Guide*, 1981; Tomes, J., *Scotland, Blue Guide*, 1980.

Ireland and Northern Ireland   Automobile Association, *Ireland: Where to Go, What to Do*, 1980; Automobile Association, *Touring Guide to Ireland*, 1976; David and Charles (publisher), *Where to Go in the North of Ireland* 1975; Hammond, R. J. W. (ed.), *Northern Ireland, Red Guide*, 1971.

Wales   Automobile Association, *Touring Guide to Wales*, 1975; Beach, R. (ed.), *Touring Guide to Wales*, 1973; Llewellyn, A., *The Shell Guide to Wales*, 1973; Tomes, J. (ed.), *Wales and the Marches, Blue Guide*, 1979.

London   Banks, F. R., *The Penguin Guide to London*, 1986; Cody, M. (ed.), *A. A. Book of London*, 1983; Piper, D., *Companion Guide to London*, 1977; Plimmer, C. and Plimmer, D., *London, A Visitor's Companion*, 1977; French, Y., *London, Blue Guide*, 1986.

For the addresses of regional and local Tourist Information Centres see: British Tourist Board, *Directory of Tourist Information Centres*, annually.

Readers can also consult the series Pevsner, N. (ed.), *Buildings of England*, listed by county on pages 8–10.

Not listed here is the series *The Victoria History of the Counties of England* published by Oxford University Press, London, facsimile editions of out of print volumes by Dawson & Sons, Folkestone.

REFERENCE

Automobile Association, *Illustrated Guide to Britain*, London, Drive Publications, 1977.

Automobile Association, *Big Atlas of Town Plans*, London, Drive Publications, 1982.

Automobile Association, *Book of British Towns*, London, Drive Publications, 1982.

Automobile Association and British Tourist Authority, *Where to Go in Britain*, London, Drive Publications, 1982.

Automobile Association, *Camping and*

Caravanning in Britain, London, Drive Publications, annually.

Automobile Association, *Self Catering in Britain*, London, Drive Publications, annually.

Automobile Association, *Touring Book of Britain*, London, Drive Publications, 1984.

Automobile Association, *Motorists' Atlas of Great Britain*, London, Drive Publications, 1984.

Automobile Association, *Second Touring Guide to Britain*, London, Drive Publications, 1985.

Automobile Association, *New Book of the Road*, London, Drive Publications, 1985.

Bartholomew (publisher), *Road Atlas Britain*, Edinburgh, 1984.

Bartholomew (publisher), *Touring Road Map of England and Wales*, Edinburgh, 1985.

Bartholomew (publisher), *Touring Road Map of Great Britain*, Edinburgh, 1985.

British Tourist Board, *Directory of Tourist Information Centres*, London, annually.

Brittain, J. (ed.), *Alternative Routes in Britain*, London, Automobile Association, 1981.

Collins (publisher), *Road Atlas Britain*, London, 1985.

Fedden, R. and Joekes, R. (comps. and eds), *The National Trust Guide*, London, Cape, 1984.

Fullard, H. (ed.), *National Road Atlas of Great Britain*, London, George Philip, 1982.

George Philip (publisher), *B. P. Road Atlas*, London, 1981.

George Philip (publisher), *Local Maps*, London (series).

George Philip (publisher), *The National Trust Atlas*, London, 1981.

George Philip (publisher), *On Route: What to See in Britain and How to Get There*, London, 1982.

George Philip (publisher), *Philip's Touring Maps*, London (series).

George Philip (publisher), *R. A. C. Navigator Atlases*, London (series).

George Philip (publisher), *R. A. C. Regional Maps*, London (series).

George Philip (publisher), *The Shell Road Atlas of Great Britain*, London, 1982.

George Philip (publisher), *The Shell Touring Atlas of Great Britain*, London, 1982.

Royal Automobile Club, *Regional Motoring Maps* (series).

GENERAL

Automobile Association, *Treasures of Britain*. London, Drive Publications, 1981.

Automobile Association, *Book of Country Walks*, London, Drive Publications, 1978.

Automobile Association, *Book of British Villages*, London, Drive Publications, 1981.

Automobile Association, *Discovering Britain*, London, Drive Publications, 1982.

Automobile Association, *Book of Town Walks*, London, Drive Publications, 1984.

Automobile Association, *Stately Homes, Castles and Gardens in Britain*, London, Drive Publications, 1984.

Automobile Association, *Illustrated Guide to Britain's Coast*, London, Drive Publications, 1985.

Automobile Association, *Illustrated Guide to Country Towns and Villages of Britain*, London, Drive Publications, 1985.

Automobile Association, *Where to Go in the Countryside*, London, Drive Publications, 1985.

Bailey, B., *The National Trust Book of Ruins*, London, Weidenfeld and Nicolson, 1984.

Bearshaw, B., *The Towpaths of England*, London, Hale, 1985.

Bell, M. (ed.), *Britain's National Parks*, Newton Abbot, David and Charles, 1975.

Burke, J., *Roman England*, London, Weidenfeld and Nicolson, 1983.

Bishop, J. (ed.), *The Illustrated Counties of England*, London, Allen and Unwin, 1985.

Boote, R. and Perring, F. (eds), *The Macmillan Guide to Britain's Nature Reserves*, London, Macmillan, 1984.

Braithwaite, L., *Exploring British Cities*, London, Black, 1986.

Brereton, P., *Through Britain on Country Roads*, London, Weidenfeld and Nicolson, 1982.

Burton, A., *The Shell Book of Undiscovered Britain and Ireland*, Newton Abbot, David and Charles, 1986.

Chamberlin, R., *The National Trust Book of English Country Towns*, Exeter, Webb and Bower, 1983.

Chamberlin, R., *English Market Towns*, London, Weidenfeld and Nicolson, 1985.

Crowl, P. A., *The Intelligent Traveller's Guide to Historic Britain*, London, Sidgwick and Jackson, 1983.

Darke, J. amd Finn, T., *What You Must See in the British Isles*, London, Marshall Cavendish, 1981.

Duerdan, F., *The Complete Rambler: A Guide to Every Aspect of Walking in Britain*, London, Granada, 1983.

Duncan, A. (ed.), *Walker's Britain: A Complete Guide to over 240 Walks and Rambles*, London, Pan, 1982.

Eperon, A., *Travellers' Britain*, London, Pan, 1981.

Fodor, E. et al. (eds), *Great Britain*, London, Hodder and Stoughton, 1984.

Forde-Johnston, J. L., *A Guide to the Castles of England and Wales*, Constable, 1981.

Foss, A., *The National Trust Country House Treasures*, London, Weidenfeld and Nicolson, 1980.

Goudie, A. and Gardner, R., *Discovering Landscape in England and Wales*, London, Allen and Unwin, 1985.

Hadfield, J. (ed.), *The Shell Book of English Villages*, London, Michael Joseph, 1980.

Hammond, R. J. W. (ed.), *Complete England, Red Guide*, London, Ward Lock, 1974.

Hogg, G., *The Shell Guide to the Viewpoints of England*, Reading, Osprey, 1975.

Hogg, G. and Tomes, J., *The Shell Book of Exploring Britain*, London, Black, 1985.

Jackson, M., *Exploring England*, London, Collins, 1979.

Jennings, P., *Paul Jennings' Companion to Britain*, London, Cassell, 1981.

Johnson, P., *The National Trust Book of British Castles*, London, Weidenfeld and Nicolson, 1978.

Kerr, N. and Kerr, M., *A Guide to the Norman Sites in Britain*, London, Granada, 1984.

Knapp, B. and Whittow, J., *Britain From the Road*, London, Allen and Unwin, 1985.

Kogan Page (publisher), *Seeing Britain on a Budget*, London, 1981.

Leeds, C. A., *England: A Traveller's Guide to History*, Ormskirk, Hesketh, 1981.

Lussey, K., *A Hitch-Hiker's Guide to Great Britain*, Harmondsworth, Penguin, 1983.

McNight, H., *Shell Book of Inland Waterways*, Newton Abbot, David and Charles, 1981.

Marriott, M., *The Mountains and Hills of Britain: A Guide to the Uplands of England, Scotland and Wales*, London, Collins, 1982.

Marriott, M., *A Concise Guide to the Footpaths of Britain*, London, Collins, 1985.

Mattingly, A., *Walking in the National Parks*, Newton Abbot, David and Charles, 1982.

Millar, T. G., *Long Distance Paths of England and Wales*, Newton Abbot, David and Charles, 1984.

Mossman, K., *The Shell Book of Rural Britain*, Newton Abbot, David and Charles, 1978.

Muir, R. and Welfare, H., *The National Trust Guide to Prehistoric and Roman Britain*, London, George Philip, 1983.

National Trust (publisher), *The National Trust Atlas, showing Plans of Historic, Architectural and Scenic*

Interest in England, Wales and Northern Ireland, London, 1981.

National Trust, *Exploring Unspoilt Britain and Northern Ireland*, London, Octopus, 1985.

Nicolson, A., *The National Trust Book of Long Walks*, London, Weidenfeld and Nicolson, 1981.

Nicolson, N., *The National Trust Book of Great Houses of Britain*, London, Weidenfeld and Nicolson, 1978.

Perrott, D., *The Ordnance Survey Guide to the Waterways*, 3 vols, London, Robert Nicholson, 1983.

Redfern, R. A., *Walking in England*, London, Hale, 1980.

Ross, A., *A Traveller's Guide to Celtic Britain*, London, Routledge & Kegan Paul, 1985.

Rossiter, S., *England, Blue Guide*, London, Benn, 1980.

Simmons, J., *A Selective Guide to England*, Edinburgh, Bartholomew, 1979.

Skyvington, W., *Great Britain Today*, London, Batsford, 1983.

Smith, R., *Wildest Britain: A Visitor's Guide to the National Parks*, London, Blandford Press, 1983.

Soper, T., *The National Trust Guide to the Coast*, Exeter, Webb and Bower, 1984.

Speaight, G., *The New Shell Guide to Britain*, London, Ebury Press, 1985.

Spence, K., *Cathedrals and Abbeys of England and Wales, Blue Guide*, London, Benn, 1984.

Stonehouse, B., *The Aerofilm Book of Britain from the Air*, London, Weidenfeld and Nicolson, 1982.

Thomas, G. S., *Gardens of the National Trust*, London, Weidenfeld and Nicolson, 1979.

Thomas, R., *Coastal Britain*, London, Batsford, 1984.

Waugh, M., *The Shell Book of Country Parks*, Newton Abbot, David and Charles, 1981.

Westacott, H. D., *The Walker's Handbook*, Harmondsworth, Penguin, 1980.

Wickers, D. and Pederson, A., *Britain at Your Feet: Backpacker's Handbook*, London, Hamlyn, 1981.

Wilson, R. J. A., *Guide to the Roman Remains in Britain*, London, Constable, 1980.

Yeadon, D., *Hidden Corners of Britain*, London, Allen and Unwin, 1981.

ENGLISH COUNTIES AND REGIONS

BEDFORDSHIRE

Bigmore, P., *Bedfordshire and Huntingdonshire Landscape*, Sevenoaks, Hodder and Stoughton, 1979.

Godber, J. and Dickinson, P. G. M., *Bedfordshire and Huntingdonshire*, Sevenoaks, Hodder and Stoughton, 1973.

Kennett, D., *Portrait of Bedfordshire*, London, Hale, 1978.

BERKSHIRE

Channer, N., *Berkshire Rambles*, Newbury, Countryside Books, 1979.

Higham, R., *Berkshire and the Vale of White Horse*, London, Batsford, 1977.

Yarrow, I., *Berkshire*, London, Hale, 1974.

BUCKINGHAMSHIRE

Camp, J., *Portrait of Buckinghamshire*, London, Hale, 1972.

Reed, M., *Buckinghamshire Landscape*, Sevenoaks, Hodder and Stoughton, 1979.

Watkins, B., *Buckinghamshire: A Shell Guide*, London, Faber, 1981.

CAMBRIDGESHIRE

Manning, S. A., *Portrait of Cambridgeshire*, London, Hale, 1978.

Mee, A., *Cambridgeshire*, Sevenoaks, Hodder and Stoughton, 1965.

Taylor, C., *The Cambridgeshire Landscape*, Sevenoaks, Hodder and Stoughton, 1973.

Taylor, C., *Cambridgeshire and Mid-Anglia, National Trust Regional History*, London, Collins, 1984.

CHANNEL ISLANDS

Eadie, P. M., *The Channel Islands, Blue Guide*, London, Benn, 1981.

Eggert, H., *The Channel Islands*, London, Hale, 1980.

Lemprière, R., *Portrait of the Channel Islands*, London, Hale, 1975.

Lemprière, R., *Customs, Ceremonies and Traditions of the Channel Islands*, London, Hale, 1976.

Mead, R., *The Channel Islands*, London, Hale, 1979.

CHESHIRE

Bethell, D., *Portrait of Cheshire*, London, Hale, 1979.

Burnley, K., *Portrait of Wirral*, London, Hale, 1981.

Dore, R. N., *Cheshire*, London, Batsford, 1977.

Ellison, N., *The Wirral Peninsula*, London, Hale, 1973.

Mee, A., *Cheshire*, Sevenoaks, Hodder and Stoughton, 1968.

CORNWALL

Balchin, W., *The Cornish Landscape*, Sevenoaks, Hodder and Stoughton, 1983.

Baring-Gould, S., *Cornwall*, Hounslow, Wildwood House, 1981.

Bates, D., *Companion Guide to Devon and Cornwall*, London, Collins, 1976.

Berry, C., *Portrait of Cornwall*, London, Hale, 1971.

Betjeman, J., *Cornwall: Shell Guide*, London, Faber, 1964.

Darke, J., *Cornish Landscapes*, London, Batsford, 1983.

Davidson, R., *Cornwall*, London, Batsford, 1978.

Ellis, P. B., *The Cornish Language and its Literature*, London, Routledge & Kegan Paul, 1974.

Hamilton-Jenkin, A. K., *Cornwall and its People*, Newton Abbot, David and Charles, 1970.

Laws, P., *A Guide to the National Trust in Devon and Cornwall*, Newton Abbot, David and Charles, 1979.

Mee, A., *Cornwall*, Sevenoaks, Hodder and Stoughton, 1967.

Mumford, C., *Portrait of the Isles of Scilly*, London, Hale, 1970.

Pyatt, E. C., *The Cornwall Coast Path: Long Distance Footpath Guide*, London, HMSO, 1977.

Ravensdale, J., *Cornwall: National Trust Regional History*, London, Collins, 1984.

Rawe, D. R., *Cornish Villages*, London, Hale, 1978.

Sidgwick and Jackson (publisher), *Cornwall, Golden Hart Guide*, London, 1983.

Ward Lock (publisher), *Complete Cornwall*, London, 1977.

Ward Lock (publisher), *West Cornwall and the Isles of Scilly*, London.

COTSWOLDS

Brill, E., *Portrait of the Cotswolds*, London, Hale, 1971.

Crosher, G. R., *Along the Cotswold Way*, London, 1976.

Drury, H. W., *Walking in the Cotswolds*, London, Hale, 1981.

Hadfield, C. and Hadfield, A. M. (eds), *The Cotswolds: A New Study*, Newton Abbot, David and Charles, 1973.

Hammond, R. J. W. (ed.), *The Complete Cotswolds and Shakespeare Country*,

Red Guide, London, Ward Lock, 1975.

Sale, R., *Visitor's Guide to the Cotswolds*, Ashbourne, Moorland Publishing, 1982.

Ward Lock (publisher), *Cheltenham and the Cotswolds*, London, 1964.

Wright, L. and Priddey, J., *Cotswold Heritage*, London, Hale, 1977.

DARTMOOR AND EXMOOR

Baring-Gould, S., *Dartmoor*, Hounslow, Wildwood House, 1982.

Burton, S. H., *Exmoor*, London, Hale, 1984.

Countryside Commission, *Dartmoor: National Park Guide*, London, HMSO, 1969.

Countryside Commission, *Exmoor National Park: National Park Guide*, London, HMSO, 1970.

Gill, C., *Dartmoor*, Newton Abbot, David and Charles, 1976.

Hemery, E., *High Dartmoor: Land and People*, London, Hale, 1983.

Peel, J. H. B., *Portrait of Exmoor*, London, Hale, 1970.

Smith, V., *Portrait of Dartmoor*, London, Hale, 1969.

Ward Lock (publisher), *North Devon and Exmoor, Red Guide*, London, 1982.

Westacott, H. D., *Dartmoor for Walkers and Riders*, Harmondsworth, Penguin, 1982.

DERBYSHIRE AND PEAK DISTRICT

Banks, F. R., *The Peak District*, London, Hale, 1975.

Bellamy, R., *The Peak District Companion*, Newton Abbot, David and Charles, 1981.

Christian, R., *The Peak District*, Newton Abbot, David and Charles, 1976.

Mee, A., *Derbyshire*, Sevenoaks, Hodder and Stoughton, 1969.

Millward, R. and Robinson, A., *The Peak District*, London, Eyre Methuen, 1975.

Porter, C. L. M., *A Visitor's Guide to the Peak District*, Ashbourne, Moorland, 1982.

Poucher, W. A., *The Peak and the Pennines*, London, Constable, 1983.

DEVON

Bates, D., *The Companion Guide to Devon and Cornwall*, London, Collins, 1976.

Born, A., *South Devon*, London, Gollancz, 1983.

Burton, S. H., *Devon Villages*, London, Hale, 1973.

Chugg, B., *Devon*, London, Batsford, 1980.

Hammond, R. J. W. (ed.), *Complete Devon, Red Guide*, London, Ward Lock, 1972.

Hoskins, W. G., *Devon and its People*, Newton Abbot, David and Charles, 1968.

Hoskins, W. G., *Devon*, Newton Abbot, David and Charles, 1972.

Jellicoe, A. and Mayne, R., *Devon*, London, Faber, 1975.

Laws, P., *Guide to the National Trust in Devon and Cornwall*, Newton Abbot, David and Charles, 1978.

Messurier, B. Le, *Visitor's Guide to Devon*, Ashbourne, Moorland Publishing, 1983.

Sidgwick and Jackson (publisher), *Devon, Golden Hart Guide*, London, 1983.

St Leger, G. D., *Portrait of Devon*, London, Hale, 1970

Westacott, H. D., *Devon South Coast Path*, Harmondsworth, Penguin, 1982.

DORSET

Jackman, B., *The Dorset Coast Path: Long Distance Footpath Guide*, London, HMSO, 1979.

Mee, A., *Dorset*, Sevenoaks, Hodder and Stoughton, 1967.

Rivers, M. P., *Dorset: A Shell Guide*, London, Faber, 1966.

Taylor, C., *Dorset*, Sevenoaks, Hodder and Stoughton 1970.

Treves, F., *Highways and Byways in Dorset*, Hounslow, Wildwood House, 1981.

Ward Lock (publisher), *Complete Dorset and Wiltshire, Red Guide*, London, 1976.

Westacott, H. D., *Dorset Coast Path*, Harmondsworth, Penguin, 1982.

Wightman, R., *Portrait of Dorset*, London, Hale, 1972.

COUNTY DURHAM

Thompson, H., *Durham Villages*, London, Hale, 1976.

Thorold, H., *County Durham: A Shell Guide*, London, Faber, 1980.

White, P., *Portrait of County Durham*, London, Hale, 1971.

ESSEX

Crouch, M., *Essex*, London, Batsford, 1969.

Manning, S. A., *Portrait of Essex*, London, Hale, 1977.

Maxwell, D., *Unknown Essex*, London, E. P. Publishing, 1970.

Mee, A., *Essex*, Sevenoaks, Hodder and Stoughton, 1966.

Scarfe, N., *Essex, Shell Guide*, London, Faber, 1968.

GLOUCESTERSHIRE

Beckinsale, R. P., *Companion to Gloucestershire and the Cotswolds*, Bourne End, Spurbooks, 1972.

Coysh, A. W. et al., *The Mendips*, London, Hale, 1977.

Finberg, H. P. R., *Gloucestershire*, Sevenoaks, Hodder and Stoughton, 1955.

Mee, A., *Gloucestershire*, Sevenoaks, Hodder and Stoughton, 1966.

Ryder, T. A., *Portrait of Gloucestershire*, London, Hale, 1972.

Verey, D., *Gloucestershire*, London, Faber, 1970.

HAMPSHIRE AND THE ISLE OF WIGHT

Barton, J., *The Visitor's Guide to Hampshire and the Isle of Wight*, Ashbourne, Moorland, 1985.

Holder, J. H., *Explore Hampshire*, Newbury, Countryside Books, 1982.

Hughes, J. P., *The Isle of Wight: A Shell Guide*, London, Faber, 1967.

Mee, A., *Hampshire, with the Isle of Wight*, Sevenoaks, Hodder and Stoughton, 1967.

O'Dell, N., *Portrait of Hampshire*, London, Hale, 1979.

Patterson, A. T., *Hampshire and the Isle of Wight*, London, Batsford, 1976.

Sibley, P., *Discovering the Isle of Wight*, London, Hale, 1977.

Wilson, L., *Portrait of the Isle of Wight*, London, Hale, 1972.

HEREFORDSHIRE

Andere, M., *Herefordshire: The Enchanted Land*, Hereford, Express Logic, 1974.

Nash, B. T. (ed.), *Herefordshire Our Heritage*, 3 vols, Hereford, Express Logic, 1975–6.

Tonkin, J. W., *Herefordshire*, London, Batsford, 1977.

HERTFORDSHIRE

Bailey, B. J., *Portrait of Hertfordshire*, London, Hale, 1978.

Healey, R. M., *Hertfordshire: A Shell Guide*, London, Faber, 1982.

Johnson, W. B., *Hertfordshire*, London, Batsford, 1970.

Mee, A., *Hertfordshire*, Sevenoaks, Hodder and Stoughton, 1965.

Munby, L., *The Hertfordshire Landscape*, Sevenoaks, Hodder and Stoughton, 1977.

KENT

Arnold, H. (ed.), *Kent*, London, Cadogan Books, 1983.

Boyle, J. and Berbiers, J. L., *Rural Kent*, London, Hale, 1976.

Burnham, C. P. and McRae, S. G., *Kent, the Garden of England*, Tenterden, Norbury, 1978.

Church, R., *Kent*, London, Hale, 1966.

Gardiner, D., *Companion to Kent*, Bourne End, Spurbooks, 1973.

Higham, R., *Kent*, London, Batsford, 1974.

Hughes, J. P., *Kent: A Shell Guide*, London, Faber, 1969.

Mee, A., *Kent*, Sevenoaks, Hodder and Stoughton, 1969.

Reynolds, K., *The Visitor's Guide to Kent*, Ashbourne, Moorland, 1985.

Spence, K., *The Companion Guide to Kent and Sussex*, London, Collins, 1973.

Ward Lock (publisher), *The Kent Coast, Red Guide*, London, 1965.

Webb, W., *Kent's Historic Buildings*, London, Hale, 1977.

Nicholson, N., *Portrait of the Lakes*, London, Hale, 1972.

Poucher, W. A., *Lakeland Peaks*, London, Constable, 1972.

Poucher, W. A., *Lakeland Fells*, London, Constable, 1985.

Rice, H. A. L., *Lake Country Towns*, London, Hale, 1974.

Sidgwick and Jackson (publisher), *Lake District, Golden Hart Guide*, London, 1984.

Slack, M., *Lakeland Discovered*, London, Hale, 1982.

Smith, K., *Cumbrian Villages*, London, Hale, 1973.

Spencer, B., *A Visitor's Guide to the Lake District*, Ashbourne, Moorland Publishing, 1981.

Taylor, C. D., *Portrait of Windermere*, London, Hale, 1983.

Unsworth, W., *The High Fells of Lakeland*, London, Hale, 1972.

LAKE DISTRICT

Barringer, J. C., *The Lake District: National Trust Regional History*, London, Collins, 1984.

Cooper, W. H., *The Lakes*, London, Warne, 1970.

Countryside Commission, *Lake District: National Park Guide*, London, HMSO, 1975.

Davies, H., *A Walk around the Lakes*, London, Weidenfeld and Nicolson, 1979.

Dunn, M., *Walking through the Lake District*, Newton Abbot, David and Charles, 1984.

Ffinch, M., *Portrait of Kendal and the Kent Valley*, London, Hale, 1983.

Marshall, J. D., *Portrait of Cumbria*, London, Hale, 1981.

Mee, A., *The Lake Counties: Cumberland and Westmorland*, Sevenoaks, Hodder and Stoughton, 1970.

Millward, R. and Robinson, A., *The Lake District*, London, Eyre and Spottiswoode, 1970.

Nicholson, N., *Greater Lakeland*, London, Hale, 1969.

LANCASHIRE

Alcock, J. P., *Discovering Lancashire*, Aylesbury, Shire Publications, 1977.

Bagley, J. J., *Lancashire*, London, Batsford, 1972.

Bagley, J. J., *A History of Lancashire*, Chichester, Phillimore, 1976.

Lofthouse, J., *Portrait of Lancashire*, London, Hale, 1977.

Lofthouse, J., *Lancashire Countrygoer*, London, Hale, 1974.

Lofthouse, J., *Lancashire Villages*, London, Hale, 1973.

Marshall, J. D., *Lancashire*, Newton Abbot, David and Charles, 1974.

Mee, A., *Lancashire*, Sevenoaks, Hodder and Stoughton, 1973.

LEICESTERSHIRE

Bailey, B. J., *Portrait of Leicestershire*, London, Hale, 1977.

Hoskins, W. G., *Leicestershire: A Shell Guide*, London, Faber, 1970.

Mee, A., *Leicestershire and Rutland*, Sevenoaks, Hodder and Stoughton, 1967.

LINCOLNSHIRE

Kaye, D., *Lincolnshire and South Humberside*, Aylesbury, Shire Publications, 1984.

Lloyd, M., *Portrait of Lincolnshire*, London, Hale, 1983.

Mee, A., *Lincolnshire*, Sevenoaks, Hodder and Stoughton, 1970.

LONDON

A-Z Map Company (publisher), *London Guide: A-Z Information*, Sevenoaks, 1984.

Bagley, W. A., *Green London Walks: Thirty Walks in London's Woodlands, Parklands, Heaths and Commons*, London, Warne, 1981.

Baker, M., *Discovering London's Statues and Monuments*, Aylesbury, Shire Publications, 1982.

Banks, F. R., *The New Penguin Guide to London*, Harmondsworth, Penguin, 1986.

Blatch, M., *A Guide to London Churches*, London, Constable, 1978.

Cassell (publisher), *Berlitz Guide to London*, London, 1980.

Clayton, R., *Portrait of London*, London, Hale, 1980.

Cody, M. (ed.), *A. A. Book of London*, London, Drive Publications, 1983.

Downes, G. et al. (eds), *Alternative London*, London, Otherwise Press, 1982.

Ebel, S. and Impey, D., *A Guide to London's Riverside*, London, Constable, 1985.

French, Y., *Blue Guide London*, London, Black, 1986.

Hatts, L., *Country Walks around London*, Newton Abbot, David and Charles, 1983.

Jenkins, S., *Companion Guide to Outer London*, London, Collins, 1981.

Jones, E. and Woodward, C., *A Guide to the Architecture of London*, London, Weidenfeld and Nicolson, 1983.

Kutcher, A., *Looking at London, Illustrated Walks Through a*

Changing City, London, Thames and Hudson, 1978.

Lawson, A., *Discover Unexpected London*, Oxford, Phaidon, 1979.

Lucas, J., *The Magic of London's Museums*, Watford, Exley Publications, 1979.

Middleditch, M., *London Map-Guide*, Harmondsworth, Penguin, 1985.

Newnes (publisher), *ABC London Street Atlas*, 1984.

Perlmutter, K., *London Street Markets*, Hounslow, Wildwood House, 1983.

Piper, D., *Companion Guide to London*, London, Collins, 1977.

Plimmer, C. and Plimmer, D., *London: A Visitor's Companion*, London, Batsford, 1977.

Rogers, M., *Museums and Galleries of London, Blue Guide*, London, Benn, 1986.

Saunders, A., *The Art of Architecture of London: An Illustrated Guide*, Oxford, Phaidon, 1984.

White, J. T., *Country London*, London, Routledge & Kegan Paul, 1984.

Williams, G., *London Walks*, London, Constable, 1978.

Wittich, J., *Discovering London's Parks and Squares*, Aylesbury, Shire Publications, 1981.

Wittich, J. and Phillips, R., *Off Beat Walks in London*, Aylesbury, Shire Publications, 1977.

NORFOLK

Dorman, B., *Norfolk*, London, Batsford, 1973.

Dymond, D., *The Norfolk Landscape*, Sevenoaks, Hodder and Stoughton, 1984.

Ellis, E. A., *The Broads*, London, Collins, 1965.

Harrod, W. and Linnell, C. L. S., *Norfolk: A Shell Guide*, London, Faber, 1966.

Kennett, D. H., *Norfolk Villages*, London, Hale, 1980.

Yaxley, D., *Portrait of Norfolk*, London, Hale, 1977.

NORTHAMPTONSHIRE

Ireson, T., *Northamptonshire*, London, Hale, 1974.

Smith, J., *Northamptonshire: A Shell Guide*, London, Faber, 1968.

Steane, J., *Northamptonshire Landscape*, Sevenoaks, Hodder and Stoughton, 1974.

Webb, P. G., *Portrat of Northamptonshire*, London, Hale, 1977.

NORTHUMBERLAND

Countryside Commission, *Northumberland National Park: National Park Guide*, London, HMSO, 1969.

Fraser, C. and Emsley, K., *Northumbria*, London, Batsford, 1978.

Godfrey, L. (ed.), *Complete Northumbria*, London, Ward Lock, 1979.

Grierson, E., *The Companion Guide to Northumbria*, London, Collins, 1976.

Newton, R., *Northumberland Landscape*, Sevenoaks, Hodder & Stoughton, 1972.

Ridley, N. G., *Portrait of Northumberland*, London, Hale, 1977.

Rowland, T. H., *Discovering Northumberland*, Newcastle-upon-Tyne, Graham, 1973.

Sharp, T., *Northumberland*, London, Faber, 1970.

Wright, G. N., *A View of Northumbria*, London, Hale, 1981.

NOTTINGHAMSHIRE

Christian, R., *Nottinghamshire*, London, Batsford, 1974.

Mee, A., *Nottinghamshire*, Sevenoaks, Hodder and Stoughton, 1970.

Thorold, H., *Nottinghamshire: A Shell Guide*, London, Faber, 1984.

OXFORDSHIRE

Bloxham, C., *Portrait of Oxfordshire*, London, Hale, 1981.

Emery, F., *The Oxfordshire Landscape*, Sevenoaks, Hodder and Stoughton, 1974.

Hindley, G., *Oxford: City and Countryside, Golden Hart Guide*, Sidgwick and Jackson, 1984.

Mee, A., *Oxfordshire*, Sevenoaks, Hodder and Stoughton, 1970.

Ward Lock (publisher), *The Thames Valley and Oxford, Red Guide*, London, 1980.

PENNINES

Buck, G., *Walking in the Lancashire Pennines*, Clapham, Dalesman, 1982.

Killick, J., *Pennine Chain*, Hebden Bridge, Littlewood Press, 1983.

Oldham, K., *Pennine Way*, Clapham, Dalesman, 1982.

Raistrick, A., *Pennine Dales*, London, Eyre Methuen, 1978.

Redfern, R. A., *Portrait of the Pennines*, London, Hale, 1969.

Redfern, R. A., *South Pennine Country*, London, Hale, 1979.

Stephenson, T., *The Pennine Way: Long Distance Footpath Guide*, London, HMSO, 1981.

Wright, C. J., *Guide to the Pennine Way*, London, Constable, 1979.

SHROPSHIRE

Bailey, B. J., *Portrait of Shropshire*, London, Hale, 1981.

Haines, G. H., *Shropshire and Herefordshire Villages*, London, Hale, 1974.

Mee, A., *Shropshire*, Sevenoaks, Hodder and Stoughton, 1968.

Moulder, M., *Shropshire: A Shell Guide*, London, Faber, 1973.

Rowley, T., *The Shropshire Landscape*, Sevenoaks, Hodder and Stoughton, 1972.

Waite, V., *Shropshire Hill Country*, London, Dent, 1970.

SOMERSET

Allen, D. J., *Somerset*, Aylesbury, Shire Publications, 1982.

Brown, M., *Somerset*, Aylesbury, Shire Publications, 1982.

Gunnell, C., *The Somerset and North Devon Coast Path: Long Distance Footpath Guide*, London, HMSO, 1981.

Havinden, M., *The Somerset Landscape*, Sevenoaks, Hodder and Stoughton, 1982.

Little, B., *Portrait of Somerset*, London, Hale, 1983.

Mee, A., *Somerset*, Sevenoaks, Hodder and Stoughton, 1968.

Westacott, H. D., *The Somerset and North Devon Coast Path*, Harmondsworth, Penguin, 1983.

STAFFORDSHIRE

Bird, V., *Staffordshire*, London, Batsford, 1974.

Mee, A., *Staffordshire*, Sevenoaks, Hodder and Stoughton, 1971.

Palliser, D. M., *The Staffordshire Landscape*, Sevenoaks, Hodder and Stoughton, 1976.

Thorold, H., *Staffordshire: A Shell Guide*, London, Faber, 1978.

SUFFOLK

Burke, J., *Suffolk*, London, Batsford, 1971.

Jobson, A., *Suffolk Villages*, London, Hale, 1971.

Jobson, A., *Portrait of Suffolk*, London, Hale, 1973.

Scarfe, N., *Suffolk: A Shell Guide*, London, Faber, 1966.

Scarfe, N. (ed.), *The Suffolk Landscape*, Sevenoaks, Hodder and Stoughton, 1972.

Smedley, N., *Life and Tradition in Suffolk and North East Essex*, London, Dent, 1976.

SURREY

Arnold, H. (ed.), *Surrey*, London, Cadogan Books, 1984.

Baker, J. L., *A Picture of Surrey*, London, Hale, 1980.

Cracknell, B. E., *Portrait of Surrey*, London, Hale, 1974.

Fraser, M., *Surrey*, London, Batsford, 1975.

Mee, A., *Surrey*, Sevenoaks, Hodder and Stoughton, 1966.

Pitt, D. and Shaw, M., *Surrey Villages*, London, Hale, 1971.

Watkin, B., *Surrey: A Shell Guide*, London, Faber, 1977.

SUSSEX

Arnold, H. (ed.), *Sussex*, London, Cadogan Books, 1984.

Brandon, P., *The Sussex Landscape*, Sevenoaks, Hodder and Stoughton, 1974.

Burke, J., *Sussex*, London, Batsford, 1974.

Darby, B., *View of Sussex*, London, Hale, 1975.

Darby, B., *The South Downs*, London, Hale, 1976.

Harrison, D., *Along the South Downs*, London, Cassell, 1975.

Mee, A., *Sussex*, Sevenoaks, Hodder and Stoughton, 1964.

Meynell, E., *Sussex*, London, Hale, 1966.

Mitchell, W. S., *East Sussex: A Shell Guide*, London, Faber, 1978.

Price, B., *Sussex: People, Places and Things*, Chichester, Phillimore, 1975.

Spence, K., *The Companion Guide to Kent and Sussex*, London, Collins, 1973.

Woodford, C., *Portrait of Sussex*, London, Hale, 1981.

259

WARWICKSHIRE

Beckinsale, R. and Beckinsale, M., *The English Heartland*, London, Duckworth, 1980.

Bunting, J., *Warwickshire*, London, Batsford, 1973.

Cave, L. F., *Warwickshire Villages*, London, Hale, 1976.

Hickman, D., *Warwickshire: A Shell Guide*, London, Faber, 1979.

Hillier, C., *The Western Midland: A Journey to the Heart of England*, London, Gollancz, 1976.

Mee, A., *Warwickshire*, Sevenoaks, Hodder and Stoughton, 1966.

Wright, L. and Priddey, J., *Heart of England*, London, Hale, 1978.

WILTSHIRE

Cheetham, J. H. and Pipes, J., *Wiltshire: A Shell Guide*, London, Faber, 1968.

Child, M., *Wiltshire*, Aylesbury, Shire Publications, 1984.

Mee, A., *Wiltshire*, Sevenoaks, Hodder and Stoughton, 1964.

Street, P., *Portrait of Wiltshire*, London, Hale, 1980.

Ward Lock (publisher), *Complete Dorset and Wiltshire, Red Guide*, London, 1976.

Whitlock, R., *Wiltshire*, London, Batsford, 1976.

Woodruffe, B. J., *Wiltshire Villages*, London, Hale, 1982.

WORCESTERSHIRE

Leatherbarrow, J. S., *Worcestershire*, London, Batsford, 1974.

Lees-Milne, J., *Worcestershire*, London, Faber, 1964.

Mee, A., *Worcestershire*, Sevenoaks, Hodder and Stoughton, 1968.

Stranz, W., *Worcestershire and Herefordshire*, Aylesbury, Shire Publications, 1972.

YORKSHIRE

Allison, K. J., *The East Riding of Yorkshire*, Sevenoaks, Hodder and Stoughton, 1976.

Bainbridge, C., *North Yorkshire and North Humberside*, Aylesbury, Shire Publications, 1984.

Barker, M., *Yorkshire: The North Riding*, London, Batsford, 1977.

Broadhead, I. E., *Portrait of the Yorkshire Ouse*, London, Hale, 1982.

Colbeck, M., *Yorkshire*, London, Batsford, 1975.

Colbeck, M., *Yorkshire: The Dales*, London, Batsford, 1979.

Colbeck, M., *Yorkshire Moorlands*, London, Batsford, 1983.

Countryside Commission, *North York Moors: National Park Guide*, London, HMSO, 1969.

Duerden, N., *Portrait of the Dales*, London, Hale, 1976.

Hammond, R. J. W., *Complete Yorkshire*, London, Ward Lock, 1973.

Hartley, M. and Ingilby, J., *Life and Tradition in the Yorkshire Dales*, London, Dent, 1968.

Hughes, G., *Millstone Grit*, London, Gollancz, 1975.

Lofthouse, J., *A Countrygoer in the Dales*, London, Hale, 1973.

Mee, A., *Yorkshire: East Riding with York*, Sevenoaks, Hodder and Stoughton, 1964.

Mee, A., *Yorkshire: North Riding*, Sevenoaks, Hodder and Stoughton, 1970.

Poucher, W. A., *The Yorkshire Dales and the Peak District*, London, Constable, 1985.

Raistrick, A., *The West Riding of Yorkshire*, Sevenoaks, Hodder and Stoughton, 1970.

Rhea, N., *Portrait of the North York Moors*, London, Hale, 1985.

Slack, M., *Portrait of West Yorkshire*, London, Hale, 1984.

Speakman, C., *Walking in the Yorkshire Dales*, London, Hale, 1982.

Spencer, B., *A Visitor's Guide to the Yorkshire Dales, Teesdale and Weardale*, Ashbourne, Moorland Publishing, 1982.

Wood, G. B., *Yorkshire Villages*, London, Hale, 1980.

Wright, G. N., *Yorkshire: The East Riding*, London, Batsford, 1976.

ENGLAND - OTHER GUIDES

Addison, W., *Portrait of Epping Forest*, London, Hale, 1977.

Andrew, K., *The Southern Upland Way: Long Distance Footpath Guide*, London, HMSO, 1984.

Bailey, B. J., *View of the Chilterns*, London, Hale, 1979.

Broadhead, I. E., *Portrait of Humberside*, London, Hale, 1983.

Cracknell, B. E., *Portrait of London River*, London, Hale, 1980.

Cull, E., *Portrait of the Chilterns*, London, Hale, 1982.

Darby, B., *The South Downs*, London, Hale, 1976.

Falconer, A., *The Cleveland Way: Long Distance Footpath Guide*, London, HMSO, 1977.

Ffinch, M., *The Howgills and the Upper Eden Valley*, London, Hale, 1983.

Forestry Commission, *Explore the New Forest*, London, HMSO, 1975.

Garner, L., *The Visitor's Guide to the Severn and Avon*, Ashbourne, Moorland, 1986.

Grimson, J., *The Channel Coasts of England*, London, Hale, 1978.

Haddon, J., *Portrait of Avon*, London, Hale, 1980.

Hammond, R. J. W., *Complete Thames and Chilterns*, London, Ward Lock, 1977.

Herbstein, D., *The North Downs Way: Long Distance Footpath Guide*, London, HMSO, 1982.

Higham, R., *Regional Guide to South East England and East Anglia*, London, Ward Lock, 1981.

Jennett, S., *The South Downs Way: Long Distance Footpath Guide*, London, HMSO, 1978.

Jennett, S., *The Ridgeway Path: Long Distance Footpath Guide*, London, HMSO, 1978.

Jones, J. B., *Offa's Dyke Path: Long Distance Footpath Guide*, London, HMSO, 1977.

Keates, J., *The Companion Guide to the Shakespeare Country*, London, Collins, 1979.

Lands, N., *Visitor's Guide to the Chilterns*, Ashbourne, Moorland Publishing, 1981.

Morland, B., *Portrait of the Potteries*, London, Hale, 1978.

Parker, D., *The West Country and the Sea*, London, Longman, 1980.

Parsons, H., *Portrait of the Black Country*, London, Hale, 1986.

Ratcliffe, R., *The Wolds Way: Long Distance Footpath Guide*, London, HMSO, 1982.

Royal Automobile Club, *Going Places 1: Southeast England*, London, Travellers Realm, 1981.

Royal Automobile Club, *Going Places 3: West Country*, London, Travellers Realm, 1981.

Royal Automobile Club, *Going Places 4: Southwest England*, London, Travellers Realm, 1981.

Royal Automobile Club, *Going Places 5: Northwest England*, London, Travellers Realm 1981.

Royal Automobile Club, *Going Places 6: Southern England*, London, Travellers Realm 1981.

Royal Automobile Club, *Going Places 7: Home Counties*, London, Travellers Realm 1981.

Royal Automobile Club, *Going Places 8: East Anglia and Essex*, London, Travellers Realm 1981.

Royal Automobile Club, *Going Places 9: Central England*, London, Travellers Realm 1982.

Royal Automobile Club, *Going Places 10: East Midlands*, London,

Travellers Realm 1982.

Seymour, J., *East Anglia, Companion Guide*, London, Collins, 1977.

Stenning, E. H., *Portrait of the Isle of Man*, London, Hale, 1983.

Stevenson, B., *Middlesex*, London, Batsford, 1972.

Storey, E., *Portrait of the Fen Country*, London, Hale, 1982.

Thompson, E. V., *Discovering Bodmin Moor*, St Teath, Bodmin, Bossiney Books, 1980.

Trewin, J. C., *Portrait of the Shakespeare Country*, London, Hale, 1970.

Tully, C., *The Visitor's Guide to East Anglia*, Ashbourne, Moorland, 1984.

Vesey-Fitzgerald, B., *Portrait of the New Forest*, London, Hale, 1977.

Waite, V., *Portrait of the Quantocks*, London, Hale, 1969.

Ward Lock (publisher), *The New Forest, Red Guide*, London, 1963.

Wright, G., *View of Wessex*, London, Hale, 1978.

SCOTLAND

Aitken, R., *The West Highland Way: Long Distance Footpath Guide*, London, HMSO, 1984.

Automobile Association, *Illustrated Road Book of Scotland*, London, Drive Publications, 1971.

Automobile Association, *Touring Guide to Scotland*, London, Drive Publications, 1978.

Automobile Association, *Scotland: Where to Go, What to Do*, London, Drive Publications, 1982.

Bain, A., *Scottish Museums and Galleries Guide*, Edinburgh, Polygon, 1986.

Bartholomew (publisher), *Historical Map of Scotland*, Edinburgh, 1985.

Bartholomew (publisher), *Touring Road Map of Scotland*, Edinburgh, 1985.

Close-Brooks, J., *The Highlands: Exploring Scotland's Heritage*, London, HMSO, 1986.

Countryside Commission for Scotland, *The Official Guide to Scotland's Countryside*, Perth, 1977.

Douglas, H., *Portrait of the Burns Country*, London, Hale, 1975.

Dymock, E. and Miller, R., *Scotland by Car*, Newton Abbot, David and Charles, 1967.

Fenwick, H., *Scotland's Historic Buildings*, London, Hale, 1974.

Fenwick, H., *Scotland's Castles*, London, Hale, 1976.

Fenwick, H., *Scotland's Abbeys and Cathedrals*, London, Hale, 1978.

Fenwick, H., *View of the Lowlands*, London, Hale, 1981.

Finlay, I., *The Central Highlands*, London, Batsford, 1976.

Frank, B., *Discover Scotland*, Edinburgh, Bartholomew, 1985.

Graham, C., *Portrait of the Moray Firth*, London, Hale, 1977.

Graham, C., *Portrait of Aberdeen and Deeside*, London, Hale, 1980.

Graham-Campbell, D., *Portrait of Argyll and the Southern Hebrides*, London, Hale, 1978.

Graham-Campbell, D., *Portrait of Perth, Angus and Fife*, London, Hale, 1979.

Grant, J. S., *Highland Villages*, London, Hale, 1977.

Hammond, R. J. W., *Complete Scottish Lowlands*, London, Ward Lock, 1974.

Hammond, R. J. W. (ed.), *Western Scotland*, London, Ward Lock, 1976.

Hammond, R. J. W., *Complete Scotland*, London, Ward Lock, 1980.

Hammond, R. J. W., *Northern Scotland*, London, Ward Lock, 1980.

House, J., *Portrait of the Clyde*, London, Hale, 1975.

Lindsay, M., *The Lowlands of Scotland: Edinburgh and the South*, London, Hale, 1977.

Lindsay, M., *Lowland Scottish Villages*, London, Hale, 1980.

Linklater, E. and Nicolson, J. R., *Orkney and Shetland*, London, Hale, 1980.

Lister, J. A., *The Scottish Highlands*, Edinburgh, Bartholomew, 1980.

Lochhead, M., *Portrait of the Scott Country*, London, Hale, 1973.

Maclaren, M. and McNie, D. L., *The New Shell Guide to Scotland*,

London, Ebury Press, 1977.

McCormick, D., *Islands of Scotland*, Reading, Osprey, 1974.

McInnes, D. and McInnes, K., *Walking through Scotland*, Newton Abbot, David and Charles, 1981.

McLean, A. C., *The Highlands and Islands of Scotland*, Glasgow and London, Collins, 1976.

Magnusson, M., *Treasures of Scotland*, London, Weidenfeld and Nicolson, 1981.

Miller, P., *Orkney*, London, Batsford, 1971.

Murray, W. H., *The Islands of Western Scotland: The Inner and Outer Hebrides*, London, Methuen, 1973.

Murray, W. H., *The Companion Guide to the West Highlands of Scotland*, Glasgow and London, Collins, 1977.

Naismith, R. J., *Buildings of the Scottish Countryside*, London, Gollancz, 1985.

Nicolson, J. R., *Shetland*, Newton Abbot, David and Charles, 1979.

Prentice, R. (ed.), *The National Trust for Scotland Guide*, London, Cape, 1981.

Read, J. and Manjon, M., *Visitor's Scotland*, London, Macmillan, 1979.

Ritchie, A., *Orkney and Shetland: Exploring Scotland's Heritage*, London, HMSO, 1985.

Royal Automobile Club, *Going Places 2: Scotland*, London, Travellers Realm, 1981.

Simpson, W. D., *Portrait of the Highlands*, London, Hale, 1972.

Simpson, W. D., *Portrait of Skye and the Outer Hebrides*, London, Hale, 1973.

Smith, R. A., *The Visitor's Guide to the Scottish Borders and Edinburgh*, Ashbourne, Moorland, 1983.

Sobel, A., *The Western Isles of Scotland*, London, New English Library, 1976.

Stevenson, J., *The Clyde Estuary and Central Region: Exploring Scotland's Heritage*, London, HMSO, 1985.

Thompson, F., *The Highlands and Islands*, London, Hale, 1974.

Thompson, F., *Scotland*, London, Ward Lock, 1983.

Tomes, J., *Scotland, Blue Guide*, London, Benn, 1980.

Tranter, N., *The Heartland of Scotland, The Queen's Scotland*, London, Hodder and Stoughton, 1971.

Tranter, N., *Portrait of the Border Country*, London, Hale, 1972.

Tranter, N., *The North East, The Queen's Scotland*, London, Hodder and Stoughton, 1974.

Tranter, N., *Portrait of the Lothians*, London, Hale, 1979.

Tranter, N., *Nigel Tranter's Scotland*, Harmondsworth, Penguin, 1983.

Weir, T., *Scottish Lochs*, London, Constable, 1972.

Weir, T., *The Western Highlands*, London, Batsford, 1973.

NORTHERN IRELAND

Appletree Press (publisher), *See Northern Ireland By Train*, Belfast, 1986.

Automobile Association, *Touring Guide to Ireland*, London, Drive Publications, 1976.

Automobile Association, *Ireland: Where to Go, What to Do*, London, Drive Publications, 1980.

Bartholomew (publisher), *Historical Map of Ireland*, Edinburgh, 1985.

Bartholomew (publisher), *Touring Road Map of Ireland*, Edinburgh, 1985.

Bartholomew (publisher), *Visitor's Map of Ireland*, Edinburgh, 1985.

Brooks, J., *National Trust in Northern Ireland: Tour of the Properties of the Ulster Heritage*, Belfast, Eason, 1978.

David and Charles (publisher), *Where to Go in the North of Ireland*, Newton Abbot, 1985.

Hammond, R. J. W. (ed.), *Northern Ireland, Red Guide*, London, Ward Lock, 1971.

Rogers, R., *Irish Walk Guide – North East: Down, Antrim, Armagh, Derry, Tyrone, Fermanagh*, Dublin, Gill and Macmillan, 1980.

Sandford, E., *Discover Northern Ireland, Belfast*, Northern Ireland Tourist Board, 1976.

WALES

Automobile Association, *Touring Guide to Wales*, London, Drive Publications, 1975.

Automobile Association, *Castles in Wales*, London, Drive Publications, 1984.

Barber, W. T., *Exploring Wales*, Newton Abbot, David and Charles, 1982.

Barber, W. T., *The Visitors' Guide to Historic Places of Wales*, Ashbourne, Moorland, 1984.

Barrett, J. H., *The Pembrokeshire Coast Path: Long Distance Footpath Guide*, London, HMSO, 1973.

Beazley, E. and Brett, L., *North Wales*, Shell Guide, London, Faber, 1971.

Beazley, E. and Howell, P., *The Companion Guide to North Wales*, London, Collins, 1975.

Condry, W., *Exploring Wales*, London, Faber, 1972.

Countryside Commission, *Brecon Beacons: National Park Guide*, London, HMSO, 1967.

Countryside Commission, *Pembrokeshire Coast: National Park Guide*, London, HMSO, 1973.

Countryside Commission, *Snowdonia: National Park Guide*, London, HMSO, 1974.

Fletcher, H. L. V., *Portrait of the Wye Valley*, London, Hale, 1968.

Gibson, P., *The Visitor's Guide to South and West Wales*, Ashbourne, Moorland, 1984.

Hammond, R. J. W. (ed.), *North Wales*, London, Ward Lock, 1971.

Hammond, R. J. W. (ed.), *The Wye Valley*, London, Ward Lock, 1975.

Hilling, J. B., *Snowdonia and Northern Wales*, London, Batsford, 1980.

Jones, J., *The Lakes of North Wales*, Hounslow, Wildwood House, 1983.

Jones, R., *Walks in Wales*, London, Hale, 1979.

Llewellyn, A., *The Shell Guide to Wales*, London, Michael Joseph, 1973.

Lockley, R. M., *Pembrokeshire*, London, Hale, 1969.

MacDonald, C., *Visitor's Guide to North Wales and Snowdonia*, Ashbourne, Moorland Publishing, 1982.

McInnes, D. and McInnes, K., *Walking through Wales*, Newton Abbot, David and Charles, 1984.

Marsh, T., *The Summits of Snowdonia*, London, Hale, 1984.

Mason, E. J., *Portrait of the Brecon Beacons*, London, Hale, 1975.

Miles, D., *Portrait of Pembrokeshire*, London, Hale, 1984.

Peel, J. H. B., *Portrait of the Severn*, London, Hale, 1980.

Poucher, W. A., *Wales*, London, Constable, 1981.

Rees, V., *South West Wales*, Shell Guide, London, Faber, 1963.

Royal Automobile Club, *Going Places 11: Wales*, London, Travellers Realm, 1982.

Senior, M., *Portrait of North Wales*, London, Hale, 1973.

Thomas, R., *South Wales Guide Book*, Edinburgh, Bartholomew, 1977.

Tomes, J. (ed.), *Wales and the Marches, Blue Guide*, London, Benn, 1979.

Vaughan-Thomas, W., *Portrait of Gower*, London, Hale, 1976.

Wales Tourist Board, *Mid-Wales: A Tourist Guide*, Cardiff, 1985.

Wales Tourist Board, *North Wales: A Tourist Guide*, Cardiff, 1985.

Wales Tourist Board, *South Wales, A Tourist Guide*, Cardiff, 1985.

Wales Tourist Board, *Wales: Castles and Historic Places*, Cardiff, 1985.

Whittow, J., *Snowdonia's Landscape*, London, Allen and Unwin, 1985.

SEE ALSO

2   Buildings and Architecture
3   Cities
11   Geography

39 WALES

For bibliographical guides to Wales, Welsh life, culture, politics, and history readers are referred to the following: Jones, S. R., *Books of Welsh Interest*, 1977; National Book League, *Reader's Guide to Wales*, 1973; Pollock, L. and McAllister, I. *A Bibliography of United Kingdom Politics: Scotland, Wales and Northern Ireland*, 3 vols, 1980; University of Wales Press (publisher), *A Bibliography of the History of Wales*, 1962.

The following books are recommended as general surveys of Wales, Welsh life and culture: British Council, *Introducing Wales*, 1978; Dodd, A. H., *Life in Wales*, 1972; Fishlock, T., *Wales and the Welsh*, 1972; Griffith, L. W., *The Welsh*, 1964; Jones, B. R. (ed.), *Anatomy of Wales*, 1972; Llewellyn, A., *Shell Guide to Wales*, 1973; Morgan, P., *Background to Wales: A Course of Studies in Modern Welsh Life*, 1968; Thomas, D. (ed.), *Wales: A New Study*, 1979.

For an introduction to contemporary Wales and Welsh affairs see: Central Office of Information, *The Welsh Office Today: Its Functions and Organisation*, 1978; Central Office of Information, *Wales*, 1981; Osmond, J. (ed.), *The National Question Again*, 1985.

The following provide useful surveys in their respective fields:

Economy   Humphreys, G., *Industrial Britain, South Wales*, 1972; Nevin, E. T. et al., *The Structure of the Welsh Economy*, 1966; Rees, G. L. et al., *Survey of the Welsh Economy*, 1974.

Geography   see page 72.

History   Jones, G. E., *Modern Wales: A Concise History, c. 1485–1979*, 1985; Morgan, K. O., *Rebirth of a Nation, 1880–1980*, 1981; Vaughan-Thomas, W., *Wales: A History*, 1985; Williams, G., *The Welsh and Their History*, 1982.

Politics   Bogdanor, V., *Devolution*, 1979; Evans, G., *A National Future for Wales*, 1976; Osmond, J., *Creative Conflict: The Politics of Welsh Devolution*, 1978; Osmond, J. (ed.), *The National Question Again*, 1985.

REFERENCE

Balsom, D. and Burch, M. (eds), *Political and Electoral Handbook for Wales*, Aldershot, Saxon House, 1980.

Blackwell (publisher), *The Dictionary of Welsh Biography down to 1940*, Oxford, 1959.

Carter, H. (ed.), *National Atlas of Wales*, Cardiff, University of Wales Press, 1981.

Davies, E. (ed.), *A Gazetteer of Welsh Place-Names*, Cardiff, University of Wales Press, 1975.

Evans, H. M. and Thomas, W. O., *Y Geiriadur Mawr, The Complete Welsh-English, English-Welsh Dictionary*, Llandysul, Gomer, 1983.

Her Majesty's Stationery Office, *Digest of Welsh Statistics*, Cardiff, annually.

Jones, B., *A Bibliography of Anglo-Welsh Literature, 1900–1965*, Swansea, Library Association, 1970.

Jones, S. R., *Books of Welsh Interest*, Aberystwyth, Welsh Book Council, 1977.

National Book League, *Reader's Guide to Wales: Selected Bibliography*, London, 1973.

Pollock, L. and McAllister, I., *A Bibliography of United Kingdom Politics: Scotland, Wales and Northern Ireland*, 3 vols, Glasgow, University of Strathclyde, 1980.

Rees, W., *An Historical Atlas of Wales from Early to Modern Times*, London, Faber, 1951.

University of Wales Press, *A Bibliography of the History of Wales*, Cardiff, 1962.

The Welsh Office, *Welsh Social Trends*, Cardiff, 1977.

GENERAL

British Council, *Introducing Wales*, London, 1978.

Carter, H., *The Towns of Wales*, Cardiff, University of Wales Press, 1965.

Central Office of Information, *Wales*, London, HMSO, 1981.

Davies, R. R. et al. (eds), *Welsh Society and Nationhood*, Cardiff, University of Wales Press, 1984.

Dodd, A. H., *Life in Wales*, London, Batsford, 1972.

Fishlock, T., *Wales*, London, Faber, 1979.

Griffith, L. W., *The Welsh*, Cardiff, University of Wales Press, 1964.

Humphreys, G., *Industrial Britain: South Wales*, Newton Abbot, David and Charles, 1972.

Jenkins, J. G., *Life and Tradition in Rural Wales*, London, Dent, 1976.

Jones, B. R. (ed.), *Anatomy of Wales*, Cardiff, Gwerin Publications, 1972.

Lewis, E. D., *The Rhondda Valleys*, London, Phoenix House, 1959.

Lockley, R. B., *Wales*, London, Batsford, 1966.

Morgan, G. (ed.), *The World of Wales*, Cardiff, University of Wales Press,
1968.

Morgan, P. *Background to Wales: A Course of Studies in Modern Welsh Life*, Swansea, C. Davies, 1968.

Morris, J. (ed.), *Wales*, London, Oxford University Press, 1982.

Morris, J., *The Matter of Wales: Epic Views of a Small Country*, London, Oxford University Press, 1985.

Nevin, E. T., et al., *The Structure of the Welsh Economy*, Cardiff, University of Wales Press, 1966.

Rees, D. B., *Chapels in the Valley: A Study in the Sociology of Welsh Non-Conformity*, Merseyside, Ffynnon Press, 1975.

Rees, G. and Rees, T. L., *Poverty and Inequality in Wales*, London, Croom Helm, 1980.

Rose, R. and McAllister, I., *United Kingdom Facts*, London, Macmillan, 1982.

Smith, P., *Houses of the Welsh Countryside*, London, HMSO, 1975.

Williams, G. (ed.), *Social and Cultural Change in Contemporary Wales*, Routledge & Kegan Paul, 1978.

HISTORY

Dodd, A. H., *The Industrial Revolution in North Wales*, Cardiff, University of Wales Press, 1971.

Dodd, A. H., *Short History of Wales: Welsh Life and Customs*, London, Batsford, 1977.

Francis, H. and Smith, D., *The Fed: A History of the South Wales Miners in the Twentieth Century*, London, Lawrence and Wishart, 1980.

Houlder, C., *Wales: An Archaeological Guide*, London, Faber, 1978.

Jack, R. Ian, *Medieval Wales*, Cambridge, Cambridge University Press, 1976.

Jones, G. E., *Modern Wales: A Concise History, c.1485–1979*, Cambridge, Cambridge University Press, 1985.

Morgan, K. O., *Rebirth of a Nation: Wales 1880–1980, History of Wales*, vol. 6, Oxford, Clarendon Press, 1981.

Roberts, G., *Aspects of Welsh History*, Cardiff, University of Wales Press, 1969.

Roderick, A. J. (ed.), *Wales Through the Ages*, 2 vols, Swansea, C. Davies, 1959.

Smith, D. (ed.), *A People and a Proletariat: Essays in the History of Wales, 1780–1980*, London, Pluto, 1980.

Thomas, H., *A History of Wales, 1485–1660*, Cardiff, University of Wales Press, 1972.

Vaughan-Thomas, W., *Wales: A History*, London, Michael Joseph, 1985.

Walker, D. (ed.), *A History of the Church in Wales*, Penarth, Church in

Wales Publications, 1976.

Williams, D., *A Short History of Modern Wales, 1485 to the Present Day*, London, John Murray, 1961.

Williams, D., *A History of Modern Wales*, London, Murray, 1977.

Williams, G. A., *When Was Wales? A History of the Welsh*, Harmondsworth, Penguin, 1985.

Williams, G., *The Welsh and their History*, London, Croom Helm, 1982.

Williams, G., *The Welsh Church from Conquest to Reformation*, Cardiff, University of Wales Press, 1968.

GOVERNMENT AND POLITICS

Balsom, D. and Burch, M. (eds), *A Political and Electoral Handbook for Wales, 1959–1979*, Aldershot, Gower, 1980.

Bogdanor, V., *Devolution*, Oxford, Oxford University Press, 1979.

Central Office of Information, *The Welsh Office Today: Its Function and Organisation*, London, 1978.

Evans, G., *A National Future for Wales*, Plaid Cymru, Carmarthen, 1976.

Foulkes, D. et al. (eds), *The Wales Veto: The Wales Act 1978 and the Referendum*, Cardiff, University of Wales Press, 1983.

Hechter, M., *Internal Colonialism: The Celtic Fringe in British National Development, 1536–1966*, London, Routledge & Kegan Paul, 1978.

James, A. J. and Thomas, J. E., *Wales at Westminster: A History of*

Parliamentary Representation of Wales, 1800–1979, Llandysul, Gomer Press, 1981.

Morgan, K. O., *Wales in British Politics, 1868–1922*, Cardiff, University of Wales Press, 1980.

Morgan, W. J., *The Welsh Dilemma*, Swansea, Davies, 1973.

Osmond, J., *Creative Conflict: The Politics of Welsh Devolution*, London, Routledge & Kegan Paul, 1978.

Osmond, J. (ed.), *The National Question Again*, Llandysul, Gomer Press, 1985.

Philip, A. B., *The Welsh Question: Nationalism in Welsh Politics, 1945–1970*, Cardiff, University of Wales Press, 1975.

Williams, C. H. (ed.), *National Separatism*, Cardiff, University of Wales Press, 1982.

CULTURE AND TRADITIONS

Blake, L., *Welsh Folk Dance and Costume*, Llangollen, Gwynn, 1954.

Conran, A. (ed.), *Penguin Book of Welsh Verse*, Harmondsworth, Penguin, 1976.

Garlick, R., *An Introduction to Anglo-Welsh Literature*, Cardiff, University of Wales Press, 1972.

Handley-Taylor, C. (ed.), *Authors of Wales Today*, London, Eddison Press, 1972.

Harris, M. C., *Crafts, Customs and Legends of Wales*, Newton Abbot, David and Charles, 1980.

Hilling, J. B., *The Historic Architecture of Wales*, Cardiff, University of Wales Press, 1976.

Jones, G., *Welsh Folklore and Folk Customs*, Woodbridge, D. S. Brewer, 1979.

Jones, G., *Welsh Legends and Folk-Tales*, Harmondsworth, Penguin, 1979.

Jones, W. R., *Bilingualism in Welsh Education*, Cardiff, University of Wales Press, 1966.

Morgan, G., *The Dragon's Tongue: The Fortune of the Welsh Language*, Cardiff, Triskel Press, 1966.

Owen, T. M., *Welsh Folk Customs*, Cardiff, National Museum of Wales, 1959.

Parry, T., *A History of Welsh Literature*, Cardiff, University of Wales Press, 1979.

Rees, D. B., *Wales: The Cultural Heritage*, Ormskirk, Hesketh, 1981.

Rowan, E. (ed.), *Art in Wales 2000 BC-AD 1850: An Illustrated History*, Cardiff, University of Wales Press, 1978.

Rowan, E. (ed.), *Art in Wales 1850–1980: An Illustrated History*, Cardiff, University of Wales Press, 1985.

Stephens, M. (ed.), *The Welsh Language Today*, Llandysul, J. D. Lewis, 1973.

Stephens, M. (ed.), *The Oxford Companion to the Literature of Wales*, Oxford, Oxford University Press, 1986.

Thomas, A. R., *The Linguistic Geography of Wales*, Cardiff, University of Wales Press, 1973.

Williams, G., *An Introduction to Welsh Literature*, Cardiff, University of Wales Press, 1978.

Williams, G., *Religion, Language and Nationality in Wales*, University of Wales Press, 1979.

SEE ALSO:

40 WOMEN

Reference guides to the literature on women and feminism are provided in: Evans, M. and Morgan, D. (eds), *Work on Women: A Guide to the Literature*, 1979; Darter, P., *The Women's Movement, Reader's Guide*, 1983; Kanner, B. (ed.), *The Women of England: From Anglo-Saxon Times to the Present: Interpretative Bibliographical Essays*, 1980; Gilbert, V. F. and Tatla, D. S. (comps.), *Women's Studies: A Bibliography of Theses and Dissertations, 1870–1982*, 1985; Ritchie, M. (ed.), *Women's Studies: A Checklist of Bibliographies*, 1980; Rosenberg M. B. and Bergstrom, L. V., *Women and Society: A Critical Review of the Literature with a Selected Annotated Bibliography*, 1975; Rowbotham, S., *Women's Liberation and Revolution: A Bibliography*, 1973.

For information on women, women's studies and women's organisations in Britain reference should be made to: Collins, W. et al., *Directory of Social Change: Women*, 1978; Faulder, C. et al., *The Women's Directory*, 1976; National Council of Social Services Women's Forum, *Women's Organisations in Great Britain*, 1975; Roberts, H. (ed.), *Doing Feminist Research*, 1981.

For introductory reading on particular fields relating to women the following are recommended:

Economic Status   Chapman, J. R. (ed.), *Economic Independence for Women: The Foundation of Equal Rights*, 1976; Her Majesty's Stationery Office, *Women and Work: A Review*, 1975; Her Majesty's Stationery Office, *Equality for Women: A Policy for Equal Opportunity*, 1974; Her Majesty's Stationery Office, *Women and Work: Sex Differences and Society*, 1974.

Feminism   Coote, A. and Gill, T., *Women's Rights: A Practical Guide*, 1974; Coote, A. and Campbell, B., *Sweet Freedom: The Struggle for Women's Liberation*, 1982; Greer, G., *The Female Eunuch*, 1970; Wandor, M. (ed.), *The Body Politic: Writings from the Women's Liberation Movement in Britain, 1969–72*, 1972.

Legal Rights   Coote, A. and Gill, T., *Women's Rights: A Practical Guide*, 1974; Lewis, J. (ed.), *Women's Welfare, Women's Rights*, 1983.

Literature   Kaplan, S. J., *Feminine Consciousness in the Modern British Novel*, 1975; Sage, L., *Contemporary Women Novelist*, 1984; Showalter, E., *A Literature of Their Own: British Women Novelists from Brontë to Lessing*, 1982.

Political Rights   Liddington, J. and Norris, J., *One Hand Tied Behind Us: The Rise of the Women's Suffrage Movement*, 1978; Fulford, R., *Votes for Women*, 1957; Ramelson, M., *Petticoat Rebellion*, 1967.

Social History   Adam, R., *A Woman's Place, 1910–1975*, 1975; Mackenzie, M., *Shoulder to Shoulder*, 1975; Stenton, D. M., *The English Woman in History*, 1978; Lewis, J., *Women in England, 1870–1950: Sexual Divisions and Social Change*, 1984.

269

REFERENCE

Banks, O., *The Biographical Dictionary of Feminists, Vol. I, 1800–1930*, Brighton, Harvester, 1985.

Beddoe, D., *Discovering Women's History: A Practical Handbook*, London, Pandora Press, 1983.

Darter, P., *The Women's Movement, Reader's Guide no. 47*, Library Association, Public Libraries Group, 1983.

Evans, M. and Morgan, D. (eds), *Work on Women: A Guide to the Literature*, London and New York, Tavistock, 1979.

Faulder, C. et al., *The Women's Directory*, London, Virago, 1976.

Gilbert, V. F. and Tatla, D. S. (comps.), *Women's Studies: A Bibliography of Theses and Dissertations, 1870–1982*, Oxford, Blackwell, 1985.

Kanner, B. (ed.), *The Women of England: From Anglo-Saxon Times to the Present: Interpretative Bibliographical Essays*, London, Mansell, 1980.

National Council of Social Services Women's Forum, *Women's Organisations in Great Britain*, London, 1975.

Norton, M., *Directory of Social Change, vol. 3, Women*, Hounslow, Wildwood House, 1978.

Ritchie, M. (ed.), *Women's Studies: A Checklist of Bibliographies*, London, Mansell, 1980.

Rosenberg, M., B. and Bergstrom, L. V., *Women and Society: A Critical Review of the Literature with a Selected Annotated Bibliography*, London, Sage, 1975.

Rowbotham, S., *Women's Liberation and Revolution: A Bibliography*, Bristol, Falling Wall Press, 1973.

Stafford, P. et al. (eds), *The Europa Bibliographical Dictionary of British Women*, London, Europa Publications, 1983.

Todd, J. (ed.), *A Dictionary of British and American Women Writers, 1660 to 1800*, London, Methuen, 1985.

GENERAL

Adam, R., *A Woman's Place, 1910–1975*, London, Chatto and Windus, 1975.

Aldred, C., *Women at Work*, London, Pan, 1981.

Barker, D. L. and Allen, S., *Sexual Divisions and Society: Process and Change*, London, Tavistock, 1976.

Beale, J., *Getting it Together: Women as Trade Unionists*, London, Pluto, 1984.

Beechey, V. and Whitelegg, E. (eds), *Women in Britain Today: Family, Employment, Education and Health*, Milton Keynes, Open University Press, 1986.

Bouchier, D., *The Feminist Challenge: The Movement for Women's Liberation in Britain and the USA*, London, Macmillan, 1984.

Brophy, J. and Smart, C., *Women-in-Law*, London, Routledge & Kegan Paul, 1985.

Byrne, E., *Women and Education*, London, Tavistock, 1978.

Chapman, J. R. (ed.), *Economic Independence for Women: The Foundation of Equal Rights*, London, Sage, 1976.

Coote, A. and Campbell, B., *Sweet Freedom: The Struggle for Women's Liberation*, London, Pan, 1982.

Coote, A. and Gill, T., *Women's Rights: A Practical Guide*, Harmondsworth, Penguin, 1974.

Coussins, J., *The Equality Report*, London, National Council for Civil Liberties, 1977.

Currell, M., *Political Women*, London, Croom Helm, 1974.

Dalla Costa, M., *The Power of Women and the Subversion of the Community*, Bristol, Falling Wall Press, 1972.

David, D., *British Women Intellectuals*, London, Macmillan, 1985.

Davies, R., *Women and Work*, London, Hutchinson, 1975.

Deem, R., *Women and Schooling*, London, Routledge & Kegan Paul, 1978.

Duelli-Klein, R. (ed.), *So Far, So Good, So What? Women's Studies in the UK*, Oxford, Pergamon, 1983.

Ellmann, M., *Thinking about Women*, London, Virago, 1979.

Evans, R. J., *The Feminists*, London, Croom Helm, 1979.

Figes, E., *Sex and Subterfuge: Women Writers to 1850*, London, Macmillan, 1982.

Gavron, H., *The Captive Wife*, London, Routledge & Kegan Paul, 1966.

Greer, G., *The Female Eunuch*, London, Macgibbon and Kee, 1970.

Hamilton, R., *The Liberation of Women*, London, Allen and Unwin, 1978.

Her Majesty's Stationery Office, *Equality for Women: A Policy for Equal Opportunity*, London, 1974.

Her Majesty's Stationery Office, *Women and Work: Sex Differences and Society*, London, 1974.

Her Majesty's Stationery Office, *Women and Work: A Review*, London, 1975.

Holland, J. (ed.), *Feminist Action*, Hounslow, Battle Axe Books, 1985.

Hughes, M. and Kennedy, M. (eds), *New Futures: Changing Women's Education*, London, Routledge & Kegan Paul, 1985.

Jackson, S., *On the Social Construction of Female Sexuality*, London, Women's Research and Resources Centre, 1978.

Joseph, G., *Women at Work: The British Experience*, Oxford, Philip Allan, 1983.

Kaplan, S. J., *Feminine Consciousness in the Modern British Novel*, Urbana, Illinois University Press, 1975.

King, J. and Stott, M. (eds), *Is this your Life? Images of Women in the Media*, London, Virago, 1977.

Klein, V., *The Feminine Character: History of an Ideology*, London, Routledge & Kegan Paul, 1946.

Kuhn, A. and Wolpe, A. M. (eds), *Feminism and Materialism*, London, Routledge & Kegan Paul, 1978.

Lewis, J. (ed.), *Women's Welfare, Women's Rights*, London, Croom Helm, 1983.

Mackenzie, M., *Shoulder to Shoulder*, Harmondsworth, Penguin, 1975.

Martin, J. and Roberts, C., *Women and Employment – A Lifetime Perspective*, London, HMSO, 1984.

Maya, M. (ed.), *Women in the Community*, London, Routledge & Kegan Paul, 1976.

Mews, H., *Frail Vessels: Woman's Role in Women's Novels from Fanny Burney to George Eliot*, London, Athlone, 1969.

Middleton, L., *Women in the Labour Movement*, London, Croom Helm, 1977.

Mitchell, J., *Women's Estate*, Harmondsworth, Penguin, 1971.

Mitchell, J. *Psychoanalysis and Feminism*, London, Allen Lane, 1974.

Mitchell, J., *Women: The Longest Revolution: Essays in Feminism, Literature and Psychoanalysis*, London, Virago, 1984.

Mitchell, J. and Oakley, A., *Women*, Harmondsworth, Penguin, 1973.

Oakeley, A., *The Sociology of Housework*, Oxford, Martin Robertson, 1974.

Oakley, A., *Housewife*, London, Allen Lane, 1984.

Pizzey, E., *Scream Quietly or the Neighbours Will Hear*, Harmondsworth, Penguin, 1974.

Reid, I. and Wormald, E., (eds), *Sex Differences in Britain*, Oxford, Grant McIntyre, 1982.

Richards, J. R., *The Sceptical Feminist*, Harmondsworth, Penguin, 1982.

Roberts, H. (ed.), *Doing Feminist Research*, London, Routledge & Kegan Paul, 1981.

Rowbotham, S., *Women's Consciousness, Man's World*, Harmondsworth, Penguin, 1973.

Rowe, M., (ed.), *Spare Rib Reader*, Harmondsworth, Penguin, 1982.

Sharpe, S., *Just Like a Girl: How Girls Learn to be Women*, Harmondsworth, Penguin, 1976.

Showalter, E., *A Literature of Their Own: British Women Novelists from Brontë to Lessing*, London, Virago, 1982.

Smart, C. and Smart, B. (eds), *Women, Sexuality and Social Control*, London, Routledge & Kegan Paul, 1978.

Smith, P. M., *Language, the Sexes and Society*, Oxford, Blackwell, 1985.

Spencer, J., *The Rise of the Woman Novelist: from Aphra Behn to Jane Austen*, Oxford, Blackwell, 1986.

Stacey, M. and Price, M., *Women, Power and Politics*, London, Tavistock, 1981.

Stubbs, P., *Women and Fiction: Feminism and the Novel, 1880–1920*, Brighton, Harvester, 1979.

Ungerson, C., *Women and Social Policy*, London, Macmillan, 1985.

Wandor, M. (ed.), *The Body Politic: Writings from the Women's Liberation Movement in Britain, 1969–1972*, London, Stage One Publications, 1972.

Westwood, S., *All Day, Every Day: Factory and Family in the Making of Women's Lives*, London, Pluto, 1984.

White, C., *Women's Magazines: A Sociological Inquiry*, London, Michael Joseph, 1970.

Wilson, E., *Only Halfway to Paradise: Women in Postwar Britain, 1945–1968*, London, Tavistock, 1980.

HISTORY

Branca, P., *Silent Sisterhood: Middle Class Women in Victorian Homes*, London, Croom Helm, 1975.

Clarke, J., *In Our Grandmothers' Footsteps: A Virago Guide to London*, London, Virago, 1984.

Davidson, C., *A Woman's Work Is Never Done: A History of Housework in the British Isles, 1650–1950*, London, Chatto and Windus, 1982.

Delamont, S. and Duffin, L., *The Nineteenth Century Woman: Her Cultural and Physical World*, London, Croom Helm, 1978.

Duffin, L. (ed.), *Women and Work in Pre-Industrial Britain*, London, Croom Helm, 1985.

Forster, M., *Significant Sisters: The Grassroots of Active Feminism, 1839–1939*, London, Heinemann, 1984.

Fulford, R., *Votes for Women: The Story of a Struggle*, London, Faber, 1957.

Garner, L., *Stepping Stones to Women's Liberty: Feminist Ideas in the Women's Suffrage Movement, 1900–1918*, Aldershot, Gower, 1984.

Harrison, B., *Separate Spheres: The Opposition to Women's Suffrage in Britain, 1867–1928*, London, Croom Helm, 1978.

Lewis, J., *Women in England, 1870–1950: Sexual Divisions and Social Change*, Brighton, Harvester, 1984.

Liddington, J. and Norris, J., *One Hand Tied Behind Us: The Rise of the Women's Suffrage Movement*, London, Virago, 1978.

McBride, T., *The Domestic Revolution*, London, Croom Helm, 1976.

Pankhurst, S., *The Suffragette Movement*, London, Virago, 1977.

Prior, M. (ed.), *Women in English Society, 1500–1800*, London, Methuen, 1985.

Ramelson, M., *Petticoat Rebellion: A Century of Struggle for Women's Rights*, London, Lawrence and Wishart, 1967.

Roberts, E., *A Woman's Place: An Oral History of Working Class Women, 1890–1940*, Oxford, Blackwell, 1985.

Rowbotham, S., *Hidden from History*, London, Pluto, 1973.

Stenton, D. M., *The English Woman in History*, New York, Schocken, 1978.

Strachey, R., *The Cause: A Short History of the Women's Movement in Great Britain*, London, Virago, 1978.

Vicinus, M. (ed.), *Suffer and Be Still: Women in the Victorian Age*, London, Methuen, 1980.

Wollstonecraft, M., *A Vindication of the Rights of Women*, London, Dent, 1970.

PART II
PERIODICALS, JOURNALS, MAGAZINES

The following is a select list of periodicals, journals and magazines under general headings relating to British life, society and culture.

For more comprehensive lists including information concerning frequency of publication, price, etc. see: Benn Publications (publisher), *Benn's Media Directory, incorporating Benn's Press Directory*, annually; Bowker (publisher), *Ulrich's International Periodicals Directory: A Classified Guide to Current Periodicals, Foreign and Domestic*, biennially; Thomas Skinner Directories (publisher), Willing's Press Guide, annually; Walford, J. (ed.), *Walford's Guide to Current British Periodicals, vol. 1, Humanities and Social Sciences*, 1985.

1 BROADCASTING AND MEDIA

Broadcast
32–4 Great Marlborough Street
London W1V 1HA

Campaign
22 Lancaster Gate
London W2 3LY

Independent Broadcasting
Independent Broadcasting Authority
70 Brompton Road
London SW3 1EY

Intermedia
International Institute of
    Communications
Tavistock House South
Tavistock Square
London WC1H 9LF

Journalist
314 Gray's Inn Road
London WC1X 8DP

The Listener
BBC Publications
35 Marylebone High Street
London W1M 4AA

London Calling
PO Box 76
Bush House
Strand
London WC2B 4PH

Media Education
Comedia
9 Poland Street
London W1V 3DG

Media, Culture and Society
Sage Publications Ltd.
28 Banner Street
London EC1Y 8QE

The Media Reporter
Brennan Publications
148 Birchover Way
Allestree
Derby DE 2RW

Media Week
20–2 Wellington Street
London WC2E 7DD

Radio Times
BBC Publications
35 Marylebone High Street
London W1M 4AA

Television
IPC Magazines Ltd
King's Reach Tower
Stamford Street
London SE1 9LS

Television Weekly
Television and Communication
Publishing Ltd
1st Floor
Consort House
Queensway
London WC2

TV Times
Independent Television Publications
247 Tottenham Court Road
London W1P 0AU

2 CURRENT AFFAIRS

Conservative Newsline (formerly
  Conservative News)
Conservative Central Office
32 Smith Square
London SW2P 3HH

Contemporary Review
61 Carey Street
London WC2 2JG

Crossbow
Bow Publications Ltd
240 Holborn
London WC1

Economist
25 St James's Street
London SW1A 1HG

Encounter
59 St Martin's Lane
London WC2N 4JS

Fabian News
Fabian Society
11 Dartmouth Street
London SW1 9BN

Guardian Weekly
Guardian Publications
164 Deansgate
Manchester M60 2RR

Illustrated London News
Elm House
10–16 Elm Street
London WC1X 0BP

International Affairs
Butterworth Scientific Ltd
Journals Division
PO Box 63
Westbury House
Bury Street
Guildford
Surrey GU2 5BH

International Socialism
Socialist Workers' Party
PO Box 82
London E2 9DS

Keesing's Contemporary Archives
Longman Group UK Ltd
6th Floor
Westgate House
The High
Harlow
Essex CM20 1NE

Labour Monthly
Unity Publications
134 Ballards Lane
London N3 2PD

Labour Research
LRD Publications Ltd
78 Blackfriars Road
London SE1 8HF

Labour Weekly
150 Walworth Road
London SE17 1JT

The Leveller: New Radical Examiner
52 Acre Lane,
London SW2 5SP

Liberal News
1 Whitehall Place
London SW1A 2HE

Liberator
c/o The National Liberal Club
1 Whitehall Place
London SW1A 2HE

Marxism Today
16 St John Street
London EC1M 4AY

New Edinburgh Review
1 Buccleuch Place
Edinburgh EH8 9LW

New Left Review
15 Greek Street
London W1E 6Q2

New Socialist
Labour Party
150 Walworth Road
London SE17 1JT

New Statesman
38 Kingsland Road
London E2 8BA

The Salisbury Review
7 Lord North Street
London SW1

Socialist Review
Socialist Workers' Party
PO Box 82
London E2 9DS

Spectator
56 Doughty Street
London WC1N 2LL

The Spokesman
Bertrand Russell House
Gamble Street
Nottingham NG 4ET

Survey of Current Affairs
HMSO
PO Box 276
London SW8 5DT

Tribune
308 Gray's Inn Road
London WC1X 8DY

3 ECONOMICS

Applied Economics
Chapman and Hall Ltd
11 New Fetter Lane
London EC4P 4EE

British Economy Survey
Oxford University Press
Education Dept
Walton Street
Oxford OX2 6DP

British Review of Economic Issues
Polytechnic of North London
129–33 Camden High Street
London NW1 7DU

Bulletin of Economic Research
Basil Blackwell Ltd
108 Cowley Road
Oxford OX4 1JF

Cambridge Economic Policy Review
Gower Publishing Co. Ltd
Gower House
Aldershot
Hants GU11 3HR

Cambridge Journal of Economics
Academic Press Ltd
24–8 Oval Road
London NW1 7DX

Capital and Class
Conference of Socialist Economists
25 Horsell Road
London N5

Contents of Recent Economic
  Journals
HMSO
PO Box 276
London SW8 5DT

Economic Affairs
MFL Publications Ltd
3–4 St Andrews Hill
London EC4V 5BY

Economic Bulletin
Gower Press
1 Westmead
Farnborough
Hampshire

The Economic Journal
Cambridge University Press
PO Box 110
Cambridge CB2 3RL

Economic Outlook
Gower Publishing Co. Ltd
Gower House
Croft Road
Aldershot
Hampshire GU11 3HR

Economic Policy Review
Department of Applied Economics
University of Cambridge
Cambridge CB3 9DE

Economic Review
Basil Blackwell Ltd
108 Cowley Road
Oxford OX4 1JF

Economic Trends
HMSO
PO Box 276
London SW8 5DT

Economica
London School of Economics and
  Political Science
Houghton Street
London WC2A 2AE

Economics
The Economics Association
Temple Lodge
South Street
Ditchling
Hassocks
Sussex BN6 8UQ

Economics Selections - An
  International Bibliography
Gordon and Breach Science
  Publishers
42 William IV Street
London WC2N 4DE

The Economist
Economist Newspaper Co. Ltd
25 St James's Street
London SW1A 1HG

Economist Advisory Group News
Economist Advisory Group Ltd
56b Tottenham Court Road
London W1P 9RE

Economy and Society
Routledge & Kegan Paul
11 New Fetter Lane
London EC4P 4EE

Finance International
Irving A. Laidlaw
70 Warren Street
London W1P 5PA

Financial Statistics
HMSO

PO Box 276
London SW8 5DT

Financial Weekly
Fleet Financial Publishing Ltd
Westgate House
9 Holborn
London EC1N 2LL

Fiscal Studies
Basil Blackwell Ltd
108 Cowley Road
Oxford OX4 1JF

Framework Forecasts For the EEC
  Economies
2–4 Tudor Street
London EC4Y

Framework Forecasts For the UK
2–4 Tudor Street
London EC4Y

History of Economic Thought
  Newsletter
Department of Economics
Queen's University
Belfast BT7 1NN

International Journal of Social
  Economics
MCB Publications Ltd
198–200 Keighley Road
Bradford BD9 4JQ

Journal of The Institute of Bankers
Institute of Bankers
10 Lombard Street
London EC3V 9AS

Monthly Digest of Statistics
HMSO
PO Box 276
London SW8 5DT

National Institute Economic Review
National Institute of Economic and
  Social Research

279

2 Dean Trench Street
Smith Square
London SW1P 3HE

Oxford Bulletin of Economics and
　Statistics
Journals Department
Basil Blackwell Ltd
108 Cowley Road
Oxford OX4 1JF

Oxford Economic Papers
Oxford University Press
Journal Subscriptions Department
Walton Street
Oxford OX2 6DP

Oxford Review of Economic Policy
Journals Department

Oxford University Press
Walton Street
Oxford OX2 6DP

Socialist Economic Review
Merlin Press Ltd
3 Manchester Road
London EC14

Socio-Economic Planning Sciences
Pergamon Press Ltd
Headington Hill Hall
Oxford OX3 0BW

Statistical News
HMSO
PO Box 276
London SW8 5DT

4 EDUCATION

British Book News
The British Council
65 Davies Street
London W1Y 2AA

British Education Index
British Library Bibliographical
  Services Division
Store Street
London WC1E 7DG

British Educational Research Journal
Carfax Publishing Co.
Haddon House
Dorchester-on-Thames
Oxford OX9 8JZ

British Journal of Educational
  Studies
Basil Blackwell Ltd
108 Cowley Road
Oxford OX4 1JF

British Journal of Educational
  Technology
Council for Educational Technology
3 Devonshire Street
London W1N 2BA

British Journal of Teacher Education
Methuen and Co Ltd
11 New Fetter Lane
London EC4P 4EE

British Library Journal
Journals Subscriptions Department
Oxford University Press
Walton Street
Oxford OX2 6DP

Bulletin of Educational Research
Newcastle Polytechnic
Department of Humanities
Ellison Place
Newcastle-upon-Tyne

Cambridge Journal of Education
Cambridge Institute of Education
Shaftesbury Road
Cambridge CB2 2BY

Collaborative Research Newsletter
Centre for Educational Sociology
University of Edinburgh
7 Buccleuch Place
Edinburgh

CORE - Collected Original
  Resources in Education
Carfax Publishing Co.
Haddon House
Dorchester-on-Thames
Oxford OX9 8JZ

Education
Longman Group UK Ltd
Longman House
Burnt Mill
Harlow
Essex CM20 2JE

Educational Research
NFER Publishing Co. Ltd
Darville House
2 Oxford Road East
Windsor
Berkshire SL4 1DF

Educational Review
Carfax Publishing Co.

Haddon House
Dorchester-on-Thames
Oxford OX9 8JZ

Educational Studies
Carfax Publishing Co.
Haddon House
Dorchester-on-Thames
Oxford OX9 8JZ

European Journal of Education
Carfax Publishing Co.
Haddon House
Dorchester-on-Thames
Oxford OX9 8JZ

Forum - For The Discussion of New
    Trends in Education
PSW Publications
11 Pendene Road
Leicester

Higher Education Current
    Awareness Bulletin
University of Aston in Birmingham
    Library
Gosta Green
Birmingham B4 7ET

Higher Education Review
Tyrrell Burgess Associates Ltd
34 Sandilands
Croydon
Surrey CR0 5DB

History of Education
Taylor and Francis Ltd
10–14 Macklin Street
London WC2B 5NF

Journal of Curriculum Studies
Taylor and Francis Ltd
10–14 Macklin Street
London WC2B 5NF

Journal of Educational
    Administration and History
The School of Education
Education Museum
Room 14
Parkinson Court
University of Leeds
Leeds LS2 9JT

Journal of Philosophy of Education
Carfax Publishing Co.
Haddon House
Dorchester-on-Thames
Oxford OX9 8JZ

New Universities Quarterly
Basil Blackwell Ltd
108 Cowley Road
Oxford OX4 1JF

Oxford Review of Education
Carfax Publishing Co.
Haddon House
Dorchester-on-Thames
Oxford OX9 8JZ

Primary Education Review
National Union of Teachers
Hamilton House
Mabledon Place
London WC1H 9BD

Research in Education
Manchester University Press
Oxford Road
Manchester M13 9PL

Secondary Education Journal
National Union of Teachers
Hamilton House
Mabledon Place
London WC1H 9BD

Sociology of Education Abstracts
Open University
Walton Hall
Milton Keynes
Buckinghamshire MK7 6AA

Studies in Adult Education
National Institute of Adult
  Education
198 De Monfort Street
Leicester LE1 7GE

Studies in Higher Education
Carfax Publishing Company
Haddon House
Dorchester-on-Thames
Oxford OX9 8JZ

The Teacher
Hamilton House
Mabledon Place
London WC1H 9BS

Times Educational Supplement
Priory House
St John's Lane
London EC1M 4BX

Times Higher Education Supplement
Priory House
St John's Lane
London EC1M 4BX

Trends in Education
HMSO
PO Box 276
London SW8 5DT

Universities Quarterly
Basil Blackwell Ltd
108 Cowley Road
Oxford OX4 1JF

Where
Advisory Centre for Education
18 Victoria Square
Bethnal Green
London E2 9PB

5 ENVIRONMENT AND GEOGRAPHY

Area
Institute of British Geographers
1 Kensington Gore
London SW7 2AR

Country Life
IPC Magazines Ltd
King's Reach Tower
Stamford Street
London SE1 9LS

The Countryman
Sheep Street
Burford
Oxford OX8 4LH

Country-Side
Thorneyholme Hall
Roughlee
Burnley
Lancashire BB12 9LH

Geo Abtracts
University of East Anglia
Norwich NR4 7JT

Geographical Journal
Royal Geographical Society
1 Kensington Gore
London SW7 2AR

Geographical Magazine
IPC Magazines Ltd
King's Reach Tower
Stamford Street
London SE1 9LS

Geography
George Philip and Sons Ltd
12–14 Long Acre
London WC2E 9LP

Journal of Geography in Higher
    Education
Oxford Polytechnic
Headington
Oxford OX3 0BP

Teaching Geography
Geographical Association
343 Fulwood Road
Sheffield S10 3BP

Transactions
Institute of British Geographers
1 Kensington Gore
London SW7 2AR

6 EUROPE

Bulletin of the European
  Communities Commission
HMSO
PO Box 276
London SW8 5DT

Common Market Signposts
European Community Information
  Services
88–90 Gray's Inn Road
London WC1

Economic Bulletin for Europe
Pergamon Press Ltd
Headington Hall
Oxford OX3 0BW

Eudised R & D Bulletin
Darville House
2 Oxford Road East
Windsor
Berkshire SL4 1DF

Europe
Commission of the European
  Communities
8 Storey's Gate
London SW1P 3AT

European Bulletin and Press
39 Stanwick Mans
Stanwick Road
London W14

European Community Information
Commission of the European
  Communities
Office for Official Publications of the
  European Communities

Boîte Postale 1003
Luxembourg

European Economic Review
European Scientific Association of
  Applied Economics
North Holland Publishing Co.
Box 211
100 AE Amsterdam
Netherlands

European Economy
HMSO
PO Box 276
London SW8 5DT

European Trends
Economist Intelligence Unit Ltd
Spencer House
27 St James's Place
London SW1A 1NT

Exploring Europe
Sussex European Research Centre
University of Sussex
Falmer
Brighton BN1 9RH

Framework Forecasts for EEC
  Economies
The Henley Centre for Forecasting
2 Tudor Street
Blackfriars
London EC4Y 0AA

Journal of Common Market Studies
Basil Blackwell Ltd
108 Cowley Road
Oxford OX4 1JF

New European
Blenheim Court Publishing
Blenheim Court
66 High Street
Whitham
Essex CM8 1AH

Parliamentary and Common Market
   News Bulletin
19 Kingsdowne Road
Surbiton KT6 6JZ

Studies in European Politics
Policy Studies Institute
1–2 Castle Lane
London SW1E 6DR

Teaching About Europe
Sussex European Research Centre
University of Sussex
Falmer
Brighton BN1 9RH

Vacher's European Companion
A. S. Kerswill Ltd
Leeder House
Erskine Road
London NW3

West European Politics
Frank Cass Ltd
Gainsborough House
11 Gainsborough Road
London E11 1RS

7 FILM AND VIDEO

Film
The British Federation of Film
  Societies
81 Dean Street
London W1V 6AA

Films and Filming
Brever Publishing Ltd
PO Box 252
2 and 4 Old Pye Street
London SW1P 2LR

Films on Screen and Video
Ocean Publications
22–4 Buckingham Palace Road
London SW1

Film Review
Old Court House
Old Court Place
Kensington
London W8 4PD

Historical Journal of Film
  Radio and Television
Carfax Publishing Co.
Haddon House
Dorchester-on-Thames OX9 8J2

Monthly Film Bulletin
British Film Institute
81 Dean Street
London W1V 6AA

Screen
SEFT
29 Old Compton Street
London W1V 5PL

Screen Digest
37 Gower Street
London WC1E 6HH

Screen International
6–7 Great Chapel Street
London W1V 3AG

Sight and Sound
British Film Institute
127 Charing Cross Road
London WC2H 0EA

Stills
Stills Publishing Co. Ltd
6 Denmark Street
London WC2H 8LP

Video - The Magazine
Link House Video Ltd
Link House
Dingwall Avenue
Croydon CR9 2TA

Video Today
Argus Specialist Publications Ltd
1 Goden Square
London W1R 3AB

8 GOVERNMENT AND ADMINISTRATION

Civic Index: A Guide to Local
  Government Literature
Humberside Libraries and Amenities
Central Library
Albion Street
Hull

County Councils Gazette
Association of County Councils
66A Eaton Square
London SW1W 9BH

Daily List of Government
  Publications
HMSO Bookshop
49 High Holborn
London WC1V 6HB

District Councils Review
Association of District Councils
25 Buckingham Gate
London SW1E 6LE

European Information Service
International Union of Local
  Authorities/Council of European
  Municipalities
36 Old Queen Street
London SW1

Government Publications Review
Pergamon Press Ltd
Headington Hill Hall
Oxford OX3 0BW

House of Commons Weekly
  Information Bulletin
Public Information Office
House of Commons
London SW1A 0AA

Journal of Public Policy
Cambridge University Press
The Edinburgh Building
Shaftesbury Road
Cambridge CB2 2RU

Knight's Local Government Reports
Charles Knight and Co. Ltd
Tolley House
17 Scarbrook Road
Croydon CR0 15Q

Local Council Review
National Association of Local
  Councils
100 Great Russell Street
London WC1B 3LD

Local Government Chronicle
Brown, Knight and Truscott Ltd
11–12 Bury Street
London EC3A 5AP

Local Government News
B and M Publications Ltd
PO Box 13
Hereford House
Bridle Path
Croydon
Surrey CR9 4NL

Local Government Policy Making
Longman Group UK Ltd
6th Floor Westgate House
The High
Harlow
Essex CM20 1NE

Local Government Review
Justice of the Peace Ltd
Little London
Chichester
Sussex PO19 1PG

Local Government Studies
Charles Knight and Co. Ltd
25 Bew Street Square
London EC4A 3JA

London Gazette
(Belfast Gazette)
(Edinburgh Gazette)
HMSO
PO Box 276
London SW8 5DT

Monthly Digest of Statistics
HMSO
PO Box 276
London SW8 5DT

Municipal and Public Services
   Journal
178–202 Great Portland Street
London W1N 6NH

Municipal Review
Association of Metropolitan
   Authorities
36 Old Queen Street
London SW1H 9JE

Parliamentary Affairs
Journal Subscriptions Dept
Oxford University Press
Walton Street
Oxford OX2 6DP

Parliamentary Debates
House of Commons–Hansard

HMSO
PO Box 276
London SW8 5DT

Parliamentary Debates
House of Lords –Hansard
HMSO
PO Box 276
London SW8 5DT

Parliamentary Index: Index to
   Parliamentary Debates
Humberside Libraries and Amenities
Central Library
Albion Street
Hull

Parliamentary Newsletter
Commonwealth Parliamentary
   Association
7 Old Palace Yard
London SW1

PSI Reports
Policy Studies Institute
1–2 Castle Lane
London SW1E 6DR

Public Administration
Royal Institute of Public
   Administration
3 Birdcage Walk
London SW1H 8JJ

Public Law
Stevens and Sons Ltd
11 New Fetter Lane
London EC4P 4EE

Red Tape
Civil and Public Services Association
215 Balham High Road
London SW17 7BN

Vacher's Parliamentary Companion
A. S. Kerswill Ltd
Leeder House
Erskine Road
London NW3 3AJ

9 HISTORY

Bulletin of the Institute of Historical
  Research
Institute of Historical Research
University of London
Senate House
Malet Street
London WC1E 7HU

Bulletin of the Society for the Study
  of Labour History
Society for the Study of Labour
  History
University of Warwick
Coventry CV4 7AL

Economic History Review
Economic History Society
London School of Economics and
  Political Science
Houghton Street
London WC2A 2AE

English Historical Review
Longman Group UK Ltd
Longman House
Burnt Mill
Harlow
Essex CM20 2JE

Guildhall Studies in London History
Guildhall Library
London EC2P 2EJ

The Historical Journal
Cambridge University Press
PO Box 110
Cambridge CB2 3RL

History
The Historical Association
59A Kennington Park Road
London SE11 4JH

History Today
History Today Ltd
83–84 Berwick Street
London W1V 3PJ

History Workshop - A Journal of
  Socialist Historians
History Workshop
PO Box 69
Oxford OX2 7XA

Journal of Contemporary History
Sage Publications Ltd
28 Banner Street
London EC1Y 8QE

Journal of Imperial and
  Commonwealth History
Frank Cass and Co. Ltd
Gainsborough House
11 Gainsborough Road
London E11 1RS

Local Historian
British Association for Local History
43 Bedford Square
London WC1B 3DP

Local History Bulletin
Forest of Dean Newspapers Ltd
Coleford
Gloucestershire

Past and Present - A Journal of
  Historical Studies
Past and Present Society
175 Banbury Road
Oxford OX2 7AW

Scottish Historical Review
The Company of Scottish History
  Ltd
c/o Aberdeen University Press
Farmers Hall
Aberdeen AB9 2XT

Social History
Methuen and Co. Ltd
11 New Fetter Lane
London EC4P 4EE

Teaching History
The Historical Association
59A Kennington Park Road
London SE11 4JH

10 INDUSTRY AND COMMERCE

Bank of England Quarterly Bulletin
Economic Intelligence Department
London EC2R 8AH

The Banker
Financial Times Business
   Information Ltd
102–8 Clerkenwell Road
London EC1M 5SA

The Bankers' Magazine
BPC (Bankers' Magazine) Ltd
Holywell House
Worship Street
London EC2A 2EN

Banking World
Maxwell House
74 Worship Street
London EC2A 2EN

British Business
HMSO
PO Box 276
London SW8 5DT

British Tax Review
Sweet and Maxwell Ltd
11 New Fetter Lane
London EC4P 4EE

Business
Business People Publications
   Ltd
234 King's Road
London SW3 5UA

Business and Government
Alan Armstrong and Associates Ltd
72 Park Road
London NW1 4SH

Business History
Frank Cass Ltd
Gainsborough House
11 Gainsborough Road
London E11 1RS

Business News
Euro Publications Ltd
Euro House
14 Pearl Street
Cardiff CF1 1HD

Business Review
SDH Publications Ltd
The Lawns
Mount Pleasant
St Albans
Hertfordshire AL3 4TJ

CBI Economic Situation Report
Confederation of British Industry
21 Tothill Street
London SW1H 9LP

CBI Industrial Trends Survey
Confederation of British Industry
21 Tothill Street
London SW1H 9LP

CBI Review
Confederation of British Industry
21 Tothill Street
London SW1H 9LP

Corporate Financial Letter
Centre for Legal and Business
   Information
Rectory Road

Great Waldingfield
Sudbury
Suffolk CO20 2TL

The Director
116 Pall Mall
London SW1Y 5ED

Economic Trends
HMSO
PO Box 276
London SW8 5DT

The Economist
25 St James's Street
London SW1A 1HG

Financial Times
Bracken House
10 Cannon Street
London EC4P 4BY

Financial Weekly
Fleet Financial Publishing Ltd
Westgate House
9 Holborn
London EC1M 2LL

Industrial Law Journal
Stevens and Sons Ltd
11 New Fetter Lane
London EC4P 4EE

Industrial Relations Journal
Business Publications Ltd
Waterloo Road
London SE1 8UL

Industrial Relations Review and
  Report
Industrial Relations Services
67 Maygrove Road
London NW6 2EJ

The Investment Analyst
The Society of Investment Analysis
211–3 High Street
Bromley BR1 1NY

Investment Markets
2–4 Tudor Street
London EC4Y 0AA

Investors Chronicle
Financial Times Business Publishing
  Ltd
Greystoke Place
Fetter Lane
London EC4A 1ND

Journal of Business Finance and
  Accounting
Basil Blackwell Ltd.
108 Cowley Road
Oxford OX4 1JF

Journal of Commerce
Journal of Commerce and Shipping,
  Telegraph Ltd
213 Tower Building
Water Street
Liverpool L3 1LN

Journal of Industrial Economics
Basil Blackwell Ltd
108 Cowley Road
Oxford OX4 1JF

London Business School Journal
London Business School
Sussex Place
Regent's Park
London NW1 4SA

Management Bibliographies and
  Reviews
MCB University Press Ltd
198–200 Keighley Road
Bradford BD9 4JQ

Management Today
Management Publications Ltd
76 Dean Street
London W1A 1BU

293

Overseas Trade Statistics of the
  United Kingdom
HMSO
PO Box 276
London SW8 5DT

Quarterly Economic Reviews
Economist Intelligence Unit
27 St James's Street
London SW1A 1NT

Small Business
The Small Business Bureau
32 Smith Square
London SW1P 3HH

Talking Points on Britain's Economy
British Overseas Trade Board
Publications Sales Unit
Export House
50 Ludgate Hill
London EC4

11 LANGUAGE

Annual Review of Applied
  Linguistics
Cambridge University Press
The Edinburgh Building
Shaftesbury Road
Cambridge CB2 2RU

Applied Linguistics
Oxford University Press
Walton Street
Oxford OX2 6DP

Applied Psycholinguistics
Cambridge University Press
The Edinburgh Building
Shaftesbury Road
Cambridge CB2 2RU

Archivum Linguisticum: A Review
  of Comparative and General
  Linguistics
Mansell Publishing Co.
3 Bloomsbury Place
London WC1A 2QA

Audio-Visual Language Journal
British Association for Language
  Teaching
80 Dene Road
Wylam
Northumberland NE41 8HB

BBC English
Mary Glasgow Publications Ltd
140 Kensington Church Street
London W8 4BN

EFL Gazette
Pergamon Press Ltd

Headington Hill Hall
Oxford OX3 0BH

English
Journals Department
Oxford University Press
Walton Street
Oxford OX2 6DP

English Language Notes
University of Colorado
Boulder CO 80309
USA

English Language Teaching Journal
Journals Department
Oxford University Press
Walton Street
Oxford OX2 6DP

English Today
Cambridge University Press
Edinburgh Building
Shaftesbury Road
Cambridge CB2 2RU

The ESP Journal
Pergamon Press Ltd
Headington Hill Hall
Oxford OX3 0BW

The Incorporated Linguist
Institute of Linguists
42A Highbury Grove
London N5 2EA

IRAL: International Review of
  Applied Linguistics in Language
  Teaching

Journals Department
Oxford University Press
Walton Street
Oxford OX2 6DP

Journal of the International Phonetic
  Association
International Phonetic Association
University College
Gower Street
London WC1E 6BY

Journal of Linguistics
Cambridge University Press
Edinburgh Building
Shaftesbury Road
Cambridge CB2 2RU

Journal of Phonetics
Academic Press Ltd
24–8 Oval Road
London NW1 7DX

Language and Speech
Kingston Press Services Ltd
28 High Street
Teddington
Middlesex TW11 8EW

Language in Society
Cambridge University Press
The Edinburgh Building
Shaftesbury Road
Cambridge CB2 2RU

Language Teaching and Linguistic
  Abstracts
Cambridge University Press
Edinburgh Building
Shaftesbury Road
Cambridge CB2 2RU

Language Testing
Edward Arnold
41 Bedford Square
London WC1B 3DQ

Linguistics
Mouton Publishers
Noordeinde 41
2514 GC
The Hague
Netherlands

Logophile: The Cambridge Journal
  of Words and Language
Logophile Press
47–9 Caledonian Road
London N1 9BU

Modern English Teacher
Modern English Publications Ltd
PO Box 129
Oxford OX2 8JU

Notes and Queries
Journals Department
Oxford University Press
Walton Street
Oxford OX2 6DP

Practical English Teaching
Mary Glasgow Publications Ltd
140 Kensington Church Street
London W8 4BN

Review of English Studies
Journals Department
Oxford University Press
Walton Street
Oxford OX2 6DP

UEA Papers in Linguistics
University of East Anglia
University Plain
Norwich NR4 7TJ

The Use of English
Scottish Academic Press Ltd
33 Montgomery Street
Edinburgh EH7 5JX

Verbatim: The Language Quarterly
Laurence Urdany
Market House
Market Square
Aylesbury
Buckinghamshire

World Language English
Pergamon Press Ltd

Headington Hill Hall
Oxford OX3 0BW

York Papers in Linguistics
Department of Language
University of York
Heslington
York YO1 5DD

12 LAW

British Journal of Law and Society
University College Cardiff Press
University College
PO Box 78
Cardiff
CF1 1XL

Bulletin of Legal Developments
British Institute of International and
    Comparative Law
17 Russell Square
London WC1B 5DR

The Cambridge Law Journal
Cambridge University Press
PO Box 110
Cambridge CB2 3RL

City of London Law Review
Department of Law
City of London Polytechnic
84 Moorgate
London EC2 6SQ

Commercial Laws of Europe
Europe Law Centre Ltd
Elm House
10–16 Elm Street
London WC1X 0PB

Common Market Law Reports
European Law Centre Ltd
Elm House
10–16 Elm Street
London WC1X 0BP

Criminal Law Review
Sweet and Maxwell
11 New Fetter Lane
London EC4P 4EE

Current Law
Sweet and Maxwell
11 New Fetter Lane
London EC4P 4EE

Eurolaw Commercial Intelligence
European Law Centre Ltd
Elm House
10–16 Elm Street
London WC1X 0BP

European Commercial Cases
European Law Centre Ltd
Elm House
10–16 Elm Street
London WC1X 0BP

European Law Digest
European Law Centre Ltd
Elm House
10–16 Elm Street
London WC1X 0BP

European Law Review
Sweet and Maxwell
11 New Fetter Lane
London EC4P 4EE

Howard Journal of Criminal Justice
Basil Blackwell Ltd
108 Cowley Road
Oxford OX4 1JF

Industrial Relations Legal
    Information Bulletin
Industrial Relations Services
67 Maygrove Road
London NW6 2EJ

Journal of Business Law
Stevens & Sons Ltd
11 New Fetter Lane
London EC4P 4EE

Journal of Criminal Law
Pageant Publishing
5 Turners Wood
London NW11 6TD

Journal of Law and Society
Basil Blackwell Ltd
108 Cowley Road
Oxford OX4 1JF

Journal of Social Welfare Law
Sweet and Maxwell
11 New Fetter Lane
London EC4P 4EE

Law Notes
25–6 Chancery Lane
London WC2A 1NB

Law Quarterly Review
Stevens & Sons Ltd
11 New Fetter Lane
London EC4P 4EE

The Law Society's Gazette
The Law Society
113 Chancery Lane
London WC2 1PL

Legal Action Group Bulletin
Legal Action Group
28a Highgate Road
London NW5 1NS

Legal Studies
Butterworth & Co.
Borough Green
Sevenoaks
Kent
TN15 81H

Managerial Law
MCB Publications Limited
198–200 Keighley Road
Bradford BD9 4JQ

The Modern Law Review
Stevens & Sons Ltd
11 New Fetter Lane
London EC4P 4EE

New Law Journal
Butterworths
88 Kingsway
London WC2B 6AB

Oxford Journal of Legal Studies
Journals Department
Oxford University Press
Walton Street
Oxford OX2 6DP

Public Law
Stevens & Sons Ltd
11 New Fetter Lane
London EC4P 4EE

The Solicitor's Journal
Oyez Longman Publishing Ltd
21–7 Lamb's Conduit Street
London WC1N 3NJ

Statute Law Review
Sweet and Maxwell
11 New Fetter Lane
London EC4P 4EE

Sweet and Maxwell's Students' Law
	Reporter
Sweet and Maxwell
11 New Fetter Lane
London EC4P 4EE

13 LITERARY STUDIES AND REVIEWS

Abstracts of English Studies
University of Calgary Press
1013 Library Tower
University of Calgary
2500 University Drive
N. W. Calgary
Alberta T2N 1NA
Canada

Books and Bookmen
Brevet Publishing Ltd
445 Brighton Road
South Croydon
Surrey
CR2 6EU

British Book News
The British Council
65 Davies Street
London W1Y 2AA

British Journal for Eighteenth
    Century Studies
British Society for Eighteenth
    Century Studies
Central Printing Unit
University of Southampton
Southampton SO9 5NH

Comparative Criticism
Cambridge University Press
The Edinburgh Building
Shaftesbury Road
Cambridge CB2 2RU

Contemporary Literature
University of Wisconsin Press
Journals Division
114 N. Murray Street

Madison
WI 53715
USA

Critical Quarterly
Manchester University Press
Oxford Road
Manchester M13 9PL

Criticism: A Quarterly for Literature
    and the Arts
Wayne State University Press
5959 Woodward Avenue
Detroit
MI 48202
USA

ELH: A Journal of English Literary
    History
Johns Hopkins University Press
Baltimore
MD 21218
USA

Encounter
59 St Martin's Lane
London WC2N 4JS

English Literary Renaissance
University of Massachusetts
Department of English
Amherst
MA 01003
USA

Index on Censorship
Writers and Scholars International
    Ltd
21 Russell Street
London WC2B 5HP

Journal of Commonwealth
  Literature
Journals Department
Oxford University Press
Walton Street
Oxford OX2 6DP

Journal of Narrative Technique
Society for the Study of Narrative
  Literature
Eastern Michigan University
Ypsilanti
Michigan 48197
USA

Journal of Women's Studies in
  Literature
Eden Press
3 Henrietta Street
London WC2E 8LU

Literary Monthly
44 Sillwood Road
Brighton
Sussex

The Literary Review
285 Madison Avenue
Madison
NJ 07940
USA

London Review of Books
6A Bedford Square
London WC1B 3RA

Modern Drama
Graduate Centre for the Study of
  Drama
University of Toronto Press
Front Campus
Toronto
Ontario M55 1A6
Canada

Modern Fiction Studies
Purdue University
Department of English

West Lafayette
IN 47907
USA

New Literary History
Johns Hopkins Press
Journals Division
Baltimore
Maryland 21218
USA

Nineteenth Century Fiction
University of California Press
Berkeley
CA 94720
USA

Oxford Literary Review
Department of English
The University
Southampton SO9 5NH

Prose Studies
Frank Cass and Co. Ltd
Gainsborough House
11 Gainsborough Road
London E11 1RS

Red Letters
16 St John Street
London EC1M 4AY

Review of English Studies
Oxford University Press
Journal Subscription Department
Walton Street
Oxford OX2 6DP

Shakespeare Quarterly
Folger Shakespeare Library
2016 Capital Street S. E.
Washington DC 20003
USA

Speculum: Journal of Medieval
  Studies
Medieval Academy of America
1430 Massachusetts Avenue

Cambridge
MA 02138
USA

Studies in English Literature
   1500–1900
PO Box 1892
Rice University
Houston
Texas 77251
USA

Studies in Philology
University of North Carolina
Box 2288
Chapel Hill
N. C. 27414
USA

Studies in Romanticism
Boston University Graduate School
236 Bay State Road
Boston
MA 02215
USA

Themes in Drama
Cambridge University Press
The Edinburgh Building
Shaftesbury Road
Cambridge CB2 2RU

Times Literary Supplement
Priory House
St John's Lane
London EC1M 4BX

Twentieth Century Literature
Hofstra University Press
Hemptsead
N. Y. 11550
USA

Victorian Studies
Department of English
University of Alberta
Edmonton
Alberta TG 2EL
Canada

14 MILITARY AND DISARMAMENT

Adelphi Papers
International Institute for Strategic
  Studies
23 Tavistock Street
London WC2E 7NQ

ADIU Report
Armament and Disarmament
  Information Unit
University of Sussex
Falmer
Brighton
Sussex BN1 9RF

Armed Forces
Ian Allan Ltd
Coomblands House
Addlestone
Weybridge
Surrey KT15 1HY

Arms Control
Frank Cass and Co. Ltd
Gainsborough House
Gainsborough Road
London E11 1RS

Army Quarterly and Defence Journal
1 West Street
Tavistock
Devon PL19 8DS

Bulletin of the Military Historical
  Society
National Army Museum
Royal Hospital Road
London SW3 4HT

Current Military Literature
The Military Press
92a Church Way
Iffley
Oxford OX4 4EF

Defence
Whitton Press Ltd
Park House
Park Street
Maidenhead
Berks SL6 1QS

European Nuclear Disarmament
  Bulletin
Bertrand Russell Peace Foundation
Gamble Street
Nottingham NT7 4EJ

Jane's Defence Weekly
Jane's Publishing Co. Ltd
238 City Road
London EC1V 2PU

The Journal of the Institute of Civil
  Defence
The Institute of Civil Defence
PO Box 229
3 Little Montague Court
London EC1P 1HN

Journal of Strategic Studies
Frank Cass and Co. Ltd
Gainsborough House
11 Gainsborough Road
London E11 1RS

Nato Review
Nato Information Services
1110 Brussels
Belgium

Navy News
HMS Nelson
Portsmouth
Hampshire PO1 3HH

Peace News
8 Elm Avenue
Nottingham NG3 4GF

RAF News
Royal Air Force
Turnstile House
97–9 High Holborn
London WC1V 6LL

Royal Air Forces Quarterly
Royal Air Forces Quarterly
   Association Ltd
43 Grove Park Road
London W4 3RU

RUSI Journal
Journal of the Royal United Services
   Institute for Defence Studies
Whitehall
London SW1A 2ET

Sanity
CND
11 Goodwin Street
Finsbury Park
London N4 3HQ

Soldier
HMSO
PO Box 569
London SE1 9NH

Survival
International Institute for Strategic
   Studies
23 Tavistock Street
London WC2E 7NQ

Warfare
Viewpoint Publications
4 Boscombe Avenue
London E10 6HY

15 MUSIC

Classical Music
52a Floral Street
London WC2E 9DA

Folk Music Journal
English Folk Dance and Song Society
2 Regent's Park Road
London NW1 7AY

Folk Music News
Goldcity Ltd
28 Gordon Mansions
Torrington Place
London WC1E 7HF

Journal of Musicological Research
Gordon and Breach Science
   Publishers Ltd
42 William IV Street
London WC2N 4DE

Melody Maker
IPC Magazines Ltd
King's Reach Tower
Stamford Street
London SE1 9LS

Music Analysis
Journals Department
Basil Blackwell Ltd
108 Cowley Road
Oxford OX4 1JF

Music Journal
Incorporated Society of Musicians
10 Stratford Place
London W1N 9AE

Music and Musicians
Brevet Publishing Ltd
445 Brighton Road
Croydon CR2 6EU

The Music Review
Heffers Printers Ltd
King's Hedges Road
Cambridge CB4 2PQ

Music Week
Spotlight Publications Ltd
40 Long Acre
London WC2E 9JT

Musical Times
8 Lower James Street
London W1R 4DN

New Musical Express
5–7 Carnaby Street
London W1V 1PG

Popular Music
Cambridge University Press
The Edinburgh Building
Shaftesbury Road
Cambridge CB2 2RU

Proceedings of the Royal Musical
   Association
The Royal Musical Association
c/o The British Library
Great Russell Street
London WC1B 3DG

Sounds
Spotlight Publications Ltd
40 Long Acre
London WC2E 9JT

16 PAINTING AND ARTS

Apollo Magazine
22 Davies Street
London W1Y 1LH

Ark
Royal College of Art
Kensington Gore
London SW7 2EU

Art and Antiques Weekly
Independent Magazines Ltd
Bridge House
181 Queen Victoria Street
London EC4V 4DD

Art and Artists
Brevet Publishing Ltd
445 Brighton Road
South Croydon
Surrey CR2 6EU

Art History
Basil Blackwell Ltd
108 Cowley Road
Oxford OX4 1JF

The Artist
The Artist Publishing Co. Ltd
102 High Street
Tenterden TN30 6HT

Burlington Magazine
Burlington Magazine Publications
   Ltd
Elm House
10–16 Elm Street
London WC1X 0BP

Connoisseur
Hearst Corporation
National Magazine House
72 Broadwick Street
London W1V 2BP

Federation of British Artists
   Quarterly
17 Carlton House Terrace
London SW1Y 5BD

Gallery
Gallery Publications
17 Pandora Road
West End Lane
London NW6 1TS

Journal of the Warburg and
   Courtauld Institutes
Warburg Institute
University of London
Woburn Square
London WC1H 0AB

Leonardo
Pergamon Press Ltd
Headington Hill Hall
Oxford OX3 0BW

The Literature of Art
Art Book Company
18 Endell Street
Covent Garden
London WC2H 9BD

The Oxford Art Journal
81 St Clements Street
Oxford OX4 1AW

The Scottish Review
Scottish Arts Council
24 George Square
Glasgow G2 1EF

Studio International
Journal of Modern Art
25 Denmark Street
London WC2H 8NJ

17 POETRY AND WRITING

Agenda
5 Cranbourne Court
Albert Bridge Road
London SW11 4PE

Ambit
Martin Bax
17 Priory Gardens
London NG6 5QY

Argo
Old Fire Station
40 George Street
Oxford OX1 2AQ

Atlas Anthology
10 Park Street
London SE1

Bananas
27 Royal Crescent
London W11

Candelabrum: A Magazine of Poetry
The Red Candle Press
19 South Hill Park
London NW3 2ST

Chapman
Chapman Magazines
35 East Claremont Street
Edinburgh EH7 4HT

Control
Control Magazine
5 London Mews
London W2

Counterpoint
Court Poetry Press
1 Rayleigh Court
Kingston-upon-Thames KT1 3NF

Equofinality
87 Lansdowne Road
Worcester WR3 8LJ

Figs
66 Oakfield Road
Finsbury Park
London N4

Forever
Michael O'Neill
Holtby House
Thwaite Street
Cottingham
Hull

Freesheet
Good Elf Publications
18 Clairview Road
London SW16 6G11

The Glasgow Magazine
The Mariscat Press
3 Mariscat Road
Glasgow G41 4ND

Global Tapestry Journal
1 Spring Bank
Salesbury
Blackburn
Lancashire BB1 9EV

Granta
Granta Publications Ltd
44a Hobson Street
Cambridge CB1 1NL

Great Works
Great Works Editions
25 Portland Road
Bishops Stortford
Hertfordshire

Iron
Iron Press
5 Marden Terrace
Cullercoats
North Shields
Tyne and Wear NE30 4PD

Kudso
7 Belle Vue Drive
Farsley
Pudsey
West Yorkshire LS28 5HG

The Little Word Machine
5 Beech Terrace
Undercliffe
Bradford
West Yorkshire BD3 0PY

Lines Review
M. Macdonald
Edgefield Road
Loanhead
Midlothian EH20 9SY

New Departures
Piedmont
Bisley
Stroud
Gloucestershire GL6 7BU

New Edinburgh Review
Edinburgh University Student
Publications Board
1 Buccleuth Place
Edinburgh EH8 9LW

New Fiction
New Fiction Society
196 Shaftesbury Ave
London WC2

New Poetry
Workshop Press
2 Culham Court
Granville Road
London N4 4JB

Ninth Decade
Oasis Books
52 Cascade Avenue
London N10

Not Poetry: Contemporary Prose
    Writing
Galloping Dog Press
45 Salisbury Gardens
Newcastle upon Tyne NE2 1HP

Outposts
Outposts Publications
77 Burwood Road
Walton-on-Thames
Surrey KT12 4QL

PN Review
208 Corn Exchange Buildings
Manchester 3BQ

Poetry Book Society Bulletin
Poetry Book Society Ltd
105 Piccadilly
London W1V 0AU

Poetry Quarterly
The Curlew Press
Harecott
Kettlesing
Harrogate

Poetry Review
The Poetry Society
21 Earl's Court Square
London SW5 9DE

The Present Tense: A Review of
  Modern Poetry
115 Princess Victoria Street
Clifton
Bristol BS8 4DD

Printers Pie
Aquila Publishing Co.
PO Box 1
Portree
Isle of Skye IV51 9BT

Prospice
Aqula Publishing Co.
PO Box 1
Portree
Isle of Skye IV51 9BT

Reality Studios
75 Balfour Street
London SE17

Rock Drill
Supranormal Cassettes
First Floor Flat
9 Hertslet Road
London N7

Slow Dancer
19 Devonshire Promenade
Lenton
Nottinghamshire

Spanner
64 Lanercost Road
London SW2 3DN

Spectacular Diseases
83b London Road
Peterborough
Cambridgeshire

Stand
179 Wingrove Road
Newcastle-upon-Tyne NE4 9DA

Words
T-F Associates
1st Floor
7 Chapel Road
Worthing
West Sussex BN11 1EG

Writing Women
19 Osborne Road
Newcastle-upon-Tyne NE2 2AH

18 POLITICAL STUDIES

British Journal of Political Science
Cambridge University Press
PO Box 110
Cambridge CB2 3RL

Commonwealth
World of Information
21 Gold Street
Saffron Waldron
Essex

Electoral Studies
Butterworth Scientific Ltd
Westbury House
Bury Street
Guildford
Surrey GU2 5BH

Government and Opposition: A
   Journal of Comparative Politics
London School of Economics and
   Political Science
Houghton Street
London WC2A 2AE

International Studies Quarterly
Butterworth Scientific Ltd
Westbury House
Bury Street
Guildford
Surrey GU2 5BH

Journal of Commonwealth and
   Comparative Politics
Frank Cass and Co. Ltd
Gainsborough House
11 Gainsborough Road
London E11 1RS

International Affairs
Butterworth Scientific Ltd
Journals Division
PO Box 63
Westbury House
Bury Street
Guildford
Surrey GU2 5BH

Keesing's Contemporary Archives
Longman Group UK Ltd
6th Floor Westgate House
The High
Harlow
Essex CM20 1NE

Parliamentary Affairs: Journal of the
   Hansard Society for
   Parliamentary Government
Oxford University Press
Walton Street
Oxford OX2 6DP

The Political Quarterly
Elm House
10–16 Elm Street
London WC1X 0BP

Political Studies
Butterworth Scientific Ltd
PO Box 63
Westbury House
Bury Street
Guildford
Surrey GU2 5BH

Politics
The Political Studies Association of
   the UK
Department of Government
University of Manchester
Manchester M13 9PL

PO Box 63
Westbury House
Bury Street
Guildford
Surrey GU2 5BU

The Round Table
The Commonwealth Journal of
   International Affairs
Butterworth Scientific Ltd

Teaching Politics
The Politics Association
16 Gower Street
London WC1E 6DP

19 PRESS

DAILY NEWSPAPERS

Daily Express
Fleet Street
London EC4P 4JT

Daily Mail
Northcliffe House
Tudor Street
London EC4Y 0JA

Daily Mirror
Holborn Circus
London EC1P 1DQ

Daily Star
Great Ancoats Street
Manchester M60 4HB

Daily Telegraph
135 Fleet Street
London EC4P 4BL

Financial Times
Bracken House
Cannon Street
London EC4P 4BY

Guardian
119 Farringdon Road
London EC1R 3ER

The Independent
40 City Road
London EC1Y 2DB

Morning Star
75 Farringdon Road
London EC1M 3JX

Sun
News Group Newpapers Ltd
30 Bouverie Street
London EC4Y 8DE

Today
70 Vauxhall Bridge Road
Pimlico
London SW1V 2RP

The Times
200 Gray's Inn Road
London WC1X 8EZ

SUNDAY NEWSPAPERS

Mail on Sunday
Northcliffe House
London EC4Y 0JA

News of the World
30 Bouverie Street
London EC4Y 8DE

Observer
8 St Andrews Hill
London EC4V 5JA

Sunday Express
Fleet Street
London EC4P 4JT

Sunday Mirror
Holborn Circus
London EC1P 1DQ

Sunday Telegraph
135 Fleet Street
London EC4P 4BL

Sunday People
9 New Fetter Lane
London EC4A 1AR

Sunday Times
200 Gray's Inn Road
London WC1X 8EZ

LOCAL NEWSPAPERS

ABERDEEN

Evening Express
Aberdeen Journals Ltd
Lang Stracht
Mastrick
Aberdeen AB9 8AF
0224 690222

Press and Journal
Aberdeen Journals Ltd
Lang Stracht
Mastrick
Aberdeen AB9 8AF
0224 690222

BATH

Bath and West Evening Chronicle
Wessex Newspapers
33–4 Westgate Street
Bath BA1 1EW
0749 63041

BELFAST

Belfast Telegraph
Belfast Telegraph Newspapers Ltd
124 Royal Avenue

Belfast BT1 1EB
0232 21242

Irish News
Irish News Ltd
113–17 Donegall Street
Belfast BT1 2GE
0232 242614

BIRMINGHAM

Birmingham Evening Mail
Birmingham Post and Mail Ltd
Colmore Circus
Birmingham B4 6AX
021 236 3366

Birmingham Post
Birmingham Post and Mail Ltd
Colmore Circus
Birmingham B4 6AX
021 236 3366

BLACKBURN

Lancs. Evening Telegraph
The North Western Newspaper Co
   Ltd
New Telegraph House

High Street
Blackburn BB1 1HT
0254 63588

BLACKPOOL

W. Lancs. Evening Gazette
Blackpool Gazette and Herald Ltd
Victoria Street
Blackpool FY1 4RG
0253 25231

BOLTON

Evening News
Northern Counties Newspapers Ltd
Mealhouse Lane
Bolton BL1 1DE
0204 22345

BRADFORD

Telegraph and Argus
Bradford & District Newspapers
Hall Ings
Bradford BD1 1JR
0274 729511

BRIGHTON

Evening Argus
Southern Publishing Co
(Westminster Press Ltd)
North Road
Brighton BN1 4AU
0273 606799

BRISTOL

Evening Post
Bristol United Press Ltd
Temple Way
Old Market

Bristol BS99 7HD
0272 20080

Western Daily Press & Times &
   Mirror
Bristol United Press Ltd
Temple Way
Old Market
Bristol BS99 7HD
0272 20080

CAMBRIDGE

Cambridge Evening News
Cambridge Newspapers Ltd
51 Newmarket Road
Cambridge CB5 8EJ
0223 358877

CARDIFF

South Wales Echo
Western Mail and Echo Ltd
Thomson House
Cardiff
0222 33022

Western Mail
Western Mail and Echo Ltd
Thomson House
Cardiff
0222 33022

COVENTRY

Coventry Evening Telegraph
Coventry Newspapers Ltd
Corporation Street
Coventry CV1 1FP
0203 25588

DERBY

Derby Evening Telegraph
Derby Daily Telegraph Ltd
Northcliffe House
Derby DE1 2DW
0332 42400

DONCASTER

Doncaster Evening Post
Doncaster Newspapers Ltd
10 North Bridge Road
Doncaster
South Yorkshire
0302 4001

DUNDEE

Courier and Advertiser
D. C. Tomson & Co. Ltd
7 Bank Street
Dundee DD1 9HU
0382 23131

Evening Telegraph and Post
D. C. Tomson & Co. Ltd
7 Bank Street
Dundee DD1 9HU
0382 23131

EDINBURGH

Evening News
The Scotsman Publications Ltd
20 North Bridge
Edinburgh EH1 1YT
031 225 2468

The Scotsman
The Scotsman Publications Ltd
20 North Bridge
Edinburgh EH1 1YT
031 225 2468

EXETER

Express and Echo
The Western Times Co Ltd
160 Sidwell Street
Exeter EX4 6RS
0392 73051

GLASGOW

Daily Record
Scottish Daily Record and Sunday
  Mail Ltd
Anderston Quay
Glasgow G3 8DA
041 248 7000

Evening Times
George Outram & Co. Ltd
195 Albion Street
Glasgow G1 1QP
041 552 6255

Glasgow Herald
George Outram & Co. Ltd
195 Albion Street
Glasgow G1 1QP
041 552 6255

GREENOCK

Greenock Telegraph (Evening
  Telegraph Greenock)
Orr, Pollock & Co Ltd
2 Crawfurd Street
Greenock PA15 1LH
Scotland
0475 23301

GRIMSBY

Grimsby Evening Telegraph
Hull and Grimsby Newspapers Ltd
80 Cleethorpe Road
Grimsby DN31 3EH
0472 59232

GUERNSEY

Guernsey Evening Press and Star
The Guernsey Press Co Ltd
Braye Road
Vale
Guernsey, C. I.
0481 45866

HALIFAX

Halifax Evening Courier
Halifax Courier Ltd
PO Box 19
King Cross Street
Halifax
West Yorkshire
0422 65711

HUDDERSFIELD

Huddersfield Daily Examiner
Huddersfield Examiner Ltd
Ramsden Street
Huddersfield HD1 2TD
0484 37444

HULL

Daily Mail
Hull and Grimsby Newspapers Ltd
Jameson Street
Hull HU1 3LF
0482 27111

IPSWICH

East Anglian Daily Times
East Anglian Daily Times Co Ltd
30 Lower Brook Street
Ipswich IP4 14N
0473 56777

JERSEY

Jersey Evening Post
W. E. Guiton & Co Ltd
PO Box 582
Five Oaks
St Saviour
Jersey, C. I.
0534 73333

LEEDS

Yorkshire Evening Post
Yorkshire Post Newspapers Ltd
Wellington Street
Leeds LS1 1RF
0532 432701

LEICESTER

Leicester Mercury
F. Hewitt & Son (1927) Ltd
St George Street
Leicester LE1 9FQ
0533 20831

LINCOLN

Lincolnshire Echo
Lincolnshire Publishing Co Ltd
St Benedict Square
Lincoln LN5 7AT
0522 26101

LIVERPOOL

Liverpool Daily Post
Liverpool Daily Post & Echo Ltd
PO Box 48
Old Hall Street
Liverpool L69 3EB
051 227 2000

317

Liverpool Echo
Liverpool Daily Post & Echo Ltd
PO Box 48
Old Hall Street
Liverpool L69 3EB
051 227 2000

Journal of Commerce
The Journal of Commerce &
   Shipping Telegraph Ltd
Fowler Buildings
7 Victoria Street
Liverpool L2 5QA
051 236 4511

LONDON

Evening News
118 Fleet Street
London EC4P 4DD

London Evening Standard
118 Fleet Street
London EC4P 4DD

MANCHESTER

The Manchester Evening News Ltd
164 Deansgate
Manchester M60 2RD
061 832 7200

NEWCASTLE

Evening Chronicle
Newcastle Chronicle & Journal Ltd
Thomson House
Groat Market
Newcastle-upon-Tyne NE99 1BO
0632 327500

Journal
Newcastle Chronicle & Journal Ltd
Thomson House
Groat Market
Newcastle-upon-Tyne NE99 1BO
0632 327500

NEWPORT

South Wales Argus
South Wales Argus Ltd
Cardiff Road
Maesglas
Newport
Gwent NPT 1QW
0633 62241

NORTHAMPTON

Chronicle and Echo (Northampton)
Northampton Mercury Co Ltd
Upper Mounts
Northampton NN1 3HR
0604 21122

NORWICH

Eastern Daily Press
Eastern Counties Newspapers Ltd
Rouen Road
Norwich NR1 1RE
0603 28311

Eastern Evening News
Eastern Counties Newspapers Ltd
Rouen Road
Norwich NR1 1RE
0603 28311

NOTTINGHAM

Evening Post
T. Bailey Forman Ltd
PO Box 99

Nottingham NG1 4AB
0602 45521

OLDHAM

Oldham Evening Chronicle
Hirst, Kidd & Rennie Ltd
Union Street
Oldham OL1 1EQ
061 633 2121

OXFORD

Oxford Mail
Osney Mead
Oxford OX2 0EJ
0865 244988

PETERBOROUGH

Peterborough Evening Telegraph
East Midland Allied Press Provincial
  Newspapers Ltd
Oundle Road
Woodston
Peterborough PE2 9QR
0733 68900 and 68301

PLYMOUTH

Western Morning News
Western Morning News Co. Ltd
Leicester Harmsworth House
65 New George Street
Plymouth PL1 1RE
0752 266626

Western Evening Herald
Western Morning News Co. Ltd
Leicester Harmsworth House
65 New George Street
Plymouth PL1 1RE
0752 266626

PORTSMOUTH

The News
Portsmouth and Sunderland News
  PLC
The News Centre
Hilsea
Portsmouth PO2 9SX
0705 664488

PRESTON

Lancashire Evening Post
Lancs Evening Post Ltd
127 Fishergate
Preston PR1 2DN
0772 54841

READING

Evening Post
Thames Valley Newspapers Ltd
8 Tessa Road
Reading RG1 8NS
0734 55833

SCARBOROUGH

Scarborough Evening News
Scarborough and District
  Newspapers Ltd
Aberdeen Walk
Scarborough YO11 1BB
0723 63631

SCUNTHORPE

Scunthorpe Evening Telegraph
Hull and Grimsby Newspapers Ltd
Telegraph House
Doncaster Road
Scunthorpe DN15 7RE
0724 843421

319

SHEFFIELD

Morning Telegraph
Sheffield Newspapers Ltd
York Street
Sheffield S1 1PU
0742 78585

Star
Sheffield Newspapers Ltd
York Street
Sheffield S1 1PU
0742 78585

SOUTH SHIELDS

Shields Gazette and Shipping
  Telegraph
Northern Press
Chapter Row
South Shields NE33 1BL
0632 554661

SOUTHAMPTON

Southern Evening Echo
Southern Newspapers Ltd
Above Bar
Southampton SO9 7BA
0703 34134

STOKE-ON-TRENT

Evening Sentinel
Staffordshire Sentinel Newspapers
  Ltd
Sentinel House
Etruria
Stoke-on-Trent ST1 5HA
0782 289800

SUNDERLAND

Echo
Portsmouth and Sunderland
  Newspapers PLC
Pennywell Industrial Estate
Sunderland SR4 9ER
0783 243011

SWANSEA

South Wales Evening Post
The Swansea Press Ltd
Adelaide Street
Swansea SA1 1QT
0792 50841

SWINDON

Evening Advertiser
Wiltshire Newspapers (Westminster
  Press Ltd)
Newspaper House
100 Victoria Road
Swindon SN1 3BE
0793 28144

TORQUAY

Herald Express
Western Times Co. Ltd
Harmsworth House
Barton Hill Road
Torquay TQ2 8JN
0803 213213

WOLVERHAMPTON

Express and Star
Midland News Association
50 Queen Street
Wolverhampton WV1 3BU
0902 22351

WORCESTER

Evening News
Berrow's West Midlands Ltd
Berrow's House
Worcester WR2 5JX
0905 423434

YORK

Yorkshire Evening Press
York & County Press
15 Coney Street
York YO1 1YN
0904 53051

20 SCIENCE AND TECHNOLOGY

Aslib Book List
Information House
26–7 Boswell Street
London WC1N 3JZ

British Medical Bulletin
Baxter's Place
Leith Walk
Edinburgh EH1 3AF

British Medical Journal
Medical Association House
Tavistock Square
London WC1H 9JR

Bulletin of Science Technology and
    Society
Pergamon Press Ltd
Headington Hill Hall
Oxford OX3 0BW

Current Technology Index
Library Association
2 Ridgmount Street
London WC1E 7AE

Endeavour
Pergamon Press Ltd
Headington Hill Hall
Oxford OX3 0BW

Ethics in Science and Medicine
Pergamon Press Ltd
Headington Hill Hall
Oxford OX3 0BW

Futures
Butterworth Scientific Ltd
Journals Division

PO Box 63
Westbury House
Bury Street
Guildford
Surrey GU2 5BH

History of Science
Science History Publications Ltd
Halfpenny Furze
Mill Lane
Chalfont St Giles HP8 4NR

Nature
Macmillan Journals Ltd
4 Little Essex Street
London WC2R 3LF

New Scientist
New Science Publications
128 Long Acre
London WC2E 9HQ

Notes and Records of the Royal
    Society
The Royal Society
6 Carlton Terrace
London SW1Y 5AG

Research in Science and
    Technological Education
Carfax Publishing Co.
PO Box 25
Abingdon
Oxon OX14 1RW

The School Science Review
Association for Science Education
College Lane
Hatfield
Herts AL10 9AA

Science Education Newsletter
Blackwell Scientific Publications
Osney Mead
Oxford OX2 0EL

Science in Parliament
Pharmaceutical Press
1 Lambeth High Street
London SE1 7JN

Science Progress
Blackwell Scientific Publications
Osney Mead
Oxford OX2 0EL

Science and Public Policy
Butterworth Scientific Ltd
Journals Division
PO Box 63
Westbury House

Bury Street
Guildford
Surrey GU2 5BH

Social Studies of Science
Sage Publications Ltd
28 Banner Street
London EC1Y 8QE

Studies in History and Philosophy of
   Science
Pergamon Press Ltd
Headington Hill Hall
Oxford OX3 0BW

Technology in Society
Pergamon Press Ltd
Headington Hill Hall
Oxford OX3 0BW

21 SOCIETY AND SOCIAL POLICY

British Journal of Social Work
Academic Press Inc. Ltd
24–8 Oval Road
London NW1 7DX

British Journal of Sociology
Routledge & Kegan Paul
11 New Fetter Lane
London EC4P 4EE

Community Development Journal
Oxford University Press
Journals Subscription Department
Walton Street
Oxford OX2 6DP

Community Digest
National Federation of Community
    Associations
8–9 Upper Street
London N1 0PQ

Ethnic Minority Digest
26 Branksome Road
Merton Park
London SW19 3AW

European Journal of Sociology
Cambridge University Press
PO Box 110
Cambridge CB2 3RL

Focus on Community Work
Journal of the Family Service Units
207 Old Marylebone Road
London NW1 5QP

Forum
International Journal of Human
    Relations
Forum Press Ltd
2 Bramber Road
London W14 9PB

Health and Social Service Journal
Macmillan Journals Ltd
4 Little Essex Street
London WC2R 3LF

Housing and Planning Bulletin
National Housing and Town
    Planning Council
Norvin House
45–55 Commercial Street
London E1 6BA

Journal for the Theory of Social
    Behaviour
Basil Blackwell Ltd
108 Cowley Road
Oxford OX4 1JF

Journal of Social Policy
Cambridge University Press
PO Box 110
Cambridge CB2 3RL

New Community
Commission for Racial Equality
Elliot House
10–12 Allington Street
London SW1E 5EH

New Society
14–16 Farringdon Lane
London EC1R 3AY

Parliament and Social Work
British Association of Social Workers
16 Kent Street
Birmingham B5 6RD

Race and Class
Institute of Race Relations
247–9 Pentonville Road
London N1 9NG

Social Policy and Administration
Basil Blackwell Ltd
108 Cowley Road
Oxford OX4 1JF

Social Science Research
Academic Press Inc.
24–8 Oval Road
London NW1 7DX

Social Science Information
Sage Publications
28 Banner Street
London EC1Y 8QE

Social Service Abstracts
HMSO
PO Box 569
London SE1 9NH

Social Science Teacher
Association for the Teaching of the
    Social Sciences
6 Battlefield Road
St Albans

Social Work Today
British Association of Social Workers
16 Kent Street
Birmingham B5 6RD

The Sociological Review
University of Keele
Keele
Staffordshire ST5 5BG

Sociology
BSA Publications Ltd
351 Station Road
Dorridge
Solihull
West Midlands BG3 8EY

22 THEATRE AND GENERAL ARTS

The Artful Reporter
North West Arts
12 Harter Street
Manchester M1 6HY

Art North
Northern Arts
10 Osborne Terrace
Newcastle-upon-Tyne NE2 1NZ

Arts Alive
Merseyside Arts
6 Bluecoat Chambers
School Lane
Liverpool L1 3BX

Arts Council Bulletin
Arts Council of Great Britain
105 Piccadilly
London W1V 0AU

Arts Diary
South East Arts Association
9–10 Crescent Road
Tunbridge Wells
Kent TN1 2LU

Arts in Action
Arts Council of Great Britain
105 Piccadilly
London W1V 0AU

Arts Report
West Midlands Arts
Brunswick Terrace
Stafford ST16 1BZ

Arts South West
South West Arts

Bradnich Place
Gandy Street
Exeter EX4 3OS

Arts Yorkshire
Yorkshire Arts Association
Glyde House
Glydegate
Bradford
Yorkshire

City Limits
313 Upper Street
London N1 2XQ

Dance and Dancers
Brevet Publishing Ltd
445 Brighton Road
South Croydon CR2 6EU

Drama
9 Fitzroy Square
London W1P 6AE

Eastword
Eastern Arts Association
8–9 Bridge Street
Cambridge CB2 1UA

Gambit: International Theatre
  Review
John Calder (Publishers) Ltd
18 Brewer Street
London W1R 4AS

London Magazine
30 Thurloe Place
London SW7 2HQ

London Theatre Record
4 Cross Deep Gardens
Twickenham
Middlesex TW1 4GU

Plays and Players
Brevet Publishing Ltd
445 Brighton Road
South Croydon CR2 6EU

The Stage and Television Today
Carson and Comerford Ltd
47 Bermondsey Street
London SE1 3XT

Théâtre International
British ITI Centre
31 Shelton Street
London WC2H 9HT

Theatre Newsletter
British Theatre Institute
30 Clareville Street
London SW7 5AW

Theatre Notebook
The Society for Theatre Research
77 Kinnerton Street
London SW1X 8ED

Theatre Research International
Oxford University Press
Journal Subscription Department
Walton Street
Oxford OX2 6DP

Time Out
Time Out Ltd
Tower House
Southampton Street
London WC2E 7HD

23 THOUGHT AND PHILOSOPHY

Analysis
Basil Blackwell Ltd
108 Cowley Road
Oxford OX4 1JF

The British Journal for the
  Philosophy of Science
British Society for the Philosophy of
  Science
Social Studies Building
University of Warwick
Coventry CV4 7AL

The Locke Newsletter
Roland Hall
Department of Philosophy
The University
York

Metaphilosophy
Basil Blackwell Ltd
108 Cowley Road
Oxford OX4 1JF

Mind: A Quarterly Review of
  Philosophy
Basil Blackwell Ltd
108 Cowley Road
Oxford OX4 1JF

New Humanist
Rationalist Press Association
88 Islington High Street
London N1 8EW

Philosophical Books
Basil Blackwell Ltd
108 Cowley Road
Oxford OX4 1JF

Philosophical Investigations
Basil Blackwell Ltd
108 Cowley Road
Oxford OX4 1JF

Philosophical Quarterly
Scottish Academic Press
33 Montgomery Street
Edinburgh EH7 5JX

Philosophy
Cambridge University Press
PO Box 110
Cambridge CB2 3RL

The Philosophy Forum
Gordon and Breach Science
  Publishers
42 William IV Street
London WC2N 4DE

Radical Philosophy
c/o Howard Feather
General Education Department
Thurrock Technical College
Woodview
Grays
Essex

Ratio
Basil Blackwell Ltd
108 Cowley Road
Oxford OX4 1JF

Seminar: Journal of the
  Philosophical Seminar
Philosophical Seminar
Philosophy Department
University College
Cork

Social Philosophy and Policy
Basil Blackwell Ltd
108 Cowley Road
Oxford OX4 1JF

Theoria to Theory: An International
Journal of Science, Philosophy
and Contemplative Religion
Gordon and Breach Science
Publishers
42 William IV Street
London WC2N 4DE

24 WOMEN

Cosmopolitan
National Magazine Co. Ltd
National Magazine House
72 Broadwick Street
London W1V 2BP

Everywomen
34 Islington Green
London N1 8EV

Spare Rib
Spare Rib Ltd
27 Clerkenwell Close
London EC1R 0AT

Townswoman
2 Cromwell Place
London SW7 2JG

Studies on Women Abstracts
Carfax Publishing Co.
PO Box 25
Abingdon
Oxon OX14 1RW

Woman
IPC Magazines Ltd
King's Reach Tower
Stamford Street
London SE1 9LS

Woman's Own
IPC Magazines Ltd
King's Reach Tower
Stamford Street
London SE1 9LS

Women's Review
Unit 1
2nd Floor
1–4 Christina Street
London EC2

Women's Studies
Gordon and Breach Science
    Publishers Ltd
42 William IV Street
London WC2N 4DE

Women's Studies International
    Forum
Pergamon Press Ltd
Headington Hill Hall
Oxford OX3 0BW

Working Woman
Wintour Publications
77 Farringdon Road
London EC1

Writing Women
19 Osborne Road
Newcastle-upon-Tyne NE2 2AH

PART III
SOURCES OF INFORMATION

The following compilation is a select list of organisations, associations and institutions with information on particular fields of British life, society and culture.

For more comprehensive lists of such organisations readers are referred to: Anderson, I. G. (ed.), *Councils, Committees and Boards: A Handbook of Advisory, Consultative, Executive and Similar Bodies in British Public Life*, Beckenham, Kent, CBD Research, 1985; Codlin, E. M. (ed.), *Aslib Directory, Vol. 1, Information Sources in Science, Technology and Commerce*, London, Aslib, 1982; Codlin, E. M. (ed.), *Aslib Directory, Vol. 2, Information Sources in the Social Sciences, Medicine and the Humanities*, London, Aslib, 1984; Henderson, G. P. and Henderson, S. P. A. (eds), *Directory of British Associations*, Beckenham, Kent CBD Research, 1986.

ORGANISATIONS AND
INSTITUTIONS

1 ARTS AND ARTS ASSOCIATIONS

ARTS

Architectural Association
34–6 Bedford Square
London WC1B 3ES
01 636 0974

Arlis
Brighton Polytechnic
Faculty of Art and Design
Grand Parade
Brighton BN2 2JY
0273 604041

Artists League of Great Britain
Bankside Gallery
48 Hopton Street
London SE1 9JH
01 928 7521

Arts Council of Great Britain
105 Piccadilly
London W1V 0AU
01 629 9495

Association of Art Institutions
Imperial Chambers
24 Widemarsh Street
Hereford HR4 9EP
0432 66453

British Acadamy
Burlington House
Piccadilly
London W1V 0NS
01 734 0457

British Arts Festivals Association
33 Rufford Road

Sherwood
Nottingham NG5 2NQ
0602 621979

British Ballet Organisation
39 Lonsdale Road
London SW13 9JP
01 748 1241

British Society of Aesthetics
c/o The School of Art and Design
Trent Polytechnic
Nottingham NG1 4BU
0602 84249 ext. 2379

Computer Arts Society
50–51 Russell Square
London WC1B 4JX
01 636 3783

Contemporary Art Society
c/o Tate Gallery
Millbank
London SW1P 4RG
01 821 5323

Council of Regional Arts
  Associations
59 St James's Street
London SW1A 1LL
01 629 9586

Courtauld Institute of Art
20 Portman Square
London W1H 0BE
01 935 9292

Crafts Council
12 Waterloo Place
London SW1Y 4AU
01 930 4811

Critics Circle
7 Lloyd Square
London WC1X 9BA
01 837 4379

Federation of British Artists
17 Carlton House Terrace
London SW1Y 5BD
01 930 6844

FPS (Free Painters and Sculptors)
15 Buckingham Gate
London SW1E 6LB
01 828 5963

Institute of Contemporary Arts
Nash House
The Mall
London SW1 5AH
01 930 0493

Inter-Action
Royal Victoria Dock
London E16 1BT
01 511 0411/2

League of Socialist Artists
The League
18 Camberwell Church Street
London SE5

National Association of Arts Centres
c/o Rick Welton
23 Woodland Terrace
Darlington
County Durham DL3 9NT
0325 483277

National Association of Decorative
  and Fine Arts
625 Grand Buildings
Trafalgar Square

London WC2N 5HN
01 930 1693

National Campaign for the Arts
Francis House
Francis Street
London SW1P 1DE
01 828 6913

National Society for Art Education
7a High Street
Corsham
Wiltshire SN13 0ES
0249 714825

New English Art Club
17 Carlton House Terrace
London SW1Y 5BD
01 930 6844

Royal Academy of Arts
Burlington House
Piccadilly
London W1V 0DS
01 734 9052

Royal Academy of Dancing
48 Vicarage Crescent
London SW11 3LT
01 223 0091

Royal Fine Art Commission
2 Carlton Gardens
London SW1Y 5AA
01 930 3935

Royal Society of Arts
6–8 John Adam Street
London WC2N 6EZ
01 839 2366

Royal Society of British Sculptors
108 Old Brompton Road
London SW1 3RA
01 373 5554

Society of Architectural Historians of
   Great Britain
Room 208
30 Warwick Street
London W1R 6AB
01 734 8144

Society of Industrial Artists and
   Designers
12 Carlton House Terrace
London SW1Y 5AH
01 839 4453

ARTS COUNCILS AND REGIONAL ARTS ASSOCIATIONS

The Arts Council of Great Britain
105 Piccadilly
London W1V 0AU
01 629 9495

The Scottish Arts Council
19 Charlotte Square
Edinburgh EH2 4DF
031 226 6051

The Welsh Arts Council
Holst House
9 Museum Place
Cardiff CF1 3NX
0222 394711

The Arts Council of Northern
   Ireland
181a Stranmillis Road
Belfast BT9 5DU
0232 663591

East Midlands Arts
Mountfields House
Forest Road
Loughborough LE11 3HU
0509 218292

Eastern Arts Association
8–9 Bridge Street
Cambridge CB2 1UA
0223 357596

Greater London Arts Association
25–31 Tavistock Place
London WC1H 9SF
01 388 2211

Lincolnshire and Humberside Arts
St Hugh's
23 Newport
Lincoln
0522 33555

and

Posterngate Gallery
6 Posterngate
Hull HU1 2JN
0482 24813

Merseyside Arts Association
8 Bluecoat Chambers
School Lane
Liverpool L1 3BX
051 709 0671

North Wales Arts Association
10 Wellfield House
Bangor
Gwynedd LL57 1ER
0248 353248

North West Arts
12 Harter Street
Manchester M1 6HY
061 228 3062

Northern Arts Association
10 Osborne Terrace
Newcastle-upon-Tyne NE2 1NZ
091 281 6334

South East Arts Association
9–10 Crescent Road

Tunbridge Wells
Kent TN1 2LU
0892 41666

South East Wales Arts Association
Victoria Street
Cwmbran
Gwent NP44 3JP
06333 67530

South West Arts
Bradninch Place
Gandy Street
Exeter EX4 3LS
0392 218188

Southern Arts Association
19 Southgate Street
Winchester
Hampshire SO23 9DQ
0962 55099

West Midlands Arts
Brunswick Terrace
Stafford ST16 1BZ
0785 59231

West Wales Arts
Dark Gate
Carmarthen
Dyfed SA31 1Q1
0267 234238

Yorkshire Arts Association
Glyde House
Glydegate
Bradford
Yorkshire BD5 0BQ
0274 723051

2 BROADCASTING

BBC

BBC
Broadcasting House
London W1A 1AA
01 580 4468

BBC Chief Press and
Publicity Officer - Radio
Broadcasting House
London W1A 1AA
01 580 4468

BBC Chief Press and
Publicity Officer - Television
Television Centre
Wood Lane
London W12 7RJ
01 743 8000

BBC Education Department
Head of Continuing Education -
  Radio
BBC Broadcasting House
London W1A 1AA
01 580 4468

BBC Education Department
Head of Continuing Education -
  Television
BBC
Villiers House
The Broadway
London W5 2PA
01 743 8000 ext. 8010

BBC External Broadcasting
PO Box 76
Bush House

Strand
London WC2B 4PH
01 240 3456

BBC Film and Videotape Library
Reynard Mills Industrial Estate
Windmill Road
Brentford
Middlesex TW8 9NF
01 567 6655

BBC Music Library
Room 409
Yalding House
156 Great Portland Street
London W1N 6AJ
01 580 4468 ext. 4880

BBC News Information Service
The Langham
Portland Place
London W1A 1AA
01 580 4468

BBC Programme Information Unit
The Langham
Portland Place
London W1A 1AA
01 580 4468 ext. 4647/4033

BBC Publications
35 Marylebone High Street
London W1M 4AA
01 580 5577

BBC Radio Drama Play Library
Broadcasting House

Portland Place
London W1A 1AA
01 580 4468

BBC Reference Library Service
The Langham
Portland Place
London W1A 1AA
01 580 4468

BBC Sound Archives
Broadcasting House
London W1A 1AA
01 580 4468

BBC Television
Television Centre

Wood Lane
London W12 7RJ
01 743 8000

BBC Television Drama Script
  Library
Television Centre
Wood Lane
London W12 7RJ
01 743 8000

BBC Written Archives Centre
Caversham Park
Reading RG4 80Z
0734 472742

BBC REGIONS

BBC East
St Catherine's Close
All Saints Green
Norwich NR1 3ND
0603 28841

BBC Midlands
Broadcasting Centre
Pebble Mill Road
Birmingham B5 7SA
021 472 5353

BBC North
Broadcasting Centre
Woodhouse Lane
Leeds LS2 9PX
0532 441188

BBC North-East
Broadcasting House
54 New Bridge Street
Newcastle-upon-Tyne NE1 8AA
0632 20961

BBC North-West
New Broadcasting House
Oxford Road

Manchester M60 1SJ
061 236 8444

BBC South
South Western House
Canute Road
Southampton SO9 1PF
0703 26201

BBC South-West
Broadcasting House
Seymour Road
Mannamead
Plymouth PL3 5BD
0752 29201

BBC West
Broadcasting House
21–33B Whiteladies Road
Clifton
Bristol BS8 2LR
0272 32211

BBC Northern Ireland
Broadcasting House
25–7 Ormeau Avenue
Belfast BT2 8HQ
0232 44400

BBC Scotland
Broadcasting House
Queen Margaret Drive
Glasgow G12 8DG
041 339 8844

BBC Wales
Llantrisant Road
Llandaff
Cardiff CF5 2YO
0222 564888

BBC LOCAL RADIO

BBC Radio Bristol
3 Tyndalls Park Road
Bristol BS8 1PP
0272 741111

BBC Radio Cambridgeshire
Broadcasting House
104 Hills Road ·
Cambridge CB2 1LD
0223 315970

BBC Radio Cleveland
PO Box 1548
Broadcasting House
Newport Road
Middlesborough
Cleveland TS1 5JA
0642 225211

BBC Radio Cornwall
Phoenix Wharf
Truro
Cornwall TR1 1UA
0872 75421

BBC Radio Cumbria
Hilltop Heights
London Road
Carlisle CA1 2NA
0228 31661

BBC Radio Devon
65 St David's Hill
Exeter EX14 4DB
0392 215651

BBC Radio Furness
Broadcasting House
Hartington Street

Barrow-in-Furness
Cumbria
0229 36767

BBC Radio Guernsey
Commerce House
Les Banques
St Peter Port
Guernsey
0481 28977

BBC Radio Humberside
63 Jameson Street
Hull HU1 3NU
0482 23232

BBC Radio Jersey
Broadcasting House
Rouge Bouillon
St Helier
Jersey
0534 70000

BBC Radio Kent
30 High Street
Chatham
Kent ME4 4EZ
0634 462843

BBC Radio Lancashire
King Street
Blackburn
Lancashire BB2 2EA
0254 62411

BBC Radio Leeds
Broadcasting House
Woodhouse Lane
Leeds LS2 9PN
0532 442131

BBC Radio Leciester
Epic House
Charles Street
Leicester LE1 3SH 0533 27113

BBC Radio Lincolnshire
Radio Buildings
10 Newport
Lincoln LN1 3EU
0522 40011

BBC Radio London
35A Marylebone High Street
London W1A 4LG
01 486 7611

BBC Radio Manchester
PO Box 90
New Broadcasting House
Oxford Road
Manchester M60 1SJ
061 228 3434

BBC Radio Merseyside
55 Paradise Street
Liverpool L1 3BP
051 708 5500

BBC Radio Newcastle
Crestina House
Archibold Terrace
Newcastle-upon-Tyne NE2 1DZ
0632 814243

BBC Radio Norfolk
Norfolk Tower
Surrey Street
Norwich
Norfolk NR1 3PA
0603 617411

BBC Radio Northampton
PO Box 1107
Abingdon Street

Northampton NN1 2BE
0604 20621

BBC Radio Nottingham
York House
Mansfield Road
Nottingham NG1 3JB
0602 415161

BBC Radio Oxford
242–54 Banbury Road
Oxford OX2 7DW
0865 53411

BBC Radio Sheffield
Ashdell Grove
60 Westbourne Road
Sheffield S10 2QU
0742 686185

BBC Radio Solent
South Western House
Canute Road
Southampton SO9 4PJ
0703 31311

BBC Radio Stoke-on-Trent
Conway House
Cheapside
Hanley
Stoke-on-Trent
Staffordshire ST1 1JJ
0782 24827

BBC Radio Sussex
Marlborough Place
Brighton BN1 1TU
0273 680231

BBC Radio West Midlands
Pebble Mill Road
Birmingham B5 7SD
021 472 5141

COMMERCIAL TELEVISION

Anglia Television
Anglia House
Norwich NR1 3JG
0603 615151

Border Television
Television Centre
Carlisle CA1 3NT
0228 25101

Central Independent Television
Central House
Broad Street
Birmingham B1 2JP
021 643 9898

Channel Four Television
56 Charlotte Street
London W1P 2AX
01 631 4444

Channel Television
The Television Centre
St Helier
Jersey 0534 73999

Grampian Television
Queen's Cross
Aberdeen AB9 2XJ
0224 646464

Granada Television
Granada Television Centre
Manchester M60 9EA
061 832 7211

HTV Wales
The Television Centre
Culverhouse Cross
Cardiff CF5 6XJ
0222 590590

Independent Broadcasting Authority
(IBA)
70 Brompton Road

London SW3 1EY
01 584 7011

London Weekend Television
South Bank Television Centre
Kent House
Upper Ground
London SW1 9LT
01 261 3434

Scottish Television
Cowcaddens
Glasgow G2 3PR
041 332 9999

Television South West
Derry's Cross
Plymouth P11 2SP
0752 663322

Thames Television
Thames Television House
306 Euston Road
London NW1 3BB
01 387 9494

TV-AM Ltd
Breakfast Television Centre
Hawley Crescent
London NW1Y 4DX
01 267 4300

TVS (Television South)
Television Centre
Northam Road
Southampton S09 5HZ
0703 34211

Tyne Tees Television
The Television Centre
City Road
Newcastle-upon-Tyne NE1 2AL
0632 610181

Ulster Television
Havelock House

Ormeau Road
Belfast BT7 1EB
0232 228122

Yorkshire Television
The Television Centre
Leeds LS3 1JS
0532 438283

COMMERCIAL RADIO

Association of Independent Radio
  Contractors
Regina House
259–69 Old Marylebone Road
London SW3 1EY
01 262 6681

ILR Aberdeen
NorthSound
45 King's Gate
Aberdeen AB2 6BL
0224 632234

ILR Ayr
West Sound
Radio House
54 Holmston Road
Ayr KA7 3BD
0292 283662

ILR Belfast
PO Box 96
Kiltonga Industrial Estate
Newtownards
Northern Ireland BT23 4ES
0247 815555

ILR Birmingham
BRMB Radio
PO Box 555
Radio House
Aston Road North
Birmingham B6 4BX
021 359 4481–9

ILR Bournemouth
Two Counties Radio
5–7 Southcote Road
Bournemouth BH1 3LR
0202 294881

ILR Bradford
Pennine Radio
PO Box 235
Pennine House
Forster Square
Bradford BD1 5NP
0274 731521

ILR Brighton
Southern Sound
Radio House
Franklin Road
Partslade
Sussex BN4 2SS
0273 422288

ILR Bristol
Radio West
PO Box 963 Watershed
Canons Road
Bristol BS99 7SN
0272 279900

ILR Bury St Edmunds
Saxon Radio
Long Brackland
Bury St Edmunds
Suffolk IP33 1JY
0284 701511

ILR Cardiff
Cardiff Broadcasting Company
Radio House
West Canal Wharf
Cardiff CF1 5JX
0222 384041

ILR Coventry
Mercia Sound
Hertford Place

Coventry CV1 3TT
0203 28451

ILR Doncaster
Radio Hallam
PO Box 194
Hartshead
Sheffield S1 1GP
0742 71188

ILR Dundee/Perth
Radio Tay
PO Box 123
Dundee DD1 9UF
0382 29551

ILR East Kent
Invicta Radio
15 Station Road East
Canterbury CT1 2RB
0227 55252

ILR Edinburgh
Radio Forth House
Forth Street
Edinburgh EH1 3LF
031 556 9255

ILR Exeter/Torbay
DevonAir Radio
The Studio Centre
35–7 St David's Hill
Exeter EX4 4DA
0392 30703

ILR Glasgow
Radio Clyde
Clydebank Business Park
Clydebank
Glasgow G81 2RX
041 941 1111

ILR Gloucester and Cheltenham
Severn Sound
PO Box 388
Old Talbot House
67 Southgate Street

Gloucester GL1 1TX
0452 423791

ILR Great Yarmouth and Norwich
Radio Broadland
St George's Plain
Colegate
Norwich NR3 1DD
0603 630621

ILR Guildford
County Sound
The Friary
Guildford
Surrey GU1 4YX
0483 505566

ILR Hereford/Worcester
Radio Wyvern
5–6 Barbourne Terrace
Worcester
0905 612212

ILR Humberside
Viking Radio
Commercial Road
Hull HU1 2SA
0482 25141

ILR Inverness
Moray Firth Radio
PO Box 271
Inverness IV3 6SF
0463 224433

ILR Ipswich
Radio Orwell
Electric House
Lloyds Avenue
Ipswich IP1 3HZ
0473 216971

ILR Leeds
Radio Aire
PO Box 362
Leeds 1LR
0532 452299

ILR Leicester
Leicester Sound
29–31 Castle Gate
Nottingham NG1 7AP
0602 581731

ILR Liverpool
Radio City
PO Box 194
8–10 Stanley Street
Liverpool L69 1LD
051 227 5100

ILR London
Capital Radio
Euston Tower
London NW1 3DR
01 388 1288

ILR London
London Broadcasting Company
Gough Square
London EC4P 4LP
01 353 1010

ILR Luton/Bedford
Chiltern Radio
Chiltern Road
Dunstable
Bedfordshire LU6 1HQ
0582 666001

ILR Maidstone and Medway
Invicta Radio
32 Earl Street
Maidstone ME14 1ND
0622 686721

ILR Manchester
Piccadilly Radio
127–31 The Piazza
Piccadilly Plaza
Manchester M1 4AW
061 236 9913

ILR Northampton
Hereward Road
PO Box 1557
73 Abington Street
Northampton NN1 2HW

ILR Nottingham
Radio Trent
29–31 Castle Gate
Nottingham NG1 7AP
0602 581731

ILR Peterborough
Hereward Radio
PO Box 225
114 Bridge Street
Peterborough
Cambridgeshire PE1 1JX
0733 46225

ILR Plymouth
Plymouth Sound
Earl's Acre
Alma Road
Plymouth PL3 4HX
0752 27272

ILR Portsmouth
Radio Victory
PO Box 257
247 Fratton Road
Portsmouth PO1 5RT
0705 827799

ILR Preston and Blackpool
Red Rose Radio
PO Box 301
St Paul's Square
Preston
Lancashire PR1 1YE
0772 556301

ILR Reading
Radio 210 Thames Valley
PO Box 210
Reading RG3 5RZ
0734 413131

ILR Reigate and Crawley
Radio Mercury
Broadfield House
Brighton Road
Crawley RH11 9BS
0293 519161

ILR Sheffield and Rotherham
Radio Hallam
PO Box 194
Hartshead
Sheffield S1 1GP
0742 71188

ILR Southend/Chelmsford
Essex Radio
Radio House
Clifftown Road
Southend-on-Sea
Essex SS1 1SX
0702 333711

ILR Stoke-on-Trent
Signal Radio
Studio 257
67–73 Stoke Road
Stoke-on-Trent
Staffordshire ST4 2SR
0782 417111

ILR Swansea
Swansea Sound
Victoria Road
Gowerton
Swansea SA4 3AB
0792 893751

ILR Swindon/West Wiltshire
Wiltshire Radio
Old Lime Kiln
High Street
Wootton Bassett
Swindon
Wiltshire SN4 7EX
0793 853222

ILR Teesside
Radio Tees
74 Dovecot Street
Stockton-on-Tees
Cleveland TS18 1HB
0642 615111

ILR Tyne and Wear
Metro Radio
Long Rigg
Swalwell
Newcastle-upon-Tyne NE99 1BB
0632 883131

ILR Wolverhampton and Black
  Country
Beacon Radio 303
PO Box 303
267 Tettenhall Road
Wolverhampton WV6 0DQ
0902 757211

ILR Wrexham and Deeside
Marcher Sound Sain-Y-Gororau
The Studios
Mold Road
Gwersyllt
Wrexham
Clwyd LL11 4AF
0978 752202

OTHER SOURCES

Broadcasters' Audience Research
  Board
Knighton House
52–66 Mortimer Street
London W1N 8AN
01 636 6866

British Academy of Film and
  Television Arts
195 Piccadilly
London W1
01 734 0022

Centre for Mass Communication
  Research
104 Regent Road
Leicester LE1 7LT
0533 555557

Independent Television Companies
  Association
Knighton House
56 Mortimer Street
London W1N 8AN
01 636 6866

Independent Television Publications
  Ltd
247 Tottenham Court Road
London W1P 0AY
01 636 3666

Local Radio Association
34 Grand Avenue
London N10 3BP
01 883 7229

Media Society
Bedford Chambers
Covent Garden

London WC2E 8HA
01 836 6541

The Media Studies Association
The School of Communication
Trinity and All Saints' College
Brownberrie Lane
Horsforth
Leeds LS18 5HD
0532 584341

Royal Television Society
Tavistock House East
Tavistock Square
London WC1H 9HR
01 387 1970

Society for Education in Film and
  Television
29 Old Compton Street
London W1V 5PM
01 734 5455

Television Training Centre
23 Grosvenor Street
London W1
01 629 6839

Women's Media Action Group
c/o A Woman's Place
Hungerford House
Victoria Embankment
London WC2
01 668 2519

Women in Media
c/o Joan Plachta
BM W1M
London WC1N 3XX
01 380 0517

3 CITIES

ABERDEEN

Aberdeen Chamber of Commerce
15 Union Terrace
Aberdeen AB9 1HF
0224 641 222

Aberdeen City Council
Town House
Aberdeen AB9 1AQ
0224 642121

Aberdeen City Libraries
Central Library
Rosemount Viaduct
Aberdeen AB9 1GU
0224 634622

BATH

Bath Chamber of Commerce
16 Abbey Churchyard
Bath

Bath City Council
Guildhall
Bath BA1 5AW
0225 61111

Bath Reference Library
Avon County Library
18 Queen Square
Bath BA1 2HP
0225 28144

BELFAST

Belfast City Council
City Hall
Belfast BT1 5GS
0232 220202

Belfast Public Library
Royal Avenue
Belfast BT1 1EA
0232 243233

Northern Ireland Chamber of
   Commerce and Industry
Chamber of Commerce House
22 Great Victoria Street
Belfast BT2 7BJ
0232 244113

BIRMINGHAM

Birmingham Chamber of Industry
and Commerce
PO Box 360
75 Harborne Road
Birmingham B15 3DH
021 454 6171

Birmingham City Council
The Council House

Victoria Square
Birmingham B1 1BB
021 235 9944

Central Library
Chamberlain Square
Birmingham B3 3HQ
021 2354511

BRADFORD

Bradford Chamber of Commerce
and Industry
Commerce House
Cheapside
Bradford BD1 4JZ
0274 728166

Bradford City Council
City Hall

Bradford BD1 1HY
0274 729577

Bradford Public Libraries
Prince's Way
Bradford BD1 1NN
0274 733081

BRISTOL

Bristol Chamber of Industry and
Shipping
16 Clifton Park
Bristol B58 3BY
0272 737373

Bristol City Council
Council House

College Green
Bristol BS1 5TR
0272 26031

Central Library
College Green
Bristol BS1 5TL
0272 276121

CAMBRIDGE

Cambridge City Council
The Guildhall
Cambridge CB2 3QJ
0223 358 977

Cambridge and District Chamber of
Commerce and Industry
Owen Webb House

1 Gresham Road
Cambridge CB1 2EP
0223 355713

Central Library
7 Lion Yard
Cambridge
0223 65252

CANTERBURY

Canterbury City Council
Council Offices
Military Road
Canterbury CT1 1WY
0227 51755

Canterbury and District Chamber of
Trade
40–1 Castle Row

Canterbury
Kent CT1 2QY
0227 69214/6

Canterbury Public Library
Kent County Library
High Street
Canterbury CT1 2JF
0227 63608

CARDIFF

Cardiff Chamber of Commerce and
Industry
101–8 The Exchange
Mount Stuart Square
Cardiff CF1 6RD
0222 481648

Cardiff City Council
City Hall

Cardiff CF1 3ND
0222 31033

County of Glamorgan Libraries
County Library Headquarters
The Hayes
Cardiff CF1 2QU
0222 22116

CHESTER

Chester City Council
Town Hall
Chester CH1 2HN
0244 40144

Cheshire Libraries and Museums
91 Hoole Road
Chester CH2 3NG
0244 20055

Chester and North Wales Chamber
of Commerce
6 Hunter Street
Chester CH1 2AU
0244 23051

COVENTRY

Coventry Chamber of Commerce
and Industry
123 St Nicolas Street
Coventry CV1 4FD
0203 51777

Coventry City Council
Council House
Coventry CV1 5RR
0203 25555

Coventry Public Library
Bayley Lane
Coventry
0203 25555

DERBY

Central Library
The Wardwick
Derby
Derbyshire DE1 1HF
0332 31111

Derby City Council
Council House

Derby DE1 2FS
0332 31111

Derby and Derbyshire Chamber of
    Commerce and Industry
4 Vernon Street
Derby DE1 1FR
0332 47031

DUNDEE

Dundee City Council
City Chambers
Dundee DD1 3BY
0382 23141

Dundee District Libraries
Central Library
The Wellgate
Dundee DD1 1DB
0382 23141

Dundee and Tayside Chamber of
    Commerce and Industry
Chamber of Commerce Buildings
Panmure Street
Dundee EE1 1ED
0382 22122

DURHAM

Durham Chamber of Commerce
Coronation Buildings
65 Quayside
Durham
0632 611142

Durham City Council
Town Hall

Durham DH1 3NW
0385 67131

Durham County Library
County Hall
Durham DH1 5TY
0385 64411

EDINBURGH

City of Edinburgh
City Chambers
High Street
Edinburgh EH1 1YJ
031 225 2424

Edinburgh Chamber of Commerce
    and Manufactures
3 Randolph Crescent

Edinburgh EH3 7UD
031 225 5851

Edinburgh City Libraries
Central Library
George IV Bridge
Edinburgh EH1 1EG
031 225 5584

350

EXETER

Exeter Central Library
Devon County Council
Castle Street
Exeter EX4 3PQ
0392 53425

Exeter City Council
Civic Centre
Dix's Field

Exeter EX1 1JN
0392 77888

Exeter and District Chamber of
    Commerce and Trade
Equitable Life House
31 Southernhay East
Exeter EX1 1NS
0392 36641

GLASGOW

City of Glasgow
City Chambers
Glasgow G2 1DU
041 221 9600

Glasgow Chamber of Commerce and
    Manufactures
30 George Square

Glasgow G2 TEQ
041 204 2121

Mitchell Library
North Street
Glasgow G3 7DN
041 221 7030

GLOUCESTER

Gloucester City Council
Guildhall
Eastgate Street
Gloucester GL1 1QG
0452 22232

Gloucester and County Chamber of
    Commerce
20 Cheltenham Road

Gloucester
0452 23383

Gloucestershire County Library
Shire Hall
Quayside Wing
Gloucester NG31 6PY
0476 3926

KINGSTON-UPON-HULL

Central Library
Albion Street
Hull HU1 3TF
0482 224040

Hull Incorporated Chamber of
    Commerce and Shipping
Samman House
Bowlalley Lane

Hull HU1 1XT
0482 24976

Kingston-upon-Hull City Council
Guildhall
Alfred Gelder Street
Kingston-upon-Hull
North Humberside HU1 2AA
0482 223111

LANCASTER

Central Library
Market Square
Lancaster LA1 1HY
0524 63266/7

Lancaster City Council
Town Hall
Lancaster LA1 1PJ
0524 65272

Lancaster Chamber of Commerce,
 Trade and Industry
St Leonard's House
St Leonardgate
Lancaster LA1 1NN
0524 39467

LEEDS

Leeds Chamber of Commerce and
 Industry
Commerce House
2 St Alban's Place
Wade Lane
Leeds LS2 8HZ
0532 430491

Leeds City Council

Civic Hall
Leeds LS1 1UR
0532 463000

Leeds City Libraries
Municipal Buildings
Calverley Street
Leeds LS1 3AB
0532 463000

LEICESTER

Leicester City Council
New Walk Centre
Welford Place
Leicester LE1 6ZG

Leicester and County Chamber of
 Commerce and Industry
4th Floor
York House
91 Granby Street

Leicester LE1 6EA
0533 551491

Leicestershire Libraries and
 Information Services
Thames Tower
2 Navigation Street
Leicester LE1 3TZ
0533 538921

LINCOLN

Lincoln City Council
City Hall
Beaumont Fee
Lincoln LN1 1DB
0522 32 151

Lincolnshire County Library
Brayford House
Lucy Tower Street

Lincoln LN1 1XN
0522 26287

Lincoln Incorporated Chamber of
 Commerce
15–16 St Mary's Street
Lincoln LN5 7EQ
0522 23713

LIVERPOOL

Liverpool City Council
Municipal Buildings
Dale Street
Liverpool L69 2DH
051 227 3911

Liverpool City Libraries
Brown, Picton and Hornby Libraries
William Brown Street

Liverpool L3 8EW
051 2072147

Merseyside Chamber of Commerce
and Industry
Number One Old Hall Street
Liverpool L3 9HG
051 227 1234

LONDON

City and Guilds of London Institute
76 Portland Place
London W1N 4AA
01 580 3050

City of London Information Centre
The Guildhall
London EC2P 2EJ
01 606 3030

Guildhall Library
Aldermanbury
London EC2
01 606 3030

London Appreciation Society
17 Manson Mews
London SW7 5AE

London Chamber of Commerce and
Industry
69 Cannon Street
London EC4N 5AB
01 248 4444

London Library
14 St James's Square
London SW1
01 930 7705

London Residuary Body
St Vincent House
30 Orange Street
London WC2H 7HH
01 930 0613

London Society
c/o The City University
Northampton Square
London EC1V 0HB
01 278 6170

London Visitor and Convention
Bureau
26 Grosvenor Gardens
Victoria
London SW1
01 730 3488

Museum of London
150 London Wall
London EC2
01 600 3699

Museum of London Library
London Wall
London EC2

MANCHESTER

Central Library
St Peter's Square

Manchester M2 5PD
061 2369422

Manchester Chamber of Commerce
   and Industry
56 Oxford Street
Manchester M60 7HJ
061 236 3210

Manchester City Council
Town Hall
Manchester M60 2JT
061 236 3377

NEWCASTLE-UPON-TYNE

Newcastle-upon-Tyne City Council
Civic Centre
Barras Bridge
Newcastle-upon-Tyne NE99 2BM
0632 328520

Newcastle-upon-Tyne Libraries
Princess Square
New Bridge Street

Newcastle-upon-Tyne NE99 1MC
0632 610691

Tyne and Wear Chamber of
   Commerce and Industry
65 Quayside
Newcastle-upon-Tyne NE1 3DS
0632 611142

NORWICH

Central Library
Bethel Street
Norwich NR2 1HJ
0603 611277

Norwich City Council
City Wall
Norwich NR2 1NH
0603 22233

Norwich and Norfolk Chamber of
   Commerce and Industry
112 Barrack Street
Norwich NR3 1UB
0603 625977

NOTTINGHAM

Nottingham City Council
The Guildhall
Nottingham NG1 4BT
0602 418571

Nottinghamshire Chamber of
   Commerce and Industry
395 Mansfield Road

Nottingham NG5 2DL
0602 624624

Nottinghamshire County Library
Central Library
Angel Row
Nottingham

OXFORD

Oxford Chamber of Commerce
6 Bank Court Chambers
Cowley Centre
Oxford
0865 772255

Oxford City Council
St Aldate's
Oxford OX1 1DS
0865 249811

Oxfordshire County Libraries
Holton Park
Oxford OX9 1QQ
08677 3766

PLYMOUTH

Central Library
Devon County Council
Drake Circus
Plymouth PL4 8AL
0752 264675

Plymouth City Council
The Civic Centre
Plymouth PL1 2EW
0752 668000

PORTSMOUTH

Central Library
Guildhall Square
Portsmouth PO1 2DX
0705 81911

Portsmouth City Council
Civic Offices
Guildhall Square

Portsmouth PO1 2AL
0705 822251

South-East Hampshire Chamber of
Commerce and Industry
27 Guildhall Walk
Portsmouth PO1 2RP
0705 825351

READING

Reading Borough Council
Civic Offices
Civic Centre
Reading RG1 7TD
0734 5591

Reading Central Library
Blagrave Street

Reading RG1 1QL
0734 590058

Reading Chamber of Commerce and
Trade
43 West Street
Reading RG1 1AT
0734 595049

SHEFFIELD

Sheffield Chamber of Commerce and
Manufactures
Commerce House
33 East Street
Sheffield S1 3FX
0742 730114

Sheffield City Council
Town Hall
Sheffield S1 2HH
0742 26444

Sheffield City Libraries
Central Library
Surrey Street
Sheffield S1 1XZ
0742 734711

SOUTHAMPTON

Southampton Chamber of
    Commerce
Bugle House
53 Bugle Street
Southampton S09 4WP
0703 23541

Southampton City Council

Civic Centre
Southampton S09 4XR
0703 23855

Southampton Divisional Library
Civic Centre
Southampton S09 4XP
0703 23855

STOKE-ON-TRENT

City Central Library
Bethesda Street
Hanley
Stoke-on-Trent
Staffordshire ST1 3RS
0782 263568

North Staffordshire Chamber of
    Commerce and Industry

Winton House
Stoke Road
Stoke-on-Trent ST4 2RL
0782 44731

Stoke-on-Trent City Council
Town Hall
Stoke-on-Trent ST4 1HH
0782 48241

SWANSEA

County Library
West Glamorgan House 12
Orchard Street
Swansea
0792 42044

Swansea Chamber of Commerce and
    Shipping
Rooms F6–F7

Burrows Chambers
East Burrows Road
Swansea SA1 1RF
0792 53297

Swansea City Council
The Guildhall
Swansea SA1 4PA
0792 50821

YORK

York City Council
Guildhall
York YO1 1QN
0904 59881

York Public Library
North Yorkshire Council
Museum Street
York Y01 2DS
0904 55631

4 COMMONWEALTH

Association of Commonwealth
  Teachers
42 Camborne Avenue
London W13
01 567 3221

Association of Commonwealth
  Universities
36 Gordon Square
London WC1H 0PF
01 387 8572

Commonwealth Arts Association
c/o Commonwealth Institute
Kensington High Street
London W8 6NQ
01 603 4535

Commonwealth Education Liaison
  Committee
Marlborough House
Pall Mall
London SW1Y 5HY
01 839 3411

Commonwealth Family and
  Friendship Association
45 Mayesbrook Road
Dagenham
Essex RM8 2EX
01 590 9425

Commonwealth Institute
Kensington High Street
London W8 6NQ
01 603 4535

Commonwealth Institute Library
Kensington High Street

London W8 6NQ
01 603 4535

Commonwealth Library Association
c/o The Library Association
7 Ridgemount Street
London WC1E 7AE
01 636 7543

Commonwealth Parliamentary
  Association
7 Old Palace Yard
Houses of Parliament
London SW1A 0AA
01 219 4666

Commonwealth Press Union
184 Fleet Street
London EC4A 2DU
01 242 1056

Commonwealth Science Council
Marlborough House
Pall Mall
London SW1Y 5HX
01 839 3411

Commonwealth Secretariat
10 Carlton House Terrace
London SW1Y 5AH
01 839 3411

Commonwealth Youth Exchange
  Council
4 Park Place
St James's Street
London SW1A 1LR

Council for Education in The
  Commonwealth
North East London Polytechnic
Long Bridge Road
Dagenham
Essex RM8 2AS
01 597 7611

English Speaking Union of the
  Commonwealth
Dartmouth House
37 Charles Street
Berkeley Square
London W1X 8AB
01 629 0104

Foreign and Commonwealth Office
Downing Street
London SW1A 2AL
01 233 3000

Institute of Commonwealth Studies
27 Russell Square
London WC1B 5DS
01 580 5876

League for the Exchange of
  Commonwealth Teachers
Seymour Mews House
2nd Floor
26–37 Seymour Mews
London W1H 9PE
01 486 284019

Royal Commonwealth Society
18 Northumberland Avenue
London WC2N 5BJ
01 930 6733

5 ECONOMICS

Board of Inland Revenue
Somerset House
London WC2R 1LB
01 438 6622

Department of Employment
Caxton House
Tothill Street
London SW1H 9NA
01 213 3000

Economic and Social Research
   Council
1 Temple Avenue
London EC4Y 0BD
01 363 5252

Economic Research Council
55 Park Lane
London W1Y 3DH
01 834 4979

Economic Study Association
12 Addison Avenue
London W11 4QR
01 602 3653

Economics Association
18 Cedar Road
Sutton
Surrey SM2 5DP
01 642 9268

Economist Intelligence Unit
Spencer House
27 St James's Place
London SW1A 1NT
01 493 6711

Economists Advisory Group
52 St Katherine's Way
London E1 9LB
01 488 9941

Her Majesty's Treasury
Parliament Street
London SW1P 3AG
01 233 3000

Institute of Economic Affairs
Lord North Street
London SW1P 3LB
01 799 3745

Institute of Economics and Statistics
Oxford University
St Cross Buildings
Manor Road
Oxford OX1 3UL
0865 49631

National Economic Development
   Council
Millbank Tower
Millbank
London SW1P 4QX
01 211 5457

National Institute of Economic and
   Social Research
2 Dean Trench Street
Smith Square
London SW1P 3HE
01 222 7665

Policy Studies Institute
1–2 Castle Lane
London SW1E 6DR
01 828 7055

Royal Economic Society
c/o Economic Journal
Department of Economics
  and Related Subjects
University of York
Heslington
York YO1 5DD

6 EDUCATION

Advisory Centre for Education
18 Victoria Park Square
London E2 9PB
01 980 4596

Association of Polytechnic Teachers
27 Elphinstone Road
Southsea
Hampshire PO5 3HP
0705 818625

Association of University Teachers
1 Pembridge Road
London W11 3HJ
01 221 4370

BBC Education Department (Radio)
Broadcasting House
London W1A 1AA
01 580 4468

BBC Education Department
  (Television)
BBC
Villiers House
The Broadway
London W5 2PA
01 743 8000 ext. 8010

British Council
65 Davies Street
London W1
01 930 8466

Campaign For Comprehensive
  Education
17 Granard Avenue
London SW15 6HH
01 788 5831

Central Bureau for Educational
  Visits and Exchanges
Seymour Mews House
Seymour Mews
London W1A 9PE
01 486 5101

Centre for Educational Technology
Civic Centre
Mold
Clwyd CH7 1YA
0352 55105 ext. 262

Committee of Vice-Chancellors and
  Principals of the Universities of
  the United Kingdom
29 Tavistock Square
London WC1H 9EZ
01 387 9231

Council for Educational Technology
  for the United Kingdom
3 Devonshire Street
London W1N 2BA
01 636 4186

Council of Subject Teaching
c/o The Historical Association
59A Kennington Park Road
London SE11 4JH
01 735 3901

Department of Education and
  Science
Elizabeth House
York Road
London SE1 7PH
01 928 922

Educational Centres Association
c/o The Chequer Institute
Chequer Street
London EC1Y 8PL
01 251 4185

Educational Television Association
86 Micklegate
York YO1 1JZ
0904 29701

Headmasters' Conference
29 Gordon Square
London WC1H 0PS
01 388 1765/6

Independent Schools Information
  Service
26 Caxton Street
London SW1 0RG
01 222 7353/0065

International Students House
229 Great Portland Street
London W1N 5HD
01 631 3223

The Library Association
7 Ridgemount Street
London WC1E 7AE
01 636 7543

Media Resources Centre
Inner London Education Authority
275 Kennington Lane
London SE11

Museums Association
34 Bloomsbury Way
London WC1A 2SF
01 404 4767

National Confederation of Parent
  Teacher Associations
43 Stonebridge Road
Northfleet
Gravesend

Kent DA11 9DS
0474 60618

National Foundation for
  Educational Research
The Mere
Upton Park
Slough
Berkshire SL1 2DQ
0753 2816

National Institute of Adult
  Education
19B De Montfort Street
Leicester LE1 7GE
0533 551451

National Reference Library of
  Schoolbooks and Classroom
  Materials
20 Bedford Way
London WC1H 0AL
01 636 1500 ext. 267

National Union of Students
461 Holloway Road
London N7 6LZ
01 272 8900

National Union of Teachers
Hamilton House
Mabledon Place
London WC1H 9BD
01 387 2442

Nuffield Foundation
Nuffield Lodge
Regent's Park
London NW1 4RS
01 722 8871

Regional Advisory Council for
  Further Education
Tavistock Square House
Tavistock Square
London WC1H 9LR
01 388 0027

School Broadcasting Council for the
UK
BBC
London W1A 1AA
01 580 4468

Schools Council for Curriculum and
Examinations
160 Great Portland Street
London W1N 6LL
01 580 0352

Skills Exchange - Ideas in Education
Falmer House
University of Sussex
Brighton BN1 9QF

Socialist Educational Association
62 Thornhill Road
Heaton Mersey
Stockport SK4 3HL

United Kingdom Council for
Overseas Student Affairs
60 Westbourne Grove
London W2 5FG
01 229 9268

University Grants Committee
14 Park Crescent
London W1N 4DH
01 636 7799

University of the Third Age
6 Parkside Gardens
London SW19 5EY
01 947 0401

Workers' Educational Association
Temple House
9 Upper Berkeley Street
London W1 8BY
01 402 5608

7 ENVIRONMENT AND GEOGRAPHY

Automobile Association
Fanum House
Basingstoke
Hampshire RG21 2EA
0256 62929

British Waterways Board
Melbury House
Melbury Terrace
London NW1 6JX
01 262 6711

Civic Trust
17 Carlton House Terrace
London SW1Y 5AW
01 930 0914

Conservation Society
12a Guildford Street
Chertsey
Surrey KT16 9BQ
09328 60975

The Conservation Trust
246 London Road
Earley
Reading RG6 1AJ
0734 663650

Council for Environmental
  Education
School of Education
University of Reading
London Road
Reading RG1 5AQ
0734 85234

Council for the Protection of Rural
  England
4 Hobart Place

London SW1W 0HY
01 235 9481

Countryside Commission
John Dower House
Crescent Place
Cheltenham GL50 3RA
0242 21381

Department of Environment
2 Marsham Street
London SW1P 3EB
01 212 3434

Field Studies Council
62 Wilson Street
London EC2A 2BU
01 583 7471

Forestry Commission
231 Corstorphine Road
Edinburgh EH12 7AT
031 334 0303

Friends of the Earth
377 City Road
London EC1V 1NA
01 837 0731

The Geographical Association
343 Fulwood Road
Sheffield 10 3BP
0742 61666

Geologists' Association
Burlington House
Piccadilly
London W1V 9AJ
01 734 2356

Greenpeace
36 Graham Street
London N1 8LL
01 251 3022/3020

The Green Party
10 Station Road
Balham High Road
London SW12 9AZ
01 673 0045

Institute of British Geographers
1 Kensington Gore
London SW7 2AR
01 584 6371

Institution of Environmental
    Sciences
14 Princes Gate
Hyde Park
London SW1 1PU
01 584 6262

National Association for
    Environmental Education
c/o Perry Common School
Faulkners Farm Drive
Erdington
Birmingham B23 7XP
021 373 1647

National Environmental Research
    Council
PO Box 18
Swindon
Wiltshire SN2 1ET
0793 26222

Nature Conservancy Council
19–20 Belgrave Square
London SW1X 8PY
01 235 3241

Ordnance Survey
Romsey Road
Maybush
Southampton SO9 4DH
0703 7755555

Ramblers' Association
1/5 Wandsworth Road
London SW8 2LJ
01 582 6878

Regional Studies Association
29 Great James Street
London WC1N 3ES
01 242 0363

Royal Automobile Club
PO Box 100
RAC House
Landsdowne Road
Croydon CR9 2JA
01 686 2525

Royal Commission on
    Environmental Pollution
Church House
Great Smith Street
London SW1P 3BL
01 212 8620

Royal Geographical Society
1 Kensington Gore
London SW7 2AR
01 589 5466

Royal Society for Nature
    Conservation
The Green
Nettleham
Lincoln LN2 2NR
0522 752326

The Royal Town Planning Institute
26 Portland Place
London W1N 4BE
01 636 9107

Town and Country Planning
    Association
17 Carlton House Terrace
London SW1Y 5AS
01 930 8903/5

8 EUROPE

E. C. AND GENERAL SOURCES

Anti-Common Market League
52 Fulham High Street
London SW6 3LQ
01 736 7393

Centre of European Governmental
  Studies
University of Edinburgh
Old College
South Bridge
Edinburgh EH8 9YL
031 6671011 ext. 4215

Commission of the European
  Community
Information Office
20 Kensington Palace Gardens
London W8 4QQ
01 721 8090

EEC Information Unit
Department of Trade
1 Victoria Street
London SW1H 0ET
01 215 5336

European Community
Press and Information Office
20 Kensington Palace Gardens

London W8 4QQ
01 727 8090

European Movement
1a Whitehall Place
London SW1A 2HA
01 839 6622

European Parliament Information
  Office
2 Queen Anne's Gate
London SW14 9AA
01 222 0411

Sussex European Research Centre
University of Sussex
Falmer
Brighton BN1 9LF
0273 606755 ext. 913

UK Centre for European Education
University of London Institute of
  Education
18 Woburn Square
London WC1H 0NS
01 636 1500 ext. 295

University Association for
  Contemporary European Studies
12a Maddox Street
London W1R 9PL

EUROPEAN DOCUMENTATION CENTRES

European Documentation Centre
University of Aberdeen
University Library
New Library

Meston Walk
Aberdeen AB9 2UB
0224 40241

European Documentation Centre
University of Bath
University Library
Claverton Down
Bath BA2 7AY
0225 6941

European Documentation Centre
Queen's University
Government Publications
  Department
The Library
Belfast BT7 1LS
0232 45133

European Documentation Centre
Birmingham Polytechnic
Commerce Centre Library
Main Library
Perry Barr
Birmingham B42 7HA
021 356 6911

European Documentation Centre
University of Birmingham
Main Library
PO Box 363
Birmingham B15 2TT
021 4721301

European Documentation Centre
University of Bradford
The Library
Richmond Road
Bradford BD7 1DP
0274 33466

European Documentation Centre
University of Sussex Library
Documents Section
Falmer
Brighton BN1 9QL
0273 66755

European Documentation Centre
University of Bristol
Law Library
Wills Memorial Building

Queens Road
Bristol BS8 1RJ
0272 24161

European Documentation Centre
University of Cambridge
University Library
West Road
Cambridge CB3 9DR
0223 61441

European Documentation Centre
University of Kent at Canterbury
The Library
Canterbury CT2 7NU
Kent
0227 66822

European Documentation Centre
Arts and Social Studies Library
University College
PO Box 78
Cardiff CF1 1XL
0222 44211

European Documentation Centre
New University of Ulster
The Library
Coleraine BT52 1SA
Londonderry
0265 4141

European Documentation Centre
Lanchester Polytechnic Library
Priory Street
Coventry CV1 5FB
0203 24011

European Documentation Centre
University of Warwick
The Library
Coventry CV4 7AL
0203 417417

European Documentation Centre
University of Dundee
Law Library
Scrymgeour Building

367

Park Place
Dundee DD1 4HN
0382 23181

European Documentation Centre
University of Durham
University Library
Palace Green
Durham DH1 3RN
0385 61262

European Documentation Centre
University of Edinburgh
Centre of European Governmental
 Studies
Old College
South Bridge
Edinburgh EH8 9YL
031 667 1011

European Documentation Centre
University of Essex
Library
PO Box 24
Colchester CO4 3UA
0206 862286

European Documentation Centre
University of Exeter
Faculty of Law
Centre for European Legal Studies
Amory Building
Rennes Drive
Exeter EX4 4RJ
0392 77911

European Documentation Centre
University of Glasgow
The University Library
Hillhead Street
Glasgow G12 8QE
041 334 2122

European Documentation Centre
University of Surrey
The Library
Guildford GU2 5XH
0483 71281

European Documentation Centre
University of Hull
Brynmor Jones Library
Cottingham Road
Hull HU6 7RX
0482 46311

European Documentation Centre
University of Keele
University Library
Keele
Staffordshire ST5 5BG
0782 621111

European Documentation Centre
University of Lancaster
University Library
Lancaster LA1 4YH
0524 65201

European Documentation Centre
University of Leeds
Faculty of Law
Leeds LS2 9JT
0532 31751

European Documentation Centre
Leeds Polytechnic Library
Calverley Street
Leeds LS1 3HE
0532 462925

European Documentation Centre
University of Leicester
University Library
University Road
Leicester LE1 7RH
0533 50000

European Documentation Centre
British Library of Political and
 Economic Science
London School of Economics and
 Political Science
10 Portugal Street
London WC2A 2HD
01 405 7686

European Documentation Centre
University of London
Queen Mary College
The Library
Mile End Road
London E1 4NS
01 980 4811

European Documentation Centre
The Polytechnic of Central London
EEC Unit
309 Regent's Street
London W1R 8AL
01 580 2020

European Documentation Centre
The Polytechnic of North London
The Library
Kentish Town
Prince of Wales Road
London NW5 3LB
01 607 2789

European Documentation Centre
Royal Institute of International
   Affairs
The Library
10 St James Square
London SW1Y 4LE
01 930 2233

European Documentation Centre
University of London
Centre for European Agricultural
   Studies
Wye College
Wye
Ashford
Kent TN25 5AH
0233 812401

European Documentation Centre
Loughborough University of
   Technology
The Library
Loughborough
Leicestershire LE11 3TU
0509 63171

European Documentation Centre
University of Manchester
John Rylands Library
Oxford Road
Manchester M13 9PP
061 273 3333

European Documentation Centre
Newcastle-upon-Tyne Polytechnic
Library
Ellison Place
Newcastle-upon-Tyne NE1 8ST
0632 326002

European Documentation Centre
University of East Anglia
University Plain
Library
Norwich NR4 7TJ
0603 56161

European Documentation Centre
University of Nottingham
University Library
Nottingham NG7 2RD
0602 56101

European Documentation Centre
University of Oxford
Radcliffe Camera
Bodleian Library
Oxford OX1 3BG
0865 44675

European Documentation Centre
Portsmouth Polytechnic
Frewen Library
Cambridge Road
Portsmouth PO1 2ST
0705 27681

European Documentation Centre
University of Reading
University Library
Whiteknights
Reading RG6 2AA
0734 84331

European Documentation Centre
University of Salford
The Library
Salford M5 4WT
061 7365843

European Documentation Centre
Sheffield City Polytechnic
The Library
Pond Street
Sheffield S1 1WB
0742 20911

European Documentation Centre
University of Southampton
Faculty of Law
Highfield
Southampton SO9 5NH
0703 559 122

Polytechnic of Wolverhampton
The Robert Scott Library
St Peter's Square
Wolverhampton WN1 1RH
0902 27371

9 FILM

British Acadamy of Film and
  Televison Arts
195 Piccadilly
London W1V 9LG
01 734 0022

British Board of Film Censors
3 Soho Square
London W1V 5DE
01 439 7961

British Film Institute
127 Charing Cross Road
London WC2H 0EA
01 437 4355

Film Artistes' Association
61 Marloes Road
London W8 6LF
01 937 4567/8

Independent Film Makers'
  Association
79 Wardour Street
London W1V 3PH
01 439 0460

National Film Archive
81 Dean Street
London W1V 6AA
01 437 4355

National Film School
South Bank
London SE1
01 928 1431

Society for Education in Film and
  Television
29 Old Compton Street
London W1V 5PM
01 734 5455

10 GOVERNMENT AND ADMINISTRATION

GOVERNMENT DEPARTMENTS, MINISTRIES AND OFFICES

Cabinet Office
70 Whitehall
London SW1A 2AS
01 273 3000

Central Statistical Office
Great George Street
London SW1P 3AQ
01 233 7584

Civil Service Department
Whitehall
London SW1A 2AZ
01 273 5577

Commission for Local
  Administration in England
21 Queen Anne's Gate
London SW1H 9BV
01 222 5622

Department of Education and
  Science
Elizabeth House
York Road
London SE1 7PH
01 928 9222

Department of Employment
Caxton House
Tothill Street
London SW1H 9NA
01 213 3000

Department of Energy
Thames House South
Millbank

London SW1P 4QJ
01 211 3000

Department of the Environment
2 Marsham Street
London SW1P 3EB
01 212 3434

Department of Health and Social
  Security
Alexander Fleming House
Elephant and Castle
London SE1 6BY
01 407 5522

Department of Trade and Industry
1 Victoria Street
London SW1H 0ET
01 215 7877

Duchy of Lancaster
Strand
London WC2E 7ED
01 836 8277

Foreign and Commonwealth Office
Downing Street
London SW1A 2AL
01 233 3000

Her Majesty's Stationery Office
St Crispins
Duke Street
Norwich NR3 1PD
0603 622211

Her Majesty's Treasury
Parliament Street
London SW1P 3AG
01 233 3000

Home Office
50 Queen Anne's Gate
London SW1H 9AT
01 218 3000

House of Commons
Westminster
London SW1A 0AA
01 219 3000

House of Commons Information
Office
House of Commons
London SW1A 0AA
01 219 4272

House of Lords
Westminster
London SW1A 0PW
01 219 3000

House of Lords Information Office
House of Lords
London SW1A 0AA
01 219 3073/4

Ministry of Agriculture, Fisheries
and Food
Whitehall Place
London SW1A 2HH
01 233 3000

Ministry of Defence
Main Building
Whitehall
London SW1A 2HB
01 218 9000

Office of the Parliamentary
Commissioner for Adminstration
Church House
St Catherine's House
10 Kingsway
London WC2B 6JP
01 242 0262

Prime Minister's Office
10 Downing Street
London SW1
01 233 3000

Privy Council Office
Whitehall SW1A 2AT
01 233 3000

Public Record Office
Chancery Lane
London WC2A 1LR
01 405 0741

CENTRAL OFFICE OF INFORMATION

Central Office of Information
Hercules Road
London SE1 7DU
01 928 2345

Central Office of Information
Overseas Visitors and Information
Studies Division
Hercules Road
London SE1 7DU
01 928 2345

Central Office of Information
North Eastern Region
Andrews House
Gallowgate
Newcastle-upon-Tyne NE1 4TB
0632 327575 ext. 540

Central Office of Information
Yorkshire and Humberside Region
City House
New Station Street

Leeds LS1 4JG
0532 438232 ext. 367

Central Office of Information
Eastern Region
Three Crowns House
72–80 Hills Road
Cambridge CB2 1LL
0223 358911

Central Office of Information
London and South Eastern Region
Atlantic House
Holborn Viaduct
London EC1N 2PD
01 583 5744

Central Office of Information
South Western Region

The Pithay
Bristol BS1 2NF
0272 291071 ext. 3468

Central Office of Information
Midland Region
Five Ways Tower
Frederick Road
Edgbaston
Birmingham B15 1SH
021 643 8191 ext. 2017

Central Office of Information
North Western Region
22nd Floor Sunley Building
Piccadilly Plaza
Manchester M1 4BD
061 832 9111 ext. 362

GOVERNMENT LIBRARIES

Department of Education and
   Science Library
Elizabeth House
York Road
London SE1 7PH
01 928 9222

Department of the Environment and
   Transport Library
2 Marsham Street
London SW1P 3EB
01 212 4847/8/50

Department of Health and Social
   Security Library
Alexander Fleming House
Elephant and Castle
London SE1 6BY
01 407 5522

Departments of Trade and Industry
   Library Services
1 Victoria Street
London SW1 0ET
01 215 7877

Foreign and Commonwealth Office
   Library
Sanctuary Buildings
Great Smith Street
London SW1P 3BZ
91 212 0663

Home Office Library
50 Queen Anne's Gate
London SW1H 9AT
01 213 3646

House of Commons Library
House of Commons
London SW1A 0AA
01 219 4272

House of Lords Library
House of Lords
London SW1A 0PW
01 219 5242

Ministry of Agriculture, Fisheries
   and Food Library
3 Whitehall Place

London SW1A 2HH
01 839 7711

Ministry of Defence (Whitehall)
  Library

Old War Office
Whitehall
London SW1A 2EU
01 218 0139

OTHER SOURCES

Association of District Councils
25 Buckingham Gate
London SW1E 6LE
01 828 7931

Association of Metropolitan
  Authorities
35 Great Smith Street
Westminster
London SW1P 3BJ
01 222 8100

British Library of Political and
  Economic Science
10 Portugal Street
London WC2A 2HD
01 405 7686

Civil and Public Services Association
215 Balham High Road
London SW17 7BQ
01 672 1299

The Hansard Society for
  Parliamentary Government
16 Gower Street
London WC1E 6DP
01 323 1131

Institute of Local Government
  Administrators
127 Lexden Road
Colchester

Essex CO3 3RJ
0206 45212

Institute of Local Government
  Studies
University of Edgbaston
Birmingham 15
021 472 1301

Local Government Reform Society
115 Aldwick Road
Bognor Regis
Sussex

National Association of Local
  Councils
100 Great Russell Street
London WC1B 3LD
01 637 1865

National Union of Ratepayers'
  Associations
47 Victoria Street
London SW1H 0EQ
01 222 6220
01 886 8144

Royal Institute of Public
  Administration
3 Birdcage Walk
London SW1H 9JJ
01 222 2248

11 HISTORY

Ancient Monuments Board for
  England
Fortress House
23 Savile Row
London W1X 2HE
01 734 6010

Ancient Monuments Society
St Andrew-by-the-Wardrobe
Queen Victoria Street
London EC4V 5DE
01 236 3934

Association of Contemporary
  Historians
c/o London School of Economics and
  Political Science
Aldwych
London WC2A 2AE
01 405 7686

Association for Studies in the
  Conservation of Historic
  Buildings
c/o Institute of Archaeology
31–4 Gordon Square
London WC1
01 387 6052

British Academy for the Promotion
  of Historical, Philosophical and
  Philological Studies
Burlington House
Piccadilly
London W1V 0NS
01 734 0457

British Archaeological Association
61 Old Park Ridings

Winchmore Hill
London N21 2ET

British Association for Local History
43 Bedford Square
London WC1B 3DP
01 636 4066

British Records Association
Master's Court
The Charterhouse
Charterhouse Square
London EC1M 6AU
01 253 0436

Cambridge Antiquarian Society
c/o University Archives
University Library
West Road
Cambridge CB3 9DR
0223 61441

Cambridge Group for the History of
  Population and Social Structure
27 Trumpington Street
Cambridge CB2 1QA
0223 35498

Civic Trust
17 Carlton House Terrace
London SW1Y 5AW
01 930 0914

Council for British Archaeology
112 Kennington Road
London SE11 2RE
01 582 0494

Economic History Society
Peterhouse
Cambridge

English Heritage
15–17 Great Marlborough Street
London W1V 1AF
01 734 6010 ext. 810

Folklore Society
c/o University College
Gower Street
London WC1E 6BT
01 387 5894

Hakluyt Society
c/o British Library Map Room
The British Library
Great Russell Street
London WC1B 3DG
025 125 4207

Her Majesty's Tower of London
London EC3N 4AB
01 709 0765 ext. 213

Heraldry Society
28 Museum Street
London WC1
01 580 5110

Historic Houses Association
38 Ebury Street
London SW1W 0LU
01 730 9419

Historical Association
59a Kennington Park Road
London SE11 4JH
01 735 3901

History Workshop Centre for Social
  History
PO Box 69
Oxford OX2 7XA

Institute of Contemporary History
  and Wiener Library Ltd
4 Devonshire Street
London W1N 2BH
01 636 7247

Institute of Historical Research
University of London
Senate House
Malet Street
London WC1E 7HU
01 636 0272

London Record Society
c/o Institute of Historical Research
Senate House
Malet Street
London WC1E 7HU
01 636 0272 ext. 215

Museums Association
34 Bloomsbury Way
London WC1A 2SF
01 404 4767

National Heritage
9a North Street
London SW4 0HN
01 720 6789

National Monuments Record
Fortress House
23 Savile Row
London W1X 1AB
01 734 6010

National Museum of Labour History
Limehouse Town Hall
Commercial Road
London E14 7HA
01 515 3229

National Trust for Places of
  Historical Interest and Natural
  Beauty
42 Queen Anne's Gate
London SW1H 9AS
01 222 9251

Public Record Office
Ruskin Avenue
Kew
Richmond
Surrey TW9 4DU
01 876 344

Royal Commission on Historical
  Manuscripts
Quality House
Quality Court
Chancery Lane
London WC2A 1HP
01 242 1198

Royal Commission on Historical
  Monuments
Fortress House
23 Savile Row
London W1X 1AB
01 734 6010 ext. 308

Royal Historical Society
c/o University College
Gower Street
London WC1E 6BT
01 387 7532

Social History Society of the United
  Kingdom
Centre for Social History
The University of Lancaster
Lancaster LA1 4YG
0524 65201

Society of Antiquaries of London
Burlington House

Piccadilly
London W1V 0HS
01 734 0193
01 737 9954

Society of Archivists
c/o South Yorkshire County Record
  Office
Ellin Street
Sheffield S1 4PL
0742 29191

Society for the Protection of Ancient
  Buildings
37 Spital Square
London E1 6DY
01 377 1644

Society for the Study of Labour
  History
Department of Politics
Salford University
Salford M5 4WT
061 736 5843

Standing Conference for Local
  History
26 Bedford Square
London WC1B 3HU
01 636 4066

The Victorian Society
1 Priory Gardens
Bedford Park
London W4 1TT
01 994 1019

12 INDUSTRIAL COMPANIES

Allied Lyons Plc
Allied House
156 St John's Street
London EC1P 1AR
01 243 9911

Barclays Bank Plc
54 Lombard Street
London EC3P 3AH
01 626 1567

Bat Industries Plc
Windsor House
50 Victoria Street
London SW1A 0NL
01 222 7979

British Aerospace Plc
100 Pall Mall
London SW1Y 5HR
01 930 1020

British Airways
Speedbird House
Heathrow Airport
Hounslow
Middlesex TW6 2JA
01 759 5511

British Coal
Hobart House
Grosvenor Place
London SW1X 7AE
01 235 2020

British Gas Corporation
Rivermill House
152 Grosvenor Road
London SW1V 3JL
01 829 1444

British Petroleum Co Plc
Britannic House
Moor Lane
London EC2Y 9BU
01 920 8000

British Railways Board
Rail House
Euston Square
PO Box 100
London NW1 2D2
01 262 3232

British Steel Corporation
9 Albert Embankment
London SE1 7SN
01 735 7654

British Telecommunications
   Corporation
2–12 Gresham Street
London EC2V 7AG
01 357 3000

Britoil Plc
150 St Vincent Street
Glasgow G2 5LJ
041 889 5988

Central Electricity Generating Board
Sudbury House
15 Newgate Street
London EC1A 7AU
01 248 1202

Courtaulds Plc
18 Hanover Square
London W1A 2BB
01 629 9080

Esso UK Plc
Victoria Street
London SW1E 5JW
01 834 6677

Ford Motor Company Ltd
Eagle Way
Brentwood
Essex CM13 3BW
0277 25300

General Electric Company Plc
1 Stanhope Gate
London W1A 1EH
01 493 8484

Guest, Keen and Nettlefolds Plc
PO Box 55
Cranford Street
Smethwick
West Midlands B66 2R2
021 558 3131

Imperial Chemical Industries Plc
Imperial Chemical House
Millbank
London SW1P 3JF
01 834 4444

Lonrho Plc
Cheapside House
138 Cheapside
London EC2V 6BL
01 606 9898

Lucas Industries Plc
Great King Street
Birmingham B19 2XF
021 554 5252

Marks and Spencer Plc
Michael House
37–67 Baker Street

London W1A 1DN
01 935 4422

Metal Box Plc
Queen's House
Forbury Road
Reading
Berkshire RG1 3JH
0734 581177

Post Office
33 Grosvenor Place
London SW1X 1PX
01 235 8000

Rio-Tinto Zinc Corporation Plc
6 St James's Square
London SW1Y 4LD
01 930 2399

Rover Group
106 Oxford Road
Uxbridge
Middlesex UB8 1EH
0895 5177

Shell UK
Shell Mex House
Strand
London WC2R 0DX
01 934 1234

Tate and Lyle Plc
Sugar Key
Lower Thames Street
London EC3R 6DQ
01 626 6525

Unilever Plc
Unilever House
Blackfriars
London EC4P 4BQ
01 822 5252

13 INDUSTRY AND COMMERCE

Advertising Association
15 Wilton Road
London SW1V 1NJ
01 828 2771

Advisory, Conciliation and
  Arbitration Service
Cleland House
Page Street
London SW1P 4ND
01 211 3000

Aslib - The Association for
  Information Management
Information House
26-7 Boswell Street
London WC1N 3J2
01 430 2671

Association of British Chambers of
  Commerce
212–24 Shaftesbury Avenue
London WC2H 8EB
01 240 5831

Association of Independent
  Businesses
108 Weston Street
London SE1 3QB
01 403 4066

Association of Stock and Share
  Dealers
7 Ludgate Broadway
London EC4V 6DX
01 248 1549

Banking Information Services
10 Lombard Street

London EC3V 9AP
01 626 8486

British Association for Commercial
  and Industrial Education
16 Park Crescent
Regent's Park
London W1N 4AP
01 636 5351

British Institute of Management
Management House
Parker Street
London WC2B 5PT
01 405 3456

British Junior Chamber
12 Regent Place
Rugby
Warwickshire CV21 2PN
0788 72795

British Overseas Trade Board
1 Victoria Street
London SW1H 0ET
01 215 5365

British Poster Advertising
  Association
41 Tothill Street
London SW1H 9LG
01 222 3156/7

British Society of Commerce
25 Bridgeman Terrace
Wigan WN1 1TD
0942 43572

British Standards Institution
2 Park Street
London W1A 2BS
01 629 9000

British Universities Industrial
  Relations Association
Oxford Centre for Management
  Studies
Kennington
Oxford
0865 735422

Business Statistics Office
Cardiff Road
Newport
Gwent NPT 1XG
0633 56111

CBD Research Ltd
154 High Street
Beckenham BR3 1EA
01 650 7745

City Business Library
Gillett House
55 Basinghall Street
London EC2
01 606 3030

Confederation of British Industry
Centre Point
103 New Oxford Street
London WC1A 1DU
01 379 7400

Consumers' Association
14 Buckingham Street
London WC2N 6DS
01 839 1222

Department of Energy
Thames House South
Millbank
London SW1P 4QJ
01 211 3000

Department of Industry
1 Victoria Street
London SW1H 0ET
01 215 7877

Department of Trade
1 Victoria Street
London SW1H 0ET
01 215 7877

Design Council
28 Haymarket
London SW1Y 45U
01 839 8000

Faculty of Teachers in Commerce
141 Bedford Road
Sutton Coldfield
West Midlands B75 6DB
021 378 1265

Henley Centre for Forecasting
2–4 Tudor Street
Blackfriars
London EC4Y 0AA
01 353 9961

HM Customs and Excise
King's Beam House
39–41 Mark Lane
London EC3R 7HE
01 626 1515

Industrial Relations Research Unit
Warwick University
Coventry CV4 7AL
0203 24011

Industrial Society
Peter Runge House
3 Carlton House Terrace
London SW1Y 5DG
01 839 4300

Institute of Administrative
  Management
205 High Street
Beckenham

Kent BR3 1BA
01 658 0171

Institute of Bankers
10 Lombard Street
London EC3V 9AS
01 623 3531

Institute of Commerce
24 Southwark Street
London SE1
01 403 0487

Institute of Directors
116 Pall Mall
London SW1Y 5ED
01 839 1233

Institute of Practitioners in
  Advertising
44 Belgrave Square
London SW1X 8QS
01 235 7020

Institute of Public Relations
1 Great James Street
London WC1N 3DA
01 405 5505

Institute of Workers' Control
Bertrand Russell House
Gamble Street
Nottingham N61 4ET
0602 74504

Labour Research Department
78 Blackfriars Road
London SE1 8HF
01 928 3649

Manpower Services Commission
Moorfoot
Sheffield S1 4PQ
0742 753275

Market Research Society
15 Belgrave Square
London SW1X 8PF
01 235 4709

Ministry of Agriculture Fisheries and
  Food
Whitehall Place
London SW1A 2HH
01 233 3000

Monopolies and Mergers
  Commission
New Court
48 Carey Street
London WC2A 2JT
01 831 6111

National Consumer Council
18 Queen Anne's Gate
London SW1H 9AA
01 222 9501

National Council of Consumer
  Groups
12 Mosley Street
Newcastle-upon-Tyne NE1 1DE
0632 618259

National Economic Development
  Council
Millbank Tower
21 Millbank
London SW1P 4QX
01 211 3000

National Economic Development
  Office
Millbank Tower
21 Millbank
London SW1P 4QX
01 211 3000

Panel on Takeovers and Mergers
PO Box 226
The Stock Exchange
London EC2P 2JX
01 628 2318

Patent Office
25 Southampton Buildings
Chancery Lane
London WC2A 1AY
01 405 8721

Royal Agricultural Society of
  England
35 Belgrave Square
London SW1X 8QN
01 235 5323

Society of Business Economists
11 Bay Tree Walk
Watford
Hertfordshire WD1 3RX
Watford 37287

The Stock Exchange
London EC2P 2JX
01 588 2355

14 INTERNATIONAL AFFAIRS

British International Studies
Association
c/o Department of International
Relations
Keele University
Keele
Staffordshire ST5 5BG
0782 621111

Council for Education in World
Citizenship
19 Tudor Street
London EC4
01 353 3353

Foreign and Commonwealth Office
Downing Street
London SW1A 2AL
01 233 3000

Overseas Development
Administration
Eland House
Stag Place
London SW1E 5DH
01 213 3000

Royal Institute of International
Affairs
Chatham House
10 St James's Square
London SW1Y 4LE
01 930 2233

United Nations Association of Great
Britain and Northern Ireland
3 Whitehall Court
London SW1A 2EL
01 930 2931

United Nations Information Centre
14–15 Stratford Place
London W1N 9AF
01 629 6411

World Development Movement
Bedford Chambers
Covent Garden
London WC2E 8HA
01 836 3672

15 LANGUAGE

Association for Literary and
  Linguistic Computing
Literary and Linguistic Computing
  Centre
Sidgwick Site
Cambridge CB3 9DA
0223 56411

Association of Recognised English
  Language Schools (ARELS)
125 High Holborn
London WC1V 6QD
01 242 3136

British Council
10 Spring Gardens
London SW1A 2BN
01 930 8466

Centre for Information on Language
  Teaching and Research (CILT)
20 Carlton House Terrace
London SW1Y 5AP
01 839 2626

Early English Text Society
c/o T. F. Hoad
St Peter's College
Oxford OX1 2DL

The English Association
1 Priory Gardens
Bedford Park
London W4 1TT
01 995 4236

English Speaking Board
32 Roe Lane
Southport

Merseyside PR9 9EA
0704 34587

Federation of English Language
  Course Organisations
218A York Street
London W1
01 935 5743

Institute of Dialect and Folklife
  Studies
University of Leeds
Leeds LS2 9JT
0532 431751

Institute of Linguists
24A Highbury Grove
London N5 2EA
01 359 7445

Institute of Modern Language
  Studies
University of Leeds
Leeds LS2 9JT
0532 31751

International Phonetic Association
University College London
Gower Street
London WC1E 6BT
01 387 7050

National Association for the
  Teaching of English
10B Thornhill Road
Edgerton
Huddersfield
West Yorkshire HD3 3AF
0484 207228

The Translators' Association
84 Drayton Gardens
London SW10 9SB
01 373 6642

The Translators' Guild
24A Highbury Grove
London N5 2EA
01 359 7445

16 LAW

Amnesty International
5 Roberts Place
London EC1 0EJ
01 251 8371

Association of Law Teachers
c/o P. Harris
Department of Public Sector
  Administration and Law
Sheffield City Polytechnic
Pond Street
Sheffield S1 1WB
0742 20911 ext. 2188

Bar Association for Commerce,
  Finance and Industry
63 Great Cumberland Place
London W1H 7LJ
01 723 9556

British Institute of Human Rights
Charles Clore House
17 Russell Square
London WC1B 5DR
01 637 0420

British Institute for International and
  Comparative Law
Charles Clore House
17 Russell Square
London WC1B 5DR
01 636 58025

British Legal Association
29 Church Road
Tunbridge Wells
Kent TN1 1HT
0892 38214

Centre for Socio-Legal Studies
Wolfson College
Oxford
0865 52968

Council of Legal Education
4 Gray's Inn Place
London WC1R 5DX
01 405 4665

Department of the Director of Public
  Prosecutions
4–12 Queen Anne's Gate
London SW1H 9AZ
01 213 3000

Gray's Inn
South Square
London WC1
01 405 4177

Haldane Society of Socialist Lawyers
35 Wellington Street
London WC2
01 836 5917

Holborn Law Society
69–73 Theobald's Road
London WC1

Home Office
50 Queen Anne's Gate
London SW1H 9AT
01 213 3000

Institute of Advanced Legal Studies
17 Russell Square
London WC1B 5DR
01 637 1731

Justice (British Section of the
  International Commission of
  Jurists)
95a Chancery Lane
London WC2A 2DT
01 405 6018

Law Centres Federation
164 North Gower Street
London NW1 2ND
01 387 8570

Law Commission
Conquest House
37–8 John Street
Theobald's Road
London WC1N 2BQ
01 242 0861

Law Notes Lending Library
25 Chancery Lane
London WC2
01 405 6151

Law Officers Department
Royal Courts of Justice
Strand
London WC2A 2LL
01 405 7641

Law Reform Committee
Lord Chancellor's Department
Neville House
Page Street
London SW1P 4LS
01 211 3000

The Law Society
The Law Society's Hall

113 Chancery Lane
London WC2A 1PL
01 242 1222

Legal Action Group
28a Highgate Road
London NW5 1NS
01 267 0048
01 485 1189

Legal Aid
The Law Society
113 Chancery Lane
London WC2A 1PL
01 242 1222

Lord Chancellor's Department
House of Lords
London SW1
01 219 3000

National Council for Civil Liberties
21 Tabard Street
London SE1 4LA
01 403 3888

Police Federation
15–17 Langley Road
Surbiton
Surrey KT6 6LP
01 399 2247

United Kingdom Association for
  European Law
c/o University of Edinburgh
Old College
South Bridge
Edinburgh

17 LITERATURE

Arts Council Poetry Library
8–9 Long Acre
London WC2E 9LH
01 379 6596

Jane Austen Society
Ivalls
Bentworth
Alton
Hampshire GU34 5JU
0420 63193

Arnold Bennett Literature Society
Bursley Leisure Centre
Market Place
Burslem
Stoke-on-Trent ST6 3DS
0782 813363

The Burns Federation
c/o Dick Institute
Elmbank Avenue
Kilmarnock
Ayrshire KA1 3BU
0563 26401

The British Science Fiction
    Association
18 Gordon Terrace
Blantyre
Lanarkshire
Scotland G72 9NA

Browning Society of London
351 Woodstock Road
Oxford
0865 55962

Byron Society
6 Gertrude Street

London SW10 0JN
01 352 5112

Carlyle Society of Edinburgh
c/o The School of Scottish Studies
University of Edinburgh
27 George Square
Edinburgh EH8 9JX
031 661 1011

Lewis Carroll Society
Clatterwick Hall
Little Leigh
Northwich
Cheshire CW8 4RJ
0606 891303

Crime Writers' Association
c/o The Press Club
76 Shoe Lane
London EC4A 3UB
01 353 2644

The Joseph Conrad Society
The English Department
Royal Holloway College
Egham Hill
Egham
Surrey TW20 0EX

The Dickens Fellowship
48 Doughty Street
London WC1N 2LF
01 405 2127

Edinburgh Sir Walter Scott Club
1 Rothesay Terrace
Edinburgh EH3 7UP
031 225 1300

Edwardian Studies Association
125 Markayte Road
Dagenham
Essex RM8 2LB

George Eliot Fellowship
71 Stepping Stones Road
Coventry CV5 8JT
0203 592231

The Incorporated Brontë Society
Brontë Parsonage
Haworth
Keighley
West Yorkshire
0535 42323

International P. E. N.
38 King Street
London WC2E 8JT
01 374 7939

Johnson Society
Johnson Birthplace Museum
Breadmarket Street
Lichfield
Staffordshire W513 6LG
05432 24972

Johnson Society of London
Round Chimney
Playden
Rye
East Sussex TN31 7UR
079 78252

Keats-Shelley Memorial Association
Keats House
Keats Grove
London NW3 2RR
01 435 2062

Kipling Society
18 Northumberland Avenue
London WC2N 5BJ
01 930 6733

Charles Lamb Society
1a Royston Road
Richmond
Surrey TW10 6LT
01 940 3837

The Library Association
7 Ridgemount Street
London WC1E 7AE
01 636 7543

Marlowe Society
193 White Horse Hill
Chislehurst
Kent BR7 6DH
01 587 7509

National Book League
45 East Hill
Wandsworth
London SW18 2QZ
01 870 9055

The Poetry Book Society
21 Earls Court Square
London SW5 9DE
01 244 9792

Poetry Society
21 Earls Court Square
London SW5 9DE
01 373 7861

Publishers Association
19 Bedford Square
London WC1B 3HJ
01 580 6321

Royal Society of Literature of the
    United Kingdom
1 Hyde Park Gardens
London W2
01 723 5104

Shakespeare Birthplace Trust
The Shakespeare Centre
Stratford-upon-Avon CV37 6QW
0789 4016

The Shakespeare Institute
PO Box 363
Birmingham B15 2TT
021 472 1301

Shakespeare Reading Society
35 Benhurst Court
Leigham Court Road
London SW16 2QN
01 769 7574

Sherlock Holmes Society of London
The Old Crown Inn
Lopen
near South Petherton
Somerset TA13 5JX
0460 40717

Shaw Society
6 Stanstead Grove
London SE6 4UD
01 690 2325

Shaviana
High Orchard
125 Markayte Road
Dagenham
Essex

Society of Authors
84 Drayton Gardens
London SW10 9SD
01 373 6642

The Tennyson Society
c/o Tennyson Research Centre
Central Library
Free School Lane
Lincoln LN2 1EZ
0522 33541

Thomas Hardy Society
8 Brooklands Road
Langport
Somerset TA10 952
0460 720 63

Tolkien Society
c/o Anne Haward
35 Amesbury Crescent
Hove
East Sussex BN3 5RD

H. G. Wells Society
Polytechnic of North London
Department of Language and
  Literature
Prince of Wales Road
London NW5 3LB
01 607 2789

Writers' Guild of Great Britain
430 Edgware Road
London W2 1EH
01 723 8074

18 MILITARY AND DISARMAMENT

Advisory Panel on Disarmament and
  Non-Proliferation
Foreign and Commonwealth Office
Arms Control Disarmament
  Research Unit
Downing Street (East)
London SW1A 2AL
01 233 5762

Bertrand Russell Peace Foundation
Bertrand Russell House
Gamble Street
Nottingham NGT 4ET
0602 784 504

Campaign Against Arms Trade
5 Caledonian Road
London N1 9DX
01 278 1976

Campaign for Nuclear Disarmament
11 Goodwin Street
London N4 3HQ
01 263 9698

Centre for Peace Studies
St Martin's College
Bowerham
Lancaster LA1 3JD
0524 37698

European Nuclear Disarmament
227 Seven Sisters Road
London N4 2DA
01 272 1236

Imperial War Museum
Lambeth Road
London SE1 6HZ
01 735 8922

Imperial War Museum Library
Lambeth Road
London SE1 6HZ
01 735 8922

International Institute for Strategic
  Studies
23 Tavistock Street
London WC2E 7NQ
01 379 7676

Military Archives - King's College
  Library
160 Strand
London WC2R 2LS
01 405 7686

Military Historical Society
National Army Museum
Royal Hospital Road
London SW3 4HT

Ministry of Defence
Main Building
Whitehall
London SW1A 2HB
01 218 9000

National Army Museum
Royal Hospital Road
London SW3 4HT
01 730 0717 ext. 49

National Peace Council
29 Great James Street
London WC1N 3ES
01 242 3228

National Defence College Library
Latimer
Chesham
Buckinghamshire HP5 1UD
02404 4433

National Maritime Library
National Maritime Museum
Romney Road
London SE10 9NF
01 858 4422

National Maritime Museum
Greenwich
London SE10 9NF
01 858 44225

NATO Information Services
Boulevard Léopold III
1100 Bruxelles
Belgium
02 241 00 40

Peace Pledge Union
6 Endsleigh Street
London WC1
01 387 5501

Royal Air Forces Association
43 Groves Park Road
London W4 3RU
01 584 5020

Royal Air Force Museum
Aerodrome Road
London NW9 5LL
01 205 2266

Royal Artillery Institution Library
Royal Military Academy
Academy Road
London SE18 4JJ
01 856 5533

Royal Naval Association
82 Chelsea Manor Street
London SW3 5RU
01 352 6764

Royal United Services Institute for
  Defence Studies
c/o Ministry of Defence
London SW1A 2ET
01 218 5062

School of Peace Studies
Bradford University
Bradford
West Yorkshire BD7 1DP
0274 33466

Stockholm International Peace
  Research Institute (SIPRI)
Sveagagen 166
S–113
46 Stockholm
Sweden

Women Oppose the Nuclear Threat
Central Contact
Box 600
Peace News
8 Elm Avenue
Nottingham

19 MINORITIES

Alcoholics Anonymous
11 Redcliffe Gardens
London SW10 9BQ
01 352 9779

All London Teachers Against Racism
and Fascism
Panther House
Room 216
38 Mount Pleasant
London WC1X 0AP
01 278 7850

Asian Women's Resource and
Refuge Centre
134 Minet Road
London NW10

Association of Gypsy and Romany
Organisations
Romani Place
Trewint Street
London SW18

Black People's Information Centre
301–3 Portobello Road
London W10

Black Women's Centre
41 Stockwell Green
London SW9

Board of Deputies of British Jews
Woburn House
Upper Woburn Place
London WC1H 0EP
01 387 4044

Campaign for Homosexual Equality
274 Upper Street
London N1 2UA
01 359 3973

Commission for Racial Equality
Elliot House
10–12 Allington Street
London SW1E 5EH
01 828 7022

Confederation of Indian
Organisations (UK)
5–5a Westminster Bridge Road
London SE1
01 929 9889

Council of Christians and Jews
48 Onslow Gardens
London SW7 3PX
01 589 8854

Gypsy Lore Society
Manor Farm
Henley Road
Coventry

Immigration Aid Unit
2 Alum Rock Road
Saltley
Birmingham B8 1JB
021 328 1272

Institute of Race Relations
257–9 Pentonville Road
London N1 9NG
01 837 0041/4

Jewish Historical Society of England
33 Seymour Place
London W1H 5AP
01 723 4404

Jewish Museum
Woburn House
Upper Woburn Place
London WC1 0EP
01 388 4525

Joint Council for the Welfare of
  Immigrants
44 Theobald's Road
London WC1 8SP
01 405 5527/8

Minority Arts Advisory Service
Beauchamp Lodge
2 Warwick Crescent
London W2
01 286 1858

Minority Press Group
9 Poland Street
London W1V 3DG
01 439 2059

Minority Rights Group
36 Craven Street
London WC2N 5NG
01 930 6659

National Association for Multiracial
  Education
86 Station Road
Mickleover
Derby DE3 5FP
0332 511751

National Association of Community
  Relations Councils
5 Tavistock Place
London WC1
01 388 3368

National Council for Civil Liberties
186 King's Cross Road
London WC1X 9DE
01 278 4575

National Gypsy Council
Greengate Street
Oldham
Greater Manchester
061 665 1924

Release
1 Elgin Avenue
London W9 3PR
01 289 1123

Research Unit on Ethnic Relations
Aston University in Birmingham
St Peter's College
College Road
Saltley
Birmingham B8 3TE
021 327 0194

Runnymede Trust
37a Gray's Inn Road
London WC1X 8PP
01 404 5266

Searchlight Publishing
37B New Cavendish Street
London W1M 8JR
01 928 9810

United Kingdom Immigrants
  Advisory Service
7th Floor
Brettenham House
Savoy Street
Strand
London WC2E 7EN
01 240 5176

Union of Muslim Organisations of
  UK and Eire
109 Campden Hill Road
London W8
01 229 0538

West Indian Women's Organisation
　Association
71 Pound Lane
Willesden
London NW10 2HU
01 451 4827/7331

20 MUSIC

Amateur Music Association
43 Renshaw Street
Liverpool L1 2SF
051 709 68 62

Association for British Music
2 Union Place
Boston
Lincolnshire PE21 6PS
0205 60541

BBC Music Library
Yalding House
156 Great Portland Street
London W1N 6AJ
01 580 4468

British Academy of Songwriters,
  Composers and Authors
148 Charing Cross Road
London WC2
01 240 2823

British Federation of Music Festivals
Festivals House
198 Park Lane
Macclesfield
Cheshire SK11 6UD
0625 28297

British Jazz Society
10 Southfield Gardens
Twickenham
Middlesex TW1 4SZ
01 892 0133

British Music Information Centre
10 Stratford Place
London W1N 9AE
01 499 8567

The Composers' Guild of Great
  Britain
10 Stratford Place
London W1N 9AE
01 499 8567

English Folk Dance and Song Society
Cecil Sharp House
2 Regent's Park Road
London NW1 7AY
01 485 2206

Gilbert and Sullivan Society
273 Northfield Avenue
London W5 4UA

Hirsch Music Library
British Library
Great Russell Street
London WC1
01 636 1544 ext. 260

International Association of Music
  Libraries
Royal Northern College of Music
124 Oxford Road
Manchester M13 9RD
061 273 6283 ext. 244

Jazz Centre Society
35 Great Russell Street
London WC1
01 580 8532

The Morris Ring
21 Eccles Road
Ipswich
Suffolk IP2 9RG
0473 682540

National Federation of Music
  Societies
Francis House
Francis Street
London SW1P 1DE
01 828 7320

Royal Academy of Music
Marylebone Road
London NW1 5HT
01 935 5461

Royal College of Music
Prince Consort Road
London SW7 2BS
01 589 3643

Royal Musical Association
10 Braggs Lane
Wrestlingworth
Sandy
Bedfordshire SG10 2ER
0223 312393 ext. 3410

Royal Philharmonic Society
10 Stratford Place
London W1N 9AE
01491 8110

Society for the Promotion of New
  Music
10 Stratford Place
London W1N 9AE
01 491 8111

Vaughan Williams Memorial Library
2 Regent's Park Road
London NW1 7AY
01 485 2206

Victoria Library - Music Lending
  Library
160 Buckingham Palace Road
London SW1

Workers' Music Association
236A Westbourne Park Road
London W11 1EL
01 727 7005

21 NORTHERN IRELAND

The Civil Service Commission
Rosepart House
Upper Newtownards Road
Belfast BT4 3NR
02318 4585

Department of Agriculture for
Northern Ireland
Dundonald House
Upper Newtownards Road
Belfast BT4 3SB
0232 650111

Department of Economic
Development Northern Ireland
Netherleigh
Massey Avenue
Belfast BT4 2JP
0232 63244

Department of Education for
Northern Ireland
Rathgael House
Ballo Road
Bangor
County Down BT19 2PR
0247 66311

Department of the Environment for
Northern Ireland
Stormont
Belfast BT4 3SS
0232 63210

Department of Finance
Parliament Buildings
Stormont

Belfast BT4 3SS
0232 63210

Department of Health and Social
Services Northern Ireland
Dundonald House
Upper Newtownards Road
Belfast BT4 3SF
0232 650111

Exchequer and Audit Department
Northern Ireland
Rosepark House
Upper Newtownards Road
Belfast BT4 3NS
02318 4585

Industrial Development Board for
Northern Ireland (IDB)
IDB House
64 Chichester Street
Belfast BT1 4JX
0232 233233

Lord Chancellor's Department
Northern Ireland
Northern Ireland Court Service
Headquarters
Windsor House
Bedford Street
Belfast BT2 7LT
0232 228594

Northern Ireland Development
Agency
Maryfield
100 Belfast Road

Holywood
County Down BT18 9QX
035281 4232

Northern Ireland Economic Council
Parliament Buildings
Stormont
Belfast BT4 3TT

Northern Ireland Information
  Service
Stormont Castle
Belfast BT4 3ST
0232 63011

Northern Ireland Office
Whitehall
London SW1A 2A2
01 273 3000

Northern Ireland Office
Government Offices
Great George Street
London SW1P 3AJ
01 233 3000

Office of the Northern Ireland
  Parliamentary Commissioner for
  Administration
33 Wellington Place
Belfast BT1 6HN
0232 233821

Public Record Office of Northern
  Ireland
66 Balmoral Avenue
Belfast BT 6NY
0232 661621

OTHER SOURCES

Arts Council of Northern Ireland
181A Stranmillis Road
Belfast BT9 5DU
0232 663591

Northern Ireland Tourist Board
48 High Street
Belfast BT1 2DS
0232 31221

Ulster Archaeological Society
c/o Department of Archaeology
Queen's University
Belfast BT7 1NN
0232 45133 ext. 255

Ulster Architectural Heritage Society
181a Stranmills Road
Belfast BT9 5DU
0232 660809

Ulster Folklife Society
c/o Ulster Folk Museum
Cultra Manor
Holywood
County Down BT18 0EU
02317 5411

Ulster Society for Irish Historical
  Studies
36 North Parade
Belfast BT7 2GG

22 POLITICAL ORGANISATIONS

POLITICAL PARTIES

Communist Party of Great Britain
16 St John Street
London EC1M 4AD
01 251 4406

Conservative and Unionist Party
32 Smith Square
London SW1P 3HH
01 222 9000

The Green Party
10 Station Road
Balham High Road
London SW12 9AZ
01 673 0045

Labour Party
150 Walworth Road
London SE17 1JT
01 703 0833

Liberal Party
1 Whitehall Place
London SW1A 2HE
01 839 4092

Plaid Cymru
51 Cathedral Road
Cardiff CF1 9HD
0222 31944

Scottish National Party
6 North Charlotte Street
Edinburgh EH2 4JH
031 226 3661

Social Democratic Party
4 Cowley Street
London SW1
01 222 7999

OTHER SOURCES

Bow Group
240 High Holborn
London WC1V 1DT
01 405 0878

Campaign Group of Labour MPs
House of Commons
Westminster
London SW1
01 219 3000

Conservative Political Centre
32 Smith Square
London SW1P 3HH
01 222 9000

Electoral Reform Society
6 Chancel Street
Southwark
London SE1 0UX
01 928 9407

Fabian Society
11 Dartmouth Street
London SW1H 9BN
01 222 8877

Labour Party Library
150 Walworth Road
London SE17 1JT
01 703 0833

Monday Club
51 Victoria Street
London SW1
01 799 5220

Marx Memorial Library
37a Clerkenwell Green

London EC1R 0DU
01 253 1485

Tribune Group
c/o Jeannette Gould
House of Commons
London SW1A 0AA

23 PRESS

DAILY NEWSPAPERS

Daily Express
121 Fleet Street
London EC4P 4JT
01 353 8000

Daily Mail
Northcliffe House
Tudor Street
London EC4Y 0JA
01 353 6000

Daily Mirror
Holborn Circus
London EC1P 1DQ
01 353 0246

Daily Star
Great Ancoats Street
Manchester M60 4HB
061 236 9575

Daily Telegraph
135 Fleet Street
London EC4P 4BL
01 353 4242

Financial Times
Bracken House
10 Cannon Street
London EC4P 4BY
01 248 8000

Guardian
119 Farringdon Road
London EC1R 3ER
01 278 2332

The Independent
40 City Road
London EC1Y 2DB
01 253 1222

Morning Star
75 Farringdon Road
London EC1M 3JX
01 405 9242

Sun
News Group Newspapers Ltd
30 Bouverie Street
London EC4Y 8DE
01 353 3030

Today
70 Vauxhall Bridge Road
Pimlico
London SW1V 2RP
01 630 1333

The Times
200 Gray's Inn Road
London WC1X 8EZ
01 837 1234

SUNDAY NEWSPAPERS

Mail on Sunday
Northcliffe House
London EC4Y 0JA
01 353 6000

Sunday Mirror
Holborn Circus
London EC1P 1DQ
01 353 0246

News of the World
30 Bouverie Street
London EC4
01 353 3030

Sunday People
9 New Fetter Lane
London EC4A 1AR
01 353 0246

Observer
8 St Andrews Hill
London EC4V 5JA
01 236 0202

Sunday Telegraph
135 Fleet Street
London EC4P 4BL
01 353 4242

Sunday Express
Fleet Street
London EC4P 4JT
01 353 8000

Sunday Times
200 Gray's Inn Road
London WC1X 8EX
01 837 1234

OTHER SOURCES

Institute of Journalists
Bedford Chambers
Covent Garden
London WC2E 8HA
01 836 6541

Press Club
76 Shoe Lane
London EC4A 3JB
01 353 2644

National Council for the Training of
  Journalists
Carlton House
Hemnell Street
Epping
Essex CM16 4NL
0378 72395

The Press Council
1 Salisbury Square
London EC4Y 8AE
01 353 1248

Newspaper Library
Colindale Avenue
London NW9 5HE
01 200 5515

National Union of Journalists
Acorn House
314–20 Gray's Inn Road
London WC1 8DP
01 278 7916

Newspaper Society
Whitefriars House
6 Carmelite Street
London EC4Y 0BL
01 583 3311

405

24 SCIENCE AND TECHNOLOGY

Advisory Council for Applied
  Research and Development
Cabinet Office
70 Whitehall
London SW1A 2AS
01 233 6139

Association of British Science
  Writers
c/o The Royal Institution
21 Albemarle Street
London W1X 4BS
01 409 2992

Association of Consulting Scientists
Owles Hall
Buntingford
Hertfordshire 5G9 9PL
0763 72665

Association of Management and
  Professional Staffs
14 Harley Street
London W1N 1AA
01 636 7021

The Association for Science
  Education
College Lane
Hatfield
Hertfordshire AL10 9AA
07072 67411

British Association for the
  Advancement of Science
23 Savile Row
London W1X 1AB
01 734 6010

British Astronomical Association
Burlington House
Piccadilly
London W1V 0NL
01 734 4145

The British Computer Society
13 Mansfield Street
London W1M 0BP
01 637 0471

British Medical Association
BMA House
Tavistock Square
London WC1H 7JP
01 387 4499

British Museum - Natural History
Cromwell Road
London SW7 5BD
01 589 6323

British Society for the History of
  Science
Halfpenny Furze
Nill Lane
Chalfont Saint Giles
Buckinghamshire HP8 4NR
02407 2509

British Society for the Philosophy of
  Science
School of Social Sciences
University of Sussex
Falmer
Brighton BN1 9AN
0273 606755

British Society for Social
  Responsibility in Science
9 Poland Street
London W1V 3DG
01 437 2728

British Technology Group
Kingsgate House 66–74
Victoria Street
London SW1E 6SL
01 828 3400

Chemical Society
Burlington House
Piccadilly
London W1V 0BN
01 734 9971

Council for Science and Society
3–4 St Andrew's Hill
London EC4V 5BY
01 236 6723

Institute of Biology
41 Queen's Gate
London SW7 5HU
01 589 9076

Institute of Information Scientists
657 High Road
Tottenham
London N17 8AA
01 808 6399

Institute of Physics
47 Belgrave Square
London SW1X 8QX
01 235 6111

Institute of Science Technology
Staple Inn Buildings South
335 High Holborn
London WC1V 7PX
01 405 9443

Intermediate Technology Group
9 King Street
Covent Garden

London WC2E 8HW
01 836 9434

The Institution of Civil Engineers
1–7 Great George Street
London SW1P 3AA
01 222 7722

The Institution of Electrical
  Engineers
Savoy Place
London WC2R 0BL
01 240 1871

Linnaean Society of London
Burlington House
Piccadilly
London W1V 0LQ
01 734 1040

Medical Research Council
20 Park Crescent
London W1N 4AL
01 636 5422

National Centre for Alternative
  Technology
Llwyngwern Quarry
Machynlleth
Powys
Wales SY20 9AZ
0654 2400

National Computing Centre
Oxford Road
Manchester M1 7ED
061 228 6333

Parliamentary and Scientific
  Committee
30 Farrington Street
London EC4A 4EA
01 236 3011 ext. 275

Research and Development Society
47 Belgrave Square
London SW1X 8QX
01 235 6111

Royal Aeronautical Society
4 Hamilton Place
London W1V 0BQ
01 499 3515

Royal Anthropological Institute
56 Queen Anne Street
London W1M 9LA
01 486 6832

Royal Astronomical Society
Burlington House
Piccadilly
London W1V 0NL
01 734 4582

Royal Institution of Great Britain
  Library
21 Albemarle Street
London W1X 4BS
01 409 2992

Royal Society of Chemistry
Burlington House
Piccadilly
London W1V 0BN
01 734 9971

The Royal Society
6 Carlton House Terrace
London SW1Y 5AG
01 839 5561

Royal Society Library
6 Carlton House Terrace
London SW1Y 5AG
01 839 5561

Science and Engineering Research
  Council
Polaris House
North Star Avenue
Swindon SN2 1ET
0793 26222

Science Museum
Exhibition Road
South Kensington
London
01 589 3456

Science Museum Library
Imperial Institute Road
South Kensington
London SW7 NH
01 589 6371

Science Policy Research Unit
Mantell Building
University of Sussex
Falmer
Brighton BN1 9RF
0273 686758

Science Reference Library
Holborn Branch
25 Southampton Buildings
Chancery Lane
London WC2A 1AW
01 405 8721 ext. 3344/5

United Kingdom Atomic Energy
  Authority
Library and Information Centre
11 Charles II Street
London SW1Y 4QP
01 930 6262 ext. 587

25 SCOTLAND

GOVERNMENT OFFICES

Crown Office
5–7 Regent Road
Edinburgh EH7 5BL
031 557 3800

Department of Agriculture and
 Fisheries for Scotland
Chesser House
500 Gorgie Road
Edinburgh EH11 3AW
031 443 4020

General Register Office (Scotland)
New Register House
Edinburgh EH1 3YT
031 556 3952

Highland and Islands Development
 Board
Bridge House
27 Bank Street
Inverness IV1 1QR
0463 234171 ext. 208

Industry Department for Scotland
New St Andrew's House
Edinburgh EH1 3TA
031 556 8400

Lord Advocate's Department
Fielden House
10 Great College Street
Westminster
London SW1P 3SL
01 212 7676

Scottish Development Department
New St Andrew's House
St James Centre
Edinburgh EH1 3SZ
031 556 8400

Scottish Economic Council
c/o Scottish Economic Planning
 Department
Scottish Office
New St Andrew's House
St James Centre
Edinburgh EH1 3TA
031 556 8400

Scottish Economic Planning
 Department
New St Andrew's House
St James Centre
Edinburgh EH1 3TA
031 556 8400

Scottish Education Department
New St Andrew's House
St James Centre
Edinburgh EH1 3SY
031 556 8400

Scottish Home and Health
 Department
St Andrew's House
Regent Road
Edinburgh EH1 3DE
031 556 8501

409

Scottish Information Office
New St Andrew's House
St James Centre
Edinburgh EH1 3TD
031 556 8400 ext. 5652

Scottish Law Commission
140 Causewayside
Edinburgh EH9 1PR
031 668 2131

Scottish Office
New St Andrew's House

St James Centre
Edinburgh EH1 3SX
031 556 8400

Scottish Office Library
Room 2–64 New St Andrew's House
Edinburgh EH1 3TG
031 556 8400 ext. 5694

Scottish Record Office
HM General Register House
Edinburgh EH1 3YY
031 556 6585

OTHER SOURCES

Ancient Monuments Board for
  Scotland
3–11 Melville Street
Edinburgh EH3 7QN
031 226 2570 ext. 204

Association of Arts Centres in
  Scotland
Braehead
Nether Anguston
Culter
Aberdeen AB1 0PN
0224 732112

Association for Scottish Literary
  Studies
c/o Department of English
Tylor Building
University
Aberdeen AB9 2UB
0224 40241

Edinburgh Bibliographical Society
c/o National Library of Scotland
George IV Bridge
Edinburgh EH1 1EW
031 226 4531

Gaelic League of Scotland
c/o Highlanders Institute
34 Berkeley Street
Glasgow G3

The Highland Association
Abertarff House
Church Street
Inverness IV1 1EU
0463 31226

Law Society of Scotland
26 Drumbsbeugh Gardens
Edinburgh EH3 7YR
031 226 7411

National Galleries of Scotland
The Mound
Edinburgh EH2 2EL
031 556 8921

National Library of Scotland
George IV Bridge
Edinburgh EH1 1EW
031 226 4531

National Trust for Scotland
5 Charlotte Square
Edinburgh EH2 4DU
031 226 5922

Royal Celtic Society
49 Queen Street
Edinburgh EH2 3NT
031 226 5084

Royal Fine Art Commission for
  Scotland
9 Atholl Crescent
Edinburgh EH3 8HA
031 229 1109

The Royal Scottish Academy
The Mound
Edinburgh EH2 2EL
031 225 6671

School of Scottish Studies
27 George Square
Edinburgh EH8 9LD
031 667 1011

Scottish Arts Council
19 Charlotte Square
Edinburgh EH2 4DF
031 226 6051

Scottish Church History Society
51 Portland Road
Kilmarnock
Ayrshire KA1 2EQ
0563 25311

Scottish Economic Society
c/o Department of Economics
Heriot-Watt University

Edinburgh EH1 2HT
031 225 8432

Scottish Gaelic Texts Society
108 Queen Victoria Drive
Glasgow G14 9BL
041 959 5090

Scottish History Society
c/o Dr Annette M. Smith
Department of Modern History
The University
Dundee DD1 4HN
0382 23181

Scottish Record Society
Scottish History Department
University of Glasgow
Glasgow G12 8QQ
041 339 8855 ext. 576

Scottish Tourist Board
23 Ravelston Terrace
Edinburgh EH4 3EU
031 332 2433

Society of Antiquaries of Scotland
c/o National Museum of Antiquities
Queen Street
Edinburgh EH2 1JD
031 556 8921

26 SOCIAL POLICY AND VOLUNTARY ORGANISATIONS

Acton Society Trust
9 Poland Street
London W1V 3DG
01 437 8954

Age Concern
40 Pitcairn Road
Mitcham
Surrey CR4 3LL
01 640 5431

Alternative Communities Movement
18 Garth Road
Bangor
North Wales

Association for Children's Play and
  Recreation
Britannia House
50 Great Charles Street
Birmingham B3 2LB
021 233 3399

Association of Community Workers
Colombo Sports and Community
  Centre
Colombo Street
Blackfriars
London SE1 8DP
01 633 0628

Association of Directors of Social
  Services
Social Services Department
County Hall
Taunton
Somerset TA1 4DY
0832 73451

Association for Independent
  Disabled Self-Sufficiency
7 Alfred Street
Bath
Avon BA1 2QU
0225 25197

Association for Neighbourhood
  Councils
50 Whetstone Close
Farquhar Road
Edgbaston
Birmingham B15 2QN

Association of Research into
  Voluntary Action and
  Community Involvement
26 Queen's Road
Wivenhoe
Essex CO7 9JH
0206 225344

Association for Self-Help and
  Community Groups
7 Chesham Terrace
Ealing
London W13 9HX
01 579 5589

Association for the Teaching of the
  Social Sciences
Allandale
Johnshill
Lochwinnoch
Renfrewshire
0505 842061

British Agencies for Adoption and
  Fostering
11 Southwark Street
London SE1 1RQ
01 407 8800

British Association for Counselling
37a Sheep Street
Rugby
Warwicks CV21 3BX
0788 78328/9

British Association of Settlements
  and Social Action Centres
13 Stockwell Road
London SW9 9AU
01 733 7428

British Association of Social Workers
16 Kent Street
Birmingham B5 6RD
021 622 3911

British Council of Churches
2 Eaton Gate
London SW1W 9BL
01 730 9611

British Institute of Management
  Foundation
Management House
Parker Street
London WC2B 5PT
01 405 3456

British Pensioners and Trade Unions
  Action Association
22 Church Lane
Woodford
Bramhall
Cheshire SK7 1RQ

British Red Cross Society
9 Grosvenor Crescent
London SW1X 7EJ
01 235 5454

British Sociological Association
10 Portugal Street
London WC2A 2HB
01 242 3388

British Sports Association for the
  Disabled
Hayward House
Ludwig Guttman Sports Centre
  for the Disabled
Stoke Mandeville
Harvey Road
Aylesbury
Bucks HP21 8PP
0296 27889

British Youth Council
57 Chalton Street
London NW1 1HU
01 387 7559/5882

Brook Advisory Centres
153A East Street
London SE17 2SD
01 708 1234/1390

Centre for Policy on Ageing
Nuffield Lodge Studio
Regent's Park
London NW1 4RS
01 586 9844/9

Charities Aid Foundation
48 Pembury Road
Tonbridge
Kent TN9 2JD
0732 356323

Child Poverty Action Group
1 Macklin Street
London WC2B 5NH
01 242 3225/9194

Children's Legal Centre
20 Compton Terrace
London N1 2UN
01 359 6251

413

Christian Aid
PO Box No 1
London SW9 8BH
01 733 5500

Church Action on Poverty
27 Blackfriars Road
Salford
Lancs M3 7AQ
061 832 5253

Church of England National Council
  for Social Aid
38 Ebury Street
London SW1W 0LU
01 730 6175

Civil Aid
'Thistledome'
Main Street
Sewstern
Grantham
Lincs
0476 860923

Commission for Racial Equality
Elliot House
10–12 Allington Street
London SW1E 5EH
01 828 7022

Community Action
PO Box 665
London SW1X

Community Projects Foundation
60 Highbury Grove
London N5 2AG
01 226 5375

Community Relations Councils
National Association of Community
  Relations Councils
5 Tavistock Place
London WC1

Community Resources Agency
Lozells Social Development Centre
173 Lozells Road
Lozells
Birmingham B19 1RN
021 523 8076

Co-operative Women's Guild
342 Hoe Street
Walthamstow
London E17 9PX
01 520 4902/521 2715

Councils for Voluntary Service -
  National Association
26 Bedford Square
London WC1B 3HU
01 636 4066

Counsel and Care for the Elderly
131 Middlesex Street
London E1 7JF
01 247 9844

Department of Health and Social
  Security
Alexander Fleming House
Elephant and Castle
London SE1 6BY
01 407 5522

Disability Alliance
25 Denmark Street
London WC2 8NJ
01 240 0806

Disablement Information Advice
  Line (Dial)
DIAL House
117 High Street
Clay Cross
Nr Chesterfield
Derbyshire S45 9DZ
0246 864498

Dr Barnado's
Tanner's Lane
Barkingside

Ilford
Essex IG6 1QG
01 550 8822

Economic and Social Science
  Research Association
177 Vauxhall Bridge Road
London SW1V 1ER
01 834 4979

Family Planning Association
Margaret Pyke House
27–35 Mortimer Street
London W1N 7RJ
01 636 7866

Family Rights Group
6 Manor Gardens
Holloway Road
London N7 6LA
01 272 4231

Family Welfare Association
501–5 Kingsland Road
London E8 4AU
01 254 6251

Fawcett Society
46 Harleyford Road
London SE11 5AY
01 587 1287

Foundation for Alternatives
The Rookery
Adderbury
Nr Banbury
Oxon
0295 810993

Gingerbread
35 Wellington Street
London WC2E 7BN
01 240 0953

Green Alliance
60 Chandos Place
Covent Garden

London WC2N 4HG
01 836 0341

Housing Centre Trust
33 Alfred Place
London WC1E 7JU
01 637 4202

Howard League
322 Kennington Park Road
London SE11 4PP
01 735 3317

Institute of Community Studies
18 Victoria Park Square
London E2 9PF
01 980 6263

Institute of Social Welfare
239 Weston Road
Acton Trussell
Stafford ST17 0SL
0785 3572

Invalid Children's Aid Association
126 Buckingham Road
London SW1W 9SB
01 730 9891

Joint Council for the Welfare of
  Immigrants
115 Old Street
London ECN 9JR
01 251 8701

Joseph Rowntree Memorial Trust
Beverely House
Shipton Road
York YO3 6RB
0904 29241

Low Pay Unit
9 Poland Street
London W1V 3DG
01 437 1780

Mental Health Foundation
8 Hallam Street

415

London W1N 6DH
01 580 0145/6

MIND
22 Harley Street
London W1N 2ED
01 637 0741

Mutual Aid Centre
18 Victoria Park Square
London E2 9PF
01 980 6263

National Association of Citizens
  Advice Bureaux
115–23 Pentonville Road
London N1 9LZ
01 833 2181

National Association of Community
  Councils
8–16 Coronet Street
London N1 6HD
01 739 6658

National Association of Round
  Tables of Great Britain and
  Ireland
Marchesi House
15 Park Road
London NW1 6XN
01 262 3071

National Association of Women's
  Clubs
5 Vernon Rise
King's Cross Road
London WC1X 9EP
01 837 1434

National Association of Young
  People's Counselling and
  Advisory Services
17–23 Albion Street
Leicester LE1 6GD
0533 554775

National Children's Bureau
8 Wakley Street
Islington
London EC1V 7QE
01 278 9441

National Council for Voluntary
  Organisations
26 Bedford Square
London WC1B 3HU
01 636 4066

National Council for Voluntary
  Youth Services
Wellington House
29 Albion Street
Leicester LE1 6GD
0533 554910

National Cyrenians
13 Wincheap
Canterbury
Kent CT1 3TB
0227 51641

National Federation of the Blind of
  the UK
45 South Street
Normanton
West Yorks WF6 1EE
0294 89 2146

National Federation of Community
  Organisations
8–9 Upper Street
London N1 0PQ
01 226 0189

National Institute for Social Work
5–7 Tavistock Place
London WC1H 9SS
01 387 9681

National League of the Blind and
  Disabled
2 Tenterden Road
London N17 8BE
01 808 6030

National Marriage Guidance
  Council
Herbert Gray College
Little Church Street
Rugby
Warwickshire CV21 3AP
0788 73241

National Playing Fields Association
25 Ovington Square
London SW3 1LQ
01 584 6445

National Society for the Prevention
  of Cruelty to Children
64–47 Saffron Hill
London EC1N 8RS
01 242 1626

National Unemployment Action
  Association
c/o Birmingham Settlement
318 Summer Lane,
Birmingham B19 3RL
021 359 3562

National Youth Bureau
17–23 Albion Street
Leicester LE1 6GD
0533 554775

Nuffield Foundation
Nuffield Lodge
Regent's Park
London NW1 4RS
01 722 8871

Office of Population Census and
  Surveys
St Catherine's House
10 Kingsway
London WC2B 6JP
01 242 0262

Outward Bound Trust
12 Upper Belgrave Street
London SW1X 8BA
01 235 4286

Patients Association
Room 33
18 Charing Cross Road
London WC2H 0HR
01 240 0671

Pensioners' Link
17 Balfe Street
London N1 9EB
01 278 5501

Policy Studies Institute
100 Park Village East
London NW1
01 387 2171

Prison Reform Trust
Nuffield Lodge
Regent's Park
London NW1 4RS
01 722 8871/586 4978

Queen's Silver Jubilee Trust
8 Buckingham Street
London WC2N 6BU
01 930 9811

Rotary International in Great Britain
  and Ireland
Sheen Lane House
Sheen Lane
London SW14 8AF
01 878 0931

Royal National Institute for the
  Blind
224 Great Portland Street
London W1N 6AA
01 388 1266

Royal National Institute for the Deaf
105 Gower Street
London WC1E 6AH
01 387 8033

Royal Society for the Prevention of
  Accidents
Cannon House

417

The Priory Queensway
Birmingham B4 6BS
021 233 2461

Salvation Army
101 Queen Victoria Street
London EC4P 4EP
01 236 5222

Samaritans Incorporated
17 Uxbridge Road
Slough
Berks SL1 1SN
0753 32713/4

Shaftesbury Society
Shaftesbury House
112 Regency Street
London SW1P 4AX
01 834 7444

Shelter
157 Waterloo Road
London SE1 8XF
01 633 9377

Simon Community
St Joseph's House
129 Malden Road
London NW5 4HS
01 485 6639

Social Aid
38 Ebury Street
London SW1W 0LU
01 730 6175

Social Care Association
23a Victoria Road
Surbiton
Surrey KT6 4JZ
01 390 6831

Social Science Research Council
1 Temple Avenue
London EC4Y 0BD
01 353 5252

Sue Ryder Foundation
Cavendish
Suffolk CO10 8AY
0787 280252

Toc H
Forest Close
Wendover
Bucks HP22 6BT
0296 623911

Volunteer Centre
29 Lower King's Road
Berkhamsted
Herts HP4 2AB
04427 73311

Women's Royal Voluntary Service
17 Old Park Lane
London W1Y 4AJ
01 499 6040

Youthaid
9 Poland Street
London W1V 3DG
01 439 8523

27 SPORT

Amateur Athletics Association
Francis House
London SW1P 1DL
01 828 9326

Amateur Boxing Association
Francis House
London SW1P 1DE
01 828 8571

Amateur Swimming Association
Derby Square
Loughborough
Leicester LE11 0AL
0509 30431

British Boxing Board of Control
Ramillies Building
Hills Place
Oxford Circus
London W1R
01 437 1475/6

British Olympics Association
1–2 John Prince's Street
London W1M 0DH
01 408 2029

Football Association
16 Lancaster Gate
London W2 3LW
01 262 4542

Football League
319 Clifton Drive South
St Annes-on-Sea
Lancashire FY8 1JG
0253 729421

Lawn Tennis Association
Barons Court
West Kensington
London W14 9EG
01 387 2366

Marylebone Cricket Club
Lord's Cricket Ground
London NW8 8QN
01 289 1611

Rugby Football League
180 Chapeltown Road
Leeds LS7 4HT
0532 624637

Rugby Football Union
Whitton Road
Twickenham
Middlesex TW2 7RQ
01 892 8161

Sports Council
16 Upper Woburn Place
London WC1
01 388 1277

28 THEATRE AND PERFORMING ARTS

British Actors Equity Association
8 Harley Street
London W1N 2AB
01 637 9311

British Theatre Association
9 Fitzroy Square
London W1P 6AE
01 387 2666

British Theatre Association Library
9 Fitzroy Square
London W1P 6AE
01 387 2666

British Theatre Institute
30 Clareville Street
London SW7 5AW
01 370 4154

British Theatre Resource Centre
Unit 33
44 Earlham Street
London WC2H 9LA

Central Council for Amateur
    Theatre
County Hall
Martineau Lane
Norwich NR1 2DL
0603 611122

Edinburgh Festival Fringe Society
170 High Street
Edinburgh EH1 1QS
031 226 5257

Edinburgh Festival Society
21 Market Street

Edinburgh EH1 1BW
031 226 4001

International Federation for Theatre
    Research
14 Woronzow Road
London NW8 6QE

Little Theatre Guild of Great Britain
19 Abbey Park Road
Grimsby
South Humberside DN32 0HJ
0472 43424

National Drama Festivals
    Association
24 Jubilee Road
Formby
Liverpool L37 2HT
07048 71292

National Operatic and Dramatic
    Association
1 Crestfield Street
London WC1H 8AU
01 837 5655

National Sound Archive
20 Exhibition Road
London SW7 2AS
01 589 6603

Royal Academy of Dancing
48 Vicarage Crescent
London SW11 3LT
01 223 0091

Royal Academy of Dramatic Art
62–4 Gower Street

London WC2E 6ED
01 636 7076

Society for Theatre Research
77 Kinnerton Street
London SW1X 8ED

Theatre Arts Society
Wyndhams Theatre
Charing Cross Road
London WC2 0DA
01 836 2671

Theatre Museum
Victoria and Albert Museum
South Kensington
London SW7 2RL
01 589 6371

Variety Club of Great Britain
3rd Floor East
Avon House
360 Oxford Street
London W1N 0DY
01 491 4521

29 THOUGHT AND PHILOSOPHY

Anthrosophical Society of Great
  Britain
Rudolf Steiner House
35 Park Road
London NW1 6XT
01 723 4400

Aristotelian Society
Philosophy Department
Bedford College
Regent's Park
London NW1
01 486 4400

Bertrand Russell Society
9 Nasebey Avenue
Higher Blackley
Manchester M9 2JJ

British Academy for the Promotion
  of Historical, Philosophical and
  Philological Studies
Burlington House
Piccadilly
London W1V 0NS
01 734 0457

British Humanist Association
13 Prince of Wales Terrace
London W8 5PG
01 937 2341

British Society for the Philosophy of
  Science
Room 0–60
Social Studies Building
University of Warwick
Coventry CV4 7AL
0203 24011

Cambridge Philosophical Society
c/o Scientific Periodicals Library
Arts School
Benet Street
Cambridge CB2 3PY
0223 358381

The Francis Bacon Society
Cannonbury Tower
Canonbury Place
Islington
London N1 2NQ
01 370 1233

Humanist Teachers' Association
13 Prince of Wales Terrace
London W8 5PB
01 937 2341

MIND Association
c/o Prof. D. Holdcroft
Department of Philosophy
University of Leeds
Leeds LS2 9JT
0532 431751 ext. 6241

The Philosophical Society of England
Victoria Institute
29 Queen Street
London EC4R 1BH
01 248 3642

Radical Philosophy
c/o Department of Sociology
University of Essex
Colchester CO4 3SQ

Radical Philosophy Group
c/o Howard Feather
Thurrock Technical College
Grays
Essex
0375 371621 ext. 352

Rationalist Press Association
88 Islington High Street
London N1 8EW
01 226 7251

Royal Institute of Philosophy
14 Gordon Square

London WC1H 0AG
01 387 4130

Thomas Paine Society
443 Meadow Lane
Nottingham NG 3GB
0602 860010

The Victorian Institute or
   Philosophical Society of Great
   Britain
29 Queen Street
London EC4R 1BH
01 248 3642

30 TRADE UNIONS

Amalgamated Union of Engineering
  Workers
110 Peckham Road
London SE15 5EL
01 703 4231

Amalgamated Union of Engineering
  Workers/Technical
  Administrative and Supervisory
  Section
Onslow Hall
Little Green
Richmond
Surrey TW9 1QN
01 948 2271

Association of Professional,
  Executive, Clerical and Computer
  Staff
22 Worple Road
London SW19 4DF
01 947 3131

Association of Scientific, Technical
  and Managerial Staffs
10–26a Jamestown Road
London NW1 7DT
01 267 4422

Civil and Public Services Association
215 High Road
London SW17 7BQ
01 672 1299

Confederation of Health Service
  Employees
Glen House
Banstead
Surrey SM7 2LH
073 73 53322

Electrical Electronic
  Telecommunications and
  Plumbing Union
Hayes Court
West Common Road
Bromley
Kent BR2 7AU
01 462 7755

National Graphical Association
Graphical House
63–7 Bromham Road
Bedford MK40 2AG
0234 51521

National and Local Government
  Officers Association
1 Mabledon Place
London WC1H 9AJ
01 388 2366

National Union of General and
  Municipal Workers
Thorne House
Ruxley Ridge
Claygate
Esher
Surrey KT10 OT1
0372 62081

National Union of Public Employees
Civic House
Aberdeen Terrace
Blackheath
London SE3 0QY
01 852 2842

National Union of Mineworkers
St James House
Vicar Lane

Sheffield 1
0742 700 388

National Union of Railwaymen
Unity House
Euston Road
London NW1 2BL
01 387 4771

National Union of Seamen
Maritime House
Old Town
London SW4 0JP
01 622 5581

National Union of Teachers
Hamilton House
Mabledon Place
London WC1H 9BD
01 387 2442

Society of Graphical and Allied
  Trades
Sogat House
274–88 London Road
Hadleigh
Benfleet
Essex SS7 2DE
0702 553131

Trades Union Congress
Congress House
23–8 Great Russell Street
London WC1B 3SL
01 636 4030

Trade Union Research and
  Information Centres
Coventry Workshop
40 Bingley Road
Coventry CV3 1JA
0203 27772

Transport and General Workers'
  Union
Transport House
Smith Square
Westminster
London SW1P 3JB
01 828 7788

Union of Communication Workers
UCW House
Crescent Lane
London SW4 9RN
01 622 9977

Union of Construction, Allied
  Trades and Technicians
Ucatt House
177 Abbeville Road
Clapham
London SW4 9RL
01 622 2442

Union of Shop, Distributive and
  Allied Workers
'Oakley'
188 Wilmslow Road
Fallowfield
Manchester M14 6LJ
061 224 2804

31 TRAVEL AND TOURISM IN BRITAIN

HOLIDAY AND TRAVEL ORGANISATIONS

Automobile Association
Fanum House
Basingstoke
Hampshire RG21 2EA
0256 20123

British Travel Centre
4–12 Lower Regent Street
London SW1
01 730 3400

British Mountaineering Council
Crawford House
Precinct Centre
Booth Street East
Manchester M13 9R2
061 273 5835

Camping Club of Great Britain and
  Ireland
11 Lower Grosvenor Place
London SE1
01 828 1012

Caravan Club
East Grinstead House
East Grinstead

Sussex RH19 1UA
0342 26944

Cyclists Touring Club
69 Meadrow
Goldaming
Surrey
Godalming 7217

Ramblers' Association
1–5 Wandsworth Road
London SW8 2LJ
01 582 6768

Royal Automobile Club
PO Box 100
RAC House
Landsdowne Road
Croydon CR9 2JA
01 686 2525

Youth Hostels Association
Trevelyan House
St Albans
Hertfordshire AL1 2DY
0727 55215

TOURIST BOARDS

British Tourist Authority
Thames Tower
Black's Road
London W6 9EL
01 846 9000

English Tourist Board
4 Grosvenor Gardens
London SW1W 0DU
01 730 3400

Northern Ireland Tourist Board
River House
48 High Street
Belfast BT1 2DS
0232 231221

Scottish Tourist Board
23 Ravelston Terrace

Edinburgh EH4 3EU
031 332 2433

Wales Tourist Board
Brunel House
2 Fitzalan Road
Cardiff CF2 1UY
0222 499909

REGIONAL TOURIST BOARDS

Cumbria
Cumbria Tourist Board
Ashleigh Holly Road
Windermere
Cumbria LA23 2AQ
096 62 4444

East Anglia (Norfolk, Suffolk, Essex,
  Cambridgeshire)
East Anglia Tourist Board
14 Museum Street
Ipswich
Suffolk IP1 1HU
0473 214211

East Midlands (Derbyshire,
  Leicestershire, Lincolnshire,
  Northamptonshire,
  Nottinghamshire)
East Midlands Tourist Board
Exchequergate
Lincoln
Lincolnshire LN2 1PZ
0522 31521/3

Heart of England (Gloucestershire,
  Herefordshire, Shropshire,
  Staffordshire, Warwickshire, West
  Midlands, Worcestershire)
Heart of England Tourist Board
Department EH
PO Box 15
Worcester WR1 2JT
0905 29511

Isle of Man
Isle of Man Tourist Board

13 Victoria Street
Douglas
Isle of Man
0624 4323

Isle of Wight
Isle of Wight Tourist Board
Department HE
21 High Street
Newport
Isle of Wight
0983 524343

London
London Tourist Board
26 Grosvenor Gardens
London SW1W 0DU
01 730 3488

North West (Cheshire, Greater
  Manchester, Lancashire,
  Merseyside, High Peak District)
North West Tourist Board
The Last Drop Village
Bromley Cross
Bolton
Lancashire BL7 9PZ
0204 591511

Northumbria (Cleveland, Durham,
  Northumberland, Tyne and
  Wear)
Northumbria Tourist Board
9 Osborne Terrace
Jesmond
Newcastle-upon-Tyne
Tyne and Wear NE2 1NT
0632 817744

South East (Kent, East Sussex,
Surrey, West Sussex)
South East England Tourist Board
1 Warwick Park
Tunbridge Wells
Kent TN2 5TA
0892 40766

Southern England (Hampshire,
Eastern Dorset)
Southern Tourist Board
Town Hall Centre
Leigh Road
Eastleigh
Hampshire SO5 4DE
0703 616027

Thames and Chilterns (Oxfordshire,
Berkshire, Bedfordshire,
Buckinghamshire, Hertfordshire)
Thames and Chiltern Tourist Board
8 The Market Place
Abingdon

Oxfordshire OX14 3UD
0235 22711

West Country (Avon, Cornwall,
Devon, Dorset, Somerset,
Wiltshire, Isles of Scilly)
West Country Tourist Board
Trinity Court
37 Southernhay East
Exeter
Devon EX1 1QS
0392 76351

Yorkshire and Humberside
(Humberside, North Yorkshire,
West Yorkshire, South Yorkshire)
Yorkshire and Humberside Tourist
Board
Department EH 82
312 Tadcaster Road
York
North Yorkshire YO2 2HF
0904 707961

LOCAL TOURIST INFORMATION

Tourist Information Centre
St Nicholas House
Broad Street
Aberdeen
Grampian
0224 632727

Tourist Information Centre
52 High Street
Belfast
County Antrim
0232 246609

Tourist Information Centre
2 City Arcade
Birmingham
West Midlands
021 6432514

Tourist Information Centre
City Hall
Bradford

West Yorkshire
0274 753682

Tourist Information Centre
Colston House
Colston Street
Bristol
Avon
0272 293891

Tourist Information Centre
Wheeler Street
Cambridge
Cambridgeshire
0223 358977

Tourist Information Centre
22 St Peter's Street
Canterbury
Kent
0227 66567

428

Tourist Information Centre
3 Castle Street
Cardiff
South Glamorgan
0222 27281

Tourist Information Centre
Town Hall
Northgate Street
Chester
Cheshire
0244 40144 ext.211/2250

Tourist Information Centre
36 Broadgate
Coventry
West Midlands
0203 20084/51717

Tourist Information Centre
Reference Library
The Wardwick
Derby
Derbyshire
0332 31111 ext. 2185/6

Tourist Information Centre
13 Claypath
Durham
County Durham
0385 43720

Tourist Information Centre
Nethergate Centre
Dundee
Tayside
0382 27723

Tourist Information Centre
Waverley Market
Edinburgh
Lothian
031 226 6591/225 8821

Tourist Information Centre
Civic Centre
Dix's Field
Exeter

Devon
0392 72434

Tourist Information Centre
George Square
Glasgow
Strathclyde
041 2217371/2

Tourist Information Centre
6 College Street
Gloucester
Gloucestershire
0452 421188

Tourist Information Centre
Central Library
Albion Street
Hull
Humberside
0482 223344

Tourist Information Centre
Central Library
Calverley Street
Leeds
West Yorkshire
0532 462454

Tourist Information Centre
12 Bishop Street
Leicester
Leicestershire
0533 556699

Tourist Information Centre
Castle Hill
Lincoln
Lincolnshire
0522 29828

Tourist Information Centre
Victoria Station Forecourt
London SW1
01 730 3488

Tourist Information Centre
29 Lime Street

Liverpool
Merseyside
051 709 3631

Tourist Information Centre
Magnum House
Portland Street
Piccadilly
Manchester
061 247 3694

Tourist Information Centre
Central Library
Princess Square
Newcastle-upon-Tyne
0632 610691

Tourist Information Centre
Augustine Steward House
14 Tombland
Norwich
Norfolk
0603 666071/2

Tourist Information Centre
18 Milton Street
Nottingham
Nottinghamshire
0602 470661

Tourist Information Centre
St Aldates
Oxford
Oxfordshire
0865 726871

Tourist Information Centre
Civic Centre
Royal Parade
Plymouth
Devon
0752 264849

Tourist Information Centre
Civic Offices
Guildhall Square
Portsmouth

Hampshire
0705 834092/3

Tourist Information Centre
Civic Offices
Civic Centre
Reading
Berkshire
0734 592388/55911

Tourist Information Centre
St Albans
37 Chequer Street
St Albans
Hertfordshire
0727 64511

Tourist Information Centre
Town Hall Extension
Union Street
Sheffield
South Yorkshire
0742 734671

Tourist Information Centre
Above Bar Precinct
Southampton
Hampshire
0703 21106

Tourist Information Centre
Central Library
Bethesda Street
Hanley
Stoke-on-Trent
Staffordshire
0782 281242

Tourist Information Centre
Singleton Street
Swansea
West Glamorgan
0792 468321

Tourist Information Centre
The Guildhall
The Broadway
Winchester

Hampshire
0962 68166

Tourist Information Centre
De Grey Rooms

Exhibition Square
York
North Yorkshire
0904 21756/7

NATIONAL PARKS

Brecon Beacons National Park
Glamorgan Street
Brecon
Powys LD3 7DP

Dartmoor National Park
'Parke'
Haytor Road
Bovey Tracey
Devon

Exmoor National Park
Visitor Services
Exmoor House
Dulverton
Somerset

Lake District National Park
Busher Walk
Kendal
Cumbria

Northumbria National Park
Eastburn
South Park
Hexham
Northumberland NE46 1BS

North York Moors National Park
The Old Vicarage
Bondgate
Helmsley
York YO6 5BP

Peak District National Park
Aldern House
Baslow Road
Bakewell
Derbyshire DE4 1AE

Pembrokeshire Coast National Park
County Offices
Haverfordwest
Dyfed

Snowdonia National Park
Penryhndeudraeth
Gwynedd

Yorkshire Dales National Park
'Colvend'
Hebden Road
Grassington
North Yorkshire BD23 5LB

NATIONAL TRUST

CORNWALL

The National Trust
Lanhydrock
Bodmin PL30 4DE
0208 4281

DEVON

The National Trust
Killerton House
Broadclyst
Exeter EX5 3LE
0392 881 691

EAST ANGLIA

The National Trust
Blickling Hall
Norwich NR11 6NF
0263 733471

EAST MIDLANDS

The National Trust
Clumber Park Stableyard
Worksop
Nottinghamshire S80 3BE
0909 486411

KENT AND EAST SUSSEX

The National Trust
Scotney Castle
Lamberhurst
Tunbridge Wells TN3 8JN
0892 890651

LONDON

The National Trust
42 Queen Anne's Gate
London W1H 9AS
01 222 9251

MERCIA

The National Trust
Attingham Park
Shrewsbury
Shropshire SY4 4TP
074 377 649

NORTH WEST

The National Trust
Rothay Holme
Rothay Road

Ambleside
Cumbria LA22 0EJ
096 633 883

NORTHUMBRIA

The National Trust
Scot's Gap
Morpeth
Northumberland NE61 4EG
067 074 691

SEVERN

The National Trust
34–6 Church Street
Tewkesbury
Gloucestershire GL20 5SN
0684 297747

SOUTHERN

The National Trust
Polesden Lacey
Dorking
Surrey RH5 6BD
0372 53401

THAMES AND CHILTERNS

The National Trust
Hughenden Manor
High Wycombe
Buckinghamshire HP14 4LA
0494 28051

WESSEX

The National Trust
Stourton
Warminster
Wiltshire BA12 6QD
0747 840560

YORKSHIRE

The National Trust
32 Goodramgate
York YO1 2LG
0904 29621

NORTHERN IRELAND

The National Trust
Rowallane House
Saintfield
Ballynahinch
County Down BT24 7LH
0238 510721

WALES

The National Trust
Trinity Square
Llandudno
Gwynedd LL30 2DE
0492 74421

The National Trust
22 Alan Road
Llandeilo
Dyfed SA19 6HU
055882 3530

SCOTLAND

The National Trust for Scotland
5 Charlotte Square
Edinburgh EH2 4DU
031 226 5922

32 WALES

Ancient Monuments Board for
  Wales
Welsh Office
New Crown Buildings
Cathays Park
Cardiff CF1 3NQ
0222 825 111

Council for the Protection of Rural
  Wales
14 Broad Street
Welshpool
Powys SY21 7JP
0938 2525

Development Board for Rural Wales
Ladywell House
Newtown
Powys SW16 1JB
0686 26965

Historical Society of the Church in
  Wales
c/o Archdeacon Owain Jones
10 Camden Crescent
Brecon
Powys
0874 4631

Historical Society of the Methodist
  Church in Wales
The Manse
Caradog Road
Aberystwyth
Dyfed SY23 3BU
0970 3351

Land Authority of Wales
11th Floor

Brunel House
2 Fitzalan Road
Cardiff CF2 1SQ
022 499077

Museum of Welsh Antiquities
Fford Gwynedd
Bangor
North Wales LL57 2UW
0248 51151 ext. 437

National Library of Wales
Aberystwyth
Dyfed SY23 3BU
0970 3816/9

National Museum of Wales
Cathays Park
Cardiff CF1 3NP
0222 397951

National Museum of Wales Library
Cathays Park
Cardiff CF1 3NP
0222 397951

Plaid Cymru
51 Cathedral Road
Cardiff CF1 9HD
0222 31944

Royal Cambrian Academy of Arts
Plas Mawr
Conwy
North Wales
0492 63 3413

Welsh Arts Council
Holst House

434

Museum Place
Cardiff CF1 3NS
0222 3947211

Welsh Bibliographical Society
c/o National Library of Wales
Aberystwyth
Dyfed SY23 3BU
0970 3816/9

Welsh Development Agency
PO Box 100
Greyfriars Road
Cardiff CF1 1WF
0222 32955

Welsh Folk Museum
St Fagans
Cardiff CF5 6XB
0222 569 441

Welsh Folk Song Society
46 Marlborough Road
Roath
Cardiff
Glamorgan

Welsh Fourth Channel Authority
Clos Sophia
Cardiff CF1 9XY
0222 43421

Welsh Language Society
5 Maes Albert
Aberystwyth
Dyfed
0970 4501

Welsh Office
Crown Buildings
Cathays Park
Cardiff CF1 3NQ
0222 825111

Welsh Office
Gwdyr House
Whitehall
London SW1A 2ER
01 233 3000

Wales Tourist Board
Brunel House
2 Fitzalan Road
Cardiff CF2 1UY
0222 49909

33 WOMEN

British Federation of University
  Women
Crosby Hall
Cheyne Walk
London SW3 5BA
01 352 5354

Campaign for Financial and Legal
  Independence
214 Stapleton Hall Road
London N4

Equal Opportunities Commission
Overseas House
Quay Street
Manchester M3 3HN
061 833 9244

Equal Pay and Opportunity
  Campaign
59 Canonbury Park North
London N1 2JU
01 379 6223

Family Planning Association
  Information Service
27–35 Mortimer Street
London W1N 7RJ
01 636 7866

Family Rights Group
6 Manor Gardens
Holloway Road
London N7 6LA
01 272 4231

Fawcett Library
City of London Polytechnic
Calcutta House

Old Castle Street
London E1 7NT
01 283 1030

Feminist Library and Information
  Centre
Hungerford House
Victoria Embankment
London WC2N 6NU
01 930 0715

Mothers' Union
24 Tufton Street
London SW1P 3RB
01 222 5533

National Advisory Centre on
  Careers for Women
Drayton House
30 Gordon Street
London WC1H 0AY
01 380 0117

National Council of Civil Liberties –
  Women's Rights Unit
21 Tabard Street
London SE1
01 403 3888

National Council of Women of
  Great Britain
36 Lower Sloane Street
London SW1W 8BP
01 730 0619

National Federation of Women's
  Institutes
39 Eccleston Street
London SW1W 9NT
01 730 7212

National Housewives Register
245 Warwick Road
Solihull
West Midlands B92 7AH
021 706 1101

National Union of Townswomen's
  Guilds
Chamber of Commerce House
75 Harborne Road
Birmingham B15 3DA
021 455 6216

Rights for Women
52–4 Featherstone Street
London EC1Y 8RT
01 251 6577

Spare Rib
27 Clerkenwell Close
London EC1R 0AT
01 253 9792

Women's Aid Federation
374 Gray's Inn Road
London WC1
01 837 9316

Women's Fightback
41 Ellington Street
London N7

Women's Information Referral and
  Enquiry Service (WIRES)
PO Box 20
Oxford
0865 240991

Women's National Commission
Government Offices
Great George Street
London SW1P 3AQ
01 233 4208

A Woman's Place
Hungerford House
Victoria Embankment
London WC2
01 668 2519

Women's Reproductive Rights
  Information Centre
52–4 Featherstone Street
London EC1Y 8RT
01 251 6332

Women's Research and Resources
  Centre
190 Upper Street
London N1
01 359 5773

MUSEUMS AND GALLERIES

The following is a select list of museums, galleries and libraries in towns and cities of the United Kingdom. For a more complete list of museums and galleries, including details of exhibited material, see: Brink, A. and Watkins, D., *The Libraries, Museums and Art Galleries Year Book*, Cambridge; Roberts, S., Cooper, A. and Gilder, L., *Research Libraries and Collections in the U.K.: A Selective Inventory and Guide*, London, 1978; Wickens, P. M. (ed.), *Museums and Art Galleries in Great Britain and Ireland*, Dunstable, annually.

ABERDEEN

Aberdeen Art Gallery and Museum
Schoolhill
Aberdeen AB9 1FQ
0224 646333

Gordon Highlanders' Regimental
   Museum
Viewfield Road
Aberdeen AB1 7HX
0224 38174

ABERYSTWYTH

Aberystwyth Arts Centre
University College of Wales
Penglais
Aberystwyth
0970 85620

National Library of Wales
Aberystwyth SY23 3BU
0970 3816/9

ALLOWAY

Burns' Cottage
Alloway
Ayr
Scotland

ARMAGH

Armagh County Museum
The Mall
Armagh
Northern Ireland BT61 9BE

AYOT ST LAWRENCE

Shaw's Corner
Ayot Street
Ayot St Lawrence
Hertfordshire
0438 820307

BANGOR

Museum of Welsh Antiquities
University College of North Wales
Bangor
Wales

BATH

Museum of Costume
Assembly Rooms
Bath
0225 61111 ext. 327

Roman Baths Museum
Stall Street
Bath
Avon
0225 61111 ext. 327

BEDFORD

Bunyan Collection
Harpur Street
Bedford
0234 56181

BELFAST

Ulster Folk and Transport Museum
Cultra Manor
Holywood BT18 0EU
02317 5411

Ulster Museum
National Museum of Northern
    Ireland
Botanic Gardens
Belfast BT9 5AB
0232 668251

BIRMINGHAM

Barber Institute of Fine Arts
University of Birmingham
Edgbaston Road
Birmingham B15 2TS
021 472 0962

City of Birmingham Museum and
    Art Gallery
Chamberlain Square

Birmingham B3 3DH
021 235 3890

Museum of Science and Industry
Newhall Street
Birmingham B3 1RZ
021 236 1022

BRADFORD

Bradford Industrial Museum
Moorside Road
Eccleshill
0274 631756

Cartwright Art Gallery and Museum
Lister Park
Bradford BD9 4NZ
0274 493313

BRISTOL

Blaise Castle House Museum
City Museum
Henbury

Bristol BS10 7QS
0272 506789

Chatterton House Museum
City Museum
Redcliffe Way
Bristol

City Museum and Art Gallery
Queen's Road
Bristol BS8 1RL
0272 299771

Georgian House
7 Great George Street
Bristol BS1 5RR
0272 299771

Red Lodge
Park Row
Bristol BS1
0272 299771

CAMBRIDGE

Cambridge and County Folk
  Museum
Castle Street
Cambridge CB3 0AQ
0223 355159

Cambridge University Archives
University Library
West Road
Cambridge CB3 9DR
0223 61441

Fitzwilliam Museum
Trumpington Street

Cambridge CB3 1RB
0223 69501–3

Kettle's Yard
University of Cambridge
Northampton Street
Cambridge CB3 0PZ

Whipple Museum of the History of
  Science
Free School Lane
Cambridge CB2 3RH
0223 358381

CANTERBURY

Coleridge Museum
St Augustine's Abbey Museum
Canterbury

Roman Pavement
Butchery Lane
Canterbury
0227 52747

Royal Museum
High Street
Canterbury
0227 52747

Westgate Museum
St Peter's Street
Canterbury
0227 52747

CARDIFF

National Museum of Wales
Cathays Park
Cardiff CF1 3NP
0222 397951

Welsh Folklore Museum
St Fagan's Castle

Cardiff CF5 6BX
0222 569441

Welsh Industrial and Maritime
  Museum
Bure Street
Cardiff CF1 6AN
0222 481919

CASTLE HOWARD

Castle Howard Costume Galleries
Castle Howard

Yorkshire YO6 7DA
065 384 333

CHALFONT ST GILES

Milton's Cottage
Deanway
Chalfont St Giles

Buckinghamshire
02407 2313

CHAWTON

Jane Austen Memorial Trust
Main Street

Chawton
Hampshire

CHELTENHAM

Chedworth Roman Villa Museum
Roman Villa

Cheltenham GL54 3LT
024 289 256

CHESTER

Grosvenor Museum
27 Grosvenor Street

Chester CH1 2DD
02244 21616

CHESTERFIELD

Revolution House
High Street
Chesterfield

Derbyshire
0246 35928

CHICHESTER

Guildhall Museum
Priory Park
Chichester
West Sussex
0243 784683

Roman Palace and Museum
Salthill Road
Chichester
West Sussex
0243 785859

CIRENCESTER

Corinium Museum
Park Street
Cirencester

Gloucestershire
0285 5611

COLCHESTER

Colchester and Essex Museum
The Castle
Colchester

Essex CO1 1TJ
0206 577475

CONISTON

Ruskin Museum
Coniston Institute
Yewdale Road

Coniston
Cumbria
096 64359

CULLODEN

Old Leanach Farmhouse
Culloden

Invernesshire
Scotland

DURHAM

Dean and Chapter Library
Monk's Dormitory Museum

The College
Durham

EDINBURGH

Gallery of the Royal Scottish
    Academy
The Mound and Princess Street
Edinburgh EH2 2EL

Lauriston Castle
2A Cramond Road South
Edinburgh
031 336 2060

Huntly House
Canongate Edinburgh
Edinburgh
031 225 1131

National Gallery of Scotland
The Mound
Edinburgh EH2 2EL
031 556 8921

John Knox's House
45 High Street
The Royal Mile
Edinburgh EH1 1SR

National Museum of Antiquities of
    Scotland
Queen Street
Edinburgh EH2 1JD
031 556 8921

Lady Stair's House
Lady Stair's Close
Lawnmarket
Edinburgh EH1 2PA
031 225 1131

Royal Scottish Museum
Chamber Street
Edinburgh EH1 1JF
031 225 7534

Lamb's House
National Trust of Scotland
Leith
Edinburgh

Scottish Arts Council Gallery
19 Charlotte Square
Edinburgh EH2 4DF
031 226 6051

443

Scottish National Gallery of Modern
  Art
Queen Street
Edinburgh EH2 1JD
031 556 8921

Scottish National Portrait Gallery
1 Queen Street
Edinburgh EH2 1JD
031 556 8921

EGHAM

Royal Holloway College Picture
  Gallery
Royal Holloway College

Egham Hill
Egham
078 43 34455

GLASGOW

Burrell Collection
Pollok Park
Glasgow
041 649 7151

Glasgow Art Gallery and Museum
Kelvingrove Park
Glasgow
041 334 1134

Hunterian Museum and University
  Art Collection
University of Glasgow
Glasgow G12 8QQ
041 339 8855

Old Glasgow Museum
Museum and Art Galleries
People's Palace
Glasgow Green
Glasgow
041 554 0223

GRASMERE

Dove Cottage and the Wordsworth
  Museum

Grasmere
Cumbria

GUILDFORD

Guildford Museum
Castle Arch
Guildford

Surrey GU1 3AJ
0483 503497

HAMPTON COURT

Hampton Court Palace
Hampton Court
East Molesey

Surrey
01 977 8441

HAWORTH

Brontë Parsonage Museum
The Old Parsonage

Haworth
0535 42323

HIGHER BROCKHAMPTON

Hardy's Cottage
Higher Brockhampton
Dorset

KILMARNOCK

Burns' Monument and Museum
Kay Park
Burgh Parks

Kilmarnock
Ayrshire KA1 3BU
0563 26401

LEEDS

Abbey House Museum
Kirkstall
Leeds LS5 3EH

City Art Gallery
Municipal Buildings
Leeds LS1 3AA
0532 462295

City Museum
Municipal Buildings
Leeds LS1 3AA
0532 462295

Museum of Industry and Science
Canal Road
Armley
Leeds
0532 637861

University Museum of the History of
Education
University of Leeds
Leeds LS2 9JT
0532 431751

LEICESTER

Leicester Museum and Art Gallery
96 New Walk
Leicester LE1 6TD
0533 554100

Museum of Technology
Corporation Road
96 New Walk

Leicester LE1 6TD
0533 61330

Newarke Houses Museum
The Newarke
96 New Walk
Leicester LE1 6TD
0533 554100

LICHFIELD

Johnson Birthplace Museum
Breadmarket Street

Lichfield
Staffordshire WS13 6LG

LINCOLN

City and County Museum
Broadgate

Lincoln LN2 1EZ
0522 30401

Usher Gallery
Lindum Road

Lincoln LN2 1NN
0522 27980

LIVERPOOL

Merseyside Maritime Museum
Pier Head
Liverpool
051 236 1492

Sudley Art Gallery and Museum
Mossley Hill Road
Liverpool
Merseyside L18 8BX

Speke Hall
The Walk
Liverpool
Merseyside L24 1XD
051 427 7231

Walker Art Gallery
William Brown Street
Liverpool
Merseyside L3 8EL
051 227 5234 ext. 2064

LONDON

Barbican Library
Barbican Centre
London EC2Y 8DS
01 638 0569

London WC2H 7HP
01 930 3274

British Library
Department of Printed Books
Department of Manuscripts
Great Russell Street
London WC1B 3DG
01 636 1544

City Business Library
Basinghall Street
London EC2V 5DU
01 638 8251/6

British Library Newspaper Library
Colindale Avenue
London NW9 5HE
01 200 5515

Courtauld Institute Galleries
Woburn Square
London WC1E 7HU
01 580 1015

British Library
Reference Division
Great Russell Street
London WC1B 3DG
01 636 1544

Cricket Memorial Gallery
Lord's Cricket Ground
St John's Wood
London NW8 8QN
01 289 1611

British Museum
Great Russell Street
London WC1B 3DG
01 636 1555

Cuming Museum
Walworth Road
London SE17 1RS
01 703 3324

Central Reference Library
St Martin's Street

Dickens' House
48 Doughty Street
London WC1N 2LF
01 405 2127

Dulwich College Picture Gallery
College Road
Dulwich
London SE21 7AD
01 693 5254

Guildhall Art Gallery
King Street
London EC2P 2ET

Guildhall Library
Aldermanbury
London EC2P 2EJ
01 606 3030

Hayward Gallery
Belvedere Road
South Bank
London SE1 BS2
01 928 3144

Holborn Library
32–8 Theobald's Road
London WC1X 8PA
01 405 2705

Horniman Museum
London Road
Forest Hill
London SE23 3PQ
01 699 2339

Imperial War Museum
Lambeth Road
London SE1 6HZ
01 735 8922

Dr Johnson's House
17 Gough Square
London EC4A 3DE
01 353 3745

Keats' House
Wentworth Place
Hampstead
London NW3 2RR
01 435 2062

Kenwood - The Iveagh Bequest
Hampstead Lane
London NW3 7JR
01 348 1286

Livesey Museum
682 Old Kent Road
London SE15 1JF
01 639 5604

London Library
14 St James's Square
London SW1Y 4LG
01 930 7705/6

Madame Tussaud's
Marylebone Road
London NW1

Museum of London
London Wall
London EC2Y 5HN
01 600 3699

National Army Museum
Royal Hospital Road
Chelsea
London SW3 4HT
01 730 0717

National Gallery
Trafalgar Square
London WC2N 5DN
01 839 3526

National Maritime Museum
Romney Road
Greenwich
London SE10 9NF
01 858 4422

National Museum of Labour History
Limehouse Town Hall
Commerical Road
London E14
01 515 3229

National Portrait Gallery
2 St Martin's Place
London WC2H 0HE
01 930 1552

National Sound Archive
29 Exhibition Road
London SW7 2AS
01 589 6603

Public Record Office Museum
Chancery Lane
London WC2A 1LR
01 405 3488 ext. 475

The Queen's Gallery
Buckingham Palace
London SW1

Royal Academy of Arts
Burlington House
Piccadilly
London W1V 0DS
01 734 9052

Royal Air Force Museum
Aerodrome Road
London NW9 5LL
01 205 2266

Royal Artillery Museum
Military Academy
London SE18 4JJ
01 856 5533

Science Museum
Exhibition Road
London SW7 5NH
01 589 3456

Science Reference Library (Holborn)
25 Southampton Buildings
Chancery Lane
London WC2A 1AW
01 405 8721

Science Reference Library (Aldwych
  Reading Room)
9 Kean Street
Drury Lane
London WC2B 4AT
01 636 1544 ext. 229

Serpentine Gallery
Kensington Gardens
London W2 3XA
01 402 6075

Sir John Soane's Museum
13 Lincoln's Inn Fields
London WC2A 3BP
01 405 2107

South London Art Gallery
Peckham Road
London SE5 8UH
01 703 6120

Tate Gallery
Millbank
London SW1P 4RG
01 821 7128

Tower of London
Tower Hill
London EC3N 4AB
01 709 0765

University of London Library
Senate House
Malet Street
London WC1E 7HU
01 636 4514

Victoria and Albert Museum
Cromwell Road
South Kensington
London SW7 2RL
01 589 6371

Wallace Collection
Hertford House
Manchester Square

London W1M 6BN
01 935 0687

Warburg Institute Library
Woburn Square
London WC1H 0AB
01 580 9663

Whitechapel Art Gallery
Whitechapel High Street

London E1 7QX
01 377 0107

William Morris Gallery and
    Brangwyn Gift
Lloyd Park
Forest Road
Walthamstow
London E17 4PP
01 527 5544

MANCHESTER

City Art Gallery
Mosley Street
Manchester M2 3JL
061 236 9422

Gallery of Modern Art
Athenaeum
Princess Street
Manchester M1 4HR
061 236 9422

Greater Manchester Museum of
    Science and Industry
Liverpool Road

Manchester
061 832 2244

Manchester Museum
The University
Oxford Road
Manchester M13 9PL
061 273 3333

Whitworth Art Gallery
Whitworth Park
Manchester M25 6ER
061 273 4865

NETHER STOWEY

Coleridge's Cottage
Nether Stowey
Somerset

NEWCASTLE-UPON-TYNE

John George Joicey Museum of
    Local History
1 City Road
Newcastle-upon-Tyne
0632 324562

Laing Art Gallery
Higham Place

Newcastle-upon-Tyne
0632 327734

Museum of Science and Engineering
Blandford House
West Blandford Street
Newcastle-upon-Tyne
0632 326789

NOTTINGHAM

The Castle Museum and Art Gallery
Nottingham NG1 6EL
0602 411881

Industrial Museum
Wollaton Park
Nottingham
0602 284602

OXFORD

Ashmolean Library
Beaumont Street
Oxford OX1 2PH
0865 512651 ext. 683

Museum of Modern Art
30 Pembroke Street
Oxford OX1 1BP
0865 722733

Bodleian Library
Broad Street
Oxford OX1 3BG
0865 244675

Museum of Oxford
St Aldates
Oxford OX1 1DZ
0865 815559

Christ Church Picture Gallery
Canterbury Quadrangle
Oxford OX1 1DP
0865 242102

Museum of the History of Science
Broad Street
Oxford OX1 3AZ
0865 243997

PORTSMOUTH

Charles Dickens Birthplace Museum
393 Commercial Road
Old Portsmouth

Hants
0705 827261

SHEFFIELD

Sheffield City Art Galleries
Surrey Street
Sheffield S1 1X2
0742 734782

Sheffield S3 8RY
0742 22106

Kelham Island Industrial Museum
Alma Street

Sheffield City Museum
Weston Park
Sheffield S10 2TP
0742 768588

SOUTHAMPTON

Maritime Museum
Wool House
Bugle Street
Southampton
0703 23941

Tudor House Museum
St Michael's Square
Southampton
0703 24216

STOKE-ON-TRENT

City Museum and Art Gallery
Broad Street
Hanley

Stoke-on-Trent
0782 29611 ext. 2173

STRATFORD-UPON-AVON

Anne Hathaway's Cottage
Shakespeare's Birthplace Trust
Shottery
Stratford-upon-Avon
0789 204016

Shakespeare's Birthplace
Shakespeare's Birthplace Trust
Stratford-upon-Avon
Warwickshire
0789 204016

Royal Shakespeare Theatre Picture
   Gallery and Museum
Waterside
Stratford-upon-Avon
Warwickshire
0789 204016

Shakespeare Centre Library
Henly Street
Stratford-upon-Avon CV37 6QW
0789 204016

SWANSEA

Glynn Vivian Art Gallery and
   Museum
Alexandra Road
Swansea
Glamorgan
0792 55006

Swansea Museum
University College of Swansea
Victoria Road
Swansea
Glamorgan SW1 1SN
0792 53763

WINCHESTER

City Museum
The Square
Winchester
Hampshire
0962 68166 ext. 269

Winchester
Hampshire
0962 698166

Westgate Museum
High Street

Winchester College Museum
Kingsgate Street
Winchester
Hampshire

WORCESTER

The Commandery
Sidbury
Worcester
0905 25371

Tudor House Museum
Friar Street
Worcester
0905 25371

451

YORK

Castle Museum York
Tower Street
York
0904 53611

Jorvik Viking Centre
Coppergate
York
0904 32342

The Heritage Centre
Castlegate
York
0904 28632

The Yorkshire Museum
Museum Gardens
York YO1 1J2
0904 29745

STUDY AND RESEARCH – UNIVERSITIES, POLYTECHNICS, COLLEGES

The following lists indicate the higher educational institutions in the United Kingdom which provide study facilities in subjects dealing with British life, society and culture. Details on the use of these facilities can be obtained from the university, polytechnic or college authorities. Addresses are listed on pages 483–497.

For further details on British institutions of higher education see: Boehm, K. and Wellings, N. (eds), *The Student Book: The Applicant's Guide to Universities, Polytechnics and UK Colleges*, London, Macmillan, annually; British Council and The Association of Commonwealth Universities; *Higher Education in the United Kingdom: A Handbook for Students and their Advisers*, London, Longman, biennially; Europa Publications (publisher), *World of Learning*, 2 vols, London, annually.

1 ART

Bath Academy of Art
Birmingham Polytechnic
Brighton Polytechnic
Bristol Polytechnic
Camberwell School of Art
Canterbury College of Art
Central School of Art and Design
Chelmer Institute of Higher
  Education
Chelsea School of Art
Coventry Polytechnic
Crewe and Alsager College
Duncan Jordanstone College of Art
Edinburgh College of Art
Exeter College of Art
Falmouth School of Art
Glasgow School of Art
Gloucestershire College of Arts
Goldsmiths' College
Gwent College of Higher Education
Hull College of Higher Education
Kingston Polytechnic
Leicester Polytechnic
Liverpool Polytechnic
Loughborough College of Art
Maidstone College of Art

Manchester Polytechnic
Middlesex Polytechnic
Newcastle University
North East London Polytechnic
North Staffs Polytechnic
Norwich School of Art
Portsmouth Polytechnic
Preston Polytechnic
Ravensbourne College of Art
Reading University
Robert Gordon's Institute of
  Technology
Royal Academy Schools
St Martin's School of Art
Sheffield Polytechnic
Slade School of Fine Art
South Glamorgan Institute of Higher
  Education
Stourbridge College of Art
Trent Polytechnic
Ulster Polytechnic
West Surrey College of Art and
  Design
Wimbledon School of Art
Winchester School of Art
Wolverhampton Polytechnic

2 ART HISTORY

Aberdeen University
Aberystwyth University
Bath Academy of Art
Birkbeck College
Bristol University
Cambridge University
Cambridgeshire College of Arts and
  Technology
Chelmer Institute of Higher
  Education
Courtauld Institute
East Anglia University
Edinburgh College of Art
Edinburgh University
Essex University
Exeter College of Art
Exeter University
Glasgow University
Goldsmiths' College
Kent University
Leeds University
Leicester Polytechnic
Leicester University
Loughborough University
Manchester Polytechnic
Manchester University

Middlesex Polytechnic
National Extension College
New College Durham
Newcastle Polytechnic
Newcastle University
North Staffordshire Polytechnic
Nottingham University
Open University
Oxford Polytechnic
Oxford University
Reading University
Roehampton Institute of Higher
  Education
St Andrews University
Sheffield Polytechnic
Slade School of Fine Art
South Glamorgan Institute of Higher
  Education
Sunderland Polytechnic
Sussex University
University College (University of
  London)
Wales Polytechnic
Warwick University
Westfield College

3 BUSINESS ECONOMICS

Buckingham University
Hull University
Middlesex Polytechnic
Preston Polytechnic
Southampton University

4 BUSINESS STUDIES

Aberystwyth University
Aston University
Bangor University
Belfast University
Birmingham Polytechnic
Birmingham University
Bradford University
Brighton Polytechnic
Bristol Polytechnic
Buckingham University
Central London Polytechnic
City of London Polytechnic
City University
Coventry Polytechnic
Dundee College of Technology
Dundee University
East Anglia University
Edinburgh University
Glasgow College of Technology
Hatfield Polytechnic
Heriot-Watt University
Huddersfield Polytechnic
Hull College of Higher Education
Hull University
Imperial College
Kent University
Kingston Polytechnic
Lancaster University
Leeds Polytechnic
Leeds University
Leicester Polytechnic
Liverpool Polytechnic
Liverpool University

London Business School
Loughborough University
Manchester Business School
Manchester Polytechnic
Manchester University
Middlesex Polytechnic
Napier College
Newcastle Polytechnic
Newcastle University
North East London Polytechnic
North London Polytechnic
North Staffordshire Polytechnic
Oxford Polytechnic
Plymouth Polytechnic
Portsmouth Polytechnic
Preston Polytechnic
Salford University
Sheffield Polytechnic
Sheffield University
South Bank Polytechnic
Stirling University
Strathclyde University
Sunderland Polytechnic
Swansea University
Teesside Polytechnic
Thames Polytechnic
Trent Polytechnic
Ulster Polytechnic
University of Manchester Institute of
    Science and Technology
Wales Polytechnic
Warwick University
Wolverhampton Polytechnic

5 ECONOMIC HISTORY

Aberdeen University
Aberystwyth University
Belfast University
Birmingham University
Bristol University
Cambridge University
Durham University
East Anglia University
Edinburgh University
Exeter University
Glasgow University
Hull University
Kent University
Lancaster University
Leeds University
Leicester University
Liverpool University
London School of Economics
Loughborough University
Manchester Polytechnic

Manchester University
Metropolitan College
Middlesex Polytechnic
National Extension College
Newcastle University
Nottingham University
Portsmouth Polytechnic
Reading University
St Andrew's University
Sheffield University
Southampton University
Stirling University
Strathclyde University
Sussex University
Swansea University
University College (University of London)
Warwick University
York University

6 ECONOMICS

Aberdeen University
Aberystwyth University
Aston University
Bangor University
Bath University
Belfast University
Birmingham Polytechnic
Birmingham University
Bradford University
Bristol Polytechnic
Bristol University
Brunel University
Cambridgeshire College of Arts and
   Technology
Cambridge University
Cardiff University
Central London Polytechnic
City of London Polytechnic
City University
Coventry Polytechnic
Dorset Institute of Higher Education
Dundee University
Durham University
Ealing College of Higher Education
East Anglia University
Edinburgh University
Essex University
Exeter University
Glasgow College of Technology
Glasgow University
Heriot-Watt University
Huddersfield Polytechnic
Keele University
Kent University
Kingston Polytechnic
London School of Economics
Lancaster University
Leeds Polytechnic
Leeds University

Leicester Polytechnic
Leicester University
Liverpool Polytechnic
Liverpool University
Loughborough University
Manchester Polytechnic
Manchester University
Metropolitan College
Middlesex Polytechnic
National Extension College
Newcastle Polytechnic
Newcastle University
North East London Polytechnic
North London Polytechnic
North Staffordshire Polytechnic
Nottingham University
Open University
Oxford Polytechnic
Oxford University
Plymouth Polytechnic
Portsmouth Polytechnic
Preston Polytechnic
Queen Mary College
Reading University
St Andrews University
Salford University
Sheffield University
Southampton University
Stirling University
Strathclyde University
Sunderland Polytechnic
Surrey University
Sussex University
Swansea University
Thames Polytechnic
Trent Polytechnic
Ulster University
University College (University of
   London)

7 EDUCATION

Aberdeen University
Aberystwyth University
Aston University
Bangor University
Bath College of Higher Education
Bath University
Bedford College of Higher Education
Belfast University
Birmingham Polytechnic
Birmingham University
Bradford College
Bradford University
Brighton Polytechnic
Bristol Polytechnic
Bristol University
Brunel University
Buckinghamshire College of Higher
  Education
Cambridge University
Cardiff University
Chelsea College
Christ Church College
City of Liverpool College
City of Manchester College
Crewe and Alsager College
Dorset Institute of Higher Education
Dundee University
Durham University
East Anglia University
Edge Hill College
Edinburgh University
Exeter University
Glasgow University
Goldsmiths' College
Gwent College of Higher Education
Huddersfield Polytechnic
Hull College of Higher Education
Hull University
Ilkley College Institute of Education

Jordanhill College
Keele University
King Alfred's College
Kingston Polytechnic
Lancaster University
Leeds Polytechnic
Leeds University
Leicester Polytechnic
Liverpool Institute of Higher
  Education
Liverpool Polytechnic
Liverpool University
Manchester Polytechnic
Manchester University
Matlock College
Middlesex Polytechnic
New College Durham
North East London Polytechnic
North London Polytechnic
North Wales Institute of Higher
  Education
Nottingham University
Open University
Oxford Polytechnic
Portsmouth Polytechnic
Roehampton Institute of Higher
  Education
Salford University
Sheffield Polytechnic
Sheffield University
South Bank Polytechnic
South Glamorgan Institute of Higher
  Education
Southampton University
Stirling University
Strathclyde University
Sunderland Polytechnic
Sussex University
Swansea University

Teesside Polytechnic
Thames Polytechnic
Trent Polytechnic
Ulster Polytechnic
Ulster University
University of Manchester Institute of
  Science and Technology
Warwick University
West Glamorgan Institute of Higher
  Education

West London Institute of Higher
  Education
West Midland College of Higher
  Education
West Sussex Institute of Higher
  Education
Wolverhampton Polytechnic
Worcester College of Higher
  Education

8 ENGLISH

Aberdeen University
Aberystwyth University
Bangor University
Bedford College
Belfast University
Birkbeck College
Birmingham Polytechnic
Birmingham University
Bristol Polytechnic
Bristol University
Buckingham University
Cambridge University
Cardiff University
Crewe and Alsager College
Dundee University
Durham University
Ealing College of Higher Education
East Anglia University
Edinburgh University
Essex University
Exeter University
Glasgow University
Goldsmiths' College
Hatfield Polytechnic
Huddersfield Polytechnic
Hull University
Keele University
Kent University
King's College
Kingston Polytechnic
Lampeter College
Lancaster University
Leeds University
Leicester Polytechnic
Leicester University
Liverpool University
Loughborough University
Manchester Polytechnic

Manchester University
Middlesex Polytechnic
New College Durham
Newcastle Polytechnic
Newcastle University
North London Polytechnic
Nottingham University
Open University
Oxford Polytechnic
Oxford University
Plymouth Polytechnic
Portsmouth Polytechnic
Preston Polytechnic
Queen Mary College
Reading University
Royal Holloway College
St Andrews University
Salford University
Sheffield Polytechnic
Sheffield University
Southampton University
Stirling University
Strathclyde University
Sunderland Polytechnic
Sussex University
Swansea University
Teesside Polytechnic
Thames Polytechnic
Trent Polytechnic
Ulster University
University College (University of
    London)
Wales Polytechnic
Warwick University
Westfield College
Wolverhampton Polytechnic
York University

9 EUROPEAN BUSINESS STUDIES

Buckinhamshire College of Higher
   Education
Kent University
Lancaster University
Middlesex Polytechnic
Swansea University

10 EUROPEAN STUDIES

Bath University
Bradford University
Brunel University
Buckingham University
Cardiff University
Coventry Polytechnic
East Anglia University
Hull University
Kent University
Lancaster University
Leeds Polytechnic
Loughborough University
Manchester Polytechnic

North London Polytechnic
Queen Mary College
Sheffield Polytechnic
Southampton College of Higher Education
Surrey University
Trent Polytechnic
Ulster University
University of Manchester Institute of Science and Technology
Warwick University
Wolverhampton Polytechnic

11 FILM STUDIES

Central London Polytechnic
Christ Church College
Coventry Polytechnic
Essex University
Exeter College of Art
Gwent College of Higher Education
Harrow College of Higher Education
Hull College of Higher Education
Kent University
Liverpool Polytechnic
London College of Printing
London International Film School
Maidstone College of Art
Middlesex Polytechnic
National Film School
North East London Polytechnic
Portsmouth Polytechnic
Sheffield Polytechnic
Stirling University
Warwick University
West Surrey College of Art and
  Design

12 GEOGRAPHY

Aberdeen University
Aberystwyth University
Bedford College
Belfast University
Birkbeck College
Birmingham University
Bradford University
Brighton Polytechnic
Bristol University
Cambridgeshire College of Arts and Technology
Cambridge University
Cardiff University
Central London Polytechnic
Christ Church College
City of Liverpool College
City of London Polytechnic
Coventry Polytechnic
Crewe and Alsager College
Dorset Institute of Higher Education
Dundee University
Durham University
Ealing College of Higher Education
East Anglia University
Edinburgh University
Exeter University
Glasgow University
Goldsmiths' College
Huddersfield Polytechnic
Hull University
Keele University
Kent University
King's College
Kingston Polytechnic
Lampeter College
Lancaster University
Leeds University
Leicester University
Liverpool Polytechnic

Liverpool University
London School of Economics
Loughborough University
Luton College of Higher Education
Manchester Polytechnic
Manchester University
Middlesex Polytechnic
National Extension College
New College Durham
Newcastle Polytechnic
Newcastle University
North London Polytechnic
Portsmouth Polytechnic
Preston Polytechnic
Queen Mary College
Reading University
Salford University
Sheffield Polytechnic
Sheffield University
Southampton University
Strathclyde University
Sunderland Polytechnic
Sussex University
Swansea University
Thames Polytechnic
Trent Polytechnic
Ulster University
University College (University of London)
Wales Polytechnic
Warwick University
West Midland College of Higher Education
West Sussex Institute of Higher Education
Wolverhampton Polytechnic
Worcester College of Higher Education

13 HISTORY

Aberdeen University
Aberystwyth University
Bangor University
Bedford College
Belfast University
Birkbeck College
Birmingham University
Bolton Institute of Technology
Bradford University
Brighton Polytechnic
Bristol Polytechnic
Bristol University
Buckingham University
Bulmershe College of Higher
 Education
Cambridgeshire College of Arts and
 Technology
Cambridge University
Cardiff University
Central London Polytechnic
Chelmer Institute of Higher
 Education
Crewe and Alsager College of Higher
 Education
Dorset Institute of Higher Education
Dundee University
Durham University
Ealing College of Higher Education
East Anglia University
Edinburgh University
Essex University
Exeter University
Glasgow College of Technology
Glasgow University
Goldsmiths' College
Hatfield Polytechnic
Heriot-Watt University
Huddersfield Polytechnic
Hull University

Keele University
Kent University
King Alfred's College
King's College
Kingston Polytechnic
Lampeter College
Lancaster University
Leeds University
Leicester Polytechnic
Leicester University
Liverpool Polytechnic
Liverpool University
London School of Economics
Loughborough University
Manchester Polytechnic
Manchester University
Middlesex Polytechnic
National Extension College
New College Durham
Newcastle Polytechnic
Newcastle University
North London Polytechnic
Nottingham University
Open University
Oxford Polytechnic
Oxford University
Plymouth Polytechnic
Portsmouth Polytechnic
Preston Polytechnic
Queen Mary College
Reading University
Roehampton Institute of Higher
 Education
Royal Hollway College
St Andrews University
Salford University
Sheffield Polytechnic
Sheffield University
Southampton University

Stirling University
Strathclyde University
Sunderland Polytechnic
Sussex University
Swansea University
Teesside University
Thames Polytechnic
Trent Polytechnic
Ulster Polytechnic
Ulster University
University College (University of
London)

Wales Polytechnic
Warwick University
West Midland College of Higher
Education
West Sussex Institute of Higher
Education
Westfield College
Wolverhampton Polytechnic
York University

14 INTERNATIONAL RELATIONS

Aberdeen University
Keele University
Kent University
London School of Economics
Open University
Reading University
St Andrews University
Southampton University
Sussex University
Warwick University

15 IRISH STUDIES

Aberystwyth University
Belfast University
Edinburgh University
Glasgow University
Manchester University
Ulster University

16 LAW

Aberdeen University
Aberystwyth University
Aston University
Belfast University
Birmingham Polytechnic
Birmingham University
Bristol Polytechnic
Bristol University
Brunel University
Buckingham University
Cambridge University
Cardiff University
Central London Polytechnic
Chelmar Institute of Higher
   Education
City of London Polytechnic
Coventry Polytechnic
Dorset Institute of Higher Education
Dundee University
Durham University
Ealing College of Higher Education
East Anglia University
Edinburgh University
Essex University
Exeter University
Glasgow University
Holborn Law Tutors
Hull University
Keele University
Kent University
King's College
Kingston Polytechnic
Lancaster University
Leeds Polytechnic
Leeds University

Leicester Polytechnic
Leicester University
Liverpool Polytechnic
Liverpool University
London School of Economics
Manchester Polytechnic
Manchester University
Metropolitan College
Middlesex Polytechnic
National Extension College
Newcastle Polytechnic
Newcastle University
North East London Polytechnic
North London Polytechnic
North Staffordshire Polytechnic
Nottingham University
Oxford Polytechnic
Oxford University
Preston Polytechnic
Queen Mary College
Reading University
Sheffield University
South Bank Polytechnic
Southampton University
Strathclyde University
Sussex University
Trent Polytechnic
University College (University of
   London)
University College Buckland
University of Manchester Institute of
   Science and Technology
Wales Polytechnic
Warwick University
Wolverhampton Polytechnic

17 LINGUISTICS

Aston University
Bangor University
Birmingham University
Cambridge University
Coventry Polytechnic
East Anglia University
Edinburgh University
Essex University
Exeter University
Glasgow University
Hatfield Polytechnic
Hull University
Lancaster University

Liverpool University
Manchester University
Newcastle University
Nottingham University
Preston Polytechnic
Reading University
St Andrews University
Sussex University
University of Manchester Institute of
  Science and Technology
University College (University of
  London)
York University

18 MANAGEMENT

Aston University
Cardiff University
Hull University
Imperial College
Kent University
Kingston Polytechnic
Lancaster University
Leeds University
London Business School
Manchester Business School
North East London Polytechnic

Queen Elizabeth College
Salford University
South Bank Polytechnic
Southampton University
Stirling University
Sussex University
Swansea University
Teesside Polytechnic
University of Manchester Institute of
  Science and Technology
Warwick University

19 MEDIA STUDIES

Central London Polytechnic
Coventry Polytechnic
Dorset Institute of Higher Education
Harrow College of Higher Education
North East London Polytechnic
Stirling University
Sunderland Polytechnic

20 MUSIC

Aberdeen University
Aberystwyth University
Bangor University
Bath College of Higher Education
Belfast University
Birmingham Polytechnic
Birmingham School of Music
Birmingham Univesity
Bristol University
Cambridge University
Cardiff University
City University
Crewe and Alsager College
Dartington College of Arts
Durham University
Ealing College of Higher Education
East Anglia University
Edinburgh University
Exeter University
Glasgow University
Goldsmiths' College
Guildhall School of Music and
  Drama
Huddersfield Polytechnic
Hull University
Keele University
King's College
Kingston Polytechnic
Lancaster University
Leeds University
Leicester University
Liverpool University

London College of Music
Manchester College (Oxford
  University)
Manchester University
Middlesex University
Newcastle Polytechnic
Nottingham University
Open University
Oxford University
Reading University
Royal Academy of Music
Royal College of Music
Royal Holloway College
Royal Northern College of Music
Royal Scottish Academy of Music
  and Drama
St Andrews University
Salford University
Sheffield University
Southampton University
Stirling University
Surrey University
Sussex University
Trent Polytechnic
Trinity College of Music
Wales Polytechnic
Warwick University
Welsh College of Music and Drama
West Midland College of Higher
  Education
York University

21 PHILOSOPHY

Aberdeen University
Aberystwyth University
Bangor University
Bedford College
Belfast University
Birkbeck College
Birmingham University
Bolton Institute of Technology
Bristol University
Cambridge University
Cardiff University
City University
Crew and Alsager College
Dundee University
Durham University
East Anglia University
Edinburgh University
Essex University
Exeter University
Glasgow University
Heythrop College (University of London)
Huddersfield Polytechnic
Hull University
Jew's College
Keele University
Kent University
King's College
Lampeter, University of Wales
Lancaster University
Leeds University
Leicester University

Liverpool University
London School of Economics
Manchester Polytechnic
Manchester University
Middlesex Polytechnic
National Extension College
Newcastle University
North London Polytechnic
Nottingham University
Open University
Oxford Polytechnic
Oxford University
Plymouth Polytechnic
Reading University
St Andrews University
St Martin's College
Sheffield University
Southampton University
Stirling University
Strathclyde University
Sunderland Polytechnic
Surrey University
Sussex University
Swansea University
Thames Polytechnic
Ulster Polytechnic
Ulster University
University College (University of London)
Wales Polytechnic
Warwick University
York University

22 POLITICAL SCIENCE

Aberdeen University
Aberystwyth University
Aston University
Bath University
Belfast University
Birmingham Polytechnic
Birmingham University
Bradford University
Bristol Polytechnic
Bristol University
Brunel University
Buckingham University
Cambridge University
Cardiff University
Central London Polytechnic
City of London Polytechnic
Coventry Polytechnic
Dorset Institute of Higher Education
Dundee University
Durham University
East Anglia University
Edinburgh University
Essex University
Exeter University
Glasgow College of Technology
Glasgow University
Huddersfield Polytechnic
Hull University
Keele University
Kent University
Kingston Polytechnic
Lancaster University
Leeds University
Leicester Polytechnic
Leicester University

Liverpool Polytechnic
Liverpool University
London School of Economics
Manchester Polytechnic
Manchester University
Metropolitan College
National Extension College
Newcastle Polytechnic
Newcastle University
North London Polytechnic
Nottingham University
Open University
Oxford Polytechnic
Oxford University
Plymouth Polytechnic
Portsmouth Polytechnic
Preston Polytechnic
Queen Mary College
Reading University
St Andrews University
Salford University
Sheffield Polytechnic
Sheffield University
Southampton University
Stirling University
Strathclyde University
Sunderland Polytechnic
Sussex University
Swansea University
Teesside Polytechnic
Thames Polytechnic
Trent Polytechnic
Ulster Polytechnic
Warwick University
York University

23 PUBLIC ADMINISTRATION

Bedford College
City of London Polytechnic
City of Manchester College
Dundee University
Durham University
Essex University
Kent University
Leeds University
Leicester Polytechnic
London School of Economics
Manchester Polytechnic
Manchester University

North London Polytechnic
Open University
Oxford Polytechnic
Robert Gordon's Institute of
 Technology
Salford University
Sheffield Polytechnic
Southampton University
Strathclyde University
Teesside Polytechnic
Trent Polytechnic

Aberdeen University
Edinburgh University
Glasgow University
St Andrews University
Stirling University

25 SOCIAL ADMINISTRATION

Bangor University
Bedford College
Birmingham University
Bristol University
Cardiff University
Central London Polytechnic
Christ Church College
City of London Polytechnic
Coventry Polytechnic
Dundee University
Durham University
East Anglia University
Edinburgh University
Essex University
Exeter University
Goldsmiths' College
Hull University
Ilkley College
Keele University
Kent University
Lancaster University
Leeds Polytechnic
Leeds University
Leicester Polytechnic
London School of Economics
Loughborough University
Manchester Polytechnic

Manchester University
Middlesex Polytechnic
Newcastle University
North East London Polytechnic
Nottingham University
Open University
Oxford Polytechnic
Plymouth Polytechnic
Portsmouth Polytechnic
Preston Polytechnic
Roehampton Institute of Higher
 Education
St Mark and St John College
Salford University
Sheffield Polytechnic
South Bank Polytechnic
Southampton University
Stirling University
Strathclyde University
Sussex University
Swansea University
Teesside Polytechnic
Trent Polytechnic
Ulster Polytechnic
Ulster University
Warwick University
York University

26 SOCIOLOGY

Aberdeen University
Aberystwyth University
Aston University
Bangor University
Bath University
Bedford College
Belfast University
Birkbeck College
Birmingham Polytechnic
Birmingham University
Bradford College
Bradford University
Bristol Polytechnic
Bristol University
Brunel University
Buckinghamshire College
Cambridgeshire College of Arts and
  Technology
Cambridge University
Cardiff University
Central London Polytechnic
City of Liverpool College
City of London Polytechnic
City University
Crewe and Alsager College
Durham University
East Anglia University
Edinburgh University
Essex University
Exeter University
Glasgow University
Goldsmiths' College
Hatfield Polytechnic
Huddersfield Polytechnic
Hull University
Keele University
Kent University
Kingston Polytechnic
Lancaster University
Leeds University

Leicester University
Liverpool Polytechnic
Liverpool University
London School of Economics
Loughborough University
Manchester Polytechnic
Manchester University
Metropolitan College
Middlesex Polytechnic
Newcastle Polytechnic
Newcastle University
North East London Polytechnic
North London Polytechnic
North Staffordshire Polytechnic
Nottingham University
Open University
Oxford Polytechnic
Oxford University
Plymouth Polytechnic
Portsmouth Polytechnic
Reading University
Roehampton Institute of Higher
  Education
Salford University
Sheffield University
South Bank Polytechnic
Southampton University
Stirling University
Strathclyde University
Surrey University
Sussex University
Swansea University
Teesside Polytechnic
Thames Polytechnic
Ulster University
Wales Polytechnic
Warwick University
Worcester College of Higher
  Education
York University

27 ADDRESSES OF UNIVERSITIES, POLYTECHNICS AND COLLEGES

UNIVERSITIES

University of Aberdeen, Aberdeen, Scotland AB9 1FX (The Secretary)

University of Aston in Birmingham, Gosta Green, Birmingham B4 7ET

University of Bath, Claverton Down, Bath BA2 7AY (The Secretary and Registrar)

The Queen's University of Belfast, Belfast, Northern Ireland, BT7 1NN (The Secretary: correspondence about admission to Admissions Officer)

University of Birmingham, PO Box 363, Birmingham, B15 2TT

University of Bradford, Richmond Road, Bradford BD7 1DP (The Registrar and Secretary)

University of Bristol, Denate House, Tyndall Avenue, Bristol, BS8 1TH

Brunel University, Uxbridge, Middlesex UB8 3PH (The Academic Registrar)

University of Buckingham, Hunter Street, Buckingham MK18 1EG

University of Cambridge, University Registry, The Old Schools, Cambridge CB2 1TN (The Registrar)

The City University, Northampton Square, London, EC1V 0HB (The Academic Registrar)

University of Dundee, Dundee, Scotland DD1 4HN (The Secretary)

University of Durham, Old Shire Hall, Durham DH1 3HP (The Registrar and Secretary)

University of East Anglia, Norwich NR4 7TJ (The Registrar and Secretary)

University of Edinburgh, Old College, South Bridge, Edinburgh, Scotland EH8 9YL (The Secretary)

University of Essex, Wivenhoe Park, Colchester, Essex, CO4 3SO

University of Exeter, Exeter EX4 4OJ (The Academic Registrar and Secretary)

University of Glasgow, Glasgow, Scotland G12 800 (The Secretary and Registrar)

Heriot-Watt University, Edinburgh, Scotland EH1 1HX (The Secretary)

University of Hull, Hull HU6 7RX

University of Keele, Keele, Staffordshire ST5 5BG

University of Kent at Canterbury, The Registry, The University, Canterbury CT2 7NZ

University of Lancaster, University House, Lancaster LA1 4YW (The Undergraduate Admissions Officer or the Graduate Studies Officer)

University of Leeds, Leeds LS2 9JT

University of Leicester LE1 7RH

University of Liverpool, PO Box 147, Liverpool L69 3BX

University of London, Senate House, Malet Street, London WC1E 7HU (The Academic Registrar)

Loughborough University of Technology, Loughborough LE11 3TU (The Academic Registrar)

University of Manchester, Manchester M13 9PL

University of Manchester Institute of Science and Technology (UMIST), PO Box 88, Sackville Street, Manchester M60 1QD

University of Newcastle-upon-Tyne, Newcastle-upon-Tyne, NE1 7RU

University of Nottingham, University Park, Nottingham NG7 2RD

The Open University, Walton Hall, Milton Keynes MK7 6AA (The Secretary)

University of Oxford, University Offices, Wellington Square, Oxford OX1 2JD

University of Reading, Whiteknights, Reading RG6 2AH

Royal College of Art, Kensington Gore, London SW7 2EU

University of St Andrews, College Gate, St Andrews, Scotland KY16 9AJ (The Secretary and Registrar)

University of Salford, Salford M5 4WT

University of Sheffield, Sheffield S10 2TN

University of Southampton, Highfield, Southampton SO9 5NH (The Secretary and Registrar; correspondence about courses and admission to The Academic Registrar)

University of Stirling, Stirling, Scotland FK9 4LA

University of Strathclyde, McCance Building, 16 Richmond Street, Glasgow, Scotland G1 1XQ (correspondence about courses and admission to The Admission Office (undergraduate) or The Postgraduate Office)

University of Surrey, Guildford, Surrey GU2 5HX (The Academic Registrar)

University of Sussex, Falmer, Brighton BN1 9RH (The Registrar and Secretary)

The New University of Ulster, Coleraine, County Londonderry, Northern Ireland BT52 1SA

University of Wales, University Registry, Cathays Park, Cardiff, CF1 3NS

University College of Wales, PO Box 2, Aberystwyth, Dyfed SY23 2AX

University College of North Wales, Bangor, Gwynedd LL57 2DG (The Secretary and Registrar)

University College, Cardiff, PO Box 78, Cardiff CF1 1XL

University College of Swansea, Singleton Park, Swansea, West Glamorgan SA2 8PP

University of Wales Institute of Science and Technology (UWIST), King Edward Avenue, Cardiff CF1 3NU (The Academic Registrar)

Welsh National School of Medicine, Heath Park, Cardiff CF4 4XN (The Registrar and Secretary)

St David's University College, Lampeter, Dyfed SA48 7ED (The Academic Registrar)

University of Warwick, Coventry CV4 7AL (The Academic Registrar)

University of York, Heslington, York YO1 5DD (The Undergraduate Admissions Office or The Graduate Office)

UNIVERSITY INSTITUTES

British Institute in Paris, 9 rue de Constantine, 75007 Paris, France (London Secretary: Woburn Square, London WC1H 0NS)

Courtauld Institute of Art, 20 Portman Square, London W1H 0BE (The Registrar and Secretary)

Institute of Advanced Legal Studies, 17 Russell Square, London WC1B 5DR

Institute of Archaeology, 31–4 Gordon Square, London WC1H 0PY

Institute of Classical Studies, 31–4 Gordon Square, London WC1H 0PY

Institute of Commonwealth Studies, 27 Russell Square, London WC1B 5DS (The Assistant Secretary)

Institute of Education, Bedford Way, London WC1H 0AL

Institute of Germanic Studies, 29 Russell Square, London WC1B 5DP (The Deputy Director)

Institute of Historical Research, University of London, Senate House, London WC1E 7HU (The Secretary and Librarian)

Institute of Latin American Studies, 31 Tavistock Square, London WC1H 9HA

Institute of United Stated Studies, 31 Tavistock Square, London WC1H 9EZ

School of Slavonic and East European Studies, University of London, Senate House, London WC1E 7HU (The Secretary-Registrar)

Warburg Institute, Woburn Square, London WC1H 0AB

NON-MEDICAL SCHOOLS

Bedford College, Inner Circle, Regent's Park, London NW1 4NS (The Registrar)

Birkbeck College, Malet Square, London WC1E 7HX

Chelsea College, Manresa Road, London SW3 6LX (The Academic Registrar)

Imperial College of Science and Technology, London SW7 2AZ (The Registrar)

Holborn Law Tutors, 200 Greyhound Road, London W14 9RY

King's College, Strand, London WC2R 2LS (The Registrar)

London School of Economics and Political Science, Houghton Street, Aldwych, London WC2A 2AE (for undergraduate courses, The Registrar; for graduate courses, The Secretary of the Graduate School).

Queen Elizabeth College, 61–7 Campden Hill Road, London W8 7AH

Queen Mary College, Mile End Road, London E1 4NS (The Registrar)

Royal Holloway College, Egham Hill, Egham, Surrey TW20 0EX (The Registrar)

Slade School of Fine Art, University College, London, Gower Street, London WC1E 6BT

POLYTECHNICS

City of Birmingham Polytechnic, Corporation Street, Birmingham B4 7DX

Brighton Polytechnic, Mithras House, Lewes Road, Maulsecoomb, Brighton BN2 4AT

Bristol Polytechnic, Coldharbour Lane, Bristol BS16 1OY

The Polytechnic of Central London, 309 Regent Street, London W1R 8AL

City of London Polytechnic, 117–19 Houndsditch, London EC3A 7BU

Coventry Polytechnic, Priory Street, Coventry CV1 5FB

Hatfield Polytechnic, PO Box 109, Hatfield, Hertfordshire AL10 9AB
Huddersfield Polytechnic, Queensgate, Huddersfield, HD1 3DH
Kilburn Polytechnic, Priory Park Road, London NW6 1YB
Kingston Polytechnic, Penrhyn Road, Kingston upon Thames KT1 2EE
Leeds Polytechnic, Calverley Street, Leeds LS1 3HE
Leicester Polytechnic, PO Box 143, Leicester LE1 9BH
Liverpool Polytechnic, Rodney House, 70 Mount Pleasant, Liverpool L3 5UX
Manchester Polytechnic, All Saints, Manchester M15 6BM
Middlesex Polytechnic, 114 Chase Side, London N14 5PN
Newcastle-upon-Tyne Polytechnic, Ellison Building, Ellison Place, Newcastle-
    upon-Tyne NE1 8ST
North East London Polytechnic, Romford Road, London E15 4LZ
Polytechnic of North London, Holloway Road, London N7 8DB
North Staffordshire Polytechnic, College Road, Stoke-on-Trent ST4 2DE
Oxford Polytechnic, Headington, Oxford OX3 0BP
Plymouth Polytechnic, Drake Circus, Plymouth PL4 8AA
Portsmouth Polytechnic, Alexandra House, Museum Road, Portsmouth PO1
    2QQ
Preston Polytechnic, Corporation Street, Preston, PR1 2TQ
Sheffield City Polytechnic, Pond Street, Sheffield, S1 1WB
Polytechnic of the South Bank, Borough Road, London SE1 0AA
Sunderland Polytechnic, Chester Road, Sunderland SR1 3SD
Teesside Polytechnic, Borough Road, Middlesbrough, Cleveland TS1 3BA
Thames Polytechnic, Wellington Street, Woolwich, London SE18 6PF
Trent Polytechnic, Burton Street, Nottingham NG1 4BU
Ulster Polytechnic, Shore Road, Newtownabbey, County Antrim, BT37 0QB
The Polytechnic of Wales, Llantint Road, Treforest, Pontypridd, Mid
    Glamorgan CF37 1DL
Wolverhampton Polytechnic, Molineux Street, Wolverhampton WV1 1SB

COLLEGES OF TECHNOLOGY, ART, COMMERCE AND EDUCATION

Aberdeen College of Commerce, Holburn Street, Aberdeen, AB9 2YT
Aberdeen College of Education, Hilton Place, Aberdeen AB9 1FA
Aberystwyth College of Further Education, Llanbadarn College, Aberystwyth
    SY23 3BP
Abingdon College of Further Education, Northcourt Road, Abingdon, Oxon
Abraham Moss Centre Open College, Cresent Road, Crumpsall, Manchester
    M8 6UH
Air Service Training, Perth Aerodrome, Perth
College of Air Training, Hamble, Southampton
Architectural Association School of Architecture, 34–6 Bedford Square,
    London WC1B 3ES
Armagh Technical College, Lonsdale Street, Armagh, County Armagh BT61
    7HN
Arnold and Carlton College of Further Education, Digby Avenue, Mapperly,
    Nottingham NG3 6DR

486

Askham Bryan College of Agriculture and Horticulture, Askham Bryan, York YO2 3PR

Avery Hill College, Bexley Road, London SE9 2PQ

Ayr Technical College, Dam Park, Ayr KA8 0EU

Barnfield College, New Bedford Road, Luton LU3 2AX

Barnsley College of Technology, Church Street, Barnsley S70 2AN

Basingstoke Technical College, Worting Road, Basingstoke, Hants

Bath Academy of Art, Corsham, Wiltshire SN13 0DB

Bath College of Higher Education, Newton Park, Bath BA2 9BN

Bedford College of Higher Education, Cauldwell Street, Bedford MK42 9AH

Belfast College of Technology, College Square East, Belfast BT1 6DJ

Bell College of Technology, Almada Street, Hamilton, Lanarkshire ML3 0JB

Benesh Institute of Choreology, 4 Margravine Gardens, Barons Court, London W6 8RH

Bingley College, Lady Lane, Bingley BD16 4AR

Birmingham College of Foods and Domestic Arts, Summer Road, Birmingham B3 1JB

Birmingham School of Music, Paradise Circus, Birmingham B3 3HG

Birmingham School of Speech Training and Dramatic Art, 45 Church Road, Edgbaston, Birmingham B15 3SW

Bishop Grosseteste College, Lincoln LN1 3DY

Blackburn College of Technology and Design, Feilden Street, Blackburn BB2 1LH

Blackpool and Fylde College of Further and Higher Education, Ashfield Road, Bispham, Blackpool FY2 0BN

Bletchley College of Further Education, Sherwood Drive, Bletchley, Milton Keynes MK3 6DR

Bolton College of Education (Technical), Chadwick Street, Bolton BL2 1JW

Bolton Institute of Technology, Deane Road, Bolton BL3 5AB

Bournemouth and Poole College of Art, Royal London House, Landsdowne, Bournemouth BH1 3JL

Bournemouth and Poole College of Further Education, North Road, Parkstone, Poole BH14 0LS

Bradford College, Great Horton Road, Bradford BD7 1AY

Bretton Hall College of Higher Education, West Bretton, Wakefield, West Yorkshire WF4 4LG

Brighton Technical College, Pelham Street, Brighton BN1 4FA

Bristol Old Vic Theatre School, 2 Downside Road, Clifton, Bristol BS8 2XF

Bromley College of Technology, Rookery Lane, Bromley, Kent BR2 8HE

Brooklands Technical College, Heath Road, Weybridge, Surrey KT13 8TT

Buchan Technical College, Argyll Road, Fraserburgh, Aberdeenshire AB4 5RF

Buckinghamshire College of Higher Education, Newlands Park, Chalfont St Giles, Bucks HP8 4AD

Bulmershe College of Higher Education, Bulmershe Court, Earley, Reading RG6 1HY

Bury Metropolitan College of Further Education, Market Street, Bury, Lancs BL9 0BG

Byam Shaw School of Art, 70 Campden Street, London W8 7EN

Camberwell School of Arts and Crafts, Peckham Road, London SE5 8UF
Camborne School of Mines, Trevenson, Pool, Redruth, Cornwall TR15 3SE
Cambridgeshire College of Arts and Technology, Cambridge CB1 3AJ
Canterbury Christ Church College, North Holmes Road, Canterbury CT1 1QU
Canterbury College of Art, New Dover Road, Canterbury CT1 3AN
Canterbury College of Technology, New Dover Road, Canterbury CT1 3AN
Carlett Park College of Technology, Eastham, Wirral, Merseyside L62 0AY
Carlisle Technical College, Victoria Place, Carlisle CA1 1HS
Carshalton College of Further Education, Nightingale Road, Carshalton, Surrey
Cassio College, Langley Road, Watford, Herts WD1 3RH
Castlereagh College of Further Education, Montgomery Road, Belfast BT6 9JD
Cauldon College of Further Education, Stoke Road, Shelton, Stoke-on-Trent ST4 2DG
Central College of Commerce, 300 Cathedral Street, Glasgow G1 2TA
Central School of Art and Design, Southampton Row, London WC1B 4AP
Central School of Speech and Drama, Embassy Theatre, Eton Avenue, London NW3 3HY
Charlotte Mason College of Education, Ambleside, Cumbria LA22 9BB
Chelmer Institute of Higher Education, Victoria Road South, Chelmsford, Essex CM1 1LL
Chelsea School of Art, Manresa Road, London SW3 6LS
Cheltenham General Hospital, School of Nursing, Sandford Road, Cheltenham, Glos GL53 7AN
Cheltenham School of Orthoptics, Cheltenham General Hospital, Cheltenham, Glos GL53 7AN
Chester College of Higher Education, Cheyney Road, Chester CH1 4BJ
Chesterfield College of Technology, Infirmary Road, Chesterfield S41 7NG
Chichester College of Technology, Westgate Fields, Chichester, Sussex PO19 1SB
Chippenham Technical College, Cocklebury Road, Chippenham, Wilts
Christ's and Notre Dame College, Duntocher Road, Bearsden, Glasgow G61 4QA
Christ's College, Woolton Road, Liverpool L16 8ND
City and East London College, Bunhill Row, London EC1Y 8LQ
City of Cardiff College of Education, Cyncoed, Cardiff
City of Leeds College of Music, Cookridge Street, Leeds LS2 8BH
City of Liverpool College of Higher Education, Liverpool Road, Prescot, Merseyside L34 1NP
City of Manchester College of Higher Education, Hathersage Road, Rusholme, Manchester M13 0JA
Clarendon College of Further Education, Pelham Avenue, Nottingham
Colchester Institute of Higher Education, Sheepen Road, Colchester, Essex CO3 3LL
Coleraine Technical College, Union Street, Coleraine

College for the Distributive Trades, 30 Leicester Square, London WC2H 7LE

College for Librarianship Wales, Llanbadarn Fawr, Aberystwyth, Dyfed SY23 3AS

College of Nautical Studies, Warsash, Southampton SO3 6ZL

College of Speech Therapists, Harold Poster House, 6 Lechmere Road, London NW2 5BU

Cooperative College, Stanford Hall, Lougborough, Leics LE12 5QR

Cordwainers' Technical College, Mare Street, Hackney, London E8 3RE

Cornwall Technical College, Redruth, Cornwall TR15 3RD

Coventry Technical College, Butts, Coventry CV1 3GD

Craigie College of Education, Ayr KA8 0SR

Craiglockhart College of Education, 219 Colinton Road, Edinburgh EH14 1DJ

Crawley College of Technology, College Road, Crawley, Sussex RH10 1NR

Crewe and Alsager College of Higher Education, Crewe, Cheshire CW1 1DU

Croydon College of Design and Technology, Fairfield, Croydon CR9 1DX

Cumbria College of Art and Design, Brampton Road, Carlisle CA3 9AY

Darlington College of Technology, Cleveland Avenue, Darlington, County Durham DL3 7BB

Dartington College of Arts, Totnes, Devon TQ9 6EJ

De La Salle College of Higher Education, Hopwood Hall, Middleton, Manchester M24 3XH

Derby Lonsdale College of Higher Education, Kedleston Road, Derby DE3 1GB

Derby School of Occupational Therapy, Highfield, 403 Burton Road, Derby DE3 6AN

Doncaster Metropolitan Institute of Higher Education, Waterdale, Doncaster DN1 3EX

Doreen Bird College of Theatre Dance, Birbeck Centre, Birbeck Road, Sidcup, Kent

Dorset House School of Occupational Therapy, 58 London Road, Headington, Oxford OX3 7PE

Dorset Institute of Higher Education, Wallisdown Road, Wallisdown, Poole, Dorset BH12 5BB

Drama Centre London, 176 Prince of Wales Road, Chalk Farm, London NW5 3PT

Dudley College of Technology, The Broadway, Dudley, West Midlands DY1 4AS

Duncan of Jordanstone College of Art, Perth Road, Dundee DD1 4HT

Dundee College of Commerce, 30 Constitution Road, Dundee DD3 6TB

Dundee College of Education, Gardyne Road, Broughty Ferry, Dundee DD7 1NY

Dundee College of Technology, Bell Street, Dundee DD1 1HG

Dunfermline College of Physical Education, Cramond, Edinburgh EH4 6JD

Dunstable College, Kingsway, Dunstable, Beds LU5 4HG

Ealing College of Higher Education, St Mary's Road, London W5 5RF

Early Music Centre, 62 Princedale Road, London W11 4NL

East Warwickshire College of Further Education, Clifton Road, Rugby

Edge Hill College of Higher Education, St Helens Road, Ormskirk, Lancashire L39 4QP

Edinburgh College of Art, Lauriston Place, Edinburgh EH3 9DF

Edinburgh School of Agriculture, West Mains Road, Edinburgh EH9 3JG

English National Opera, Camperdown House, Half Moon Passage, Aldgate, London E1

Erith College of Technology, Tower Road, Belvedere, Kent DA17 6JA

Evesham College of Further Education, Cheltenham Road, Evesham, Worcs WR11 6LP

Exeter College of Art and Design, Earl Richards Road North, Exeter EX2 6AS

F. L. Calder College, Dowesfield Lane, Liverpool L18 3JJ

Falkirk College of Technology, Grangemouth Road, Falkirk FK2 9AD

Falmouth School of Art, Woodlane, Falmouth, Cornwall TR11 4RA

Farnborough College of Technology, Boundary Road, Farnborough GU14 6SB

Galashiels College of Further Education, 8 Melrose Road, Galashiels TD1 2AF

Gateshead Technical College, Durham Road, Gateshead NE9 5BN

Glasgow Central College of Commerce, 300 Cathedral Street, Glasgow G1 2TA

Glasgow College of Building and Printing, 60 North Hanover Street, Glasgow G1 2BP

Glasgow College of Food Technology, 230 Cathedral Street, Glasgow G21 2TG

Glasgow College of Technology, Cowcaddens Road, Glasgow G4 0BA

Glasgow School of Art, 167 Renfrew Street, Glasgow G3 6RQ

Glasgow School of Occupational Therapy, 29 Sherbrooke Avenue, Glasgow G41 4ER

Goldsmiths' College, New Cross, London SE14 6NW

Grimsby College of Technology, Nuns Corner, Grimsby, South Humberside DN34 5BQ

Guildford County College of Technology, Stoke Park, Guildford, Surrey GU1 1EZ

Guildford School of Acting and Drama Dance Education, Bellairs Centre, Millbrook, Guildford, Surrey

Guildhall School of Music and Drama, Barbican, London EC2Y 8DT

Gwent College of Higher Education (Art and Design), Clarence Place, Newport, Gwent NPT 0UW; (Management, Science), Allt-yr-yn Avenue, Newport, Gwent NPT 5XA; (Education), College Crescent, Caerleon, Newport, Gwent NP6 1XJ

Hamilton College of Education, Bothwell Road, Hamilton, Lanarkshire ML3 0BD

Hammersmith and West London College, Baron's Court, Gliddon Road, London W14 9BL

Harlow Technical College, College Gate, The High, Harlow CM20 1LT

Harper Adams Agricultural College, Newport, Shropshire TF10 8NB

Harrow College of Higher Education, Northwich Park, Harrow, HA1 3TP

Hastings College of Further Education, Archery Road, St Leonards-on-Sea, East Sussex TN38 0HX

Herefordshire Technical College, Folly Lane, Hereford HR2 6LL

Hertfordshire College of Art and Design, Hatfield Road, St Albans, Herts AL1 3RS

Hertfordshire College of Building, St Peter's Road, St Albans, Herts AL1 3RX

Hertfordshire College of Higher Education, Wall Hall, Aldenham, Warford, Herts WD2 8AT

Highbury College of Technology, Corsham, Portsmouth PO6 2SA

Homerton College, Cambridge CB2 2PH

Hugh Baird College of Further Education, Balliol Road, Bootle, Merseyside L20 7EW

Hull College of Higher Education, Queen's Gardens, Hull HU1 3DH

L. M. Marsh College of Physical Education, Barkhill Road, Liverpool L17 6BD

Ilkley College, Wells Road, Ilkley, West Yorkshire LS29 9RD

Imperial Society of Teachers of Dancing, Euston Hall, Birkenhead Street, London WC1H 8BE

Inverness Technical College, Longman Road, Inverness

Institute for Choreology, 4 Margravine Gardens, Baron's Court, London W8 8RH

Jew's College, 11 Montagu Place, Montagu Square, London W1H 2BA

Jordanhill College of Education, Southbrae Drive, Glasgow G13 1PP

Kent College for the Careers Service, College Road, Hextable, Swanley, Kent BR8 7RN

Kidderminster College, Hoo Road, Kidderminster, Worcs DY10 1LX

King Alfred's College, Sparkford Road, Winchester SO22 4NR

Kingston College of Further Education, Kingston Hall Road, Kingston upon Thames, Surrey KT1 2AQ

Kirkcaldy College of Technology, St Brycedale Avenue, Kirkcaldy, Fife

La Sainte Union College of Higher Education, The Avenue, Southampton SO9 5HB

Laban Centre for Movement and Dance, Goldsmith's College, New Cross, London SE14 6NW

Lancashire College of Agriculture, Myerscough Hall, Bilsborrow, Preston PR3 0RY

Leek College of Further Education, Stickwell Street, Leek, Staffs ST13 6DP

Lewis Castle College, Stornoway, Isle of Lewis, Western Isles PA86 0XR

Lincoln College of Technology, Cathedral Street, Lincoln LN2 5HQ

Lipton Orthoptic Institute, Glasgow Eye Infirmary, 3 Sandyford Place, Glasgow

Lisburn Technical College, Castle Street, Lisburn, County Antrim BT27 4SU

Liverpool College of Occupational Therapy, Victoria Road, Huyton, Liverpool L36 5SB

Liverpool Institute of Higher Education (Christ's and Notre Dame), Woolton Road, Liverpool L16 8ND

Llandrillo Technical College, Llandudno Road, Ross-on-Sea, Colwyn Bay,

Clwyd LL28 4HX

London Academy of Music and Dramatic Art, Tower House, 226 Cromwell Road, London SW5 0SR

London Bible College, Green Lane, Northwood, Middlesex HA6 2UW

London College of Dance and Drama, 100 Marylebone Lane, London W1

London College of Fashion, 20 John Prince's Street, Oxford Street, London W1M 9HL

London College of Furniture, 41 Commercial Road, London E1 1LA

London College of Music, Great Marlborough Street, London W1V 2AS

London College of Printing, Elephant and Castle, London SE1 6SB

London Graduate School of Business Studies, Sussex Place, Regents Park, London NW1 4SA

London International Film School, 24 Shelton Street, London WC2H 9HP

London School of Contemporary Dance, 17 Duke's Road, London WC1

London School of Occupational Therapy, 55 Eton Avenue, London NW3 3ET

Loughborough College of Art and Design, Radmore, Loughborough, Leics LE11 3BT

Loughborough Technical College, Radmore, Loughborough, Leics LE11 3BT

Loughry College of Agriculture and Food Technology, Cookstown, County Tyrone BT80 9AA

Luton College of Higher Education, Park Square, Luton LU1 3JU

Mabel Fletcher Technical College, Sandown Road, Liverpool L15 4JB

Maidstone College of Art, Oakwood Park, Oakwood Road, Maidstone, Kent ME16 8AG

Management College, Greenlands, Henley on Thames, Oxon RG9 3AU

Manchester Business School, Booth Street West, Manchester M15 6PB

Manchester Royal Eye Hospital, Oxford Road, Manchester M13 9WH

Matlock College of Higher Education, Matlock, Derbyshire DE4 3FW

Matthew Boulton Technical College, Sherlock Street, Birmingham M5 7DB

Melton Mowbray College of Further Education, Asfordby Road, Melton Mowbray LE13 0HJ

Merton Technical College, Morden, Surrey SM4 5LZ

Mid-Cornwall College of Further Education, Palace Road, St Austell, Cornwall

Mid-Kent College of Higher and Further Education, Horsted, Maidstone Road, Chatham, Kent ME5 9UQ

Mid-Warwickshire College of Further Education, Warwick New Road, Leamington Spa CV32 5JE

Midland Orthoptic Training School, Birmingham and Midland Eye Hospital, Church Street, Birmingham B3 2NS

Millbank College of Commerce, Bankfield Road, Liverpool L13 0BQ

Monkwearmouth College of Further Education, Swan Street, Sunderland SR5 1EB

Moray College of Further Education, Hay Street, Elgin, Grampian Region JV30 2NW

Moray House College of Education, Holyrood Road, Edinburgh EH8 8AQ

Mountview Theatre School, 104 Crouch Hill, London N8

Napier College of Commerce and Technology, Colinton Road, Edinburgh EH10 5DT

National Extension College, 18 Brooklands Avenue, Cambridge CB2 2HN

National Film School, Beaconsfield Film Studios, Station Road, Beaconsfield, Bucks HP9 1LG

National Hospitals College of Speech Sciences, 59 Portland Place, London W1N 3AJ

Nene College, Moulton Park, Northampton NN2 7AL

New College, Framwellgate Moor, Durham DH1 5ES

Newcastle-upon-Tyne College of Arts and Technology, Maple Terrace, Newcastle-upon-Tyne NE4 7SA

Newman College, Bartley Green, Birmingham, B32 3NT

Newry Technical College, Newry, County Down BT35 8DN

Nonington College of Physical Education, Nonington, Dover, Kent CT15 4HH

Normal College, Bangor, North Wales

North Cheshire College, Fearnhead, Warrington, Lancs WA2 0DB

North East Surrey College of Technology, Reigate Road, Ewell, Epsom, Surrey KT17 3DS

North East Wales Institute of Higher Education, Kelsterton College, Connah's Quay, Clwyd CH5 4BR

North Gloucestershire College of Technology, The Park, Cheltenham, Glos DL50 2RR

North Hertfordshire College, Cambridge Road, Hitchin, Herts SG4 0JD

North London School of Physiotherapy of the Visually Handicapped, 10 Highgate Hill, London N19 5ND

North Oxfordshire Technical College and School of Art, Broughton Road, Banbury, Oxon OX16 9QA

North Riding College of Education, Filey Road, Scarborough, North Yorkshire YO11 3AZ

North of Scotland College of Agriculture, 581 King Street, Aberdeen AB9 1UD

North West Kent College of Technology, Miskin Road, Dartford

North Wirral College of Technology, Borough Road, Birkenhead, Merseyside L42 9QD

North Worcestershire College, Bromsgrove, Worcs B60 1PQ

Northampton School of Occupational Therapy, St Andrew's Hospital, Northampton NN1 5DG

Northern College of Speech and Drama, Thorn Bank, Werneth Hall Road, Werneth, Oldham OL8 1QZ

Northumberland College of Education, Ponteland, Newcastle-upon-Tyne NE20 0AB

Norwich City College of Further and Higher Education, Ipswich Road, Norwich, Norfolk NR2 2LJ

Norwich School of Art, St George Street, Norwich, Norfolk NR3 1BB

Oak Hill College, Southgate, London N14 4PS

Oldham College of Technology, Rochdale Road, Oldham, Lancs OL9 6AA

Paisley College of Technology, High Street, Paisley, Renfrewshire PA1 2BE

Park Lane College of Further Education, Park Lane, Leeds LS3 1AA

Perth College of Further Education, Brahan Estate, Creiff Road, Perth PH1 2NA

Peterborough Technical College, Park Crescent, Peterborough, Cambs PE1 4DZ

Plymouth College of Further Education, King's Road, Devenport PL1 5QG

Queen's College, 1 Park Drive, Glasgow G3 6LP

Queen Margaret College, 36 Clerwood Terrace, Edinburgh EH12 8TS

Rambert School of Ballet, The Place, 17 Duke's Road, London WC1H 9AB

Ravensbourne College of Art and Design, Walden Road, Chislehurst, Kent BR7 5SN

Redditch College, Peakman Street, Redditch, Worcs B98 8DW

Redhill Technical College, Gatton Point, Redhill, Surrey RH1 2JX

Reid Kerr College, Renfrew Road, Paisley PA3 4DR

Reigate School of Art and Design, 127 Blackborough Road, Reigate, Surrey RH2 7DE

Richmond College of Further Education, Spinkhill Drive, Sheffield S13 8FD

Richmond-upon-Thames College, Egerton Road, Twickenham, Middlesex TW2 7SJ

College of Ripon and York St John, Lord Mayor's Walk, York YO3 7EX

Robert Gordon's Institute of Technology, Schoolhill, Aberdeen AB9 1FR

Roehampton Institute of Higher Education, Roehampton Lane, London SW15 5PJ

Rolle College, Exmouth, Devon EX8 2AT

Rose Bruford College of Speech and Drama, Lamorbey Road, Sidcup, Kent DA15 9DF

Royal Academy of Arts (Schools), Burlington Gardens, London W1

Royal Academy of Dancing, 48 Vicarage Crescent, London SW11 3LT

Royal Academy of Dramatic Art, 62–4 Gower Street, London WC1E 6ED

Royal Academy of Music, Marylebone Road, London NW1 5HT

Royal Agricultural College, Cirencester, Glos GL7 6JS

Royal College of Music, Prince Consort Road, London SW7 2BS

Royal College of Nursing, Henrietta Place, Cavendish Square, London W1M 0AB

Royal National College for the Blind, College Road, Hereford HR1 1EB

Royal Northern College of Music, 124 Oxford Road, Manchester M13 9RD

Royal Scottish Academy of Music and Drama, St George's Place, Glasgow G2 1BS

St Alban's College, 29 Hatfield Road, St Alban's, Herts AL1 3RJ

St Andrew's School of Occupational Therapy, St Andrew's Hospital, Northampton NN1 5DG

St John's College of Further Education, Lower Hardman Street, Deansgate, Manchester M3 3FP

St Joseph's College of Education, Trench House, Belfast BT11 9GA

St Katherine's College, Stand Park Road, Liverpool L16 9JD

College of St Mark and St John, Derriford Road, Plymouth PL6 8BH

St Martin's College, Lancaster, Lancs LA1 3JD

St Martin's School of Art, 107 Charing Cross Road, London WC2H 0DU

St Mary's College, Waldegrave Road, Strawberry Hill, Twickenham TW1 4SX

St Mary's College of Education, 191 Falls Road, Belfast BT12 6FE

St Mary's College of the Sacred Heart, Fenham, Newcastle-upon-Tyne, NE4 9YH

College of St Paul and St Mary, The Park, Cheltenham, Glos GL50 2RH

Salford College of Technology, Frederick Road, Salford M6 6PU

Salisbury College of Technology, Southampton Road, Salisbury, Wilts SP1 2LW

Scarborough Technical College, Lady Edith's Drive, Scarborough, North Yorkshire YO12 5RN

Scottish College of Textiles, Galashiels, Borders Region TD1 3HF

Seale-Hayne Agricultural College, Newton Abbot, Devon TQ12 6NQ

Shoreditch College, Englefield Green, Egham, Surrey TW20 0JZ

Shrewsbury College of Arts and Technology, London Road, Shrewsbury, Shropshire

Shuttleworth College, Old Warden Park, Biggleswade, Beds SG18 9DX

Slough College of Higher Education, Wellington Street, Slough, Bucks SL1 1YG

Solihull College of Technology, Blossomfield Road, Solihull B91 1SB

Somerset College of Arts and Technology, Wellington Road, Taunton, Somerset

South Bristol Technical College, Marksbury Road, Bristol BS3 5JL

South Cheshire College of Further Education, Dane Bank Avenue, Crewe CW2 8AB

South Devon Technical College, Newton Road, Torquay, Devon TQ2 5BY

South Dorset Technical College, Newstead Road, Weymouth, Dorset DT4 0DX

South East London College, Lewisham Way, London SE4 1UT

South Glamorgan Health Authority (Teaching), 14th Floor, Pearl Assurance House, Greyfriars Road, Cardiff CF1 3RT

South Glamorgan Institute of Higher Education, Western Avenue, Llandaft, Cardiff CF5 2YB

South Gwent College of Further Education, Nash Road, Newport, Gwent NP6 2BR

South London College, Knights Hill, London SE27 0TX

South Shields Marine and Technical College, St George's Avenue, South Shields, Tyne and Wear

South West London College, Tooting Broadway, London SW17 0TQ

Southall College of Technology, Beaconsfield Road, Southall, Middlesex UB1 1DP

Southampton College of Higher Education, East Park Terrace, Southampton SO9 4WW

Stafford College of Technology, Wellington Road, South, Stockport, Greater Manchester SK1 3UQ

Stourbridge College of Technology and Art, Church Street, Stourbridge, West Midlands DY8 1LY

Stranmillis College, Stranmillis Road, Belfast BT9 5DY

School for the Study of Disorders of Human Communication, 86 Blackfriars Road, London SE1 8HA

Suffolk College of Higher and Further Education, Rope Walk, Ipswich, Suffolk 1P4 1LT

Swindon College, Regent Circus, Swindon SN1 1PT

Telford College of Further Education, Crewe Toll, Edinburgh EH4 2NZ

Thanet Technical College, Ramsgate Road, Broadstairs, Kent CT10 1PT

Thomas Danby College, Roundhay Road, Sheepscar, Leeds LS7 3BG

Thomson Foundation Television College, Kirkhill House, Newton Mearns, Glasgow G77 5RH

Tottenham College of Technology, High Road, London N15 4RU

Tresham College (Kettering Centre), St Mary's Road, Kettering, Northants NN15 7BS

Trinity College, Carmarthen, Dyfed

Trinity and All Saints' Colleges, Brownberrie Lane, Horsforth, Leeds LS18 5HD

Trinity College of Music, Mandeville Place, London W1M 6AQ

University Hospital of Wales, Heath Park, Cardiff CF4 4XW

Wakefield College of Technology and Arts, Margaret Street, Wakefield, West Yorkshire WF1 2DH

Waltham Forest College, Forest Road, London E17 4JB

Warley College of Technology, Crocketts Lane, Smethwick, Warley, West Midlands B66 3BU

Watford College, Hempstead Road, Watford, Herts WD1 3EZ

Webber Douglas Academy of Dramatic Art, 30–6 Clareville Street, London SW7 5AW

Welsh College of Librarianship, Llanbadarn Fawr, Aberystwyth, Dyfed SY23 3AS

Welsh College of Music and Drama, Castle Grounds, Cathays Park, Cardiff

Welsh School of Occupational Therapy, University Hospital of Wales, Heath Park, Cardiff CF4 4XW

West Bromwich College of Commerce and Technology, Wednesbury, West Midlands WS10 9ER

West Glamorgan Institute of Higher Education, Townhill Road, Townhill, Swansea SA2 0UT

West London Institute of Higher Education, Lancaster House, Borough Road, Isleworth, Middlesex TW7 5DU

West Midlands College of Higher Education, Gorway, Walsall, West Midlands SW1 3BD

West of Scotland Agricultural College, Auchincruive, Ayr KA6 5HW

West Surrey College of Art and Design, Falkner Road, The Hart, Farnham, Surrey GU9 7DS

West Sussex Institute of Higher Education, Upper Bognor Road, Bognor Regis, Sussex PO21 1HR

Westhill College, Weoley Park Road, Selly Oak, Birmingham B29 6LL

Westminster College, Battersea Park Road, London SW11 4JR

Westminster College, North Hinksey, Oxford OX2 9AT

Willesden College of Technology, Denzil Road, London NW10

Wimbledon School of Art, Merton Hall Road, Wimbledon, London SW19 3QA

Winchester School of Art, Park Avenue, Winchester, Hants SO23 8DL

Worcester College of Higher Education, Henwick Grove, Worcester WR2 6AJ

Worcester Technical College, Deansway, Worcester

Writtle Agricultural College, Writtle, Chelmsford, Essex CM1 3RR

York College of Arts and Technology, Dringhouses, York YO2 1UA

Ystrad Mynach College of Further Education, Twyn Road, Ystrad Mynach, Hengoed, Glamorgan

PART IV
TEACHING RESOURCES

1 PUBLISHERS

This select list of the main publishers in the United Kingdom indicates which areas their post-school programmes cover: Arts – Geography – History – Literature – Politics – Society – Thought. Most publishers will provide information concerning current publications in particular fields. For a more comprehensive list of British publishers readers are referred to Black (publisher), *Writers' and Artists' Yearbook*, London, annually.

	ARTS	GEOGRAPHY	HISTORY	LITERATURE	POLITICS	SOCIETY	THOUGHT
Allen & Unwin Ltd Ruskin House 40 Museum Street London WC1A 1LU	•	•	•		•	•	•
Allen (W. H.) & Co. Plc 44 Hill Street London W1X 8BL	•		•	•	•	•	
Allison & Busby 6a Noel Street London W1V 3RB			•	•	•	•	
Arnold (Edward) Ltd 41–2 Bedford Square London WC1B 3DQ	•	•	•	•	•	•	•
Athlone Press Ltd 44 Bedford Row London WC1R 4LY	•	•	•	•	•	•	•
Barrie & Jenkins Ltd 17–21 Conway Street London W1P 6JD	•		•	•			
Bartholomew & Son Ltd 12 Duncan Street Edinburgh EH9 1TA		•					
Batsford Ltd 4 Fitzhardinge Street Portman Square London W1H 0AH	•	•	•			•	
Blackie & Son Ltd Bishopbriggs Glasgow G64 2NZ			•			•	
Blackwell, Basil, Ltd 108 Cowley Road Oxford OX4 1JF			•	•	•	•	•

	ARTS	GEOGRAPHY	HISTORY	LITERATURE	POLITICS	SOCIETY	THOUGHT
Bodley Head Ltd 30 Bedford Square London WC1B 3RP			•	•	•	•	
Boyars, Marion, Ltd 24 Lacy Road London SW15 1NL	•			•		•	
Calder, John, Ltd 18 Brewer Street London W1R 4AS	•			•	•	•	
Cambridge University Press The Edinburgh Building Shaftesbury Road Cambridge CB2 2RU	•	•	•	•	•	•	•
Cape, Jonathan, Ltd 30 Bedford Square London WC1B 3EL			•	•	•	•	
Cass, Frank & Co Ltd Gainsborough House 11 Gainsborough Road London E11 1RS	•		•	•	•	•	
Cassell Ltd 1 Vincent Square London SW1P 2PN	•			•	•	•	
Chatto & Windus Ltd 40–2 William IV Street London WC2N 4DF	•		•	•	•	•	
Collins, William, Sons & Co. Ltd 8 Grafton Street London W1X 3LA	•	•	•	•	•	•	•
Constable & Co. Ltd 10 Orange Street London WC2H 7EG		•	•	•	•	•	

	ARTS	GEOGRAPHY	HISTORY	LITERATURE	POLITICS	SOCIETY	THOUGHT
Croom Helm Ltd Provident House Burrell Row Beckenham Kent BR3 1AT	•	•	•	•	•	•	•
David & Charles Ltd Brunel House Forde Road Newton Abbot Devon TQ12 2PU	•		•		•	•	
Dent (J. M.) & Sons Ltd Aldine House 33 Welbeck Street London W1M 8LX		•	•				
Deutsch, André, Ltd 105 Great Russell Street London WC1B 3LJ	•		•	•	•	•	
Duckworth & Co. Ltd The Old Piano Factory 43 Gloucester Crescent London NW1 7DY			•	•	•	•	•
Faber & Faber Ltd 3 Queen Square London WC1N 3AU	•	•	•	•	•	•	•
French (Samuel), Ltd 52 Fitzroy Street London W1P 6JR				•			
Geographia Ltd 17 Conway Street London W1P 6JD		•					
Gollancz (Victor) Ltd 14 Henrietta Street London WC2E 8QJ	•		•		•	•	

	ARTS	GEOGRAPHY	HISTORY	LITERATURE	POLITICS	SOCIETY	THOUGHT
Gower Ltd Gower House Croft Road Aldershot Hampshire GU11 3HR					•	•	
Granada Publishing Ltd 8 Grafton Street London W1X 3LA		•	•	•	•	•	
Hale, Robert, Ltd Clerkenwell House 45–7 Clerkenwell Green London EC1 0HT			•	•	•		
Hamilton, Hamish, Ltd Garden House 57–9 Long Acre London WC2E 9JZ	•		•	•	•	•	
Harvester Press Ltd 16 Ship Street Brighton Sussex BN1 1AD			•	•	•	•	•
Heinemann, William, Ltd 10 Upper Grosvenor Street London W1X 9PA	•	•	•	•	•	•	
Her Majesty's Stationery Office St Crispins Duke Street Norwich NR3 1PD	•	•	•		•	•	
Hodder & Stoughton Ltd Mill Road Dunton Green Sevenoaks Kent TN13 1YA	•	•	•	•	•	•	

	ARTS	GEOGRAPHY	HISTORY	LITERATURE	POLITICS	SOCIETY	THOUGHT
Hogarth Press Ltd William IV Street London WC2N 4DG			•	•		•	
Hutchinson Books Ltd 17–21 Conway Street London W1P 6JD		•	•	•	•		
Joseph, Michael, Ltd 44 and 45 Bedford Square London WC1B 3DU	•		•	•	•	•	
Kimber, William, & Co. Ltd 100 Jermyn Street London SW1Y 6EE		•	•		•	•	
Knight, Charles & Co. Ltd Tolley House 17 Scarbrook Road Croydon Surrey CR0 1SQ					•	•	
Kogan Page Ltd 120 Pentonville Road London N1 9JN					•	•	
Lawrence & Wishart Ltd 39 Museum Street London WC1A 1LQ			•	•	•	•	•
Longman Group UK Ltd 5 Bentinck Street London W1M 5RN	•	•	•	•	•	•	•
Lutterworth Press 7 All Saints Passage Cambridge CB2 3LS	•		•	•		•	
Macdonald & Evans Ltd Estover Road Estover Plymouth PL6 7PZ		•	•		•	•	

	ARTS	GEOGRAPHY	HISTORY	LITERATURE	POLITICS	SOCIETY	THOUGHT
Macmillan Publishers Ltd 4 Little Essex Street London WC2R 3LF	•	•	•	•	•	•	•
Manchester University Press Oxford Road Manchester M13 9PL			•		•	•	•
Merlin Press Ltd 3 Manchester Road London E14 9BD					•	•	•
Methuen Ltd 11 New Fetter Lane London EC4P 4EE	•	•	•	•	•	•	•
Murray, John, Ltd 50 Albemarle Street London W1X 4BD	•	•	•	•	•	•	•
New English Library Ltd 47 Bedford Square London WC1B 3DP		•	•	•	•	•	
Open University Press 12 Cofferidge Close Stony Stratford Milton Keynes MK11 1BY	•	•	•	•	•	•	
Oxford University Press Walton Street Oxford OX2 6DP	•	•	•	•	•	•	
Oyez Longman Ltd 21–7 Lamb's Conduit Street London WC1N 3NJ					•	•	
Pan Books Ltd Cavaye Place London SW10 9PG				•			

	ARTS	GEOGRAPHY	HISTORY	LITERATURE	POLITICS	SOCIETY	THOUGHT
Penguin Books Ltd Bath Road Harmondsworth Middlesex UB7 0DA	•	•	•	•	•	•	•
Pergamon Press Ltd Headington Hill Hall Oxford OX3 0BW	•	•	•		•	•	
Phaidon Press Ltd Littlegate House St Ebbes Street Oxford OX1 7BD	•		•				
Pinter, Frances Ltd 25 Floral Street London WC2E 9DS					•	•	
Pluto Press 105a Torriano Avenue London NW5 2RX	•		•	•	•	•	•
Quartet Books Ltd 27–9 Goodge Street London W1P 1FD					•	•	
Routledge & Kegan Paul Ltd 11 New Fetter Lane London EC4P 4EE	•	•	•	•	•	•	•
Scolar Press 13 Brunswick Centre London WC1N 1AF	•		•	•			
Secker, Martin & Warburg Ltd 54 Poland Street London W1V 3DF	•		•	•	•	•	
Sidgwick & Jackson Ltd 1 Tavistock Chambers Bloomsbury Way London WC1A 2SG			•	•	•	•	•

	ARTS	GEOGRAPHY	HISTORY	LITERATURE	POLITICS	SOCIETY	THOUGHT
Thames & Hudson Ltd 30–4 Bloomsbury Street London WC1B 3QP	•		•				
University Tutorial Press 842 Yeovil Road Slough SL1 4JQ		•	•	•	•	•	
Van Nostrand Reinhold (UK) Co. Ltd Molly Millars Lane Wokingham Berkshire RG11 2PY	•		•	•	•	•	•
Verso Ltd 15 Greek Street London W1V 5LF	•				•	•	•
Virago Press 41 William IV Street London WC2N 4DB	•		•	•	•	•	•
Weidenfeld, George & Nicolson 91 Clapham High Street London SW4 7TA	•	•	•	•	•	•	•
Woburn Press Gainsborough House 11 Gainsborough Road London E11 1RS			•	•	•	•	

2 FILM DISTRIBUTORS

Listed below are some of the main suppliers of commercial or educational 16mm films in areas relevant to British Studies. Conditions of loan or purchase in the UK and abroad vary considerably. Most distributors indicate rates and conditions of loan or purchase in their catalogues. For a comprehensive list of British film distributors see British Film Institute, *Film and Television Yearbook*.

BBC Enterprises
Guild House
Oundle House
Peterborough PE2 9PZ

British Film Institute
81 Dean Street
London W1V 6AA

British Films Ltd
Carlye House
235 Vauxhall Bridge Road
London SW1

Central Film Library
Government Building
Bromyard Avenue
Acton
London W3 7JB

CFM Distribution
Pottery Lane House
Pottery Lane
London W11 4LZ

Children's Film Foundation Ltd
6–10 Great Portland Street
London W1N 6JN

Chiltern Consortium
Chiltern Resources Library
Wall Hall
Aldenham
Watford
Hertfordshire

Columbia-EMI-Warner Distributors
135 Wardour Street
London W1V 4AP

Concord Films Council
201 Felixstowe Road
Ipswich
Suffolk IP3 9BJ

Connoisseur Films Ltd
167 Oxford Street
London W1R 2DX

Contemporary Films Ltd
55 Greek Street
London W1V 6DB

CTVC Film Library
Foundation House
Walton Road
Bushey
Watford

Education and Television Films
247a Upper Street
London N1 1RU

EMI Audio Visual Services
5 Dean Street
London W1

Film Distributors Associated
Building No 9
GEC Estate
East Lane
Wembley
Middlesex HA9 7QB

Films Department
The British Council
11 Portland Place
London W1N 4EJ

Golden Films
Stewart House
Frances Road
Windsor
Berkshire SL4 3AF

Granada Television Film Library
Granada Television Network Ltd
Television Centre
Quay Street
Manchester M60 9EA

Guild Sound and Vision Ltd
Woodston House
85–129 Oundle Road
Peterborough

511

Independent Film-Makers'
Association
79 Wardour Street
London W1V 3PA

Independent Television
ITN House
48 Wells Street
London W1P 4DE

Intercontinental Films
2b Queen Street
Bridgend
Mid-Glamorgan CF31 1HX

London Film-Makers Co-Operative
42 Gloucester Avenue
London NW1

Millbank Films
Thames House North
Millbank
London SW1P 4QG

Multilink Film Library Ltd
12 The Square
Vicarage Farm Road
Peterborough
PE1 5TS

National Audio-Visual Aids Library
Paxton Place
Gipsy Road
London SE27 9SR

Open University
c/o Guild Sound and Vision Ltd
Woodston House
85–129 Oundle Road
Peterborough PE2 9PY

Other Cinema
79 Wardour Street
London W1V 3TH

Pegasus Films
5 Sycamore Villas
West View

Mold
Clwyd
North Wales

Peter Darvill Associates
280 Chartridge Lane
Chesham
Buckinghamshire

Random Film Library Ltd
25 The Burroughs
Hendon
London NW4 4AT

Rank Film Library
PO Box 70
Great West Road
Brentford
Middlesex TW8 9HR

Scottish Central Film Library
Dowanhill
74 Victoria Crescent Road
Glasgow G12 9JN

Services Kinema Corporation
Chalfont Grove
Narcot Lane
Chalfont St Peter
Gerrard's Cross
Buckinghamshire SL9 8TN

Shell Film Library
25 The Burroughs
Hendon
London NW4 4AT

Stewart Film Distributors Ltd
107–15 Long Acre
London WC2 9NU

Technicolor Audio Visual Systems
Ltd
PO Box 7
Bath Road
West Drayton
Middlesex UB7 QDB

Video Arts Ltd
Dumbarton House
68 Oxford Street
London W1N 9LA

Viscom
Parkhall Road Trading Estate
Dulwich
London SE21 8EL

Welsh Arts Council
Museum Place
Cardiff CF1 3NX

World Wide Pictures Ltd
21–5 St Anne's Court
London W1V 3AS

3 VIDEO WORKSHOPS

The following is a list of video workshops or centres which will loan or hire video cassettes for group study or other activities. Conditions of loan and hire vary considerably.

Action Space
16 Chenies Street
London WC1
01 637 7664

The Basement Project
St George's Town Hall
Cable Street
London E1
01 790 4020

Belfast Film Workshop
37 Queen Street
Belfast BT1 6EA
0232 226661

Birmingham Film and Video
  Workshop
60 Holt Street
Birmingham B7
021 359 5545/4192

Brighton Film and Video Workshop
c/o Watts Building
Brighton Polytechnic
Moulsecoomb
Brighton BN2 4GJ

Bristol Film Workshop
37–9 Jamaica Street
Bristol BS2 8JP
0272 426 199

Central Film Library
Government Building
Bromyard Avenue
Acton
London W3 7JB
01 743 5555

Clockwork Video Unit
Media Workshop
'D' Block
Middlesex Polytechnic
Trent Park
Cockfosters
Barnet
Hertfordshire

Counter Image
19 Whitworth Street West
Manchester M1 5WG
061 228 3551

Electric Newspaper
21 Trentishoe Mansions
90 Charing Cross Road
London WC2
01 836 5391

Fantasy Factory Video
42 Theobald's Road
London WC1 8XNW
01 405 6862

Film Workshop Trust
17 Great King Street
Edinburgh EH3 6QW
031 556 2078

Glasgow University Media Group
Department of Sociology
University of Glasgow
Glasgow G12 8QQ
041 339 8855

Glasgow Film and Video Workshop
Glasgow Arts Centre
12 Washington Street
Glasgow G3 8AZ

Hull Film and Video Workshop
Outreach Community Arts
Northumberland Avenue
Hull HU2 0LN
0482 226420

Interaction Trust Ltd
15 Wilkin Street
Kentish Town
London NW5
01 485 0881

London Video Arts
23 Frith Street
London W1
01 437 2786

515

Manchester Film and Video
  Workshop
5 James Leigh Street
Manchester M60 1SX
061 236 6953

Newcastle Media Workshops
5 Saville Place
Newcastle upon Tyne NE1
0632 322410

Newham Community Video
c/o 123 Prince Regent Lane
London E13
01 474 5556

Reel TV
West London Media Workshop
The Base
St Thomas's Church Hall
East Row
London W10
01 969 1020

Sheffield Video Workshop
8 Kearsley Road
Sheffield S2 4TE
0742 583524

TV Studio Workshop
Highbury Station Road
London N1 1SB
01 226 9143

Walworth and Aylesbury
  Community Arts Trust
Shop 8
Taplow
East Street
Aylesbury Estate
London SE17
01 701 9010

Women's International Video
  Exchange Service
c/o The Albany
Creek Road
Deptford
London SE8
01 692 0231

4 AUDIO-VISUAL SUPPLIERS

The following is a list of audio-visual suppliers who offer software relevant to the study or teaching of major areas of British Studies: Arts – Geography – History – Literature – Politics – Society – Thought. Conditions of loan or purchase vary considerably. Most suppliers give indications of rates and conditions of loan or purchase in their catalogues. For a more comprehensive list of audio-visual suppliers see NAVAC, *Audio-Visual Handbook*, London, 1980.

	AUDIO CASSETTE	FILM	FILM LOOP	FILM STRIP	SLIDE	VIDEO	WALLCHART
Arts Council of Great Britain 105 Piccadilly London W1V 0AU							
Arts		•				•	
Arnold-Wheaton Educational Publishers Butterley Street Leeds LS10 1AX							
Geography							
Social Studies	•			•			•
Audio Arts 6 Briarswood Wood London SW4 9PX							
Arts	•						
Audio Learning Ltd Sarda House 183–9 Queensway London W2							
Arts	•						
Economics	•						
Geography	•						
Literature	•						
Politics	•						
Social Studies	•						
Audio Visual Library Services 10–13 Powdrake Road Grangemouth Stirlingshire FK3 9UT Scotland							
Arts				•	•		
Geography				•	•		
History				•	•		
Literature	•						
Politics	•						
Social Studies	•				•		

519

	AUDIO CASSETTE	FILM	FILM LOOP	FILM STRIP	SLIDE	VIDEO	WALLCHART
Audio Visual Productions Hocker Hill House Chepstow Gwent NP6 5ER							
Arts	•			•	•		
Geography	•			•	•		
History	•			•	•		
Literature	•						
Politics	•			•	•		
Social Studies	•			•	•		
Boulton Hawker Films Ltd Hadleigh Near Ipswich Suffolk IP7 5BG							
Arts		•					
Geography		•					
History		•					
Social Studies		•					
British Council 10 Spring Gardens London SW1A 2BN							
Arts	•	•			•	•	
Economics	•	•			•	•	•
Geography	•	•			•	•	•
History	•	•			•	•	•
Literature	•	•			•	•	•
Philosophy	•	•			•	•	•
Politics	•	•			•	•	•
Social Studies	•	•			•	•	•
British Universities Film **Council** 81 Dean Street London W1V 6AA							
Arts		•			•		
Economics		•			•		
Geography		•			•		
History		•			•		
Literature		•			•		
Philosophy		•			•		
Politics		•			•		
Social Studies		•			•		

	AUDIO CASSETTE	FILM	FILM LOOP	FILM STRIP	SLIDE	VIDEO	WALLCHART
Caedmon Spoken Word Recordings							
Gower Publishing Co. Ltd							
Gower House							
Croft Road							
Aldershot							
Hants GU11 3HR							
Arts	•						
History	•						
Literature	•						
Philosophy	•						
Cambridge University Press							
The Pitt Building							
Trumpington Street							
Cambridge CB2 1RP							
Geography	•				•		•
History					•	•	
Literature	•				•		
Concord Films Council							
201 Felixstowe Road							
Ipswich							
Suffolk 1P3 9BJ							
Arts		•				•	
Economics		•				•	
Philosophy		•				•	
Politics		•				•	
Social Studies		•				•	
Educational Productions Ltd							
Bradford Road							
East Arsdley							
Wakefield							
Yorkshire							
Arts				•		•	
Economics				•			•
Geography				•		•	
History				•		•	
Literature	•			•			
Social Studies	•			•		•	•

	AUDIO CASSETTE	FILM	FILM LOOP	FILM STRIP	SLIDE	VIDEO	WALLCHART
Edward Patterson Associates							
68 Copers Cope Road							
Beckenham							
Kent							
Arts	•	•			•	•	
Geography	•	•			•	•	
History	•	•		•	•	•	
Literature		•		•		•	
Philosophy					•		
Social Studies	•	•			•	•	
Eothen Films Ltd							
EMI Studios							
Shenley Road							
Borehamwood							
Hertfordshire WD6 1JG							
Arts		•	•				•
Philosophy		•					•
Faber & Faber Ltd							
3 Queen Square							
London WC1N 2AU							
Literature	•						
Fergus Davidson Associates Ltd							
376 London Road							
West Croydon							
Surrey							
Arts	•	•	•	•	•	•	•
Economics	•			•		•	
Geography	•	•	•	•	•	•	•
History	•	•		•		•	
Literature	•	•				•	
Politics		•				•	
Social Studies		•		•		•	

	AUDIO CASSETTE	FILM	FILM LOOP	FILM STRIP	SLIDE	VIDEO	WALLCHART
Focal Point Audio Visual Ltd 251 Copnor Road Portsmouth PO3 5EE							
Arts	•			•	•		
Geography	•			•	•		
History	•			•	•		
Social Studies	•			•	•		
George Philip 12–14 Long Acre London WC2E 9LP							
Geography							•
Geoslides Production Services 4 Christian Fields London SW163JZ							
Geography	•				•		
Holmes McDougall Ltd Allander House 137–41 Leith Walk Edinburgh EH6 8NS							
Geography						•	
History	•			•	•		
Hugh Baddeley Productions 64 Moffats Lane Brookmas Park Hatfield Hertfordshire AL9 7RU							
Arts		•				•	
Geography		•		•	•	•	
Film		•		•	•	•	
Politics				•	•		
Social Studies		•		•	•	•	

	AUDIO CASSETTE	FILM	FILM LOOP	FILM STRIP	SLIDE	VIDEO	WALLCHART
Hulton Educational Publications Raans Road Amersham Buckinghamshire HP6 6JJ							
Geography							•
History							•
Ivan Berg Associates 35a Broadhurst Gardens London NW6 3QT							
Arts	•						
History	•						
Literature	•						
London Television Service Hercules Road London SE1 7DU							
Arts						•	
History						•	
Social Studies						•	
Longman Group UK Ltd 5 Bentinck Street London W1M 5RN							
Arts				•			
Geography				•			
History				•			
Literature	•			•			
Social Studies				•			
Mary Glasgow Publications Ltd Brookhampton Lane Kineton Warwickshire CV35 0JB							
Arts	•			•			
Economics	•			•			
Geography	•			•			
History	•			•			
Literature	•			•			
Politics	•			•			
Social Studies	•			•			

	AUDIO CASSETTE	FILM	FILM LOOP	FILM STRIP	SLIDE	VIDEO	WALLCHART
The National Audio-Visual Aids Library Paxton Place Gipsy Road London SE27 9SR							
Arts	•	•	•	•	•	•	
Economics	•	•	•	•	•	•	
Geography	•	•	•	•	•	•	
History	•	•	•	•	•	•	
Literature	•	•	•	•	•	•	
Philosophy	•	•	•	•	•	•	
Politics	•	•	•	•	•	•	
Social Studies	•	•	•	•	•	•	
British Coal Film Branch Hobart House Grosvenor House Grosvenor Place London SW1							
Arts		•					
Economics		•					
Geography		•					
History		•					
Social Studies		•					
Thomas Nelson and Sons Ltd Nelson House Mayfield Road Walton-on-Thames Surrey KT12 5PL							
Geography					•		•
Norwich Tapes Ltd Wakefield House Caldbec Hill Battle Sussex TN33 0JS							
Literature	•						

	AUDIO CASSETTE	FILM	FILM LOOP	FILM STRIP	SLIDE	VIDEO	WALLCHART
Open University Educational Enterprises Ltd							
12 Cofferidge Close							
Stony Stratford							
Milton Keynes							
Bedfordshire							
Arts	•	•					•
Economics	•	•					•
Geography	•	•					•
History	•	•					•
Literature	•	•					•
Philosophy	•	•					•
Politics	•	•					•
Social Studies	•	•					•
Pictorial Charts Educational Trust							
27 Kirchen Road							
London W13 0UD							
Economics							•
Geography							•
History							•
Philosophy							•
Social Studies							•
Audio Visual Rank							
PO Box 20							
Great West Road							
Brentford							
Middlesex							
Geography		•		•			•
History		•		•			•
Literature		•		•			•

BRITISH SOURCES OF INFORMATION